"Brilliant, precise color at a price that is affordable."

MW01397463

COLOR PRINTER SPECIAL

We sell a wide variety of Color Printer to meet every Hi-Speed color, up to 20 pages per minute Photo quality with paper sizes up to 13" x 19" Leases as low as $65 per month

Call Now To Try Out Our Awesome Pri • Phone: (651) 778-1324 • Fax: (651) 776-2651

PRINTER SERVICE PROFESSIONALS

SERVICE • SALES • SUPPLIES

We are the local Color and Network Printer & Copier Specialists! When you need quality Service, Sales or Supplies support, Call us to see why Printer Pros is the best in town!

OUR CUSTOMERS SAY WE'RE THE BEST IN TOWN! CALL NOW TO SEE WHY

Printer Pros offers provides specialized support on all types of printers and we are authorized by the following Companies.

- Xerox
- QMS
- Minolta
- Lexmark
- Zebra
- Kyocera
- Okidata
- Hewlett Packard
- Canon
- Ricoh
- Printek
- and more....

www.printerservicepros.com

1412 Arcade St. • St. Paul, MN 55106

ACCELERATED MEDIA**SOLUTIONS**, INC
digital media systems integrators

www.createdvds.com

DVD/CD AUTHORING SYSTEMS
spruce technologies

ENCODING & COMPRESSION
spruce technologies . zapex . wired . terran
canopus . heuris

VIDEO TO DVD TRANSFER
spruce technologies

SINGLE AND MULTI-DISC DVD BURNERS
pioneer . ultera . hoei sangyo

CD/DVD DUPLICATORS & PRINTERS
primera . mediaFORM . microtech . hoei sangyo
rimage . CeDaR . microboards

STREAMING MEDIA
carbonwave . terran . real networks

NLE SYSTEMS - ONLINE/MPEG/DV/FILM
fast . dps . canopus . matrox . pinnacle . trakker
avid

EFFECTS COMPOSITING
adobe . bigfx . boris . pinnacle . ultimatte

FIBRE & SCSI STORAGE
rorke data . transoft . medea

ERGONOMIC WORKSTATIONS
winsted . nightingale

minneapolis
612.377.3100

chicago
312.595.9100

nationwide
877.725.0575

sales . rentals . training . support

The Gold Book™

For 20 years Penco has been taking orders from the Twin Cities Professional Design Community, now we have added one more way to take them.

ArtSuppliesOnline.com

is our very own, e-commerce web site. With over 30,000 items in the database, you are sure to find what you are after.

NOW SELLS ONLINE AT
artsuppliesonline.com

- Using latest Secure technology from Verisign, the leader in web safe transactions
- Payment options include Major Credit Cards, or net 30 for established Penco account holders
- Custom Shopping list for quick and easy ordering of staple items • Huge product database
- Easy to navigate, clear, clean design • Shop by categories, popular products, or key word search

Retail store open 7 days a week
Close to Downtown business center
Easy access from all directions
Great prices, selection and service

Penco Artists' Supply Warehouse
718 Washington Ave North
Minneapolis, MN 55401

Call 612-333-3330 x 1 for orders and customer service
or 800-967-7367 x1 outside metro area   Fax 612-333-0200

We are proud to be celebrating our 20th year in business!

FOREWORD

Welcome to the 20th annual edition of *THE GOLD BOOK*, the definitive directory of the creative services industry of Minnesota.

The 2001-2002 edition contains many new firms — as well as some entirely new service categories — while retaining all of the traditional convenience of *THE GOLD BOOK* as a desktop reference guide. New this year is *THE GOLD BOOK ONLINE*. Check it out at **gogoldbook.com!**

The continuing growth of creative services in the Twin Cities has made it the fourth largest center in the nation for this important and influential industry.

We have again this year attempted to identify, locate and contact every firm engaged in the industry in each of the major activity or service categories, and through telephone interviews and questionnaires, compile detailed current information on them. Because we rely on the information furnished to us, we assume that the data as provided and published is correct, but Prime Publications, inc. and *THE GOLD BOOK* are not responsible for the accuracy or completeness of the information as supplied.

As in the past, we welcome the suggestions of users and listees. Our goal is to provide this dynamic and rapidly evolving industry — and those businesses and individuals who rely on its services — with the most comprehensive, current and accurate resource guide available. We continue to rely heavily on your cooperation, interest and support.

The Publishers.

Published by
Prime Publications, Inc.

Duffy Busch
Publisher

Jennifer Busch
Associate Publisher/
Managing Editor

Colleen Moren
Editorial Assistant

Peggy White
Julie Diaz
Production Assistants

The Gold Book

THE GOLD BOOK
title and format
Copyright
Prime Publications, Inc.
All rights reserved.
Address editorial and
advertising inquiries to

Prime Publications, Inc.
318 Groveland Avenue
Minneapolis, MN 55403
Tel: (612) 872-7700
Toll Free: (888) 590-3965
e-mail: info@primepub.com
web: www.primepub.com

Reproduction of
the contents of
this book for
any purpose is
strictly prohibited.

Information contained in listings has been provided by the listed firm. The information as furnished and published is assumed to be accurate, but Prime Publications, Inc. and THE GOLD BOOK assume no responsibility for the accuracy or completeness of the information supplied, nor is any recommendation or endorsement implied or intended by inclusion of the firm or individual listed in this directory.

ISBN 0-932053-22-X
$19.95

CONTENTS

Advertising Agencies 11
Advertising Agencies -
    Classified & Yellow Pages .. 55
Advertising, Publishers & Media Reps . 56
Animation 58
Art Directors 63
Artist & Photographer Representatives 66
Artists & Art Studios 70
Audio Visual Services 83
Awards   92
Bindery Services 93
Branding & Brand Development 94
Broadcast Media 101
Business Research 105
Business Support 107
Cartography 109
Celebrity Acquisition 110
Computer Graphics & Digital Imaging 111
Corporate Advertising &
    PR Departments 123
Corporate Communications, Meeting,
    Satellite & Teleconferencing 125
Desktop Publishing 130
Direct Marketing/Database Marketing 134
Direct Marketing/Direct Response ... 136
Direct Marketing/Fulfillment 150
Direct Marketing/Telemarketing 147
Direct Marketing/Tracking 149
Displays, Exhibits & Banners 151
Editors & Editorial Services 160
Education & Training 167
Electronic Graphics 174
Electronic Prepress 179

CONTENTS

Entertainment Agencies 183
Event Planning 184
Executive Search Services 190
Film & Video Producers 191
Film & Video Support 218
Film Processing 248
Game, Puzzle & Toy Designers 250
Graphic Designers 251
Graphics Consultants 275
Graphics Temporaries 280
Indoor Advertising & Signage 283
Industrial & Product Designers 284
Industry Organizations 286
Legal Services 290
Libraries: Photo, Slide, Film & Music . 292
Licensing Agents 298
Literary Agents 299
Location Scouting 300
Marketing Agencies 301
Marketing Communications 313
Marketing Consultants 331
Marketing Research 344
Media Planning & Buying 357
Mergers & Acquisitions 360
Model & Talent Agencies 361
Music & Jingles 369
Naming Services 378
Outdoor Advertising & Signage 379
Package Designers 384
Photo Stylists 389
Photographers 392
Photographers - Advertising 394
Photographers - Architectural 420

Photographers - Industrial 424
Photographers - News & PR 426
Photomechanical Services 427
Point of Purchase 428
Premium & Specialty Advertising 431
Presentation Services 438
Printing Services 440
Production Management 453
Props & Costumes 454
Public Relations 461
Publications 476
Publishers 476
Publishers - Books 496
Publishers - Custom 501
Publishers - Periodical 503
Radio 509
Recording & Sound Services 514
Retail Promotion 525
Retouching Services 527
Sales Promotion & Incentives 530
Schools 535
Screen Printers 536
Set Design/Set Styling 537
Slides 540
Speakers & Speakers Bureaus 543
Sports & Entertainment Marketing ... 545
Sweepstakes & Contest Designers .. 546
Telemarketing Consultants &
    Service Bureaus 547
Teleprompters 548
Television - Broadcast 549
Television - Cable Access 550
Temporary Staffing 551
Translators 554
Typesetting & Typographers 558
Voice Talent 560
Writers 563
Writers - Advertising 571
Writers - Editorial 583
Writers - Technical 590

ON THE WEB AT

gogoldbook.com

Advertising Agencies

A

A B DILLON — 612-349-2706
333 N. Washington Avenue #404 — Minneapolis 55401
FAX: 612-349-2707
CONTACT: William Andrews
E-MAIL: wandrews@dillonagency.com
WWW: dillonagency.com
CAPABILITIES: A B provides full advertising, multi-media web sites. This involves TV, radio, print, sales promotion, direct response and web site development.
CURRENT/RECENT CLIENTS/PROJECTS: American Express, Gelco, Lunds/Byerly's, Syntegra

A LIGHT COMMUNICATIONS — 612-781-3879
PO Box 18015 — Minneapolis 55418
FAX: 612-781-0922
CONTACT: Adele Bergstrom
E-MAIL: lightcom@uswest.net
SERVICES: Advertising copywriting and design: direct mail; business-to-business; community and customer newsletters; press releases; brochures; directories; specialty advertising pieces. "One bright idea deserves another."
CAPABILITIES: Developing creative strategies based on an overall marketing plan that delivers a cohesive message while making the most of your advertising dollars.
SPECIALTIES: From initial concept to file on disk; Mackintosh platform; Illustrator, PhotoShop, Quark experience. Samples available on request.
PRESIDENT/CEO/OWNER: Adele Bergstrom

ADAMS' PRODUCE — 763-553-1714
2664 Shenandoah Lane — Plymouth 55447
CONTACT: Toni Adams
SERVICES: Art direction: concept development through finished piece. Associated staff of account executives with consumer and business-to-business experience. Additional associated staff includes writers, designers, illustrators and a media buyer.
CAPABILITIES: Over 20 years experience in advertising, designed marketing, promotion and direct mail, Macintosh and traditionally trained with the latest equipment and upgrades. Products produced include: Ads, collateral, direct mail packages, web ready graphics and copy.
CURRENT/RECENT CLIENTS/PROJECTS: Previous experience working with Ad Agencies on consumer and business experience and currently working with national, global corporate and industrial accounts.

ALLOUT MARKETING, INC. — 952-404-0800
742 Twelve Oaks Center — Wayzata 55391
15500 Wayzata Blvd.
FAX: 952-404-0900
CONTACT: Christine Mignogna, Director of First Impressions/Cheryl Schwanke, Marketing Guru
E-MAIL: marketing@alloutmarketinginc.com

12 / Advertising Agencies

CAPABILITIES: Full-service strategic marketing firm which identifies, develops, plans and implements effective, revenue-generating global marketing visions for technology-based, high-tech, and biotechnology/medical companies. AOM offers a comprehensive portfolio of services including Marketing Consulting, Market Research, Internet Marketing, Graphic Design, Event Management and Public Relations. This wide range of offerings, backed by extensive experience in business development, provides a powerful combination for AllOut Marketing clients. AOM clients benefit from a focused analysis of their current business environment that leads to clear cut global strategies for revenue growth.
SPECIALTIES: Business-to-Business; Technology-based; High-tech; Biotechnology/Medical
PRESIDENT/CEO/OWNER: Ruth R. Lane

ANDERSON-MADISION ADVERTISING, INC.   612-835-5133
7710 Computer Avenue   Minneapolis 55435
FAX: 612-835-4977
CONTACT: Christopher J. Madison
SERVICES: Advertising and public relations, communication and marketing of leading edge manufacturing technologies through effective advertising publicity strategies.
CAPABILITIES: Full service capabilities for new and traditional media.

ANIMUSE.COM   612-823-2880
3152 Elliot Avenue South   Minneapolis 55407
FAX: 612-823-2880
CONTACT: Bill Dobbs
E-MAIL: bdobbs@animuse.com
WWW: animuse.com
SERVICES: Advertising and design for individuals and small businesses; Animation and CD-ROM's; Website design and programming; Illustration; Logos; Print & internet advertising.
CURRENT/RECENT CLIENTS/PROJECTS: Another Land Travel; Bernafon Hearing Aids; Blues Buster Light Bulbs; Embodied Arts; Great Plains TV; Gladwin Machinery; KTCA-TV; The Kydd Group; Patrick's Cabaret; RAM Automated Equipment; Rotary International; St. Paul Chamber Orchestra; Science Museum of Minnesota; Sovran Companies; StarTribune; Talisman Silks; and Trend Enterprises.

ARMOUR PHOTOGRAPHY   612-341-2858
212 N. 3rd Avenue #290   Minneapolis 55401
FAX: 612-341-2384
CONTACT: Hope Armour
E-MAIL: japhoto@bitstream.net
SERVICES: Conceptual still life and super clean product representation.
CAPABILITIES: Commercial photography created for the advertising and design community. Our happy and talented staff includes two full time photographers, production coordinator and studio manager.
CURRENT/RECENT CLIENTS/PROJECTS: Peterson Milla Hooks, Martin Williams, Kerker, Hunt Adkins, Carmichael Lynch, GraphiCulture, Group Design, Prospera & Target.
PRESIDENT/CEO/OWNER: Jake Armour

Advertising Agencies / 13

THE ARNOLD GROUP   612-339-0714
105 5th Avenue South #450   Minneapolis 55401
FAX: 612-339-2440
CONTACT: Dan Arnold
E-MAIL: info@arnoldgroup.com
WWW: arnoldgroup.com
SERVICES: A full-service, integrated marketing agency specializing in developing strategies that build brands, strengthen relationships and drive sales. Strategic planning, collateral and sales support materials, catalogs, advertising, point-of-purchase materials, new media (web sites and CD-ROM), packaging, annual reports and direct marketing.
CAPABILITIES: Outdoor recreation, home improvement, medical and technical.

THE ART FARM ADVERTISING, INC.   651-293-0162
310 Sherman Street   St. Paul 55102
FAX: 651-293-0204
CONTACT: Pat Salkowicz, Mark Gates
E-MAIL: artfarm@bitstream.net
SERVICES: Full-service advertising and marketing agency specializing in retail, consumer, publishing, direct mail and sales promotion.

AVA GROUP INC.   651-766-9500
480 W. Highway 96, #100   St. Paul 55126
CONTACT: Pam Miller
E-MAIL: jpedalty@avagroup.com
CAPABILITIES: Full-service marketing communications firm devoted to medial, health care and wellness businesses. We offer a full spectrum of services from consultation through produced materials in many mediums including the web.
SPECIALTIES: Help medical and health care businesses position their companies and their products, develop strategies and messages that reach and motivate the target audience. We bring clients decades of experience in the medical device, HMO, hospital home health care and wellness industries.

B

BARD ADVERTISING, INC.   612-340-1100
540 Lumber Exchange Building   Minneapolis 55402
10 South 5th Street
FAX: 612-340-1199
CONTACT: Barbra Stabno
SERVICES: Full service marketing communications agency focusing on co-marketing consumer promotions, trade promotions, corporate identity and advertising awareness campaigns.
PRESIDENT/CEO/OWNER: Barbra Stabno

BBDO MINNEAPOLIS   612-338-8401
150 South 5th Street   Minneapolis 55402

14 / Advertising Agencies

OFFICERS: Bob Thacker, President/CEO; Tom Keating, SVP/Mgmt Supv'r; Wes Crawford, SVP/Mgmt Supv'r; Steve Hayes, SVP/Mgmt Supv'r; Dennis Haley, EVP/Exec. CD; Nancy Rice, SVP/Group CD; Jeff Harrington, VP/Bus Development; Carolyn Hubbartt, VP/Media Director
ACCOUNT SUPERVISORS: Gary Hohman, Peter Murphy, Sue Perkins, Evonne Groves, Bryan Ojala, Lisa Greenberg, Tim Buggy, Penny Utecht, Mike Alberts
CURRENT/RECENT CLIENTS/PROJECTS: Dodge Dealers Assoc.; Hormel Foods Corporation; Buffets, Inc.; TCF Bank; Fiserv, Dain Rauscher
BILLINGS: $100 million

THE BENYAS AD GROUP INC

Advertising + Design

THE BENYAS AD GROUP, INC.	**612-340-9804**
126 North Third Street, Suite 300	**Minneapolis 55401**

FAX: 612-334-5950
CONTACT: Bradley A. Benyas
E-MAIL: benyas@visi.com
SPECIALTIES: Results-oriented marketing support materials, product literature, capabilities brochures, print advertising. Specialized fields include: high technology, development/construction, education, financial, insurance, business-to-business, manufacturer-to-distributor.

BLAZE MARKETING GROUP, INC.	**651-602-0499**
380 South Lafayette Freeway #210	**St. Paul 55107**

FAX: 651-602-0779
CONTACT: Stephen R. Smith
E-MAIL: don@blazemarketing.com
WWW: blazemarketing.com
SERVICES: Full service ad agency/marketing firm specializing in small to medium size businesses. Development and implementation of long term strategic marketing plans. Mediums include: television, radio, print, e-commerce and web sites, industrial videos.
CAPABILITIES: We specialize in medium to small businesses and work on a result oriented basis.
CURRENT/RECENT CLIENTS/PROJECTS: All Glass Minnesota; Batteries Plus; Lakeland Medical Academy; Now Bikes & Fitness; Cheapo Records and Tapes; Mach 1
PRESIDENT/CEO/OWNER: Don J. Schulz

THE BOB PETERSON GROUP	**952-473-1501**
15500 Wayzata Blvd, #911	**Wayzata 55391**

FAX: 952-475-1756

Advertising Agencies / 15

CONTACT: Mike Peterson
E-MAIL: mikebpg@2z.net
SPECIALTIES: Assisting the corporate marketing effort by providing creative support for all phases of product promotion and company identification. Agency role varies from developing total market strategies to specific project involvement, all within a personal and highly responsive agency environment. Specialized fields include: forestry, industrial, construction equipment and building materials, chemicals, food, dairy, agriculture, automotive, and recreational/fitness products.
CURRENT/RECENT CLIENTS/PROJECTS: Accessory Research Engineering, Allied Equipment, Brush Technology, Carlson Tractor & Equipment, Cimline, Inc., Easy Auger, FEC/Food Engineering Corporation, Gamet Manufacturing, Garlock Equipment Company, Govesan, Jacobson LLC, Native American Tubcraft, Nu-Con Equipment, Tioga Inc., Vendtronics LLC, Waconia Manufacturing.
PRESIDENT/CEO/OWNER: Michael Peterson, P; Kristi Johnson, VP

BOZELL KAMSTRA
612-371-7500
100 North 6th Street #800A
Minneapolis 55403
FAX: 612-371-7540
CONTACT: Bill Coontz
WWW: bozellkamstra.com
SERVICES: Consumer packaged goods, consumer products and services, business branding.
CAPABILITIES: Full service public relations, advertising (print and broadcast), yellow page advertising, business and technical, interactive.
SALES CONTACT: Officers: Dean Buresh, President; Bill Coontz, Partner, General Manager; Claire Canavan, Chief Financial Officer; Ron Anderson, VC & Exe. Creative Director; David Dasenbrock, Partner in Charge, Media; Katherine Johnson, Partner, Director of Client Services; Jack Stanton, Partner, Director of Strategic Planning. Bob Kay, Partner, Creative Director. Connie McCaffrey, Partner, Director of Public Relations.
CURRENT/RECENT CLIENTS/PROJECTS: Billy Graham Evangelical Association; Cargill Foods; Ceridian Employer Services; Deluxe Corp; eFunds; General Mills, Inc.'; GOVT.com; Hurd Millwork Company; North Star Steel; Schwan's Grocery Products Division; Wagner Spray Tech.
AFFILIATED OFFICES: Austin, TX; Boston, MA; Cleveland, OH; Dallas, TX; New York, NY; Pittsburgh, PA

BROWNE & BROWNE MARKETING, INC.
612-341-3008
275 Market Street #541
Minneapolis 55405
International Market Square
FAX: 612-341-0965
CONTACT: Timothy Browne
E-MAIL: tim@jgic.com
SERVICES: Full-service national marketing communications firm. The agency has a 13 year track record of delivering innovative marketing solutions with proven market share increases for both Fortune 500 and regional companies including consumer products, packaged goods, retail, automotive, sports manufacturers, broadcast media, optical, high-tech and financial.
SPECIALTIES: Promotional marketing, strategic planning, business-to-business, event marketing, sponsorships, dealer association advertising, Affinity Marketing Plus, Marketing Services Audit, Measurement and analysis.
CURRENT/RECENT CLIENTS/PROJECTS: Walman Optical; Chrysler Motors Corporation; Vinyl Art; Minneapolis-St. Paul Dodge Dealers; 3M; Midwest Sports Channel; Green Eagle Sports; Human Life Alliance, Inc.; Cedarcrest Academy.

16 / Advertising Agencies

PRESIDENT/CEO/OWNER: Timothy P. Browne, P; Colleen M. Ohrbeck, EVP and Creative Director

C

Campbell | Mithun

CAMPBELL MITHUN   **612-347-1000**
222 South Ninth Street   **Minneapolis 55402**
FAX: 612-347-1515
CONTACT: Ann Baxter, New Business Manager
OFFICERS: Bill Dunlap, Chairman & CEO; Les Mouser, President & COO; John Hurst, EVP/Chief Creative Officer; Rick Gibson, EVP, Associate Creative Officer; George Halvorson, EVP, Deputy Creative Officer; Patricia Cameron, EVP, Director of Strategic Planning; Richard Lynch, EVP/Director of Account Planning; Earl Herzog, EVP/Contact Planning Director; Peter Bach, EVP/ Chief Financial Officer; Rich Rosengren, EVP/Director of Business Development
CREATIVE DIRECTOR: Jim Bosha, EVP/Executive Creative Director; David Duncan, SVP/Executive Creative Director; Cathy Grisham, SVP/Executive Creative Director; Steve Jankowski, SVP/Executive Creative Director; Bob Brihn, VP/Creative Director; John Bussjager, VP/Creative Director; Harry Gonnella, VP/Creative Director; Kelly Gothier, VP/Creative Director; Bill Johnson, VP/Creative Director; Carl Kidd, Creative Director; Steve Maresch, SVP/Creative Director; Christy Martin, SVP/Creative Director; Barb Meeker, VP/Creative Director; Chris Mihock, VP/Creative Director; Greg Prokop, SVP/Creative Director; Rob Wallace, SVP/Creative Director; Scott Webster, VP/Creative Director; Mark Wildenhaus, Creative Director; David Weinstock, SVP/Director of Design
GROUP ACCOUNT MANAGERS: Roxann Goertz, SVP/Group Account Manager; Don Kvam, EVP/Group Account Manager - Package Goods; Beth Miller, SVP, Group Account Manager; Rich Rosengren, EVP/Group Account Manager; Virginia Vonckx, EVP/Group Account Manager - Retail 2000; Steve Wehrenberg, EVP/Group Account Manager - Technology & Service
MEDIA DIRECTOR: Lee Baker, SVP/Group Media Director; Mary Gelderman, VP/Associate Media Director; Alan Gersten, SVP/Group Media Director; Earl Herzog, Media Director; Mia Hoagberg, Associate Media Director; Rebecca Hoeppner, Associate Media Director; Tom McCarthy, VP/Media Operations Director; John Rash, SVP/Director of Broadcast Negotiations; Jim Romlin, SVP/Group Media Director; Julia Tangeman, VP/Associate Media Director

Advertising Agencies / 17

ACT PLANNING/COMM GROUP/DIGITAL RES: Research and Planning: Patricia Cameron, EVP/Director of Strategic Planning; Richard Lynch, EVP/Director of Account Planning. Promotion Marketing: Tom Tessman, SVP/Director of Promotion; Joe Rossini, VP/Director of Planning. Direct Marketing: Michelle Arntzen, VP/Director of Direct Marketing; Charles Lecrone, Director of Broadcast Media Services. Public Relations: Paula Baldwin, SVP/Director of Public Relations. Digital Resources: Brian Sullivan, SVP/Director of Graphic Services. Autonomous Operating Units: Cash Plus, Inc. Dick Hurrelbrink, CEO; Pedersen Gest, Brian Buldoon, President
CURRENT/RECENT CLIENTS/PROJECTS: ADC, Agrilink Foods (Birds Eye), Alberto Culver, Andersen Corporation, American Academy of Dermatology, BlueLight.com, Bordon, Inc., Celestial Seasonings, CNS, Inc., DoTheGood.com, Eli Lilly, Fanball.com, Frigidaire, General Mills, H&R Block, HoMedics, Interstate Bakeries Corporation, Jr-s.com, KB Gear Interactive, KeyCorp, Kimberly-Clark, Kmart Corporation, Land O'Lakes, Minnesota Department of Health, Minnesota Public Radio, Minnesota Wild, MoneyGram Payment Systems, Inc., National Easter Seals, Novartis Seeds, Pactiv, Qwest, RedTag.com, Resealworld.com, Schwan's, Specialty Brands, The St. Paul Companies, The Toro Company, United HealthCare, ValueVision, Verio, Verizon Wireless (formely AirTouch)
BILLINGS: $960 million at year-end 1999. Offices: Irvine, CA; New York, NY; Seattle, WA; Detroit, MI
SPECIALTIES: Market Segment Specialties: Campbell Mithun KidCom tm: Lynne Robertson, VP/General Manager; Campbell Mithun Health & Wellness: Beth Miller, SVP/Director

CANTON COMMUNICATIONS, INC.   612-925-5873
6075 Lincoln Drive #104   Minneapolis 55436
CONTACT: John Canton
SERVICES: All areas of advertising with strong emphasis on broadcast media, radio-TV production. AFTRA Signator services.
CURRENT/RECENT CLIENTS/PROJECTS: Metro Bowling Proprietors Assn. (Gold Pin Bowling Centers); Sea Note Cruises; AMF Bowling Centers; Danger Recording Studio; Nokomis Lanes Bowling Center; Boca Chica Restaurant; Saint Croix National Golf Course; MN House DFL Caucus; Pearson Candy Company; Silver Springs Golf Course; Tedd Hoyt (Lincoln Financial Advisors); Carousel Shows; Cartier Lighting; William Flaskamp, Attorney; Piguin Bowling Centers.

CARLSON CUNICO, INC.   651-292-1992
405 Sibley Street #115   St. Paul 55101
FAX: 651-224-1162
CONTACT: Jayne Dumas
WWW: ekquehl.com
SERVICES: Carlson Cunico has been acquired by e.k. Quehl Company. See that listing for information concerning services and specialties.

CARMICHAEL LYNCH, INC.   612-334-6000
800 Hennepin Avenue   Minneapolis 55403
FAX: 612-334-6090
CONTACT: John Colasanti
E-MAIL: firstinitial,lastname@clynch.com
WWW: carmichaellynch.com
CAPABILITIES: Full service advertising agency with PR, design and interactive divisions.

18 / Advertising Agencies

CURRENT/RECENT CLIENTS/PROJECTS: A.T. Cross; American Standard, Inc.; babyCenter.com; Big Idea Productions, Inc.; Brown-Forman Beverages Worldwide; Capella University; Cargill Corporation; Caribou Coffee Company, Inc.; Department 56; ezgov.com; Formica Corporation; Gibson Guitars; Harley-Davidson Motor Company; The HoneyBaked Ham Company; Minnesota Office of Tourism; Rapala Normark Group, Inc.; Northwest Airlines; Porsche Cars North America, Inc.; Sunbeam Corporation; The Trane Company; Trex Company, Inc.; Volvo Trucks North America; White Wave, Inc.; ZapMedia.

CHANCE/NELSON & ASSOCIATES, INC.   952-941-9660
7201 West 78th Street #230   **Minneapolis 55439**
FAX: 952-941-3460
CONTACT: Russ Chance or Carl Nelson
E-MAIL: carroll@chancenelson.com
CAPABILITIES: Advertising Agency.
SPECIALTIES: A full-service agency with special emphasis in financial, health care and business-to-business marketing communications.
CURRENT/RECENT CLIENTS/PROJECTS: Thermo King, Wells Fargo, Copeland Buhl CPA's, St. Francis Regional Medical Center, Sick, Inc., Wells Fargo Investment & Trust Services.

CITY'S BEST MARKETING, INC.   952-888-1174
10740 Lyndale Avenue S #15E   **Minneapolis 55420**
FAX: 952-888-2764
CONTACT: Linda E. Kelley, Lynn Adler
WWW: c-b-m.com
SERVICES: Full service marketing communications and design firm. Creative/Design/Print Services, Marketing Strategy development. Corporate identity development. Target/Direct Marketing (business-to-business and consumer), Website Design, Media Negotiation/Placement, Package Design.
CURRENT/RECENT CLIENTS/PROJECTS: Firstel Federal Credit Union; 3M; Karastan Floor Design Gallery; Southview Design & Landscaping; Packnet; Tecnifoam Manufacturing; Minneapolis Convention Center; Minnesota Department of Transportation; Minnesota Wire and Cable; ECI Corp.; Construction Services; Newman Financial; Uptime Computer Service; Coit
PRESIDENT/CEO/OWNER: Linda E. Kelly, P; Lynn Adler, VP Sales

CLARITY
COVERDALE
FURY

CLARITY COVERDALE FURY, INC.   612-339-3902
120 S 6th Street #1300   **Minneapolis 55402**

Advertising Agencies / 19

FAX: 612-359-4399
WWW: ccf-ideas.com
OFFICERS: Tim B. Clarity, CEO, P; Jac Coverdale, EVP; Jerry Fury, VP; Gary Hellmer, VP; Bob Schulke, VP; Diane Ethier, VP.
CREATIVE DIRECTOR: Jac Coverdale
MEDIA DIRECTOR: Diane Ethier
ACCOUNT SUPERVISORS: Gary Hellmer, Marcy Little, Ann Wiessner, Sarah Guilday, Rob Rankin, Patrick Daugherty
BILLINGS: $67 million.
CURRENT/RECENT CLIENTS/PROJECTS: The Malt-O-Meal Company; Perry Italian Sausage; Belvedere Vodka; ReliaStar Financial; Chopin Vodka; University of St. Thomas; HealthSystem Minnesota; Galleria Shopping Center; Mercedes-Benz Automobiles; Altru Health System; DBI/SALA; Harmon AutoGlass; Michael Foods; Crystal Farms; Johnsonville Sausage; Juut SalonSpa; Pillsbury Bakeries and Foodservice.

COMO CONSORTIUM, LTD.   763-521-4955
2933 Quail Avenue North   **Golden Valley 55422**
FAX: 763-632-2380
CONTACT: Lance Como
CAPABILITIES: Free-agent creative, graphic design and production, specializing in print media with the bulk of our work being ads, annual reports, brochures, direct mail, packaging and outdoor for national and regional accounts (samples of our work at www.comoltd.com).
SPECIALTIES: Digital file distribution and no bullshit graphic production for award-winning clients. We always achieve our goals by satisfying our clients. We always satisfy our clients by doing things right--the first time.
CURRENT/RECENT CLIENTS/PROJECTS: 99' include AlphaBetas, Inc., St. Paul, MN; Americsan MedTech, St. Paul, MN; American Safety Technologies, Roseland, NJ; Billboards, Eden Prairie, MN; Famous Dave's of America, Eden Prairie, MN; Grand Pines Resorts, Hayward, WI; Kaufman Marketing Group, Jackson, WY; La Pura Ujungla, Satra Cruz, Costa Rica; Merita NordBanken, New York, NY
PRESIDENT/CEO/OWNER: Lance Comp, President

CONCEPT GROUP INC.   651-221-9710
192 West Ninth Street   **St. Paul 55102**
FAX: 651-227-4591
CONTACT: Brad Moore
E-MAIL: info@conceptgroup.com
WWW: conceptgroup.com
SERVICES: Full-service marketing communications; strategic communications planning; account management; concept and creative development; design; computer illustration; copywriting; production; post production coordination and implementation; photography studio.
CAPABILITIES: Print advertising; collateral; direct marketing; brand and identity development; sales promotion and incentive programs; public relations; video concepting and scripting; interactive and electronic media; including web site planning, design, development and implementation; CD-ROM development
CURRENT/RECENT CLIENTS/PROJECTS: High tech, low tech and "no tech" clients - B to B and B to C.
PRESIDENT/CEO/OWNER: John Ruddy, P, Brad Moore, EVP, Jay Troe, VP/AD; Mike Davis, CD; Vicki Giefer, Director of Account Services; Mike Brunner, Director of Strategic Planning and Marketing; George Ramsay, Director of New Business Development; Paul Larson, Interactive Services Manager.

20 / Advertising Agencies

CRC, INC. 952-937-6000
6321 Bury Drive #10 Eden Prairie 55346
FAX: 952-937-5155
CONTACT: Cindy Owens, New Business Specialist
WWW: crc-inc.com

CREATIVE COMMUNICATIONS 612-338-5098
CONSULTANTS, INC.
111 3rd Avenue South #390 Minneapolis 55401
FAX: 612-338-1398
CONTACT: Susan McPherson
E-MAIL: smcpherson@cccinc.com
WWW: cccinc.com
SERVICES: Integrated marketing approach for business-to-business communications.
BILLINGS: Billings: $7.5 million
CURRENT/RECENT CLIENTS/PROJECTS: Business-to-business; transportation; plastics; recreation/leisure; communications; industrial; packaging; building products; utilities; hi-tech; machinery; process control.
PRESIDENT/CEO/OWNER: Susan McPherson, P/CEO; Claire Cunningham, VP, Acct. Services; Deb Hyden, Med. Director; Linda Franey, Production Manager; Claire Cunningham, Account Supervisor; Kevin Deshler, Laura Dockery, Dyan Padgett, Account Executives

CREATIVE RESOURCE CENTER/CRC, INC. 952-937-6000
6321 Bury Drive #10 Eden Prairie 55346
FAX: 952-937-5155
CONTACT: Cindy Owens, New Business Specialist
WWW: crc-inc.com
SERVICES: A full-service integrated marketing communications agency with 20 years experience in strategic communications planning across a range of delivery forms. Services include planning and implementation of strategic marketing communications, internet presence, sales promotion, relationship marketing, internet list development and maintenance, and development of full-scale e-commerce web stores. Full in-house planning and creative teams for both print and internet development include experts in planning, design, copy, content management, database design and development, website development, management, hosting and serving. In-house photography studio.
SPECIALTIES: Integrated marketing communications planning and implementation, internet business strategy, sales promotion including sales materials, collateral, POS, full integration of promotion on the internet including interactive relationship marketing. Corporate and brand identity programs, package design, business-to-business and consumer advertising, and direct mail.
CURRENT/RECENT CLIENTS/PROJECTS: CNS Interactive; FSMC; Graco; Haagen-Dazs Interactive, Interactive Learning Group (Video Buddy); Loffler Business Systems; McGlynn's Retail Bakeries; Multifoods Bakery Products; NK Lawn & Garden; Old Dutch; Pillsbury Interactive; Primera Technology; Rosemount Office Systems Interactive; Sargento Foods, Inc.; 3M Intranet.
PRESIDENT/CEO/OWNER: Michael Lundeby, CEO; Elizabeth Petrangelo, EVP; Joe Andrews, VP; Troy Braun, Creative Director

Advertising Agencies / 21

THE
cullinan
GROUP

AN INTEGRATED MARKETING AGENCY

1128 harmon place, suite 304
minneapolis, mn 55403

THE CULLINAN GROUP   **612-338-7636**
1128 Harmon Place, #304   **Minneapolis 55403**
FAX: 612-338-8173
CONTACT: Wayne Cullinan, Carol Miletti
E-MAIL: amenzel@cullinangroup.com; Wayne Cullinan - wcullinan@cullinangroup.com; Carol Miletti - cmiletti@cullinangroup.com
WWW: cullinangroup.com
SERVICES: Full service integrated marketing communications agency practicing strategic marketing in the disciplines of advertising, sales promotion and direct response. Additional services include retail marketing, point-of-purchase, merchandising, multi-media and event production. Billings: 20 million
CURRENT/RECENT CLIENTS/PROJECTS: GreenMountain.com; Orion Food Systems/Hot Stuff Pizza; Smash Hit Subs; Thinsulate/3M; Georgia Pacific/Vinyl Siding Divisions; Hearth Technologies/Heat-N-Glo Fireplaces; Pillsbury Foodservice/Bakery Division; General Mills/Yoplait Division
PRESIDENT/CEO/OWNER: Wayne A. Cullinan, P/CEO; Lynne Cullinan, COO; Jerry Little, VP/CD; Gary Scott, VP; Julie Bain, VP Account Planning & Interactive; Ron Signorelli, Gary A. Scott, Management Supervisors; Dana Misner, Shari Bell, Account Supervisor; Barb Shelstad, Nate Koepsell, Cheryl Turk, Gina Parker, Acct. Executives; Lori Haugesag, Manager of Production; Jerry Little, Lisa Proctor, Terri Wykle, Jim Davis, Matt Howd, Willie Ford, Wendy Lukaszewski, Creative.

D

D.S. ADV. ETC.   **952-595-8042**
5775 Wayzata Boulevard #960   **Minneapolis 55416**
FAX: 952-591-1932
CONTACT: David Schmieg
E-MAIL: dschmieg@concentric.net
CAPABILITIES: Advertising, design, art direction.

D.W. ET AL.   **612-339-7848**
400 First Avenue North #316   **Minneapolis 55401**
The Wyman Building
CONTACT: Dan Wallace
WWW: dwetal.com

22 / Advertising Agencies

CAPABILITIES: D.W. et al. Ltd. works with B2B firms to build businesses and brands. As consultants, we craft strategies and write plans. As marketing agents, we implement plans through a network we've cultivated since 1986. Core deliverables: strategic marketing plans, positioning and brand plans, company brochures, web sites and advertising campaigns. Extended capabilities are available through allied advisors and specialists.
SPECIALTIES: Business-to-business firms.
CURRENT/RECENT CLIENTS/PROJECTS: Alliant Consulting; The Bureau Electronics Division; Carlson School of Management IRC; City of Minneapolis ITS; e-fortunecookie.com; Fredrikson & Byron; GTE; hrtomorrow.com; Honeywell; IBM; KruegerWright; Norberg Management; NRG; personallitigation.com; PDI; Palamino Euro Bistro; Pro Group; Research Resources; Serving Software; The Collaborative; Wilson Learning; and Winona Research.

TODD DANIELS MARKETING & ADVERTISING 651-291-8074
26 East Exchange Street #610   St. Paul 55101
FAX: 651-297-6548
CONTACT: Dan Foote
E-MAIL: danf@todd-daniels.com
WWW: todd-daniels.com
SERVICES: Full-service marketing and advertising agency. Specialties include: strategic planning, corporate identities, point-of-purchase, literature development, public relations, ad design, media placement, event planning, direct mail, website design. Product positioning, tradeshow execution, and merchandising.
PRESIDENT/CEO/OWNER: Dan Foote, Todd Butzer

JEFFREY DARREL ADVERTISING 651-464-8960
PO Box 261   Forest Lake 55025
CONTACT: Jeff Brooks
E-MAIL: jdthegreat@aol.com
SERVICES: Full-service agency. Full advertising campaigns, media planner, publicity, radio production, public relations, promotions, consultant, jingle writer.
CURRENT/RECENT CLIENTS/PROJECTS: Deer Creek Cedar Homes; Coffee & Bytes Coffee Shop; Katie's K-9 Television Show on Pax TV.
PRESIDENT/CEO/OWNER: Jeff Brooks

DEMOTT ADVERTISING 763-498-7910
9800 Garden Lane   Rogers 55374
FAX: 763-498-7777
SERVICES: Full service ad agency specializing in business-to-business and high tech. Services include media selection and placement; creative for ads and collateral; direct mail; publicity and feature stories; sales incentive programs and more.
CONTACT: Garret DeMott

DESIGNSTEIN 612-339-0690
800 Washington Avenue North #205   Minneapolis 55401
FAX: 612-339-5895
CONTACT: Bill Helgeson
E-MAIL: info@designstein.com
WWW: designstein.com

Advertising Agencies / 23

SERVICES: Web building, site design, internet marketing, world wide web presence and content provider. Specializing in full-service solutions from content analysis through site design to back-end programming. Internet strategy, marketing and promotion.
CAPABILITIES: Full service web design agency. Innovative, results-based web site design and development. Emphasis on creativity and communication of corporate or brand identity.
CURRENT/RECENT CLIENTS/PROJECTS: Clairol; 3M; Faegre & Benson, LLP; Ceridian Corporation; Kopp Investment Advisors; Fairview Health Services; Wilson Learning Corporation; U.S. Bank; St. Paul Technical College; Minnesota Film Board; U.S. Department of Education; University of St. Thomas; Hospitality Minnesota.

DK&Y   **612-798-4070**
6009 Penn Avenue South   **Minneapolis 55419**
FAX: 612-798-4071
CONTACT: Brian Dahl
E-MAIL: sales@dkandy.com
WWW: dkandy.com
SERVICES: Integrated marketing and advertising agency offering account, creative, production and media services.
CURRENT/RECENT CLIENTS/PROJECTS: Winnebago Industries, The Toro Company, General Mills, International Home Foods, CTC Distribution Direct, Imani Sports, HEI, Uromedica.
PRESIDENT/CEO/OWNER: John Denn, Mark Yaeger; Mike Dobies, Mark Yaeger, Creative Directors; John Denn, Brian Dahl, Todd E. Scott, Account Supervisors

E

E. K. QUEHL COMPANY   **651-224-2423**
405 Sibley Street #115   **St. Paul 55101**
FAX: 651-224-1164
CONTACT: Jayne Dumas
WWW: ekquehl.com
SERVICES: For over three decades, we have provided a comprehensive array of integrated strategies, from marketing, design and digital imaging, advertising, and public relations to printing, promotional products and website development.
SPECIALTIES: Corporate identity and branding, business collateral, graphic design, direct mail, photography, copywriting, media placement, website design, construction and maintenance.
PRESIDENT/CEO/OWNER: Jayne Dumas, P; Patrick Siegrist, Mktg. Director; Kevin Hecimovich, AE; Kim Becker, AD; Tom Jestus, CD

E. LIVINGSTON & ASSOCIATES   **952-835-4080**
3305 Shepherd Hills Drive   **Bloomington 55431**
CONTACT: Edward Livingston
CAPABILITIES: Business-to-business advertising, public relations and sales promotion.
CURRENT/RECENT CLIENTS/PROJECTS: National manufacturers and marketers of industrial and technical products.

24 / Advertising Agencies

ELLIOTT HOUSE ADVERTISING GROUP   651-698-3083
PO Box 65782   St. Paul 55165
FAX: 651-695-0886
CONTACT: James Brooks
E-MAIL: irish@mn.state.net
SERVICES: Advertising media on college campuses in the Midwest and Central states.
PRESIDENT/CEO/OWNER: James Brooks

F

FABER SHERVEY ADVERTISING   952-944-5111
8101 Lea Road   Bloomington 55438
CONTACT: Paul Shervey
CREATIVE: Paul Shervey, Creative Director
ACCOUNT SUPERVISORS: Paul Shervey, Jay Huebsher
SPECIALTIES: Business-to-business, construction and industrial.

FALLEK AND ASSOCIATES   612-545-7001
7515 Wayzata Boulevard   Minneapolis 55426
FAX: 612-545-7020
E-MAIL: aisbofmn@aol.com
SERVICES: Specializes in education and industrial advertising and direct marketing.
CURRENT/RECENT CLIENTS/PROJECTS: DeskTop Labels; Meyers Printing Company; American Institute of Small Business; Forest and Floral Garden Center; National Shooting Sports Foundation.
PRESIDENT/CEO/OWNER: Max Fallek

THE FALLS AGENCY   612-872-6372
2550 Blaisdell Avenue South   Minneapolis 55404
FAX: 612-872-1018
CONTACT: Peggy Arnson
E-MAIL: s.lund@fallsagency.com

Advertising Agencies / 25

SPECIALTIES: Full service agency with print, broadcast and web capabilities. Comprehensive, marketing-based approach to local and national advertising, including trade, retail and specialized dealer programs; for clients in recreational/outdoor products, e-commerce, restaurants, banking, publishing and real estate.
OFFICERS: Robert Falls, CEO; Sharon Lund, President
ACCOUNT SUPERVISORS: Toni Baraga, Melissa Carraher
CREATIVE DIRECTOR: Peggy Arnson
BILLINGS: $13 million

FOX COMMUNICATIONS, INC.   952-546-8488
2340 Daniels Street Suite B   Long Lake 55356
FAX: 952-546-8756
CONTACT: Connie Piepho
E-MAIL: cpiepho@foxcommunications.com

CAPABILITIES: Full-service agency, specializing in business-to-busines and multi-location retail, with advertising, marketing, direct response and direct mail, yellow pages, print, outdoor and broadcast media expertise.
CURRENT/RECENT CLIENTS/PROJECTS: Dental Services Group; Distribution Services, Inc.; Sterling Optical; Plymouth Plumbing; Benson-Orth Associates.
PRESIDENT/CEO/OWNER: Connie Piepho

FREELANCE CONSORTIUM   612-824-5398
5728 12th Avenue South   Minneapolis 55417
CONTACT: Stephanie Fox

SERVICES: Advertising in creative print and collateral material including internal and external publications, collateral material, newsletters and annual reports, PR writing and events.
CURRENT/RECENT CLIENTS/PROJECTS: Health One; Mr. Tire; Lyndale Hardware; Ludlow, Inc.; The Chaconnes; American Chemical; Ellerbe Becket; Prodea Inc.; Cloudwalk Women's Wellness Center; TundraWare; Veronica Casey Law Offices; US Federal Credit Union.

G

GABRIEL DIERICKS RAZIDLO

GABRIEL DIERICKS RAZIDLO 612-547-5000
900 Second Avenue South #1770 Minneapolis 55402
FAX: 612-547-5090
CONTACT: Tom Gabriel
OFFICERS: Tom Gabriel, P & CD; Marianne Diericks, Client Services/GM; Mark Razidlo, Client Services/CFM
CURRENT/RECENT CLIENTS/PROJECTS: Black Forest Inn; DuPont Corian®; DuPont Zodiaq; Eat Street; HEWI, Inc.; Hunter Douglas Window Fashions; Irish Setter Boots; Library Foundation of Hennepin County; Phillips Beverage Company; Red Wing Shoes; Science Museum of Minnesota; Star Tribune; Target; The Thymes Limited; US Bancorp Piper Jaffray; Vasque Boots.

GEOFFREY CARLSON GAGE, LLC 952-401-7660
500 Lake Street #100 Excelsior 55331
FAX: 952-401-7662
CONTACT: Geoff Gage
E-MAIL: info@gcgage.com
WWW: gcgage.com

Advertising Agencies / 27

SERVICES: Advertising Services: consulting, strategic planning, creative concepting and development, media planning and buying, production coordination. Internet Services: Consulting and existing site analysis, strategic planning, creative concepting and site development, electronic development/programming, ongoing site maintenance, online web site search engine visibility promotion.
CAPABILITIES: Geoffrey Carlson Gage is a strategically creative Internet and advertising solutions agency, whose mission is to grow our client's business, sell their products and/or services and build their brands in an affordable manner. There are five major points-of-difference separating us from our competitors. 1) Our ability (based on our background and expertise) as a small advertising agency to create, develop, and deliver an integrated combination of breakthrough traditional media advertising and interactive advertising/web site development. 2) Our ability as a small advertising agency to create, develop, and deliver creative, multi-disciplined, value driven web sites based on a balance of advertising, marketing and technology practices and principles. 3) Our ability to create, develop, and deliver a combination of traditional advertising and online search engine visibility promotion to drive traffic to sites. 4) Our tremendous flexibility centered on client needs, and 5) Our partnership with local and national Internet service provider, US Internet.
CURRENT/RECENT CLIENTS/PROJECTS: Condor Corporation; Stars of Aspen; Gage Marketing Group; Milestone Motorsports; The Minnesota Wild; Craig Young/Coldwell Burnet Realty; Bob Jasper/Fleet Corporate Aircraft Leasing; Metromark; CEPCO Management, Inc.; US Internet; Gage In-store Marketing; Midwave Corporation.
PRESIDENT/CEO/OWNER: Geoff Gage

GALLAGHER MEDIA, INC.   **952-853-2266**
2626 East 82nd Street #201   **Minneapolis 55425**
FAX: 952-853-2262
CONTACT: Anne Gallagher, Carrie DeNet
E-MAIL: anne.gmi@manleygroup.com
SERVICES: Since 1972, a flexible and collaborative approach to clients' needs, especially budgeting, media planning and placement, negotiation, marketing, political planning and placement.
CURRENT/RECENT CLIENTS/PROJECTS: Bachman's; Home Valu; Drexel; Taco John's; Mail Boxes Etc.; Kawasaki; Minnesota Department of Agriculture; Minnesota Business Partnership; Minnesota Beef Council; Parts Plus, and political candidates and issues nationwide.

GRAF ADVERTISING   **612-881-0031**
8609 Lyndale Avenue South   **Minneapolis 55420**
FAX: 805-753-8030
CONTACT: Rick Graf
E-MAIL: rickgraf@grafadvertising.com
WWW: grafadvertising.com
SERVICES: Graphic arts design, copywriting, web site design, digital animation, HTML writing, GUI design, banner ads, HTML newsletters, e-marketing, opt-in e-mail, e-zine sponsorships, event planning, media placement for print, radio, out-of-home, online ads and sponsorships, strategic marketing communications planning and consulting.
CAPABILITIES: Business marketing communications since 1980. Experience includes work with local, regional and national companies.
CURRENT/RECENT CLIENTS/PROJECTS: Fairview Hiawatha Pharmacy direct mail marketing campaign and out-of-home advertising; Vista Productions Web site and event marketing; Novartis Seeds, Inc's. Pro Shield point of purchase counter display; Minnesota American Marketing Assn. web site, HTML newsletter and e-marketing communications; Road Rescue national print ad campaign.

28 / Advertising Agencies

GRAPHIC RELIEF 612-386-8088
15207 94th Place North Maple Grove 55369
CONTACT: Tony Rubasch
E-MAIL: tonyr@graphicrelief.com
WWW: inet-serv.com/~tonyr
SPECIALTIES: A relief designer with strong emphaiss in retail direct mail catlaogs and web site creation for general consumer merchandise. Along with creative marketing communications for industrial manufacturing, food industry, retail clothing, recreation providers and health care.
CURRENT/RECENT CLIENTS/PROJECTS: Major advertising and marketing communication agencies in the Twin Cities location.

GRUGGEN BUCKLEY 612-321-0744
430 1st Avenue N. Suite 470 Minneapolis 55401
FAX: 612-321-0646
CONTACT: Terry Gruggen
E-MAIL: terry@gruggen.com or gordy@gruggen.com
WWW: gruggen.com
SERVICES: The agency specializes in the design and production of collateral materials. These include point-of-sale displays, in-store graphics, signage, brochures, newsletters, flyers, custom display pieces and retail maps. We are especially strong in retail applications that require fast turnaround and low costs.
CURRENT/RECENT CLIENTS/PROJECTS: AT&T Corporate; AT&T Wireless Services; Best Buy; CellularOne; Cincinnati Bell; Cincinnati Bell Wireless; Circuit City; Corporate Learning Center; Dobson Communications; Greene Holcomb & Fisher; Giant Eagle; iwireless; Lucent Technologies; McDonald's; Metrocall; Minnesota Timberwolves; Polaris; Office Depot; Red Cross; Rollerblade; Ronald McDonald House Charities; SFX Entertainment; SunCom; Target; Triton PCS; Valvoline Oil Company

H

HATLING & THOMAS 320-259-7976
1529 West St. Germain St. Cloud 56301
FAX: 320-259-0082
CONTACT: Joe Gibbons
E-MAIL: info@halting.com

Advertising Agencies / 29

WWW: hatling.com
SERVICES: Full service advertising and business communications.
CURRENT/RECENT CLIENTS/PROJECTS: Various 3M divisions; Stearms, Inc. (various divisions); Campbell's Soup Company; St. Cloud Convention & Visitor Bureau; Dezurik; Marco; St. Cloud Hospital.
PRESIDENT/CEO/OWNER: Bill Hatling

HEALTH CARE COMMUNICATIONS, INC.   651-436-1557
489 Quinnell Avenue North   Lakeland 55043
FAX: 651-436-3520
CONTACT: Sandra M. Hansen-Tollefson
SPECIALTIES: Full-service agency specializing in all aspects of medical product advertising, promotion and marketing communications.
CURRENT/RECENT CLIENTS/PROJECTS: Medical product companies, hospitals and other health-related businesses.
PRESIDENT/CEO/OWNER: Sandra M. Hansen-Tollefson

HEDSTROM/BLESSING, INC.   763-591-6200
8301 Golden Valley Road #300   Minneapolis 55427
FAX: 763-591-6232
CONTACT: Julie Pearl
E-MAIL: info@hb-inc.com
WWW: www.hb-inc.com
OFFICERS: Steve Blessing, Chm/CEO; Brenda Spanier, Pres/COO; Tom Blessing, VP; Julie Pearl, VP
SPECIALTIES: Consumer and business-to-business advertising and direct marketing; sales support including collateral, promotion, point-of-purchase, and presentations; identity and packaging graphics; interactive and website design.
CURRENT/RECENT CLIENTS/PROJECTS: Selected accounts include 3M; Bachman's; Carlson Leisure Group; Fabcon; Intellisol International; Interactive Learning Group; Land O'Lakes; Pillsbury; Target.

HENDLER - JOHNSTON, LLC   952-346-9258
9448 Lyndale Avenue South #222   Bloomington 55420
FAX: 952-346-9259
CONTACT: Adam Johnston
E-MAIL: ajohnston@hjmarketingdesign.com
WWW: hjmarketingdesign.com

30 / Advertising Agencies

SERVICES: Full range of corporate identity including the following: annual reports, direct mail, brochures, advertising, catalogs, packaging, posters, logos, collateral and much more. Web design and implementation of your site including e-business solutions.
CAPABILITIES: Industrial, financial, consumer branding of products or services. Clients retain H & J because they are seeking innovative solutions to their marketing needs.
CURRENT/RECENT CLIENTS/PROJECTS: Thermo King; Gingiss Formalwear; Dolan Media Company; Commerce Financial Group; Café Chateau, Donatelle Plastics, Inc. and Wireless Ronin Technologies, Inc.
PRESIDENT/CEO/OWNER: Adam Johnston, Chris Hendler

HUNT ADKINS, INC.   **612-339-8003**
15 South 5th Street - 3rd Floor   **Minneapolis 55402**
FAX: 612-339-8104
CONTACT: Kathy McCuskey
SERVICES: Marketing communications agency: strategic planning, account management, creative (traditional and new media), development, production, web design, graphic design, part of the ogilvy syndicate - access to world wide resources - media planning and buying, direct marketing, interactive, promotion.
CURRENT/RECENT CLIENTS/PROJECTS: StoryBox, MLT Vacations, MN Twins, Northwest Airlines, Ogilvy & Mather - The Syndicate, PGA -2002, POPZ Popcorn, Radio K, Dublin Publications, Westlaw, Mr. Binks Super Global Lottery

I

INFINITY DIRECT, INC.   **763-559-1111**
13220 County Road 6   **Plymouth 55441**
FAX: 763-553-1852
CONTACT: Mike Boyle
WWW: infinitydirect.com
SPECIALTIES: Full service capabilities. Consumer and business-to-business direct marketing programs.
CREATIVE SERVICES: Collateral development, brand/identity programs, concept design, brochures, promotion development, planning and execution, copywriting, graphic design, interactive--CD ROM/DVD, web page and web response.
PRODUCTION SERVICES: Printing, lettershop, fulfillment. Interactive--CD-ROM/DVD processing and personalization services.
PRESIDENT/CEO/OWNER: Thomas L. Harding, CEO/Owner

INITIO, INC.   612-339-7195
212 Third Avenue North #510   Minneapolis 55401
FAX: 612-333-0632
CONTACT: Geoff Grassle
E-MAIL: initio-online.com
OFFICERS: Paul Chapin, Scott Sample., Geoff Grassle
CREATIVE DIRECTOR: Paul Chapin, Scott Sample, Ruth Harvey
ACCOUNT SUPERVISORS: Todd Retzlaff
MEDIA DIRECTOR: Rebecca Illingworth
BILLINGS: $12 million
CAPABILITIES/SPECIALTIES: Full service ad agency. Integrated marketing solutions, consumer products, retail and business-to-business.

Advertising Agencies / 31

CURRENT/RECENT CLIENTS/PROJECTS: Bremer Financial, U-Care, West Health, Broadband Broadcasting, Connexus Energy, US Department of Health, Deloitte & Touche, Jackpot Junction Casino, Metacom, AgStar, HNT Brands.

INTERNATIONAL & ETHNIC COMMUNICATIONS, INC.
4215 Winnetka Avenue North #255
FAX: 763-535-9574
CONTACT: Ricardo Paul Vallejos
E-MAIL: info@intl-ethnic.com
WWW: intl-ethnic.com

612-359-8390

Minneapolis 55428

TYPES OF WRITING: Multicultural concepting and creative for consumer and business-to-business print, packaging, collateral, direct response, broadcast, web sites, video, press releases, corporate communications. Also copy translation/adaptation and transcreation. Interview, feature stories for US Hispanic Market.
SPECIALTIES: Hispanic marketing, Latino advertising, print, radio, collateral, print, video.
WRITTEN FOR: US companies and agencies marketing products and services to international and US ethnic markets.

INTERSECT, INC.
824 Meadow Lane South
FAX: 612-374-9616
CONTACT: Lance P. Nelson
E-MAIL: rochrad@aol.com

612-377-6066

Golden Valley 55416

SERVICES: Market analysis, strategy and plan development, ad campaign development, and persuasive execution of advertising and promotion programs.
CAPABILITIES: Specializing in the health and fitness industry, food industry, new products, and new ventures.
CURRENT/RECENT CLIENTS/PROJECTS: Charles Atlas, IBid Live USA, Infinite Power Workout, Ivanko Barbell Company, Landice Treadmills, Urban Rebounding.

32 / Advertising Agencies

J

JAM ADVERTISING, INC.　　　　　　　　　　　763-784-1060
9200 University Avenue NW　　　　　　　　　Coon Rapids 55448
FAX: 763-784-1021
CONTACT: Jason Potts
E-MAIL: info@jamadvertising.com
WWW: jamadvertising.com
SERVICES: Full-service marketing communications including strategic planning; advertising; sales collateral and presentations; POS materials; direct mail; trade show support; media planning; package design; photography; website development; logo development.
CAPABILITIES: Provide effective marketing communications at a good value.
PRESIDENT/CEO/OWNER: Jason Potts, P; Chuck Wallace, VP; Mike O'Connor, CEO; Jean O'Connor, CFO

JGI COMMUNICATIONS　　　　　　　　　　612-341-0814
275 Market Street #541　　　　　　　　　　　Minneapolis 55405
FAX: 612-341-0965
CONTACT: Thom Johnson
CAPABILITIES: JGI Communications is the Marketing Communications division of the Johnson Grossfield Corporation. JGI specializes in business-to-business and consumer marketing communication programs, including print and interactive media, advertising campaigns, collateral design, corporate identity, POP, sales support material, catalogs, trade show materials, annual reports, research and market planning. 10 employees.
CURRENT/RECENT CLIENTS/PROJECTS: H B Fuller; Graco, Inc.; Horton Holding; ReliaStar; Arden Architecture; Powermation, Inc.; Integrated Inc.; Telex; Medtronic; Hormel Foods; Geneva; TLC Inc.; Blackhawk Inc.; Pyramid Trim; Noran Neurologic; QBF, Inc.; Ecolab, Inc.
PRESIDENT/CEO/OWNER: Thom Johnson, Co-P; Mark Grossfield, CO-P

JOHNSON ADVERTISING, INC.　　　　　　　612-339-6514
121 South 8th Street #825　　　　　　　　　Minneapolis 55402
FAX: 612-252-6001
CONTACT: Jerri Johnson
SERVICES: Consumer and business-to-business print advertising and graphic design. Agency background/experience in all media. Ads, collateral, direct mail and corporate identity.
CAPABILITIES: Freelance art direction.

K

KENNEDY & COMPANY　　　　　　　　　　　612-447-0188
16677 Duluth Avenue SE #202　　　　　　　　Prior Lake 55372
FAX: 612-447-0190
CONTACT: Patricia Kennedy
E-MAIL: pkennedy@pioneerplanet.infi.net

Advertising Agencies / 33

SERVICES: Works with a consortium of local advertising talent on a freelance basis, dependent upon the needs of a specific project or client's needs.
SPECIALTIES: Media planning and buying; marketing, retail, direct response, internet, political.
CURRENT/RECENT CLIENTS/PROJECTS: Chuck & Don Pet Food Outlets; Prior Lake Water Ski Association; Petplanet.com; American Agco; MN Wic/Department of Health.
PRESIDENT/CEO/OWNER: Pat Kennedy

KERKER MARKETING COMMUNICATIONS 952-835-7922
7701 France Avenue South #600 **Minneapolis 55435**
FAX: 952-835-2232
CONTACT: Charles H. Kelly
E-MAIL: results@kerker.com
WWW: kerker.com
OFFICERS: Charles H. Kelly, President; Laurin L. Leih, EVP/Med. Dir.; Phil Wendorf, EVP/CFO; Mike Gray, VP/Direct Marketing; Diane Norman, VP/Business Development; Chris Preston, EVP/CD; Liz Warren, VP/Production; Gary Young, VP/PR Dir.
FOCUS: Kerker is in the business of creating customers via strategic brand strategies. The firm utilizes integrated marketing to achieve superior results for its clients.
SPECIALTIES: Kerker is a full-service marketing communications firm serving consumer, business-to-business and retail accounts. Clients include Fortune 100 corporations seeking global marketing programs, as well as regional companies seeking advertising and public relations.
CURRENT/RECENT CLIENTS/PROJECTS: 3M Adhesives; Bonding Systems; Packaging Systems; Industrial Tapes; Industrial Markets Group; Protective Materials (Scotchgard™ Protection); American Medical Systems; Baldwin Hardware; Central Research Laboratories; Eco Water Systems; Health Care Minneapolis Grand Hotel; North Memorial Health Care; Race for the Cure; Sico; Stratasys; Sub-Zero Freezer Company; Thermo King; United Sugars; Wolf Gourmet; Target Stores; Zonetrader.com

L

LABELLE & ASSOCIATES 612-541-0310
7601 Wayzata Boulevard #200 **St. Louis Park 55426**
FAX: 612-541-1805
E-MAIL: billelabelleassociates.com
SERVICES: Full service marketing communications.

34 / Advertising Agencies

CURRENT/RECENT CLIENTS/PROJECTS: Paper Warehouse, Inc.; Armtec Defense Products; The Fireplace Center; Personnel Strategies, Inc.
PRESIDENT/CEO/OWNER: William LaBelle

LANCE LEWEY ADVERTISING AND PHOTOGRAPHY
3005 James Avenue South
FAX: 612-821-1115
CONTACT: Lance Lewey
E-MAIL: lewey@bpsi.net

612-821-1114

Minneapolis 55408

SPECIALTIES: We are dedicated to quality—producing powerful images, and promoting the success of our industrial and professional services clients. Specialties include print projects—especially color brochures, ads and annual reports—and interactive, such as CD presentations and web sites. In-house capabilities in photography, writing, design and research.
CURRENT/RECENT CLIENTS/PROJECTS: Manufacturers, industrial clients, and professional services films.
PRESIDENT/CEO/OWNER: Lance Lewey, President

LARSON & ASSOCIATES
3225 Lafayette Ridge Court
CONTACT: John Larson

952-471-0343

Wayzata 55391

SPECIALTIES: Industrial, consumer products or business-to-business; foods and food service, agricultural and products in general; market planning; create and produce advertising for all media; concept design; copy and layout; packaging and corporate identification; media planning, placement and consultation.

LUDLOW ADVERTISING
9801 Dupont Avenue South #300
FAX: 612-881-2266
CONTACT: Patricia Ludlow
WWW: ludlow-adv.com

612-881-4411

Minneapolis 55431

SPECIALTIES: Recruitment advertising solutions and communications.
PRESIDENT/CEO/OWNER: Cargill; Norwest Banks; Toro; DataCard; Fingerhut; TCF Financial Corp.; United Defense.
PRESIDENT/CEO/OWNER: Patricia Ludlow, Owner

LYNCH JARVIS JONES, INC.
119 North Fourth Street #301
FAX: 612-371-0459
CONTACT: Kevin Lynch
E-MAIL: kevinlynch@ljj.com
WWW: ljj.com

612-371-0014

Minneapolis 55401

SERVICES: Business analysis, marketing research, strategic planning, mass communications and public education, for growing, ethical organizations which offer products, services, ideas and issues fundamental to the fulfillment, happiness and wellness of the human race and the planet earth.

Advertising Agencies

CURRENT/RECENT CLIENTS/PROJECTS: Fairview Health Service; Minnesota Department of Health; Minnesota Department of Public Safety; Minnesota Department of Children, Families and Learning; The Minneapolis Foundation; Minnesota Center for Health Promotion; Minneapolis Public Schools; Loantech; Centers for the Application of Prevention Technologies; Minnesota State Colleges, and Universities; Wedge Community Co-op.
PRESIDENT/CEO/OWNER: Kevin Lynch, CEO; Gregg Byers, CD; Paul Engebretson, Director of Operations

M

MAGNETO COMMUNICATIONS   952-352-0787
801 Main Street   Hopkins 55343
CONTACT: Matt Farley
WWW: magnetocom.com
ACCOUNT SUPERVISORS: Matt Farley, Account Services Director
CREATIVE DIRECTOR: Arik Nordby, Jeff Ess
CAPABILITIES/SPECIALTIES: Advertising, Marketing & Design. Concise copy. Fun Ideas.
CURRENT/RECENT CLIENTS/PROJECTS: Clients must be completely lost with no compass. It will be easier to make you look good. Nonetheless, we will consider taking your account if you have a sense of humor and a insatiable desire to see your business succeed.

MAINSTREET GROUP, INC.   651-631-1416
900 Long Lake Road #200   St. Paul 55112
FAX: 651-631-0208
CONTACT: Scott Bakken
E-MAIL: scott@mainstreetgroup.com
WWW: mainstreetgroup.com
SERVICES: Full service advertising and marketing agency, offering TV, radio, and direct mail, plus daily on-line reports of direct response campaigns.
SPECIALTIES: Exclusive provider of MainTrax (direct response campaign results with daily updates).
CURRENT/RECENT CLIENTS/PROJECTS: AT&T; Time Warner Cable; Charter Communications; HBO; MediaOne; MSC; Comcast Cable; Cox Cable; Montgomery Cable; Bell Industries; Delta Dental of Minnesota; Deluxe Corporation; Adelphia; Cable One.

MAMMOTH MARKETING COMMUNICATIONS   612-623-8000
2710 NE Summer Street   Minneapolis 55413
FAX: 612-623-4810
CONTACT: Jeff Johnson
E-MAIL: jj@bigideas.com
WWW: bigideas.com
SERVICES: Business-to-business, all service ad agency. Web design, media buying, print advertising, collateral design, strategic marketing, video and radio production, sales presentations, interactive media.
CAPABILITIES: Extensive experience with business-to-business marketing for manufacturers, assemblers, converters and distributors.
CURRENT/RECENT CLIENTS/PROJECTS: Bergquist, Land O' Lakes, Hubbard Broadcasting, TiVo, DirecTV, Hosokawa Bcpex, Gentra Systems, Serac, Conwed, Carla Corp, UFE.

36 / Advertising Agencies

MARKETRAIN 651-297-6000
26 East Exchange Street #610 St. Paul 55101
FAX: 651-297-6548
CONTACT: Todd Butzer
E-MAIL: toddb@marketrain.com
WWW: marketrain.com
SERVICES: Customized marketing and advertising for small businesses on a budget. All work is project-based, and prices include all creative, copywriting and design. Specialties include: logos, direct mail, ID packages, flyers, brochures, websites, and ad campaigns.
PRESIDENT/CEO/OWNER: Todd Butzer, Dan Foote

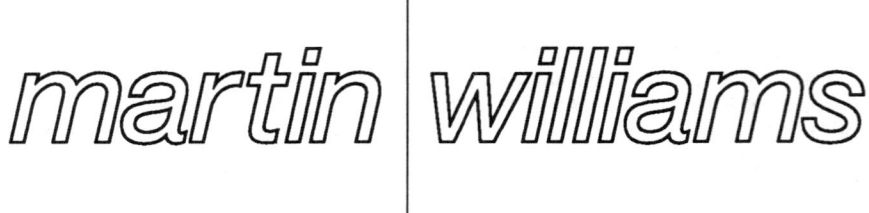

MARTIN/WILLIAMS ADVERTISING 612-340-0800
60 South 6th Street #2800 Minneapolis 55402
FAX: 612-342-9700
CONTACT: Mike Gray
WWW: martinwilliams.com
OFFICERS: David D. Floren; Chairman, Steve Collins, President; Tim Frojd, Vice Chair, CFO; Mike Gray, EVP; Tom Kelly, EVP, Creative Director; Dan Woodbury, EVP. New Business Contact: Mike Gray
CURRENT/RECENT CLIENTS/PROJECTS: Abbot Northwestern Hospitals, Allina Health System, American Humane Society, Cargill, Catholic Charities, Gold 'n Plump, Lexington Home Furnishings, Marvin Windows, Mervyn's, Novartis, Polaris, Powertel, Rubbermaid, Steelcase, Target Corporation, 3M, US Bank, Virtual Ink, Bruegger's Bagels, Lincoln Financial Group, Rooster.com, and Victory motorcycles. Subsidiaries: Creo, International and Cross Cultural Communications; Karwoski & Courage, Public Relations, (i) Group, Interactive, design, direct, and sales promotion.

MEDIATECH 651-646-0166
2003 Ashland Avenue #2 St. Paul 55104
FAX: 612-397-8662
CONTACT: Thomas Malone
SERVICES: Strategic planning, media buying and negotiations for television, radio, print and outdoor advertising, market research, promotion planning and implementation.
SPECIALTIES: Developing effective Media plans for a wide variety of retail, national and business-to-business accounts. Specialties include casino advertising and promotions for regional casinos, building product accounts and hospitality.
CURRENT/RECENT CLIENTS/PROJECTS: Shooting Star Casino & Hotel; Dairyland Power Cooperatives; EnPower, Touchstone; Medical Institute of Minnesota; JPMP; Wallace Marx & Associates; Miller Marketing.

Advertising Agencies / 37

MEDVEC·EPPERS
advertising

MEDVEC-EPPERS ADVERTISING, LTD. **651-429-1001**
4441 Lake Avenue South **St. Paul 55110**
FAX: 651-429-3812
CONTACT: Jason Medvec
E-MAIL: jason-m@medvec-eppers.com
WWW: medvec-eppers.com
SERVICES: Fresh, intrusive and memorable communications. Strategic planning for consumer, retail and e-business clients; concept development and production of advertising; comprehensive web site development, implementation and marketing; broadcast concept and production; collateral, direct mail and promotional programs.
CAPABILITIES: Offering recommendations regarding all aspects of the marketing communications process; web(in)Site, our strategic system for optimizing Internet communications; impatience with communications that don't communicate; elimination (yes, elimination) of mark-ups on all outside charges including media, printing and production.
CURRENT/RECENT CLIENTS/PROJECTS: Old Home Foods, Northern States Power Company (NSP), Bruegger's Bagels, Slumberland Stores, Hardware Hank/Trustworthy Hardware Stores, Uptown Art Fair, Banc Midwest Corp, Aerosim Technologies, Air-Serve, Auto Glass Plus, Caribou Highlands Lodge, County Banks, Digisource, Mammoth Outfitters, Outdoor Viewing Systems, Oxboro Medical, Shavlik Technologies, Southview Banks, Twin Cities Marathon, White Rock Banks, Zaud Squad (Edina Realty.)
OFFICERS: Jason T. Medvec, P; Shawn Lee Eppers, VP; Randy Phillips, CFO
ACCOUNT SUPERVISORS: Alex Heiser
CREATIVE DIRECTOR: Christine Howey

38 / Advertising Agencies

J. T. MEGA, INC.
4020 Minnetonka Boulevard
FAX: 952-929-5417
CONTACT: Jay Mega
E-MAIL: info@jtmega.com
WWW: jtmega.com
CAPABILITIES: Foodservice and food processing industries.
CURRENT/RECENT CLIENTS/PROJECTS: Land O' Lakes Food Ingredients; Brakebush Brothers; Automatic Products; Michael Foods; Amana; Frigoscandia; National City Bank; Ecolab; Hormel Foodservice.
BILLINGS: $17 million
PRESIDENT/CEO/OWNER: Jay Mega, President; Phil Lee, VP Director Client Services

952-929-1370
Minneapolis 55416

MEIROVITZ & COMPANY
212 Third Avenue North #579
FAX: 612-338-8730
CONTACT: Michael B. Meriovitz
SERVICES: Financial, legal, consumer service, non-profit.

612-338-2559
Minneapolis 55401

MEYER MARKETING, LTD.
14 Seventh Avenue North
FAX: 320-656-4187
CONTACT: Ross Handahl
E-MAIL: rhandahl@meyerhd.com
WWW: meyerhd.com
SERVICES: Corporate identity, logos, audio-visual presentations, exhibits, direct mail, POP displays, magazine publications, creative advertising and collateral services (brochures, newsletters, etc.), complete computer graphics and typesetting facilities, media research and placement. Focus group facility on premises. Market surveys, prospecting, opinion polls, selling, public appeals and analysis of data by computer, includes 40 - 50 national WATS.
SPECIALTIES: Industrial, commercial, financial, political, medical, professional, educational and property and real estate areas.
PRESIDENT/CEO/OWNER: Officers: Larry Meyer, CEO; Peg Meyer, P; Tom Caprio, P-Telemarketing; Creative Director: Tim Mortensen; Media Director: Frank Frush; Account Supervisors: Peg Meyer, Ross Handahl, Murdock Johnson, Trudy Gluth, Gina Martens-Nutter.

320-656-4111
St. Cloud 56303

Advertising Agencies / 39

MIRAGE ADVERTISING (FORMERLY RUDISILL ADVERTISING, INC.)
2585 Hamline Avenue North #C
FAX: 651-636-0346
CONTACT: Lynn Warner, Jen Nelson
CREATIVE: Beth Heapy
MEDIA: Nicci Braasch, Kjel Carlstrom
E-MAIL: mirageadvertising.com

651-636-0345

Roseville 55113

CAPABILITIES: Full-service agency providing marketing services for both consumer retail advertising and business-to-business assignments. Services include: client planning and positioning; complete media planning and buying; creative development and execution; TV and radio production services; corporate identity programs; direct mail and point-of-sale promotions; on site promotions and coordination; web site development and web advertising placement. All assignments are results driven.
SPECIALTIES: Serving companies of all sizes with full agency services or on a project by project basis. Clients benefit from our innovative "partner in success" philosophy.

MTM ADVERTISING
125 Main Street SE #341
FAX: 612-331-2845
CONTACT: Ladd Conrad
E-MAIL: ladd@mtmad.com

612-331-2502

Minneapolis 55424

SERVICES: Full service advertising, marketing, public relations, publicity and promotional firm. Specializing in the medical and health, home building and development, hospitality and tourism, retail professional services industries.
CAPABILITIES: Planing, graphic design, ad design, corporate identity, logos, exhibits, direct mail, displays, media research, media.
CURRENT/RECENT CLIENTS/PROJECTS: Hotel Sofitel; Ridgeview Medical Center; Vida Helathcare; Minnesota Occupational Health; Preservation Development; Data communication Solutions; HuntGregory; The Siska Group; Woodland Capital; Performance Computer Forms.
PRESIDENT/CEO/OWNER: Ladd Conrad

N

NEMER, FIEGER & ASSOCIATES, INC.
6250 Excelsior Blvd #203
CONTACT: James Fieger

952-925-4848

Minneapolis 55416

SERVICES: Full-service advertising, marketing, public relations, publicity, promotions and special events with heavy emphasis on hospitality, entertainment, leisure and fast food industries plus various local retail products and services. Billings: $23.2 million.
CAPABILITIES/SPECIALTIES: Directors: Rex Thompson & Allen Jorgenson, Co-Directors, Motion Picture Adv.; Jan Crownover, Dir., Reciprocal Trade Division; Jan Sandhoefner, Office Manager; Juli Gilles, Media Director.

40 / Advertising Agencies

CURRENT/RECENT CLIENTS/PROJECTS: Associated Hotels; Capital Hotel Group; Aggregate Industries, Inc.; Championship Auto Shows; Dangerfield's Restaurant; Fine Line Features; Goodfellow's Restaurant; Grant Thornton LLP; Hampton Inn Airport/Richfield; Hollywood Pictures; Ivories Restaurant; Justus Lumber; Medco; Metro-Goldwyn Mayer; Minnesota Street Rod Association; New Line Cinema; Paramount Pictures; Samuel Goldwyn Co.; Sea Note Cruises; Subway Sandwich Shops/16 markets; Tejas Restaurant; Touchstone Pictures; Tri-Mark Pictures; Universal Pictures; Walt Disney Pictures; Zuhrah Shrine Circus.

PRESIDENT/CEO/OWNER: Officers: James Fieger, CEO; June Fieger, EVP; Jon Woestehoff, COO; Dan Lechelt, CFO; J. Marie Fieger, Sr. VP; Tony Harris, EVP; Eric Loeffler, VP Mkt Comm.

NITEWRITER ADVERTISING
2006 W. 54th Street
612-926-2350
Minneapolis 55419

CONTACT: Jerry Haine
E-MAIL: jhaines@visi.com

SERVICES: Types of writing: Advertising and collateral, including print, radio, TV, brochures, direct mail and point-of-purchase.

CAPABILITIES: Hunting, fishing, camping, hiking. Also automotive aftermarket, business-to-business.

CURRENT/RECENT CLIENTS/PROJECTS: Warner Manufacturing; Sportsman's Guide; US Feeds; Red Wing Shoe; Minnkota; Johnson Fishing; Eureka!Tent; Camp Trails; Old Town Canoe; Stearns; ITT Meyer; Thexton Tools; Supersweet Feeds.

NORTH WOODS ADVERTISING
200 Textile Building
119 North Fourth Street
612-340-9999
Minneapolis 55401

FAX: 612-340-0857
CONTACT: Bill Hillsman, Greta Unowsky, John Blackshaw
WWW: northwoodsadvertising.com

SERVICES: Integrated marketing communications, advertising, and public relations; marketing strategy and research; media strategy, planning and buying; creative direction, copywriting, design and art direction; interactive media/website design; broadcast and print production; brand valuation, brand extension and strategic planning; political strategy and communications.

CAPABILITIES: Retail, sports marketing, enthusiast products, politics, law and government, public service, non-profits, publishing, higher education, food (organic and health), professional services, book and motion picture promotion, emerging technology, turnaround situations and crisis communications.

CURRENT/RECENT CLIENTS/PROJECTS: Mall of America; Harper Collins; American Oats; Jesse Ventura for Governor (MN); Ciresi for US Senate (MN); Christabella, Inc.; Airline Pilots Assn.; Wellstone for US Senate; Center for a Sustainable Economy; American Iron & Supply; Earth Day 2000; Canterbury Park; Robins Kaplan Miller & Ciresi LLP; Mahoney Ulbrich Christiansen Russ; Carleton College; Minnesota State Colleges & Universities; Logan for US Senate (FL); Minnesota Outdoor Heritage Assn.; Boyd for Governor (OK); International Assn. of Machinists & Aerospace Workers; Jacob Wetterling Foundation; Ventura for Minnesota, Inc.; SpeakOut.com.

PRESIDENT/CEO/OWNER: Bill Hillsman, Owner/Chief Creative Officer; John Blackshaw, President

NYGARD DIMENSIONS
1414 Marshall Street N.E.
612-371-9228
Minneapolis 55413

Advertising Agencies / 41

FAX: 612-371-9232
CONTACT: Ben Wallace, Director of Account Services
E-MAIL: id@brandcommunications.com
WWW: brandcommunications.com
SERVICES: Brand-based marketing communications: brand strategy and identity development, integrated marketing communications planning, creative development, design, production, implementation, measurement and management through all media: Print: literature, stationery, direct mail, advertising, sales tools, packaging, sales kits; Digital: Websites (internet/intranet/extranet), online promotion, sales tools/software, product demos, video presentations, kiosks, online brand identity management; Environmental: themed events, stage sets, exhibits, displays/POP.
CAPABILITIES: Brand identity systems, including naming, logo, brand elements and guidelines. Unique approach to brand identity strategy, design development and management through all points of stakeholder contact to create the "whole brand experience." Sister companies Nygard Set Design and Harmony Box contribute to brand experience creation. Industries: information technology/e-business, healthcare/pharmaceuticals, financial services, manufacturing, retail and more.
CURRENT/RECENT CLIENTS/PROJECTS: 3M Company; Auxilium Software; Compass Productions; Conseco Finance; Larson Manufacturing; Lawson Software; Lutheran Brotherhood; MedIntelligence; nQuire Software; Pharmaceutical Care Network (PCN); Proliant (formerly AMPC, Inc.); Qtech Systems, Inc.; Sales Force 2000 Software; Safe Reflections; Sunrise Community Banks (formerly Franklin Bancorp), U.S. Magnetix; U of M Physicians.
PRESIDENT/CEO/OWNER: Jim Nygard, P

O

DENNIS P O'LEARY, INC.   612-529-5090
PO Box 29073   Brooklyn Center 55429
FAX: 612-529-1559
CONTACT: Dennis O'Leary
E-MAIL: dennis.oleary3@gte.net
SERVICES: Retail advertising services including radio, television, print and direct mail creation and placement.
CAPABILITIES: Specializing in automotive and political advertising.
CURRENT/RECENT CLIENTS/PROJECTS: GSTA Rod and Custom Show; Iten Chevrolet; Jim Lupient Auto Mall; Buerkle Acura/Isuzu; Buerkle Buick/Honda; Mary Kiffmeyer for Secretary of State.

OLSON AND COMPANY   612-339-1974
126 North Third Street #200   Minneapolis 55401
FAX: 612-339-5788
CONTACT: John Olson
E-MAIL: email@oco.com
WWW: oco.com
SERVICES: Strategic Planning, Research, Media Planning and Buying, Creative Development and Production including: Television, Radio, Print, Out-of-Home, Design, and Interactive/Website Development.
CAPABILITIES: Strategic creative that profoundly affects consumer thinking and behavior; the know-how to create opportunities and the passion to bring ideas to life; ideas that sing through every hallway of the brand, from television to the Internet, promotion to direct mail. An Internet sophistication that reflects our belief that new media are transforming communications on every level.

42 / Advertising Agencies

CURRENT/RECENT CLIENTS/PROJECTS: American Lung Association of Minnesota; Datalink; Dynamic Information Systems; Gedney Pickles; Greater Minneapolis Convention & Visitors Association; HealthEast; Koch Petroleum Group; Mall of America; Minnesota Wild NHL Hockey; Old Dutch Foods; Ordway Center for the Performing Arts; Par Aide Golf Products; Retek Inc./Retail.com; Rainbow Foods; ShopPogo.com; University of Minnesota Women's Athletics.

KRUSKOPF OLSON
417 First Avenue North, 4th Floor
612-338-3870
Minneapolis 55401
FAX: 612-630-5158
CONTACT: Sue Kruskopf
E-MAIL: skruskopf@kruskopfolson.com
WWW: kruskopfolson.com
SERVICES: Strategic planning, advertising and promotion, design (corporate identity, logo, collateral systems), integrated marketing, print and broadcast production.
CAPABILITIES: Brand development, retail.
CURRENT/RECENT CLIENTS/PROJECTS: Mystic Lake Casino & Hotel, GN Resound, McGlynn Bakeries, Minnesota History Center, InVision, Target Corporation, Fuji Ya Restaurant.

OMNI ADVERTISING, INC.
640 Gun Club Road
651-423-3422
Eagan 55123
FAX: 651-423-4320
CONTACT: Wm. Schoenecker
E-MAIL: omni@omnishop.net
WWW: omnishop.net
SERVICES: Media placement, computer graphics, photography (location and studio), publicity, copywriting, project management for brochures, ads, websites.
CAPABILITIES: We specialize in small to medium size companies - business-to-business and agriculture manufacturers - advertising and public relations.
CURRENT/RECENT CLIENTS/PROJECTS: NMC-Wollard; Reese Enterprises; CFR Corporation; R.J. Manufacturing; Lor*Al Products, Inc.; Raven Industries; Kahler Corporation; Bernard-Dalsin Manufacturing; National Agri-Services, Inc.; Railroad Services, Inc.

ORANGESEED DESIGN
800 Washington Ave. N., Suite 461
612-252-9757
Minneapolis 55401-1196
FAX: 612-252-9760
CONTACT: Damien Wolf
E-MAIL: info@orangeseed.com
WWW: orangeseed.com
SERVICES: Providing great ad concepts, copy, art direction and production when you don't need the overhead and hassles of a full-service ad agency.
SPECIALTIES: Smart business communications solutions. See our ad under Graphic Designers for more information.
CURRENT/RECENT CLIENTS/PROJECTS: Andersen Windows, West Group, ReliaStar, NSP/Xcel Energy, Grand Casino Corp., Newcourt Financial/The CIT Group, MI-Assistant Software, LawOffice.com, InsSites.com, Lundgren Brothers Construction.

Advertising Agencies / 43

P

PARACHUTE DESIGN   612-340-0333
120 South 6th Street #1300   Minneapolis 55402
FAX: 612-359-4390
CONTACT: Marcia Miller
E-MAIL: miller@parachute-design.com
WWW: parachute-design.com
SERVICES: Strategic, non-mass media, brand building tools such as packaging, corporate identities, point-of-sale, sales support systems and collateral.
CURRENT/RECENT CLIENTS/PROJECTS: Toro: Chopin Vodka; Belvedere Vodka; Harmon AutoGlass; Target; DBI/SALA; Lawn-Boy; Childrens Hospitals & Clinic Foundation; Crystal Farms; Galleria Shopping Center; Juut SalonSpa; Michael Foods; Pillsbury Bakeries & Food Service; Redline HealthCare; Altru Health System.

PARACHUTE DESIGN   612-340-0333
120 South 6th Street #1300   Minneapolis 55402
FAX: 612-359-4390
CONTACT: Marcia Miller
E-MAIL: miller@parachute-design.com
WWW: parachute-design.com
SERVICES: Strategic, non-mass media, brand building tools such as packaging, corporate identities, point-of-sale, sales support systems and collateral.
CURRENT/RECENT CLIENTS/PROJECTS: Toro: Chopin Vodka; Belvedere Vodka; Harmon AutoGlass; Target; DBI/SALA; Lawn-Boy; Childrens Hospitals & Clinic Foundation; Crystal Farms; Galleria Shopping Center; Juut SalonSpa; Michael Foods; Pillsbury Bakeries & Food Service; Redline HealthCare; Altru Health System.

PETERSON MILLA HOOKS   612-349-9116
1315 Harmon Place   Minneapolis 55403
FAX: 612-349-9141
CONTACT: Brian Hooks, EVP/Client Services; Dave Peterson, Joe Milla, Creative Directors; Betsy Treinen, Lisa Nelson, Kennedy Zakeer, Account Staff.
E-MAIL: bhooks@pmhadv.com
SERVICES: Consumer services, retail and business-to-business categories.
CAPABILITIES: Full-service advertising agency focused on high-caliber strategic planning and distinctive creative. Annual billings: $25M.

44 / Advertising Agencies

CURRENT/RECENT CLIENTS/PROJECTS: Target Stores; Dayton's; NetRadio.com; Mattel, Inc.; Edina Realty; Club Sports International/Northwest Athletic Club; Valleyfair; Junior Achievement.
PRESIDENT/CEO/OWNER: Dave Peterson, P/CD; Brian Hooks, EVP/Client Services; Joe Milla, VP/CD

R

RAINBOW MARKETING, INC.   612-926-0401
5405 Opportunity Court   Minnetonka 55343
CONTACT: James Van Hercke
CAPABILITIES: Providing advertising and marketing services for small to medium size retail, business-to-business and health care organizations.
SPECIALTIES: Retail, business-to-business and health care promotions.
OFFICERS: James & Verna Van Hercke

KRISTI K. RAZINK   612-722-8156
4609 30th Avenue South   Minneapolis 55406
FAX: 612-722-1101
CONTACT: Kristi K. Razink
E-MAIL: razink@aol.com
SERVICES: Advertising and media planning, buying, negotiation, and presentation. Expertise with all media including print, TV, radio, out-of-home, direct mail and advertising online. Assistance in all media efforts including competitive research, new business pitches, new product introductions, sales promotions, co-op, ethnic, international, PR and special events. Industries: automotive, building, education, financial, food, health care, health and beauty, high tech, hospitality, manufacturing, medical, packaged goods, retail and travel.

RILEY HAYES   612-338-7161
333 South First Street   Minneapolis 55116
FAX: 612-338-7344
CONTACT: Judy Jossi
E-MAIL: jjossi@rileyhayes.com
SERVICES: Full service agency providing consumer and business-to-business advertising, direct marketing, media planning and buying.
CURRENT/RECENT CLIENTS/PROJECTS: Marquette Financial Companies; Northwest Airlines; Wireless North; 3M Scotchtint Window Film; 3M Fire Protection Products; 3M Protective Materials Division; 3M Personal Safety Products; Woodwinds Health Campus; Dunn Brothers Coffee.
PRESIDENT/CEO/OWNER: Tom Hayes, Owner; Judy Jossi, President

RISDALL LINNIHAN ADVERTISING   651-286-6700
2475 15th Street NW   New Brighton 55112
FAX: 651-631-2561
CONTACT: John Risdall, Chairman
E-MAIL: getwired@risdall.com
WWW: risdall.com

Advertising Agencies / 45

SERVICES: Full service advertising agency offering marketing strategy and planning, marketing research, advertising, direct response, promotion, collateral, publicity/PR and business strategy and planning in the traditional and interactive arenas.
CAPABILITIES: Specializing in the educational, medical, institutional, retail, computer and environmental industries. Internet expertise from site design to site development to marketing planning and implementation.
CURRENT/RECENT CLIENTS/PROJECTS: Aeration Industries; Agribank; Allegheny Power; Alliance Water Resources; American Guidance Service; Applied Technology Consultants; ATG Laboratories, Inc.; Bang Printing; Birchwood Casey; Blanks USA; Brown Wilbert Vault Company; City of New Brighton; Clinch-On Products; Clique Capital; Cocola Palm; cranespharmacy.com; Curative; Decker Publications; Digital River; Diversity Village; EBP HealthPlans, Inc.; Electrosonic; EMPI; E. W. Blanch; Paragon; UniSure; Finnleo Sauna; Fox River; Funeral.com; Galyans; GunVault; Highland Banks; HomeRight; Honeywell; House of Hope, Hubler Family Business Consultants; Innsbruck Jewelers; Isaksen Promotional Specialties; Kinney & Lange; Learning Outfitters; Lease Point.com; Lemna Corporation; Liquid Dynamics; 3M Industrial Mineral Products Division; 3M Traffic Control Materials; 3M Dental Products; 3M Healthcare; 3M Industrial Tapes and Specialties; Magnum Research; Medtronic (Neurological Division); Micom Circuits, Inc.; Morries Automotive Group; Mounds View School District; Normark Rapala; Northern States Power; Norwest Equity Partners, Novartis, Onan Corporation; Photos, Inc.; Pillsbury; Premier Mounts; Printing Industry of MN; Progressive Marketing; Pur (Recovery Engineering); Purus, Inc.; Rainforest Café; RSR Wholesale Guns; Ramsey County Library; Rottlund Homes; SafeWater Anywhere LLC; Schoolbell.com; Schoonover Bodyworks, Inc.; Smith Foundry Company; Smith System Manufacturing, Inc.; Summit Envirosolutions; Target; Tertronics, Inc.; The TPA; Time Savers; Uni-Hydro, Inc.; Upsher-Smith Laboratories; US Filter-Autocon; USFilter-Consolidated Electric; USFilter-Control Systems; USFilter Corporate; USFilter-CPC; USFilter-General Filter; USFilter-Filterite; USFilter-Recovery Services; USFilte- Seitz; USF Johnson (France); USF Johnson Screens; Verdant Brands; VerticalNet; Vista Technologies; WalMart; Water Pollution Control Corp.; Waterworld; Western Bank.

GORDON ROBINSON & ASSOC., INC. 612-831-4666
7701 Normandale Road #110   Minneapolis 55435
FAX: 612-831-7908
CONTACT: Gregory Robinson
SPECIALTIES: Business-to-business; medical; high-tech and international.
CURRENT/RECENT CLIENTS/PROJECTS: American Industrial Refrigeration; Charlotte Fabrics; Checker Flag Parts; Furniture Industries; Nu-Way Torches; Par-Aide; St. Croix Marine Products; The King Company; Ziegler, Inc.; Lake Engineering; Park Upholstery; Energy Alternatives; Phoenix Global Distribution.
BILLINGS: Billings: $2.5 million.
PRESIDENT/CEO/OWNER: Gregory A. Robinson, P; Michael Morson, Creative Director; David DeRemer, Art Director; Mary Woell, Copywriter.

RUDISILL ADVERTISING, INC. (NOW MIRAGE ADVERTISING)   651-636-0345
2585 Hamline Avenue North #C   Roseville 55113
FAX: 651-636-0346
WWW: mirageadvertising.com

46 / Advertising Agencies

RUSSELL & HERDER   218-829-3055
315 E. River Road   Brainerd 56401
FAX: 218-829-2182
CONTACT: Carol Russell
E-MAIL: carol@russellherder.com
WWW: russellherder.com
SERVICES: Full-service integrated communications firm serving national and international clients in the health care, marine, tourism, telecommunications, forest products, higher education, financial services, manufacturing and professional services industries.
CAPABILITIES: The only communications firm in Greater Minnesota and St. Paul elected into the American Association of Advertising Agencies. Over 70-person staff specializes in creative development, advertising, public relations, strategic planning, media placement, market research and interactive development. We have offices in Duluth, St. Paul, St. Cloud and Brainerd.
CURRENT/RECENT CLIENTS/PROJECTS: St. Mary's Duluth Clinic Health Systems; Genmar; Betty Crocker; Michigan Tech University; Potlatch; Structural Board Association; College of St. Scholastica; Larsen Boats; Midwest Wireless Communications; Wellcraft Marine

S

SAGA ADVERTISING & MARKETING   612-378-0200
43 Main Street SE #509   Minneapolis 55414
FAX: 612-378-0213
CONTACT: Mark Junkersfeld
OFFICERS: Mark Junkersfeld, President
SPECIALTIES: Industrial; business-to-business; commercial; real estate; video multi-media; print.

THE SANDCASTLE GROUP   612-399-0290
212 Third Avenue No #400   Minneapolis 55401
FAX: 612-399-0264
CONTACT: Kathy Curry
E-MAIL: kcurry@sandcastlegroup.com
WWW: sandcastlegroup.com
SERVICES: 360 degrees of marketing communications; research, planning, print, broadcast, direct marketing, 1 on 1 marketing, interactive, promotions, public relations.
CAPABILITIES: Full service advertising agency, specializing in the mature market.
CURRENT/RECENT CLIENTS/PROJECTS: American Express; Choice Hotels; Medica; United HealthGroup; Starkey Hearing Aids, Mn; Department of Health; Omron HealthCare; Advolife
PRESIDENT/CEO/OWNER: John Nielson, President; Scott Moncrieff, GM

SCHULTZ-WARD PRENTICE   612-321-0500
411 Washington Avenue North #207   Minneapolis 55401
FAX: 612-321-0510
CONTACT: John Ward

Advertising Agencies / 47

SERVICES: Strategic marketing communications including: advertising, collateral, package design, web design, media planning.

CURRENT/RECENT CLIENTS/PROJECTS: Bethel College & Seminary, Bloomington CVB, Carbonair, Cargill, Delta Dental, Deluxe, Glad Corn, Grove City College, Naniboujou Lodge, Patrol Bike Systems, Pinnacle Engineering, ZH Computer.

PRESIDENT/CEO/OWNER: John Ward, Brian Prentice, Bruce Schultz

SCIDMORE, HERSOM & OTHERS 763-476-4976
1115 Vicksburg Lane #18 Plymouth 55447
CONTACT: Linda Hersom
OFFICERS: James Scidmore, Linda Hersom
CREATIVE DIRECTOR: James Scidmore
MEDIA DIRECTOR: Linda Hersom
SPECIALTIES: International, consumer/industrial and business-to-business advertising, media placement and collateral materials, electronic graphics, internet and www.

SENSE OF DESIGN 952-935-8827
5800 Baker Road Minnetonka 55345
FAX: 952-935-8726
CONTACT: Paula J. Jeske, Director of Sales & Marketing
TOLL FREE: 1-800-557-1723
E-MAIL: info@senseofdesign.com
WWW: senseofdesign.com
SERVICES: Multi-channel direct marketing and creative agency specializing in catalogs, circulars, direct mail and interactive media (web sites, online catalogs, CD-ROM). Design, art direction, copy writing, production, photography, project management and consulting; concepts to pre-press production and printing. Direct marketing experience that translates into the right creative for your audience.
SPECIALTIES: Catalogs, both print and interactive. Creative facilities in Minneapolis and Chicago. Photography studio both digital and conventional. Turnkey production or complement to in-house.
CURRENT/RECENT CLIENTS/PROJECTS: Consumer and business-to-business; direct marketers and retailers. National clientele, from Fortune 500 companies to start-ups. Sears, Fingerhut, LA Loving; Best Buy; American Dental Association; Target
PRESIDENT/CEO/OWNER: Lynda Dahlheimer, Kelly Marshik

7·30 CREATIVE 612-333-2322
100 North Sixth Street #302A Minneapolis 55403
FAX: 612-333-0767
CONTACT: Tom Harris·
E-MAIL: harris@730creative.com
WWW: www.730creative.com
SERVICES: Get results! In print or on-line, we get you and your services noticed! 7· 30 Creative's team of advertising professionals uses a proven process of combining image and message to produce print advertising, direct mail, web sites and marketing materials that get award-winning results—for B-2-B or consumer markets. We're a full-service agency, so we're with you from market research to concept to press or launch.
CAPABILITIES: Full, in-house pre-press capabilities. Scanning, photo retouch. Linotronic 560 imagesetter, 3M Matchprint and 4X CD writer.

48 / Advertising Agencies

SPECIALTIES: Corporate identity programs, print advertising, web site development/design, media buying, market research, graphic design, copywriting, account management and concept development.
CURRENT/RECENT CLIENTS/PROJECTS: International, national and regional clients in the manufacturing, medical, health care, software, print, high-tech, finance and educational industries.
OFFICERS: Tom Harris, President; DJ Harris, VP/CFO; Tom (T.O.) Oberg, VPO, CD

SHOULTZ & ASSOCIATES ADVERTISING, INC.   651-653-0849
2344 Tenth Street   White Bear Lake 55110
FAX: 651-407-7976
CONTACT: Barry Shoultz
E-MAIL: shoultz@idt.net
SERVICES: Trade publication advertising planning, development and execution for manufacturers of high tech products and software wishing to reach vertical markets, public relations/press release writing/dissemination to same markets. Print advertising for small retail and business-to-business in Minneapolis/St. Paul market.
CAPABILITIES: Twenty five years advertising experience in print advertising for retail and consumer services in Minneapolis/St. Paul market. Ten years experience in high tech business-to-business trade advertising, public relations and collateral development.
PRESIDENT/CEO/OWNER: Barry Shoultz

SIDE BY SIDE MARKETING   612-943-1451
7315 Stewart Drive   Eden Prairie 55346
FAX: 612-395-9222
CONTACT: Dan Seidler
E-MAIL: sbsm@www.com
WWW: geocities.com/sidebysidemarketing
SERVICES: A full service agency, blah, blah, blah... If you're looking for creative copy, campaign strategy, TV and Radio production that excels--on a budget-- you've found it. Media buying, strategic planning and full print and collateral production are our gig.

SMYTH COMPANIES   651-646-4544
1085 Snelling Avenue North   St. Paul 55108
FAX: 651-646-8949
CONTACT: Chuck Stone
WWW: smythco.com
SERVICES: Smyth Companies combine to integrate the primary disciplines of advertising, trade, and promotion to enhance a product's perceived value through its package by use of core capabilities of primary labels and product identification, point-of-sale and promotional packaging, package centered promotions and labeling solutions for strategic implementation.

Advertising Agencies / 49

PRESIDENT/CEO/OWNER: Smyth Companies, Inc., product lines include litho labels, pressure sensitive labels, beverage labels, box wraps, convolute labels, combination labels, and in-mold labels. Smyth manufactures point-of-sale and promotional packaging of pre-packaged self shippers, dump bins, counter top displays, pop-open displays, sidekick/power wing displays, presentation cases, sample mailer boxes, in-store signage, shelf talkers and danglers, multi-product merchandisers, peg-hook displays, mobiles and retail package design. Package centered promotions are available for on-pack/in-pack, product and shelf danglers, booklets, dry peel coupons, one-ply and two-ply coupons and game pieces. The company designs and manufacture's labeling equipment, placing equipment, and product handling systems through Smyth Systems.

STUDE-BECKER ADVERTISING & COMMUNICATIONS
332 Minnesota Street
Suite East 100 First Bank

651-293-1393
St. Paul 55101

CONTACT: Michael Dunn
SPECIALTIES: Full service advertising and business communications.
CURRENT/RECENT CLIENTS/PROJECTS: Healthcare, education, manufacturing, insurance, banking.com and e-commerce
BILLINGS: 3.5 million
PRESIDENT/CEO/OWNER: Michael Dunn, Steve Peterson

T

TAD WARE & COMPANY, INC.
716 North First Street

612-338-4686
Minneapolis 55401

FAX: 612-337-5502
CONTACT: Rhonda Vicknair
OFFICERS: Tad Ware, P; Ann Ware, Executive VP; Susan Christian, VP Finance and Operations
CREATIVE DIRECTOR: Tad Ware
ACCOUNT SUPERVISORS: Susan Schectman, Dory Skartvedt, Court Queen, Kim Johsnon, Beth Heinemann
SPECIALTIES: Custom publications and photography, consumer sales promotion and package design.

TANAKA ADVERTISING
One Main Street SE #209

612-378-3928
Minneapolis 55414

FAX: 612-378-3927
CONTACT: Lisa Lundmark
E-MAIL: lundmark@tanakainc.com
WWW: jtanaka@tanakainc.com
SERVICES: Advertising: awareness, brand, diversity, recruitment, trade and retail. Alternative media (including out-of-home). Corporate collateral: Annual reports, brochures, corporate identity, POS, sell sheets and trade show materials. Direct mail. Internet and intranet development. Marketing/Strategy: Planning, communications, media, positioning and research. Packaging/Environmental: Interior and exterior signage, POP packaging and signage, fleet design, and 3D rendering.

50 / Advertising Agencies

CAPABILITIES: At Tanaka Advertising, we specialize in creating and producing a wide variety of advertising and marketing materials. We partner with our clients in creating and planning strategies for their communications efforts. Our project managers, while skilled at guiding a project through production, are also tasked with becoming experts on each client's services and products.
CURRENT/RECENT CLIENTS/PROJECTS: Northwest Airlines; US Bancorp; Minnesota Twins; Timber Lodge Steakhouse Restaurants; Telex Communications; Deluxe Corporation; and various others.
PRESIDENT/CEO/OWNER: Jodie Tanaka

TARTAN MARKETING   **952-473-7575**
15500 Wayzata Blvd, Suite 1000   **Wayzata 55391**
Twelve Oaks Center
CONTACT: James J. MacLachlan
E-MAIL: jim@tartanmarketing.com
WWW: tartanmarketing.com
FOCUS: Tartan Marketing helps business-to-business clients form long-term strategies for creating, revitalizing and leveraging strong brands. Core competency in multi-tactical program development, carried out with strong creative articulation. Media-neutral approach, with tactical recommendations based on most effective strategies for addressing clients' unique needs, issues and opportunities.
CAPABILITIES: Quantitative/qualitative research & discovery, market and brand planning, naming and identity development, communications planning. Integrated execution (collateral, advertising, interactive, custom publications, direct response, promotions, sales programs.) Market Segment Expertise: Food marketing: foodservice/bakery/deli/distribution. High tech: e-business/intellectual properties. Financial: banking/insurance.
OFFICERS: James J. MacLachlan, CEO/Margie D. MacLachlan, VP Creative
ACCOUNT SUPERVISORS: Account Services: Terri Juranek, AE; Gina Wifler, AE; Justin Erickson, AE
BILLINGS: $7 million
YEARS IN BUSINESS: 14

THAMAN & ASSOCIATES, INC.   **612-544-3987**
12200 Golden Acre Drive   **Minnetonka 55305**
FAX: 612-544-8868
CONTACT: Robert Thaman
E-MAIL: thamaninc@aol.com

Advertising Agencies / 51

SERVICES: Retail advertising/marketing for local and regional multi-market chains with emphasis on campaign planning; television, radio, prior, direct mail advertising; in-store promotions, merchandising and signage. Established in 1988.
PRESIDENT/CEO/OWNER: Robert Thaman

TRIPP ADVERTISING 763-591-1666
10700 Hwy 55 West #150 **Plymouth 55441**
FAX: 763-591-1654
CONTACT: Howard Tripp
WWW: trippadvertising.com
OFFICERS: Howard Tripp, President; Jim Arnost, Director of Account Management; Dan Hauser, Director of Public Relations; Jim Kanters, Creative Director; Tom Martineau, Assoc. Creative Director; Patti Pulisfer, Director of Production
CURRENT/RECENT CLIENTS/PROJECTS: Abu Garcia, Alberta Flyway Outfitters, Bell Canoe Works, Commission Junction, Federal, Fenwick, National Fishing Week, Pure Fishing, Outers, USL/Bear River, Weaver, Volvo Penta
SPECIALTIES: Full Service Advertising Agency, Public Relations, E-Commerce, Interactive Media, Direct Marketing, Strategic Marketing & Planning, Collateral

U

ULTRA CREATIVE, INC. 612-338-7908
920 Second Avenue South #1200 **Minneapolis 55402**
FAX: 612-337-8178
CONTACT: Dave Biebighauser
E-MAIL: dave@ultracreative.com
CAPABILITIES: Planning and positioning, creative development, graphic design and production. Project based creative marketing firm for corporate communications; print, direct, packaging, POP, identity and collateral.
SPECIALTIES: Food products, retail, kid marketing, new products, and brand equity maintenance.
CURRENT/RECENT CLIENTS/PROJECTS: General Mills, Inc.; The Pillsbury Company; Campbell's Foods, Inc.; Marigold Foods; Gymamerica.com; Govt.com.
PRESIDENT/CEO/OWNER: Dave Biebighauser, President; Gino Perfetti, Vice President

52 / Advertising Agencies

UNO HISPANIC ADVERTISING DESIGN
1515 East Lake Street #204
FAX: 612-728-5410
CONTACT: Carolina Ornelas
E-MAIL: luis@unoonline.com
WWW: unoonline.com

612-728-5411
Minneapolis 55407

CAPABILITIES: Uno is an award winning international firm specializing in creating and producing strategic visual communication programs for the Hispanic/Latino market. Uno services include: corporate/brand identity, collateral material, corporate signature programs. Hispanic event marketing, brand analysis and strategy, Hispanic marketing communication programs, retail, graphic communication programs. New product development. Packaging and merchandising, product naming.

SPECIALTIES: Uno is the only international renowed advertising design consulting firm located in Minneapolis specializing in the Hispanic Latino market. We are a certified minority business, and have a non-equity strategic alliance with Javier Romero Design Inc, In New York City; Chavez and Associates, Inc. in San Diego, CA; Hispanic Independent products in Hollywood, CA and Fritz Torrez Publicidad, Mexico.

CURRENT/RECENT CLIENTS/PROJECTS: MTV Latino, Quantum Axcess, Target Stores, Jose Cuervo Tequila, Univision, Chivas Regal, Garcia Lks., Cartel Creativo, Casanova Pedril Publicidad, Alcone Marketing Group, and Bates USA

W

WELLAND LAIKE COMMUNICATION
255 E Kellogg Blvd #103
FAX: 651-224-9566
CONTACT: Steve Miller
E-MAIL: slm@welland-laike.com

651-224-9554
St. Paul 55101

SERVICES: Strategic development of marketing & advertising campaigns, design and production of promotional material, media buying, internet marketing and web site design, public relations.

CAPABILITIES: Corporate identities, logos, public relations and advertising for regulated industries; legal, financial and health care.

CURRENT/RECENT CLIENTS/PROJECTS: Sieben, Grose & Von Holtum; Brovillette Greater Metro Insurance; Nile Healthcare; Nichols Financial Services Company; Beverly Healthcare; United Bankers Bank; Oasis Markets.

PRESIDENT/CEO/OWNER: Steven L. Miller, APR

dig·i·tal·peo·ple (dĭj'ĭ-təl-pē'pəl) 1. graphic design. 2. layout/production. 3. presentation graphics. 4. web design. 5. graphics tech support. 6. copywriting. 7. editing/proofreading. 8. typesetting. 9. media. 10. account services. 11. multi-media design. 12. document processing. 13. marketing. 14. prepress

WE'RE REDEFINING CREATIVE STAFFING.

www.digitalpeople.net

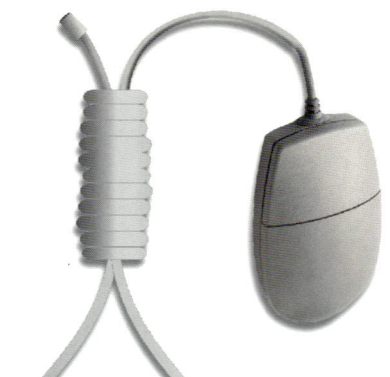

BEFORE YOU WRAP
THE MOUSE CORD AROUND
YOUR NECK AND END IT ALL,
GIVE US A CALL.

At DigitalPeople, we've got a much more productive way to resolve your creative and internet staffing issues. We've been there before and understand the pressures of finding solid talent to produce exceptional work – on time and within budget. With a deep pool of carefully screened and thoroughly tested applicants, we're well armed to provide you with the most qualified and competent person for your project. So, whether you're searching for temporary, temporary-to-hire, contract employment or full-time placements, we've got your creative solution. Visit our web site to learn more.

952.842.8359   digitalpeople®   www.digitalpeople.net

Advertising Agencies / 53

WHITNEY MORSE
420 North 5th Street #740
FAX: 612-338-1994
CONTACT: Mark Morse
E-MAIL: mark@whitneymorse.com
WWW: whitneymorse.com

612-338-1992
Minneapolis 55401

SERVICES: Full-service problem solving agency; strategic marketing and branding consult, communications, print, broadcast, custom music, web development, multimedia, on-line marketing, direct mail, public relations, research and media buying/planning.
CAPABILITIES: Growing a client's business through creative problem detection, solution development and integrated implementation.
CURRENT/RECENT CLIENTS/PROJECTS: Baltimore Sun, Digi International, Augustine Medical, AKG Acoustics, E-Color, Yamaha.

WILHIDE & COMPANY
3019 West 43rd Street
FAX: 612-920-4428
CONTACT: Doug Wilhide
E-MAIL: wilhide@skypoint.com

612-926-3939
Minneapolis 55410

SERVICES: We provide creative and consulting services for marketing communications: concepting, creative direction, copywriting, art direction/design, project management for ads, brochures, direct mail packages, etc.
CAPABILITIES: Special expertise in business-to-business advertising; direct marketing - strategic planning for programs and creative services for implementation. Industry expertise in financial, education, manufacturing, software systems.
CURRENT/RECENT CLIENTS/PROJECTS: IBM; Lawson Software; Lotus; Data Myte/Rockwell Automation; Personnel Decisions International; ROI Systems; Gillette Children's Specialty Healthcare; Minneapolis Public Schools; Crisis Connection; University of St. Thomas; Duplication Factory; Cargill; 3M; American Express; Norwest/Wells Fargo.
PRESIDENT/CEO/OWNER: Doug Wilhide

WISE BUY MEDIA
2585 Hamline Avenue North #C
FAX: 651-636-0346
CONTACT: Lynn Warner, Jen Nelson
CREATIVE: Beth Heapy
MEDIA: Nicci Braasch, Kjel Carlstrom
E-MAIL: wisebuymedia.com

651-636-0345
Roseville 55113

CAPABILITIES: Full-service Media placement agency providing marketing services for both consumer retail advertising and business-to-business assignments. Services include: client planning and positioning; complete media planning and buying; complete demo research; TV and radio production services; direct mail and point-of-sale promotions; outdoor placements; on site promotions and coordinating; web advertising placement; PR support; provide a presence at key trade shows; maximize plan impact through utilization of merchandising and added value opportunities. All assignments are results driven.
SPECIALTIES: Serving companies of all sizes with complete media strategies, placement and promotions. Clients benefit from our 20+ years of expertise in media buying.

54 / Advertising Agencies

Z

THE ZIMMERMAN GROUP 612-341-1100
701 Fourth Avenue South #1330 Minneapolis 55415
FAX: 612-341-0323
CONTACT: Jim Zimmerman
E-MAIL: zgroup@goldengate.net
SERVICES: Food products, consumer package good, new product development.
BILLINGS: Billings: $10 million
CURRENT/RECENT CLIENTS/PROJECTS: ACT II Microwave Popcorn; Country Hearth Bread; Essence of India Foods; Faribault Foods; Floating Arms Ergonomic Products; Grand Metropolitan USA; John I. Has Hops; Land O' Lakes; Magnavox Home Security Products; Merlin Development; Norwesco, Inc Group; Ralston Analytical Lab; Sawatdee Bar & Cafe Seneca Foods; Standard Fusee; ST Specialty Foods; Toro Oil Products; Wildlife Forever.
PRESIDENT/CEO/OWNER: Jim Zimmerman, President; Kathy Ashpole, VP/Administration & Production

Advertising Agencies - Classified & Yellow Pages

D

DIS MEET PEOPLE   612-424-4266
PO Box 200   Osseo 55369
FAX: 612-315-3066
CONTACT: Gerry Knudson
E-MAIL: dismeetpeo@aol.com
SERVICES: Personal ads, calendar of events, clubs and groups, editorials, classifieds, display ads.

L

LUDLOW ADVERTISING   612-881-4411
9801 Dupont Avenue South #300   Minneapolis 55431
FAX: 612-881-2266
CONTACT: Patricia Ludlow
WWW: ludlow-adv.com
SPECIALTIES: Recruitment advertising solutions and communications.
PRESIDENT/CEO/OWNER: Cargill; Norwest Banks; Toro; DataCard; Fingerhut; TCF Financial Corp.; United Defense.
PRESIDENT/CEO/OWNER: Patricia Ludlow, Owner

Advertising, Publishers & Media Reps

B

BENSON COMMUNICATIONS, INC.   612-974-0014
17554 Bearpath Trail   Eden Prairie 55347
FAX: 612-974-0015
CONTACT: Tom Benson
E-MAIL: bensoncom@uswest.net
SERVICES: Travelhost Twin Cities is a monthly magazine distributed only in hotel rooms of selected Twin Cities hotels. Total monthly audience exceeds 100,000 Twin Cities visitors, which provides advertisers the opportunity to reach them directly with information about dining, shopping, entertainment and vacation ideas. Travelhost Twin Cities can also publish customized, sponsored maps and coupon booklets.
CAPABILITIES: Our special strength is to assist marketers in finding and influencing Twin Cities visitors to do business with them, thereby generating incremental revenue not otherwise possible. Customized maps and coupon books, as well as special magazine inserts, provide additional creative marketing opportunities for advertisers. Via 70 Travelhost editions nationally, we also provide regional and national advertising opportunities to this same 100% traveler audience.
CURRENT/RECENT CLIENTS/PROJECTS: Current advertisers include a wide range of restaurants, travel marketers and retailers who benefit from the opportunity to efficiently reach Twin Cities visitors in the privacy of their own hotel rooms. (100,000+ each month.)

C

CABLE IZ   612-533-8196
6900 Winnetka Avenue No   Brooklyn Park 55428
FAX: 612-533-1346
CONTACT: Dave Kiser
E-MAIL: dkiser@nwct.org
WWW: cableiz.com
SERVICES: Cable television advertising time and production of commercial to the 13 Northwest suburbs of Minneapolis.
CAPABILITIES: Professional, commercial production for advertising clients. Digital production equipment.
CURRENT/RECENT CLIENTS/PROJECTS: Numerous local advertising clients.
PRESIDENT/CEO/OWNER: Greg Moore

D

TOM DEVENY & ASSOCIATES   612-926-2624
3803 Thomas Avenue South   Minneapolis 55410
FAX: 612-925-9564
CONTACT: Tom Deveny
E-MAIL: tomdeveny@aol.com
SERVICES: Independent magazine Publishers Rep. Advertising consulting (sales).
CAPABILITIES: Newspaper, magazine 30 years experience.

Advertising, Publishers & Media Reps / 57

CURRENT/RECENT CLIENTS/PROJECTS: Maple Communications - Fleet Equipment Magazine Transport Technology Today. MPHA Pharmacist.

M

MEDIA NETWORKS, INC.   612-338-0348
706 Second Avenue South #276   Minneapolis 55402
FAX: 612-338-0752
CONTACT: Beth Martinson, Pam Nelson
E-MAIL: beth.martinson@medianetworks.com or pamela.nelson@medianetworks.com
WWW: medianetworks.com
CAPABILITIES: Media Networks, Inc. provides a powerful way to reach your prime prospects in local markets. MNI is the only advertising vehicle that gives you access to 27 of the most prestigious national magazines on a local market basis, grouped into Networks for additional market reach--the News, Executive, Men's and Home Networks. Through our exclusive relationships with 13 of the most respected publishing companies in the magazine industry today, MNI enables you to reach top-quality, targeted audiences in over 300 Network markets across the country.
CURRENT/RECENT CLIENTS/PROJECTS: We work with local, regional and national companies located in the Twin Cities, and offer advertising opportunities in the following magazines on a local market basis across the country. Time, Newsweek, US News & World Report, Business Week, Entrepreneur, Fortune, Kiplinger's Personal Finance, Money, Mutual Funds, FSB, American Homestyle, Bon Appetit, This Old House, Traditional Home, Metropolitan Home, Car and Driver, Field & Stream, Esquire, Outdoor Life, Road & Track, Sports Afield, Sports Illustrated, and People Magazine.
PRESIDENT/CEO/OWNER: Mark Ford, President; Time Inc., Owner

MINNESOTA NEWSPAPER ASSOCIATION   612-332-8844
12 South 6th Street #1120   Minneapolis 55402
FAX: 612-342-2958
CONTACT: Lisa Hills
E-MAIL: mnaadv@visi.com
WWW: mnnewspapernet.org
SERVICES: MNA is the trade association owned and operated by Minnesota Newspapers. We offer a one order, one bill newspaper advertising placement service for all daily, weekly and shopper publications in Minnesota. MNA also can coordinate regional and national ad placements. MNA does not charge a fee for its service. Classified (MCAN) and display ad networks also available. Complete newspaper directory and press release service available. Electronic ad delivery capabilities available at no extra charge.
PRESIDENT/CEO/OWNER: Linda Falkman, Executive Director

Animation

A

ADTECH COMMUNICATIONS GROUP   952-944-6347
8220 Commonwealth Drive #201   Eden Prairie 55344
FAX: 952-944-5643
CONTACT: Maureen Lundberg
E-MAIL: sales@adtechinc.com
WWW: adtechinc.com

SERVICES: Since 1982 we've been bringing technology, creativity and artistry together in a synergistic way to create award-winning graphics and animation for video, multimedia, web and other emerging electronic technologies. We'll take your graphics/animation from concept through completion. Visit our web site or call to see our demo reel - you'll see award wining animations using leading edge technology including multiple SGI super Unix and NT based workstations and NT based high end Hoodini (read very powerful), Synergy Custom and Adtech Proprietary Software covering a wide range of 2D and 3D software, Pandemonium, additional paint systems and Discreet's Edit Plus non-linear editing. Output is to all electronic media. Technical capabilities include organic terrain growth, organic plant growth, hair and beard growth, kaleidoscope generation, magnetics, particle systems and generation, image morphing, blob metamorphosis, natural phenomenon such as fog and water, lattice deformations, magnets, collisions, ray tracing with reflection, refraction and shadows, rotoscoping, bump mapping, texture mapping, environmental mapping, object metamorphosis, inverse kinematics, programmable painterly effects, multiple digital overlays, airbrush effects, object deformations, fractals, etc. - we've got it all!

SPECIALTIES: Concept driven, high end 2D and 3D identity design services, character animation, and dynamic integration of animation with live footage. Award winning animation and design for film, video, web, multimedia, and emerging electronic visual media. Providing integrated design solutions across all your electronic media.

CURRENT/RECENT CLIENTS/PROJECTS: Honeywell, 3M, Minnesota Power, Fisher-Rosemount, Hormel Foods, General Mills, National Car Rental, Datacard, Control Data, Minnegasco, Anderson Windows, Caterpillar Inc., GMAC-RFC, Lutheran Brotherhood, Texas Instruments, Graco, KMSP-TV, Northern States Power, Alpine Industries and more under construction! To discuss ways Adtech can go to work for you, contact Maureen Lundberg at 952-944-6347.

ANIMUSE.COM   612-823-2880
3152 Elliot Avenue South   Minneapolis 55407
FAX: 612-823-2880
CONTACT: Bill Dobbs
E-MAIL: bdobbs@animuse.com
WWW: animuse.com

SERVICES: Cel animation; CD-ROM and Web site interactives (Director, GIF, and Flash); HTML and JavaScript; Storyboarding; Cartooning; Caricatures and Character design.

SPECIALTIES: Character animation; internet interactive animation. Humorous and technical subjects. Intelligent animated art and programming expertise. Available for independent projects or as part of your team.

CURRENT/RECENT CLIENTS/PROJECTS: Carlson Marketing Group; Gage Marketing; Gatorade; General Electric; Great Plains TV; IBM; KTCA-TV; The Kydd Group; Land-O-Lakes; Levi's; Mike Jones Film; NFLA; NHL; Northland Inn; Proctor & Gamble; Quaker Oats; Reelworks Animation; Sears; StarTribune; Tandem Computer and Trend Enterprises.

Animation / 59

C

CRASH & SUES
510 Marquette Avenue #600
FAX: 612-338-4601
CONTACT: Crash Medin
E-MAIL: crash@crash-sues.com
WWW: crash-sues.com

612-338-7947
Minneapolis 55402

SERVICES: C-Reality Film to tape transfer system with Da Vinci 2K color correction system; fire HD and D1 online edit; Inferno HD graphics and compositing; 2D/3D CGI; closed captioning; videoboards, and duplication/traffic; NTSC/PAL; various multi-media capabilities; Echoboys original music, sound design and mix.
CAPABILITIES: Expertise in television commercials, music videos.

H

HDMG DESIGN, POST & EFFECTS
6573 City West Parkway
FAX: 952-943-1957

952-943-1711
Eden Prairie 55344

CONTACT: Design/Animation: Angella Kassube, Andy Reynolds, Brian Olson; Editors/Compositors: Jamie Heuton, Greg Mattern, Michael Guncheon, Jessie Yerama; Assistant Editor: John Gleim; DVD Author: Mike Faustgen; Location Production: Jamie Heuton; Accounts: Mona Cifaldi; Scheduling: Marci Meyocks; Traffic: Kim Schafer
E-MAIL: info@hdmg.com
WWW: www.hdmg.com
SERVICES: HDMG is an organization of people who love what we do. We have fun doing great work with intelligent clients (yes, that would be you) in a joint bursting with cool equipment. We are a producer-support service that promotes a direct partnership between producers and operators. We provide digital editing, design, paint, animation, special effects and compositing, DVD authoring and Avid non-linear offline in a relaxed, creative environment. We are an operator-run facility, with all owners and operators directly responsible for developing client relationships and maintaining our facility. Since we have no account reps, every client receives direct operator contact throughout their project. Cool!
EQUIPMENT: Fire, 2 Digital Editing suites mastering to Digital Betacam, 2 Avid Offlines, Flint, 2 DF/X Composium Graphics/Animation suites, Intergraph running 3D Studio Max, MacLab with PhotoShop, After Effects and Illustrator, Ultimatte 8, Insert stage with Ultimate Memory Head, Sonic Solutions DVD Creator with 5.1 Dolby Digital surround, and many tape formats including Digital Betacam, D5, D2, DV/DVC Pro, DV Cam, MII, Beta SP, 3/4", 1", Hi-8, S-VHS, VHS (including international formats), DAT and DA88. Co-located with PostAudio, Inc., a sync mix facility featuring 2 digital audio suites.

60 / Animation

I

INTERACTIVE PERSONALITIES, INC.   612-332-7625
708 North First Street #241   Minneapolis 55401
FAX: 612-332-2046
CONTACT: David Seckinger
E-MAIL: info@iperson.com
WWW: iperson.com
SERVICES: Develop corporate group presentations which incorporate the principles of accelerated learning, group dynamics, persuasion and performance theater. Venues include tradeshows, company meetings, live public relations events, and product launches.
CAPABILITIES: Real-time animation, computer enhanced corporate mascots, and characters, interactive branding, live theatrical performance, and corporate gameshows featuring audience response technology.
CURRENT/RECENT CLIENTS/PROJECTS: Ameritech; BellSouth; Burson Marstellar; Cargill; Compaq; General Motors; Hewlett Packard; IBM; M&M Mars; Mitsubishi Motors; Mobil Oil; Procter & Gamble; Pfizer; Sony; US West; Whirlpool.
PRESIDENT/CEO/OWNER: President, Dan Yaman; General Manager, Joan Nelson.

P

PIXEL FARM, INC.   612-339-7644
251 First Avenue North #600   Minneapolis 55401
FAX: 612-339-7551
CONTACT: Stacey Ranum
E-MAIL: stacey@pixelfarm.com
WWW: pixelfarm.com
SERVICES: High-end digital post-production facility specializing in visual effects, 3D, 2D animation, on/off-line editorial, and film transfer for commercial broadcast, feature film, music videos and corporate markets.
CAPABILITIES: Discreet logic flame and inferino. Quantel Infinity, Editbox, Hal Express and Paintbox Express. AVID Symphony and AVID off-line. Two 3D workstations running Maya. SoftImage, Eddie, Pandemonium and more. URSA Film transfer with daVinci color corrector.

PRECISION POWERHOUSE   612-333-9111
911 Second Street South   Minneapolis 55415
FAX: 612-332-9200
CONTACT: Dan Piepho, Paul Sunberg, Gene Gunderson
E-MAIL: dan@power-house.com; pauls@power-house.com or geneg@power-house.com
WWW: precisionpowerhouse.com
SPECIALTIES: Video and Interactive Media marketing via direct mail; video and multimedia sales presentations. DVD authoring and Interactive media software development for retail and corporate products; training presentation; commercials (TV and Radio) web pages for businesses; web publishing; infomercials; e-business and direct response; audio, video and CD audio/ROM/DVD replication.

Animation / 61

R

REELWORKS ANIMATION STUDIO 612-333-5063
318 Cedar Avenue South #300 Minneapolis 55454
FAX: 612-333-7970
CONTACT: Bruce McFarlan
E-MAIL: reelwork@reelworks.com
WWW: reelworks.com
SERVICES: 20 years experience in creating award winning animation for commercials, long format and animation for the web. With a vast array of animation styles ranging from classic cel to digital 2-D and 3-D and a client list that includes DDB Needham Worldwide, Foote Cone Belding, Ketchum, BBDO, Fallon McElligott and DMB & B, Reelworks has produced memorable, eye catching commercials for Coca-Cola, Time Magazine, Hershey's, Alka-Seltzer, New York Times and M.T.V. to name a few.
PRESIDENT/CEO/OWNER: Bruce McFarlan

THE RICHARD DIERCKS COMPANY, INC. 612-334-5900
420 North 5th Street #300 Minneapolis 55401
FAX: 612-334-5907
CONTACT: Michael Perkins
CONTACT: graphics@digitalite.com
SERVICES: 3D and 2D graphics and animation for spot, corporate, industrial and legal applications. DVD, multimedia, interactive development, web development.
CAPABILITIES: TDI/Wavefront/SGI, Kinemation, Dynamation, complete title development, 3D Studio Max. Long form animation, children's, legal/forensic.
CURRENT/RECENT CLIENTS/PROJECTS: Better Homes & Gardens; Lintus, NY; Simitar; Quality Video; Legos; Caswell International.
PRESIDENT/CEO/OWNER: Richard A. Diercks

S

SHA-KAR 9 ANIMATION 612-522-6373
3337 Halifax Avenue North Minneapolis 55422
FAX: 612-522-7481
CONTACT: Steffin Griswold
E-MAIL: masada@sk9.com
WWW: sk9.com
SERVICES: Storyboarding, screen plays, 2D character animation, digital cel compositing, 3D modeling/animation, video special effects, CD-ROM and website interactions using Director and Flash.
SPECIALTIES: Storyboarding, character design, plot development and interactive media.

STUDIO Z IMAGERY 612-337-0031
123 North 3rd Street #205 Minneapolis 55401
FAX: 612-359-6056
CONTACT: Fred Zlock

62 / Animation

E-MAIL: webmaster@studiozimagery.com
WWW: studiozimagery.com
CAPABILITIES: 3D computer animation and 3D modeling for corporate, industrial and legal applications.
SPECIALTIES: CD-Rom projects. Technical and architectural animations. Auto CAD training video content.

Art Directors

B

THE BENYAS GROUP   612-340-9804
126 North Third Street, Suite 300   Minneapolis 55401
FAX: 612-334-5950
CONTACT: Bradley A. Benyas
E-MAIL: benyas@visi.com
CAPABILITIES: Art direction, photo direction; print supervision; development of primary marketing support materials.
SPECIALTIES: Print production and supervision. The Benyas Group is a results-oriented firm specializing in printed communications that advance our clients, their companies, and their products.

BOWEN CREATIVE COMPANY   952-837-9850
3300 Edinborough Way #115   Edina 55435
FAX: 952-837-9861
CONTACT: Laura Justus
E-MAIL: guy@bowencreative.com
SERVICES: Complete graphic design and art direction services for print and electronic media. Formats include catalogs, publications, recipe booklets, cookbooks, consumer packaging, brochures, posters, web pages.
CAPABILITIES: Concepting, design, layout, photo direction, logo and identity design, and pre-press print production supervision. Full electronic design and production capabilities, with expertise in various graphic software applications.
PRESIDENT/CEO/OWNER: Guy Bowen, Barbara Bowen

C

JEANETTE CARRELL ART DIRECTOR   651-481-4948
3187 Park Overlook Drive   Shoreview 55126
FAX: 651-483-5748
CONTACT: Jeanette Carrell
E-MAIL: jcarrel@bitstream.net

CHARLIE WALBERG CREATIVE SERVICES   651-213-0012
27421 Quinlan Avenue   Lindstrom 55045
FAX: 651-213-0508
CONTACT: Charlie Walberg
E-MAIL: dobe@fishnet.com
WWW: walberg.net
SERVICES: Design and art direction, concept and photo illustration.
CAPABILITIES: Design and art direction from a professional with over 20 years experience in a wide variety of business categories.

JEAN CHURILLA, ADVERTISING ARTIST   952-953-0633
8276 173rd Street West   Lakeville 55044

64 / Art Directors

CONTACT: Jean Churilla
E-MAIL: churilla@aol.com
SERVICES: Corporate identity design, logos, ads, newsletters, brochures, catalogs and annual reports.
CAPABILITIES: Concept, design, layout, photo direction, and art direction.
PRESIDENT/CEO/OWNER: Jean Churilla

D

DAVIES DESIGN   612-544-9789
6505 Glenwood Avenue   Golden Valley 55427
CONTACT: Laura E. Davies
CAPABILITIES: Creative layout and graphic design services for small to large companies from concept to print.
SPECIALTIES: Logos, brochures, direct mail, catalogs, business stationery, photo direction, and scanning/photo manipulation.
PRESIDENT/CEO/OWNER: Laura E. Davies

G

GOOSE GRAPHICS   613-385-4002
333 North Washington Avenue   Minneapolis 55401
FAX: 612-349-2707
CONTACT: David J. Van Gieson
CAPABILITIES: All types of art direction, story boards, concept boards.
SPECIALTIES: Consumer promotion; creative and art direction.

GRAPHIC RELIEF   612-386-8088
15207 94th Place North   Maple Grove 55369
CONTACT: Tony Rubasch
E-MAIL: tonyr@graphicrelief.com
WWW: inet-serv.com/~tonyr
SPECIALTIES: A relief designer with strong emphaiss in retail direct mail catlaogs and web site creation for general consumer merchandise. Along with creative marketing communications for industrial manufacturing, food industry, retail clothing, recreation providers and health care.
CURRENT/RECENT CLIENTS/PROJECTS: Major advertising and marketing communication agencies in the Twin Cities location.

LAURIE GROSS   612-865-1796
1500 Jackson Street #431   Minneapolis 55413
FAX: 612-788-2211
CONTACT: Laurie Gross
CAPABILITIES: Conceptual art direction and design. Experience in all media.
SPECIALTIES: Colorful solutions for creating and building a strong corporate and product identity.

R

BARBARA REDMOND DESIGN, INC.   612-339-3861
120 South 6th Street #2025   Minneapolis 55402
FAX: 612-339-5918
CONTACT: Barbara Redmond
E-MAIL: redmonddesign@uswest.net
CAPABILITIES: Graphic design, graphic consultant. Design communications company specializing in design consultation and communications for corporate identity, literature design systems, brochures, annual reports and multi-lingual design systems.
PRESIDENT/CEO/OWNER: Barbara Redmond

S

SHANNON DESIGNS   651-426-0202
2629 South Shore Boulevard   White Bear Lake 55110
FAX: 651-426-0205
CONTACT: Alyn Shannon
E-MAIL: alyn@dgi.net

T

SCOTT TONEY/CREATIVE ALLIANCE   612-823-4405
4405 Park Avenue South   Minneapolis 55407
FAX: 612-823-4405
CONTACT: Scott Toney
E-MAIL: scott.toney@adpartners.com
CAPABILITIES: Print advertising (consumer/business-to-business), digital design, collateral, direct mail, display and packaging. Electronic capabilities include Mac and PC.
SPECIALTIES: Print advertising, corporate and product identity.

Artist & Photographer Representatives

A

ART REP SERVICES   612-823-1120
4859 Aldrich Avenue South   Minneapolis 55409
CONTACT: Chip Nadeau, Nancy South
E-MAIL: chip@artrepinc.com
CAPABILITIES: Representatives for photography and Illustration services.
SPECIALTIES: Minneapolis: Tony Kubat Photography: romantic, illustrative still live/food, photographers - Tony Kubat, Mete Nielsen.

B

NANCY BACHER, ARTIST REPRESENTATIVE   763-786-1200
2654 Rodeo Drive NE   Blaine 55449
FAX: 763-786-1200
E-MAIL: nbacher@visi.com
WWW: nancybacher.com
SERVICES: Individuals represented: Bryan Anderson: Ink, brush and MAC, all subject matter; Jeffrey Anderson: complete generated 3D illustration and animation; Mary Bergherr: pastel, pencil and charcoal, food product and editorial; Jan-Willem Boer: airbrush, painting, pen /ink and color wash - technical product, editorial and fine art; Derek Brigham: computer montages, photo manipulation, creative concepting, web and homepage design. Typography, logos and technical art; Bret Meredith: painting with acrylics, scratch board; Adam Turner: scratchboard with computer.
CAPABILITIES/SPECIALTIES: Commercial illustration in all areas including advertising, editorial, technical, product, fashion, annual reports, etc. All illustrators very capable of concepting, designing and turning the clients ideas into an amazing piece of illustration.
PRESIDENT/CEO/OWNER: Nancy Bacher

D

DIMENSION CREATIVE   612-884-4045
9801 Dupont Avenue South #168   Minneapolis 55431
FAX: 612-884-3450
CONTACT: Joanne Koltes
E-MAIL: dimensioncreative.com
WWW: jkoltes@visi.com
SERVICES: A viable resource of creative and production support for both ad agencies and corporations. Dimension offers illustration, photography, design and complete web site development services. Emphasis in the national publishing and greeting card/giftbag market.

Artist & Photographer Representatives / 67

F

JENNIFER CLARK FROST -   651-690-9631
PHOTOGRAPHERS REPRESENTATIVE
1909 Sargent Avenue   St. Paul 55105
FAX: 651-690-1443
CONTACT: Jennifer Clark Frost
SERVICES: I represent 4 talented thriving studios in Minneapolis - Gallop Studios; Susan Gilmore Photography; Ellie Kingsbury Pictures; Treleven Photography. They offer a wide range of styles and specialties and advertising, corporate and editorial markets.
CAPABILITIES: Categories represented: electronic media (digital capture, quick time, etc.), interior/architectural, people (location and studio), product illustration (all scales), sets and a variety of location photography. Stock also available.

K

KLP, INC.   612-332-5635
233 Park Avenue, Third Floor   Minneapolis 55415
FAX: 612-332-5637
CONTACT: Karyn Kopecko
E-MAIL: karynlp@isd.net
WWW: karynlp.com
CAPABILITIES: A full-service group representing and marketing national and regional commercial photographers. Klp's production team can assist with any request, enduring success from concept to execution on all photography assignments.

M

MASON ILLUSTRATION   612-729-1774
3810 Edmund Boulevard   Minneapolis 55406
FAX: 612-729-0133
CONTACT: Jerry or Marietta Mason
E-MAIL: mason@uswest.com
SERVICES: Area Represented: Illustration; storyboards, advertising, design, corporate, editorial and cartoon. Traditional and digital style, technique and applications. High-end digital imaging; includes scanning, retouching, compositing and photo restoration. Mac or Windows platforms, various output services provided.

68 / Artist & Photographer Representatives

CAPABILITIES: Illustrators: Neal Aspinall, graphic humor/editorial; Kenn Backhaus, mixed medium; Paul Fricke, storyboards/cartoon; Patrick Faricy, airbrush; Glenn Gustafson, airbrush/digital; Joe Heffron, graphic/mixed; Dan Lotts, mixed medium; Jeff Meyer, pastels; Mark Mille, airbrush/fantasy; Chris Monroe, humor; Randy Rogers, airbrush/digital; Tom Rosborough, watercolor/color pencil. Prepress: JKL Studios, Kurt Lang; (see Electronic Prepress, Computer Graphics or Retouching Services.) Additional Artist Associates: Peter Krause, storyboards; Franklyn Margasak, storyboards; Gordon Purcell, storyboards; Harlan Scheffler, scratchboard; Dan Wiemer, watercolor/scratchboard.

O

ROBIN OGDEN REPRESENTS   612-925-4174
4409 Washburn Avenue So   Minneapolis 55410
FAX: 612-925-2135
CONTACT: Robin Ogden
E-MAIL: rjoreps@aol.com
SERVICES: Photographers represented: John Reed Forsman, studio and still life; Jeff Johnson, people, fashion, lifestyle; Richard Hamilton Smith, location. Illustrators represented: Kelly Hume, logo and hand lettering design; Dianne Bennett, cut paper illustration; Lisa Sims, full color comps and storyboards.

S

SECRET AGENT MAN   612-753-1115
16421 Olivine Street NW   Ramsey 55303
FAX: 612-753-1114
CONTACT: Jeff Cerise
E-MAIL: cerise@bitstream.net
SERVICES: Representing commercial photographers: Bob McNamara, Paul Westbrook and Perry Hanson in Minneapolis. Also digital illustration firm called Electric Soup in Hollywood, California.
CAPABILITIES: Over 10 years experience.
CURRENT/RECENT CLIENTS/PROJECTS: Wells Fargo Annual Report; Stars on Ice; Iams; Regis; Target; Wilsons Leather; Harley-Davidson; The Barbers; BVD; Fruit of the Loom.

DEBORAH SNYDER, CREATIVE   612-922-3462
REPRESENTATIVE
5321 West 62nd Street   Edina 55436
FAX: 612-922-0357
CONTACT: Deborah Snyder
E-MAIL: debs@debsnyder.com
WWW: debsnyder.com
CAPABILITIES: Illustration line art, four color, technical to cartoon with a good range in between. Individuals represented: Illustrators such as Scott Buchscacher, Mike Carina, John Clarke, Margo De Paulis, Doug Horne, Mark Jarman, Steve Mark, Glenn Quist, Mike Wohnoutka, Keith Wong.

Artist & Photographer Representatives / 69

W

JAN WILLEM BOER   763-780-4085
2654 Rodeo Drive NE   Blaine 55449
FAX: 763-786-1200
E-MAIL: jboer@visi.com
SERVICES: The new Dutch Master with greencard and multiple personality disorder, driven to draw on any white piece of paper. Person 1: precise, specializing in high-tech and cutaways, exceptionally intelligent airbrush illustrator. Person 2: wild, uncontrolled, scribbly pen and splashes of color artist.
CAPABILITIES/SPECIALTIES: Either an airbrush or pen/ink with color wash capability to produce illustrations for product, technical, corporate reports, editorial or whatever your need may be.
CONTACT: Represented by Nancy Bacher - 763-786-1200

Artists & Art Studios

A

ANIMUSE.COM   612-823-2880
3152 Elliot Avenue South   Minneapolis 55407
FAX: 612-823-2880
CONTACT: Bill Dobbs
E-MAIL: bdobbs@animuse.com
WWW: animuse.com
CAPABILITIES: Complete website design and programming; interactive animation; illustration; internet consulting.
SPECIALTIES: Character animation, illustration, cartoons, caricatures, and design. Director, GIF, Flash, HTML and JavaScript; Illustrator and PhotoShop. Available for independent projects or as part of your team.
CURRENT/RECENT CLIENTS/PROJECTS: BBDO; Bolin Agency; Carlson Marketing Group; Gage Marketing; Gatorade; General Electric; General Mills; Great Plains TV; IBM; KTCA-TV; The Kydd Group; Land O' Lakes; Levi's; Martin Williams; Mike Jones Film; NFLA; NHL; Northland Inn; Proctor & Gamble; Quaker Oats; Reelworks Animation; Rotary International; Science Museum of Minnesota; Sears; StarTribune; Tandem Computer; and Trend Enterprises.

NEIL APPLEQUIST   612-533-6343
4207 62nd Avenue North   Brooklyn Center 55429
CONTACT: Neil Applequist
E-MAIL: applequist@uswest.net
SERVICES: Complete pre-press services. Design, scanning color and black and white. Using QuarkXPress, PhotoShop, Illustration. With 20 years experience.
CAPABILITIES: Freelance artist for 10 years. Specializing in packaging, catalogs, brochures, manuals, and corporate publications.

ARCHITECTURAL ART BY KOHLRUSCH   763-784-9475
4038 86th Lane NE   Circle Pines 55014
CONTACT: Mike Kohlrusch
SERVICES: Colored, pen and ink renderings, perspective or front views, logos, ink floor plans, cartoons, miscellaneous art services.
SPECIALTIES: Residential, commercial and display renderings.

ASI IMAGE STUDIOS   612-379-7117
10 Second Street NE #214   Minneapolis 55413
FAX: 612-331-5769
CONTACT: Bill Gensch
E-MAIL: bill@a-s-i.com
WWW: a-s-i.com
SERVICES: Graphic Design, layout, custom electronic artwork production services for a wide range of applications, i.e. print, multimedia, web and interactive. 3D, illustration design and rendering of text, logos, objects and environments, special effects and photo/illustration composites.
CAPABILITIES: For over 20 years providing the finest in Graphic Design, composites, special effects and custom electronic artwork services. Also providing custom graphics for web and interactive prospects.

B

B J LARSON   612-471-0343
3225 Lafayette Ridge Court   Wayzata 55391
CONTACT: B J Larson
E-MAIL: Jtbdlars@aol.com
SERVICES: Recreations of paintings of the classic master painters in oil or on canvas, portraits; illustrations in B&W. Illustrations for newspaper, magazines or collateral; story book illustrations.

BAU, INC.   952-912-0191
5511 Bristol Lane   Minnetonka 55343
FAX: 952-933-0295
CONTACT: Douglas Johnson
E-MAIL: johns93@bitstream.net
SERVICES: We are the graphics bureau to the Twin Cities. The most capable center for scanning, retouching, photo-manipulation, illustration, and illustration integrated with design. We have years of experience in working seamlessly with business and design schedules. Call for our free, clearly understandable pricing and information booklet.
CAPABILITIES: No better scanning or retouching can be found in the Twin Cities area. We can work with any item from 8mm film to the side of a building. All can be saved in any file format needed, to a variety of convenient storage media. True photographic printing is available also - and always an index print. Our art department brings illustration and design to a higher level of effectiveness by being able to integrate the two into a more communicative whole. We have many styles at our disposal to meet any clients needs.
CURRENT/RECENT CLIENTS/PROJECTS: American Medical Systems; Adult Option in Education; Banc; Campbell Mithun Esty; Carlson Marketing Group; Chez Francoise; La Flame; Photo Quick; VRB Art; Wellington Windows.
PRESIDENT/CEO/OWNER: Douglas Johnson

THE BEAUDRY GROUP   612-940-3244
3402 Hennepin Avenue South   Minneapolis 55408
FAX: 612-338-2732
CONTACT: Steve Beaudry
E-MAIL: bg@2z.net
SERVICES: 3- dimensional illustration, miniature sets, ad props.

DOUG BEKKE   612-338-5417
2436 34th Avenue South   Minneapolis 55406
FAX: 612-729-8416
SERVICES: Airbrush illustrations and line art.
PRESIDENT/CEO/OWNER: Doug Bekke

72 / Artists & Art Studios

THE BENYAS GROUP   **612-340-9804**
126 North Third Street, Suite 300   **Minneapolis 55401**
FAX: 612-334-5950
CONTACT: Bradley A. Benyas
E-MAIL: benyas@visi.com
TYPE OF WORK: Full-service graphic arts from concept and layout, through production and printing; in-house resources include artwork, illustration, scans, page composition, color mock-ups. Expert abilities to graphically depict what client wants to communicate to audience.
SPECIALIZATION: Design and development of primary marketing support materials include capabilities brochures, print ads, product graphics and literature, corporate identity.

JAN WILLIAM BOER   **6763-780-4085**
2654 Rodeo Drive NE   **Blaine 55449**
FAX: 763-786-1200
CONTACT: Nancy Bacher, Art Rep.
E-MAIL: jboer@visi.com
SERVICES: Type of Work: 4/c graphic and airbrush illustration for technical and product; specializing in hi-tech and cutaways, graphic and editorial illustration; understanding of European design.
SPECIALTIES: Airbrush and technical illustration.

ROBERT BUCKNER DESIGNS & SUCH   **651-458-9722**
8332 Hemingway Avenue South   **Cottage Grove 55016**
CONTACT: Robert Buckner
E-MAIL: buckyart@aol.com
WWW: buckyart.com
CAPABILITIES: Corporate brochures and other printed media design from concept to finish. Creative 2D and 3D design.
SPECIALTIES: Logo design and presentation; sketches; corporate brochures; B&W line art; illustration and computer-generated design.
PRESIDENT/CEO/OWNER: Robert Buckner

Artists & Art Studios / 73

C

CBIG (CHILDRENS BOOK ILLUSTRATORS GUILD)
880 Laurel Avenue
651-224-0544
St. Paul 55104
CONTACT: Vicki Deutsch
E-MAIL: vldeu@yahoo.com
SERVICES: We showcase artists talents and make it possible for them to share creative work with other artists. Our guild continues to gather to share techniques, ideas and information. Our meetings are informal and may include; sharing portfolio's, demonstrations of techniques, guest lectures, visits to printing plants and children's book stories, etc. And, we share updates on various art news. Our meetings are held monthly with pre-notification.
CAPABILITIES: As a group we've been able to promote our artist's through Illustration gallery shows and include our members in various advertising books for artists. We have published children's book illustrators within the group who offer helpful advise to beginning of illustration. We've sponsored projects including: Illustration conferences, promotional guild calendars, a children's activity book, illustration gallery shows and library displays and had our "StoryLines" Illustration show touring statewide.
CURRENT/RECENT CLIENTS/PROJECTS: In the near future, we hope to design another member directory with illustrations which will again be sent to various businesses and book stores. We are working to complete a new web site for members to advertise their art under children's books and CBIG sites on the internet. We are competing our last artists speaker session for the summer of 2000 and hope to begin it again this fall. We constantly have clients who have heard of our guild, through various contacts, and are looking for artists within our group.
PRESIDENT/CEO/OWNER: Vicki Deutsch

JUDITH CONNER DESIGN
2502 Beverly Road
651-645-7010
St. Paul 55104
FAX: 651-646-4561
SERVICES: Art direction, design, photo direction
PRESIDENT/CEO/OWNER: Judith Connor

GLORIA COOPER CALLIGRAPHY & DESIGN
5527 Malibu Drive
612-822-5709
Minneapolis 55436
E-MAIL: chai1701@mn.uswest.net
SERVICES: Calligraphy--hand lettering in English or Hebrew. Many styles available. Also illustration and art services, painting, water color quacke, colored pencil, pastel. Commissioned pieces done such as signs, poems, quotes, frontice pieces, hand addressed envelopes, design innovations of all types.
CAPABILITIES/SPECIALTIES: Design Kitabbot (Hebrew wedding documents); lettered by hand with fully illustrated and painted borders.
CURRENT/RECENT CLIENTS/PROJECTS: Taught at workshops for Minneapolis Institute of Art in conjunction with the Succot project. Included in group show of women artists at St. John's University, Collegeville, MN commissioned work by Ted Deckel, Fingerhut Co.
CONTACT: Gloria Cooper

74 / Artists & Art Studios

CYD WICKER STUDIO   612-617-9111
1701 E. Hennepin #285   Minneapolis 55414
CONTACT: Cyd Wicker
E-MAIL: cwicker939@earthlink.net
SERVICES: Fine paintings in oil traditional. Specialize in portraiture, interiors, still lifes, imaginative and landscapes.
CAPABILITIES: Operates her studio in Minneapolis and will arrange portrait sittings at her studio or travel to location.
CURRENT/RECENT CLIENTS/PROJECTS: Cyd has painted over 75 commissioned portraits including Presidential portraits of Ronald Reagan, Jimmy Carter, and Bill Clinton

D

DICK BOBNICK ILLUSTRATION, INC.   952-890-7833
3412 Barbara Lane   Burnsville 55337
FAX: 952-890-6984
CONTACT: Dick Bobnick
WWW: theispot.com/artist/bobnick or bobnick.com
SERVICES: Premier quality realistic advertising and portrait illustration (painted or airbrush), creative layout concepts and tight comps. Over thirty years experience, nationally and internationally published.
CAPABILITIES: People, portraiture, celebrities, sports, action-adventure, historical, entertainment, glamour, children, and animal subjects in full color, hard line or grahite pencil. Clientele includes national publishers, ad agencies, corporations and PR firms.
CURRENT/RECENT CLIENTS/PROJECTS: Internationally marketed collectibles, prints, federal stamps for foreign governments, book covers, album covers, celebrity portrait commissions for promotional programs on TV, films and endorsements as well as biographical book covers.

E

ESCHER ILLUSTRATIONS   651-722-4648
808 Montana Avenue East   St. Paul 55106
CONTACT: Linda Escher
E-MAIL: L_escher@yahoo.com
SERVICES: Illustrations and original fine art available. Portfolio available upon request.
CAPABILITIES: Natural Science Illustration; children's book illustrations, humorous cartoon characters.
CURRENT/RECENT CLIENTS/PROJECTS: Minnesota Zoological Gardens; education publishers; Museums; parks and wildlife organizations.

EVOLUTIONARY ILLUSTRATION & DESIGN STUDIOS   763-493-4842
9081 Larch Lane North   Maple Grove 55369

Artists & Art Studios / 75

E-MAIL: redtail@mn.uswest.net
WWW: firetruck.net/evostudio/index.htm
CONTACT: Shawn Wallace

F

STEVE FASTNER 612-338-0959
529 S 7th Street #445 Minneapolis 55415
FAX: 612-338-0959
CONTACT: Steve Fastner
SERVICES: Illustration for book covers, posters, magazine covers and general illustration.
CAPABILITIES: Airbrush illustration.
CURRENT/RECENT CLIENTS/PROJECTS: SQP, Inc.; Malt-O-Meal; Scholastic Books.

FRETHEIM & FRIENDS 763-494-4564
8677 Zinnia Way North Maple Grove 55369
CONTACT: Kristine Fretheim
E-MAIL: kfretheim@earthlink.net
SERVICES: Type of work: Advertising and graphic design, concept to finish. Services include design, copywritng, photography, illustration, production coordination. Macintosh technology is used to create logos, annual reports, brochures, catalogs, sales literature, newsletters, packaging, direct mail, and print advertising.
CAPABILITIES: Creative design and dependable service at moderate rates.

H

HSC SCENIC SERVICES, LTD 612-521-1673
2800 North 2nd Street Minneapolis 55411
FAX: 612-521-1801
CONTACT: Philip Hinz
E-MAIL: hscscenic@aol.com
SERVICES: Custom design/build and installation. Sculpting and mold making, metal working, wood working, urethane hardcoating system - FRP capabilities. Design, AutoCAD 14, and engineering services.
CAPABILITIES: We create Visual Eco-systems from design to installation, we make the unique 3D elements, facades and murals for exciting public places; retail, theme parks, restaurants, museums, children's hospitals, and corporations.
CURRENT/RECENT CLIENTS/PROJECTS: MN Historical Society; Shea Architects; BWBR; Children's Hospital; Lutheran Children's Hospital; Heritage Exhibits; Ellerbe Becket; MN Department of Env. Asst.; Stein Design; General Mills; Taylor Displays

76 / Artists & Art Studios

J

JACKIE URBANOVIC, ILLUSTRATION   612-339-7055
RKB Studios, 420 N 5th Street #920   Minneapolis 55401
FAX: 612-339-8689
CONTACT: Diane Larson or Paul Smith
WWW: rkbstudios.com
CAPABILITIES: Light hearted illustration in a variety of styles. For advertising, editorial and children's work.
SPECIALTIES: Sequential illustration; picture books, comic strips, simple animation and character creation.
CURRENT/RECENT CLIENTS/PROJECTS: Kemps, Malt-O-Meal, Target (Archer Farms), Midwest Living Magazine, Publishers Weekly Magazine, Kopp Mutual Funds, Minneapolis Children's Hospital.

JOHNNYS ILLUSTRATIVE DESIGN   612-869-2861
5937 12th Avenue South   Minneapolis 55417
FAX: 612-869-2861
CONTACT: Johnny Hanson
SERVICES: Experienced illustration and design services - complete from raw conceptualization to final production. Strong graphic solutions in bold illustrative styles.
CAPABILITIES: Twenty-seventh year in business primarily designing for print media. B & W and color work, realistic and cartoony, vintage retro-toons and clip-arty, dynamic silhouetting, product embellishment, hand-rendered fonts and distinctive logo design. All rendered in a variety of traditional media - pen and ink, pencil, paint, airbrush. Also complete computer and typography skills.
CURRENT/RECENT CLIENTS/PROJECTS: Wide range of clients - retail and editorial, the entertainment business - music promotional materials - ads, posters, CD packages, point-of-sale and product packaging. Beer labels and graphics, Renaissance Festivals nationwide, recent concert posters for Bob Dylan, Los Lobos, The Radiators and many more.
PRESIDENT/CEO/OWNER: Johnny Hanson

K

KNITTIG DESIGN, INC.   612-870-3753
322 Groveland Avenue   Minneapolis 55403
FAX: 612-870-0059
CONTACT: Denny Knittig, Betsy Nagle
E-MAIL: bjnagle@knittigdesign.com
SERVICES: Type of Work: Creative design services with total project management from concept through print production depending on individual client needs.
SPECIALTIES: Creative solutions to marketing communications needs including packaging, brochures, point-of-sale, annual reports, cookbook and editorial publications, photo art direction.
PRESIDENT/CEO/OWNER: Denny Knittig, Betsy Nagle

Artists & Art Studios / 77

IRV KNOWLEN DESIGN/ILLUSTRATION
4824 Hampshire Avenue North
763-537-7349
Crystal 55428
E-MAIL: irvk@spacestar.net
SERVICES: Layout, design, line illustration, color illustration quark, freehand, illustrator, PhotoShop.
PRESIDENT/CEO/OWNER: Irv Knowlen

BILL KROLL
901 82nd Avenue North
763-561-5407
Brooklyn Park 55444
FAX: 763-561-0577
CONTACT: Bill Kroll
SERVICES: Lettering, type design, calligraphy.

L

TOM LOCHRAY INC.
5645 10th Avenue South
612-823-7630
Minneapolis 55417
FAX: 612-824-8421
CONTACT: Tom Lochray
E-MAIL: tomlochray@tomlochray.com
WWW: tomlochray.com
SERVICES: Illustration for print and interactive media. Stock illustration available.
CAPABILITIES: Creating illustration for annual reports, point of purchase, newspaper, magazine, presentation, web-ready art. Interactive game art and packaging. Conceptual imagery, cover art, spot illustration.
PRESIDENT/CEO/OWNER: Tom Lochray

M

MIKE REED ILLUSTRATION
1314 Summit Avenue
612-374-3164
Minneapolis 55403
FAX: 612-374-3164
CONTACT: Mike Reed
E-MAIL: mikelr@winternet.com
WWW: mikereedillustration.com
CAPABILITIES: Illustration.
SPECIALTIES: Editorial, commercial children's books, traditional and digital mediums.

78 / Artists & Art Studios

N

LISA NANKIVIL   651-644-3508
2145 Dudley Avenue   St. Paul 55108
CONTACT: Lisa Nankivil
E-MAIL: lisanank@aol.com
WWW: trafficzone.com
SERVICES: Fine art oil painting, suitable for advertising illustration. Stylistic range from old masters to surrealism.
CAPABILITIES: Also do painted scenic backdrops. 15 years in advertising. 10 years as fine arts oil painter.
CURRENT/RECENT CLIENTS/PROJECTS: Paintings in national collections, many exhibitions local and national. Advertising clients include Target, Daytons, and Regis.

C A NOBENS ILLUSTRATION & DESIGN, INC.   612-935-9130
3616 Rhode Island Avenue South   St. Louis Park 55426
CONTACT: Cheryl Nobens
SERVICES: Illustration for children's books and products for children. Whimsical art for adults.
CAPABILITIES: 20 years experience taking products from concept through graphic design and illustration; extensive experience in educational art; published children's author.

O

OASIS ART STUDIO   612-860-1701
952 Medina Road   Wayzata 55391
FAX: 952-449-4956
CONTACT: Nancy Capetz
CAPABILITIES: Illustration for advertising, annual reports, package design, etc.
SPECIALTIES: Realistic airbrush and oil, conceptual work, loose pastel, computer illustration.
CURRENT/RECENT CLIENTS/PROJECTS: Nabisco, LifeTouch, Kemps, Federal Express

OTTO'S ART STUDIOS AND GALLERY   612-421-4179
15400 Rose Street NW   Andover 55304
CONTACT: Otto Henry Pfeiffer
SERVICES: Celebrity artist - Otto Henry Pfeiffer portraits of people and pets. Complete framing service Gallery.
CAPABILITIES: Since 1944 - Art of all kinds. Prints - limit editions and mural painting.

Artists & Art Studios / 79

P

TYLER PAGE   612-872-2224
4849 Emerson Avenue South   Minneapolis 55409
CONTACT: Tyler Page
E-MAIL: tylerpage@yahoo.com
SERVICES: Illustration and Graphic design, specializing in comics-related work/styles. Illustration in any media and any style. I work with oil paint, watercolor, colored pencil and pen and ink. Graphic Design games cater towards fun and youth oriented campaigns.
CAPABILITIES: 10 years experience with illustration and publication of comic books. 4 years of experience in designing CD artwork in the music industry for national and international performances. Proficient in traditional media as well as Mac & PC with Illustrator, PhotoShop and Quark. I also have prepress and print experience.
CURRENT/RECENT CLIENTS/PROJECTS: Dementia Comics; St. Olaf College; St. Olaf Orchestra; Boldt Entertainment; Surprises Magazines.

PAPAS ART STUDIO   612-920-3979
6106 Excelsior Blvd.   St. Louis Park 55416
SERVICES: People and pet portraits, illustrations, cartoons. Caricatures, architectural renderings, patent and trademark drawings, maps, retouching, lettering.
CAPABILITIES: Pen and ink, airbrush, watercolor, oil.
PRESIDENT/CEO/OWNER: Al Papas

PENSCRIPTIONS   651-645-4223
1896 Albert Street No.   St. Paul 55113
CONTACT: Judy Dodds
E-MAIL: jdpens@worldnet.att.net
SERVICES: Original work for private or corporate setting to become framed art work, artist's book; work for camera ready art; hand lettered designs for mission statements; annual reports; invitations; recognitions; certificates; brochures; packaging; cards.
CAPABILITIES: Custom hand lettered calligraphy; designs created with pointed or broad edged pen or brush; watercolor washes; collage; variety of alphabets.
CURRENT/RECENT CLIENTS/PROJECTS: University of St. Thomas; University of Minnesota; William Mitchell College of Law; St. Paul Chamber Orchestra; ELCA; Lungblomsten Foundation; Rivertown Trading Company; Macalester College; The Bibelot Shop; Denarius Advisors; Montage; Kramer Lothrop Brewer Financial; Mt. Carmel Ministries.

MARY PERKINS   651-436-8578
4042 River Road   Afton 55001
FAX: 651-646-5303
CONTACT: Mary Perkins
WWW: clickweddingphotographer.com
SERVICES: Photojournalism, fine art photography.
CAPABILITIES: Photojournalist, candid, human interest, fine art, manipulated Polaroids.

80 / Artists & Art Studios

CURRENT/RECENT CLIENTS/PROJECTS: 3M; Corporate Newspaper; contract assignments; photojournalistic weddings; fine art weddings.

R

RURIK   651-221-9047
300 Broadway Street #509   St. Paul 55101
CONTACT: Rurik Hover
WWW: isd.net/rhover
CAPABILITIES: Fine art and commercial illustration; portraits; indoor murals.
SPECIALTIES: Photo-realistic portraits, in acrylic or graphite.
CURRENT/RECENT CLIENTS/PROJECTS: First Union Management, St. Cloud, MN; Ragel Eyewear, Eagan, MN; Department 56, Eden Prairie, MN

S

FREDERICK SHORT   763-441-7254
16651 Kangaroo Circle   Ramsey 55303
CONTACT: Fred Short
SERVICES: Sculpture.
CAPABILITIES: Clay, wood, rock, bronze and soft sculpture. Life, surrealism and abstract.
CURRENT/RECENT CLIENTS/PROJECTS: Self-motivated, independent/John Deere, Bobcat, Chevrolet, Dayton-Hudson and confidential.

SPECTRUM STUDIO, INC.   612-332-2361
1503 Washington Avenue South   Minneapolis 55454
FAX: 612-332-2364
CONTACT: Renae Lefebvre
E-MAIL: rep@spectrumstudio.net
ALTERNATE PHONE: 1-800-500-1394
SERVICES: Spectrum Studio is in its twenty-fifth year providing high quality illustration. Our clients include corporations, package design firms, graphic design firms, advertising agencies and publishers worldwide.
CAPABILITIES: Talent: Lisa Brooks, production art, desktop publishing; Martin Harris, Illustration, digital; Anthony Hilscher, Illustration, airbrush, mixed medium, digital; Mark Jensen, Illustration, airbrush, mixed medium; Jack Johnson, Illustration, caricatures; Roger Lundquist, Illustration, mixed medium, watercolor; Preston Palmer, Illustration, digital, 3D; Jim Rownd, Illustration, airbrush, oil, mixed medium; Larry Ruppert, Illustration, airbrush, mixed medium, marker comps, digital; John Schreiner, Illustration, airbrush, oil, mixed medium, digital.
PRESIDENT/CEO/OWNER: Renae Lefebvre

STEVEN LINDER PHOTO   952-884-8134
10824 River Terrace Drive   Bloomington 55431
FAX: 952-884-9876
CONTACT: Steven Linder

Artists & Art Studios / 81

E-MAIL: slinder@pioneerplanet.infi.net
WWW: linderphoto.com
CAPABILITIES: Stock photography, Aeriel photography, Commercial photography.

KATHY A. STEWART	612-729-2440
4533 Cedar Avenue South	Minneapolis 55407

SERVICES: Prop and set design (some fabrication); specialty panting--murals, faux finishes; model building; product coordinator.
CAPABILITIES/SPECIALTIES: Ten years of experience working on feature film and commercials, industrials, and theatrical productions. Plus two years working on museum installations as project coordinator.
PRESIDENT/CEO/OWNER: Kathy Stewart

STUDIO ONE, INC.	612-831-6313
7300 Metro Blvd. #400	Edina 55439

FAX: 612-831-6529
CONTACT: David Kuettel
E-MAIL: systems@studio1.com
WWW: studio1.com
SERVICES: Illustration and graphic design.
SPECIALTIES: A 40 year tradition in airbrush and other mediums for technical, line and digital illustration. See our portfolio online or call to set up a portfolio showing.
PRESIDENT/CEO/OWNER: David Kuettel

T

GLENN TERRY, FINE ARTIST	612-413-1991
PO Box 151	Cedar 55011

CONTACT: Glenn Terry
E-MAIL: greatart@skypoint.com
WWW: skypoint.com/~greatart
SERVICES: Design and creation of bronze and marble statues, fountains, sculptural groups, architectural sculpture, mural painting.
CAPABILITIES: Large figurative sculpture and fountains. Design of homes and offices.
CURRENT/RECENT CLIENTS/PROJECTS: 9 - 1/2 foot tall bronze statue of St. Paul to be placed at the entry to the Cathedral of St. Paul. 33 foot tall futuristic water display in stairway court of large private residence. Murals and wall treatments for Tooth By the Lake Dental Office in Hopkins, Steamworks, Inc. Coffee House in Minneapolis. Design of Law Office and life-size bronze statue/fountain of justice in Maplewood.

CRAIG THIESEN	651-228-0482
308 Prince Street #210	St. Paul 55101

FAX: 651-228-0843
CONTACT: Craig Thiesen
E-MAIL: craig@studio210.com
WWW: studio210.com

82 / Artists & Art Studios

SERVICES: Hand colored and digitally colored photographs, specializing in Minnesota and European landscapes. Computer graphics - consulting and production, including digital manipulation, image database management, Macintosh system trouble shooting, and website construction.
CURRENT/RECENT CLIENTS/PROJECTS: James Page Brewing, Northwest Canoe Company, Cavdozo Photo Gallery, Saint Paul Art Crawl, Department of Natural Resources.
PRESIDENT/CEO/OWNER: Craig Thiesen

CHRISTINE TIERNEY
1700 East 116th Street

612-890-2536
Burnsville 55337

CONTACT: Christine Tierney
E-MAIL: cmtart@aol.com
SERVICES: Classical illustration. Specializing in children's art, nature, fashion, and menu illustration. Watercolor, oil, pastel pen and ink, and Graphite. Whimsical story and book illustration; technical illustration; Posters, T-shirts, greeting cards; Traditional portraits and still lifes.

ANDREE TRACEY
1341 Flag Avenue South

612-541-1858
Minneapolis 55426

FAX: 612-541-1858
CONTACT: Andree Tracey
SERVICES: Storyboards, illustrations, concept boards, comp layouts and animatics.
CAPABILITIES: Marker renderings of food, people, animal, sports and products, including automotive and technological. Concept planning and new business presentation experience. Will work on or off-site.
CURRENT/RECENT CLIENTS/PROJECTS: Fallon McElligott; CME; BBDO; Peterson Milla Hooks; Nelson-Henry and many other agencies both large and small.

U

UNCLE PETE'S COLORING BOOK
2205 California Street NE #502

612-782-9185
Minneapolis 55418

CONTACT: Pete Driessen
E-MAIL: elroydog@bitstream.net
SERVICES: Visual arts/painting; acrylic on canvas, paper, collage and found object.
CAPABILITIES: Contemporary/social political interpretation.

Audio Visual Services

A

ACTORS PLUS/VOICE PLUS   651-426-9400
1564 5th Street   St. Paul 55110
CONTACT: Debbie Klemmer Rush
TOLL FREE: 877-426-9500
E-MAIL: agency@voiceplustalent.com
WWW: voiceplustalent.com
SERVICES: Since 1972, providing professional voice and on-camera actors and narrators; men, women, children, ethnic and earprompted talent; foreign language translators and narrators. Photos, audio clips, resumes, resources and other topics of interest are available on our website. CD's and audition arrangements available.
CAPABILITIES: We represent highly qualified Voice talent and on-camera actors for broadcast commercials, industrials, educational videos, documentaries, IVR systems, voicemail, CD-ROM's, actors and spokespersons for live training programs, trade shows, conventions, sales meetings and award dinners. Real people models for print.
CURRENT/RECENT CLIENTS/PROJECTS: Honda (1986 - present) Commercial; Mayo Clinic (1990 - present) Industrial; Best Buy (1985 - present) Industrial and Commercial; Many advertising agencies, A/V production studios, Independent producers, Broadcast stations and Corporate media departments.
PRESIDENT/CEO/OWNER: Linda Klemmer

ADVANCED AUDIO VISUAL   952-881-4500
8801 Lyndale Avenue So #100   Bloomington 55420
FAX: 952-881-4770
CONTACT: Larry Pierce
CAPABILITIES: Portable computer presentation support. Complete audio-visual, video and audio support. Show coordination and equipment rental, both nationally and locally.
SPECIALTIES: Offering computer presentation and comprehensive audio-visual support to small and medium sized businesses.
PRESIDENT/CEO/OWNER: Larry Pierce, Ed Koskie

ALPHA VIDEO   612-896-9898
7711 Computer Avenue   Edina 55435
FAX: 612-896-9899
CONTACT: Rick Risch
E-MAIL: webmaster@alphavideo.com
WWW: alphavideo.com
SERVICES: Alpha Video is a professional video systems dealer of HDTV, DV, Non-linear, Digital and NT Technology, Alpha specializes in the design, configuration, installation, support and training of these video systems in broadcast, cable, corporate, production and education markets. Rental capabilities range from event support to broadcast rental equipment. Services include delivery and set up, camera operation for onsite shoots, fully equipped linear and non-linear edit suites, tape digitizing, and full tape duplication capabilities. SVHS, DCVPRO and BETA SP.
PRESIDENT/CEO/OWNER: Stan Stanek
SALES CONTACT: Rick Risch, Rental Manager; Kevin Groves, Broadcast Sales; Jim Morical, Educational Sales

84 / Audio Visual Services

ALTERNATIVE VIDEO SOLUTIONS　　　　　　　　　　　　651-631-2426
2023 West County Road C　　　　　　　　　　　　　　Roseville 55113
FAX: 651-631-3070
CONTACT: Rob Thill
E-MAIL: info@avs-us.com
WWW: avs-us.com
CAPABILITIES: In support of business shows, staging, trade show. Complete A/V rental/service company. Show coordination, equipment rental and technical support.
SPECIALTIES: Large screen video. LED screens, Videowalls, super bright Projection and Plasma screens. Multi camera systems and other goodies for your business meetings, product launches, conventions and trade shows.
CURRENT/RECENT CLIENTS/PROJECTS: US and International - Dayton's Fashbash, 11 x 16 feet tall LED screen. 3M 2000 stockholders meetings, 18 x 24 digital projection screen. Guidant national sales meeting, projection, laser show and audience response system. NBA - Videowall for commercial shoot. Quark 4 x 4 videowall with 4 computer screens.

B

P. H. BRINK INTERNATIONAL　　　　　　　　　　　　763-591-1977
6100 Golden Valley Road　　　　　　　　　　　　　Golden Valley 55442
FAX: 763-542-9138
CONTACT: Greg Brink or Bob Dungan
E-MAIL: gregb@phbrink.com
CAPABILITIES: Foreign language audio visual services from concept through production film, videotape, and slides in all major languages.
SPECIALTIES: Language adaptations of English scripts for voice-over or on-camera shooting. Complete graphic replacement and post production services. All talent are natives of your target market and have English as a second language.

Audio Visual Services / 85

C

CONUS PRODUCTIONS & SATELLITE SERVICES 651-642-4477
3415 University Avenue   Minneapolis 55414
FAX: 651-642-4551
CONTACT: Brian Tuttle
CAPABILITIES: Single and multi-camera video production service. Mobile and fixed satellite uplinks, and full production crews available for event broadcast.
EQUIPMENT: Sony CCD cameras, modular control rooms. Chyron graphics. Support Beta SP video tape format 4 uplink trucks, tape playback.
SPECIALTIES: Mobile uplink and multi-camera video production.
PRESIDENT/CEO/OWNER: Terry O'Reilly, GM

F

FLYING COLORS INCORPORATED   612-752-0200
917 North 5th Street   Minneapolis 55401
CONTACT: Bob Sullivan, VP; Rick Cornish, CD
CAPABILITIES: Complete AV program concepting, design and coordination; from analysis of your needs and your audience; to implementing a creative solution, production, distribution and presentation, to evaluating the program's impact.
SPECIALTIES: Highly creative, innovative programs that are on-target, on-time, and on-budget. We're experienced specialists in video, multimedia, events and original music.

FREESTYLE PRODUCTIONS, INC.   763-417-9575
6112 Olson Memorial Highway   Minneapolis 55422
FAX: 763-417-9576
CONTACT: Dale Kivimaki, Mark Hulsey
E-MAIL: dale@freestyle-productions.com
WWW: freestyle-productions.com
CAPABILITIES: Freestyle Productions provides video and multimedia communication services with a specialized focus on high-profile, live-event productions including corporate meetings, trade shows, conventions and concerts. Complete array of broadcast equipment: multi-camera field packages, post production/mobile, non-linear edit suites, switcher/effects & graphic systems, large-format video and data projection, front & rear screens and videowalls.
SPECIALTIES: Over 10 years of national and international experience producing all types of live and special events shows. Freestyle provides an intuitive understanding of how to best communicate their client's message to impact large and small audiences.
CURRENT/RECENT CLIENTS/PROJECTS: Fox Sports Net, Coca-Cola, Lucent Technologies, Apple Computer, Northwest Airlines, Promise Keepers, Carlson Companies, Lutheran Brotherhood, US West, Minnesota State Fair, Universal Studios Hollywood.

86 / Audio Visual Services

G

GREATAPES CORPORATION 612-872-8284
1523 Nicollet Avenue Minneapolis 55403
FAX: 612-872-0635
CONTACT: Robert M. McCarthy
TOLL FREE: 1-800-879-8273
CAPABILITIES: We can develop your project from concept to completion, or just polish a piece of it. GT Media offers digital audio/video production and post. Our facilities feature digital audio recording and editing, sweetening for video and a complete sound effects and music library. GT Media has its own on-staff producers, engineers and composers. We offer both high-speed and real time audio cassette duplication and transferring capabilities (most formats), small and large quantity CD replication. GT Media offers on-line and off-line video edits suites, Macintosh-based and Flint SGI-based graphics and compositing, studio and remote video production and video duplication. We also offer blank audio and video tape stock.
EQUIPMENT: Audio: Sonic Solutions digital audio workstation, ISDN digital patch, time code R-dat, full analog support (4-track and 1/4 track). Gauss, Magnafax and Omegatech high speed duplication systems. KABA real time, Hoei CD-R replicator. On-line: Sony digital switcher, Sony DME 3000 Digital effects, Abekas A-72 Digital CG, Flint Graphics, Video Explorer, Digital Betacam, Component Beta SP, 1", Hi-8, S-VHS. Non-linear: ImMIX VideoCube. In-house 35 x 30 video studio, ikegami cameras, full production support.
SPECIALTIES: Broadcast and educational audio and video productions. Corporate image, training, language translation, commercial, multimedia programs, duplication and packaging of all audio and video products and styles. Media Express printing/copy center.

THE GREENE SHEET 763-560-3292
3009 74th Avenue North Brooklyn Park 55444
FAX: 763-560-6647
CONTACT: Sam Howard
E-MAIL: unclegeo@bpsi.net
WWW: bstock.com
SERVICES: Uncle Geo's Greene Sheet is a brokerage firm specializing in used and B-stock production equipment. We serve the video, film, audio and multimedia industries. There are no fees for listing, only when we sell your gear. Staffed by experienced production professionals, the Greene Sheet is the oldest equipment brokerage on the web. Over 15 years of system design experience is available to help our customers make informed decisions about buying and selling used gear.
CAPABILITIES: System appraisals available for production companies, banks and leasing companies.
PRESIDENT/CEO/OWNER: George F. Greene

Audio Visual Services / 87

INHOUSE MEDIA
800 N. Washington Avenue #307
FAX: 612-341-4063
CONTACT: Jim Gustafson
E-MAIL: jimg@inhousegroup.com
WWW: inhousegroup.com

612-341-4010
Minneapolis 55401

SERVICES: Meetings and Events: Business theater and staging services; motion graphics and 2D/3D animation; on-site event management; speaker support production; theme development and speech writing; video production and non-linear post-production. Computer Based Training: Deliverable on CD-ROM, DVD, Internet or Intranet. Sales Presentations: Corporate ID and logo design, E-commerce applications; Interactive kiosk design; web design, site development and hosting.
CAPABILITIES: InHouse Media wants to be your production company. Our years of experience help you exceed your presentation needs in any media. InHouse Media makes you a hero!
CURRENT/RECENT CLIENTS/PROJECTS: We serve current and future Fortune 500 companies.
PRESIDENT/CEO/OWNER: Joel DesLauriers/Jim Gustafson

world-class ebusiness results

IPARES, LTD.
5000 Union Plaza
FAX: 612-215-2310
CONTACT: Tom Harold
E-MAIL: info@ipares.com
WWW: ipares.com

612-215-2300
Minneapolis 55401

CAPABILITIES: Integration of marketing, design and technology.
SERVICES: Internet Professional Services: Providing Fortune 1000 corporations with Internet, Intranet, Extranet, Sales Force Automation, Kiosk and Database Marketing solutions. Multimedia Related Services: Design/concepting, consulting, writing/instructional design and programming. Internet/Intranet: In-house design and programming including secure E-commerce solutions and web-based training.
CAPABILITIES/SPECIALTIES: Graphic design services for brochures, catalogs, ads, display and packaging. Complete prepress production services.
PRESIDENT/CEO/OWNER: Lon Bencini/Tom Harold

88 / Audio Visual Services

L

LIFETOUCH VIDEO CREATIONS   612-826-4389
11000 Viking Drive, Suite 300   Eden Prairie 55344
FAX: 612-832-5665
CONTACT: Brian Dellis
SERVICES: Full service video production from pre-production through post-production. Including conception, script writing, talent, planning, crew and equipment for location shooting, sound recording, mixing and editing on Betacam SP. Rental and duplication available.
EQUIPMENT: Sony & Hitachi Betacam chip cameras, video studio and 2 on-line edit suites. Duplication also available.
SPECIALTIES: Corporate, industrial, broadcast video production.
PRESIDENT/CEO/OWNER: Director of Operations, Brian Dellis; Senior Producer, Tim Johnson; Producer, Donnie Koshiol.

LONG RUN PRODUCTIONS, LTD.   612-673-9729
245 2nd Avenue North   Minneapolis 55401
FAX: 612-673-9469
CONTACT: Jud Williams
CAPABILITIES: Filling the technical needs of producers and directors - DP, engineer and video production equipment. Triax-controlled Ikegami HL-57 and HL-55A cameras. BVW-50, BVW-35, BVV-5 VTRS, all Betacam SP. Fully-equipped 1-ton support truck. Lighting, shooting and engineering.
PRESIDENT/CEO/OWNER: Thomas Ingledew, Jud Williams

M

MAINSTREAM COMMUNICATIONS, INC.   952-888-9000
9555 James Avenue South #235   Bloomington 55431
CONTACT: Garry Krebs, Bob Ewert
E-MAIL: gkrebs@mainstreamcom.net
WWW: mainstreamcom.net
SERVICES: Mainstream concepts and stages corporate events of all kinds including meetings, trade shows, and special events. Our staff includes the professionals who know how to navigate the challenges of meeting rooms, conventional halls, and trade show floors. Our inventory includes a vast array of audio visual equipment; video and data projection, front and rear screens. Intelligent lighting, and multi-channel sound systems with effects. We warehouse existing sets which are available for rent or we can custom design and build one for you. We also provide live talent and nationally known acts to make your event special.
CAPABILITIES/SPECIALTIES: We are a turnkey video production environment. Location video crews include Beta SP equipment and complete location lighting and sound recording. Our 1,200 s.f. sound stage includes a lighting package along with available sets. We offer 4 edit suites: Digital Betacam complete with DME, 2 non-linear including DVE, and a portable Beta SP AB-Roll Edit Suite which can be used in-studio or for location events. Other in-house services include 3D animation featuring Softimage software and a sound recording studio with multiple music libraries.

Audio Visual Services / 89

MEDIA LOFT, INC.   612-375-1086
333 Washington Avenue North #210   Minneapolis 55401
FAX: 612-375-0913
CONTACT: David Kelsey
SERVICES: Award-winning full service communications company; script to screen concepting and production for video, film business theatre, corporate meetings and events.
PRESIDENT/CEO/OWNER: Engenio H. DiLorenzo

MEDIA MAXX COMMUNICATIONS   612-332-1047
127A South Drive   Circle Pines 55014
CONTACT: Jeff Gearhart
E-MAIL: mediamaxx@unique-software.com
WWW: creativefrontiers.net/mediafest/mediafest.htm
CAPABILITIES: Dynamic media solutions for non-linear editing, compact disc and digital versatile disk, authoring, audio visual camera acquisition and recording, studio switching, distribution and broadcast. Full service graphics, animation, audio and video production services. Production system design, integration, installation and training.
SPECIALTIES: Founder and host of Mediafest Digital Workshops. Workshops sponsored by Internet providers, hardware and software companies, publishers, international communications organizations and local media.
CURRENT/RECENT CLIENTS/PROJECTS: State Universities and Colleges, Broadcast, Cable Access, Local Government, US West Communications, Geospan, Floe International, Arctic Cat, Polaris, National Car Rental and The Burton Report.

MOTION PICTURE PROJECTIONISTS AND VIDEO TECHNICIANS   612-378-2153
312 Central Avenue SE #367   Minneapolis 55414
CONTACT: Davin C. Anderson, Business Representative
E-MAIL: iatse219@mtn.org
WWW: mtn.org/iatse219
CAPABILITIES: Camera assistant, equipment rental, projectionist services. Union: IATSE local 219.
SPECIALTIES: Projectionist services (film and video) audio visual services, camera operators, photographers, equipment rental and installation, teleconferencing, computer projection, multi-image, conventions, reasonable rates, over 100 employees.

O

OAKWOOD PRODUCTIONS   651-631-9518
PO Box 120699   St. Paul 55112
FAX: 651-639-1969
CONTACT: Joseph Ferraro
E-MAIL: jfproducer@aol.com
WWW: oakwoodproductions.com
SERVICES: Complete video production: Business services (marketing product introduction, duplication, seminars). Weddings, legal, special events, sports.

90 / Audio Visual Services

P

PRECISION POWERHOUSE   612-333-9111
911 Second Street South   Minneapolis 55415
FAX: 612-332-9200
CONTACT: Dan Piepho, Paul Sunberg, Gene Gunderson
E-MAIL: dan@power-house.com; pauls@power-house.com or geneg@power-house.com
WWW: precisionpowerhouse.com
SERVICES: Full service communications company specializing in award-winning sales, marketing and training videos, audio and Interactive media production and post-production. Video sales presentation, product marketing presentations, video news releases, video/floppy disk/CD-ROM/DVD, annual reports, Interactive media training programs, video/audio/CD-ROM, catalogs, etc.
EQUIPMENT: 40 x 60 production soundstage, full-scale complete digital audio post production suite, full-scale complete digital/video post production suite, digital/analog video post production suite, SFI 3D animation suite, Interactive media workstations, DVD surround sound authoring suite, complete internet services, class five thousand clean-room, large scale audio/video duplication, CD and DVD replication, package designers on staff, worldwide shipping services, producer/director services, writers, technicians.
SPECIALTIES: We do everything under one roof with electronic tools for corporate sales, marketing and training in video, audio, Interactive media, DVD, e-business and the internet.

R

R.E.M. VIDEO & EVENT COMPANY   612-788-9221
1828 NE Jefferson Street   Minneapolis 55418
FAX: 612-788-7712
CONTACT: Roger Miller
E-MAIL: info@remvideoevent.com
WWW: remvideoevent.com
SERVICES: Full service production house for video, events/presentations, audio, multimedia. Our focus is in business to business communications delivered live or on media. We have in-house presentation expertise and equipment for TVL, Powerpoint (advanced), Astound and SCALA. Video productions on Betacam and DV formats. Non-linear broadcast and non-broadcast editing. Non-linear audio production for audio CD video and film sweetening and music production scoring.
SPECIALTIES: Historical productions commemorating companies and places. Business-to-business marketing and training. Original music.
PRESIDENT/CEO/OWNER: Roger Miller, Presentations & Video; Michael Loonan, Audio & Multimedia; Pat Miller, Production Management

Audio Visual Services / 91

T

TAG TEAM FILM & VIDEO, INC.   651-917-0058
2375 University Avenue West #200   St. Paul 55114
FAX: 651-917-0368
CONTACT: Jeff Byers
E-MAIL: jeff@tagteamfilmvideo.com
SERVICES: Digital Betacam and Betacam SP video production, 16 mm film production, off-line and on-line non-linear editing.
EQUIPMENT: Field production - complete crew and equipment packages featuring Sony BVP-570/550 digital cameras with 16 x 9 capability. Sony DVW-250 digital Betacam VTR, BVW-50 and BVV-5 Betacam SP VTRs. Extensive audio, lighting, grip and monitoring equipment. Single camera and live-switched multi-camera configurations. Aaton LTR-7 16mm camera pkg. Post production - SoftImage DS and Avid 1000.
SPECIALTIES: Providing independent, corporate and broadcast producer/directors with comprehensive, professional production and post-production services.
CURRENT/RECENT CLIENTS/PROJECTS: The St. Paul Companies; Corporate Video; ABC; Novartis; The Producers Consortium; Honeywell; Shandwick; Mayo Clinic; General Mills; Falls Agency; ESPN; Fleishman-Hillard; A & E.
PRESIDENT/CEO/OWNER: Thomas G. Krohn, Jeffrey J. Byers

TAKE 1 PRODUCTIONS   952-831-7757
9969 Valley View Road   Eden Prairie 55344
CONTACT: Rob Hewitt
SERVICES: Full service video and multimedia production company. Complete scripting, studio and location shooting, digital non-linear editing, computer generated graphics, 3D animation, digital video effects, multimedia authoring, MPEG encoding, video/CD-ROM duplication.
SPECIALTIES: Presentations for sales, training, and product demonstrations.
PRESIDENT/CEO/OWNER: Teri Murphy

Awards

T
TRILOGY MARKETING GROUP
944 Cobb Road
FAX: 651-482-8270
CONTACT: James D. Lemke
E-MAIL: trilogymktg@aol.com

651-482-8270
Shoreview 55126-3804

SERVICES: Creative design and development of custom awards that match the recipient, event, budget, accomplishment and/or environment where the awards will be displayed.
CAPABILITIES: Resourcing unique and extra-ordinary awards using a combination of different ideas/materials to help generate high recipient impact and perceived value. Other services: Personalization; packaging and distribution; warehousing provide at no charge; fulfillment services available.
PRESIDENT/CEO/OWNER: James D. Lemke

Bindery Services

C

CG BOOK PRINTERS
PO Box 8800
FAX: 507-386-6350
CONTACT: Dan Kvasnicka
E-MAIL: cgbooks@corpgraph.com

507-388-3300
North Mankato 56003

SERVICES: Complete book printer and manufacturer: creative book design services, drum scanning, electronic prepress, up to 8 color sheet fed printing, side sewn casebinding, perfect binding, saddle stitch binding, hard and soft cover capabilities.
CAPABILITIES: CG Book printers specializes in children's books (hardcase, juvenile sized, reinforced library bound.) We also have the capabilities to produce products with padded board material.
PRESIDENT/CEO/OWNER: Joe Keenan

THE COLLATORS, INC.
7107 Medicine Lake Road
FAX: 763-591-9757
CONTACT: Wayne Nelson
E-MAIL: collator@uswest.net

763-591-0541
Golden Valley 55427

CAPABILITIES: Distribution and fulfillment; storage; word processing; address labels; mailing and shipping - UPS. USPS, and others; computerized inventory reporting; shrink-wrapping; pickup and delivery.
SPECIALTIES: Hand collation and light assembly.

Branding & Brand Development

D

D.W. ET AL.　612-339-7848
400 First Avenue North #316　Minneapolis 55401
The Wyman Building
CONTACT: Dan Wallace
WWW: dwetal.com
CAPABILITIES: D.W. et al. Ltd. works with B2B firms to build businesses and brands. As consultants, we craft strategies and write plans. As marketing agents, we implement plans through a network we've cultivated since 1986. Core deliverables: strategic marketing plans, positioning and brand plans, company brochures, web sites and advertising campaigns. Extended capabilities are available through allied advisors and specialists.
SPECIALTIES: Business-to-business firms.
CURRENT/RECENT CLIENTS/PROJECTS: Alliant Consulting; The Bureau Electronics Division; Carlson School of Management IRC; City of Minneapolis ITS; e-fortunecookie.com; Fredrikson & Byron; GTE; hrtomorrow.com; Honeywell; IBM; KruegerWright; Norberg Management; NRG; personallitigation.com; PDI; Palamino Euro Bistro; Pro Group; Research Resources; Serving Software; The Collaborative; Wilson Learning; and Winona Research.

E

ECLECTIC MUSIC/MARKETING &　651-690-4999
PUBLISHING
585 Warwick Street　St. Paul 55116
FAX: 651-690-4999
CONTACT: Don Wozniak
SERVICES: Marketer of music and entertainment products specializing in affordable brand building campaigns for musicians (bands of all musical styles) and content companies. We build marketing communications and promotion plans to help channel your music or creative expression to the proper end user.
SPECIALTIES: We produce awareness and image campaigns, electronic press kits and outdoor and in-store events.
CURRENT/RECENT CLIENTS/PROJECTS: Ingram/LeBrun Music, Inc. and Northword Sound.

F

FRANKE + FIORELLA　612-338-1700
401 North 3rd Street, Suite 380　**Minneapolis 55401**
FAX: 612-338-2300
CONTACT: Deb Fiorella
E-MAIL: deb@frankefiorella.com
WWW: frankefiorella.com
CAPABILITIES: Logo design, corporate identity development, brand strategy, strategic planning, positioning and naming. Concept/design exploration and project management through production of final files.

Branding & Brand Development / 95

SPECIALTIES: Developing brand identity systems for new and existing products, services and companies.
PRESIDENT/CEO/OWNER: Craig Franke, Deborah Fiorella

G

GEOFFREY CARLSON GAGE, LLC　　　　　　　　　　　952-401-7660
500 Lake Street #100　　　　　　　　　　　　　　　　**Excelsior 55331**
FAX: 952-401-7662
CONTACT: Geoff Gage
E-MAIL: info@gcgage.com
WWW: gcgage.com
SERVICES: Advertising Services: consulting, strategic planning, creative concepting and development, media planning and buying, production coordination. Internet Services: Consulting and existing site analysis, strategic planning, creative concepting and site development, electronic development/programming, ongoing site maintenance, online web site search engine visibility promotion.
CAPABILITIES: Geoffrey Carlson Gage is a strategically creative Internet and advertising solutions agency, whose mission is to grow our client's business, sell their products and/or services and build their brands in an affordable manner. There are five major points-of-difference separating us from our competitors. 1) Our ability (based on our background and expertise) as a small advertising agency to create, develop, and deliver an integrated combination of breakthrough traditional media advertising and interactive advertising/web site development. 2) Our ability as a small advertising agency to create, develop, and deliver creative, multi-disciplined, value driven web sites based on a balance of advertising, marketing and technology practices and principles. 3) Our ability to create, develop, and deliver a combination of traditional advertising and online search engine visibility promotion to drive traffic to sites. 4) Our tremendous flexibility centered on client needs, and 5) Our partnership with local and national Internet service provider, US Internet.
CURRENT/RECENT CLIENTS/PROJECTS: Condor Corporation; Stars of Aspen; Gage Marketing Group; Milestone Motorsports; The Minnesota Wild; Craig Young/Coldwell Burnet Realty; Bob Jasper/Fleet Corporate Aircraft Leasing; Metromark; CEPCO Management, Inc.; US Internet; Gage In-store Marketing; Midwave Corporation.
PRESIDENT/CEO/OWNER: Geoff Gage

96 / Branding & Brand Development

H

HEDSTROM/BLESSING, INC.

HEDSTROM/BLESSING, INC.   763-591-6200
8301 Golden Valley Road #300   Minneapolis 55427
FAX: 763-591-6232
CONTACT: Julie Pearl
E-MAIL: info@hb-inc.com
WWW: www.hb-inc.com
OFFICERS: Steve Blessing, Chm/CEO; Brenda Spanier, Pres/COO; Tom Blessing, VP; Julie Pearl, VP
SERVICES: Brand development and stewardship including brand strategies, positioning, naming, identity development and implementation.
CAPABILITIES: Corporate and product brand identity development and stewardship. New product launches. Full complement of services including naming, logo design, packaging design, advertising, direct marketing, promotion, collateral, point-of-purchase, interactive and website design.
CURRENT/RECENT CLIENTS/PROJECTS: Selected accounts include 3M; Bachman's; Carlson Leisure Group; Fabcon; Intellisol International; Interactive Learning Group; Land O'Lakes; Pillsbury; Target.

L

LEAPFROG ASSOCIATES   612-332-0132
2950 Dean Parkway #2404   Minneapolis 55416
FAX: 612-377-FROG
CONTACT: Diane Page
E-MAIL: leapfrogtwo@aol.com
SERVICES: New product concept ideation. Name generation, brand positioning and repositioning, line extensions, trend tracking.
CAPABILITIES: Fast track process: Results of an ideation plus written and illustrated concept boards plus focus group insights - all within 48 hours.
CURRENT/RECENT CLIENTS/PROJECTS: 3M; ConAgra; Unipak; Pillsbury; Gold N' Plump.

Branding & Brand Development / 97

M

MAGNETO COMMUNICATIONS 952-352-0787
801 Main Street Hopkins 55343
CONTACT: Matt Farley
WWW: magnetocom.com
ACCOUNT SUPERVISORS: Matt Farley, Account Services Director
CREATIVE DIRECTOR: Arik Nordby, Jeff Ess
SERVICES: Creatives with the brains for business. We'll learn your business inside and out to help build a detailed plan for developing your brand.
CAPABILITIES: Provide clients with a clear and concise approach to brand development through focused research, strategy, design and implementation.
SPECIALTIES: Corporate ID and logo development, annual reports and marketing collateral.

N

NYGARD DIMENSIONS 612-371-9228
1414 Marshall Street N.E. Minneapolis 55413
FAX: 612-371-9232
CONTACT: Ben Wallace, Director of Account Services
E-MAIL: id@brandcommunications.com
WWW: brandcommunications.com
SERVICES: Brand-based marketing communications: brand strategy and identity development, integrated marketing communications planning, creative development, design, production, implementation, measurement and management through all media: Print: literature, stationery, direct mail, advertising, sales tools, packaging, sales kits; Digital: Websites (internet/intranet/extranet), online promotion, sales tools/software, product demos, video presentations, kiosks, online brand identity management; Environmental: themed events, stage sets, exhibits, displays/POP.
CAPABILITIES: Brand identity systems, including naming, logo, brand elements and guidelines. Unique approach to brand identity strategy, design development and management through all points of stakeholder contact to create the "whole brand experience." Sister companies Nygard Set Design and Harmony Box contribute to brand experience creation. Industries: information technology/e-business, healthcare/pharmaceuticals, financial services, manufacturing, retail and more.

98 / Branding & Brand Development

CURRENT/RECENT CLIENTS/PROJECTS: 3M Company; Auxilium Software; Compass Productions; Conseco Finance; Larson Manufacturing; Lawson Software; Lutheran Brotherhood; MedIntelligence; nQuire Software; Pharmaceutical Care Network (PCN); Proliant (formerly AMPC, Inc.); Qtech Systems, Inc.; Sales Force 2000 Software; Safe Reflections; Sunrise Community Banks (formerly Franklin Bancorp), U.S. Magnetix; U of M Physicians.
PRESIDENT/CEO/OWNER: Jim Nygard, P

P

KENDALL PURDY GROUP 952-471-8210
1975 Fagerness Pt. Road Wayzata 55391
FAX: 952-471-9712
CONTACT: John Purdy
E-MAIL: kenpurgrp@aol.com
SERVICES: Brand Centric Planing for consumer and business-to-business companies. Facilitated planning meetings to collectively define brand vision and marketing strategies. Qualitative and quantitative research support to define and better understand customer attitudes, perceptions, motivations and feelings toward a brand in the context of its product or service category. Agency search and/or resource identification and selection for the execution of brand marketing communications.
CAPABILITIES: Objective and means-neutral consulting for defining effective brand strategies and plans. Over 25 years of experience with a wide variety of consumer and business-to-business clients as a brand development director with leading Twin Cities advertising agencies and as an independent consultant.
CURRENT/RECENT CLIENTS/PROJECTS: Clients served as an independent consultant include: 3M Corporate Communications; 3M Home Care Division; Radisson Hotels Wolrldwide; United Sugars (American Crystal Sugar); California Olive Industry; C K Witco Corp.; Shearson Publishing; TryAngle Marketing Clarity Coverdale Fury Advertising.
PRESIDENT/CEO/OWNER: John Purdy

Branding & Brand Development / 99

T

TARTAN MARKETING
15500 Wayzata Blvd, Suite 1000
Twelve Oaks Center

952-473-7575
Wayzata 55391

CONTACT: James J. MacLachlan
E-MAIL: jim@tartanmarketing.com
WWW: tartanmarketing.com
FOCUS: Tartan Marketing helps business-to-business clients form long-term strategies for creating, revitalizing and leveraging strong brands. Core competency in multi-tactical program development, carried out with strong creative articulation. Media-neutral approach, with tactical recommendations based on most effective strategies for addressing clients' unique needs, issues and opportunities.
CAPABILITIES: Quantitative/qualitative research & discovery, market and brand planning, naming and identity development, communications planning. Integrated execution (collateral, advertising, interactive, custom publications, direct response, promotions, sales programs.) Market Segment Expertise: Food marketing: foodservice/bakery/deli/distribution. High tech: e-business/intellectual properties. Financial: banking/insurance.
OFFICERS: James J. MacLachlan, CEO/Margie D. MacLachlan, VP Creative
ACCOUNT SUPERVISORS: Account Services: Terri Juranek, AE; Gina Wifler, AE; Justin Erickson, AE
BILLINGS: $7 million
YEARS IN BUSINESS: 14

##

WATERS MOLITOR
1000 Shelard Parkway #600

952-797-5000
Minneapolis 55426

FAX: 952-797-5001
CONTACT: Dori Molitor
E-MAIL: dmolitor@watersmolitor.com
WWW: watersmolitor.com

100 / Branding & Brand Development

SERVICES: Brand positioning, communications platform and go-to-market strategies. Strategy development, brand events, co-marketing. Promotion planning and execution. Creative development, interactive communications, post-event analysis.

CAPABILITIES: Marketing brands to women. Strengthening the bond between brand and consumer to create Brand Enthusiasm®. Building an emotional connection between brand and consumer leading to competitive differentiation and long-term loyalty. Winner of 5 best in the World PRO Awards of Excellence, unprecedented in the industry.

CURRENT/RECENT CLIENTS/PROJECTS: Dunkin/ Donuts, Gerber, Innuity.com, Malt-O-Meal, Nabisco, Respond.com, Sargenton, SuperValu, Tone Brothers Spices, US Bank, WomenVenture.

Broadcast Media

C

CABLE12/NORTHWEST COMMUNITY TELEVISION 763-533-8196
6900 Winnetka Avenue North Brooklyn Park 55428
FAX: 763-533-1346
CONTACT: David Kiser
GEOGRAPHICAL AREA COVERED: NW Suburbs of Minneapolis
HOURS: Channel 12; Hours: 24 hours
RATE INFORMATION: Local ad sales available
FORMAT: DVC-PRO, S-VHS, 3/4 inch, VHS.
FACILITIES: 1 Production van, 2 studios, editing suites
ACCOUNT SUPERVISORS: General Manager: Mike Johnson, News Director: Anne Angerer; Advertising Director: David Kiser

K

KLBB/KLBP AM 612-321-7200
331 11th Street South Minneapolis 55404
FAX: 612-321-7202
CONTACT: Chris Olsen
GEOGRAPHICAL AREA COVERED: Minneapolis/St. Paul.
RADIO BAND LOCATION: 1400/1470.
NETWORK AFFILIATION: MN Radio Networks.
HOURS: 24 hours.
FORMAT: Adult standards.
PRESIDENT/CEO/OWNER: Tim Shears, President; James Rasmussen, VP of Programming; Jim Lowe, Network Sales Manager; Lisa Schinstine, Radio Stations Sales Manager; Reed Hagen, Program Director; Chris Olsen, Marketing & Promotion Director

M

THE MINNEAPOLIS TELECOMMUNICATIONS NETWORK 612-331-8575
125 SE Main Street Minneapolis 55414
FAX: 612-331-8578
CONTACT: John Akre
GEOGRAPHICAL AREA COVERED: City of Minneapolis. Channel Number: 32, 33, 58 on Time Warner Cable. Network Affiliation: Time Warner Cable
HOURS: 5 - midnight
RATE INFORMATION: Free for citizens and non-profits
FORMAT: 3.4 inch and S-VHS
CAPABILITIES/SPECIALTIES: Training on television production equipment access to community television channels. Media literacy training, Internet service provide for non-profit, government organizations. Web design training. Dial up Internet accounts and web hosting for non-profit organizations.

102 / Broadcast Media

CURRENT/RECENT CLIENTS/PROJECTS: MTN was voted best TV station by City Pages in Spring of 2000.
FACILITIES: Special Facilities: Portable equipment, studios and editing suite, Internet training
PRESIDENT/CEO/OWNER: General Manager-President: Pamela Colby; Sales Manager: Karrie Cable-Spratt; News Director: John Akre

THE MNN RADIO NETWORKS INC.   612-321-7200
331 11th Street South   **Minneapolis 55404**
FAX: 612-321-7202
SERVICES: The MNN Radio Networks, Inc. (MNN) provides radio stations in the upper Midwest with news, sports, weather, lifestyle features, agriculture programming as well as wire service and distribution services for professional and U of M sports.
PRESIDENT/CEO/OWNER: Tim Shears
CONTACT: Laura Niemi

R

RELAY HOUSE, INC.   763-972-8008
9277 Meridian Avenue South   **Montrose 55363**
FAX: 763-972-8018
CONTACT: Randy Johnson
PAGER: 800-641-8071 (no pin # required)
E-MAIL: relayhouse@worldnet.att.net
WWW: relayhouse.com
CAPABILITIES: Uplink services: Ku Uplink truck featuring dual path transmission ability with full redundancy. Separate Beta-SP edit bay and intercom system with IFB. Downlink services: Eight (8) C&Ku downlink antenna systems. Relay House also provides projection and audio systems.
SPECIALTIES: Satellite uplink and downlink services for the broadcast industry and business community.

RUMJUNGLE MEDIA, INC.   612-476-9900
17309 Bay Lane   **Wayzata 55391**
FAX: 612-476-0909
CONTACT: Kathy Ross
E-MAIL: rumjungle@rumjungle.com
WWW: rumjungle.com
SERVICES: Internationally experienced DP Camera Crews (Betacam SP, Digital Betacam, Mini DV & HDTV) with top-notch support crews, including producers and production assistants for broadcast, commercial and corporate clientele. RumJungle Media has an extensive database of satellite up-link services, grips, gaffers, make-up artists and teleprompter operators.
CAPABILITIES: Rumjungle has equipment packages featuring a wide array of gear for every situation. We offer Sony BVW-D600 cameras with 16:9 wide screen capability with comprehensive lighting and wireless audio packages. Expect superb lighting design, inventive production techniques, rock-steady hand-held camera operation and efficient set-up.
CURRENT/RECENT CLIENTS/PROJECTS: 1998 National News Emmy Award for NBC; 1999 National News Emmy Award for ABC; 1999 Telly Award for "Fish!".

# Broadcast Media / 103

W

WCCO-TV 612-339-4444
90 South 11th Street Minneapolis 55403
CONTACT: Greg Keck
GEOGRAPHICAL AREA COVERED: 80 - 100 mile radius of the Twin Cities
NETWORK AFFILIATION: CBS; Channel 4
HOURS: 24 hours, Sunday through Thursday 5:00 AM - 1:30 AM; Friday & Saturday 6:00 AM - 2:30 AM.
OFFICERS: Station Manager: Greg Keck; News Director: Ted Canova, Vice President & General Manager

WFTC-TV 612-379-2929
1701 Broadway Street NE Minneapolis 55413
FAX: 612-379-2900
CONTACT: Susan Groh
WWW: fox29.com
GEOGRAPHICAL AREA COVERED: Minneapolis-St. Paul
NETWORK AFFILIATION: Fox; Channel 29
HOURS: 24 hours.
RATE INFORMATION: Call for rates.
CAPABILITIES: Tape: BetaSp, Beta, 1-inch; Special features: full-studio, non-linear editing, 3D animation, digital effects.
OFFICERS: General Manager: Steve Spendlove; Sales Manager: Tom Bourassa; Studio Booking-Production Manager: Susan Groh

WHITEWOLF ENTERTAINMENT, INC. 612-754-5680
11610 Jay Street #B Minneapolis 55448
FAX: 612-755-4297
CONTACT: Douglas Hajicek
ALTERNATE PHONE: 612-239-6293
E-MAIL: dhajicek@usinternet.com
SERVICES: Full service production company, specializing in documentaries, TV shows, and specials with network experience. Full editing both off-line, online, non-linear. Difficult outdoor shooting a specialty. All services A-Z scripting, shooting, editing.
CAPABILITIES: Custom equipment design for any type of video production from infrared to water and weatherproof, remote cameras time lapse. Formats range from high def to mini dv cannon LX1, Hidden Cameras, etc. Also 16 x 19 ratio production (wide screen) digital Betacam. BetacamSP, and 35mm film. Plus all other formats. Also studio shoots and interviews, on location or studio, Broll shooting for out-of-state production companies accepted.
CURRENT/RECENT CLIENTS/PROJECTS: Discovery Channel/"The Man That Walks with Bears" 1999; Animal Planet; "Brotherwolf" Jim Brandenburg 1999; "On the Heels of Crime"; Dayton Hudson Corp. 1999; Discovery Online/"Bear Cam" 1999; Tremendous Entertainment/"Secrets of the Mayan Underworld 1999.
PRESIDENT/CEO/OWNER: Douglas Hajicek

WMNN NEWSRADIO 1330 612-321-7200
331 11th Street South Minneapolis 55404

104 / Broadcast Media

FAX: 612-321-7222
SERVICES: WMNN News Radio 1330 brings the Twin Cities the most comprehensive news, business updates, weather, sports and traffic reports from Minnesota's largest radio news gathering organization. On WMNN, you're never more than 10 minutes away from a newscast.
PRESIDENT/CEO/OWNER: Tim Shears
CONTACT: Laura Niemi
ALTERNATE PHONE: Newsroom: 612-321-7211; Admin. 321-7202

Business Research

B

BUSINESS AND INDUSTRIAL MARKET RESEARCH CORPORATION
814 Hague Avenue
651-224-0619
St. Paul 55104
CONTACT: V.B. Colaiuta, Ph.D.

SERVICES: Market potential studies, concept testing, competitive analyses, industry and market overviews, customer satisfaction surveys and image surveys.

TYPES OF RESEARCH: Full-line primary and secondary market research, particularly for manufacturing industries and high-tech industries such as electronics, plastics, dairy, computers, software, factory automation and automotive; research can be done at market. Industry, company and product/service levels of focus.

RESEARCH & TESTING METHODS: Telephone surveys, mail surveys, intercepts, panels, focus groups; secondary methods include acquisition and analysis of public/private documents, electronic database searching, etc.

I

INFORM RESEARCH SERVICES
300 Nicollet Mall
612-630-6020
Minneapolis 55401
FAX: 612-630-6030
CONTACT: Ted Hathaway, Manager
E-MAIL: inform@mpls.lib.mn.us
WWW: mpls.lib.mn.us/inform.asp

SERVICES: Research using online (Internet) resources, published information, library resources, and professional organizations. Document delivery using library resources and online services.

CAPABILITIES: Online (Internet) searching of information resources.

INTERNATIONAL RESEARCH & EVALUATION (IRE)
21098 Ire Control Center
952-888-9635
Eagan 55121
FAX: 952-888-9124
CONTACT: Rick Kenrick, Comm. Dir.
E-MAIL: ireittn@gte.net
WWW: ire-ittn.com

CAPABILITIES: Collecting, storing and disseminating information online, on demand through the information and technology transfer network. In-depth research probes and studies to improve the decision support process.

SPECIALTIES: Market research and analysis; premium testing; feasibility studies; design and development of client desired topic/subject embedded interactive multimedia platforms.

PRESIDENT/CEO/OWNER: Randall L. Voight, CEO

P

ANN POTTER & ASSOCIATES 612-338-5750
1614 Harmon Place Minneapolis 55403
CONTACT: Ann Potter
E-MAIL: acpotter@tc.umn.edu
TYPES OF RESEARCH: Strategic planning and marketing support; industry analysis; market trend and segmentation ID; competitive intelligence.
RESEARCH & TESTING METHODS: Comprehensive database and web searches, custom telephone research and related fieldwork, executive interviews, quick primary studies.
SPECIALTIES: Alternative distribution networks, niche markets, international work, specialty products.

Business Support

E

EXECUTIVE TYPING SERVICES   763-503-0167
7732 Riverdale Drive   Minneapolis 55444
FAX: 763-503-0166
CONTACT: Julie Diaz
E-MAIL: exectyping@aol.com
SERVICES: Database Management/Maintenance; Word Processing; Tape Transcription (micro & standard size cassettes). For more information or a free quote, give us a call.

P

POTTER PRODUCTION SERVICES   612-825-9998
4231 Grand Avenue   Minneapolis 55409
FAX: 612-825-0368
CONTACT: Greg Potter
E-MAIL: greg@duckcap.com
SERVICES: Providing bookkeeping services for the small business. Quickbooks specialist.
CAPABILITIES: Familiarity with the creative community comes from working for 20 + years in film production.
CURRENT/RECENT CLIENTS/PROJECTS: Filmmakers; Twist; Artstarts; New French Café.

THE PROSPER GROUP, INC.   612-825-4305
50 Luverne Avenue   Minneapolis 55419
FAX: 612-825-2930
CONTACT: Marlys Tamte
E-MAIL: mtamte@visi.com
SERVICES: Consulting to small and medium-sized agencies on areas of growth, profitability, operations, HR, morale, and strategic planning. We help agencies improve their bottom lines and position themselves for growth.
CAPABILITIES: Database of resumes of talented AE's, project managers, art directors and freelancers, available for review by agencies at no charge.
PRESIDENT/CEO/OWNER: Marlys Tamte

W

WORD TECH SECRETARIAL SERVICE
6825 York Place
FAX: 612-549-0796
CONTACT: Patty Mesenbrink
E-MAIL: wordtec000@aol.com

612-349-9214
Brooklyn Center 55429

SERVICES: Database management, direct mail fulfillment, desktop publishing, generate mailing lists, mailing labels, personal and business clerical, press kit assembly, tape transcription from standard or micro cassette machines, transcribing focus groups, interviews, meetings, conference calls, dictation, word processing, repetitive letters.

CAPABILITIES: Multi-faceted business office support service. We handle your overflow, special projects and day to day office support. Pick up and delivery with prior arrangements.

CURRENT/RECENT CLIENTS/PROJECTS: Production companies, producers, large and small businesses, marketing departments, public relations firms, advertising agencies, non-profits, etc.

Cartography

B

BUSINESS INFORMATION TECHNOLOGIES, INC. 612-820-0255
4640 W. 77th Street #262 Edina 55435
FAX: 612-820-0232
E-MAIL: rbyers@bit-co.com
WWW: bit-co.com
SERVICES: Software - mapping. Marketing, bank compliance. Custom Mapping - Trade areas, zip codes, customer profiling. Lists - Direct mail and telemarketing. Databases - Demographics, geographic boundaries. Marketing.
PRESIDENT/CEO/OWNER: Gary Mertz, P
CONTACT: Richard Byers

Celebrity Acquisition

H

THE HOLLYWOOD-MADISON GROUP 818-762-8008
11684 Ventura Blvd #258 Studio City 91604
FAX: 818-762-8089
CONTACT: Jonathan Holiff, President
E-MAIL: info@hollywood-madison.com
WWW: hollywood-madison.com
SERVICES: The Hollywood-Madison Group is the nation's leading procurer of celebrities. The Hollywood-Madison Group (HMG) is the only full-service agency specializing in celebrity endorsements and Hollywood tie-ins. With our exclusive Fame Index™, we can help you search over 10,000 celebrities - from actors to athletes - to find every performer who matches your unique requirements. And, we can rank them by their fees and popularity too! Simply the best access to celebrities!
CAPABILITIES: Talent Casting, Celebrity Endorsements, Personal Appearances, Hollywood Tie-Ins; Celebrity P.S.A.S/Celebrity "Seeding", Research, Licensing, Video News Releases (VNRs), Satellite Media Tours (SMTs), Special Events, Television Production, Parties, Premieres, Merchandising, Focus Groups/Consumer Testing, Event Management, Marketing and Consulting.
CURRENT/RECENT CLIENTS/PROJECTS: Aspen Club; Bal Harbour Shops, Florida; Cinemax; Disney (Disney Online); Drugstore.com; Eli-Lilly & Co. (Humalog); Fetzer Wines; General Motors Corporate; The Gillette Company; Hanes Hosiery; Hewlett-Packard, Inc.; Johnson & Johnson (Motrin, Concerta); Kellogg USA, Inc.; Mattel, Inc. (Cabbage Patch Kids); Pharmacia/Upjohn; Phillips Consumer Electronics; Pizza hut; Pontiac (Axtek); Proctor & Gamble (Pringles, ThermaCare; Fixodent; Charmin; Bounty; Swiffer); Prudential Insurance Corporation.

Computer Graphics & Digital Imaging

A

ACCI   **612-975-1989**
6585 Edenvail Boulevard   **Eden Prairie 55346**
FAX: 612-975-0397
CONTACT: Bill Grambsch
E-MAIL: sales@goacci.com
WWW: goacci.com
SERVICES: Large format digital sales, service and supplies 24" x 60" digital printers from Encad, Raster Graphics. Epson and HP, AGL Greie and Seal Laminators. All media, ink and lamination, supplies stocked in ACCI Minneapolis warehouse.
CAPABILITIES: Large format digital printing and laminating equipment. Local sales, service and supplies. Training seminars for printing and laminating.
CURRENT/RECENT CLIENTS/PROJECTS: Only show room in Midwest with Encad, Raster Graphics and Epson printers.
PRESIDENT/CEO/OWNER: Richard Grambsch/Bill Grambsch

ADTECH COMMUNICATIONS GROUP   **952-944-6347**
8220 Commonwealth Drive #201   **Eden Prairie 55344**
FAX: 952-944-5643
CONTACT: Maureen Lundberg
E-MAIL: sales@adtechinc.com
WWW: adtechinc.com
SERVICES: Since 1982 we've been bringing technology, creativity and artistry together in a synergistic way to create award-winning graphics and animation for video, multimedia, web and other emerging electronic technologies. We'll take your graphics/animation from concept through completion. Visit our web site or call to see our demo reel - you'll see award wining animations using leading edge technology including multiple SGI super Unix and NT based workstations and NT based high end Hoodini (read very powerful), Synergy Custom and Adtech Proprietary Software covering a wide range of 2D and 3D software, Pandemonium, additional paint systems and Discreet's Edit Plus non-linear editing. Output is to all electronic media. Technical capabilities include organic terrain growth, organic plant growth, hair and beard growth, kaleidoscope generation, magnetics, particle systems and generation, image morphing, blob metamorphosis, natural phenomenon such as fog and water, lattice deformations, magnets, collisions, ray tracing with reflection, refraction and shadows, rotoscoping, bump mapping, texture mapping, environmental mapping, object metamorphosis, inverse kinematics, programmable painterly effects, multiple digital overlays, airbrush effects, object deformations, fractals, etc. - we've got it all!
SPECIALTIES: Concept driven, high end 2D and 3D identity design services, character animation, and dynamic integration of animation with live footage. Award winning animation and design for film, video, web, multimedia, and emerging electronic visual media. Providing integrated design solutions across all your electronic media.
CURRENT/RECENT CLIENTS/PROJECTS: Honeywell, 3M, Minnesota Power, Fisher-Rosemount, Hormel Foods, General Mills, National Car Rental, Datacard, Control Data, Minnegasco, Anderson Windows, Caterpillar Inc., GMAC-RFC, Lutheran Brotherhood, Texas Instruments, Graco, KMSP-TV, Northern States Power, Alpine Industries and more under construction! To discuss ways Adtech can go to work for you, contact Maureen Lundberg at 952-944-6347.

112 / Computer Graphics & Digital Imaging

AS SOON AS POSSIBLE, INC.   **952-564-2727**
3000 France Avenue South   **St. Louis Park 55416**
FAX: 952-564-2720
CONTACT: George West, 952-564-2621
E-MAIL: gwest@asap.net
WWW: asap.net
CAPABILITIES: A.S.A.P. is a Marketing Communications Production Company that offers prepress Services (Mac & PC), Printing (digital, offset, and direct-to-plate), Large Trade Show/Display Prints, and Internet & Interactive Multimedia. For more information, call George West today at 952-564-2621 or visit our web site at www.asap.net.
EQUIPMENT: Imagesetters, Canons, Agfa Chromapress, Heidelberg Quickmaster DI's, Xerox Doc 40, Micropress, Offset Presses, Iris, Rainbow, Scanners, and Ink Jet and Electrostatic Large Format Printers. Pick-up and delivery available.

B

BAU, INC.   **952-912-0191**
5511 Bristol Lane   **Minnetonka 55343**
FAX: 952-933-0295
CONTACT: Douglas Johnson
E-MAIL: johns93@bitstream.net
SERVICES: We are the graphics bureau to the Twin Cities. The most capable center for scanning, retouching, photo-manipulation, illustration, and illustration integrated with design. We have years of experience in working seamlessly with business and design schedules. Call for our free, clearly understandable pricing and information booklet.
CAPABILITIES: No better scanning or retouching can be found in the Twin Cities area. We can work with any item from 8mm film to the side of a building. All can be saved in any file format needed, to a variety of convenient storage media. True photographic printing is available also - and always an index print. Our art department brings illustration and design to a higher level of effectiveness by being able to integrate the two into a more communicative whole. We have many styles at our disposal to meet any clients needs.
CURRENT/RECENT CLIENTS/PROJECTS: American Medical Systems; Adult Option in Education; Banc; Campbell Mithun Esty; Carlson Marketing Group; Chez Francoise; La Flame; Photo Quick; VRB Art; Wellington Windows.
PRESIDENT/CEO/OWNER: Douglas Johnson

Computer Graphics & Digital Imaging / 113

BEYLERIAN DESIGN
3329 Garfield Street NE
FAX: 612-781-1832
CONTACT: Edwin Beylerian
E-MAIL: beyle002@maroon.tc.umn.edu
612-781-1748
Minneapolis 55418

SERVICES: Graphic design, publication design, interface design for multimedia, web design, animation.
CAPABILITIES: Unique creative solutions, strong conceptualization capabilities, interdisciplinary approach, communications in education, medicine and the arts.
CURRENT/RECENT CLIENTS/PROJECTS: Computer User, University of Minnesota Department of Surgery, Microscopy Society of America, Intermedia Arts.

C

CASWELL PHOTOGRAPHY
700 Washington Avenue North #308
FAX: 612-340-1538
CONTACT: George or Karin
E-MAIL: george@caswellphoto.com
WWW: caswellphoto.com
612-332-2729
Minneapolis 55401

SERVICES: Photo illustrator creating dynamic visual images utilizing traditional and digital techniques for the advertising, corporate and graphic design communities. Color, humor and whimsy are combined with exceptional technical skills resulting in strong visuals that sell products and services.
PRESIDENT/CEO/OWNER: George Caswell

COLORHOUSE
13010 County Road 6
FAX: 763-550-3600
CONTACT: William Klocke
E-MAIL: info@colorhouse.com
WWW: colorhouse.com
763-553-0100
Minneapolis 55441

SERVICES: Colorhouse has spent three and a half decades perfecting our specialty--prepress. So whenever you come to Colorhouse, you can depend on the highest quality and efficiency for all we have to offer: image acquisition/scanning, color separations, creative retouching, electronic page assembly, digital asset management. Digital proofing, CTP capabilities, high-speed electronic file transfer, flexographic plates, and short-to-medium run offset printing. Progressive technology and fast turnaround have become dependable hallmarks of our service. The end result is color separations or electronic files that meet the very highest standards of quality--delivered on-time and within budget.
SPECIALTIES: Large state-of-the-art facility offering high-quality prepress for ads, packaging and collateral. Best known for our progressive technology, creative retouching, unparalleled service and quick turnaround.

114 / Computer Graphics & Digital Imaging

EQUIPMENT: Workstations include 40-Mac Power PCs, 5 Barco stations, Proofing: 4 Kodak Approvals, DuPont Waterproof, 3M Matchprint, Kodak large format printer, Doc12 color copier. Output: Scitex Dolevs, Barco megasetter. Data Mgmt: 3 terabytes RAID on Sun Server, Kodak Optical Jukebox. File Transfer: T1, ISDN, Wam!Net, PDF, Internet. Press: 28" 4/c Akiyama.
PRESIDENT/CEO/OWNER: William Klocke

CRASH & SUES   **612-338-7947**
510 Marquette Avenue #600   **Minneapolis 55402**
FAX: 612-338-4601
CONTACT: Heidi Habben
E-MAIL: crash@crash-sues.com
WWW: crash-sues.com
SERVICES: C-Reality Film to tape transfer system with Da Vinci 2K color correction system; fire HD and D1 online edit; inferno HD graphics and compositing; 2D/3D CGI; closed captioning; videoboards, and duplication/traffic; NTSC/PAL; various multi-media capabilities; Echoboys original music, sound design and mix.
CAPABILITIES: Expertise in television commercials, music videos.

D

DIGIGRAPHICS, INC.   612-721-2434
2639 Minnehaha Avenue So   Minneapolis 55406
FAX: 612-721-4855
CONTACT: Joe Sodomka
WWW: digidigi.com
SERVICES: Digital imaging and design services for professional illustration and presentation programs, Macintosh and Windows. Creative design, high-resolution scanning, photo retouch and compositing; direct digital output to photographic media (48" x 96"), photographic film (35mm, 4 x 5, 8 x 10). Large format color inkjet display prints (60" x 240"). Other digital services include: high volume Canon laser copies, digital overheads, Fujix prints, CD-R mastering and volume CD-R duplication. Full in-house traditional photographic services including volume 35mm slide duplication quantity R3 prints and overheads, custom color prints/transparencies to 50" x 144", and quantity B&W prints. Complete mounting, laminating and custom finishing services.
SPECIALTIES: Design, create, image large format high-resolution digital files for tradeshows and other display purposes. Fast Service Available: Yes. Pickup and Delivery : Yes

DIGITAL REFLEXIONS   612-835-3411
9300 Collegeview Road #319   Bloomington 55437
FAX: 612-835-3411
CONTACT: Andrew Grivas
E-MAIL: prints@mn.uswest.net
WWW: digitalreflexions.com
SERVICES: Illustration and archival quality digital printing. See web site for gallery of artwork. Password protected entry for individual client jobs.
CAPABILITIES: High quality medical illustration for all media. Award-winning illustration in 3-D modeling, cover art, line art, photo-compositing and electronic retouching. 15 years' experience. Fujix pictrography digital printing.

H

HDMG DESIGN, POST & EFFECTS 952-943-1711
6573 City West Parkway Eden Prairie 55344
FAX: 952-943-1957
CONTACT: Design/Animation: Angella Kassube, Andy Reynolds, Brian Olson; Editors/Compositors: Jamie Heuton, Greg Mattern, Michael Guncheon, Jessie Yerama; Assistant Editor: John Gleim; DVD Author: Mike Faustgen; Location Production: Jamie Heuton; Accounts: Mona Cifaldi; Scheduling: Marci Meyocks; Traffic: Kim Schafer
E-MAIL: info@hdmg.com
WWW: www.hdmg.com
SERVICES: HDMG is an organization of people who love what we do. We have fun doing great work with intelligent clients (yes, that would be you) in a joint bursting with cool equipment. We are a producer-support service that promotes a direct partnership between producers and operators. We provide digital editing, design, paint, animation, special effects and compositing, DVD authoring and Avid non-linear offline in a relaxed, creative environment. We are an operator-run facility, with all owners and operators directly responsible for developing client relationships and maintaining our facility. Since we have no account reps, every client receives direct operator contact throughout their project. Cool!
EQUIPMENT: Fire, 2 Digital Editing suites mastering to Digital Betacam, 2 Avid Offlines, Flint, 2 DF/X Composium Graphics/Animation suites, Intergraph running 3D Studio Max, MacLab with PhotoShop, After Effects and Illustrator, Ultimatte 8, Insert stage with Ultimatte Memory Head, Sonic Solutions DVD Creator with 5.1 Dolby Digital surround, and many tape formats including Digital Betacam, D5, D2, DV/DVC Pro, DV Cam, MII, Beta SP, 3/4", 1", Hi-8, S-VHS, VHS (including international formats), DAT and DA88. Co-located with PostAudio, Inc., a sync mix facility featuring 2 digital audio suites.

I

ILLUSION GRAPHICS & COMMUNICATIONS 763-546-0228
2849 Louisiana Avenue No. Minneapolis 55427
FAX: 763-546-8908
CONTACT: Carol Irish/Larry Kluge
E-MAIL: illusion@illusiongraphics.com
WWW: illusiongraphics.com
SERVICES: Full service electronic design firm working with local and international clients on a wide variety of creative and production projects ranging from corporate image and digital through print production design. Services include creative and production design, art direction, writing/editing, photography, scanning, photo enhancement, complete digital preparation of press-ready files, print management, and CD-ROM creation.
SPECIALTIES: High-end digital graphics and design creation and production backed by a solid foundation in traditional design and print process, and an in-depth knowledge of current and future trends in digital design production. Areas of specialization encompass digital illustration and design, photo enhancement, design for multi-language publications, CD-ROM creation and print management.

116 / Computer Graphics & Digital Imaging

CURRENT/RECENT CLIENTS/PROJECTS: Thermo King; Donaldson Company; Wagner Spray Tech; Dahlberg Sciences-Canada; Griffiths Corporation; Kelly Promotions; Audio Medical-England; Hansation Akustik-Germany.
PRESIDENT/CEO/OWNER: Carol J. Irish

IMAGETECH SOLUTIONS, INC.   **612-379-0699**
958 East Hennepin Avenue   Minneapolis 55414
FAX: 612-379-2229
CONTACT: Terry Nelson
E-MAIL: itsolutions@earthlink.net
SERVICES: Photographic services: E-6 and C-41 and black and white dip and dunk film processing, custom and quantity color and black and white printing, transparency duplicating, trade show prints and transparencies, complete mounting and print finishing services, Rush service available. Digital Imaging services: Scanning low to high resolution, creative image manipulation, film recording 4" x 5" to 8" x 10", direct digital ink-jet outputs, preproofs.
PRESIDENT/CEO/OWNER: David Lundberg, Terry Nelson

INFOJO   **612-922-8780**
3146 West Calhoun Blvd #409   Minneapolis 55416
FAX: 612-922-8780
E-MAIL: jobaecker@aol.com
WWW: infojo.net
SERVICES: Graphic Design: Specializing in industrial/commercial brochures/catalogs as well as small run jobs. Logos, trade show graphics, vinyl signs. Consulting & Training: For smaller offices wishing to develop in-house graphic departments and/or print projects. Will teach skills for PhotoShop, Corel and Quark software. Advertising Agent: Services for print ad buying. Photography: A wide range of photographic services, specializing in industrial/commercial products and portrait work. Technical & Creative Writing: For instruction manuals, annual reports, etc.
CAPABILITIES/SPECIALTIES: Native German speaker. Able to translate into/out of German. Portable lighting system for on-location photography. 35mm and medium format photography available. Writing background provides material for all kinds of publications. Experience as advertising agent for clients advertising in international trade publications.
CURRENT/RECENT CLIENTS/PROJECTS: 4-color company catalogs; Conversions to PDF (electronic format); CD artwork; Vinyl banners; Backlit display graphics for trade shows; Website design; Graphics for novelty items.
PRESIDENT/CEO/OWNER: Joe Baecker

INTERFACE GRAPHICS   **612-338-TYPE**
241 1st Avenue North   Minneapolis 55401
FAX: 612-338-8647
CONTACT: Gary Hansen

IPARES, LTD.   **612-215-2300**
5000 Union Plaza   Minneapolis 55401
FAX: 612-215-2310
CONTACT: Tom Harold
E-MAIL: info@ipares.com
WWW: ipares.com

Computer Graphics & Digital Imaging / 117

FOCUS: Integration of marketing, design and technology.
SERVICES: Internet Professional Services: Providing Fortune 1000 corporations with Internet, Intranet, Extranet, Sales Force Automation, Kiosk and Database Marketing solutions. Multimedia Related Services: Design/concepting, consulting, writing/instructional design and programming. Internet/Intranet: In-house design and programming including secure E-commerce solutions and web-based training.
CAPABILITIES/SPECIALTIES: Graphic design services for brochures, catalogs, ads, display and packaging. Complete prepress production services.
PRESIDENT/CEO/OWNER: Lon Bencini/Tom Harold

J

JKL STUDIOS	612-729-1774
3810 Edmund Boulevard	Minneapolis 55406

FAX: 612-729-0133
CONTACT: Jerry or Marietta Mason; Kurt Lang
ALTERNATE PHONE: 651-653-0811
E-MAIL: jklstudios@tcinternet.net
SERVICES: High-end digital imaging; includes scanning, retouching, compositing and photo restoration. Mac or Windows platforms, various output services provided.
CAPABILITIES: 16 plus years experience photo/digital manipulation working with large files, photo composition and assembly on high-end equipment in the print industry. Complete understanding of reproduction capabilities of CMYK process on press.
CURRENT/RECENT CLIENTS/PROJECTS: Produced and continues to produce digital "magic" for all major agencies in the Twin Cities.
PRESIDENT/CEO/OWNER: Kurt Lang

JUNTUNEN MEDIA GROUP	612-341-3348
708 North First Street	Minneapolis 55401

FAX: 612-341-0242
CONTACT: John Gorski
ALTERNATE PHONE: 800-535-4366
E-MAIL: mjuntunen@juntunen.com
WWW: juntunen.com
SERVICES: Discover Juntunen and "see what's on your mind". Our design, graphics, 3D animation, and special effects artists infuse energy and creativity into our clients' graphic visions. Whether concepting, storyboarding, 2D and 3D animation, special effects and multi-layer compositing, paint, file transfer, character generation, "plussing" a project is our passion. Supporting you and our artists is our complete production facility, original, hybrid, or needle drop music, sound design, directors of photography, editors and duplication.
CAPABILITIES: Our graphics team is led by Tom Wiener, Art Director, formerly of Betelgeuse in New York. Tom brings expertise, spectacular, fresh imaging to TV spots, promotions, and corporate film and video production. Juntunen Media 2000: DVD authoring. Full digital video support. Webcasting. Visual web-based library: catalog and store all your brand assets. Retrieve from anywhere in the world and repurpose.
CURRENT/RECENT CLIENTS/PROJECTS: Major national and international corporations; sports and entertainment organizations; government organizations.
PRESIDENT/CEO/OWNER: Bill Juntunen

118 / Computer Graphics & Digital Imaging

M

MCARTLAND 763-421-1313
2420 4th Avenue North Anoka 55303
CONTACT: Tom McFarland
E-MAIL: tommyfar@aol.com
WWW: mcartland.com
SERVICES: Providing a variety of computer-based media solutions including; animation, digital imaging, compositing, multimedia design, SFX, video post-production and website design.
CAPABILITIES: 20 years experience providing content for film, television and computer screens.
EQUIPMENT: Apple Computers with Radius and Media 100 video boards - running After Effects, Flash, GoLive, Illustrator, LightWave 3D, PhotoShop and Premiere.
CURRENT/RECENT CLIENTS/PROJECTS: Carlson Media Services; Interactive Personalities; Media Craft; Post Card Productions; R.E.M. Video & Event Co.; River City Video; Science Museum of MN; University of Rochester, NY.

P

PHOTOGRAPHIC SPECIALTIES 612-522-7741
1718 Washington Avenue North Minneapolis 55411
FAX: 612-522-1934
CONTACT: Rick Schuenemann
E-MAIL: drewkal@photospec.com
SERVICES: P.S. is a full service custom photo lab and digital imaging service. We specialize in large runs of prints and transparencies for visual merchandising, POP, Trade Show Exhibits and museums. We have in-house graphic designers, a stock photo library and shipping and kitting capabilities.
CAPABILITIES: Two Light Jet 5000 Digital photo images for true photographic images up to 48" x 96" in one piece. Drum and flatbed scanning, LVT 8 x 10 film recorder, and Repri and Ellegro scan/retouch system. Color span Inkjet printers (4) and full mounting and laminating capabilities up to 80" wide. 4 traditional mural rooms with wall easels, prints and trans up to 72" x 16' one piece.
CURRENT/RECENT CLIENTS/PROJECTS: Large nationwide retail chains, display and store design firms.
PRESIDENT/CEO/OWNER: Drew Kalman

PHOTOLAB IMAGING CORPORATION 763-525-5900
5900 Olson Memorial Highway Golden Valley 55422
FAX: 763-525-0190
CONTACT: Jeff Ferrazzo, VP Sales
E-MAIL: sales@p-i-c.com
WWW: p-i-c.com

Computer Graphics & Digital Imaging / 119

CAPABILITIES: Complete photographic and digital display print products and imaging services from high-resolution drum and flatbed scanning, image manipulation, retouching and photocomposition, to direct digital photographic, high-resolution film or Ink Jet digital output. Maximum printing capabilities include Lambda Digital photographic printing up to 50" wide, traditional Photographic printing up to 72" wide, Cibachrome printing up to 50" wide, Ink Jet printing up to 50" wide, Arizona 6-color Ink Jet graphics (including 3M products) up to 52" wide and cut-vinyl graphics up to 48" wide.
PRESIDENT/CEO/OWNER: Charles W. Specht

PIXEL FARM, INC.   612-339-7644
251 First Avenue North #600   Minneapolis 55401
FAX: 612-339-7551
CONTACT: Stacey Ranum
E-MAIL: stacey@pixelfarm.com
WWW: pixelfarm.com
SERVICES: High-end digital post-production facility specializing in visual effects, 3D, 2D animation, on/off-line editorial, and film transfer for commercial broadcast, feature film, music videos and corporate markets.
CAPABILITIES: Discreet logic flame and inferno. Quantel Infinity, Editbox, Hal Express and Paintbox Express. AVID Symphony and AVID off-line. Two 3D workstations running Maya. SoftImage, Eddie, Pandemonium and more. URSA Film transfer with daVinci color corrector.

POINT CLOUD, INC.   763-551-1950
13220 County Road 6   Plymouth 55441
FAX: 763-551-1961
CONTACT: Tom Campbell
SERVICES: Point Cloud is a leading provider of interactive 3D product imaging for e-commerce businesses and has developed a revolutionary software technology that transfers standard 20 video images into interactive 3D images used for showcasing products on the internet.
CAPABILITIES: Point Cloud utilizes a digital camera, turntable and personal computer along with the software we developed to capture 3D images. Our technology is unique because it is low file size, high resolution and inexpensive.
CURRENT/RECENT CLIENTS/PROJECTS: Point Cloud has been diligently developing our technology for launch.
PRESIDENT/CEO/OWNER: Robert Bodor, CEO/Founder

POPULAR FRONT STUDIO, INC.   612-362-0900
605 Central Avenue NE   Minneapolis 55414
FAX: 612-362-0999
CONTACT: Sarah Bratnober
E-MAIL: studio@popularfront.com
WWW: popularfront.com
SERVICES: Strategic design solutions delivered via traditional and new media - print, video, photography, CD-ROM, DVD, and web. Complete photo studio for creation of images with both film and filmless photography. Capabilities include: content strategy, design, photography, retouching, visual special effects, web site design and programming, multimedia, video editing, and motion special effects. View print, photo, interactive, and motion samples on our web site.

120 / Computer Graphics & Digital Imaging

CURRENT/RECENT CLIENTS/PROJECTS: Amerimark, Beautopia International Haircare, Blu Dot Design & Manufacturing, Conwed Plastics, Fallon McElligott, Imation Corporation, Jasc Software, KTCA Television, Life Time Fitness, Malt-O-Meal Company, Microsoft Sidewalk, PBS, Starkey Laboratories, TriSense Software, Ltd., WAM!NET, William Mitchell College of Law.
PRESIDENT/CEO/OWNER: Michael Keefe, Laurence Bricker

PRECISION POWERHOUSE
911 Second Street South
612-333-9111
Minneapolis 55415

FAX: 612-332-9200
CONTACT: Dan Piepho, Paul Sunberg, Gene Gunderson
E-MAIL: dan@power-house.com; pauls@power-house.com or geneg@power-house.com
WWW: precisionpowerhouse.com
SERVICES: 2D and 3D Alias/Wavefront animation, Autodesk Animator, compositing on DDR, morphing and digital effects. Authorware Professional, Macromedia Director, Microsoft Visual Basic Visual C++, Java, JavaScript, Cold Fusion, Robo Help, scanning.
EQUIPMENT: Silicon Graphics maximum impact indigo 2 with Allias/Wavefront 2D and 3D software Maya, Accom 5 minute digital disk recorder, Pinnacle Aladdin digital effects, DVE and CG, Autodesk Animator workstation, Macromedia's Director, Flo and Morph Software, Adobe PhotoShop, Adobe Illustrator, DeBabelizer, Macromodel CoreDraw5, Barco Paint, Maximum Impact.
SPECIALTIES: Video and Interactive Media marketing via direct mail, video and multimedia sales presentations. DVD authoring and Interactive media software development for retail and corporate products; training presentation; commercials (TV and radio) web pages for businesses; web publishing; infomercials; e-business and direct response; audio, video and CD audio/ROM/DVD replication.

PROFESSIONAL COLOR SERVICE, INC.
909 Hennepin Avenue South
612-673-8900
Minneapolis 55403

FAX: 612-673-8988
CONTACT: Tim Doe
E-MAIL: procolor@procolor.com
WWW: procolor.com
CAPABILITIES: Soup-to-nuts digital imaging. Digital manipulation, retouching, composites, printing, archiving, award-winning graphic design capabilities, 'over-the-shoulder' computer services for those who would rather point than click. Our one-stop-shop line of products and services Includes: new 3D lenticular display prints, digital display photographs and transparencies, as well as a complete range of scanning services, including those from our high res drum, Photo CD, and Dicomed digital camera. Fine art IRIS reproduction. Short-run digital 4-color printing on our Heidelberg DI and Docucolor systems. Color laser copies and Bubblejet copies up to 24" x 36". Film processing 24 hours a day Monday through Friday and 8:30 to 11:30 on Saturday. Pick up and delivery.
SPECIALTIES: One-stop shop imaging services.
OFFICE HOURS: Monday through Friday 7:30 am to 8:00 pm; Saturday 8:30 to 2:00 pm.

PUSH MEDIA GROUP
411 Washington Avenue North #209
612-339-8294
Minneapolis 55401

FAX: 612-339-8296
CONTACT: Danny Schmidt/James Curry
E-MAIL: dan@pushgroup.com
WWW: pushgroup.com

Computer Graphics & Digital Imaging / 121

CAPABILITIES: Web, film and video production.
SPECIALTIES: Motion graphics utilizing 2D and 3D animation, special effects, and compositing.
CURRENT/RECENT CLIENTS/PROJECTS: NSP, VH1, General Motors, Nike, Paisley Park, Minnesota Vikings
PRESIDENT/CEO/OWNER: Danny Schmidt

T

CRAIG THIESEN   651-228-0482
308 Prince Street #210   St. Paul 55101
FAX: 651-228-0843
CONTACT: Craig Thiesen
E-MAIL: craig@studio210.com
WWW: studio210.com
SERVICES: Hand colored and digitally colored photographs, specializing in Minnesota and European landscapes. Computer graphics - consulting and production, including digital manipulation, image database management, Macintosh system trouble shooting, and website construction.
CURRENT/RECENT CLIENTS/PROJECTS: James Page Brewing, Northwest Canoe Company, Cavdozo Photo Gallery, Saint Paul Art Crawl, Department of Natural Resources.
PRESIDENT/CEO/OWNER: Craig Thiesen

TOP FLIGHT MARKETING   651-793-8334
18214 127th Street SE #200   Big Lake 55309
FAX: 651-793-8335
CONTACT: Christopher Nalty
E-MAIL: info@topflightmarketing.com
WWW: topflightmarketing.com
SERVICES: Full line of web, design and marketing services including: desktop publishing, company sponsored newsletters, guerilla marketing, niche and database marketing, product and company positioning, direct response, business promotion and photography.
CAPABILITIES: Our specialties include: developing complete immersive imaging experiences (360 degrees panoramic walkthroughs) for use on the web and multi-media. This technology allows a user to view on their PC what previously could only be seen in person. Specific industry applications include: Real Estate, Resorts, City Tours, Industrial Walkthroughs, Stadiums, Arenas and Concert Halls, Auto Dealers, Museums, Online stories and any other area where a visual tour is applicable. Top Flight Marketing can also develop any object into an interactive 360 degree virtual object that can be "picked up" and examined from any angle. 360 degrees surround sound can be added for enhanced realism.
CURRENT/RECENT CLIENTS/PROJECTS: Our current client list includes: Honeywell Federal Credit Union; Edina Realty; Acucraft Fireplace Systems; Innovative Laser Technologies; Moorhead State University; Trinity Baptist Church and Heart Note Productions.

U

UPFRONT PRODUCTIONS 651-633-5299
2350 County Road C #120 St. Paul 55113
FAX: 651-633-5197
CONTACT: Tricia Nordby Hamrin/Chris Hamrin
WWW: hoopjumping.com
CAPABILITIES: Organizational Communications Solutions Center. A Spectrum. A Synergy. Concept Development, Copywriting, Graphic Design, Illustration, Document Production, Web Site Creation, Scanning, Photo Retouching, Pre-press, Offset Printing, Digital B&W Printing, Color Copies, Posters, Displays, Signs, Custom Assembly, Inventory, Distribution, Corporate Compass® MIS, VantagePoint™, Hoop Jumping™.
SPECIALTIES: Choose your hoop. We'll jump through it™.
OFFICERS: Tricia Nordby Hamrin/Chris Hamrin

Corporate Advertising, Marketing & PR Depts.

I

ISA PROMOTIONS, INC. 651-439-1339
206 Mariner Way Bayport 55003
FAX: 651-439-4512
CONTACT: Maralee Meissner
E-MAIL: isapromo@ix.netcom.com
WWW: isapromo.com
PRESIDENT/CEO/OWNER: Susan J. Larimer

M

MINNESOTA CLIPPING SERVICE 612-672-9141
12 South 6th Street #1237 Minneapolis 55402
FAX: 612-672-9174
CONTACT: Debbie Friez
E-MAIL: mnclip@visi.com
WWW: burrelles.com
SERVICES: Providing complete local, regional, national, and international media monitoring including newspapers, magazines, broadcast media, wire services and the Internet. Additional services include electronic clipping, media directory, PR evaluation, clip mounting, fax service and advertising analysis services.
CAPABILITIES: Burrelle's Information Office (BIO), our complete software package, efficiently manages all types of media clips. Receive, store, display, organize, search, share and report on all monitored media quickly and digitally. Clip book presentations can be prepared in minutes.

P

PROSPERA DESIGN 952-832-5588
8400 Normandale Lake Blvd #500 Minneapolis 55437
FAX: 952-831-9191
CONTACT: Heidi Libera
E-MAIL: info@prospera.com
WWW: prospera.com
SERVICES: Prospera Design offers inventive solutions to help your company thrive and prosper as you invest in new methods of design, marketing and global communications. Prospera is owned by Shandwick International, a leader in public relations, offering clients a global network of resources with over 100 offices worldwide.
SPECIALTIES: Prospera specializes in corporate identity, material audits, graphic standards, publications, marketing collateral, annual reports, video, environmental graphics and print management.
CURRENT/RECENT CLIENTS/PROJECTS: Deluxe Corp.; Greater Minneapolis Chamber of Commerce; Merck-Medco; University of Minnesota; Minnesota State University Mankato; Lawson Software; Lutheran Brotherhood; Novartis; Seagate Technology; SCIMED
PRESIDENT/CEO/OWNER: Heidi Libera, Senior Vice President, Design Director; Todd Spichke, Design Director; Lawrence Sahulka, Design Director

124 / Corporate Advertising, Marketing & PR Depts.

S

SKYLINE DISPLAYS INC   651-234-3228
3355 Discovery Road   Eagan 55121
CONTACT: Bob Bossert
CAPABILITIES: Skyline Displays, Inc. is North America's leading designer of money-saving portable displays, reconfigurable modular exhibits and quality graphics. With a new 300,000 square foot facility at our Eagan headquarters, we can offer unmatched graphic design and production capabilities and vast architectural choices.
SPECIALTIES: Started in 1908, and twice honored as an Inc. 500 company for rapid growth, Skyline and its distributors now employ over 1,200 people worldwide. With over 115 sales and service locations worldwide, Skyline offers you turnkey exhibit services, including exhibit design, installation and dismantle, storage, refurbishing, leasing and rental. We can ease your workload and provide a helping hand wherever your exhibit.
EDITORS: Bob Bossert

U

UPFRONT PRODUCTIONS   651-633-5299
2350 County Road C #120   St. Paul 55113
FAX: 651-633-5197
CONTACT: Tricia Nordby Hamrin/Chris Hamrin
WWW: hoopjumping.com
CAPABILITIES: Organizational Communications Solutions Center. A Spectrum. A Synergy. Concept Development, Copywriting, Graphic Design, Illustration, Document Production, Web Site Creation, Scanning, Photo Retouching, Pre-press, Offset Printing, Digital B&W Printing, Color Copies, Posters, Displays, Signs, Custom Assembly, Inventory, Distribution, Corporate Compass® MIS, VantagePoint™, Hoop Jumping™.
SPECIALTIES: Choose your hoop. We'll jump through it™.
OFFICERS: Tricia Nordby Hamrin/Chris Hamrin

US BANCORP PIPER JAFFRAY   612-303-0000
800 Nicollet Mall   Minneapolis 55402
CONTACT: Chris Roberts
ACCOUNT SUPERVISORS: Advertising Manager: Earl Johnston; Public Relations Manager: Chris Roberts
PRESIDENT/CEO/OWNER: Andrew Duff

Corporate Communications, Meeting, Satellite & Teleconferencing Services

C

CONUS PRODUCTIONS & SATELLITE   **651-642-4477**
SERVICES
3415 University Avenue   **Minneapolis 55414**
FAX: 651-642-4551
CONTACT: Brian Tuttle
CAPABILITIES: Single and multi-camera video production service. Mobile and fixed satellite uplinks, and full production crews available for event broadcast.
EQUIPMENT: Sony CCD cameras, modular control rooms. Chyron graphics. Support Beta SP video tape format 4 uplink trucks, tape playback.
SPECIALTIES: Mobile uplink and multi-camera video production.
PRESIDENT/CEO/OWNER: Terry O'Reilly, GM

F

FREESTYLE PRODUCTIONS, INC.   **763-417-9575**
6112 Olson Memorial Highway   **Minneapolis 55422**
FAX: 763-417-9576
CONTACT: Dale Kivimaki, Mark Hulsey
E-MAIL: dale@freestyle-productions.com
WWW: freestyle-productions.com
CAPABILITIES: Freestyle Productions provides video and multimedia communication services with a specialized focus on high-profile, live-event productions including corporate meetings, trade shows, conventions and concerts. Complete array of broadcast equipment: multi-camera field packages, post production/mobile, non-linear edit suites, switcher/effects & graphic systems, large-format video and data projection, front & rear screens and videowalls.
SPECIALTIES: Over 10 years of national and international experience producing all types of live and special events shows. Freestyle provides an intuitive understanding of how to best communicate their client's message to impact large and small audiences.
CURRENT/RECENT CLIENTS/PROJECTS: Fox Sports Net, Coca-Cola, Lucent Technologies, Apple Computer, Northwest Airlines, Promise Keepers, Carlson Companies, Lutheran Brotherhood, US West, Minnesota State Fair, Universal Studios Hollywood.

I

INHOUSE MEDIA   **612-341-4010**
800 N. Washington Avenue #307   **Minneapolis 55401**
FAX: 612-341-4063
CONTACT: Jim Gustafson
E-MAIL: jimg@inhousegroup.com
WWW: inhousegroup.com

126 / Corporate Communications, Meeting, Satellite & Teleconferencing Services

SERVICES: Meetings and Events: Business theater and staging services; motion graphics and 2D/3D animation; on-site event management; speaker support production; theme development and speech writing; video production and non-linear post-production. Computer Based Training: Deliverable on CD-ROM, DVD, Internet or Intranet. Sales Presentations: Corporate ID and logo design, E-commerce applications; Interactive kiosk design; web design, site development and hosting.
CAPABILITIES: InHouse Media wants to be your production company. Our years of experience help you exceed your presentation needs in any media. InHouse Media makes you a hero!
CURRENT/RECENT CLIENTS/PROJECTS: We serve current and future Fortune 500 companies.
PRESIDENT/CEO/OWNER: Joel DesLauriers/Jim Gustafson

J

JUNTUNEN MEDIA GROUP 612-341-3348
708 North First Street Minneapolis 55401
FAX: 612-341-0242
CONTACT: Mike Vinup
ALTERNATE PHONE: 800-535-4366
E-MAIL: mjuntunen@juntunen.com
WWW: juntunen.com
SERVICES: Seasoned production experts. Digital studio and facilities. In-studio and/or on-site crews. Our team has supported meetings and events for more than 15 years, providing creative consultation; project management; camera crews; audio support: transition cues; custom effects; stage lighting and effects; projection; satellite or fiber optic transmission -- national and international sites; playback; tvl/powerpoint/speaker support; image magnification; video walls; 16 x 9 format; and interactive meetings. For large events we'll provide one of our 53-foot digital productions trucks, complete with digital control rooms and cameras. (See Juntunen Mobile Television in Film and Video Support Services.)
CAPABILITIES: Broadband expertise: webcasting for the latest in interactive meetings and events. Live remote production: cameras, crews equipment onsite providing total technical support and creative for meetings. Live-to-tape: recording your meetings for later production and archiving. Studios and total production support for live business television production and transmission. Satellite and fiber optic transmission to delivery your media around the world. Juntunen Media 2000: DVD authoring. Full digital video support. Webcasting. Visual web-based library: catalog and store all your brand assets. Retrieve from anywhere in the world and repurpose.
CURRENT/RECENT CLIENTS/PROJECTS: Major national and international corporations; sports and entertainment organizations; government organizations.
PRESIDENT/CEO/OWNER: Bill Juntunen

M

MACHINE DREAMS INCORPORATED 612-371-4428
800 LaSalle Avenue #107 Minneapolis 55402
FAX: 612-371-0010
CONTACT: Shawn Ottmar
E-MAIL: shawn@machine-dreams.com

Corporate Communications, Meeting, Satellite & Teleconferencing Services

WWW: machine-dreams.com
SERVICES: Machine Dreams provides a complete range of advanced technologies for corporate and association meetings and events. Services include: wireless audience response systems, game shows, web broadcasts, interactive kiosks, registration systems and 3D graphics.
CAPABILITIES: Wireless Audience Response Systems, game shows and market research serving 20-2000 people. High quality video conferencing systems, web broadcasts, web training systems and web communities. Interactive kiosks using high bandwidth links and powerful navigation and display technologies. Game show modeled after Jeopardy, Who Wants to Be a Millionaire and more.
CURRENT/RECENT CLIENTS/PROJECTS: Clients for Wireless electronic voting, game shows and web broadcasts include 22 or the nation's largest companies and a wide range of non-profit and government organizations.
PRESIDENT/CEO/OWNER: Alan Yelsey

MAINSTREAM COMMUNICATIONS, INC.
9555 James Avenue South #235

952-888-9000
Bloomington 55431

CONTACT: Garry Krebs, Bob Ewert
E-MAIL: gkrebs@mainstreamcom.net
WWW: mainstreamcom.net
SERVICES: Mainstream concepts and stages corporate events of all kinds including meetings, trade shows, and special events. Our staff includes the professionals who know how to navigate the challenges of meeting rooms, conventional halls, and trade show floors. Our inventory includes a vast array of audio visual equipment; video and data projection, front and rear screens. Intelligent lighting, and multi-channel sound systems with effects. We warehouse existing sets which are available for rent or we can custom design and build one for you. We also provide live talent and nationally known acts to make your event special.
CAPABILITIES/SPECIALTIES: We are a turnkey video production environment. Location video crews include Beta SP equipment and complete location lighting and sound recording. Our 1,200 s.f. sound stage includes a lighting package along with available sets. We offer 4 edit suites: Digital Betacam complete with DME, 2 non-linear including DVE, and a portable Beta SP AB-Roll Edit Suite which can be used in-studio or for location events. Other in-house services include 3D animation featuring SoftImage software and a sound recording studio with multiple music libraries.

MARTIN/BASTIAN PRODUCTIONS
105 Fifth Avenue So #150

612-375-0055
Minneapolis 55401

FAX: 612-342-2348
CONTACT: Amy Oriani
E-MAIL: amyo@martinbastian.com
WWW: martinbastian.com
SERVICES: Martin/Bastian Productions offers creative development, execution and project management for corporate meetings and events, including staging services, business theater, speaker support, film and video production, and speakers and entertainment. We create integrated events from concept through execution, as well as offer individual meeting elements in an a la carte fashion, such as sourcing and booking speakers and entertainment.

128 / Corporate Communications, Meeting, Satellite & Teleconferencing Services

CAPABILITIES: Martin/Bastian has been in business for nearly 20 years, and we have 18 employees on staff, including meeting and event producers, video producers, graphic designers, writers, and account management. We're housed in the renovated, turn-of-the century, Crown Roller Mill in downtown Minneapolis, complete with a video facility (including on-line Media 100 post-production), a digital sound recording studio, theater, computer graphic workstations, speaker and entertainment video library, and other technical, creative, and account services.

CURRENT/RECENT CLIENTS/PROJECTS: We currently produce meetings, events, videos, and book speakers and entertainment for some of the top companies in the Midwest, and have won numerous awards for our film and video work. Recent entertainment acts we've produced for corporate clients include Bill Cosby, Bruce Hornsby, Kenny Loggins, The Neville Brothers, and Lyle Lovett and His Large Band.

PRESIDENT/CEO/OWNER: Al Soukup

MULTIMEDIA	952-931-2112
1011 First Street South #300	Hopkins 55343

FAX: 952-935-1318
CONTACT: Dianne Thill
WWW: multimedia-inc.com
SERVICES: Production of video presentations, interactive CD-ROM development, web page design, multi-image and live musical shows.
EQUIPMENT: Betacam video location and studio equipment, edit suite, multi-image programming.
SPECIALTIES: Sales meetings, sales training, marketing presentations.

P

POINT2POINT COMMUNICATION SOLUTIONS, INC.	651-223-7399
235 East Sixth Street, 4th Floor	St. Paul 55101

FAX: 651-223-7390
CONTACT: Dave Herman
WWW: pt2pt.com
CAPABILITIES: Studio and remote video production, single and multi-camera, video post, digital graphics, audio recording, editing and sweetening, studio and remote satellite uplink/downlink. Experienced staff includes directors, producers, production management and full crews.

EQUIPMENT: Two large production studios (82' x 52' and 52' x 52' - 20' high lighting grids) with state-of-the-art equipment and individual control rooms. Six studio cameras. Also insert/uplink studio (27' x 19'). Dressing rooms. Green room. Scene shop, freight elevator, loading dock. Full post-production services featuring integrated AVID non-linear on-line editing. ProTools Digital Audio Workstation, off-line edit, as well as multi-format video edit suites. Dubner Halo graphics. Adobe After Effects graphic compositing and digital 3D animation. Digital Beta, BetaSP & 1" video tape formats, 5 remote vans.

SPECIALTIES: Single source responsibility for satellite videoconferencing, satellite media tours, press conferences, meeting and convention support videos, corporate and organizational videos, training programs, employee communications, dedicated business television networks.

R

RUMJUNGLE MEDIA, INC.　　　　　　　　　　**612-476-9900**
17309 Bay Lane　　　　　　　　　　　　　　**Wayzata 55391**
FAX: 612-476-0909
CONTACT: Kathy Ross
E-MAIL: rumjungle@rumjungle.com
WWW: rumjungle.com

SERVICES: Internationally experienced DP Camera Crews (Betacam SP, Digital Betacam, Mini DV & HDTV) with top-notch support crews, including producers and production assistants for broadcast, commercial and corporate clientele. RumJungle Media has an extensive database of satellite up-link services, grips, gaffers, make-up artists and teleprompter operators.

CAPABILITIES: Rumjungle has equipment packages featuring a wide array of gear for every situation. We offer Sony BVW-D600 cameras with 16:9 wide screen capability with comprehensive lighting and wireless audio packages. Expect superb lighting design, inventive production techniques, rock-steady hand-held camera operation and efficient set-up.

CURRENT/RECENT CLIENTS/PROJECTS: 1998 National News Emmy Award for NBC; 1999 National News Emmy Award for ABC; 1999 Telly Award for "Fish!".

Desktop Publishing

A

ALT BUSINESS SERVICES   763-476-4223
13805 1st Avenue North #500   Plymouth 55441
CONTACT: Loretta Tischer Strom
SERVICES: Desktop publishing, word processing and mailing list maintenance.
PICK UP & DELIVERY: Available.
PRESIDENT/CEO/OWNER: Loretta Tischer Strom

NEIL APPLEQUIST   612-533-6343
4207 62nd Avenue North   Brooklyn Center 55429
CONTACT: Neil Applequist
E-MAIL: applequist@uswest.net
SERVICES: Complete pre-press services. Design, scanning color and black and white. Using QuarkXPress, PhotoShop, Illustration. With 20 years experience.
CAPABILITIES: Freelance artist for 10 years. Specializing in packaging, catalogs, brochures, manuals, and corporate publications.

ARTESIAN CREATIVE COMPUTER SERVICES   612-904-0649
514 North 3rd Street, #201   Minneapolis 55401
FAX: 612-338-3452
SERVICES: Complete computer pre-press services by experienced typographer, books, catalogs, all kinds of advertising materials, typographic consulting, type design, book design and production, multimedia using QuarkImmedia.
EQUIPMENT: Macintosh computers, CD-ROM, SyQuest, Zip, Jaz, Modem, QuarkXPress, Adobe Illustrator and PhotoShop, Microsoft PowerPoint, QuarkImmedia.
PRESIDENT/CEO/OWNER: Corey Sevett

AS SOON AS POSSIBLE, INC.   952-564-2727
3000 France Avenue South   St. Louis Park 55416
FAX: 952-564-2720
CONTACT: George West, 952-564-2621
E-MAIL: gwest@asap.net
WWW: asap.net
CAPABILITIES: A.S.A.P. is a Marketing Communications Production Company that offers prepress Services (Mac & PC), Printing (digital, offset, and direct-to-plate), Large Trade Show/Display Prints, and Internet & Interactive Multimedia. For more information, call George West today at 952-564-2621 or visit our web site at www.asap.net.
EQUIPMENT: Imagesetters, Canons, Agfa Chromapress, Heidelberg Quickmaster DI's, Xerox Doc 40, Micropress, Offset Presses, Iris, Rainbow, Scanners, and Ink Jet and Electrostatic Large Format Printers. Pick-up and delivery available.

AVALLO MULTIMEDIA & CREATIVE SERVICES   763-577-1630
9905 45th Avenue No #115   Plymouth 55442
FAX: 763-577-1632
CONTACT: Julie Hamilton

Desktop Publishing / 131

E-MAIL: info@avallo.com
WWW: avallo.com
SERVICES: Design for brochures, newsletters, product packaging, promotional mailers, magazine and newspaper ads, logos and signs, customer illustrations, art director for photography and video, copywriting, catalogs, press releases and media kits.
CAPABILITIES: Interactive: website design, animation, CD-ROM, catalogs and presentations. Print: layout and design, PDF conversions, art direction. Mac & PC platform
PRESIDENT/CEO/OWNER: B. A. Dunham

B

THE BENYAS GROUP   612-340-9804
126 North Third Street, Suite 300   **Minneapolis 55401**
FAX: 612-334-5950
CONTACT: Bradley A. Benyas
E-MAIL: benyas@visi.com
CAPABILITIES: From simple, half-page one-color ads to complex, 840+ page four-color technical guides, expertly composed and prepped for publishing.
SERVICES: Typesetting, scanning, image editing, electronic pre-press, trapping, color proofing, mock-ups, proofreading, data archiving, file translation, bar code creation, foreign language typography. High quality and fast turnaround.

BUSINESS EXPRESSIONS, INC.   612-473-4504
17420 30th Avenue North   **Plymouth 55447**
FAX: 612-476-3997
CONTACT: Ann L. Barnes
E-MAIL: annlbarnes@aol.com
SERVICES: Business Expressions creates marketing collateral using desk-top publishing and printing services. From concept to on-the-shelf!

C

CLEAN LINE GRAPHICS, LLC   651-459-6271
7905 Hemingway Avenue South   **Cottage Grove 55016**
CONTACT: Kathryn Barsness
CAPABILITIES: Production of brochures, corporate sales, catalogs, ads, annual reports, business forms. Layout, scanning, project coordination. Graphic production consultation and planning upon request.
SPECIALTIES: Graphic production, desktop publishing, layout with minimal design, four color...specializing in two color.

COLORHOUSE   763-553-0100
13010 County Road 6   **Minneapolis 55441**
FAX: 763-550-3600
CONTACT: William Klocke
E-MAIL: info@colorhouse.com

132 / Desktop Publishing

WWW: colorhouse.com
SERVICES: Colorhouse has spent three and a half decades perfecting our specialty--prepress. So whenever you come to Colorhouse, you can depend on the highest quality and efficiency for all we have to offer: image acquisition/scanning, color separations, creative retouching, electronic page assembly, digital asset management. Digital proofing, CTP capabilities, high-speed electronic file transfer, flexographic plates, and short-to-medium run offset printing. Progressive technology and fast turnaround have become dependable hallmarks of our service. The end result is color separations or electronic files that meet the very highest standards of quality--delivered on-time and within budget.
SPECIALTIES: Large state-of-the-art facility offering high-quality prepress for ads, packaging and collateral. Best known for our progressive technology, creative retouching, unparalleled service and quick turnaround.
EQUIPMENT: Workstations include 40-Mac Power PCs, 5 Barco stations, Proofing: 4 Kodak Approvals, DuPont Waterproof, 3M Matchprint, Kodak large format printer, Doc12 color copier. Output: Scitex Dolevs, Barco megasetter. Data Mgmt: 3 terabytes RAID on Sun Server, Kodak Optical Jukebox. File Transfer: T1, ISDN, Wam!Net, PDF, Internet. Press: 28" 4/c Akiyama.
PRESIDENT/CEO/OWNER: William Klocke

D

DOWNING COMMUNICATIONS 651-699-3901
421 Pascal Street South St. Paul 55105

SERVICES: Macintosh electronic publishing and computer graphics. 1200 dpi laser output, photo-quality color proofs, or straight to film. In-house graphic design, writing and editing.
CAPABILITIES/SPECIALTIES: Ads, newsletters, catalogs, stationery, brochures, etc. Featuring Quark Xpress, Photoshop, Adobe Illustrator. Special expertise in agriculture and government affairs.
PRESIDENT/CEO/OWNER: David W. Downing

O

OMNI ADVERTISING, INC. 651-423-3422
640 Gun Club Road Eagan 55123

FAX: 651-423-4320
CONTACT: Wm. Schoenecker
E-MAIL: omni@omnishop.net
WWW: omnishop.net
SERVICES: Media placement, computer graphics, photography (location and studio), publicity, copywriting, project management for brochures, ads, websites.
CAPABILITIES: We specialize in small to medium size companies - business-to-business and agriculture manufacturers - advertising and public relations.
CURRENT/RECENT CLIENTS/PROJECTS: NMC-Wollard; Reese Enterprises; CFR Corporation; R.J. Manufacturing; Lor*Al Products, Inc.; Raven Industries; Kahler Corporation; Bernard-Dalsin Manufacturing; National Agri-Services, Inc.; Railroad Services, Inc.

W

WBCS, INC.
5421 Tamarack Circle
CONTACT: Ward Barnett
E-MAIL: wbcs@uswest.net

952-380-0920
Minnetonka 55345

SERVICES: Concept to camera-ready prepress and typesetting. Macintosh hardware, software, and systems consultation, training, installation, and troubleshooting (on-site and by telephone). File conversion. Color scanning and proofs. Custom templates.

EQUIPMENT: Media formats include 100MB Zip, 120 GB SuperDisk, 44MB SyQuest, 88MB SyQuest, 270MB SyQuest, 540MB SyQuest, 650MB optical 1.3 GB optical, 1GB Jaz, 2GB Jaz, CD-ROM, DVD.

SPECIALTIES: Product packaging, catalogs, long documents, and repetitive-format projects. Training in all aspects of the prepress process from system setup to disk prep for accurate film output.

PRESIDENT/CEO/OWNER: Ward Barnett

Direct Marketing - Database Marketing

C

CMS, INC. 651-636-6265
300 Second Street NW St. Paul 55112
FAX: 651-636-0879
CONTACT: Mike Talbott, VP Sales & Marketing
SERVICES: Helps catalogers and e-tailers first identify the people most likely to respond, and then reach them cost-effectively through the mail and via e-mail. CMS service categories include marketing database, analytical and consulting services, list processing, and e-mail processing, including address integrity, merge/purge, postal optimization and inkjet formatting services.
PRESIDENT/CEO/OWNER: R. Kenmore Johnson, CEO/Owner; Pat Minton, President

I

IPARES, LTD. 612-215-2300
5000 Union Plaza Minneapolis 55401
FAX: 612-215-2310
CONTACT: Tom Harold
E-MAIL: info@ipares.com
WWW: ipares.com
FOCUS: Integration of marketing, design and technology.
SERVICES: Internet Professional Services: Providing Fortune 1000 corporations with Internet, Intranet, Extranet, Sales Force Automation, Kiosk and Database Marketing solutions. Multimedia Related Services: Design/concepting, consulting, writing/instructional design and programming. Internet/Intranet: In-house design and programming including secure E-commerce solutions and web-based training.
CAPABILITIES/SPECIALTIES: Graphic design services for brochures, catalogs, ads, display and packaging. Complete prepress production services.
PRESIDENT/CEO/OWNER: Lon Bencini/Tom Harold

Direct Marketing - Database Marketing / 135

P

PRO/PHASE MARKETING, INC. 952-974-1100
6550 Edenvale Blvd. **Eden Prairie 55346-2554**
FAX: 952-974-7874
CONTACT: Elliot B. Eskin
TOLL FREE: 800-969-6400
E-MAIL: e_eskin@prophase.net

SERVICES: Relational database management; computerized list maintenance, file preparation for laser personalization including upper/lower case conversion and gender/title coding; address standardization (CASS certified) postal presort processing (PAVE certified) for maximum postage savings; merge/purge (duplicate elimination); geo-coding and demographic/psychographic overlays; data entry; payment processing/order entry; literature/subscription fulfillment; mail processing (lettership); list research/development; high resolution laser printing/personalization; inkjet addressing; wafer sealing (tabbing); impact printing; target marketing via geographic/demographic/psychographic segmentation; mag tape/floppy disk/modem file transfer/conversion capabilities.

EQUIPMENT: Hewlett Packard 3000 (series 988); midrange Xerox 4635, 4650; videojet System 4000; ProFold Wafer Seal Application System; Chesire 539/525 label application system; Phillipsburg 6 station and 4 station inserters; Baum folder; hand collating, folding and inserting; metering; affix pre-canceled stamps; UPS shipments.

SPECIALTIES: Customized computer market analysis and management reporting for direct marketing programs; customer loyalty/frequency marketing programs; sales incentive programs processing; order entry/payment processing systems (on-line, real-time) response tracking/analysis; list brokering/consumer and business lists available.

PRESIDENT/CEO/OWNER: Elliot B. Eskin

Direct Marketing - Direct Response

A

ACTION MAILING SERVICES, INC.   612-557-6767
2440 Fernbrook Lane   Plymouth 55447
FAX: 612-557-9115
CONTACT: Mitch Porter
E-MAIL: mail@actionmailing.com
WWW: actionmailing.com
SERVICES: Ink jet addressing, letter and jumbo inserting, folding, tabbing, cut sheet laser printing, full postal data processing, literature and product fulfillment, handwork projects. Total mail processing services with a focus on customer service.
CAPABILITIES: Jumbo inserting and high quality ink jet addressing up to 600 dpi.
PRESIDENT/CEO/OWNER: Tony Zirnhelt

ALDATA   612-432-6900
7000 W 151st Street   Apple Valley 55124
FAX: 612-432-7064
E-MAIL: mharris@aldata.com
WWW: aldata.com
SERVICES: Direct marketing consultants, lead generation program specialists, mail/telemarketing list broker, database creative and maintenance and direct marketing computer services.
PRESIDENT/CEO/OWNER: Mike Harris
CONTACT: Terri Yahnke

AMUNDSON MARKETING   612-333-7700
10 South Fifth Street #580   Minneapolis 55402
FAX: 612-333-7701
CONTACT: Kathleen J. Amundson
CAPABILITIES: Amundson Marketing is a strategically-driven marketing agency focused on building the value of our clients' organizations through the development of valuable relationships with their customers. Our expertise encompasses the full array of marketing disciplines including strategic planning, positioning and branding, relationship marketing, direct and database marketing, frequency and loyalty marketing and promotional marketing. Our team is experienced in developing solutions based on the needs of clients and their customers, doing so in a manner that helps our clients stay ahead of their business while delivering a powerful return on investment.
SERVICES: Strategic and tactical planning, primary and secondary research, program design, management and fulfillment, creative services, production management, economic modeling, customer segmentation, modeling and profiling, partner negotiations, measurement and analysis.
CURRENT/RECENT CLIENTS/PROJECTS: National and international clients in the telecommunications, utility, high-tech, business-to-business, consumer products and service industries.

Direct Marketing - Direct Response / 137

C

COLLEEN SZOT WONDERFUL WRITER, INC.   **763-557-7116**
13615 61st Avenue North   **Minneapolis 55446**
FAX: 763-551-4831
CONTACT: Colleen Szot
TOLL FREE: 888-557-7116
E-MAIL: colleenszot@aol.com
WWW: colleenszot.com
TYPES OF WRITING: Clio award-winning writer of more than 100 direct response/infomercials (CNN's Cold War, George Foreman, Orlimar Trimental, Tony Little, Select Comfort, David Dikeman Command Performance) plus TV commercials (Wendy's, Walt Disney, Kraft, Nutri-Grain cereal), Corporate and Training Videos (Dayton-Hudson Corporation, 3M), and all print (ads, brochure, direct mail collateral). Author of best-selling book (Christian Wives), writer for cable television, 22 years experience with J. Walter Thompson, Foote, Cone & Belding, and Campbell-Mithun-Esty.
WRITTEN FOR: CNN, George Foreman, Target, Walt Disney Pictures, Troy-Bilt, HomeRight (PaintStick), 3M, Select Comfort, Tony Little and more.
SPECIALTIES: All broadcast, plus corporate videos/film, cable television.

RAPP COLLINS WORLDWIDE   **612-373-3000**
901 Marquette Avenue - 17th Floor   **Minneapolis 55402**
FAX: 612-373-3063
CONTACT: George Benson
E-MAIL: gbenson@rcwmpls.com
WWW: rappcollins.com
SERVICES: RCW operates five full-service agencies and six "centers of excellence" in North America that are committed to helping clients build and manage more profitable relationships with their customers. RCW's Customer Value Management strategies enable clients to develop one-to-one communications for individual customers via multiple points of contact. RCW's world-class capabilities include brand planning (for direct print, broadcast and interactive), direct mail, teleservices, interactive marketing, media planning and buying (online and offline), database development and management, data warehousing, decision sciences (including data mining, analytics and customer modeling), enabling technology, employee relationship management and consumer/retail promotions.

138 / Direct Marketing - Direct Response

CURRENT/RECENT CLIENTS/PROJECTS: A sampling of RCW clients includes Mercedes Benz, Pfizer, Dell Computer, 3M, Target Corporation, US Navy, and Schwan's. RCW is a division of Omnicom.
PRESIDENT/CEO/OWNER: Patrick Furey, President - Mpls Office

CONCEPT GROUP INC.   **651-221-9710**
192 West Ninth Street   **St. Paul 55102**
FAX: 651-227-4591
CONTACT: Brad Moore
E-MAIL: info@conceptgroup.com
WWW: conceptgroup.com
SERVICES: Full-service marketing communications; strategic communications planning; account management; concept and creative development; design; computer illustration; copywriting; production; post production coordination and implementation; photography studio.
CAPABILITIES: Print advertising; collateral; direct marketing; brand and identity development; sales promotion and incentive programs; public relations; video concepting and scripting; interactive and electronic media; including web site planning, design, development and implementation; CD-ROM development
CURRENT/RECENT CLIENTS/PROJECTS: High tech, low tech and "no tech" clients - B to B and B to C.
PRESIDENT/CEO/OWNER: John Ruddy, P, Brad Moore, EVP, Jay Troe, VP/AD; Mike Davis, CD; Vicki Giefer, Director of Account Services; Mike Brunner, Director of Strategic Planning and Marketing; George Ramsay, Director of New Business Development; Paul Larson, Interactive Services Manager.

E

EAGLE DIRECT/EAGLE GRAPHICS, INC.   **952-471-8531**
3701 Shoreline Drive #100   **Wayzata 55391**
FAX: 952-471-8031
CONTACT: Kathie Strand, Dir. of Operations
SERVICES: Full-service production agency. Consulting/package design/all aspects of print production and letter shop (distribution).
CAPABILITIES: Wayzata based agency for Regional/National Direct Marketers-retail, mail order, business-to-business, publication clients.
FACILITIES: Consulting for effective package (physical layout) designs.
SPECIALTIES: Marketing strategies/techniques, total print/mail coordination, effective marketing via direct mail.
PRESIDENT/CEO/OWNER: Mark Oestreich, P

G

GENERAL LITHO SERVICES, INC. **763-535-7277**
6845 Winnetka Circle **Minneapolis 55428**
FAX: 763-535-7322
CONTACT: Gary Garner
TOLL FREE & WWW: 888-646-7277; www.genlitho.com
SERVICES: It is the dedication to details that make the difference between acceptable and exceptional project management. From the first creative idea to arriving in the hands of your customers, GLS has the expertise to make it happen. Call today and discover all of the services that provide Integrated Communication Solutions(*!).
CREATIVE: Our award winning designs cover a wide range of projects from logos, brochures, ads and web pages, to complete corporate identities.
PREPRESS: We offer full electronic prepress capabilities such as punched film output, in-house scanning, and digital proofing. In addition to film output, we provide image enhancement, color correction and file manipulation services.
DIGITAL & CONVENTIONAL PRESSES: We operate state-of-the-art presses; Docutech NP-135 digital printer, 14 x 20 2 - color Heidelberg, 25 1/4 x 36 2-color Heidelberg, 20 x 28 5-color Heidelberg with coater, 20 x 28 6-color Heidelberg with coater, 28 x 40 5-color Heidelberg Perfector, 28 x 40 6-color Heidelberg CD with coater, 12 x 18 Halm Superjet 2-color perfecting envelope press.
BINDERY: Complete bindery featuring Stahl folders with in-line gluing. Muller Martini and ITOH saddle stitchers with cover feeders, 12 x 18, 20 x 26, and 28 x 40 diecutting presses, automated collating, binding, gluing and converting, along with miscellaneous machinery for special finishing applications.
DATA PROCESSING: We have highly-skilled programmers and a powerful PC-based network to handle the most complex data processing and mailing projects with ease. We have a 9-track reel tape system - 1650 or 6250 BPI. From inkjet to laser personalized components, to address standardization and postal presort optimization, merge/purge, database management and file manipulation, GLS has the direct response capabilities to maximize your results.
LETTERSHOP: Phillipsburg 6 x 9 and 9 x 12 inserters, GBR smart folder feeder for intelligent document processing. Getting your project into the mail is the goal. With a fully equipped lettership and an on-site United States Post Office. GLS can move your project out the door in rapid time.

GRAPHIC RELIEF **612-386-8088**
15207 94th Place North Maple Grove 55369

140 / Direct Marketing - Direct Response

CONTACT: Tony Rubasch
E-MAIL: tonyr@graphicrelief.com
WWW: inet-serv.com/~tonyr
SPECIALTIES: A relief designer with strong emphaiss in retail direct mail catlaogs and web site creation for general consumer merchandise. Along with creative marketing communications for industrial manufacturing, food industry, retail clothing, recreation providers and health care.
CURRENT/RECENT CLIENTS/PROJECTS: Major advertising and marketing communication agencies in the Twin Cities location.

H

HEINRICH ENVELOPE CORPORATION
925 Zane Avenue North
763-544-3571
Minneapolis 55422

FAX: 763-544-6287
CONTACT: Wesley Clerc
E-MAIL: artwork@heinrichenvelope.com
WWW: heinrichenvelope.com
SERVICES: Full line custom envelope manufacturer and printer. Hold for release program allows our customers to take advantage of large volume pricing without the problem of inventory. Stock over 200 commercial and open end envelopes for immediate shipment or to fill your imprinting needs. Free metro delivery on most orders.
CAPABILITIES: Latex sealing of envelopes. In-line banding web equipment. Clasp closure of envelopes. String and button closure of envelopes. Affiliate of one of the largest printers in the nation, giving us tremendous resources to draw upon.
PRESIDENT/CEO/OWNER: Bill Berkner

HIGH POINT CREATIVE, LLC
4583 Shady Lane
651-426-4012
St. Paul 55110

FAX: 651-426-6699
CONTACT: Kate Huebsch
E-MAIL: kate@highpointcreative.com
WWW: highpointcreative.com
SERVICES: Copywriting and full project management for business-to-business and consumer brochures, catalogs, direct mail, websites, newsletters, speeches and presentations, PowerPoint shows, special events, marketing and internal communication pieces. A special interest in "translating" high-tech products and services into compelling and effective copy for non-technical readers.
CAPABILITIES: Marketing communications with an emphasis on strategic development and effective writing.
CURRENT/RECENT CLIENTS/PROJECTS: 12 years in business serving financial services companies, industrial manufacturers, health care organizations and community not-for-profit organizations.
PRESIDENT/CEO/OWNER: Kate Huebsch, President/Owner; Maiya Willits, Creative Director

HOLDEN GRAPHIC SERVICES
607 North Washington Avenue
612-339-0241
Minneapolis 55401

CONTACT: George T. Holden

Direct Marketing - Direct Response / 141

FACILITIES: High-speed 4C process rotary offset presses OCR and MICR, invisible inks, ultraviolet (dry tapping inks and heat set inks.) Creative Facilities: Art, keylining, lithroprep.
SPECIALTIES: Snap-a-part and continuous data processing forms. Computer letters, latent (invisible) ink products for educational computer - oriented promotional materials, mini-computer and word processing forms, direct mail, lettershop, fulfillment, and teleservices.

I
INDEPENDENT DELIVERY SERVICE 651-487-1050
440 W. Minnehaha Avenue St. Paul 55103
FAX: 651-487-1807
CONTACT: Mike Tierney, Paul Overson
E-MAIL: idsstpaul@aol.com
WWW: independentdel.com
SERVICES: Door-to-door delivery of door hangers, newspapers, catalogs, flyers, brochures and phone books. Product sample delivery.
CAPABILITIES: Covering entire twin city area. Largest door-to-door delivery service in Minnesota. Member AAPS delivery of 5,000 - 1,100,000 homes available.
CURRENT/RECENT CLIENTS/PROJECTS: Minnesota Suburban, Lillie News, Focus, Smart pages, Highland Village, Southwest Journal, St. Paul Voice, Community Reporter, Savers Edge, Grand Gazette, North End News, Bugle, Merriam Park Post, AOL and other newspapers, sample and flyer delivery customers.
PRESIDENT/CEO/OWNER: Michael Depe

INFINITY DIRECT, INC. 763-559-1111
13220 County Road 6 Plymouth 55441
FAX: 763-553-1852
CONTACT: Mike Boyle
WWW: infinitydirect.com
SPECIALTIES: Full service capabilities. Consumer and business-to-business direct marketing programs.
CREATIVE SERVICES: Collateral development, brand/identity programs, concept design, brochures, promotion development, planning and execution, copywriting, graphic design, interactive--CD ROM/DVD, web page and web response.
PRODUCTION SERVICES: Printing, lettershop, fulfillment. Interactive--CD-ROM/DVD processing and personalization services.
PRESIDENT/CEO/OWNER: Thomas L. Harding, CEO/Owner

142 / Direct Marketing - Direct Response

IRRESISTIBLE INK, INC. 612-339-3899
126 N Third Street #412 Minneapolis 55401
FAX: 612-339-3788
CONTACT: Doris Hammeke, Senior VP Business Development
SERVICES: Irresistible Ink provides personalization services for clients whose needs include creating and enhancing the relationship with their customers. Services include genuine handwriting, inkjet personalization utilizing hand-scripted fonts and strategic consultation. Whether it is using greeting cards or letters for acquisition, recognition, or appreciation, Irresistible Ink brings a unique, personal touch to customer communications. Powerfully effective. Results-oriented. Memorable. Award winning.
CAPABILITIES: Genuine Handwriting; Customized Font Development; Penmanship printing - Inline printing of cursive and non-cursive handwritten fonts; Inline matching and mailing fulfillment; Consulting service for database management and personalized direct marketing campaigns.
CURRENT/RECENT CLIENTS/PROJECTS: National marketers who value personalized customer communications. Our clients include companies from the following industries: financial service, insurance hospitality, retail, catalog, telecommunications, non-profit, credit card, collections, internet and healthcare.
PRESIDENT/CEO/OWNER: Jon C. Petters, President

L

JAMES M. LAING & ASSOCIATES 612-474-1138
440 Union Place Excelsior 55331
CONTACT: James Laing
SERVICES: More effective, lower cost direct mail and general printing.

M

MAINSTREET GROUP, INC. 651-631-1416
900 Long Lake Road #200 St. Paul 55112
FAX: 651-631-0208
CONTACT: Scott Bakken
E-MAIL: scott@mainstreetgroup.com
WWW: mainstreetgroup.com
SERVICES: Full service advertising and marketing agency, offering TV, radio, and direct mail, plus daily on-line reports of direct response campaigns.
SPECIALTIES: Exclusive provider of MainTrax (direct response campaign results with daily updates).
CURRENT/RECENT CLIENTS/PROJECTS: AT&T; Time Warner Cable; Charter Communications; HBO; MediaOne; MSC; Comcast Cable; Cox Cable; Montgomery Cable; Bell Industries; Delta Dental of Minnesota; Deluxe Corporation; Adelphia; Cable One.

MARK*NET 651-221-0702
420 Summit Avenue St. Paul 55102
FAX: 651-222-3490

Direct Marketing - Direct Response / 143

CONTACT: Dennis Kelly
E-MAIL: kelly@marketnet.online.com
CAPABILITIES: Direct marketing communications research, program design, concept creative, management and execution, including direct mail, direct response, and interactive.
FACILITIES: Advertising print/AV, internet, telemarketing.
SPECIALTIES: Program development for CRM, frequency and club marketing.
CURRENT/RECENT CLIENTS/PROJECTS: National Car Rental, American Express, Gannet, IBM, Hilton Hotels, Rayovac, 3M, US Olympics, Home Depot

MARTIN/WILLIAMS - I GROUP　　　　　　　　　　**612-340-0800**
520 Marquette Avenue #800　　　　　　　　　　**Minneapolis 55402**
FAX: 612-342-4375
CONTACT: Gregg Sampson, Managing Director
WWW: martinwilliams.com
CAPABILITIES: Interactive design, front-end and back-end development, online advertising, direct marketing, e-mail marketing, graphic design.
SPECIALTIES: Website development and marketing, customer acquisition and retention, graphic design and promotional marketing.
CURRENT/RECENT CLIENTS/PROJECTS: 24k.com, 3M, AIGA Creatives, Allina/Mediva, Avenet, Berkline, Blake Schools, Brueggers, Cargill, Catholic Charities, Churchill, Datalink, Dayton's Downtown Council, Gold 'n Plump, Henredon, Homebytes.com, Homehaven/LFI, iPool, Kozy Hat, Lincoln Financial, The Loft, Marvin Windows, Mervyn's, Novartis, Polaris, Victory, Powertel, R-Tech, rooster.com, Rubbermaid, Scots, Search 401k,.com, target, US Bank, Virtual Ink/Mimio, Zonetrader.

P

PRO/PHASE MARKETING, INC.　　　　　　　　**952-974-1100**
6550 Edenvale Blvd.　　　　　　　　　　　　**Eden Prairie 55346-2554**
FAX: 952-974-7874
CONTACT: Elliot B. Eskin
TOLL FREE: 800-969-6400
E-MAIL: e_eskin@prophase.net

144 / Direct Marketing - Direct Response

SERVICES: Relational database management; computerized list maintenance, file preparation for laser personalization including upper/lower case conversion and gender/title coding; address standardization (CASS certified) postal presort processing (PAVE certified) for maximum postage savings; merge/purge (duplicate elimination); geocoding and demographic/psychographic overlays; data entry; payment processing/order entry; literature/subscription fulfillment; mail processing (lettership); list research/development; high resolution laser printing/personalization; inkjet addressing; wafer sealing (tabbing); impact printing; target marketing via geographic/demographic/psychographic segmentation; mag tape/floppy disk/modem file transfer/conversion capabilities.

EQUIPMENT: Hewlett Packard 3000 (series 988); midrange Xerox 4635, 4650; videojet System 4000; ProFold Wafer Seal Application System; Chesire 539/525 label application system; Phillipsburg 6 station and 4 station inserters; Baum folder; hand collating, folding and inserting; metering; affix pre-canceled stamps; UPS shipments.

SPECIALTIES: Customized computer market analysis and management reporting for direct marketing programs; customer loyalty/frequency marketing programs; sales incentive programs processing; order entry/payment processing systems (on-line, real-time) response tracking/analysis; list brokering/consumer and business lists available.

PRESIDENT/CEO/OWNER: Elliot B. Eskin

PROMOTIONAL SYSTEMS GROUP, INC. 1-800-726-8396
2020 O'Neil Road Hudson 54016
PO Box 226

FAX: 715-381-3123
CONTACT: Craig Beemer
E-MAIL: cbeemer@promotionalsystems.com
WWW: promotionalsystems.com

SERVICES: A promotional products and fulfillment company that is focused on providing cost-effective marketing solutions to the consumer packaged goods industry. Services include promotional product design and production, warehousing and inventory management, product inquiry response fulfillment, telemarketing, inbound 800 service, sample fulfillment, and sales material fulfillment.

CAPABILITIES: Systems: Microsoft BackOffice Small Business Server, MAS90 Inventory Management Software, Norstar-PLUS Prelude ACD Phone System, Norstar Voice Mail Model 2 and 11,276 square feet Office/Warehouse.

CURRENT/RECENT CLIENTS/PROJECTS: General Mills; Procter & Gamble; Old Home Foods; Land O'Lakes; PUR Drinking Water Products

T

TARTAN MARKETING 952-473-7575
15500 Wayzata Blvd, Suite 1000 Wayzata 55391
Twelve Oaks Center
CONTACT: James J. MacLachlan
E-MAIL: jim@tartanmarketing.com
WWW: tartanmarketing.com
FOCUS: Tartan Marketing helps business-to-business clients form long-term strategies for creating, revitalizing and leveraging strong brands. Core competency in multi-tactical program development, carried out with strong creative articulation. Media-neutral approach, with tactical recommendations based on most effective strategies for addressing clients' unique needs, issues and opportunities.
CAPABILITIES: Quantitative/qualitative research & discovery, market and brand planning, naming and identity development, communications planning. Integrated execution (collateral, advertising, interactive, custom publications, direct response, promotions, sales programs.) Market Segment Expertise: Food marketing: foodservice/bakery/deli/distribution. High tech: e-business/intellectual properties. Financial: banking/insurance.
OFFICERS: James J. MacLachlan, CEO/Margie D. MacLachlan, VP Creative
ACCOUNT SUPERVISORS: Account Services: Terri Juranek, AE; Gina Wifler, AE; Justin Erickson, AE
BILLINGS: $7 million
YEARS IN BUSINESS: 14

146 / Direct Marketing - Direct Response

V

VAL-PAK OF MINNESOTA   651-603-0603
2550 University Avenue North #301N   St. Paul 55114
CONTACT: Cindy Smoot, Patt Erickson
SERVICES: Complete shared-mail programs for consumer-oriented businesses who want to communicate by neighborhood or city-wide; solo mail programs for new movers, grand openings and other selects.
FACILITIES: Complete package of consultation, design and typesetting. Layout is included in program costs. Response evaluation and tracking program is included also.
SPECIALTIES: Cooperative, low-cost direct mail to home in the Twin Cities area and throughout North America. Zones cover immediate neighborhoods or the nation. Business-to-business mailing also available.

W

WHITNEY WORLDWIDE, INC.   651-749-5000
1845 Buerkle Road   White Bear Lake 55110
FAX: 651-748-4000
CONTACT: Les Layton
E-MAIL: 1layton@whitneyworld.com
WWW: whitneyworld.com
SERVICES: 17-year old Direct Response and Marketing Research company that has worked for many Fortune 500 and other leading companies in Minnesota. We offer experienced writers, designers and strategists who have obtained superior response rates and beaten many companies controls. We also can handle many projects completely in-house. Having acquired 3M's Direct Response Marketing business unit 14 years ago, we also "practice what we preach". Our MarketMaster® lead-generation survey system produce higher response rates and better-quality leads than many companies have ever experienced before.
CAPABILITIES: Lead generation of higher-quality leads via direct mail or the Internet and super research surveys done via the same media--not on the phone. Staff has held top corporate marketing jobs, been department heads at largest agencies, been Pulitzer Prize finalist and run their own graphic design agency.
CURRENT/RECENT CLIENTS/PROJECTS: 3M, Lawson Software, Pioneer Press, Firstar, St. Paul Companies, Cargill, Minnesota Twins, Tousley Ford, Community Credit, United Way

Direct Marketing - Telemarketing

A

A & N CRIST COMPANY, INC.
3835 Colgate Avenue
612-473-5313
Minnetonka 55345
CONTACT: Arch Christ
SERVICES: Advertising/Marketing consulting business specializing in services to small businesses, start-up and in-business.

C

CONTACT INK CORPORATION
222 3rd Avenue NE
612-623-3393
Minneapolis 55413
FAX: 612-623-9099
CONTACT: Kathie A Blea
E-MAIL: kblea@uswest.net
WWW: contactink.uswestdex.com
SERVICES: Qualify potential customers, market surveys, secondary research, data tabulation and analysis, database development and clean-up, focus group recruitment, follow-up trade show leads, customer satisfaction surveys.
CAPABILITIES: Business-to-business telephone projects.

S

SALES BY PHONE, INC.
1621 Sumter Avenue North
763-593-9419
Minneapolis 55427
CONTACT: Dick Salzer
E-MAIL: salesphone@aol.com
SERVICES: All aspects of a proactive, outbound telemarketing campaign for business-to-business and business-to-consumer appointment setting and lead generation. This includes, but is not limited to, assistance in identification of targeted markets, script writing, response writing, training our own qualified, professional telemarketers, making the calls, especially those cold calls, through written or oral reports and response tallies.
CAPABILITIES: Appointment setting, sales, qualifying leads, personalized follow-up to direct mail.
Area: Local, regional, national.

V

VOLKART MAY & ASSOCIATES
630 Interchange Tower
600 South Highway 169, #630
952-525-4900
Minneapolis 55426
FAX: 952-525-4910
CONTACT: Jon Pitton

148 / Direct Marketing - Telemarketing

CAPABILITIES: Volkart May & Associates, is committed to helping companies achieve growth by increasing companies' sales and marketing effectiveness with strategically designed fully integrated marketing programs including; business-to-business database construction and management; lead generation; lead qualification; integrated direct marketing; market research; customer satisfaction surveys; event support; inbound response and customer service; recruitment.

SPECIALTIES: Companies look to VMA to increase the productivity of their sales force with strategically designed "closed loop" lead management systems and pilot programs that have measurable results.

PRESIDENT/CEO/OWNER: Bruce Volkart, CEO; Janet May, President

Badiyan

BRINGING VISION TO REALITY

Dynamic Solutions For Training And Marketing Through Interactive Media and Video

- *25 years of Award-Winning Experience*
- *Vendor of choice to many Fortune 500 companies*
- *International Experience on six continents*
- *Total in-house capabilities*
- *From concept to completion*

720 West 94th Street
Bloomington, MN 55420
952-888-5507
e-mail: info@badiyan.com

Creative Marketing and Training Solutions through Merging Technology!

**720 West 94th Street
Bloomington, MN 55420
952-888-5507**

e-mail: info@badiyan.com

Video · Interactive media · DVD

Direct Marketing - Tracking

M

MAINSTREET GROUP, INC. 651-631-1416
900 Long Lake Road #200 St. Paul 55112
FAX: 651-631-0208
CONTACT: Scott Bakken
E-MAIL: scott@mainstreetgroup.com
WWW: mainstreetgroup.com
SERVICES: Full service advertising and marketing agency, offering TV, radio, and direct mail, plus daily on-line reports of direct response campaigns.
SPECIALTIES: Exclusive provider of MainTrax (direct response campaign results with daily updates).
CURRENT/RECENT CLIENTS/PROJECTS: AT&T; Time Warner Cable; Charter Communications; HBO; MediaOne; MSC; Comcast Cable; Cox Cable; Montgomery Cable; Bell Industries; Delta Dental of Minnesota; Deluxe Corporation; Adelphia; Cable One.

MONTAGE 651-633-1955
2200 W County Road C Roseville 55113
FAX: 651-633-2072
CONTACT: Dick Moberg
E-MAIL: ramoberg@montagenet.com
WWW: montagenet.com
SERVICES: Montage provides customer relationship management services: A customer care center to handle 1-800 calls, e-mails, web visitors, faxes and mail received by our clients; Sales lead management; E-commerce; Outbound telemarketing; Assembly, fulfillment and mailing; Sales seminar administration; Rebate processing; Database marketing.
CAPABILITIES: Montage has been providing marketing services to the business community since 1972. We specialize in programs that build customer relationships with professional, technical and managerial audiences. We specialize in turn-key systems that are tailored to client needs.
CURRENT/RECENT CLIENTS/PROJECTS: 3M Company; Allied Signal; BASF; Carpet One; Century Mfg.; Colder Products Co.; Cuddle Ewe Co.; Dyneon, Inc.; Fujitsu; Horton, Inc.; Medtronic, Inc.; Nexen Group; Norwest Corp; Rockwell Automation; Prometric, Inc.
PRESIDENT/CEO/OWNER: Ken Ehling

Direct Marketing Fulfillment

IMPACT MAILING 612-521-6245
4600 Lyndale Avenue North Minneapolis 55412
FAX: 612-521-1349
CONTACT: Mark Anderson
CAPABILITIES: Medium to high-volume mailing services for retail (consumer) direct marketing, business-to-business and other business-to-consumer projects. Complete data processing, laser printing, lettershop, bindery, and fulfillment services.
FACILITIES: Modern 90,000 SF production facility, Automatic high-speed inkjet and labeling equipment; high-speed continuous form mechanical inserters; metering and stamping (mechanical and hand); complete handwork department.
EQUIPMENT: Special equipment: inkjet; laser and direct impression personalize addressing capabilities. Catalog stitching with inside and outside inkjetting.
SPECIALTIES: Medium to long run inserting, inkjetting with shrink-wrapping, label-aire, in-line tabbling, automated 3M post-it note application.
PICK UP & DELIVERY: Yes
PRESIDENT/CEO/OWNER: Mark Anderson

Displays, Exhibits & Banners

A

ABF DISPLAY COMPANY 651-647-0598
889 Vandalia Street St. Paul 55114
FAX: 651-647-1008
CONTACT: Mary Pat Fleck
E-MAIL: abfinfo@yahoo.com
WWW: abfdisplay.com
SERVICES: Complete trade show services, complete graphic services include design and production. Point of sale displays. Lobby and building interior design and production. Nimlok distributor.
CURRENT/RECENT CLIENTS/PROJECTS: Warehousing, Graphics, Design, Servicing of all trade shows. (26 years experience.)

BRUCE S. ALLEN, INC. 612-341-0660
1018 North Fifth Street Minneapolis 55411
FAX: 612-333-2278
CONTACT: Bruce S. Allen
CAPABILITIES: Complete scenic studio.
SPECIALTIES: Custom design and fabrication in all media. Miniature to giant size sets and props for still, video, film. Displays and exhibits.

ART-TECH PRODUCTIONS, INC. 612-379-4840
1331 Water Street NE Minneapolis 55413
FAX: 612-379-1447
CONTACT: Nancy Teel
E-MAIL: fab@art-tech.net
WWW: art-tech.net
SERVICES: A design/production company that specializes in themed retail environments. Retail display fixtures, tradeshow booths, 3D signage and sculpture, theatrical props, theme painting, kiosks and showroom design.
CAPABILITIES: 20,000 sq. ft workshop area filled with the best crafts people in town. Will work with any client to design and produce a unique and distinctive product. All work is done on-site. We work on jobs both locally and nationally.

152 / Displays, Exhibits & Banners

CURRENT/RECENT CLIENTS/PROJECTS: Creative Kidstuff Toystores - retail display fixtures and store design production; Manhattan Toy - trade show booth and display fixtures; Knotts Camp Snoopy - 3D signage, retail fixtures, props, sculpture; Wirsbo - trade show display unit; Howie G's Steakhouse - 3 D statues, caricature paintings; Cleveland MetroParks Zoo - Theme painting of Australian Outback
PRESIDENT/CEO/OWNER: Carey W. Thornton

B

BUSINESS & TECHNOLOGY GRAPHICS 612-332-1555
718 N. Washington Avenue   Minneapolis 55401
FAX: 612-332-1556
CONTACT: Sandy Resig
SERVICES: Reprographic services: enlarging and reducing of large format black and white and color originals using high quality copiers. Also, 8-1/2 x 11 and 11 x 17 color copies. Mounting on foamboard and gatorboard. Laminating, encapsulating and shrinkwrapping. Servicing: corporations, ad agencies, architectural and law firms since 1965.
CAPABILITIES: Fast and reasonable.

C

CENTRAL CONTAINER CORP.   **612-425-7444**
PO Box 43310   **Minneapolis 55443**
FAX: 612-425-7917
CONTACT: Steven Braun
E-MAIL: sbraun@centralcontainer.com
WWW: centralcontainer.com
SERVICES: Designs created by an award winning structural design team. From promotional packaging and point-of-sale shelf cartons, to protective, cushioned shipping containers, we provide complete prototyping and engineered solutions. Point-of-purchase displays and "club pack" designs are turned out in minimal time. Full color mock-ups of proposed art are produced on our 54" H. P. Color Plotter. Sophisticated warehousing and logistics management within our 175,000 square foot state of the art production facility, coupled with our in-house fulfillment group, allow for true "turnkey" project management.
CAPABILITIES: Litho/label mounting on 2 automatic mounters. Substrates from corrugated to foam core. 4 color flexo press capable of process work as well as vibrant, rich solid color and line work. Precision die cutters - 2 flat bed and 2 rotary presses. Standard cartons from our flexo/folder/gluers, and specialty boxes with intricate glue patterns for "crash bottoms," 6 corner trays, and internal parts - all glued on computer automated systems.
PRESIDENT/CEO/OWNER: James E. Haglund

Displays, Exhibits & Banners / 153

D

DIGIGRAPHICS, INC.   612-721-2434
2639 Minnehaha Avenue So   Minneapolis 55406
FAX: 612-721-4855
CONTACT: Joe Sodomka
WWW: digidigi.com
SERVICES: Digital imaging and design services for professional illustration and presentation programs, Macintosh and Windows. Creative design, high-resolution scanning, photo retouch and compositing; direct digital output to photographic media (48" x 96"), photographic film (35mm, 4 x 5, 8 x 10). Large format color inkjet display prints (60" x 240"). Other digital services include: high volume Canon laser copies, digital overheads, Fujix prints, CD-R mastering and volume CD-R duplication. Full in-house traditional photographic services including volume 35mm slide duplication quantity R3 prints and overheads, custom color prints/transparencies to 50" x 144", and quantity B&W prints. Complete mounting, laminating and custom finishing services.
SPECIALTIES: Design, create, image large format high-resolution digital files for tradeshows and other display purposes. Fast Service Available: Yes. Pickup and Delivery : Yes

E

EXHIBITS PLUS   612-378-6570
2211 Broadway Street NE   Minneapolis 55413
FAX: 612-378-6577
CONTACT: Colleen Brandt
WWW: brede.com
SERVICES: A variety of modular light weight exhibits, table-top or tradeshow regulation size. Photo mural and fabric exhibits, with rental availability.
CAPABILITIES: Facilities: design production and graphics. Warehousing: Limited warehousing.
SPECIALTIES: Showcase your company at tradeshow and corporate events. Customize your exhibit with upgraded furniture and graphics. A full line of modular exhibits, furniture, and carpet for rent.
PRESIDENT/CEO/OWNER: William C. Casey III

G

GRAPHIC EXHIBITS, INC.   651-225-1678
185 West Pennsylvania Avenue   St. Paul 55103
FAX: 651-225-1665
SERVICES: Graphic Exhibits, Inc. has offered full service convention decorating since 1971 and is locally owned and operated. We are distributors for INTEX Brand Exhibit Systems as well as Valley Forge Flag Company and DA-LITE Presentation Products. Graphic Exhibits, Inc. provides full graphic services using 3M vinyl lettering for signs, banners and interior sign graphics.

154 / Displays, Exhibits & Banners

CAPABILITIES/SPECIALTIES: Convention Service Equipment (Pipe and Drape) as well as Freight and Warehouse facilities only one mile from RiverCentre in St. Paul.
CURRENT/RECENT CLIENTS/PROJECTS: 3M Community Affairs Projects; City of St. Paul and The St. Paul Public Schools and Chamber of Commerce Job Fairs ETC: EcoWater, U of M and MN-SCU Job Fairs and other events. INTEX Portable Exhibit Sales.
PRESIDENT/CEO/OWNER: Gary L. Murphy
CONTACT: Lance Konze/Dale Gardner

H

HARRIS WAREHOUSE & CANVAS SALES
501 30th Avenue SE

612-331-1829
Minneapolis 55414

FAX: 612-331-6651
CONTACT: Marc or Sigmund Harris
E-MAIL: harrismchy501@aol.com
SERVICES: Sewing facilities for fabrication to order repairs - many materials in stock - art work for banners.
CAPABILITIES: We do work in our workrooms and have experienced sewers.
PRESIDENT/CEO/OWNER: Marc Harris

HSC SCENIC SERVICES, LTD
2800 North 2nd Street

612-521-1673
Minneapolis 55411

FAX: 612-521-1801
CONTACT: Philip Hinz
E-MAIL: hscscenic@aol.com
SERVICES: Custom design/build and installation. Sculpting and mold making, metal working, wood working, urethane hardcoating system - FRP capabilities. Design, AutoCAD 14, and engineering services.
CAPABILITIES: We create Visual Eco-systems from design to installation, we make the unique 3D elements, facades and murals for exciting public places; retail, theme parks, restaurants, museums, children's hospitals, and corporations.
CURRENT/RECENT CLIENTS/PROJECTS: MN Historical Society; Shea Architects; BWBR; Children's Hospital; Lutheran Children's Hospital; Heritage Exhibits; Ellerbe Becket; MN Department of Env. Asst.; Stein Design; General Mills; Taylor Displays

M

MODERNISTIC, INC.
169 Jenks Avenue

651-291-7650
St. Paul 55117

FAX: 651-291-2571
CONTACT: Deb Olson
E-MAIL: info@modernisticinc.com
WWW: modernisticinc.com
SERVICES: Full service screenprinter and print finisher. Services offered; Foil stamping, embossing, die cutting, mounting, finishing, UV coating, strip taping, die making and specialty screen printing including glow-in-the-dark printing, scratch off printing, scented ink printing, and glitter printing.

Displays, Exhibits & Banners / 155

CAPABILITIES: Products we offer: Point-of-purchase signage, floor graphics, window graphics, clip strips, temporary displays, fleet graphics, prototyping, banners.
PRESIDENT/CEO/OWNER: Keith Wilson

N

NORTHCOTT BANNER CORPORATION   612-722-1733
3020 East 28th Street   Minneapolis 55406
FAX: 612-722-5622
CONTACT: Millie Northcott
WWW: northcottbanner.com
SERVICES: Types of Displays: Custom printed fabric banners. Dye-sublimation and surface printing on a variety of fabrics for every application. Event, promotional and permanent merchandising banners.
FACILITIES: 15,000 sq. ft. production facility.
DESIGN FEE ARRANGEMENTS: Customer supplied or estimated per job.
SPECIALTIES: Banners in short runs or large roll-outs for: point-of-purchase, retail merchandising, special events, corporate identity, seasonal promotions, mall and boulevard décor.
PRESIDENT/CEO/OWNER: Millie Northcott

NORTHWEST COMPUTER SERVICES   651-659-9680
227 North Snelling Avenue   St. Paul 55104
FAX: 651-659-9581
CONTACT: Mike Thomas, New Business Development Manager
E-MAIL: info@nwcomputer.com
WWW: nwcomputer.com
SERVICES: Large Format Output - Image areas up to 59 inches wide x 100 feet long. Stocks - RC paper, backprint and backlit film, canvas. Laminating - Gloss, matte. Mounting - Foamcore, Sintra, Plexi, Gator board. Finishing - Trimming, framing, rounded corners, sculpted outlines. Fasteners - Velcro loop and hook, grommets. Digital Printing - Image areas up to 11.5 inches x 17.5 inches. Stocks - Cover weights in 60# to 80#. Scanning - High resolution to 8000 pixels. Enlargement up to 2500%. Reflective and Transparent art. 3D objects.
CAPABILITIES: Large Format Imaging - Trade Show and Convention booth images and graphics. Event banners. Retail and Restaurant Signage. Indoor Advertising. Murals for architects, engineers, malls, corporate and hotel lobbies. Party and event themes. Short Run Imaging - Posters, bulletins, countertop and sign cards. Complete finishing services.
SPECIALTIES: Through the expertise of our in-house technicians we have refined the RIP for our ENCAD Novajet 700 Pro 42e, resulting in some of the highest quality large format images available in the Twin Cities. Pickup & Delivery - In-house dispatch, pickup and delivery.
PRESIDENT/CEO/OWNER: Gabe Freund

156 / Displays, Exhibits & Banners

NYGARD DIMENSIONS

NYGARD DIMENSIONS　　　　　　　　　　　　　　　**612-623-8150**
1414 Marshall Street N.E.　　　　　　　　　　　　**Minneapolis 55413**
FAX: 612-623-8147
CONTACT: Luis Ferreiro, General Manager
E-MAIL: events@stagesets.com
WWW: stagesets.com
SERVICES: Custom design, fabrication, installation of themed environments including special events; trade show exhibits; stage sets for meetings, film, video and photography; corporate and point-of-purchase displays and more. Creative development and design, computer renderings and 3D modeling, site inspection, on-site management and other event planning/management capabilities.
CAPABILITIES: Specializes in dimensional environments that create the "whole brand experience", integrating brand and creative theme through all media. Brand identity and design available through sister company, Nygard & Associates. State-of-the-art 60' x 80' x 31' sound stage on-location (Harmony Box).
CURRENT/RECENT CLIENTS/PROJECTS: 3M, ADC Telecommunications, American Express Financial Advisors, Larson Manufacturing, Lawson Software, Lutheran Brotherhood, Minnesota Department of Agriculture, Minnesota Mutual Insurance, Musicland, nQuire Software, and Target Stores.

P

PHOTOGRAPHIC SPECIALTIES　　　　　　　　　　**612-522-7741**
1718 Washington Avenue North　　　　　　　　　**Minneapolis 55411**
FAX: 612-522-1934
CONTACT: Rick Schuenemann
E-MAIL: drewkal@photospec.com
SERVICES: P.S. is a full service custom photo lab and digital imaging service. We specialize in large runs of prints and transparencies for visual merchandising, POP, Trade Show Exhibits and museums. We have in-house graphic designers, a stock photo library and shipping and kitting capabilities.
CAPABILITIES: Two Light Jet 5000 Digital photo images for true photographic images up to 48" x 96" in one piece. Drum and flatbed scanning, LVT 8 x 10 film recorder, and Repri and Ellegro scan/retouch system. Color span Inkjet printers (4) and full mounting and laminating capabilities up to 80" wide. 4 traditional mural rooms with wall easels, prints and trans up to 72" x 16' one piece.
CURRENT/RECENT CLIENTS/PROJECTS: Large nationwide retail chains, display and store design firms.
PRESIDENT/CEO/OWNER: Drew Kalman

Displays, Exhibits & Banners / 157

PHOTOLAB IMAGING CORPORATION   763-525-5900
5900 Olson Memorial Highway   Golden Valley 55422
FAX: 763-525-0190
CONTACT: Jeff Ferrazzo, VP Sales
E-MAIL: sales@p-i-c.com
WWW: p-i-c.com
CAPABILITIES: Complete photographic and digital display print products and services. Digital photographic (Lambda), traditional photo and Ink Jet graphic panels for any portable, pop-up display system. Display hardware and graphic packages offered include Banner-Up™ Instant Presentations, Power Tower™ & Power Counter™ Backlit Displays and Floor and Counter Graphic Mats, for all trade show and commercial use. Custom 6-color Ink Jet banners, floor and wall graphics, vinyl graphics and 3M graphics also available. Complete digital imaging services include high-resolution scanning, image manipulation, retouching, photocomposition and CD recording.
SPECIALTIES: We've been a nationwide leading supplier of trade show graphics for over 25 years! If you have a display graphic need, we have the solution.
PRESIDENT/CEO/OWNER: Charles W. Specht

PRISM STUDIOS, INC.   612-331-1000
2505 Kennedy Street NE   Minneapolis 55413
FAX: 612-331-4106
CONTACT: Gary Duncan
TOLL FREE: 1-800-659-2001
E-MAIL: email@prismstudios.com
WWW: prismstudios.com
SERVICES: Types of Displays: Design, photography, computer graphics, digital imaging, display prints and transparencies. Full mounting, laminating and kitting.
FACILITIES: Complete photographic and digital imaging services in 30,000 square foot facility able to handle large volume with rapid turnaround.
SPECIALTIES: Sophisticated, affordable display graphics for all applications. Retail and tradeshow display prints, transparencies.

PROFESSIONAL COLOR SERVICE, INC.   612-673-8900
909 Hennepin Avenue South   Minneapolis 55403
FAX: 612-673-8988
CONTACT: Tim Doe
E-MAIL: procolor@procolor.com
WWW: procolor.com
CAPABILITIES: Four feet wide to just about any length, beautiful photographic Lambda prints for the price you've been paying for Inkjets. The Lambda outputs knock-their-socks-off trade show graphics. Need a display to hang them on? We can provide Display One portable display units. Our one-stop-shop line of products and services includes: new 3D lenticular display prints, digital display photographs and transparencies, as well as a complete range of scanning services, including those from our high res drum, Photo CD, and Dicomed digital camera. Fine art IRIS reproduction. Short-run digital 4-color printing on our Heidelberg DI and Docucolor systems. Color laser copies and Bubblejet copies up to 24" x 36". Film processing 24 hours a day Monday through Friday and 8:30 to 11:30 on Saturday. Pick up and delivery.
SPECIALTIES: One-stop shop imaging services.
OFFICE HOURS: Monday through Friday 7:30 am to 8:00 pm; Saturday 8:30 to 2:00 pm.

158 / Displays, Exhibits & Banners

S

SIGNTIFIC 651-688-8070
1285 Corporate Center Drive #180 Eagan 55121
FAX: 651-688-0458
CONTACT: Thomas Trutna
E-MAIL: signtific@ibm.net
SERVICES: We are a large format graphics producer. When you need posters, banners, signage or promotional materials, we are the place to call. From concept to product selection, production through delivery, we are the experts. Full-color, full-graphic pieces in quantity from 1-100 and beyond can now be yours quickly and inexpensively. Trade shows, events, POP, floor graphics, outdoor banners, short-run posters are our specialty.
CAPABILITIES: Over 10 years experience serving corporate customers with superior service and product knowledge. We print and laminate up to 60" wide and 150' in length. Pieces can be tiled for infinite size possibilities. Print materials include, paper, PVC, canvas, silk, transparent films, floor graphics and much more.
PRESIDENT/CEO/OWNER: Thomas Trutna

STUDIOCRAFTS, INC. 612-331-7884
451 Taft Street NE Minneapolis 55413
FAX: 612-331-2057
CONTACT: Greg Cornell
E-MAIL: studiocr@bitstream.net
SERVICES: Custom design and fabrication of scenery, props, display and tradeshow exhibits.
CAPABILITIES: Full service scenic facility. We have the people, the experience, and the facilities to take your idea to reality on time, and on budget.
CURRENT/RECENT CLIENTS/PROJECTS: Best Buy Television Commercial, 1999; General Mills National Sales Meeting, 1998, 1999, 2000; Guthrie Theater, Feb. 2000.
PRESIDENT/CEO/OWNER: Greg Cornell, Chris Johnson

U

UPFRONT PRODUCTIONS 651-633-5299
2350 County Road C #120 St. Paul 55113
FAX: 651-633-5197
CONTACT: Tricia Nordby Hamrin/Chris Hamrin
WWW: hoopjumping.com
CAPABILITIES: Organizational Communications Solutions Center. A Spectrum. A Synergy. Concept Development, Copywriting, Graphic Design, Illustration, Document Production, Web Site Creation, Scanning, Photo Retouching, Pre-press, Offset Printing, Digital B&W Printing, Color Copies, Posters, Displays, Signs, Custom Assembly, Inventory, Distribution, Corporate Compass® MIS, VantagePoint™, Hoop Jumping™.
SPECIALTIES: Choose your hoop. We'll jump through it™.
OFFICERS: Tricia Nordby Hamrin/Chris Hamrin

V

VEE CORPORATION   612-378-2561
504 Malcolm Avenue SE #200   Minneapolis 55414
FAX: 612-378-2635
CONTACT: Bonnie Ehlers
E-MAIL: bonniee@vee.com
WWW: vee.com
SERVICES: Concept, design and construction of special scenic elements and props within an exhibit booth; specialty displays; interactive exhibits. Unusual Items: Design, fabricated and installed interactive games and exhibits for NBA Jam Session.
SPECIALTIES: Scenic art, sculpting, aluminum and steel fabrication.
PRESIDENT/CEO/OWNER: Vincent E. Egan, P; Jack Pence, Mrg.

Editors & Editorial Services

B

MARK BRADLEY   651-636-1127
1851 West Shryer Avenue   Roseville 55113
CONTACT: Mark Bradley
SERVICES: Copy editing, substantive editing and rewriting of all types of copy, from video scripts to scholarly articles; transcribing and editing speeches and interviews. Experience: Fifteen years freelance writer. Ten years newsletter editor.
SPECIALTIES: Saving failing projects; re-working, re-thinking and revising projects from concept to final product, focusing ideas without destroying client's individual style.

C

DAWN CARLSON   612-920-1563
4953 Upton Avenue South   Minneapolis 55410
CONTACT: Dawn Carlson
E-MAIL: dcwritedit@aol.com
SERVICES: All levels of editing, including rewriting, substantive editing, copyediting and proofreading. Experience: 5 years.
SPECIALTIES: Newsletters, magazines and cookbooks.
CURRENT/RECENT CLIENTS/PROJECTS: Minnesota Monthly; Midwest Home & Design; Pillsbury Publications and others.

CHARS WORDSHOPPE   651-426-8601
89 Wildwood Bay Drive   Mahtomedi 55115
FAX: 651-426-7448
CONTACT: Charlotte S. Gulden
SERVICES: Copy editing and proofreading all forms of written communications.
CAPABILITIES: 16 years of experience editing and proofreading for business clients in a wide variety of media types. Specializing in advertising (ads, brochures, direct mail, catalogs) and publishing (textbooks, cookbooks, magazines.) PC expertise as well as proven knowledge of well-known style manuals.
CURRENT/RECENT CLIENTS/PROJECTS: Wessels; Arnold Henderson; General Mills; Target Corp.; U of M Landscape Arboretum; Minnesota Suburban Newspapers; American Asset Management; Miller Publishing; Cooking Pleasures Magazine; CVN; Reach Organization; McGraw Hill; Paradigm Publishing; Cowles Creative Publishing; Sense of Design; Williams Publications; Best Buy

THE CONCISE WORD   651-456-9596
4525 Alicia Drive   Inver Grove Heights 55077
FAX: 651-456-9596
CONTACT: Cheryl Crockett
E-MAIL: crockett@fullywired.org
WWW: fullywired.org
SERVICES: Editing, web page design and maintenance, resumes, help with self-publishing, desktop publishing, scanning, individualized mailings.

Editors & Editorial Services / 161

CAPABILITIES: Prepare print-ready copy for book manuscripts (edit, scan/incorporate pictures, layout); edit and correct medical software; design, format and edit newsletters, annual reports, cookbooks, and manuals; custom-design and print brochures, invitations, and business cards; design and print resumes, cover letters and stationery packages.
CURRENT/RECENT CLIENTS/PROJECTS: Edina Realty; Church Ad Project; Minnesota Homeschoolers' Alliance; Pointed Printing Services; St. Paul Area Synod (ELCA); and numerous self-publishers.

D

DEBNER PUBLICATIONS
3517 Widgeon Way
FAX: 651-683-9709
CONTACT: Claudia Debner
E-MAIL: debnerpub@msn.com

651-683-9709
Eagan 55123

SERVICES: Twenty years' experience in editing books, magazines, and corporate training materials; managing publication projects and schedules; training in editing/proofreading' and Microsoft Word; online editing and formatting.
CAPABILITIES: Substantive and style editing, teaching/training, formatting of electronic files, project organization, indexing.
CURRENT/RECENT CLIENTS/PROJECTS: Carlson Marketing Group, Wilson Learning Corporation, Honeywell.

CHERYL DRIVDAHL
1205 Lia Drive
CONTACT: Cheryl Drivdahl

507-663-1579
Northfield 55057

CAPABILITIES: Copy editing, line editing, development editing, manuscript analysis, bibliographies, proofreading, rewriting, technical writing.
SPECIALTIES: Online editing, Macintosh, Word 98, Educational materials, secondary and college levels, fiction and non-fiction trade books.
CURRENT/RECENT CLIENTS/PROJECTS: Saint Mary's Press, West Publishing Company, Motorbooks International.
PRESIDENT/CEO/OWNER: Cheryl Drivdahl

JANE DUGAN EDITORIAL SERVICES
2928 Dean Pkwy #4D
CONTACT: Jane Dugan
E-MAIL: dugan@iaxs.net
WWW: iaxs.net/~dugan/JDES/JDES.htm

612-924-0743
Minneapolis 55416

SERVICES: Editing/proofreading technical and non-technical material. Books, chapters, journal articles, manuals, reports, proposals, marketing communications.
CAPABILITIES/SPECIALTIES: Medicine/science, advertising. 18 years experience (self-employed since 1991.)

G

GREENHOUSE GROUP   763-572-9194
5770 Washington Street NE   Fridley 55432
FAX: 763-572-9194
CONTACT: Lora Polack Oberle
E-MAIL: jgoberle.com
SERVICES: Both editing and writing services are available. Types of editing, copyediting, substantive editing, development editing, series editing, proofreading. Types of writing: educational materials, research, re-writing, video scripts, newsletter copy, juvenile nonfiction, parenting.
CAPABILITIES: Experienced in managing large, multi-faceted projects. Experienced as an independent publisher in all aspects of publishing, 1997 award winner for editing from Mid-America Publishers Association. M.A. in Teaching English as a Second Language. Particular expertise in editing educational, parenting, and testing materials; also experienced in editing and writing juvenile nonfiction, sports, newsletters, general nonfiction, humor. Computers used: Macintosh Performa (QuarkExpress, Claris Works); IBM compatible (Windows, Word Perfect.)
CURRENT/RECENT CLIENTS/PROJECTS: American Guidance Service; Captstone Press; Dillion Press; Free Spirit Publishing; Insurance Testing Corporation; Minnesota Timberwolves; Minnesota Lynx; Pioneer Packaging and Printing; Zip Sort. Inc.

H

PATRICIA C HASWELL   651-690-5452
1297 Pinehurst Avenue   St. Paul 55116
CONTACT: Patricia C Haswell
E-MAIL: haswelltodd@compuserve.com
SERVICES: Copyediting and proofreading.
CAPABILITIES: 20 years' experience.
CURRENT/RECENT CLIENTS/PROJECTS: University of Minnesota Press; U of M Department of Work, Community and Family Education.

RALPH W. HENN, PUBLIC RELATIONS,   952-881-1246
EDITORIAL & MARKETING
COMMUNICATIONS SERVICES
9931 Elliott Avenue South   Bloomington 55420
FAX: On request
CONTACT: Ralph Henn
E-MAIL: rwhenn@winternet.com
WWW: winternet.com/~rwhenn
CAPABILITIES: Writing, editing, publications: news releases, publications (internal, external, sales and marketing, newsletters, newspapers, magazines, brochures, copywriting, editing, fitting, type specs, layouts, speeches, presentations, proposals (including visuals), announcements (internal and external), fact sheets, profiles, letters, www site development, research (secondary), non-technical writing and editing. Media relations: media list development and news release distribution, media contacts and placement, editorial calendar targeting, media kits (corporate, product, event). Program, production and publications management (sourcing and management of resources and suppliers to meet objectives): design, photography, print production, (electronic publishing/typesetting, printing, binding, distribution, etc.)

Editors & Editorial Services / 163

CURRENT/RECENT CLIENTS/PROJECTS: Carlson Companies (Carlson Wagonlit Travel and Carlson Marketing Group), Northwest Airlines/MLT, Presbyterian Church (USA), Intemark, Marketing Communications, National Lodging Companies, Psychological and Career Consultants, U.S. Tennis Assn., World Marketing Group/Pacific World, Future Systems Consulting, Nymax.

M

JOY MCCOMB 651-484-4553
3215 Richmond Avenue Shoreview 55126
CONTACT: Joy McComb
CAPABILITIES: Proofreading and light copyediting of books, journals, monographs. Experience: 3 years of proofreading and copyediting, technical and non-technical. Teach proofreading workshop for current and potential freelancers and companies; word processor experience; very familiar with Chicago Manual of Style.
SPECIALTIES: Technical: mathematics, physics, chemistry, geography, biochemistry, plant pathology, genetics, phy ed, law, medicine, religion, agriculture. Home economics. Non-technical including cookbooks.
CURRENT/RECENT CLIENTS/PROJECTS: Augsburg Fortress Publishers; Minnesota Extension Service; MBI Publishing Company; Minnesota History Center; Capstone Press; Paradigm Publishing; Hazelden Information and Educational Services; Hanley-Wood Custom Publishing; American Associate of Cereal Chemists; American Phytopathological Society.

MGRAPHICS 952-404-0052
3627 Druid Lane Minnetonka 55345
CONTACT: Mary Brandenburg
CAPABILITIES: Proofreading and editing.
SPECIALTIES: Collateral, advertising, and technical literature. Thorough, thoughtful work.

P

PROFESSIONAL EDITORS NETWORK OF MN 651-690-0881
(PEN)
PO Box 19265 Minneapolis 55419
CONTACT: Molly McBeath - 651-690-0881 or Barbara Schue - 651-690-5577
CAPABILITIES: Organization of staff and freelance editors, writers and allied professionals who meet to share professional knowledge and experience; group also serves as a clearinghouse for information about job and educational opportunities, and publishes a directory of freelance editors, writers, and proofreaders.
SPECIALTIES: Membership requirements: Annual fee covers expenses and meetings. Meetings: Informally organized: monthly (except July and August) on the second Tuesday of the month. 100 members, approximately.

164 / Editors & Editorial Services

S

SANDRA R. SABO   651-681-9262
2230 Bent Tree Lane   Mendota Heights 55120
FAX: 651-681-1591
CONTACT: Sandra R. Sabo
E-MAIL: srsabo@aol.com
SERVICES: Copy editing, rewriting for clarity and turning confusing language into plain English.
CAPABILITIES: Award-winning writer and editor with 20 years' experience working with non-profit organizations and corporate clients.
SPECIALTIES: Magazines, books; marketing and training materials.
CURRENT/RECENT CLIENTS/PROJECTS: Medtronic, American Society of Association Executives, Society of National Association Publications, American Gas Association, American Association of Medical Assistants, American Public Communications Council

SPOTNIK   612-377-7903
227 Colfax Avenue North   Minneapolis 55405
120 South 6th Street #2190
FAX: 612-377-1056
CONTACT: Ed Hewitt
E-MAIL: cut@spotnikcuts.com
SERVICES: Creative offline editing, primarily TV commercials, from pre-production through finish.
CAPABILITIES: Two Minneapolis locations with 5 Avid edit suites. Experienced editors.
CURRENT/RECENT CLIENTS/PROJECTS: K-Mart; Target; Ralston Purina; Toro; Perkins.

T

TECHNICAL WRITING AND EDITING   651-484-3288
426 West Sextant Avenue   St. Paul 55113
CONTACT: Robert D. Wray
CAPABILITIES: Copy editing, substantive editing, writing, rewriting, writing seminars, specialize in the field of natural resources. Experience: Bachelors and Masters degrees in forestry, 30 plus years research writing/editing for US. For service, co-author of 2 books, magazine article and column writing, teaching technical writing.
SPECIALTIES: Natural resources.
CURRENT/RECENT CLIENTS/PROJECTS: US Forest Service, University of Minnesota
PRESIDENT/CEO/OWNER: Robert D. Wray

SYLVIA TIMIAN   612-924-9139
4115 Raleigh Avenue   St. Louis Park 55416
FAX: 612-924-9139
CONTACT: Sylvia Timian

Editors & Editorial Services / 165

E-MAIL: timmy93@gateway.net
SERVICES: Editing, indexing, and proofreading services.
CAPABILITIES: 17 years experience as staff editor and freelance editor; previously medical librarian familiar with Chicago Manual of Style and AMA Manual of Style. Subjects I've worked on include: medicine, health, and nutrition, self-help, social science, education, geography and environmental awareness for elementary and middle school students. Biographies, automotive and aviation history, religious texts, general interest.
CURRENT/RECENT CLIENTS/PROJECTS: McGraw Hill Healthcare, Allina Health System, Lerner Publications, Capstone Press, Sunrise River Press, International Diabetes Center, Fairview Press, Augsburg Fortress, Education Strategies, Hazelden Publishing.
PRESIDENT/CEO/OWNER: Sylvia Timian

W

WORDSCAPE COMMUNICATION 612-823-0759
3401 Colfax Avenue South #318 Minneapolis 55408
FAX: 612-823-0536
CONTACT: Kaye Henry
E-MAIL: wordscape@juno.com
SERVICES: Copy editing, rewriting, writing, proofreading. 12 years' experience as reporter/writer, copy editor, editorial assistant and proofreader, working on news and feature articles, advertising, product description, newsletters, college publications, brochures, manuals, directories, catalogs, books and booklets.
CURRENT/RECENT CLIENTS/PROJECTS: Colle & McVoy Marketing Communications; Federal Reserve Bank of Minneapolis; Skyway Publications; Siren Media; Fallon McElligott; Access Press; Krass Monroe; Ava Group; Holistic America.
PRESIDENT/CEO/OWNER: Kaye Henry

WORKING WORDS 763-422-0648
2900 Yosemite Avenue South Minneapolis 55416
FAX: 763-422-0204
CONTACT: Karin B. Miller
E-MAIL: workwords@aol.com
SERVICES: Corporate communications and marketing communications, internal and external publications, brochures and special projects. Magazine writing for consumer, corporate and trade publications. Editing, copyediting.
CURRENT/RECENT CLIENTS/PROJECTS: Ecolab; Midwest Living; Star Thrower Distribution; Target Corporation; and the University of Minnesota.

Y

MARGARET LABASH YOUNG 612-933-5062
313 Farmdale Road Hopkins 55343
CONTACT: Margaret Labash Young
ALTERNATE PHONE: 612-305-5208
SERVICES: Copy editing, rewriting, proofreading, indexing, research, design of questionnaires, international business project management.
CAPABILITIES: Business and corporate history, science, engineering and technology, European community, art, social sciences. 20 years experience in directory publishing at Gale Research. Developed three business and scientific directories, Expert indexing of cookbooks. Member of PEN (Professional Editors Network), Special Libraries Associate and American Society of Indexers.
CURRENT/RECENT CLIENTS/PROJECTS: Ford Motor Company; Minnesota Project Innovation, Inc.; Norwest Corporation; East West Press; American Liberty Publishers; Institute of Corporate Diversity and KPMG (Accountants and Consultants).

Education & Training

A

AMERICAN SOCIETY FOR TRAINING AND DEVELOPMENT
1821 University Avenue West #S256
FAX: 651-917-1835
CONTACT: Kendra Lee Myers
E-MAIL: office@astd-smc.org
WWW: astd-smc.org

651-917-6248
St. Paul 55104

SERVICES: Non-profit professional association providing education, professional development and networking opportunities to the Southern Minnesota Training and Development community, including the Twin Cities metro area. We provide our services through monthly meetings, special events, special interest groups, a monthly newsletter and an interactive web site.

CAPABILITIES: Training and development, organizational development, technical training, facilitation, performance management, process management, public speaking, instructional design, distance education, computer based training, career development, leadership, executive coaching.

PRESIDENT/CEO/OWNER: Grayce Belvedere Young, P; Jim Arnold, P Elec.; Gayle Noakes, Past P.

B

BADIYAN INC.
720 West 94th Street
FAX: 952-888-5250
CONTACT: Janiece Haglund
E-MAIL: fbadiyan@badiyan.com
WWW: badiyan.com

952-888-5507
Bloomington 55420

CAPABILITIES: At Badiyan, we're committed to creative communications which bring vision to reality, vividly and with great impact. Award-winning, full-service corporate communications for training and marketing, corporate communications, product introduction, sales and marketing, training and public relations. In media such as video, DVD and interactive media. Fully staffed to provide complete concept development, scripting, production, post-production, and distributing services.

168 / Education & Training

SPECIALTIES: Creative communications problem solving using all types of dynamic visual media. Minnesota's most experienced production company, including products in Europe, Australia, India, the Far East, the Middle East, and South and Central America. IBM Business Partner (recommended multimedia program developer.)
EQUIPMENT: Complete in-house studio and sound stage facilities for video production. Fully equipped grip truck, location equipment, and post-production digital editing suite. IBM multimedia technology.
CURRENT/RECENT CLIENTS/PROJECTS: Fortune 500 companies; health care; insurance and financial services; manufacturing; agriculture; retail; high-tech; computers; and food.
PRESIDENT/CEO/OWNER: Fred Badiyan

E

EFFECTING CREATIVE CHANGE IN ORGANIZATIONS (ECCO)   651-636-0838
1519 McClung Drive   St. Paul 55112-1908
FAX: 651-636-0958
E-MAIL: amy@eccointernational.com
WWW: eccointernational.com
CAPABILITIES: ECCO focuses on consulting and training services including: organization development, cross cultural/diversity training, management development, train-the-trainer workshops, video production and satellite videoconferencing. All products and services are custom-designed to meet specific goals and situations. Retain pool of professionals with diverse expertise to meet client needs.
SPECIALTIES: Managing change in the organization, global organization development, customized training offered via many delivery systems (classroom, video conferencing, etc.), team building, diversity interventions, executive speech coaching and video training production. Available for speaking engagements.
PRESIDENT/CEO/OWNER: Amy S. Tolbert, Ph.D., President/Owner

H

THE HOLTON GROUP   612-338-6984
2 Greenway Gables   Minneapolis 55403
CONTACT: Rick Holton
E-MAIL: fsholton@mn.uswest.net
SERVICES: Provide communications consulting, writing, and training services to agencies, industry, and government. Write marketing and sales materials, including marketing brochures, product descriptions, sales proposals, trade journal articles, and conference papers. Also write business plans, industry analyses, speeches, and technical reports. Provide training in business and technical writing, proposal writing, and oral presentation skills.
SPECIALTIES: Business plans, sales proposals, marketing materials, and training. Have specialist industry knowledge in financial services and energy.
CURRENT/RECENT CLIENTS/PROJECTS: Alliant Industrial Services, DPRA Environmental, James J. Hill Group, NSP, Karwoski & Courage, Tunheim Group, US Bank, Wells Fargo & Company.

Education & Training / 169

I

iPares™
world-class ebusiness results

IPARES, LTD.   **612-215-2300**
5000 Union Plaza   **Minneapolis 55401**
FAX: 612-215-2310
CONTACT: Tom Harold
E-MAIL: info@ipares.com
WWW: ipares.com
FOCUS: Integration of marketing, design and technology.
SERVICES: Internet Professional Services: Providing Fortune 1000 corporations with Internet, Intranet, Extranet, Sales Force Automation, Kiosk and Database Marketing solutions. Multimedia Related Services: Design/concepting, consulting, writing/instructional design and programming. Internet/Intranet: In-house design and programming including secure E-commerce solutions and web-based training.
CAPABILITIES/SPECIALTIES: Graphic design services for brochures, catalogs, ads, display and packaging. Complete prepress production services.
PRESIDENT/CEO/OWNER: Lon Bencini/Tom Harold

J

JUNTUNEN MEDIA GROUP   **612-341-3348**
708 North First Street   **Minneapolis 55401**
FAX: 612-341-0242
CONTACT: Mike Vinup
ALTERNATE PHONE: 800-535-4366
E-MAIL: mjuntunen@juntunen.com
WWW: juntunen.com

170 / Education & Training

SERVICES: Video and television production support for education/training business television programs and webcast training. Seasoned experts, broadband, digital studio and facilities, and remote crews and support for: webcasting, live production, live-to-tape, satellite transmission and fiber optic. Our team has supported corporate training departments for more than 15 years - including events that must be satellite broadcast to international locations. We provide: creative consultant; project management; camera crews; audio support: transition cues; custom effects; stage lighting and effects; projection; satellite or fiber optic; transmission - national and international sites; playback; tvl/powerpoint/speaker support; image magnification; video walls, 16 x 9 format; interactive meetings; 53 foot digital production trucks with digital control rooms and cameras for large events. (See also Juntunen Mobile Television in Film and Video Support Services.)

CAPABILITIES: Broadband experts: webcasting expertise for the latest in interactive meetings and events. Live remote production: cameras, crews equipment on-site providing total technical support and creative for meetings. Live-to-tape: recording your meetings for later production and archiving. Studios and total production support for live business television production and transmission. Satellite and fiber optic transmission to deliver your media around the world. Juntunen Media 2000: Broadband, DVD authoring. Full digital video support. Webcasting. Visual web-based library: catalog and store all your brand assets. Retrieve from anywhere in the world and repurpose.

CURRENT/RECENT CLIENTS/PROJECTS: Major national and international corporations; sports and entertainment organizations; government organizations.

K

KDG INTERACTIVE 612-861-8890
1720 East 66th Street Richfield 55423
FAX: 612-861-8967
CONTACT: Steven Haas
E-MAIL: shaas@kdg.com
WWW: kdg.com

SERVICES: With over 150 years combined (in-house) experience, KDG InterActive is an e-business and enterprise learning outfitter recognized as a major player in their industry. They combine sophisticated strategies, award-winning design capabilities and cutting-edge technology solutions to assist today's progressive companies in their strategic migration to the e-business edge. They offer: strategic planning, marketing consulting, interactive design and production services, e-commerce site development and software development and have served a variety of global brand leaders such as 3M, Honeywell, US Bancorp, Carlson Marketing Group and Disney Online.

CAPABILITIES: KDG InterActive is fully equipped with a state-of-the-art interactive multimedia development studio and hosts an innovative team of designers, developers and programmers who create online and disk-based programs for: Information Kiosks; CBT (computer-based training); TEST (technology enabled sales tools); EPSS (electronic performance support systems). Their specialties include: Authorware, Director, programming in C++, HTML, CGI, Java, Lotus Notes, Microsoft Office Suite, PhotoShop, Premiere, Painter, Illustrator, After Effects, Infini-D, 3D Studio Max, StrataVision, etc.

Education & Training / 171

CURRENT/RECENT CLIENTS/PROJECTS: American Express, (information kiosks and training presentation); 3M, (software interface design); Business Incentives, (assorted projects); Carlson Marketing Group, (laptop sales presentations); Cray Research, (3D modeling); Disney Online, (assorted online animations); Honeywell, (electronic brochure); US Bancorp, (web based training); US West Communications, (training program); Q Tech Systems, (electronic performance support software); The Saint Paul Companies, (speaker support); Wilson Learning, (consumer self-improvement CD ROM); Minnesota Historical Society, (information kiosks); Ronald Reagan Library, (electronic cabinet room); St. Croix Medical, (computer-based training/online clinical trials); The Great Lakes Aquarium, (information kiosks.)

M

MASTER COMMUNICATIONS GROUP, INC.   952-835-6164
7805 Telegraph Road #100   Bloomington 55438
CONTACT: Christine Dean
WWW: mastcom.com
CAPABILITIES: Full service electronic communications. Complete video production services from concept and scripting through post production. BetacamSp. Media 100, non-linear editing (Boris Effects, Adobe After Effects, Commotion) 2D and 3D animation, lightWave. Audio production. Web development (adobe Go Live, Dream Weaver, Flash/Live Motion) and interactive multimedia authoring and development (authorware, Director, iShell and others.)
SPECIALTIES: Education, training and marketing for medical, technical, foreign language translations and voiceovers, and ESL/EFL.
CURRENT/RECENT CLIENTS/PROJECTS: ADP Hollander, Augustine Medical, Cambridge University Press, Evangelical Lutheran Church in America, Lutheran Church--Missouri Synod, Seagate, RSM McGladrey, Syracuse Language Systems.

MINNESOTA SCHOOL OF COMPUTER   612-861-2000
IMAGING
1401 West 76th Street   Richfield 55423
FAX: 612-861-5548
CONTACT: Admissions Department, MN School of Business, Richfield 861-2000. Brooklyn Center 566-7777; Globe College 651-730-5100; or Oakdale 730-5100
WWW: msbcollege.com or globecollege.com
SERVICES: Minnesota School of Computer Imaging, a division of the Minnesota School of Business and Globe College is comprised of a team of specialists in the computer imaging field. Students have the opportunity to master interrelated skill sets, including CD-ROM Production, Graphic Design, Multimedia broadcast animation and Website Development. Graduates are qualified to interview for positions in traditional print graphics, multimedia production animation and website development. Classes are available in three Twin Cities location. Degrees: Associate in Applied Science (AAS) in Animation Design; Associate in Applied Science (AAS) in Multimedia/Computer Graphics production, Associate in Applied Science E-Commerce Design.
CAPABILITIES: G3 and G4 workstations - SGI workstations - NT workstations. Software: PhotoShop - Illustrator - QuarkXPress - Director - Dreamweaver - Flash - HTML - Cold Fusion - Final Cut - After Affects - Softimage - Maya.
PRESIDENT/CEO/OWNER: Terry Myhre

172 / Education & Training

MULTIMEDIA
1011 First Street South #300
FAX: 952-935-1318
CONTACT: Dianne Thill
WWW: multimedia-inc.com

952-931-2112
Hopkins 55343

SERVICES: Production of video presentations, interactive CD-ROM development, web page design, multi-image and live musical shows.
EQUIPMENT: Betacam video location and studio equipment, edit suite, multi-image programming.
SPECIALTIES: Sales meetings, sales training, marketing presentations.

N

NEVILLE & ASSOCIATES
4975 Sleepy Hollow Road #100
FAX: 612-470-4063
CONTACT: John Neville
E-MAIL: jneville@sea-group.com
WWW: sea-group.com

612-470-4407
Excelsior 55331

CAPABILITIES: Offer the full spectrum from research through creative design, writing, production supervision with experience in internet/intranet/CBT, video, film and printed materials. Produce projects for training, corporate culture, community relations, internal and external communications.
SPECIALTIES: Environmental health & safety and regulatory affairs, corporate culture. Specialize in a creative, problem-solving approach to meeting clients communication objectives within schedule and budget.
CURRENT/RECENT CLIENTS/PROJECTS: Responsible Care & EHS projects for 3M, Honeywell, Cargill, Burlington Northern, Florida State, Toro, Environmental Reporting or 3M, Honeywell, Corporate Culture for HB Fuller, Hirshfields, Piper Jaffray, 3M.

S

SALES EFFECTIVENESS TRAINING
8871 Basswood Road
CONTACT: Harold W. Freeman
E-MAIL: hwfree@juno.com

612-941-4896
Eden Prairie 55344

SERVICES: Sales performance management through selection, training and reinforcement. Will train or teach others. Can write and produce custom sales training programs. Also teach and market interpersonal skills "Social Style" programs. Over 28 years training experience with Fortune "500" companies.
SPECIALTIES: Audio and video sales training packages: Seminar or self-study. Validated sales selection tests that are over 80 percent predictive and conform to EEOC requirements.
PRESIDENT/CEO/OWNER: Harold W. Freeman

Education & Training / 173

T

TRAINING DYNAMICS   612-926-7292
4131 Vincent Avenue South   Minneapolis 55410
FAX: 612-926-1145
CONTACT: Jane Keer-Keer
E-MAIL: jane@trainwithjane.com
WWW: trainwithjane.com
SERVICES: Customized software training at client site. Training for print and web. QuarkXpress, Illustrator, Photoshop, ImageReady, Goline, Dreamweaver. Also web site design.
CAPABILITIES: Web site design and site design training for Mac or Windows.

U

UNIVERSITY OF MINNESOTA COLLEGE OF   612-624-3422
CONTINUING EDUCATION
1994 Buford Avenue   St. Paul 55108
352 Classroom Office Building
FAX: 612-624-6225
CONTACT: Program Secretary - 612-624-4273
E-MAIL: infotech@cce.umn.edu
WWW: cce.umn.edu/infotech
CAPABILITIES: The College of Continuing Education at the University of Minnesota offers non-credit information technology courses in the areas of Web Design, Web Programming, Java, eBusiness, Analysis & Strategy, Unix System and C/C++ Certification, Client/Server Technology Certification and Oracle. The 104-hour Web Designer Institute is an intensive and interactive computer lab-based program offering the following web design skills: PhotoShop principles for web design, layout, and imaging; WYSIWYG web authoring skills; a solid foundation in HTML fundamentals; career issues for professionals; and more. The Enterprise Java Developer Program includes five 40-hour courses that give students the skills to architect and develop object-oriented software using the Java language. Students will acquire the skills necessary to become Enterprise Java Developers. Students should review the curriculum, which is frequently updated at the EJDP web site. All courses are taught in a highly interactive, hands-on environment by industry professionals. For more information including registration materials, call (612) 624-4273 or 1-800-336-9051 or checkout our web site.
SPECIALTIES: Unix System and C/C++ Certification, Client/Server Technology Certification and Oracle are offered through the Technical Education Center in Edina. There are two accelerated enrollment options for these programs. The UNIX System and C/C++ program gives students a comprehensive knowledge of the UNIX operating system environment. In the Client/Server Technology program, students learn how to design graphical user interfaces and how to develop event-driven programs using Visual Basic, through producing a Windows-based Client/Server application using Powerbuilder. Students in the Oracle program will complete a real world application project while preparing for certification exams through test simulations and intensive topic reviews. For more information, please contact 612-627-7787.

Electronic Graphics

A

ACCI AMERICAN CUSTOM COMPUTER   952-946-8925
7679 Washington Avenue South   Edina 55439
FAX: 952-946-8967
CONTACT: Tom Jungroth
E-MAIL: tj@goacci.com
WWW: goacci.com
SERVICES: Large format printers, and laminators, service and supplies. Epson, Encad, Cannon, HP, Raster Graphics Arizona and Bellise, AGL Greie laminators, seal laminators, ACCI, Encad, OCE, Mactac, Seal, 3M, Avery and Raster media and supplies. All media, ink and laminating supplies stocked in Minneapolis.
CAPABILITIES: Larger format printing and laminating sales, service, supplies and training. Demo and training room on site.
CURRENT/RECENT CLIENTS/PROJECTS: The Midwest's only large format digital printer dealer offering Encad, Epson 7500 and 9500, Cannon. Raster Arizona, Bellise and Carolina printers and AGL Greie laminators all in one show room.
PRESIDENT/CEO/OWNER: Bill Grambash

AS SOON AS POSSIBLE, INC.   952-564-2727
3000 France Avenue South   St. Louis Park 55416
FAX: 952-564-2720
CONTACT: George West, 952-564-2621
E-MAIL: gwest@asap.net
WWW: asap.net
CAPABILITIES: A.S.A.P. is a Marketing Communications Production Company that offers prepress Services (Mac & PC), Printing (digital, offset, and direct-to-plate), Large Trade Show/Display Prints, and Internet & Interactive Multimedia. For more information, call George West today at 952-564-2621 or visit our web site at www.asap.net.
EQUIPMENT: Imagesetters, Canons, Agfa Chromapress, Heidelberg Quickmaster DI's, Xerox Doc 40, Micropress, Offset Presses, Iris, Rainbow, Scanners, and Ink Jet and Electrostatic Large Format Printers. Pick-up and delivery available.

B

BOWEN CREATIVE COMPANY   952-837-9850
3300 Edinborough Way #115   Edina 55435
FAX: 952-837-9861
CONTACT: Laura Justus
E-MAIL: guy@bowencreative.com
SERVICES: Complete graphic design and art direction services for print and electronic media. Formats include catalogs, publications, recipe booklets, cookbooks, consumer packaging, brochures, posters, web pages.
CAPABILITIES: Concepting, design, layout, photo direction, logo and identity design, and pre-press print production supervision. Full electronic design and production capabilities, with expertise in various graphic software applications.
PRESIDENT/CEO/OWNER: Guy Bowen, Barbara Bowen

C

COLORHOUSE   763-553-0100
13010 County Road 6   Minneapolis 55441
FAX: 763-550-3600
CONTACT: William Klocke
E-MAIL: info@colorhouse.com
WWW: colorhouse.com
SERVICES: Colorhouse has spent three and a half decades perfecting our specialty--prepress. So whenever you come to Colorhouse, you can depend on the highest quality and efficiency for all we have to offer: image acquisition/scanning, color separations, creative retouching, electronic page assembly, digital asset management. Digital proofing, CTP capabilities, high-speed electronic file transfer, flexographic plates, and short-to-medium run offset printing. Progressive technology and fast turnaround have become dependable hallmarks of our service. The end result is color separations or electronic files that meet the very highest standards of quality--delivered on-time and within budget.
SPECIALTIES: Large state-of-the-art facility offering high-quality prepress for ads, packaging and collateral. Best known for our progressive technology, creative retouching, unparalleled service and quick turnaround.
EQUIPMENT: Workstations include 40-Mac Power PCs, 5 Barco stations, Proofing: 4 Kodak Approvals, DuPont Waterproof, 3M Matchprint, Kodak large format printer, Doc12 color copier. Output: Scitex Dolevs, Barco megasetter. Data Mgmt: 3 terabytes RAID on Sun Server, Kodak Optical Jukebox. File Transfer: T1, ISDN, Wam!Net, PDF, Internet. Press: 28" 4/c Akiyama.
PRESIDENT/CEO/OWNER: William Klocke

I

ILLUSION GRAPHICS & COMMUNICATIONS   763-546-0228
2849 Louisiana Avenue No.   Minneapolis 55427
FAX: 763-546-8908
CONTACT: Carol Irish/Larry Kluge
E-MAIL: illusion@illusiongraphics.com
WWW: illusiongraphics.com
SERVICES: Full service electronic design firm working with local and international clients on a wide variety of creative and production projects ranging from corporate image and digital through print production design. Services include creative and production design, art direction, writing/editing, photography, scanning, photo enhancement, complete digital preparation of press-ready files, print management, and CD-ROM creation.
SPECIALTIES: High-end digital graphics and design creation and production backed by a solid foundation in traditional design and print process, and an in-depth knowledge of current and future trends in digital design production. Areas of specialization encompass digital illustration and design, photo enhancement, design for multi-language publications, CD creation and print management.
CURRENT/RECENT CLIENTS/PROJECTS: Thermo King; Donaldson Company; Wagner Spray Tech; Dahlberg Sciences-Canada; Griffiths Corporation; Kelly Promotions; Audio Medical-England; Hansation Akustik-Germany.
PRESIDENT/CEO/OWNER: Carol J. Irish

176 / Electronic Graphics

INFINITY DIRECT, INC. 763-559-1111
13220 County Road 6 Plymouth 55441
FAX: 763-553-1852
CONTACT: Mike Boyle
WWW: infinitydirect.com
SPECIALTIES: Full service capabilities. Consumer and business-to-business direct marketing programs.
CREATIVE SERVICES: Collateral development, brand/identity programs, concept design, brochures, promotion development, planning and execution, copywriting, graphic design, interactive--CD ROM/DVD, web page and web response.
PRODUCTION SERVICES: Printing, lettershop, fulfillment. Interactive--CD-ROM/DVD processing and personalization services.
PRESIDENT/CEO/OWNER: Thomas L. Harding, CEO/Owner

M

MANUAL-MATIC, INC. 612-537-3627
4461 Independence Avenue North New Hope 55428
FAX: 877-219-3256
CONTACT: Bob Newman
E-MAIL: info@tekartbob.com
WWW: tekartbob.com
SERVICES: Manual-matic, Inc., founded by Bob Newman, has been supplying industries in Midwestern USA with custom product documentation since 1961. If your product needs to be installed, put together, operated safely and correctly serviced properly or needs replacement parts, we can write and illustrate it promptly and at Midwest prices.
CAPABILITIES: All types of technical illustration on the PC platform using CorelDraw, Photopaint, Paintshop Pro and Photofinish. Desktop publishing with Adobe PageMaker.
CURRENT/RECENT CLIENTS/PROJECTS: National Mower Company; Ciprico, Inc.; Skyline Industries; Mgs Machine Corporation.

MULTI-AD SERVICES, INC. 952-944-7933
7668 Golden Triangle Drive Eden Prairie 55344
CONTACT: Caroline Gray
OFFICERS: Caroline Gray, Prepublishing Manager
MEDIA DIRECTOR: Mark Atkinson, CD; Amy Schneider, Production Director.
CAPABILITIES: One-stop resource for custom advertising support systems. Concept becomes reality through services offered in conceptual development, illustration, design, copy, keylining, digital capture and imaging. Also offers website & multi-media design, development and management. Complete electronic services available as well as traditional illustration.
SPECIALTIES: High-end illustration, content development and/or management of client materials, production and delivery of custom advertising support systems in print and electronic mediums.
CURRENT/RECENT CLIENTS/PROJECTS: Pillsbury; General Mills; Ford; Toyota; Toro; Polaris; CASE; Mercury Marine; Simplicity; Andersen Windows; Campbell Mithun Esty; Martin Williams; Wildlife Forever; Hormel; J. Walter Thompson.
PRESIDENT/CEO/OWNER: Caroline Gray

P

PHOTOGRAPHIC SPECIALTIES   612-522-7741
1718 Washington Avenue North   Minneapolis 55411
FAX: 612-522-1934
CONTACT: Rick Schuenemann
E-MAIL: drewkal@photospec.com
SERVICES: P.S. is a full service custom photo lab and digital imaging service., We specialize in large runs of prints and transparencies for visual merchandising, POP, Trade Show Exhibits and museums. We have in-house graphic designers, a stock photo library and shipping and kitting capabilities.
CAPABILITIES: Two Light Jet 5000 Digital photo images for true photographic images up to 48" x 96" in one piece. Drum and flatbed scanning, LVT 8 x 10 film recorder, and Repri and Ellegro scan/retouch system. Color span Inkjet printers (4) and full mounting and laminating capabilities up to 80" wide. 4 traditional mural rooms with wall easels, prints and trans up to 72" x 16' one piece.
CURRENT/RECENT CLIENTS/PROJECTS: Large nationwide retail chains, display and store design firms.
PRESIDENT/CEO/OWNER: Drew Kalman

PHOTOLAB IMAGING CORPORATION   763-525-5900
5900 Olson Memorial Highway   Golden Valley 55422
FAX: 763-525-0190
CONTACT: Jeff Ferrazzo, VP Sales
E-MAIL: sales@p-i-c.com
WWW: p-i-c.com
CAPABILITIES: Complete photographic and digital display print products and imaging services from high-resolution drum and flatbed scanning, image manipulation, retouching and photocomposition, to direct digital photographic, high-resolution film or Ink Jet digital output. Maximum printing capabilities include Lambda Digital photographic printing up to 50" wide, traditional Photographic printing up to 72" wide, Cibachrome printing up to 50" wide, Ink Jet printing up to 50" wide, Arizona 6-color Ink Jet graphics (including 3M products) up to 52" wide and cut-vinyl graphics up to 48" wide.
PRESIDENT/CEO/OWNER: Charles W. Specht

T

TAJ STUDIOS   763-536-8483
5536 Xenia Avenue   Crystal 55429
FAX: 763-536-8483
CONTACT: Tom Jungroth
E-MAIL: tjungroth@yahoo.com
SERVICES: Stock photo library over 8,000 images. Digital photography for web catalogs and sites. Small product and location photography. I take "tradigital" photographs for use on the web or press.
CAPABILITIES: Table top photography digital and traditional retouch old photos to digital output quick flyers.
PRESIDENT/CEO/OWNER: Tom "TJ" Jungroth

U

UPFRONT PRODUCTIONS 651-633-5299
2350 County Road C #120 St. Paul 55113
FAX: 651-633-5197
CONTACT: Tricia Nordby Hamrin/Chris Hamrin
WWW: hoopjumping.com
CAPABILITIES: Organizational Communications Solutions Center. A Spectrum. A Synergy. Concept Development, Copywriting, Graphic Design, Illustration, Document Production, Web Site Creation, Scanning, Photo Retouching, Pre-press, Offset Printing, Digital B&W Printing, Color Copies, Posters, Displays, Signs, Custom Assembly, Inventory, Distribution, Corporate Compass® MIS, VantagePoint™, Hoop Jumping™.
SPECIALTIES: Choose your hoop. We'll jump through it™.
OFFICERS: Tricia Nordby Hamrin/Chris Hamrin

Electronic Prepress

A

AS SOON AS POSSIBLE, INC.   952-564-2727
3000 France Avenue South   St. Louis Park 55416
FAX: 952-564-2720
CONTACT: George West, 952-564-2621
E-MAIL: gwest@asap.net
WWW: asap.net
CAPABILITIES: A.S.A.P. is a Marketing Communications Production Company that offers prepress Services (Mac & PC), Printing (digital, offset, and direct-to-plate), Large Trade Show/Display Prints, and Internet & Interactive Multimedia. For more information, call George West today at 952-564-2621 or visit our web site at www.asap.net.
EQUIPMENT: Imagesetters, Canons, Agfa Chromapress, Heidelberg Quickmaster DI's, Xerox Doc 40, Micropress, Offset Presses, Iris, Rainbow, Scanners, and Ink Jet and Electrostatic Large Format Printers. Pick-up and delivery available.

C

COLORHOUSE   763-553-0100
13010 County Road 6   Minneapolis 55441
FAX: 763-550-3600
CONTACT: William Klocke
E-MAIL: info@colorhouse.com
WWW: colorhouse.com
SERVICES: Colorhouse has spent three and a half decades perfecting our specialty--prepress. So whenever you come to Colorhouse, you can depend on the highest quality and efficiency for all we have to offer: image acquisition/scanning, color separations, creative retouching, electronic page assembly, digital asset management. Digital proofing, CTP capabilities, high-speed electronic file transfer, flexographic plates, and short-to-medium run offset printing. Progressive technology and fast turnaround have become dependable hallmarks of our service. The end result is color separations or electronic files that meet the very highest standards of quality--delivered on-time and within budget.
SPECIALTIES: Large state-of-the-art facility offering high-quality prepress for ads, packaging and collateral. Best known for our progressive technology, creative retouching, unparalleled service and quick turnaround.
EQUIPMENT: Workstations include 40-Mac Power PCs, 5 Barco stations, Proofing: 4 Kodak Approvals, DuPont Waterproof, 3M Matchprint, Kodak large format printer, Doc12 color copier. Output: Scitex Dolevs, Barco megasetter. Data Mgmt: 3 terabytes RAID on Sun Server, Kodak Optical Jukebox. File Transfer: T1, ISDN, Wam!Net, PDF, Internet. Press: 28" 4/c Akiyama.
PRESIDENT/CEO/OWNER: William Klocke

E

EMERALD GRAPHICS   612-382-1149
2672 Wilshire Boulevard   Mound 55364
FAX: 612-472-5107

180 / Electronic Prepress

CONTACT: Jim Kinney
E-MAIL: jkinney@visi.com
SERVICES: High quality scanning and image manipulation.
CAPABILITIES: Color correction, retouching, image compositing, prepress consulting.
CURRENT/RECENT CLIENTS/PROJECTS: Ad Agencies, Corporations, Graphic Designers, Printers

G

GV GRAPHICS, INC.   763-542-8330
2730 Nevada Avenue North   Minneapolis 55427
FAX: 763-542-8309
CONTACT: John Hagenstein
E-MAIL: sjh@gvgraphics.com
WWW: gvgraphics.com
SERVICES: Prepress, production management and printing services featuring the best in today's equipment and staffing. Utilizing the Heidelberg Quickmaster digital press and Kodak approval in its workflow. Come to us for all your print needs.
CAPABILITIES: Heidelberg Quickmaster Digital Imaging Press Kodak approval.
CURRENT/RECENT CLIENTS/PROJECTS: MSP Publications, General Mills, Zomax, Bachman's, Tiger Oak Publications, Northrup King, International Home Foods and Navarre.
PRESIDENT/CEO/OWNER: S. John Hagenstein

J

JKL STUDIOS   612-729-1774
3810 Edmund Boulevard   Minneapolis 55406
FAX: 612-729-0133
CONTACT: Jerry or Marietta Mason; Kurt Lang
ALTERNATE PHONE: 651-653-0811
E-MAIL: jklstudios@tcinternet.net
SERVICES: High-end digital imaging; includes scanning, retouching, compositing and photo restoration. Mac or Windows platforms, various output services provided.
CAPABILITIES: 16 plus years experience photo/digital manipulation working with large files, photo composition and assembly on high-end equipment in the print industry. Complete understanding of reproduction capabilities of CMYK process on press.
CURRENT/RECENT CLIENTS/PROJECTS: Produced and continues to produce digital "magic" for all major agencies in the Twin Cities.
PRESIDENT/CEO/OWNER: Kurt Lang

Electronic Prepress / 181

N

NORTHWEST COMPUTER SERVICES   651-659-9680
227 North Snelling Avenue   St. Paul 55104
FAX: 651-659-9581
CONTACT: Mike Thomas, New Business Development Manager
E-MAIL: info@nwcomputer.com
WWW: nwcomputer.com
CAPABILITIES: Mac and Windows integrated services for front-end to back-end print or online media support for designers, marketing agencies, in-house corporate advertising departments, printing and display alliances. Digital photoshoots for cost-effective captured images that can be repeatedly repurposed and output to a variety of desired formats. Scanning for design and layout placement files or for final production of catalogs, newsletters, direct marketing and sales collateral pieces, as well as, for online formats. Color management that ensures a high degree of image consistency from software to monitor, to printer and through proofs and film. Digital and traditional production for proofing and litho film. On-demand short-run reproduction of brochures, training packets, presentation materials and table-top signage. Large format imaging for displays and event banners. Complete finishing services.
SERVICES: Conversions - Mac and Windows cross-platform. Scanning - high resolution to 8000 pixels, low-resolution FPO's, including Zip, Jaz, Dat, Optical and Syquest supported formats. Imaging - retouching, manipulation. Imagesetting - imposition, process color, spot color, trapping, applied varnishes, flexographic film. Color Management- technical support in calculated color compensation, calibration, measuring, profiling. Proofing - Matchprint, docucolor, Rainbow, Dylux, laser. Digital Printing - short-run including trimming, scoring, folding, drilling, padding, shrink wrapping. Large Format Signage - RC stock, backprint film, backlit film and canvas, including laminating, mounting, fastening. Digital Photography - Photo shoots, camera package rentals, file processing.
SPECIALTIES: Through the expertise of our in-house technicians we have refined the RIP for our ENCAD Novajet 700 Pro 42e, resulting in some of the highest quality large format images available in the Twin Cities. Pickup & Delivery - In-house dispatch, pickup and delivery.
PRESIDENT/CEO/OWNER: Gabe Freund

NORTHWOODS COLOR   612-424-3077
10467 93rd Avenue North   Maple Grove 55369
FAX: 612-424-2519
CONTACT: Amy Gottlieb
E-MAIL: email@nwcolor.com
CAPABILITIES: Complete pre-press facilities, including high quality color separations, electronic retouching, and pre-press tripping on Scitex high end systems. Macintosh desktop publishing. Tektronix digital proofing, pre-press proofing and 4/C conventional shipping. Large format output up to 32.5" x 40.5" ISDN availability.
SPECIALTIES: We offer the highest quality color separations, flexibility, fast turn around, pickup and delivery.
PRESIDENT/CEO/OWNER: Roger and Leslie Blavat

T

TECHNICAL REPRODUCTIONS   612-331-3955
2101 Broadway Street NE   Minneapolis 55413
FAX: 612-331-3958
CONTACT: Robert Kemmet
E-MAIL: triminn@aol.com
CAPABILITIES: Line negs, halftone negs, digital negs, large film positives, stats, diazo prints, large format Xerox prints, inkjet display prints, print mounting and laminating.
SPECIALTIES: Services for printers, silk screeners, architects, engineers, land surveyors, trade show exhibitors and POP displayers.
PRESIDENT/CEO/OWNER: Robert L. Kemmet, P; Wallace Cornelius, Plant Manager

U

UPFRONT PRODUCTIONS   651-633-5299
2350 County Road C #120   St. Paul 55113
FAX: 651-633-5197
CONTACT: Tricia Nordby Hamrin/Chris Hamrin
WWW: hoopjumping.com
CAPABILITIES: Organizational Communications Solutions Center. A Spectrum. A Synergy. Concept Development, Copywriting, Graphic Design, Illustration, Document Production, Web Site Creation, Scanning, Photo Retouching, Pre-press, Offset Printing, Digital B&W Printing, Color Copies, Posters, Displays, Signs, Custom Assembly, Inventory, Distribution, Corporate Compass® MIS, VantagePoint™, Hoop Jumping™.
SPECIALTIES: Choose your hoop. We'll jump through it™.
OFFICERS: Tricia Nordby Hamrin/Chris Hamrin

Entertainment Agencies

C

CLASSIC IMPRESSIONS 612-926-8742
5705 France Avenue Edina 55410
E-MAIL: classicatmr.net
WWW: 92music.com
PRESIDENT/CEO/OWNER: Lou Fishbein

D

DOWN ON THE FARM 651-433-5640
17220 Keystone Avenue Hugo 55038
FAX: 651-433-4806
E-MAIL: lneamy@hotmail.com
SERVICES: We offer pony rides, petting zoo, our place or yours.
CONTACT: Lea Ann Neamy

L

LARKSPUR STRINGS 612-861-2954
6125 Morgan Avenue South Minneapolis 55419
E-MAIL: james@wildgypsy.com
WWW: larkspurstrings.com
SERVICES: Fine string music for special events.
CAPABILITIES: Strolling ensembles, string quartets, jazz combos, strolling violinists, country, ethnic and jazz fiddlers and bands. Guitarists, mandolinists, harmonicists. Established in 1986.
CURRENT/RECENT CLIENTS/PROJECTS: General Mills; Design Group; General Re-insurance; Cub Foods; The Chart House; Rolling Green Country Club.
PRESIDENT/CEO/OWNER: James Plattes

N

NED KANTAR PRODUCTIONS, INC. 612-926-5655
3430 St. Paul Avenue Minneapolis 55416
FAX: 612-920-8482
CONTACT: Ned Kantar
E-MAIL: ned@nedkantar.com
WWW: nedkantar.com
SERVICES: Live musical talent - Jazz Trios a specialty.
CAPABILITIES: 25 years in business.
CURRENT/RECENT CLIENTS/PROJECTS: Book and produce local and national talent.

Event Planning

C

CONFERENCE COORDINATORS INTERNATIONAL   612-920-4971
5128 Sheridan Avenue South   Minneapolis 55410
FAX: 612-926-9096
CONTACT: Kay Bixby
CAPABILITIES: Experienced meeting and special event planners, local and out of town.
SPECIALTIES: Out-of-town meetings, special events and creative trade show receptions including site selection, themes, décor, entertainment and on-site coordination. All production aspects handled by our professional staff.
PRESIDENT/CEO/OWNER: Kay A. Bixby

CORPORATE MEETINGS CONSULTING   612-444-8036
24746 University Avenue NW   Isanti 55040
CONTACT: Cynthia Phillips
E-MAIL: chelming@pclink.com
SERVICES: Full-service meeting and special event management company specializing in meetings, conferences, conventions and incentive programs. Over 20 years of combined industry experience to assist clients in designing a program that produces results.
SPECIALTIES: Customized meeting, event planning and complete inbound/outbound services, strategic planning, training and development services.

D

TODD DANIELS MARKETING & ADVERTISING   651-291-8074
26 East Exchange Street #610   St. Paul 55101
FAX: 651-297-6548
CONTACT: Dan Foote
E-MAIL: danf@todd-daniels.com
WWW: todd-daniels.com
SERVICES: Full-service marketing and advertising agency. Specialties include: strategic planning, corporate identities, point-of-purchase, literature development, public relations, ad design, media placement, event planning, direct mail, website design. Product positioning, tradeshow execution, and merchandising.
PRESIDENT/CEO/OWNER: Dan Foote, Todd Butzer

DAYTOURS & CREATIVE EVENTS   612-333-3833
401 N 3rd Street #675   Minneapolis 55401
FAX: 612-333-5255
CONTACT: Larry Shiller
E-MAIL: daytours@fishnet.com
WWW: daytoursmn.com
SERVICES: Transportation, custom and pre-designed tours, event design, planning and management, gala and theme parties, décor design and installation, staging and production, visitor services.

Event Planning / 185

CAPABILITIES: With over 21 years' experience as the Twin Cities' leading destination management company, our staff and guides strive to offer you and your guests an activity program or event that is perfect in every way.
PRESIDENT/CEO/OWNER: Larry Shiller

F

FREESTYLE PRODUCTIONS, INC.   763-417-9575
6112 Olson Memorial Highway   Minneapolis 55422
FAX: 763-417-9576
CONTACT: Dale Kivimaki, Mark Hulsey
E-MAIL: dale@freestyle-productions.com
WWW: freestyle-productions.com
CAPABILITIES: Freestyle Productions provides video and multimedia communication services with a specialized focus on high-profile, live-event productions including corporate meetings, trade shows, conventions and concerts. Complete array of broadcast equipment: multi-camera field packages, post production/mobile, non-linear edit suites, switcher/effects & graphic systems, large-format video and date projection, front & rear screens and videowalls.
SPECIALTIES: Over 10 years of national and international experience producing all types of live and special events shows. Freestyle provides an intuitive understanding of how to best communicate their client's message to impact large and small audiences.
CURRENT/RECENT CLIENTS/PROJECTS: Fox Sports Net, Coca-Cola, Lucent Technologies, Apple Computer, Northwest Airlines, Promise Keepers, Carlson Companies, Lutheran Brotherhood, US West, Minnesota State Fair, Universal Studios Hollywood.

J

JALIVAY & ASSOCIATES   651-322-1405
4821 Weston Hills Drive   Eagan 55123
FAX: 651-322-4813
CONTACT: Kathy Jalivay
E-MAIL: kathy@jalivay.com
WWW: jalivay.com
CAPABILITIES: Event production, planning, coordinating, writing and distribution press releases, advertising placement and creative consulting, marketing communication planning and executing.
SPECIALTIES: Marketing communications including press releases, direct mail pieces, brochures, sales materials, event and trade show planning.
CURRENT/RECENT CLIENTS/PROJECTS: USTA, Mall of America, D.E.A.F., Gourmet Express, Fresh Paint, Inc., Clubkid, Learning Curve Toys, ATT Broadband, MAEF.

K

FRED KELLER COMMUNICATIONS   612-929-4477
4829 Minnetonka Blvd #202   Minneapolis 55416
FAX: 612-929-4488

186 / Event Planning

CONTACT: Fred Keller
SERVICES: Special events, general publicity.
CURRENT/RECENT CLIENTS/PROJECTS: McDonalds Restaurants of Minnesota; Disetronic Medical Systems; Source Food Technology.

L

WADE C. LUNEBURG 612-824-1931
3535 Pillsbury Avenue South Minneapolis 55408
CONTACT: Wade C. Luneburg
ALTERNATE PHONE: 612-281-9954 Cell
CAPABILITIES: Full range planning/execution of special events, large or small, location scouting expert.
SPECIALTIES: Working with non-profit corporations, communications/planning staffs, film companies.

M

MAINSTREAM COMMUNICATIONS, INC. 952-888-9000
9555 James Avenue South #235 Bloomington 55431
CONTACT: Garry Krebs, Bob Ewert
E-MAIL: gkrebs@mainstreamcom.net
WWW: mainstreamcom.net
SERVICES: Mainstream concepts and stages corporate events of all kinds including meetings, trade shows, and special events. Our staff includes the professionals who know how to navigate the challenges of meeting rooms, conventional halls, and trade show floors. Our inventory includes a vast array of audio visual equipment; video and data projection, front and rear screens. Intelligent lighting, and multi-channel sound systems with effects. We warehouse existing sets which are available for rent or we can custom design and build one for you. We also provide live talent and nationally known acts to make your event special.
CAPABILITIES/SPECIALTIES: We are a turnkey video production environment. Location video crews include Beta SP equipment and complete location lighting and sound recording. Our 1,200 s.f. sound stage includes a lighting package along with available sets. We offer 4 edit suites: Digital Betacam complete with DME, 2 non-linear including DVE, and a portable Beta SP AB-Roll Edit Suite which can be used in-studio or for location events. Other in-house services include 3D animation featuring SoftImage software and a sound recording studio with multiple music libraries.

CHAR MASON & ASSOCIATES 651-698-2678
2136 Ford Parkway #104 St. Paul 55116
FAX: 651-698-2672
E-MAIL: char@charmason.com
WWW: charmason.com
SERVICES: Full-service strategic marketing and event consulting from a creative professional experienced in corporate and public events & meetings, marketing programs, non-profit & association management, communications, fund-raising, and project management. View a complete client list, biography, projects, references and links at the above web address.

Event Planning / 187

CAPABILITIES: Char Mason, a Saint Paul native and University of Minnesota graduate, launched Char Mason & Associates, an event strategy and marketing consulting firm in 1999. For four years prior, Char served as Executive Director of the Grand Avenue Business Association, a 200 member retail/restaurant/professional association, and festival Director of Grand Old Day, the Midwest's largest one-day street festival. Before her time on Grand Avenue, she spent eight years with International Market Square in Minneapolis directing events and marketing for the design and home furnishings industry.

CURRENT/RECENT CLIENTS/PROJECTS: Eastside Neighborhood Development Company: Event Planning Development; Grand Avenue Business Association: Grand Old Day and General Consulting Assignment; Great Northern Communications, Saint Patrick's Day Events Year 2000 Sponsorship Development; Macalester College Scottish Fair: Sponsorship Development; Saint Paul Area Chamber of Commerce: Interim Executive Director, Saint Paul Transportation Management Organization; Saint Paul Riverfront Corporation: Grand Excursion Development; West End Business Revitalization Corporation: Banner Program Development

PRESIDENT/CEO/OWNER: Char Mason

MATT BLAIR'S CELEBRITY PROMOTIONS, INC.
308 Dearborn Court

952-908-0374

Edina 55343

FAX: 952-908-0253
CONTACT: Sara Otto, Jessica Rolf, Special Event Coordinator
E-MAIL: mblair@skypoint.com
WWW: mattblair.com
SPECIALTIES: Event Management and planning.
SERVICES: Specializing in golf tournaments, corporate events, corporate travel to major sporting events including the Super bowl, Master, Pro Bowl, and US Open. We are a licensed and bonded professional fundraiser with 10 years of experience. We can provide local and national athletes and celebrities for any type of event, speeches, appearances television and radio commercials. Call to book the Matt Blair's Minnesota Vikings Traveling Basketball and Softball Teams. Or call for more information on Matt Blair's Corporate Golf Academy for women. Bring your event to us and we will make it work.
PRESIDENT/CEO/OWNER: Matt Blair

MEDIA LOFT, INC.
333 Washington Avenue North #210

612-375-1086

Minneapolis 55401

FAX: 612-375-0913
CONTACT: David Kelsey
SERVICES: Award-winning full service communications company; script to screen concepting and production for video, film business theatre, corporate meetings and events.
PRESIDENT/CEO/OWNER: Engenio H. DiLorenzo

MEDIA PRODUCTIONS, INC.
125 SE Main Street #100

612-379-4678

Minneapolis 55414

FAX: 612-379-7988
CONTACT: Chad Ohlinger, Lori Greenberg
SERVICES: Comprehensive meeting and event services, including creative concepting, consultation, strategic planning and a full array of production and technical services.
SPECIALTIES: Medical device industry, occupational health and safety.

188 / Event Planning

PRESIDENT/CEO/OWNER: Judy Kessel, P; Jerrold Gershone, EVP; Jerry Kolb, VP

MEETING PROFESSIONALS INTERNATIONAL 651-917-6243
1821 University Avenue West #S256 St. Paul 55104
FAX: 651-917-1835
CONTACT: Jennifer Dark
E-MAIL: mpimn@nonprofitsolutions.com
WWW: mnmpi.org
SERVICES: MPI leads the meeting industry by serving the diverse needs of all people with a direct interest in the outcome of meetings, educating and preparing members from their changing roles and validating relevant knowledge and skills, as well as demonstrating a commitment to excellence in meetings.
CAPABILITIES: Professional association consisting of meeting planners and suppliers to the meeting industry. Membership: Contact office for information kit.

O

OEU'VRE CREATIVE SERVICES 651-322-7280
4980 Dodd Road Eagan 55123
FAX: 651-322-7281
CONTACT: Michelle Kraemer
E-MAIL: michelle@oeuvrecreative.com
WWW: oeuvrecreative.com
SERVICES: We offer complete special event planning services, including theme parties, product launches, award/recognition goals, and corporate anniversaries. Our services include logo and theme development, venue selection, creative writing, event and stage design and full scale production.
CAPABILITIES: At OeuVre Creative, every event begins with a blank page. It is our philosophy that each event is different, each one a unique expression of your needs and goals, and we design your event to specifically meet those criteria. Our mission is to continually deliver one of a kind productions that exceed all expectations.
CURRENT/RECENT CLIENTS/PROJECTS: Disney Productions, Musicland, RMS Titanic Society, Micron Electronics, MediaOne, Coldwell Banker Burnet Classic.
PRESIDENT/CEO/OWNER: Michelle Kraemer

S

SPORT EVENTS, LTD. 952-473-6500
15500 Wayzata Boulevard #1028 Wayzata 55391
FAX: 952-473-7186
CONTACT: Steve Briggs
E-MAIL: sbriggs@eventsltd.com
WWW: eventsltd.com
PRESIDENT/CEO/OWNER: Brian Schultz

Event Planning / 189

T

TADPOLE PARADE — 651-458-3445
10532 E Point Douglas Road South — Cottage Grove 55016
CONTACT: Will Hale
E-MAIL: willhale@uswest.net
WWW: angelfilre.com/mn/willhale
SERVICES: Provide original music entertainment for children and family events. Full 4 - 5 piece band or solo performances.
CAPABILITIES: Also experimental workshops to develop creativity and imagination as tools for resourceful solutions.

TROUPE AMERICA, INC. — 612-333-3302
528 Hennepin Avenue #206 — Minneapolis 55403
FAX: 612-333-4337
CONTACT: Curt Wollan, Producer
E-MAIL: cwollan@mninter.net
WWW: troupeamerica.com
CAPABILITIES: Types of Talent: Singers, dancers, actors, theatrical designers, directors and technicians.
SPECIALTIES: Producing musicals and plays; national bus and truck tours; convention entertainment and industrial shows; all occasions and any space.
PRESIDENT/CEO/OWNER: Curt Wollan, Producer

Executive Search Services

N
THE NYCOR GROUP 952-831-6444
4930 W 77th Street #300 Minneapolis 55435
FAX: 952-835-2883
CONTACT: Lynn M. Florell
E-MAIL: info@nycor.com
WWW: nycor.com

CAPABILITIES: Nycor Consulting candidates posses Information Technology, Web Design, Animation, E-Commerce, Multimedia, Software Design, Documentation, Implementation and Deployment, ASP, Java, Object-Oriented Platforms, and Order Fulfillment expertise.

NYCOR SEARCH, INC.: Nycor Search, Inc. is a Technical Search Firm specializing in Information Technology, Engineering, Telecommunications, Architecture, Product Development, Technical Management, and Executive-level positions.

NYCOR CONTRACT SERVICES, INC.: Nycor Contract Services, Inc. provides contract services for Information Technology, Engineering, Telecommunications, Architecture, Drafting & Design, and Technical Writing.

NYCOR TECHNICAL, INC.: Nycor Technical, Inc. provides contract services for skilled labor areas including CNC, drafting, biomedical, and technical specialties.

SPECIALTIES: Extensive database of over 45,000 experienced and pre-screened technical professionals. Established and financially sound business for 43 years.

PRESIDENT/CEO/OWNER: John F. Nymark

Film & Video Producers

A

ACCENT PRODUCTIONS   612-377-4242
35 Groveland Terrace   Minneapolis 55403
FAX: 612-377-4244
CONTACT: Julie Sadeghi
E-MAIL: julie@agcot.com
CAPABILITIES: Film and video production company for broadcast, non-broadcast and interactive.

AMT COMMUNICATIONS/ANN M. THOMPSON   651-430-0908
PO Box 267   Stillwater 55082
FAX: 651-430-0908
CONTACT: Ann M. Thompson
E-MAIL: amt_communications@compuserve.com
CAPABILITIES: Video writer, producer, director.
SPECIALTIES: Corporate communications, marketing communications, employee communications (benefit, recruitment, orientation, video news for employees), medical communications.
CURRENT/RECENT CLIENTS/PROJECTS: General Mills, Inc.; Northwest Airlines, Inc.; Dayton Hudson; State of Minnesota; McCoy & Associates; Media Loft; Edina Realty; University of Minnesota; Mahtomedi School District; Mayo Clinic; CME Video & Film; Greatapes; United Way of Minneapolis Area; Catholic Charities
PRESIDENT/CEO/OWNER: Ann M. Thompson

ARIA PRODUCTIONS   612-840-0196
119 North 4th Street #410   Minneapolis 55401
CONTACT: Dave Coleman
SERVICES: Direction: Film and video - commercials and industrials: i.e. sales, promotion and image, documentary, training. Over 20 years in the business.
SPECIALTIES: Humor, drama, motivational. Matching the right approach to the right audience.
PRESIDENT/CEO/OWNER: Dave Coleman

AUDIO/VIDEO PRODUCTIONS   612-721-8984
3845 35th Avenue South   Minneapolis 55406
FAX: 612-728-7008
CONTACT: Jim Worley
SERVICES: Full service video production.
CAPABILITIES: Documentaries, events, training, seminars.

AURORA PICTURES   612-338-2825
2525 East Franklin Avenue   Minneapolis 55406
FAX: 612-338-2617
CONTACT: Bob Foucault, Steve Kahlenbreck
E-MAIL: aurora@aurorapictures.com
WWW: aurorapictures.com

192 / Film & Video Producers

SERVICES: Full service video and film production as well as production support services, TV spots, corporate training and marketing, international distribution of business and educational videotapes, CD's and DVD's. Full Multimedia post production capabilities - CD/DVD/Web delivery. 3D animation and graphics.
CAPABILITIES: Camera crews and support crews, Betacam SP, digital, HDTV - experienced 16mm and 35mm DP's and camera operators, international travel experience, digital non-linear editing suite. On-location production of documentaries, VNR's, training and educational films and video tapes, international distribution system.
CURRENT/RECENT CLIENTS/PROJECTS: Corporate government, ad agencies and non-profit. Client list available on request.

B

BLUE EARTH PICTURES, INC.   612-337-3232
275 Market Street   **Minneapolis 55405**
International Market Square #901
FAX: 612-337-3226
CONTACT: James Ankeny, Lucinda Winter, Lee Kanten
E-MAIL: bepics@bepics.com
WWW: bepics.com
CAPABILITIES: Develops and produces film, video and new media projects. We help our clients create emotionally compelling commercial, corporate and entertainment programs. Whatever the distribution method, Broadcast TV, CD-ROM, DVD, VHS or encoded files for the Web, we deliver a high-end product for your communication needs. Our innovative and creative programming have led to numerous awards and flowing references.

BOOKER COMMUNICATIONS   651-644-5541
1249 Ashland Avenue   **St. Paul 55104**
FAX: 651-644-5541
E-MAIL: steveb@tt.net
WWW: tt.net/gbvc
SERVICES: We offer full service digital video and audio production. We specialize in documentaries, industrial videos, video television commercials and video presentations for non-profit organizations. Our music production department (The Jingle Guys) specializes in jingle production for radio and television, and original music for video productions.

Film & Video Producers / 193

CAPABILITIES: Over ten years experience in video and audio production. We've won nine national awards. We currently have a non-linear video production system using Adobe Premier and Pinnacle Systems DC-50. We can also update your old video productions and/or put them onto CD ROM.
CURRENT/RECENT CLIENTS/PROJECTS: Recent clients include Homes By Owner USA, Metro Minneapolis, YMCA, Erickson Marketing, Radisson Hotels, Breezy Point Lodge, Northern Lights Casino and the Goodman Group.
PRESIDENT/CEO/OWNER: Steve Bucher
CONTACT: Amy Fingerhut Behr, Marketing Director

DARRELL BRAND/MOVING IMAGES, INC.   612-922-3308
3308 St. Paul Avenue   Minneapolis 55416
FAX: 612-922-3802
CONTACT: Darrell Brand
E-MAIL: dbrandmii@aol.com
SERVICES: Camera, directing and editing services for commercial, industrial, documentary films and videotape.
SPECIALTIES: Special emphasis on the sensitive/personal approach to documentary style. Broadcast-quality location video packages, with or without crew.
PRESIDENT/CEO/OWNER: Darrell Brand

C

CANTWELL COMMUNICATIONS   612-826-0011
7701 Pickfair Drive   Bloomington 55438
FAX: 612-826-0022
CONTACT: Kermit Cantwell
E-MAIL: cantwell@pclink.com
SERVICES: Writing, producing and directing for film and video production.
CAPABILITIES: Sales promotion, meeting support, employee communications. Extensive travel experience.
PRESIDENT/CEO/OWNER: Kermit Cantwell

CAPTIONMAX, INC.   612-341-3566
530 North 3rd Street #210   Minneapolis 55401
FAX: 612-341-2345
CONTACT: Derek Hines
E-MAIL: paige@captionmax.com
WWW: captionmax.com
SERVICES: High quality realtime and offline captioning, foreign language subtitling and captioning, web cast captioning and transcription.
CAPABILITIES: Digitally encoded caption masters means no generation loss. All tape formats including D1, D2, Digital Betacam, Beta SP, etc. Fast turnaround.
CURRENT/RECENT CLIENTS/PROJECTS: A & E Networks; MTV Networks; Columbia TriStar; Mayo Clinic; Best Buy Corporation; Hazelden; Mac Hammond Ministries; TNN; USA Network.
PRESIDENT/CEO/OWNER: Max Duckler

194 / Film & Video Producers

CHARTHOUSE INTERNATIONAL LEARNING CORPORATION
221 River Ridge Circle
FAX: 952-890-0505
CONTACT: Mark Davis
E-MAIL: john@charthouse.com
WWW: charthouse.com/fishphilosophy.com

952-890-1800
Burnsville 55337

SERVICES: Complete film and video production services. Worldwide on-location production capabilities. Sony digital Betacam and Arriflex super 16mm film equipment. AVID editing equipment. Production of management films, documentaries, and safety films. Creation of films that reflect the heart of our authors.
CAPABILITIES: Creator of FISH! Sticks. FISH! Has been named the #1 selling business training film.

CLEARVISION PRODUCTIONS
Fox 29, 1701 Broadway Street NE
FAX: 612-379-2900
E-MAIL: sueg@fox29.com
WWW: clearvisionprod.com

612-362-3808
Minneapolis 55413

SERVICES: ClearVision Productions, a service of Fox 29 TV, is a fully equipped media production company offering complete video, audio, graphics and animation services. Capabilities include shooting on location or in-studio; linear and non-linear online edit suites; 3D animation; digital special effects and digital audio editing. In addition, our nationally recognized staff includes professionals with extensive writing and producing experience, and we can provide full creative services for your project.
CAPABILITIES: Over the last three years, Fox 29's ClearVision Productions has been honored with four national Vision Awards, two Minnesota Broadcasters Media Best Awards and a national Telly Award. Special capabilities include 3D animation using Lightwave 3D, and digital special effects including Boris FX and Digital Fusion. Studios are also available for rental.
PRESIDENT/CEO/OWNER: Susan Groh

COMMUNICATIONS UNLIMITED VIDEO PRODUCTIONS
3619 85th Avenue North
FAX: 763-493-4325
CONTACT: Joseph A.Casella
E-MAIL: jcasella@proteon.inet-serv.com

763-493-4300
Brooklyn Park 55443

SERVICES: Complete award winning video production from program concept to location shooting, script writing, non-linear editing, narration, foreign language translation and narration and duplication. Nationwide service.
CAPABILITIES: Sales, training, trade show, and corporate image videos for machinery manufacturers, industry and high tech companies.
CURRENT/RECENT CLIENTS/PROJECTS: Bosch, Alcote 1, Badger Technology, Valspar, Cub Foods, Thiele Technologies, Timesavers, MGS Machine, Portola Packaging, EX Tech Industries, Rose Forgrove Ltd.
PRESIDENT/CEO/OWNER: Joseph A.Casella

Film & Video Producers / 195

COMMUNICATIONS™

CONUS PRODUCTIONS & SATELLITE SERVICES   **651-642-4477**
3415 University Avenue   **Minneapolis 55414**
FAX: 651-642-4551
CONTACT: Brian Tuttle
CAPABILITIES: Single and multi-camera video production service. Mobile and fixed satellite uplinks, and full production crews available for event broadcast.
EQUIPMENT: Sony CCD cameras, modular control rooms. Chyron graphics. Support Beta SP video tape format 4 uplink trucks, tape playback.
SPECIALTIES: Mobile uplink and multi-camera video production.
PRESIDENT/CEO/OWNER: Terry O'Reilly, GM

CORPORATE MEDIA SERVICES   **612-881-8081**
9801 Dupont Avenue South #250   **Bloomington 55431**
CONTACT: Earl Teproten
CAPABILITIES: Video productions for sales, training, motivation, advertising, fundraising and corporate overview. In-house services include: creative concepting, scripting, design, production, studio, computer graphics, editing of video and audio.
CURRENT/RECENT CLIENTS/PROJECTS: Ashland Oil, Dupont Corporation, General Dynamics/Ft. Worth, Pratt Whitney Aircraft, General Electric, Metalcasters of Minnesota, Bloomington Chamber of Commerce, Mona Meyer McGrath & Gavin, Computer Network Technology, Ecolab, PDR Marketing & Advertising, Camax Systems, Road Rescue, Hitchcock Industries, Children's Home Society, Children Are People Support Groups, Head Start School, Proctor & Gamble, State of Minnesota.
SPECIALTIES: Award-winning video productions.

THE CREATIVE EDGE FILM & VIDEO PRODUCTIONS, INC.   **651-552-7979**
5945 Carmen Avenue   **Inver Grove Heights 55076**
FAX: 651-552-0997
CONTACT: Philip A. Lawrence III
E-MAIL: crtvedge@aol.com
SERVICES: Full-service film and video production company. Services include: concept development, script writing, award-winning videography, award-winning edition, 3D graphics, DVD authoring, packaging and duplication.
EQUIPMENT: BetaCam SP field gear, media-100 non-linear digital edit system, and Sonic Solutions DVD authoring.

196 / Film & Video Producers

SPECIALTIES: Corporate/Industrial training and marketing.

CUSTOM BUSINESS VIDEO, INC.   612-379-2336
416 University Avenue NE   Minneapolis 55413
FAX: 612-378-4943
CONTACT: Dennis Karlstad
SERVICES: Goal clarification, concept development, scriptwriting, shooting, editing, graphics, music and narration.
SPECIALTIES: 20 years experience. Special capabilities for multiple and remote location shooting, interviewing and narration.

D

DANGER STUDIOS   612-338-2510
1219 Marquette Avenue #111   Minneapolis 55403
FAX: 612-338-8735
CONTACT: C. David Erbele
E-MAIL: dangerstudios@imez.com
WWW: dangerstudios.com
SERVICES: Video and audio production, digital editing, tape duplication, original music creation, production music, web design, web hosting, email and FTP services.
CAPABILITIES: 22 years in the business of audio and video production; now with our own server and complete internet services available.

STEVE DOYLE PRODUCTIONS   612-471-0811
2554 Arcola Lane   Minneapolis 55391
FAX: 612-471-0833
CONTACT: Keely Doyle
E-MAIL: sdoyle19@idt.net or keelly@idt.net
WWW: stevedoyleproductions.com
SERVICES: Creative, pre-production, producer and director, scriptwriter, male on-camera and voiceover talent for corporate and broadcast video production.
CAPABILITIES: Corporate image, marketing, new product launch, employee education and training, point-of purchase, video news release, recruitment, fundraising; linear or DVD capability.
CURRENT/RECENT CLIENTS/PROJECTS: Regis Corporation; Pfizer; 3M; Bayer Pharmaceutical; Mallinckrodt; Waterford Crystal; US Filters; US West; Valuevision/Snap TV; CME Advertising; Colle & McVoy Marketing; Shandwick; American Red Cross; WCCO Television
PRESIDENT/CEO/OWNER: Steve Doyle

E

EIII PRODUCTIONS, INC.   612-925-2442
5606 Concord Avenue   Edina 55424
FAX: 612-925-3898
CONTACT: Eddy Nelson

Film & Video Producers / 197

CAPABILITIES: Film and video production. Original music composition, arrangement and production.
SPECIALTIES: Television commercials and corporate programs. Music and sound design for television commercials and radio jingles.
PRESIDENT/CEO/OWNER: Eddy Nelson

F

FARINACCI & ASSOCIATES, INC.   651-647-1978
1640 Como Avenue   St. Paul 55108
FAX: 651-647-9479
CONTACT: Robert Farinacci
E-MAIL: farinacci@wavefront.com
SERVICES: Full service film and video production company.
CAPABILITIES: In business since 1973, the company has received numerous national awards for a variety of productions ranging from training films and videos to documentaries on Olympic Boxing and Nascar Racing.
CURRENT/RECENT CLIENTS/PROJECTS: Mammoth, Inc. - Training, product awareness, national meetings; Temtrol Inc. - Training, product awareness; Heidelberg USA; Imation; Xerox - Pre-DRUPA documentary and DRUPA 2000/International trade show documentary to be completed in May of 2000. Distributed to print trade worldwide.

FARROW MEDIA SERVICES   651-484-5367
3488 Edgerton Street   Vadnais Heights 55127
FAX: 651-484-2655
CONTACT: Charles Farrow
E-MAIL: cfphoto@earthlink.net
SERVICES: Digital video production for documentaries, video news releases, PSAs, fundraising, educational programming, desktop non-linear editing, video on CD-ROM, for software applications and the web, and consulting.
CURRENT/RECENT CLIENTS/PROJECTS: MN Army National Guard; Baptist General Conference.

FREESTYLE PRODUCTIONS INCORPORATED

FREESTYLE PRODUCTIONS, INC.   763-417-9575
6112 Olson Memorial Highway   Minneapolis 55422
FAX: 763-417-9576

198 / Film & Video Producers

CONTACT: Dale Kivimaki, Mark Hulsey
E-MAIL: dale@freestyle-productions.com
WWW: freestyle-productions.com
CAPABILITIES: Freestyle Productions provides video and multimedia communication services with a specialized focus on high-profile, live-event productions including corporate meetings, trade shows, conventions and concerts. Complete array of broadcast equipment: multi-camera field packages, post production/mobile, non-linear edit suites, switcher/effects & graphic systems, large-format video and data projection, front & rear screens and videowalls.
SPECIALTIES: Over 10 years of national and international experience producing all types of live and special events shows. Freestyle provides an intuitive understanding of how to best communicate their client's message to impact large and small audiences.
CURRENT/RECENT CLIENTS/PROJECTS: Fox Sports Net, Coca-Cola, Lucent Technologies, Apple Computer, Northwest Airlines, Promise Keepers, Carlson Companies, Lutheran Brotherhood, US West, Minnesota State Fair, Universal Studios Hollywood.

H

MARK HUFFINGTON PRODUCTIONS   651-686-4994
1894 Bear Path Trail   **Eagan 55122**
FAX: 651-686-4994
CONTACT: Mark Huffington
E-MAIL: markh79@idt.net
SERVICES: Full-service corporate video production. Concepting, scripting, shooting, editing, duplication.
CAPABILITIES: 23 years experience. Hourly rates. Canon XL-1 Mini DV Camera, Lowel lights, edit DV non-linear editor, music library.
CURRENT/RECENT CLIENTS/PROJECTS: 3M, Target

I

IMPRESSIONS   612-472-7617
5758 Elm Road   **Mound 55364**
CONTACT: Rob Jones
E-MAIL: brccjones@aol.com
SERVICES: Television program and video production facility. Single camera, documentary style shooting. Macintosh based non-linear video editing system. 3D animations and digital video effects.
CAPABILITIES: Our main focus is documenting live events such as sports, concerts and award ceremonies. We also produce music videos, commercials, corporate training and promotional videos. Sony digital video cameras and tape with Mac based, non-linear editor.
CURRENT/RECENT CLIENTS/PROJECTS: Coon Rapids High School; Mound - Westonka High School.
PRESIDENT/CEO/OWNER: Becky L. Jorgensen

J

J R CASTING 612-288-0505
212 3rd Avenue North #160 Minneapolis 55401
FAX: 612-288-0511
CONTACT: Jean Rohn
SERVICES: Casting Director, C.S.A.
CAPABILITIES: Feature film, commercials, industrial film print. Union and non-union. 1,200 sq. ft. casting studio. 3/4" and 1/2" taping capabilities. Dubbing also available.

JUNTUNEN MEDIA GROUP 612-341-3348
708 North First Street Minneapolis 55401
FAX: 612-341-0242
CONTACT: John Gorski
ALTERNATE PHONE: 800-535-4366
E-MAIL: mjuntunen@juntunen.com
WWW: juntunen.com
SERVICES: Full production and post-production support including: broadband services, video or film production, editing, finishing, animation, compositing, graphic design and visual effects, audio recording, music scoring and sound design, studio, duplication and trafficking. Fiber optic distribution. We tailor our services to fit your needs. From shoot through trafficking, or anything in between, our team can produce and post-produce your project-providing you efficient, one-stop shopping.
CAPABILITIES: Ask for our Executive Producer who leads our network of creative producers to match clients' communication goals with production and subject matter expertise. Juntunen Media 2000: DVD authoring. Full digital video support. Webcasting. Visual web-based library: catalog and store all your brand assets. Retrieve from anywhere in the world and repurpose.
CURRENT/RECENT CLIENTS/PROJECTS: Corporate clients; sports and entertainment organizations; total digital facility support or a la carte for producers.
PRESIDENT/CEO/OWNER: Bill Juntunen

K

KAT WOMAN PRODUCTIONS 651-293-9700
3100 1st National Bank West St. Paul 55101
332 Minnesota Street
FAX: 651-222-6169
CONTACT: Katherine Lenaburg
E-MAIL: katwomanpr@aol.com
SERVICES: A full-service video production company. Services include concept design, scriptwriting, state-of-the-art video production, on-camera and voice-over talent, duplication. Kat Woman Productions keeps the price reasonable by utilizing award-winning professionals and maintaining tight production deadlines and low overhead.

200 / Film & Video Producers

CAPABILITIES: Kat Woman Productions was founded in 1994 by Katherine Lenaburg, who has more than 15 years of experience in television production. Kat is a former anchor and reporter, and is presently adjunct faculty at Brown Institute of Broadcasting in Mendota Heights. Associates of Kat Woman Productions enjoy success in many areas of film and television production throughout the United States.
CURRENT/RECENT CLIENTS/PROJECTS: Adaytum Software; Behavior Health Service, Inc.; Brown Institute; City of Saint Paul; Minnesota Corporate Credit Union; Wit at Work; Metro Cable Network; U of St. Thomas; Secretary of State Office.

KITCHENER PRODUCTIONS 612-470-5221
20500 Linwood Road Deephaven 55331
FAX: 612-470-5221
CONTACT: John Kitchener
E-MAIL: kitch@bitstream.net
SERVICES: Complete video and film production services, from concepting and scriptwriting through post. Over 12 years experience with clients and projects large and small. Also provide just scriptwriting on project basis. Call, we'll talk, we'll have coffee, I'll buy.
CAPABILITIES: Fun concepts, humor, highly creative solutions for sales, marketing, training, etc.
CURRENT/RECENT CLIENTS/PROJECTS: Video's, CD-ROMs, Webcast, Video Streaming, Websites, Meetings, A veritable cornucopia of communication.

DAVID KLAUSSEN 218-226-3500
6456 Highway 61 Little Marais 55614
CONTACT: David Klaussen

KOSKINEN VIDEO INC. 612-648-3663
5008 Yvonne Terrace Edina 55436
FAX: 952-920-5628
CONTACT: John Koskinen
E-MAIL: jannboy@aol.com
SERVICES: Director of Photography - video and film/complete field production crews. Sony 550 Beta SP and Sony 400 Beta/SP - ArriFlex 16 mm cameras and digital Betacam.
CAPABILITIES: Strong handheld and cinema Verite style, Betacam SP and digital Betacam 16:9 video production, 16 mm and Super 16 mm film production. Strong location lighting. 27 years shooting national sports, magazine features, news VNRS, behind scenes, corporate and industrial, products, capabilities and promotions.
EQUIPMENT: Eng & EFP Sony BVP 550 Digital Beta/SP, Sony BVW-400-lighting, audio, grip equipment and GMC Suburbans. Arri 16 mm film cameras.
CURRENT/RECENT CLIENTS/PROJECTS: NFL Films; NBA Entertainment; CTV - Canada; BBC; CBS; HBO; Fox Sports and News; CNN; Animal Planet; Speedvision; PBS; 3M; Anheuser Busch; ESPN; Ford; HGTV; Outdoor Life Disney - "I'm Going to Disney World"; Super Bowl Sports; General Mills.

Film & Video Producers / 201

L

LAPINSKI PRODUCTIONS, LTD.   612-843-4297
1828 Jefferson Street NE   Minneapolis 55418
CONTACT: Patrick Lapinski
E-MAIL: lapinski@minn.net
SERVICES: Complete video production and post production services for corporate and industrial communications. Multi-media project management and creative development.
CAPABILITIES: Industrial maritime training and marketing video production and still photography.
CURRENT/RECENT CLIENTS/PROJECTS: 3M; Digi International; Seaway Port of Duluth; Lake Carriers' Association; American Steamship Company.

LEE PICTURES, INC.   612-509-0955
13225 55th Avenue North   Minneapolis 55442
FAX: 612-509-0956
CONTACT: Lee Kanten
E-MAIL: leepictures@usinternet.com
SERVICES: 26 years experience creating employee communication, marketing, training, and corporate image videos and films. A sensitive interview style and expert talent direction bring credibility to our productions. In meetings, our exceptional organization gets us to your core message quickly. Then we collaborate with you to create a compelling and effective communication tool. That we are fun to work with is a bonus!
CAPABILITIES: AVID McExpress non-linear editing.
CURRENT/RECENT CLIENTS/PROJECTS: Lawson Software - external communications; Domestic Violence Awareness - Health Partners; Pfizer Pharmaceuticals - sales training.

LEHMANN PRODUCTION SERVICES   612-822-1240
3301 Garfield Avenue South   Minneapolis 55408
FAX: 612-822-1248
CONTACT: Kate Lehmann
E-MAIL: katel3317@aol.com
SERVICES: Producing, line producing, production management and consulting services for film and video production.
CAPABILITIES: Feature film experience, extensive TV experience.
CURRENT/RECENT CLIENTS/PROJECTS: CH 2, Public Radio Intl., MN Film Board

LIFETOUCH VIDEO CREATIONS   612-826-4389
11000 Viking Drive, Suite 300   Eden Prairie 55344
FAX: 612-832-5665
CONTACT: Brian Dellis
SERVICES: Full service video production from pre-production through post-production. Including conception, script writing, talent, planning, crew and equipment for location shooting, sound recording, mixing and editing on Betacam SP. Rental and duplication available.
EQUIPMENT: Sony & Hitachi Betacam chip cameras, video studio and 2 on-line edit suites. Duplication also available.

202 / Film & Video Producers

SPECIALTIES: Corporate, industrial, broadcast video production.
PRESIDENT/CEO/OWNER: Director of Operations, Brian Dellis; Senior Producer, Tim Johnson; Producer, Donnie Koshiol.

LINN UNLIMITED, A PRODUCTION COMPANY   612-949-2505
6951 Raven Court   **Eden Prairie 55346**
FAX: 612-949-2075
CONTACT: Dennis Linn
E-MAIL: linnultd@aol.com
SERVICES: Television commercials, short films, motion pictures.
CAPABILITIES: 35mm television commercials.
PRESIDENT/CEO/OWNER: Dennis Linn

LIONOWL FILMS   612-544-9262
Box 27447   **Minneapolis 55427**
FAX: 612-546-8954
CONTACT: Barry ZeVan
E-MAIL: bnz1@aol.com
SERVICES: Production (conceptualization, scripting, directing, organizing, producing.)
CAPABILITIES: Three Emmy nominations for foreign location documentaries; specializes in narration, inspiration and motivational travel and leisure docs, promotional and public relations-oriented videos.

M

MAHONEY MEDIA GROUP, INC.   612-915-9502
6900 West Lake Street   **Minneapolis 55426**
FAX: 612-915-9926
CONTACT: Timothy P. Mahoney
WWW: mahoneymedia.com
CAPABILITIES: Experienced in film and video broadcast production, 35mm, 16mm, Betacam Sp location and studio, offline and online editing. Graphics, animation, interactive and duplication.
SPECIALTIES: Storytelling, dramatic, humorous, corporate, emotional and sensitive subjects, sports and outdoor, medical, non-profits, marketing, PSA's, commercials, documentary, inspirational.

Film & Video Producers / 203

OFFICERS: Timothy P. Mahoney, President; Timothy P. Mahoney, Sales; Joe Morin, Production Manager; Chad Greene, Editor.

MARTIN/BASTIAN PRODUCTIONS   612-375-0055
105 Fifth Avenue So #150   Minneapolis 55401
FAX: 612-342-2348
CONTACT: Amy Oriani
E-MAIL: amyo@martinbastian.com
WWW: martinbastian.com
SERVICES: Martin/Bastian Productions offers creative development, execution and project management for corporate meetings and events, including staging services, business theater, speaker support, film and video production, and speakers and entertainment. We create integrated events from concept through execution, as well as offer individual meeting elements in an a la carte fashion, such as sourcing and booking speakers and entertainment.
CAPABILITIES: Martin/Bastian has been in business for nearly 20 years, and we have 18 employees on staff, including meeting and event producers, video producers, graphic designers, writers, and account management. We're housed in the renovated, turn-of-the century, Crown Roller Mill in downtown Minneapolis, complete with a video facility (including on-line Media 100 post-production), a digital sound recording studio, theater, computer graphic workstations, speaker and entertainment video library, and other technical, creative, and account services.
CURRENT/RECENT CLIENTS/PROJECTS: We currently produce meetings, events, videos, and book speakers and entertainment for some of the top companies in the Midwest, and have won numerous awards for our film and video work. Recent entertainment acts we've produced for corporate clients include Bill Cosby, Bruce Hornsby, Kenny Loggins, The Neville Brothers, and Lyle Lovett and His Large Band.
PRESIDENT/CEO/OWNER: Al Soukup

MASTER COMMUNICATIONS GROUP, INC.   952-835-6164
7805 Telegraph Road #100   Bloomington 55438
CONTACT: Christine Dean
WWW: mastcom.com
CAPABILITIES: Full service electronic communications. Complete video production services from concept and scripting through post production. BetacamSp. Media 100, non-linear editing (Boris Effects, Adobe After Effects, Commotion) 2D and 3D animation, lightWave. Audio production. Web development (adobe Go Live, Dream Weaver, Flash/Live Motion) and interactive multimedia authoring and development (authorware, Director, iShell and others.)
SPECIALTIES: Education, training and marketing for medical, technical, foreign language translations and voiceovers, and ESL/EFL.
CURRENT/RECENT CLIENTS/PROJECTS: ADP Hollander, Augustine Medical, Cambridge University Press, Evangelical Lutheran Church in America, Lutheran Church--Missouri Synod, Seagate, RSM McGladrey, Syracuse Language Systems.

MATRIX VIDEO, INC.   612-837-1852
7300 France Avenue South #203   Edina 55435
CONTACT: Peter M. Ellingson
CAPABILITIES: Editing, film transfer (16mm, 8mm & Super8), & video dupes of formats. (S-VHS, VHS, 8mm, HI-8, Digital8mm, BetaSP, DV, D-9). Basic cuts only linear editing and AB roll editing with Toaster NT and Flyer. VHS conversions., Video tape to prints, CD & DVD. D-9, Digital8, DV and S-VHS production cameras.

204 / Film & Video Producers

SPECIALTIES: Photos and slides with pan and zooms and non-linear production to most to and from most tape formats. Power Point shows to video tape. Audio tape and records to CD-ROM.
CURRENT/RECENT CLIENTS/PROJECTS: 3M, Best Buy, KTCA, KARE, WCCO, Super Value, Graco, Volunteers of America, Anagram Intl, Garlock Equipment, Carlson Companies, A1 Vending, Dolphin Temps, Carleton College, Children Cancer Research Fund, Mayo Clinic, Allied Vaughn, Hey City Theatre, Wilson's, Cargill, Stein Ind., Rainforest Café, National Museum Horseracing, CBS, Rosemount Schools, Pitney Bowes, Mpls. Fire Dept., White Bear Yacht Club, Evalu Med, Spilka, Medtronic and Hammer Residences.

MCCOY & ASSOCIATES, INC.   **612-627-9253**
17 Melbourne Avenue SE   **Minneapolis 55414**
FAX: 612-378-1283
CONTACT: Ron McCoy
E-MAIL: ron@realmccoy.com
WWW: realmccoy.com
SERVICES: Ron McCoy works with individuals that want to communicate their messages more effectively through video and companies that want to translate their message into new media applications. Ron is an independent producer resource to help you build the best creative and technical team possible to meet your client's expectations in a timely and cost effective manner.
CAPABILITIES: Program design and development services including front-end concepting, resource management and visual storyboarding. Project management and line producer services. A unique compression planning service helps group creative decision-making by providing a neutral informative facilitator. Visual pin boards with big picture design within a small group combining a creative brainstorming session with an analytical phase that addresses the What, Why issues before addressing the How and When strategy.
CURRENT/RECENT CLIENTS/PROJECTS: New media applications including DVD design and development. Traditional video program development and production. DVD commercial Library Project. 175 spot resource director for major retailer. Sales training and employee communications projects for major financial services and healthcare firms in the Twin Cities areas. Teleconferencing and business meetings for major corporations. Direct Response Broadcast projects for major retailer. Annual meetings and business communications for non-profits.

MEDIA PRODUCTIONS, INC.   **612-379-4678**
125 SE Main Street #100   **Minneapolis 55414**
FAX: 612-379-7988
CONTACT: Judy Kessel
SERVICES: Award-winning full service production company offering producing, writing, directing, editing, graphics and duplication services. Our comprehensive communication services including project consulting, strategic planning and marketing communications, including computer-based media and print production services.
SPECIALTIES: Medical device industry, occupational health and safety.
PRESIDENT/CEO/OWNER: Judy Kessel, P; Jerrold Gershone, EVP; Jerry Kolb, VP

MENTEN MUSIC, INC.   **612-333-4650**
10 South 5th Street #835   **Minneapolis 55402**
FAX: 612-333-5231
CONTACT: Dale Menten
E-MAIL: dmenten@visi.com

Film & Video Producers / 205

SERVICES: Film/video scoring and sound design. Radio and TV composing, lyric writing, arranging and production.
CURRENT/RECENT CLIENTS/PROJECTS: Adm, Miller Lite, Cheerios, Musicland, Dayton's, Sprint, Land O' Lakes, Mercury Marine, Starbucks, Ralston Purina, Polaris, MN Medical Foundation.

MESSAGE IN MOTION 218-226-3500
6456 Highway 61 Little Marais 55614
FAX: 218-226-3535
CONTACT: David Klassen
ALTERNATE PHONE: 800-681-6161
E-MAIL: dklassen@mimotion.com
SERVICES: The Whole Show. Full-service video and interactive media production for national and international clients. Award-winning writer, producer, director specialized in clear, compelling communication for marketing, public relations, training and broadcast. 25 years experience completing complex projects from script, through production, to translation and international distribution on critical deadlines.
CAPABILITIES: Script & creative services. Producer/director for studio and field locations. Digital, non-linear, no-compression video editing. Interactive media production. Transcription. Translation services and international distribution.
CURRENT/RECENT CLIENTS/PROJECTS: Technology, manufacturing, automotive, finance, agriculture, mining, government, utilities and health.

METROPOLITAN HODDER GROUP 612-333-1025
510 First Avenue North #410 Minneapolis 55403
FAX: 612-359-3636
CONTACT: Barbara Hammer
E-MAIL: barbh@metrotv.com or marka@metrotv.com
WWW: metrotv.com
SERVICES: Creative film and video production company specializing in the development of impactful programming for marketing, corporate image and employee communications. Other services include commercial production, broadcast television programming, web design and creative DVD authoring through our new facility, Digital Bucket.
PRESIDENT/CEO/OWNER: Kent Hammer
SALES CONTACT: Barbara Hammer and Mark Arfmann, Business Development

MIKE JONES FILM CORP. 952-835-4490
5280 West 74th Street Minneapolis 55439
FAX: 952-835-3413
CONTACT: Judy Super
E-MAIL: judy@mikejonesfilm.com
SERVICES: Character animation for TV commercials and short films complete from design through audio.
CURRENT/RECENT CLIENTS/PROJECTS: Owens Corning, Tom Thumb, Kroger, St. Croix Casino, Indiana Tobacco Free Partnership
PRESIDENT/CEO/OWNER: Mike Jones

MINNESOTA FILM BOARD 612-332-6493
401 N 3rd Street #460 Minneapolis 55401

206 / Film & Video Producers

FAX: 612-332-3735
CONTACT: Eric Mueller
E-MAIL: info@mnfilm.org
WWW: mnfilm.org
SERVICES: The Minnesota Film Board is a non-profit organization dedicated to making Minnesota one of the top five film/video production markets in the US. The Film Board offers professional production services and creates programs to boost the state's film community.
CAPABILITIES: Snowbate 5% rebate for features and TV series, Minnesota Independent Film Fund, Jerome Screenwriters Mentorship, Sales tax exemptions for TV commercials, Digitized photo location library, Minnesota Production Guide, Websites: www.mnfilm.org, New Media Conference.
CURRENT/RECENT CLIENTS/PROJECTS: Fox Here On Earth; New Line Cinema Sugar & Spice; Paramount - A Simple Plan.

MOTION PICTURES, INC.   612-332-6518
310 North Second Street   Minneapolis 55401
FAX: 612-337-0210
CONTACT: William Card, Daniel Polsfuss
CAPABILITIES: Film and video production.
SPECIALTIES: Commercial, music video and corporate/industrial production.

MULTIMEDIA   952-931-2112
1011 First Street South #300   Hopkins 55343
FAX: 952-935-1318
CONTACT: Dianne Thill
WWW: multimedia-inc.com
SERVICES: Production of video presentations, interactive CD-ROM development, web page design, multi-image and live musical shows.
EQUIPMENT: Betacam video location and studio equipment, edit suite, multi-image programming.
SPECIALTIES: Sales meetings, sales training, marketing presentations.

N

PETER NEUBECK VIDEO   612-377-6027
1504 South Tyrol Trail   Golden Valley 55416
CONTACT: Peter Neubeck
E-MAIL: peter@pnvideo.com
WWW: pnvideo.com
SERVICES: Complete video production and post production for lawyers. Video litigation support. Video settlement programs and Day In The Life Programs.
CAPABILITIES: Over 20 years providing video services for lawyers. BetaCam SP, DU CAM, Media 100 post production.
CURRENT/RECENT CLIENTS/PROJECTS: Most major Minnesota law firms.

Film & Video Producers / 207

P

PERIMETER PRODUCTIONS, LTD.
1312 Tyrol Trail
612-374-9072
Minneapolis 55416
FAX: 612-381-2711
CONTACT: Robert Hammel
E-MAIL: perimpro@bitstream.net
SERVICES: A creative services company that conceives and produces films, videos, multimedia, business theatre, and video walls for corporations, museums and the educational marketplace.
CAPABILITIES: Corporate image, training, documentaries and educational media. Video wall design for trade shows and public spaces.
CURRENT/RECENT CLIENTS/PROJECTS: Major Corporations, Government Organizations, Advertising Agencies. Recently completed point of sale video, "Parenting Teenagers - The Danger Zone" for Target Stores.
PRESIDENT/CEO/OWNER: Michele Blanchard, President/Writer/Producer

PINNACLE VIDEO PRODUCTIONS, INC.
9201 East Bloomington Freeway #Z
952-888-3332
Bloomington 55420
FAX: 952-888-3375
CONTACT: Scott Hoffman
PAGER: 800-539-6877
SERVICES: Full-service - concepting and scripting, film 16mm & 35mm, digital and BetacamSP video, location or our studio, post-production digital non-linear editing, compositing, effects and graphics design, media compression for web and CD-ROM, and video duplication/packaging, Foreign PAL and SECAM conversion.
EQUIPMENT: Sony Digital Beta DVW90 and Sony BetacamSP camera packages, HMI and Tungsten lighting packages, 26' 5 ton grip truck with quick loading speed rail head carts and taco carts, 12' to 30' camera crane with remote head, 2 Media 100 digital SDI & component non-linear editing suites, 2D and 3D compositing with Effetto Pronto & Iced After Effects & Commotion motion tracking.
CAPABILITIES: Formats: Digital Beta, BetacamSP, DVD, 3/4" U-Matic, SVHS, HI-8 and 8mm, VHS, PAL and SECAM. MAC & IBM/PC, Zip, Jazz and CD-ROM.
SPECIALTIES: Commercials, marketing and new product, training instruction programs, video conversion for web and multimedia CD-ROM programs.

POINT2POINT COMMUNICATION SOLUTIONS, INC.
235 East Sixth Street, 4th Floor
651-223-7399
St. Paul 55101
FAX: 651-223-7390
CONTACT: Dave Herman
WWW: pt2pt.com
CAPABILITIES: Studio and remote video production, single and multi-camera, video post, digital graphics, audio recording, editing and sweetening, studio and remote satellite uplink/downlink. Experienced staff includes directors, producers, production management and full crews.

208 / Film & Video Producers

EQUIPMENT: Two large production studios (82' x 52' and 52' x 52' - 20' high lighting grids) with state-of-the-art equipment and individual control rooms. Six studio cameras. Also insert/uplink studio (27' x 19'). Dressing rooms. Green room. Scene shop, freight elevator, loading dock. Full post-production services featuring integrated AVID non-linear on-line editing. ProTools Digital Audio Workstation, off-line edit, as well as multi-format video edit suites. Dubner Halo graphics. Adobe After Effects graphic compositing and digital 3D animation. Digital Beta, BetaSP & 1" video tape formats, 5 remote vans.

PROMEDIA PRODUCTIONS, INC.   651-631-3681
2593 Hamline Avenue North   Roseville 55113
CONTACT: Steve Keller
SERVICES: Full service film and video production company. Formats include DVCAM, Digital BetaCam, BetaCamSP, D2, 1", 3/4" SP, SVHS and Hi8. Provide creative services, in-studio or on location (single or multi-cam) shooting, post production including: two Avid online suites, two DVCAM nonlinear suites, and one multi-format online suite, Maya and SGI based 3-D animation and streaming audio and video for the Web. Audio studio offers ProTools III Digital Audio Workstation. Complete audio, video, CD/CD-ROM and DVD duplication services and international standards conversions.
CAPABILITIES: With 20 years experience in corporate and industrial videos, broadcast television, TV commercials and multi-media, ProMedia has extensive knowledge of every phase of the production process from ala carte items to full scale productions. We believe in complete customer satisfaction and our staff will work hard to give you the best possible footage, outstanding creative direction, great visuals and a finished product you'll be proud of.
CURRENT/RECENT CLIENTS/PROJECTS: ProMedia Productions, Inc. has experience with a wide range of organizations of varying sizes and industries, from Fortune 100 companies to small, privately held firms. With our strong customer base, Promedia serves as a vital resource for new trends in technology and creativity.
PRESIDENT/CEO/OWNER: Steve Keller

PROMOTIVISION, INC.   612-933-6445
5929 Baker Road #460   Minnetonka 55345
FAX: 612-933-7491
CONTACT: Executive Producer: Bill Cobbs; Producer: Bill Benedict or Nancy Greene
E-MAIL: promo460@aol.com
SERVICES: Full-service video and film production company, all work accomplished in-house. Script to screen, write, direct, shoot and edit TV spots, industrial, corporate image, training, legal or medical film or video.
EQUIPMENT: Sony cameras with BetaCam SP field player recorders, digital BetCam, 1600 sq. ft. sound conditioned studio with Cyc. Avid nonlinear Edit Suite, interformat Edit Suite, Beta SP, one-inch Grass Valley Editor and Switcher, ADO, Dubner, color camera on insert stand, 16-channel mixer, narration booth. 16 mm Arri and ACL cameras, full edit rooms.
PRESIDENT/CEO/OWNER: Michael & Nancy Greene

PUSH MEDIA GROUP   612-339-8294
411 Washington Avenue North #209   Minneapolis 55401
FAX: 612-339-8296
CONTACT: Danny Schmidt/James Curry
E-MAIL: dan@pushgroup.com
WWW: pushgroup.com

CAPABILITIES: Web, film and video production.
SPECIALTIES: Motion graphics utilizing 2D and 3D animation, special effects, and compositing.
CURRENT/RECENT CLIENTS/PROJECTS: NSP, VH1, General Motors, Nike, Paisley Park, Minnesota Vikings
PRESIDENT/CEO/OWNER: Danny Schmidt

R

R.E.M. VIDEO & EVENT COMPANY   **612-788-9221**
1828 NE Jefferson Street   **Minneapolis 55418**
FAX: 612-788-7712
CONTACT: Roger Miller
E-MAIL: info@remvideoevent.com
WWW: remvideoevent.com
SERVICES: Full service production house for video, events/presentations, audio, multimedia. Our focus is in business to business communications delivered live or on media. We have in-house presentation expertise and equipment for TVL, Powerpoint (advanced), Astound and SCALA. Video productions on Betacam and DV formats. Non-linear broadcast and non-broadcast editing. Non-linear audio production for audio CD, video and film sweetening and music production scoring.
SPECIALTIES: Historical productions commemorating companies and places. Business to business marketing and training. Original music.
PRESIDENT/CEO/OWNER: Roger Miller, Presentations & Video; Michael Loonan, Audio & Multimedia; Pat Miller, Production Management.

DAVE RESTUCCIA PRODUCTIONS   **612-377-7560**
2012 Queen Avenue South   **Minneapolis 55405**
FAX: 612-377-7561
CONTACT: Dave Restuccia
E-MAIL: daverest@aol.com
SERVICES: Corporate film and video production with fresh ideas, clear messages, exceptional attention to detail, and on-time/on-budget delivery. Concept through scriptwriting, production management, direction, editing, graphics composition, musical scoring and duplication.
CAPABILITIES: Location direction and production; in-town, two counties over, or 14 time zones away! Getting those impossible shots and making the ordinary exciting.
CURRENT/RECENT CLIENTS/PROJECTS: Corn harvest in southern Minnesota; tofu shops in Tokyo; Little League in rural Illinois; genetic engineering at Research Triangle Park; Underwater ballet at the U of M; grain barges down the Mississippi; orange juice production in Brazil; Freight trains through the Southwest; sports cars on the beach at Daytona; coca-making in Amsterdam.

RICH IMAGE VIDEO, INC.   **612-805-8827**
5148 Abercrombie Drive   **Edina 55439**
FAX: 612-942-0471

210 / Film & Video Producers

CONTACT: Rich Rumppe
E-MAIL: richimage@aol.com
SERVICES: Videographer/Director. Award winning video photography with over 25 years of News and Corporate video production experience. Complete Beta SP field production services. Digital camera, full lighting, audio, and monitoring. Experienced in News, Documentary, Health Care, Hi-tech, Training, Industrial, and Consumer products.
CAPABILITIES: The ability to move efficiently while maintaining a standard of quality that my clients deserve.
CURRENT/RECENT CLIENTS/PROJECTS: Networks, Fortune 500 companies, Public relations organization.

THE RICHARD DIERCKS COMPANY, INC.   612-334-5900
420 North 5th Street #300   Minneapolis 55401
FAX: 612-334-5907
CONTACT: Willie Powe, Jr.
CONTACT: richard@diercks.com
WWW: dvdauthor.com
SERVICES: Licensed and sponsored home video, sport, corporate, children's multimedia, interactive, CD-ROM, DVD-video, DVD-ROM, web/DVD.
CAPABILITIES: Digital Betacam. BetaCamSP, Arri 16, Digibeta SP edit suite, 16 track audio record, location sound, non-linear, digital off-line, MPEG, edit non-linear, Sonic Solution DVD(3.) Interactive training, corporate marketing, fitness, children's, outdoor. Marketing background with full distribution, Over 350 DVD titles, DVD-ROM.
CURRENT/RECENT CLIENTS/PROJECTS: Better Homes & Gardens; US Marine Corps; Lintus, NY; Federal Cartridge; Caswell Int.; Methode Jeanne Piaubert; Legos; Simitar; Unapix; Target; Honeywell.

ROBBINS ISLAND MUSIC   651-762-8123
PO Box 3452   Minneapolis 55403
FAX: 651-762-8140
CONTACT: Bradley Joseph
E-MAIL: bjoseph@bradleyjoseph.com
WWW: bradleyjoseph.com
CAPABILITIES: TV movies, commercials, corporate/industrial, documentaries, music videos, broadcast multimedia.
SPECIALTIES: Full orchestral original music, lower budget electronic scores, narada records artist with vast experiences in various mediums. Countless credits and services, multi-media scores.
CURRENT/RECENT CLIENTS/PROJECTS: "Yanni Live at the Acropolis" - Composer/Performer; Sheena Easton/"The Tonight Show" - Musical Director/Performer; ABVC World New Now; Lives of the Children Radio Series; Super Valu

DIANE ROBINSON   612-941-8797
9240 West Bush Lake Road   Bloomington 55438
FAX: 612-942-9815
CONTACT: Diane Robinson
E-MAIL: drobinsonmn@worldnet.att.net
SERVICES: Full-service production services in video, film and multimedia.
CAPABILITIES: High impact, award-winning corporate and non-profit communications, training, sales/marketing, public relations.

Film & Video Producers / 211

Call RumJumgle Media, see listing for detail!

RUMJUNGLE MEDIA, INC.   612-476-9900
17309 Bay Lane   **Wayzata 55391**
FAX: 612-476-0909
CONTACT: Kathy Ross
E-MAIL: rumjungle@rumjungle.com
WWW: rumjungle.com
SERVICES: Internationally experienced DP Camera Crews (Betacam SP, Digital Betacam, Mini DV & HDTV) with top-notch support crews, including producers and production assistants for broadcast, commercial and corporate clientele. RumJungle Media has an extensive database of satellite up-link services, grips, gaffers, make-up artists and teleprompter operators.
CAPABILITIES: Rumjungle has equipment packages featuring a wide array of gear for every situation. We offer Sony BVW-D600 cameras with 16:9 wide screen capability with comprehensive lighting and wireless audio packages. Expect superb lighting design, inventive production techniques, rock-steady hand-held camera operation and efficient set-up.
CURRENT/RECENT CLIENTS/PROJECTS: 1998 National News Emmy Award for NBC; 1999 National News Emmy Award for ABC; 1999 Telly Award for "Fish!".

S

SCHALL PRODUCTIONS   612-476-2472
1607 Oakways   **Wayzata 55391**
FAX: 612-476-4109
CONTACT: Caryn Schall Myers
E-MAIL: schallprod@aol.com
SERVICES: Complete video production services, with the benefit of ala carte personnel match-ups. We individually tailor your production crew to match your program topic and budget. Low overhead keeps your production costs down, while ensuring you the best team of production professionals for your particular project. Twenty years of experience - you name your video need and we'll fit it!

RON SCHARA   612-545-9471
6005 Wayzata Blvd #125   **Minneapolis 55416**
CONTACT: Kelly Jo McDonnell-Weiner

212 / Film & Video Producers

E-MAIL: ron@mnbound.com
WWW: mnbound.com
SERVICES: Film & video production services. Production of broadcast quality video from concept to completion, outdoor related documentaries, commercial spots.
EQUIPMENT: Beta SX, Avid non-linear editing.
SPECIALTIES: Any outdoor related production of broadcast quality video for environmental, fishing, hunting, nature, wildlife from educational to entertaining, script writing, production, post production.
CURRENT/RECENT CLIENTS/PROJECTS: ESPN; ESPN2; KARE11/NBC; The Outdoor Channel; The Outdoor Life Network; Wharf Cable in Hong Kong; Polish TV/Poland; TTN/S Korea.

SHAMROCK PICTURES, INC.	**612-619-3796**
4043 York Avenue South	Minneapolis 55410

FAX: 612-927-9681
CONTACT: Kevin Galligan
SERVICES: 16 mm film and video photography, lighting for broadcast, documentary, magazine, corporate and commercial accounts.
CAPABILITIES: Stedicam.
CURRENT/RECENT CLIENTS/PROJECTS: Target; MTV; VH-1; Fox Sports; Comedy Central; Paramount Pictures; The University of Minnesota.

GREG STIEVER	**612-333-0965**
160 North Glenwood	Minneapolis 55405

FAX: 612-397-7989
CONTACT: Greg Stiever
CAPABILITIES: Corporate image films, sales and business training videos for corporate communications.
SPECIALTIES: Directing actors and highly stylized cinematography.

STONE CIRCLE PRODUCTIONS	**612-843-4292**
1828 Jefferson Street NE	Minneapolis 55418

FAX: 612-843-4291
CONTACT: Richard Stachelek
SERVICES: Editors and editorial facilities, motion graphic design, and animation.
CAPABILITIES: Write, design, produce educational, corporate and documentary film and video.
PRESIDENT/CEO/OWNER: Richard Stachelek

T

TAG TEAM FILM & VIDEO, INC.	**651-917-0058**
2375 University Avenue West #200	St. Paul 55114

FAX: 651-917-0368
CONTACT: Jeff Byers
E-MAIL: jeff@tagteamfilmvideo.com
SERVICES: Digital Betacam and Betacam SP video production, 16 mm film production, off-line and on-line non-linear editing.

Film & Video Producers / 213

EQUIPMENT: Field production - complete crew and equipment packages featuring Sony BVP-570/550 digital cameras with 16 x 9 capability. Sony DVW-250 digital Betacam VTR, BVW-50 and BVV-5 Betacam SP VTRs. Extensive audio, lighting, grip and monitoring equipment. Single camera and live-switched multi-camera configurations. Aaton LTR-7 16mm camera pkg. Post production - SoftImage DS and Avid 1000.
SPECIALTIES: Providing independent, corporate and broadcast producer/directors with comprehensive, professional production and post-production services.
CURRENT/RECENT CLIENTS/PROJECTS: The St. Paul Companies; Corporate Video; ABC; Novartis; The Producers Consortium; Honeywell; Shandwick; Mayo Clinic; General Mills; Falls Agency; ESPN; Fleishman-Hillard; A & E.
PRESIDENT/CEO/OWNER: Thomas G. Krohn, Jeffrey J. Byers

TAKE 1 PRODUCTIONS   952-831-7757
9969 Valley View Road   Eden Prairie 55344
CONTACT: Rob Hewitt
SERVICES: Full service video and multimedia production company. Complete scripting, studio and location shooting, digital non-linear editing, computer generated graphics, 3D animation, digital video effects, multimedia authoring, MPEG encoding, video/CD-ROM duplication.
SPECIALTIES: Presentations for sales, training, and product demonstrations.
PRESIDENT/CEO/OWNER: Teri Murphy

TELE-PRODUCERS, INC.   612-941-2988
10300 Valley View Road #111   Eden Prairie 55344
FAX: 612-941-2733
CONTACT: Harlan Meyer
SERVICES: Full-service creative and technical resources for corporate and commercial production. From concept development, creative design, scripting and studio or location production through final edit.

TIMELINE COMMUNICATIONS, INC.   715-381-0190
701 2nd Street   Hudson 54016
FAX: 715-381-0195
CONTACT: Ron Johnson
E-MAIL: timeline@spacestar.net
SERVICES: Complete production services from concept to completion. On location or in-studio, at your business or across the globe. We provide everything you need to complete your film or video productions. Experienced staff of writers, producers, editors, graphic artists using state-of-the-art equipment and facilities. Located 20 minutes from the airport on the scenic St. Croix River.
CAPABILITIES: Projects range from corporate marketing and training films, television commercials, music videos, documentaries and infomercials. Principals with over 3 decades of experience and a staff of experienced, qualified professionals. Film and Beta SP formats for acquisition, out put to any format including CD. Avid media composer on/offline edit suite, 2D and 3D animations, custom music packages with a complete recording studio on site! Travel not a problem.
CURRENT/RECENT CLIENTS/PROJECTS: John Deere, ABC Good Morning America, Medtronic, JJ Keller & Associates, Jerome Foods, Rebecca's Garden, Hallmark Cards and the St. Paul Companies.
PRESIDENT/CEO/OWNER: Ron Johnson

214 / Film & Video Producers

TUNDRA FILMS   651-433-4499
PO Box 205, 101 Judd Street   Marine on St. Croix 55047
FAX: 651-433-3543
CONTACT: Gayle Knutson
E-MAIL: tundrafilm@aol.com
WWW: grandfathersbirthday.com
CAPABILITIES: Producer/Director - film.
SPECIALTIES: Motion picture.
PRESIDENT/CEO/OWNER: Gayle Knutson, Producer/Director

TUNHEIM GROUP   952-851-1600
1100 Riverview Tower   Minneapolis 55424
8009 34th Avenue South
FAX: 952-851-1610
CONTACT: Kathy Tunheim
E-MAIL: email@tunheim.com
WWW: tunheim.com
SERVICES: Public relations and communications management in areas of sports, entertainment, technology, retail, consumer products, business-to-business, institutional, professional services, regulated industries, financial services.
CAPABILITIES: Positioning, Media Relations, Community Relations, Special Events, Crisis Communications Management, Public Affairs, Sponsorship Marketing.
CURRENT/RECENT CLIENTS/PROJECTS: American Express, Andersen Corp., Chicago Motor Speedway, Chip Ganassi Racing, CART, Delta Dental Plan of Minnesota, Edgemail.com, e-Intelligence Inc., Fanball.com, DARE America, Jase Software, Met Council, Metris Companies, Microsoft North Central District, Medtronic, Inc., Multifoods, Rain Bird, Target Corporation, Barclays Global Investors, Gelco Promotional Network, Iowa Assn. of Independent Colleges and Universities, Mystic Lake Casino, Ranier Technology, Seren Innovations.
PRESIDENT/CEO/OWNER: Kathy Tunheim-President/COE; John Harden-Chief Operating Officer; Ellie Lucas, Executive Vice President; Angela Collins-Senior Vice President; Mark Andrew- Senior Vice President; Robert Bausch-Senior Vice President

U

UNIVERSITY MEDIA RESOURCES   612-624-6079
540 Rarig Center   Minneapolis 55409
330 21st Avenue South
FAX: 612-625-5022
CONTACT: Mary Kelley
E-MAIL: kelle020@tc.umn.edu
WWW: umrtv.cee.umn.edu/
SERVICES: Video and multi-media production company with award-winning staff available to assist with project design, script writing, production and editing.
CAPABILITIES: UMR facilities include: broadcast production studies, electronic classrooms, Beta-SP and S-VHS editing suites, EFP and Digital camera packages. Ability to originate satellite teleconferences from its studies or designated campus locations.
CURRENT/RECENT CLIENTS/PROJECTS: Service to University departments, government agencies, non-profits and private sectors.

Film & Video Producers / 215

PRESIDENT/CEO/OWNER: Regents of the University of Minnesota.

V

VANBAR PRODUCTIONS 612-544-9262
PO Box 27447 Minneapolis 55427
FAX: 612-546-8954
CONTACT: Barry ZeVan
E-MAIL: bnz1@aol.com

VENUS DIRECTIONS 651-636-0838
1519 McClung Drive Arden Hills 55112
FAX: 651-636-0958
CONTACT: Andres A. Parra
E-MAIL: andresdp@aol.com
CAPABILITIES: Bilingual Director (Spanish/English). Director of photography specializing in documentaries, corporate image and human interest pieces; full BetaCam-SP package available 16:9 capabilities. Offer state-of-the-art multi-language Computerized Teleprompting Service for video, film and presidential-style live presentations. Executive speech coaching available. All products and services are custom-designed to meet your specific goals and objectives. Voice-over and on-camera talent in Spanish.
SPECIALTIES: Creating images that move your message. International expertise.
PRESIDENT/CEO/OWNER: Andres A. Parra, President/Owner

VIDEO HOME SERVICES 612-721-2333
5216 33rd Avenue South Minneapolis 55417
FAX: 612-721-4004
CONTACT: Alan Naumann
E-MAIL: anaumann1@compuserve.com
WWW: videohomeservices.com
SERVICES: Video tape duplication; Event shooting - single or multi-camera, live mixing, all formats. All production services. No project is too small. I work on each aspect, from concept to completion. I make "repeating" video tapes of promo or corporate videos to be used at trade shows. Consulting services, seminars, speeches. Editing of your video footage - all formats. Photo collage on video with music and graphics.
CAPABILITIES: I have three non-linear editing systems, one of which is uncompressed video, so if you can imagine it, we can product it. One non-linear system I use for "on location video editing" for conferences, retreats, etc. I also supply all the camera work for the event and am able to produce high quality daily videos of the event. I have been in business since 1988 and enjoy working with individuals, small businesses, or non-profit organizations. I work in all formats - VHS, SVHS, 8mm, Hi-8, Beta SP, Mini DV, DVCPro, DVCam.
CURRENT/RECENT CLIENTS/PROJECTS: Greater Minneapolis Chamber of Commerce (GMCC); Grace Church - Edina; Evangelical Free Church of America; Compaq Computer Corporation; Campus Crusade for Christ; Continental Airlines; Excel Corporation; Howbrite Solutions (Educational & Training Videos).

216 / Film & Video Producers

VIDEOMED, INC.   612-938-6994
5109 Ridge Road   Minneapolis 55436
FAX: 612-938-6994
CONTACT: K.Y. Terry
E-MAIL: kaimaterry@aol.com
SERVICES: 10 years track record in custom production service for global companies and healthcare industry.
CAPABILITIES: Capable of producing culturally sensitive programs (include idea and message development, scripting, providing ethnic characters) in foreign languages: Chinese, Spanish and Hmong. Extensive experience in health information productions, present complete business concepts or technology in clear, understandable and persuasive manner.
CURRENT/RECENT CLIENTS/PROJECTS: University of Minnesota; Boeing; Computing Device International; American Assoc. Pediatric Ophthalmology Society.

W

WG COMMUNICATIONS   612-377-7900
227 Colfax Avenue North   Minneapolis 55405
FAX: 612-377-1056
CONTACT: Fritz Basgen
E-MAIL: fritz@wilsongriak.com
WWW: wgcommunications.com
SERVICES: We're a full service video and film production company. We create entire programs--writing, producing, directing--from conception to duplication. We're known for programs that have a focussed message, along with engaging and memorable creative.
CAPABILITIES: We've had a lot of experience ad success working with senior executives. We excel working on location, both domestic and overseas. And we work in a variety of mediums: film, video, DVD video, DVD-ROM and CD-ROM.

GARY WICKS   612-595-9196
13423 Larkin Drive   Minnetonka 55305
CONTACT: Gary Wicks
E-MAIL: gljwicks@earthlilnk.net
SERVICES: Provide strategies and solutions to clients regarding how to best meet their communication needs. Provide project management of interactive programs for presentation, training, and marketing purposes and web site development. Produce/direct corporate video programs and business meetings.
CURRENT/RECENT CLIENTS/PROJECTS: Media Productions; MN Department of Children; Families and Learning; MN Video Productions; The St. Paul Companies; 3M; Lawson Software; Compass Media; Media Loft; Champion Auto Stores.

WILSON GRIAK   612-377-7900
227 Colfax Avenue North   Minneapolis 55405
FAX: 612-377-1056
CONTACT: Ridge Henderson
E-MAIL: film@wilsongriak.com
WWW: wilsongriak.com
SERVICES: Film production company.

CAPABILITIES: Television commercials. Television programming.

WILSON PRODUCTIONS 952-943-0774
10300 Valley View Road #111 Eden Prairie 55344
FAX: 952-943-0838
CONTACT: Dick Kohl
E-MAIL: wilsonproductions@uswest.net
CAPABILITIES: Corporate and broadcast video services, displays/exhibit systems, meeting/events.

Film & Video Support Services

A

ADTECH COMMUNICATIONS GROUP
8220 Commonwealth Drive #201
FAX: 952-944-5643
CONTACT: Maureen Lundberg
E-MAIL: sales@adtechinc.com
WWW: adtechinc.com

952-944-6347
Eden Prairie 55344

SERVICES: Since 1982 we've been bringing technology, creativity and artistry together in a synergistic way to create award-winning graphics and animation for video, multimedia, web and other emerging electronic technologies. We'll take your graphics/animation from concept through completion. Visit our web site or call to see our demo reel - you'll see award wining animations using leading edge technology including multiple SGI super Unix and NT super workstations and NT based high end Hoodini (read very powerful), Synergy Custom and Adtech Proprietary Software covering a wide range of 2D and 3D software, Pandemonium, additional paint systems and Discreet's Edit Plus non-linear editing. Output is to all electronic media. Technical capabilities include organic terrain growth, organic plant growth, hair and beard growth, kaleidoscope generation, magnetics, particle systems and generation, image morphing, blob metamorphosis, natural phenomenon such as fog and water, lattice deformations, magnets, collisions, ray tracing with reflection, refraction and shadows, rotoscoping, bump mapping, texture mapping, environmental mapping, object metamorphosis, inverse kinematics, programmable painterly effects, multiple digital overlays, airbrush effects, object deformations, fractals, etc. - we've got it all!

SPECIALTIES: Concept driven, high end 2D and 3D identity design services, character animation, and dynamic integration of animation with live footage. Award winning animation and design for film, video, web, multimedia, and emerging electronic visual media. Providing integrated design solutions across all your electronic media.

CURRENT/RECENT CLIENTS/PROJECTS: Honeywell, 3M, Minnesota Power, Fisher-Rosemount, Hormel Foods, General Mills, National Car Rental, Datacard, Control Data, Minnegasco, Anderson Windows, Caterpillar Inc., GMAC-RFC, Lutheran Brotherhood, Texas Instruments, Graco, KMSP-TV, Northern States Power, Alpine Industries and more under construction! To discuss ways Adtech can go to work for you, contact Maureen Lundberg at 952-944-6347.

AKERLIND & ASSOCIATES CASTING
212 3rd Avenue North #250
FAX: 612-339-6507
CONTACT: Kat Rapheal, Michelle Masera, Curt Akerlind

612-339-6141
Minneapolis 55401

SERVICES: Casting for features, industrials, commercials, voiceovers, and print ads. On set baby wrangling and youth talent coaching. Wrangling for large extra scenes. Coaching for live talent bookings.

EQUIPMENT: 2,200 square foot studio space, two casting rooms, 3/4" & 1/2" decks. Space rental available.

CURRENT/RECENT CLIENTS/PROJECTS: Films: Sugar & Spice, Drop Dead Gorgeous, Sixth Sense, Stepmom, Ed TV, Jingle All the Way, Mighty Ducks, Mighty Ducks II, Mighty Ducks D3, and Equinox. Commercial and/or Print: Walt Disney World, Coca Cola, Marie Callender's, Midol, Huggies, Leap Frog, Target, Pampers, Pillsbury, National Egg Board, Miller Light, MCI, Timex and Centrum.

PRESIDENT/CEO/OWNER: Curt Akerlind

Film & Video Support Services / 219

BRUCE S. ALLEN, INC.   612-341-0660
1018 North Fifth Street   Minneapolis 55411
FAX: 612-333-2278
CONTACT: Bruce S. Allen
CAPABILITIES: Complete scenic studio.
SPECIALTIES: Custom design and fabrication in all media, miniature to giant size sets and props for still, video, film, displays and exhibits.

ALPHA VIDEO   612-896-9898
7711 Computer Avenue   Edina 55435
FAX: 612-896-9899
CONTACT: Rick Risch
E-MAIL: webmaster@alphavideo.com
WWW: alphavideo.com
SERVICES: Alpha Video is a professional video systems dealer of HDTV, DV, Non-linear, Digital and NT Technology, Alpha specializes in the design, configuration, installation, support and training of these video systems in broadcast, cable, corporate, production and education markets. Rental capabilities range from event support to broadcast rental equipment. Services include delivery and set up, camera operation for onsite shoots, fully equipped linear and non-linear edit suites, tape digitizing, and full tape duplication capabilities. SVHS, DCVPRO and BETA SP.
PRESIDENT/CEO/OWNER: Stan Stanek
SALES CONTACT: Rick Risch, Rental Manager; Kevin Groves, Broadcast Sales; Jim Morical, Educational Sales

ARIA PRODUCTIONS   612-840-0196
119 North 4th Street #410   Minneapolis 55401
CONTACT: Dave Coleman
SERVICES: Direction: Film and video - commercials and industrials: i.e. sales, promotion and image, documentary, training. Over 20 years in the business.
SPECIALTIES: Humor, drama, motivational. Matching the right approach to the right audience.
PRESIDENT/CEO/OWNER: Dave Coleman

220 / Film & Video Support Services

B

BABS CASTING 612-332-6858
420 North Fifth Street #312 Minneapolis 55401
FAX: 612-332-6728
CONTACT: Barbara Shelton
CAPABILITIES: Casting of talent.
SPECIALTIES: Casting director for commercials, feature films, industrials and print. Union and non-union.

BASSETT CREEK STUDIO 612-374-0424
1010 Second Avenue North Minneapolis 55405
FAX: 612-377-1056
CONTACT: Phil Sims
WWW: bassettcreekstudio.com
SERVICES: A purpose-built production studio for film, video or still photography. Studio is 92' x 96', not including support space, 2 bathrooms, wardrobe and make-up rooms, 7 telephones, modem connection, fax, copier, camera room, full production kitchen, 2400 amps 120/208 power. On site Grip and Lighting package available.

THE BEAUDRY GROUP **612-940-3244**
3402 Hennepin Avenue South **Minneapolis 55408**
FAX: 612-338-2732
CONTACT: Steve Beaudry
E-MAIL: bg@2z.net
SERVICES: 3- dimensional illustration, miniature sets, ad props.

BLUE MOON PRODUCTIONS, INC. 612-339-7175
212 3rd Avenue No. #390 Minneapolis 55401
FAX: 612-339-4272
CONTACT: John Dehn, Will Hommeyer, Jeff Sylvestre, Danielle Barr
E-MAIL: mail@bluemoonpro.com
CAPABILITIES: Projects range from fundraising and marketing videos to television and radio spots to documentary and educational programs. Blue Moon is committed to working in partnership with organizations that are dedicated to people, the arts and the environment.
EQUIPMENT: Complete Betacam SP camera package includes Arri fresnel lights; component Betacam SP editing suite.
SPECIALTIES: Creative media programs that portray a personal expression. Location documentary video, scriptwriting and original music composition.

C

CANDYLAND PONY SERVICE   **218-568-5680**
4893 Tree Farm Road   Pequot Lakes 56472
FAX: 218-568-5680
CONTACT: Brenda Myers
E-MAIL: bmyers@uslink.net
SERVICES: Children's activities: live pony carousel - we provide pony rides on a pony ring for children under 85 pounds. Candyland ponies have entertained children at many company promotions, company picnics, festivals, events, rodeos and community celebrations. Pony activity and petting coral also available where children can pet, brush, and interact with ponies. Children's games such as toddler horseshoes, ball toss, and stick horse relay races also.
CAPABILITIES: Candyland Pony Service is an affiliate business of Meadow Ridge Industries which includes Meadow Ridge Pony Farm, Meadow Ridge guest house and a wholesale/retail distribution business. The pony service is operated by a family unit, Brad, Brenda and Brooke Myers. The ponies are well trained and are used in other programs at the Farm including Pony Partners and Equine Encounters.
CURRENT/RECENT CLIENTS/PROJECTS: Minnesota Horse Expo; Minnetonka Summer Fest; Ralph Lauren Polo Classic; High Ball Ranch Rodeo; Austin Medical Center; Liberty Savings Bank; Deep Haven Centennial; Universal Pensions; St. Joseph Medical Center; Rainbow Food Stores; Byerly's Grocery; Mills Motors; Bean Hole Days - Pequot Lakes

BRENT CASEY, INC. PHOTO/FILM STYLING   **612-822-7676**
4312 First Avenue South   Minneapolis 55409
FAX: 612-822-7673
CONTACT: Brent Casey
PAGER: 651-229-5625
SERVICES: Production, project coordination, set design/set dressing, props, wardrobe, and creative direction. Clothing and accessories; both on and off figure. 15+ years' photo styling and adjunct experience. Accomplished in studio or location (multiple room sets through small sets.)
CAPABILITIES: Creative approach with nearly all aspects of project including stretching budgets. Discounts for portfolio building photo/film/video. Portfolio and references available.

CINE SERVICE   **952-945-9999**
4015 Auburn Drive   Minnetonka 55305
FAX: 952-945-9444
CONTACT: Matthew Quast, C.A.S.
CAPABILITIES: Production sound mixer/recordist for film and video production. 25 years experience in feature, commercial and documentary production.
EQUIPMENT: Magra IVSTC (stereo with time code). Nagra 4.2L Fostex PD/4 Time Code DAT; Sennheiser, Neumann, Sony, Schoeps, Tram and E-V Microphones; Cooper 6-channel and Shure FP32A mixer; Lectrosonics wireless mics; playback system; numerous accessories.
PRESIDENT/CEO/OWNER: Matthew Quast, C.A.S.

222 / Film & Video Support Services

CINE SOUND 2   612-866-5049
6461 Lyndale Avenue South   Richfield 55423
CONTACT: Dennis O'Rourke
CAPABILITIES: Two full-service audio studios for commercial, industrial, television programs and feature films. Features: AMS/NEVE Logic 3 Digital Console with moving fader automation & surround sound for mixing. Re-recording, ADR, foley and narration.
SERVICES: All digital audio mixing/recording/editing from any combination of source material from all video formats listed 35mm, RDAT, DA88 and timecode 1/4". Sound design, complete ADR/Looping stage. Lay-up/lay-back from /to all formats listed. Online interformat video editing. We have an extensive music and sound effects library.
FORMAT: Video: Digital Betacam, D2, 1", Beta SP, 3/4", SVHS, Hi8, Audio: RDAT, DA88, timecode 1/4", 35mm, 16mm optical and 16mm mag.
SPECIALTIES: Over 25 years experience in film and video sound design (editing and mixing for feature film, commercial, industrial, documentary and network television programs).
PRESIDENT/CEO/OWNER: Dennis O'Rourke

COLLEEN SZOT WONDERFUL WRITER, INC.   763-557-7116
13615 61st Avenue North   Minneapolis 55446
FAX: 763-551-4831
CONTACT: Colleen Szot
TOLL FREE: 888-557-7116
E-MAIL: colleenszot@aol.com
WWW: colleenszot.com
TYPES OF WRITING: Clio award-winning writer of more than 100 direct response/infomercials (CNN's Cold War, George Foreman, Orlimar Trimental, Tony Little, Select Comfort, David Dikeman Command Performance) plus TV commercials (Wendy's, Walt Disney, Kraft, Nutri-Grain cereal), Corporate and Training Videos (Dayton-Hudson Corporation, 3M), and all print (ads, brochure, direct mail collateral). Author of best-selling book (Christian Wives), writer for cable television, 22 years experience with J. Walter Thompson, Foote, Cone & Belding, and Campbell-Mithun-Esty.
WRITTEN FOR: CNN, George Foreman, Target, Walt Disney Pictures, Troy-Bilt, HomeRight (PaintStick), 3M, Select Comfort, Tony Little and more.
SPECIALTIES: All broadcast, plus corporate videos/film, cable television.

Film & Video Support Services / 223

CONUS PRODUCTIONS & SATELLITE SERVICES
3415 University Avenue
651-642-4477
Minneapolis 55414
FAX: 651-642-4551
CONTACT: Brian Tuttle
CAPABILITIES: Single and multi-camera video production service. Mobile and fixed satellite uplinks, and full production crews available for event broadcast.
EQUIPMENT: Sony CCD cameras, modular control rooms. Chyron graphics. Support Beta SP video tape format 4 uplink trucks, tape playback.
SPECIALTIES: Mobile uplink and multi-camera video production.
PRESIDENT/CEO/OWNER: Terry O'Reilly, GM

CRASH & SUES
510 Marquette Avenue #600
612-338-7947
Minneapolis 55402
FAX: 612-338-4601
CONTACT: Crash Medin
E-MAIL: crash@crash-sues.com
WWW: crash-sues.com
SERVICES: C-Reality Film to tape transfer system with Da Vinci 2K color correction system; fire HD and D1 online edit; inferno HD graphics and compositing; 2D/3D CGI; closed captioning; videoboards, and duplication/traffic; NTSC/PAL; various multi-media capabilities; Echoboys original music, sound design and mix.
CAPABILITIES: Expertise in television commercials, music videos.

D

JACKIE DALTON
PO Box 1857
612-934-9554
Minnetonka 55345
CONTACT: Jackie Dalton
SERVICES: Voice work/voiceover for on-hold messages and film. Actress for commercial work, industrial film, television and motion pictures.
CAPABILITIES: Accents: New York, Southern. British, Irish (does a younger voice and an old voice). Enjoys comedy.
CURRENT/RECENT CLIENTS/PROJECTS: Voiceovers for on-hold messaging. Clients included Babies-R-Us, Williamson-Dickie, Corp., Domino's Pizza, Holiday Inn and other companies throughout the US.

224 / Film & Video Support Services

MELISSA DALTON
PO Box 1857

612-934-9554
Minnetonka 55345

CONTACT: Melissa Dalton
SERVICES: Actress for commercial work; industrial film; motion pictures and television; including voice work/voiceover.
CAPABILITIES: Comedy, improvization, accents/dialects, soprano voice, dance experience and musical theatre.
CURRENT/RECENT CLIENTS/PROJECTS: Summer Stock Theatre 1999 Alexandria, MN; 1999 Training Video for Master Communications, Minneapolis, MN; 2000 Acting and Directing, St. Cloud State University Theatre Dept., St. Cloud, MN

SHARON DAVIS MAKE UP ARTIST
3636 Fairlawn Drive

952-475-2501
Minnetonka 55345

FAX: 612-538-8887
CONTACT: Sharon Davis
E-MAIL: sharondavis@juno.com
SERVICES: Freelance makeup and hair for film, video, still photography, and live events since 1984. Natural to character look. Extensive kit including special effects. Wig and facial hair collection, Sanitary makeup application.
CAPABILITIES: Multi-tasks if requested: script notes, logsheets, teleprompter operation, wardrobe, etc. Experienced in accident and illness simulation, likenesses and transformations, prostethic and hair goods application.
PRESIDENT/CEO/OWNER: Sharon Davis

DIGITAL PICTURES, INC.
212 N. 2nd Street

612-371-4515
Minneapolis 55401

FAX: 612-371-4527
CONTACT: Shelby Zavoral
E-MAIL: shelby@digitalpictures.com
WWW: digitalpictures.com or targacine.com
SERVICES: Computer system integration, training and consultation for adding digital video editing, 3D modeling and digital content creation to your services. We also offer 3D animation production services.
SPECIALTIES: Authorized resellers and trainers for Autodesk 3D products, Discreet, Pinnacle, Matrox, Alias/Wavefront, Intergraph, IBM, Apple, Adobe.
PRESIDENT/CEO/OWNER: Tom Grotting

ANDREA J. DUCANE
1169 Ashland Avenue

651-645-9922
St. Paul 55104

FAX: 651-527-5464
CONTACT: Andrea Ducane
CAPABILITIES: Freelance makeup for film, video, B & W and color photography. Experienced in application and maintenance of corrective, dramatic, fashion and "no-makeup" look.
SERVICES: Experience includes: feature films, commercials, P.S.A.'s, television programs, Industrial films, magazine covers and stories and print ads.
CURRENT/RECENT CLIENTS/PROJECTS: Bill Cosby, Sandy Duncan, Anthony Edwards, Gordon Jump, Estelle Getty, Joan Rivers, Olympia Dukakis, Amy Madigan, Chloe Webb, Vikings: Anthony Carter, Christ Carter. Client list available upon request.

Film & Video Support Services / 225

DUPLICATION FACTORY, INC.   612-448-9912
4275 Norex Drive   Chaska 55318
CONTACT: Mitch Waters
SERVICES: Complete video duplication services including duplication in all formats, conversion in all standards, time based correction, monitored by a state of the art quality control system. Ancillary services including package design consulting, high-speed automated packaging, individual fulfillment and warehousing.
SPECIALTIES: Large quantity, fast turn-around duplication manufactured above industry standards in a complete clean room environment.

E

ELECTRONIC INTERIORS, INC.   651-292-1035
40 Mackubin Street   St. Paul 55102
FAX: 651-292-1063
CONTACT: Kate O'Reilly
E-MAIL: info@electronicinteriors.com
WWW: electronicinteriors.com
SERVICES: Professional consultants and designers for state-of-the-art presentation spaces and technical facilities; complete planning and design services as well as total project administration services; creatively design technology into user-friendly environments; independent of all equipment manufacturers and vendors; assist client in equipment selection.
CURRENT/RECENT CLIENTS/PROJECTS: Target Headquarters; U of Minnesota; Key Investments; Metris Companies.
PRESIDENT/CEO/OWNER: Dickson Stewart/Kate O'Reilly

F

BILL FELKER   612-339-7803
4802 Quail Avenue North   Crystal 55429
CONTACT: William H. Felker
PAGER: 612-374-6797
E-MAIL: felkerfam@earthlink.net
SERVICES: Director of camera, and lighting for 35mm, 16mm, and videotape; macro, time-lapse, motion control, go motion, slow motion and creative editing. Film off-line facilities, camera for rent; lighting/camera expertise.
SPECIALTIES: High-speed, time-lapse, macro, tabletop, sets and locations. Food, people and exteriors.

FILM FOOD   612-781-1412
550 39th Avenue NE #115   Minneapolis 55421
FAX: 612-781-1931
SERVICES: Catered meals for film and video production. Homemade, nutritious meals for hardworking crews.
CAPABILITIES/SPECIALTIES: In the studio or on location.
PRESIDENT/CEO/OWNER: Kim Christensen

226 / Film & Video Support Services

MOE FLAHERTY
PO Box 580821
CONTACT: Deborah Fiscus
CAPABILITIES: Camera assistant.

612-339-7329
Minneapolis 55458

FLYING COLORS INCORPORATED　　　　　　　612-752-0200
917 North 5th Street　　　　　　　　　　　　Minneapolis 55401
CONTACT: Bob Sullivan, VP; Rick Cornish, CD
CAPABILITIES: Complete concepting, design, and production services. From analysis of your needs and your audience, to implementing a creative solution, to broadcast-quality production, distribution, and presentation...to evaluating the program's impact.
SPECIALTIES: Highly creative, innovative programs that are on-target, on-time, and on-budget. We're experienced specialists in video, multimedia, events and original music.

KIMBERLY FRANSON MODEL/ACTOR　　　　　612-386-5588
AGENCY
1300 Nicollet Mall #220C　　　　　　　　　　Minneapolis 55403
FAX: 612-338-1411
CONTACT: Kimberly Franson
E-MAIL: kfa@kimberlyfranson.com
WWW: kimberlyfranson.com
TYPES OF TALENT: Actors, on and off camera; voice; specialty; men, women, children of all ages and sizes; hair and make-up artists.
TYPES OF MODELS: Fashion, character, real people, celebrity, men, women, and children of all ages and sizes.
SPECIALTIES: Providing models and actors for all types of industry work. Preparing and conducting castings for clients.
CURRENT/RECENT CLIENTS/PROJECTS: Farouk Systems, Toni & Guy, Shandwick International, Spiderman Movie Casting, Wella Corporation, Maxim Magazine, Target, Ford Motor Company, Hoyle, Regis Corporation, Scruples, Procter & Gamble.

STEVE FRIEDERICHSEN, INC.　　　　　　　　　952-928-9354
6228 Oxford Street　　　　　　　　　　　　　St. Louis Park 55416
FAX: 952-928-9354
CONTACT: Steve Friederichsen

Film & Video Support Services / 227

E-MAIL: fps@mn.state.net
WWW: state.net/fps
SERVICES: Director of Photography/cameraman. Lighting and camera work for commercials, corporate film/video and broadcast.
CAPABILITIES: Film and video, all formats. Arri SR2 and Sony Betacam camera packages.

LINDA FROILAND	651-866-0021
190 Rose Street	Marine 55047

FAX: 651-433-3279
CONTACT: Linda Froiland
E-MAIL: lfroiland@aol.com
SERVICES: Stylist, Production Designer Costumes. Wardrobe, sets, props and make-up. Background - theatre museum television commercials industrials feature films.
SPECIALTIES: Design skills for customer.
CURRENT/RECENT CLIENTS/PROJECTS: Setterholm Productions, Wilson Griak, Maki Strunc, Judy Olausen Cognito

G

KENNETH GAMMELL	612-788-7594
3307 Lincoln Street NE	Minneapolis 55418

CONTACT: Kenneth Gammell
E-MAIL: kgprophet@aol.com
SERVICES: Editor/Post production supervisor: film, Video, Sound, Music.
CAPABILITIES: Complete post production services including Avid non-linear editing, Pro-Tools, 32 track digital recording studio. Graphics, sound effects, music. Broadcast, industrial, features. Nineteen years in business.
CURRENT/RECENT CLIENTS/PROJECTS: General Mills, 3M, Shandwick, Minneapolis Auto Dealers Assoc., several independent short films, 35 mm Feature "Acid Snow."

GREATAPES CORPORATION	612-872-8284
1523 Nicollet Avenue	Minneapolis 55403

FAX: 612-872-0635
CONTACT: Robert M. McCarthy
TOLL FREE: 1-800-879-8273
CAPABILITIES: We can develop your project from concept to completion, or just polish a piece of it. GT Media offers digital audio/video production and post. On-line and off-line video edit suites, 2D and 3D Macintosh based graphics and paint box, studio and remote video production, video duplication, digital audio recording and editing, sweetening for video, complete sound effects and music library. On-staff producer, director and composer. Complete video/audio graphics and packaging needs.
EQUIPMENT: On-line: Sony digital switcher, Sony DME 3000 Digital effects, Abekas A-72 Digital CG, Flint Graphics, Video Explorer, Digital BetaCam, Component Beta SP, 1" HI-8, S-VHS, Sonic Solutions audio workstation, ISDN digital patch, serial R-DAT, Non-linear: ImMIX Video Cube. In-house 35 x 30 video studio, Ikegami cameras, full production support.
SPECIALTIES: Innovative, inspirational, broadcast and educational video and audio productions. Corporate image, training, language translation, commercial, multimedia programs.

228 / Film & Video Support Services

GREATAPES CORPORATION
1523 Nicollet Avenue
FAX: 612-872-0635
CONTACT: Robert M. McCarthy
TOLL FREE: 1-800-879-8273

612-872-8284
Minneapolis 55403

CAPABILITIES: We can develop your project from concept to completion, or just polish a piece of it. Digital video/audio production and post. On-line and off-line video edit suites, Macintosh-based and Flint SGI-based graphics and compositing, studio and remote video production, video duplication, digital audio recording and editing, sweetening for video and a complete sound effects and music library. GT Media has its own on-staff producers, engineers and composers. We can also provide complete video/audio graphics and packaging needs.

EQUIPMENT: On-line: Sony digital switcher, Sony DME 3000 Digital effects, Abekas A-72 Digital CG, Flint Graphics, Video Explorer, Digital BetaCam, Component Beta SP, 1" HI-8, S-VHS, Sonic Solutions audio workstation, ISDN digital patch, serial R-DAT, Non-linear: ImMIX Video Cube. In-house 35 x 30 video studio, Ikegami cameras, full production support.

SPECIALTIES: Innovative, inspirational, broadcast and educational video and audio productions. Corporate image, training, language translation, commercial, multi-media programs.

GREEN MAN PYROTECHNICS
8118 Vincent Avenue South
CONTACT: David Hall
E-MAIL: pyro@pioneerplanet.infi.net
WWW: pioneerplanet.infi.net/~pyro

612-881-5758
Bloomington 55431

SERVICES: Licensed pyrotechnician specializing in living fireworks and other pyrotechnic special effects.

THE GREENE SHEET
3009 74th Avenue North
FAX: 763-560-6647
CONTACT: Sam Howard
E-MAIL: unclegeo@bpsi.net
WWW: bstock.com

763-560-3292
Brooklyn Park 55444

SERVICES: Uncle Geo's Greene Sheet is a brokerage firm specializing in used and B-stock production equipment. We serve the video, film, audio and multimedia industries. There are no fees for listing, only when we sell your gear. Staffed by experienced production professionals, the Greene Sheet is the oldest equipment brokerage on the web. Over 15 years of system design experience is available to help our customers make informed decisions about buying and selling used gear.

CAPABILITIES: System appraisals available for production companies, banks and leasing companies.

PRESIDENT/CEO/OWNER: George F. Greene

GULENCHYN, INC.
3425 34th Avenue South
CONTACT: Mike Gulenchyn

612-724-1722
Minneapolis 55406

Film & Video Support Services / 229

SERVICES: Labor: gaffer; lighting director; electrician; rigger; key grip; weapons specialist. Equipped with electrical distribution, rigging, lighting and grip.
CAPABILITIES: 30 years in the motion picture industry. Competent, experienced, and well equipped.
CURRENT/RECENT CLIENTS/PROJECTS: James Productions/Internet TV Commercial; Young and Company/Mercury Outboards; Young & Company/Eureka Vacuums; Young & Company/Porsche; Movie: "Here on Earth", 20th Century Fox; Movie: "Sugar and Spice."

GUTHRIE THEATER COSTUME RENTALS 612-375-8722
3100 California Street NE Minneapolis 55418
FAX: 612-375-8733
CONTACT: Deb Murphy
E-MAIL: costumes@guthrietheater.org
WWW: guthrietheater.org/act-II/costume-rental.htm
CAPABILITIES: Rental of classical theatrical period costumes ranging from Gothic to contemporary, including hats, shoes, and accessories, designed for the Guthrie stage.
PRESIDENT/CEO/OWNER: Joe Dowling. Artistic Director

H

HARMONY BOX 612-331-2699
1414 Marshall Street N.E. Minneapolis 55413
FAX: 612-623-8147
CONTACT: Kathy Nygard
E-MAIL: stage@harmonybox.com
WWW: harmonybox.com
SERVICES: Sound stage for film, video and photography.
CAPABILITIES: 60' x 80' x 31' clear, state-of-the-art facility designed specifically for film and commercial video production industry needs. 25' x 60' cover wall, 10' x 20' x 8' special effects pit and 50' x 35' loading/staging area. Drive-in loading and stage access, 2 dressing rooms. Makeup area, 2 production offices with dedicated phones with fax and copy capabilities, bathroom with showers, and foodservice staging area. Scissors lift, 3000 amp service. Off-street parking for up to 70 vehicles. On-site set design, fabrication and installation for film, video, photography, and meetings available through Nygard Set Design.
CURRENT/RECENT CLIENTS/PROJECTS: Film and video production including commercial television advertising, corporate video and music video production. Best Buy Company, Inc. commercial featuring Alanis Morissette and Tori Amos, Columbia Records/DNA Inc. Aerosmith music video, Gold'n Plump Chicken commercial, Sears Roebuck & Company commercial. Production Companies/Agencies: A Band Apart/Harder-Fuller Films, Area 51, Hallau Shoots & Company, Buck Holzemer Productions, Juntunen Media Group Inc., Twist Production, Two Popes, Voodoo Films and Young & Company.

HDMG DESIGN, POST & EFFECTS 952-943-1711
6573 City West Parkway Eden Prairie 55344
FAX: 952-943-1957

230 / Film & Video Support Services

CONTACT: Design/Animation: Angella Kassube, Andy Reynolds, Brian Olson; Editors/Compositors: Jamie Heuton, Greg Mattern, Michael Guncheon, Jessie Yerama; Assistant Editor: John Gleim; DVD Author: Mike Faustgen; Location Production: Jamie Heuton; Accounts: Mona Cifaldi; Scheduling: Marci Meyocks; Traffic: Kim Schafer
E-MAIL: info@hdmg.com
WWW: www.hdmg.com
SERVICES: HDMG is an organization of people who love what we do. We have fun doing great work with intelligent clients (yes, that would be you) in a joint bursting with cool equipment. We are a producer-support service that promotes a direct partnership between producers and operators. We provide digital editing, design, paint, animation, special effects and compositing, DVD authoring and Avid non-linear offline in a relaxed, creative environment. We are an operator-run facility, with all owners and operators directly responsible for developing client relationships and maintaining our facility. Since we have no account reps, every client receives direct operator contact throughout their project. Cool!
EQUIPMENT: Fire, 2 Digital Editing suites mastering to Digital Betacam, 2 Avid Offlines, Flint, 2 DF/X Composium Graphics/Animation suites, Intergraph running 3D Studio Max, MacLab with PhotoShop, After Effects and Illustrator, Ultimatte 8, Insert stage with Ultimatte Memory Head, Sonic Solutions DVD Creator with 5.1 Dolby Digital surround, and many tape formats including Digital Betacam, D5, D2, DV/DVC Pro, DV Cam, MII, Beta SP, 3/4", 1", Hi-8, S-VHS, VHS (including international formats), DAT and DA88. Co-located with PostAudio, Inc., a sync mix facility featuring 2 digital audio suites.

HOUSE OF CINEMAGRAPHICS	612-339-7803
4802 Quail Avenue North	Minneapolis 55429

CONTACT: William Felker
PAGER: 612-374-6797
SERVICES: Camera and lighting direction for 35mm, 16mm, and videotape, macro, time-lapse, motion control, go motion, slow motion experience in table tops to large sets and locations. 5mm, 16mm off-line facilities. Lighting/camera expertise. Aerial cinematography.
CAPABILITIES: Camera and lighting for tabletops, sets and locations, high speed to time lapse. Food, people and exteriors.

MELINDA HUTCHINSON	612-920-2884
2913 Toledo Avenue South	St. Louis Park 55416

CONTACT: Melinda Hutchinson
SERVICES: Food styling for print and motion. 15 years experience.

I

INDEPENDENT FEATURE PROJECT/NORTH	612-338-0871
401 N. 3rd Street #450	Minneapolis 55401

FAX: 612-338-4747
CONTACT: Jane Minton
E-MAIL: word@ifpnorth.org
WWW: ifp.org

Film & Video Support Services / 231

SERVICES: Quarterly newsletter, MN Independent film fund. McKnight screenwriting fellowship, weekly e-mail update, monthly film showcase & Bryant Lake Bowl, low-budget crew database, many screening opportunities, IFP/North resource center, overall support of filmmakers at every level.
CAPABILITIES: IFP/North supports and promotes promising MN independent filmmakers, producers, writers, directors and anyone who has a passion for film and filmmaking.
CURRENT/RECENT CLIENTS/PROJECTS: IFP/North has over 300 members active in the film/video world.
PRESIDENT/CEO/OWNER: Jane Minton, Executive Director

J

JAGGED EDGE
311 1st Avenue North #304
612-332-4440
Minneapolis 55401
FAX: 612-332-4441
CONTACT: Joe Martin
CAPABILITIES: At Jagged Edge creativity, talent and experience come before extravagance and inflated pricing. We offer fully uncompressed AVID off-line/on-line, digibeta, web services and more.
SPECIALTIES: Commercials, music videos, and corporate.
PRESIDENT/CEO/OWNER: Dan Jagunich

DAN JAGUNICH
311 1st Avenue North #304
612-332-4440
Minneapolis 55401
FAX: 612-332-4441
CONTACT: Joe Martin
CAPABILITIES: At Jagged Edge creativity, talent and experience come before extravagance and inflated pricing. We offer fully uncompressed AVID off-line/on-line, digibeta, web services and more.
SPECIALTIES: Commercials, music videos, and corporate.
PRESIDENT/CEO/OWNER: Dan Jagunich

JOHMAR FARMS
14330 Ostrum Trail North
651-433-5312
Marine on St. Croix 55047
FAX: Same - call first
CONTACT: John or Mary Block
E-MAIL: johmar@onvoymail.com
SERVICES: Animals, props.
CAPABILITIES: Animals: domestic or exotics. Props: buggies, carriages, sleighs, cars, trucks or any hard to find items.
CURRENT/RECENT CLIENTS/PROJECTS: Feature film, ad agencies, production companies, corporate in-house, film studios, photographers, TV, festivals, corporate events, plays and productions.

JUNTUNEN MEDIA GROUP
708 North First Street
612-341-3348
Minneapolis 55401
FAX: 612-341-0242
CONTACT: John Gorski
ALTERNATE PHONE: 800-535-4366

232 / Film & Video Support Services

E-MAIL: mjuntunen@juntunen.com
WWW: juntunen.com
SERVICES: Discover Juntunen and "see what's on your mind." Total production support and services in a fully-integrated, digital facility. Our staff includes seasoned directors of photography, editors, design artists, visual and sound designers. Our combination of imagination, equipment and service, turns your vision into reality. Our creative images and sound design result in effective communications products for your corporate video, television, advertising, or public relations. Juntunen Media 2000: Broadband services. DVD authoring. Full digital video support. Webcasting. Visual web-based library: catalog and store all your brand assets. Retrieve from anywhere in the world and repurpose.
CURRENT/RECENT CLIENTS/PROJECTS: Clients include commercial and corporate producers; corporate marketing; brand identity and communications directors; sports and entertainment marketers.
PRESIDENT/CEO/OWNER: Bill Juntunen

JUNTUNEN MOBILE TELEVISION
708 N. First Street
612-798-0538
Minneapolis 55401
FAX: 612-798-0547
CONTACT: Bob Rohde or Erich Manwarren
E-MAIL: brohde@juntunen.com or emanwarren@juntunen.com
WWW: juntunen.com
SERVICES: When your event requires experts accustomed to large-scale television production, Juntunen's team cannot be equaled. With two 53-foot digital production mobile units at their disposal, our professionals serve television networks, corporate or organization clients-broadcasting large meetings, news, sporting or entertainment events. Each truck, containing a digital television control room has a 12 camera capacity. Depending on the size and type of event, each truck can accommodate up to a 20 person staff. Juntunten Mobile is the only Minnesota-based business offering large-scale digital broadcast production vehicles.
CURRENT/RECENT CLIENTS/PROJECTS: 3M Annual Meeting; NWA Service Banquet; CBS and ABC News Primary coverage; NBA and Major League Baseball; ValueVision "wine.com", Bobby McFerrin at the Guthrie, VH-1 "Opening Night Live."

K

THE KEEP, INC.
245 2nd Avenue North
612-673-9469
Minneapolis 55401
FAX: 612-673-9668
CONTACT: Jud Williams
E-MAIL: jud@keep-inc.com
WWW: keep-inc.com
CAPABILITIES: Climate-controlled computer driven storage vault for film magnetic media, flat art, heroes and props. For the computer and software industry, system backups and software (Source Code), escrow services are available. Organization, rapid retrieval, inventorying, duping and distribution.
PRESIDENT/CEO/OWNER: Thomas Ingledew

KING PRODUCTIONS
2877 Holmes Avenue South
612-824-3171
Minneapolis 55408
FAX: 612-822-5813

Film & Video Support Services / 233

CONTACT: Bob King
E-MAIL: kingbob@bigfoot.com
PAGER: 612-613-1090
SERVICES: Location cameraman with equipment (video). Location soundman with equipment (film and video). Location crew with equipment (video).
CAPABILITIES: Specializing in documentary, corporate communications, commercials, dramatic film and direct-sale video. My professional background includes writing, producing, directing and both film and video editing. Broadcast-grade Betacam/lighting/audio equipment package includes clear scan camera, internal focus lenses, matte box and filters, eight lighting instruments and wireless audio.
CURRENT/RECENT CLIENTS/PROJECTS: ABC News, CBS News, NBC News, CNN, A & E Network, Discovery Channel, Court TV, numerous corporate and commercial clients, and short films "Cottonwood" and "A Day with Andrew Hiskler".
PRESIDENT/CEO/OWNER: Bob King

L

DEBORAH LAKE/WITTA MAKE-UP ARTIST   612-823-6762
4625 1st Avenue South   Minneapolis 55409
FAX: 612-823-6762
CONTACT: Deborah Lake/Witta
PAGER: 650-2881
E-MAIL: dlakewit@isd.net
SERVICES: "Key" makeup and hair for film, photo, video, movies, fashion and people. Resume available.
SPECIALTIES: Diverse in all skin tones. Specializing in difficult shoots and people. Over 15 years in the industry. Areas Operated in: local, regional, national.
CURRENT/RECENT CLIENTS/PROJECTS: "The Tipical Mary Ellen Show" - HGTV; Meredith Baxter-Birney - CH 9 News; Real Sex, HBO; "Thank God I found You" Video Mariah Carey; 98 Degrees - Pop Singing Group, "Joe", Pop recording artist; Life Fitness; Target.
PRESIDENT/CEO/OWNER: Deborah Lake/Witta

LAPINSKI PRODUCTIONS, LTD.   612-843-4297
1828 Jefferson Street NE   Minneapolis 55418
CONTACT: Patrick Lapinski
E-MAIL: lapinski@minn.net
SERVICES: Complete video production and post production services for corporate and industrial communications. Multi-media project management and creative development.
CAPABILITIES: Industrial maritime training and marketing video production and still photography.
CURRENT/RECENT CLIENTS/PROJECTS: 3M; Digi International; Seaway Port of Duluth; Lake Carriers' Association; American Steamship Company.

LAWRENCE FRIED   1-800-417-2480
1109 Xerxes Avenue South   Minneapolis 55405
CONTACT: Lawrence Fried
CAPABILITIES: Production sound recordist/sound equipment rental for film production.

234 / Film & Video Support Services

EQUIPMENT: Complete location recording packages including time code DAT's, stereo time code Nagras; smart slates, comteks, various wireless and shotgun microphones, boompoles, soundcarts, etc.
PRESIDENT/CEO/OWNER: Lawrence Fried

LIGHTHOUSE, INC.   612-627-9080
816 Ninth Street SE Minneapolis   Minneapolis 55414
FAX: 612-627-9789
CONTACT: Mitch Thompson
WWW: lominn.net/~lthouse
SERVICES: Lighthouse is a full service production equipment rental, sales, and repair company. We supply lighting, grip, electrical and motion picture camera equipment featuring our area's largest expendable and equipment inventories. Our rental department has studio packages, 10 ton, 5 ton, 3 ton, and 1 ton grip trucks, Fisher and Chapman camera dollies, Crawford and Honda generators. NEC power Distribution, Xenotech Xenons, Kino Flo's, and Cameras by Otto Nemenz.
CAPABILITIES: Mole Richardson Master Dealer. Also Dealer for Altman, American Studio Equipment, Arriflex, Bogen Cine, Chapman, Chimera, Desisti, Kino Flo, Koto, Lee Filters, Lowell Lighting, LTM/Lightmaker, Mathews Studio Equipment. Osram/Sylvania, Proltyle Trussing, Rosco Labs, Strand Lighting, Ushio and Videssence.

LIGHTING IN A JAR STUDIOS   952-942-7842
6840 Washington Avenue South   Eden Prairie 55344
FAX: 952-942-7842
CONTACT: Howard Lambert

LIGHTS ON MINNEAPOLIS   612-331-6620
61 Bedford Street SE   Minneapolis 55414
FAX: 612-331-6601
CONTACT: Kolin Mark
E-MAIL: mpls@lightson.com
WWW: lightson.com
SERVICES: Rental, sales and repair of lighting, grip, electrical and support equipment for film, video and still photography.
CAPABILITIES: Grip trucks from corporate to Super 5-ton packages, generators, dollies, daylight and tungsten - balanced lights from 100 to 20,000 watts, chromakey screens and a full line of expendables. Complete stage package at Energy Park Studios.
CURRENT/RECENT CLIENTS/PROJECTS: ABC News; Best Buy; NFL Films; CBS.
PRESIDENT/CEO/OWNER: David Boe

LOCATION AND BACK, LTD.   952-937-2985
15381 Trillium Circle   Eden Prairie 55344
FAX: 952-937-5194
CONTACT: Randy Berglin
E-MAIL: labltd@hotmail.com

Film & Video Support Services / 235

SERVICES: Location and back provides technical and hardware support services to producers, corporate production departments, ad agencies, production companies and producers of business theatre events. With over 30 years experience in video, LAB features HD/4x3 - 16x9 SDTV capabilities. We also offer specialty rental items including FUJINON 70X and 36X lens. Remote pan/tilt compact camera system with 8-preset shot memory. Folsom 9700XL scan converter and DVW-250 Digital Betacam field VTR. Complete multi-camera systems. Ranging from broadcast to high-end industrial cameras. Our continued commitment to quality has become the benchmark for video production and technical services in the upper midwest.

PRESIDENT/CEO/OWNER: Randy Berglin/Lori Berglin, CEO/CFO

M

DAVID MADERICH	**612-721-1462**
5421 29th Avenue South	Minneapolis 55417

CONTACT: David Maderich
ALTERNATE PHONE: 212-505-3553
E-MAIL: nezawithaz@yahoo.com
SERVICES: Makeup and hair for film, video, and print.
CAPABILITIES: 15 years experience in all forms of makeup and hair. New York City based, but travel to Minnesota frequently.
CURRENT/RECENT CLIENTS/PROJECTS: Salem Cigarettes; German Vogue; 3M; Pillsbury; Paisley Park and Prince; Tommy Hilfiger; Donna Karan; Coors Beer; Dove Soap; Matrix Hair.

MAGNETIC PICTURES	**612-341-0632**
121 Washington Avenue South #1618	Minneapolis 55401

FAX: 612-341-0632
CONTACT: Robert Vaaler
E-MAIL: vaaler@magneticpictures.com
SERVICES: Broadcast and corporate video production. ENG/EFP field/location shooting.
CAPABILITIES: Digital Betacam, Betacam SP.

MAINSTREAM COMMUNICATIONS, INC.	**952-888-9000**
9555 James Avenue South #235	Bloomington 55431

CONTACT: Garry Krebs, Bob Ewert
E-MAIL: gkrebs@mainstreamcom.net
WWW: mainstreamcom.net
SERVICES: Mainstream concepts and stages corporate events of all kinds including meetings, trade shows, and special events. Our staff includes the professionals who know how to navigate the challenges of meeting rooms, conventional halls, and trade show floors. Our inventory includes a vast array of audio visual equipment; video and data projection, front and rear screens. Intelligent lighting, and multi-channel sound systems with effects. We warehouse existing sets which are available for rent or we can custom design and build one for you. We also provide live talent and nationally known acts to make your event special.

236 / Film & Video Support Services

CAPABILITIES/SPECIALTIES: We are a turnkey video production environment. Location video crews include Beta SP equipment and complete location lighting and sound recording. Our 1,200 s.f. sound stage includes a lighting package along with available sets. We offer 4 edit suites: Digital Betacam complete with DME, 2 non-linear including DVE, and a portable Beta SP AB-Roll Edit Suite which can be used in-studio or for location events. Other in-house services include 3D animation featuring SoftImage software and a sound recording studio with multiple music libraries.

MATNEY & ASSOCIATES, INC.   507-663-1048
8651 Spring Creek Road   Northfield 55057
FAX: 507-663-7053
CONTACT: Ed Matney
E-MAIL: ematney@microassist.com
SERVICES: Film and tape documentary production.
CAPABILITIES: Ikegami HL-V59W Betacam, complete HMI lighting and audio. Custom field packages.
CURRENT/RECENT CLIENTS/PROJECTS: ABC; CBS; NBC; HBO; Discovery.

MATRIXVIDEO, INC.   952-837-1852
7300 France Avenue #203   Edina 55435
CONTACT: Pete Ellingson
E-MAIL: matrixpete@hotmail.com
WWW: matrixv.com
CAPABILITIES: Editing, film transfer (16mm, 8mm, & Super 8) video duplication of formats: Hi-8, S-VHS, 8mm, Beta SP, DV, D-9 to VHS, S-VHS, Hi-8, DV & 8mm. Basic cuts only linear editing and ABC roll non-linear editing with Toaster NT and flyer. VHS Pal conversions. Video tape to prints, CD ROM & DVD. Digital 8, DV and S-VHS production cameras.
SPECIALTIES: Photos and slides with pan and zooms to most tape formats, non-linear production to and from most tape formats, Power Point show to video tape, audio tape and records to a CD ROM.
CURRENT/RECENT CLIENTS/PROJECTS: 3M, Best Buy, KTCA, WCCO, Kare 11, SuperValu, Graco, Volunteers of America, Garlock Equipment Company, Carlson Companies, A/J Vending, Dolphin Temps, Carleton College, Children's Cancer Research Fund, Becker Arena Prod., Mayo Clinic, Ikon Office Solutions, Hey City Theatre, Wilson's, Cargill, AnaGram Inc, Arcadia Financial, Stein Ind., RainForest Café, National Museum of Horseracing, CBS TV, Rosemount Schools, Pitney Bowes.

MEDIA LOFT, INC.   612-375-1086
333 Washington Avenue North #210   Minneapolis 55401
FAX: 612-375-0913
CONTACT: David Kelsey
SERVICES: Award-winning full service communications company; script to screen concepting and production for video, film business theatre, corporate meetings and events.
PRESIDENT/CEO/OWNER: Engenio H. DiLorenzo

MEDIAONE   651-312-5000
10 River Park Plaza #400   St. Paul 55107
FAX: 651-312-5317
CONTACT: Mark Neuman-Scott

Film & Video Support Services / 237

E-MAIL: mneuman-scott@mediaone.com
SERVICES: Production facilities include a fully equipped 6 camera 24' production truck with slo-mo, DVE, Chyron graphics and generators, studio, non-linear edit suites, DVCPro portable equipment and graphics stations. Creative services include scripting, editing, graphics creation, shooting of commercial, program and industrial productions.

MENTZER MAKE-UP & HAIR DESIGN
8705 Boone Court

763-545-3481
Minneapolis 55426

FAX: 763-545-3481
CONTACT: Sue Mentzer Grey
E-MAIL: cgreyart@mm.com
SERVICES: Naturalistic make-up for film, print, and video.
CAPABILITIES: Twenty years experience including projects for CBS Entertainment, NBC Sports, PBS American Playhouse, Independent Filmmakers, award-winning commercial production companies, award-winning photographers and corporate communications departments.
CURRENT/RECENT CLIENTS/PROJECTS: Notables: Robert Urich, Chynna Phillips, Lindsay Wagner, Colleen Dewhurst, Gary Collins, Ronny Cox, Arnold Palmer, Stanley Marcus, Former Senator Dave Durenburger, Former Governors Elmer L. Anderson and Cecil Anrus, Skip Humphrey, Alan Page, Honeywell CEO Mike Bonsignore, News 11 anchors, and more.
PRESIDENT/CEO/OWNER: Sue Mentzer Grey

MIDWEST MEDIA ARTISTS ACCESS CENTER
2388 University Avenue West

651-644-1912
St. Paul 55114

FAX: 651-644-5708
CONTACT: Andrew Welken, Robin Harris
E-MAIL: mmaac@mtn.org
WWW: mtn.org/mmaac
SERVICES: Independent film producer's source for 16mm cameras/lighting/audio and flat bed editing. We offer workshops to train beginning producers the fine art of film making. Watch for our "Digital Filmmaking" workshops and equipment in the summer of 2000.
SPECIALTIES: Arri 16mm cameras/Steenbeck editing tables/Twin Cities' largest black and white photography darkroom.
CURRENT/RECENT CLIENTS/PROJECTS: Independent films produced through MMAAC: "Go to Hell"; "Madison on Tour", "Welcome to Alaska;" "Welcome to Cosmos;" "Pagan God; The Documentary;" "Access;" "Forbidden City;" "Martin."
PRESIDENT/CEO/OWNER: Andrew Welken/Robin Harris

MUSIC AUDIO SOUND SERVICES
4151 Wentworth Avenue South

612-823-3333
Minneapolis 55409

CONTACT: Loren Deutz
CAPABILITIES: Completely equipped location sound records/mixer for film and video with twenty years of credits including: documentaries, features, commercials, music videos, broadcast TV and albums.
SPECIALTIES: Sound mixing and recording.
CURRENT/RECENT CLIENTS/PROJECTS: Best Buy Company, Inc.; Northwest Teleproduction; McCoy & Associates, Inc.; JigSaw Pictures; Harder-Fuller Films; The Minneapolis Institute of Arts; Lee Pictures Inc.; Longrun Productions; Media Loft, Inc.; Matre Productions; Hennepin County Public Affairs Department; James Production; Voodoo Films.

238 / Film & Video Support Services

N

RAYMOND NIEMI PRODUCTION SERVICES   651-291-2892
431 W. Annapolis Street #12   St. Paul 55118
CONTACT: Raymond Niemi
PAGER: 612-622-9348
SERVICES: Producer-Director (creative). Camera, lighting, sound, grip, teleprompter (technical). Production management, coordinator (business and management).
CAPABILITIES: Above and below the line capability in video, film and audio production support. Studio and location.
SPECIALTIES: Working with actors, music related productions. Active, natural productions for the corporate, consumer and entertainment markets.
PRESIDENT/CEO/OWNER: Raymond Niemi, Production Services

O

OLD ARIZONA   612-871-0050
2821 Nicollet Avenue   Minneapolis 55408
FAX: 612-871-0355
CONTACT: Darcy Knight, Elizabeth Trumble
E-MAIL: oldaznew@mtn.org
WWW: oldarizona.com
SERVICES: Main Studio: A 2,000 sq. ft. production space ideal for tabletop, still production, music videos, set construction and rehearsal. 43' ceiling with Prolyte truss at 20'. 12' electric garage door, makeup/wardrobe studio. 1,200 amp service with camlock connectors. Backstage annex: 900 sq. ft. rehearsal space ideal for smaller projects. 8' garage door. Dance Studio: 1,100 sq. ft. hardwood floors, mirrored walls, two changing rooms. A coffee house/cafe and bookstore are also available to clients.
CURRENT/RECENT CLIENTS/PROJECTS: Target; Best Buy; Live Theatre; Live Dance; Corporate Parties; Boys to Men; Paula Abdul; Sinead O'Connor.

SUSAN OLSON FOOD STYLIST   612-920-3991
5200 Knox Avenue South   Minneapolis 55419
FAX: 612-925-9526
CONTACT: Susan Olson
E-MAIL: smofoodstylist@uswest.net
SERVICES: Food styling for film and prints; prop styling; floral styling; cookbook/recipe development, new product testing and consulting.
CAPABILITIES: 15 years experience.
CURRENT/RECENT CLIENTS/PROJECTS: Hormel recipe development and styling for mini-cookbooks, 7-00. Schwan's Mealtime TV Cooking Show, 7-00. Capt. Ken's package photography, 7-00. Watkin's catalog photography, 5-00, Baja Tortilla Grill, 30 sec. SD & T 4-00.

Film & Video Support Services / 239

PRODUCTIONS, INC.

ONLINE PRODUCTIONS, INC.   **612-881-1106**
5525 River Bluff Curve   **Minneapolis 55437**
CONTACT: Erik Prentnieks
CAPABILITIES: Video production services for corporate, commercial, educational and broadcast applications.
EQUIPMENT: Sony BVW-D600, Sony BVW-300A and Sony BVP-7 cameras, Beta SP "cuts only" editing system.
SPECIALTIES: ENG/EFP style production services, overseen by a professional with two Emmy nominations and twenty years of national network experience.

P

PASSION FRUIT COMPANY   612-822-7639
4446 Wentworth Avenue South   Minneapolis 55409
FAX: 612-822-7639
CONTACT: Mark K. Tang
WWW: passionfruitfilms.org
CAPABILITIES: Motion picture and broadcast television producer. Film and video crew support.
SPECIALTIES: Director of photography and assistant camera support for features, music videos, broadcast documentaries and public service announcements. Editor for long film features and documentaries, broadcast television programs.
CURRENT/RECENT CLIENTS/PROJECTS: Offline editor for 2000-2001 season (52 episodes); Yan Can Cook (Half hour weekly cooking program on PBS).

JAN PETERSON   651-483-9572
2730 Griggs Street North   Roseville 55113
CONTACT: Jan Peterson
ALTERNATE PHONE: Cell Phone: 612-325-3738
E-MAIL: janis.peterson@att.net
SERVICES: Independent make-up artist with over 20 years of experience. Energetic personality who helps talent feel at ease on set.
CAPABILITIES: Corporate, ethnic, beauty, corrective and natural "no make-up" look.
CURRENT/RECENT CLIENTS/PROJECTS: Charles Osgood, Jimmy Jam, Vince Gill, Harmon Killebrew, Governor Jesse Ventura.

240 / Film & Video Support Services

PIXEL FARM, INC.   612-339-7644
251 First Avenue North #600   Minneapolis 55401
FAX: 612-339-7551
CONTACT: Stacey Ranum
E-MAIL: stacey@pixelfarm.com
WWW: pixelfarm.com
SERVICES: High-end digital post-production facility specializing in visual effects, 3D, 2D animation, on/off-line editorial, and film transfer for commercial broadcast, feature film, music videos and corporate markets.
CAPABILITIES: Discreet logic flame and inferno. Quantel Infinity, Editbox, Hal Express and Paintbox Express. AVID Symphony and AVID off-line. Two 3D workstations running Maya. SoftImage, Eddie, Pandemonium and more. URSA Film transfer with daVinci color corrector.

PRECISION POWERHOUSE   612-333-9111
911 Second Street South   Minneapolis 55415
FAX: 612-332-9200
CONTACT: Dan Piepho, Paul Sunberg, Gene Gunderson
E-MAIL: dan@power-house.com; pauls@power-house.com or geneg@power-house.com
WWW: precisionpowerhouse.com
SERVICES: Production services, scriptwriting, art direction and photography, 40 x 60 x 20 fully sound proof and floating sound stage, 2-wall cyc. Serial component digital post-production, interformat post production, studio production Interactive media production, DVD authoring, 2D and 3D Alias/Wavefront animation and compositing, digital BetaCam compositing, audio production, complete CD music and sound effects library, audio sweetening, remote recording, audio, video duplication and CD audio/CD-ROM/DVD replication, blank tape sales.
EQUIPMENT: Sony DME 3000, Silicon Graphics Maximum Impact Indigo 2 with Alias/Wavefront 2D and 3D software, ACCOM 5 minute digital disk recorder, Pinnacle Aladdin digital effects, DVE and CG, Audio studio featuring Sonic Solutions. High Resolution 96/24 DVD/Surround Sound ready digital/audio workstation. Interactive media video digitizing workstation, Autodesk Animator workstation.
SPECIALTIES: Video and multimedia marketing via direct mail, video and multimedia sales presentations, multimedia software development for retail and corporate products, training presentation, commercial (TV and Radio), web pages for businesses. We produce infomercials, e-business websites and direct response, audio, video and CD. DVD products and audio/video duplication and CD-ROM/DVD replication.

PROPAGANDA   612-341-0660
1018 North Fifth Street   Minneapolis 55411
FAX: 612-333-2278
CONTACT: Bruce S. Allen
CAPABILITIES: Complete scenic studio.
SPECIALTIES: Custom design and fabrication in all media. Minature to giant-size sets and props for still, video, film, displays and exhibits.

PUSH MEDIA GROUP   612-339-8294
411 Washington Avenue North #209   Minneapolis 55401
FAX: 612-339-8296
CONTACT: Danny Schmidt/James Curry
E-MAIL: dan@pushgroup.com

Film & Video Support Services / 241

WWW: pushgroup.com
CAPABILITIES: Web, film and video production.
SPECIALTIES: Motion graphics utilizing 2D and 3D animation, special effects, and compositing.
CURRENT/RECENT CLIENTS/PROJECTS: NSP, VH1, General Motors, Nike, Paisley Park, Minnesota Vikings
PRESIDENT/CEO/OWNER: Danny Schmidt

R

REAL PRODUCTIONS 651-646-9472
1821 University Avenue #N-187 St. Paul 55104
FAX: 651-646-1842
CONTACT: Robert J. Schuster
WWW: realproductions.com
SERVICES: A full service video production company including conception, scriptwriting, storyboarding, planning, crew and equipment for studio and location shooting. On and off camera talent, sound recording and mixing and post-production, digital and analog editing. Rental and duplication available.
SPECIALTIES: Corporate image training, motivational, and sales marketing videos. Tailor both to needs and budget - specializing in the medical and high-tech industries.
PRESIDENT/CEO/OWNER: Robert J. Schuster

REALGOOD CREATIVE 952-470-0232
5101 Thimsen Avenue Minnetonka 55345
FAX: 952-470-9547
CONTACT: Jane Henderson
E-MAIL: jane@realgood.com
WWW: realgood.com
SERVICES: Creative serviced for advertising and advertisers.
CAPABILITIES: Audio production, video production, web creation, graphic design, copywriting, product development, digital audio station, digital video station.
PRESIDENT/CEO/OWNER: Kyrl Henderson

PENNY RICH GALINSON 612-544-4792
2230 Quebec Avenue South Minneapolis 55426
CONTACT: Penny Rich Galinson
SERVICES: Twenty years experience in make-up and hair styling for film, video, print advertising and special occasions, extensive specialty experience in para-medical camouflage make-up and natural look, fashion and corporate looks.
CAPABILITIES: Make-up, hair styling; licensed esthetician; facials, hair removal.
CURRENT/RECENT CLIENTS/PROJECTS: Resume, client list available on request.

ROBERT J. RIESBERG ANTIQUES 651-457-1772
343 Salem Church Road St. Paul 55118
FAX: 651-450-6014
CONTACT: Robert J. Riesberg

242 / Film & Video Support Services

CAPABILITIES: Props
SPECIALTIES: Dealing in period 17th, 18th, 19th century antiques for rent or purchase as props. By appointment only.

RUMJUNGLE MEDIA, INC.   **612-476-9900**
17309 Bay Lane   **Wayzata 55391**
FAX: 612-476-0909
CONTACT: Kathy Ross
E-MAIL: rumjungle@rumjungle.com
WWW: rumjungle.com
SERVICES: Internationally experienced DP Camera Crews (Betacam SP, Digital Betacam, Mini DV & HDTV) with top-notch support crews, including producers and production assistants for broadcast, commercial and corporate clientele. RumJungle Media has an extensive database of satellite up-link services, grips, gaffers, make-up artists and teleprompter operators.
CAPABILITIES: Rumjungle has equipment packages featuring a wide array of gear for every situation. We offer Sony BVW-D600 cameras with 16:9 wide screen capability with comprehensive lighting and wireless audio packages. Expect superb lighting design, inventive production techniques, rock-steady hand-held camera operation and efficient set-up.
CURRENT/RECENT CLIENTS/PROJECTS: 1998 National News Emmy Award for NBC; 1999 National News Emmy Award for ABC; 1999 Telly Award for "Fish!".

S

SATIN STITCHES, LTD.   **763-323-9507**
11894 Reisling Blvd NW   **Minneapolis 55433**
FAX: 612-323-9507
CONTACT: Deb Nelson
E-MAIL: deborah@satinstiches.com
WWW: satinstitches.com
SERVICES: Costume design, costume production, costume alterations.
CAPABILITIES: 2,600 sq. ft of showroom/production space with 8 full time employees. President has BFA degree in fashion design Company in business since 1978 doing custom costume making.
SPECIALTIES: Performance costuming including dance, skate, entertainers.
CURRENT/RECENT CLIENTS/PROJECTS: NBA dance teams such as Orlando Magic, NY Knicks, Portland Trailblazers. Singer/dancers for Tony Sandler pilot.

SCC ON LOCATION   **651-426-7338**
2460 E Cty Road F   **White Bear Lake 55110**
FAX: 651-426-0997
CONTACT: Judy Skeie-Voss
E-MAIL: judy@scctv.org
WWW: visi.com/accesstv
SERVICES: Community events coverage for cable TV, access programming on access channels. Community bulletin board channel for events listings. Video production training, portable equipment and studio access. Education on/about community television.
CAPABILITIES: Mobile production truck; Three camera studio; S-VHS and DVC Pro camera checkout; Media 100 editing suite; VHS/SVHS editing suites.

Film & Video Support Services / 243

CURRENT/RECENT CLIENTS/PROJECTS: Serving the communities of Birchwood Village, Dellwood, Grant, Lake Elmo, Mahtomedi, Maplewood, North St. Paul, Oakdale, Vadnais Heights, White Bear Lake, White Bear Township, Willernie.

SENNSATION TELEPROMPTER LLC	**763-531-8297**
4601 Independence Avenue North Suite 105	**Minneapolis 55428**

FAX: 763-504-1088
CONTACT: Beth A. Senn
ALTERNATE PHONE: Mobile phone: 763-986-5397
E-MAIL: bethsenn@aol.com
WWW: sennsation.com
SERVICES: Owner/operator of on-camera and presidential podium equipment. Over 15 years in business, 11 of those doing live news. Telescript software.
CURRENT/RECENT CLIENTS/PROJECTS: Julie Andrews/Orchestra Hall Lecture Series; Pillsbury National Sales Meeting; "State of the State" Address/Governor Jesse Ventura

MICHAEL R. SEVERSON	**952-435-8520**
17343 Ithaca Lane	**Lakeville 55044**

FAX: 952-892-7191
CONTACT: Mike Severson
PAGER: 888-625-3443
E-MAIL: seversound@aol.com
SERVICES: Freelance audio services for film and video production. 24 years experience in professional audio location sound mixer/recordist. From ENG to full commercial production.
CAPABILITIES: HHB Timecode DAT recorder with Smart Slate Schoeps, Sonotrim. Shure, Beyerdynamic, and E-V microphones. Shure FP-32A and FP-33 mixers. Lectrosonics UHF and VHF wireless mics. Gentner Telephone interface.
CURRENT/RECENT CLIENTS/PROJECTS: Rebecca's Garden - show mixer since 1996; Dateline NBC - several assignments; ABC; CBS; FOX; ESPN; CNN; MTV; National Geographic, NBA Entertainment.
PRESIDENT/CEO/OWNER: Michael R. Severson

SF PRODUCTIONS	**651-429-3350**
1890 Center Street	**Hugo 55038**

FAX: 651-653-0015
CONTACT: Rich Tuomi
E-MAIL: rich@simplyfishing.com
WWW: simplyfishing.com
SERVICES: Full-service video production; broadcast television, commercials, corporate, feature videos. On location; indoors/outdoors, Beta SP, 3/4". Post production: Beta SP, 3/4", S-VHS, DVE, graphics, animation. 10 years experience shooting TV and outdoor events.
PRESIDENT/CEO/OWNER: Bob Mehsikomer

SIGHTLINES	**800-948-2410**
22399 Oak Hill Road NW	**Evansville 56326**

FAX: 218-948-2383
CONTACT: Jackie Henning
SERVICES: Custom painted backgrounds and roomsets. Faux finishing and wall art. Murals.

244 / Film & Video Support Services

SPECIALTIES: Twenty years of experience painting for theatre, commercial photographers, interior residential and business centers.
PRESIDENT/CEO/OWNER: Jackie Henning

SOLDIER BRANE 612-571-3700
667 45th Avenue NE Minneapolis 55421
CONTACT: Ron Cadieux
E-MAIL: roncadux@yahoo.com
WWW: home.earthlink.net/~cadux/
SERVICES: Antique toys sales. Props for film and advertising.
CAPABILITIES: Antique toys - 30's - 50's to present. Military, cars, trains, boats and toy soldiers.

SOUNDBITES/MICHAEL R. SEVERSON 952-435-8520
17343 Ithaca Lane Lakeville 55044
FAX: 952-892-7191
CONTACT: Michael R. Severson
PAGER: 888-625-3443
E-MAIL: seversound@aol.com
CAPABILITIES: Location sound mixer/recordist for film and video production. 25 years experience recording audio for various applications.
EQUIPMENT: HHB Timecode DAT recorder with Denecke Smart Slate; Schoeps, Shure, Sonotrim. Shure and E-V microphones; Lectro Sonics UHF and VHF wireless mics; Shure FP33 and FP32A mixers; Gentner telephone interface; numerous accessories.
CURRENT/RECENT CLIENTS/PROJECTS: "Rebecca's Garden", nationally-syndicated TV show; Dateline NBC; National Geographic

GREG STIEVER 612-333-0965
160 North Glenwood Minneapolis 55405
FAX: 612-397-7989
CONTACT: Greg Stiever
CAPABILITIES: Director/cinematographer
SPECIALTIES: Directing actors and highly stylized cinematography.

STONE CIRCLE PRODUCTIONS 612-843-4292
1828 Jefferson Street NE Minneapolis 55418
FAX: 612-843-4291
CONTACT: Richard Stachelek
SERVICES: Editors and editorial facilities, motion graphic design, and animation.
CAPABILITIES: Write, design, produce educational, corporate and documentary film and video.
PRESIDENT/CEO/OWNER: Richard Stachelek

no piece of technology can match the power of a single great individual

Knowing this, we at Aquent are dedicated to bringing you together with these individuals. Individuals with unique abilities. Brilliance. Internal fire. And we continually provide them with new skills, new training, new sources of motivation — so they can constantly produce *extraordinary* business results for you.

If you want to bring the power of Aquent talent to your organization, or if you're a talented professional looking to put your powers to work, call **1-877-PARTNER** (1-877-727-8637) or visit **aquent.com**.

AQUENT
the official *AIGA* talent agency

- Creative & Design
- Web Programming & Development
- Production & Presentations
- Technical Support

43 Main Street SE, Suite 413 • Minneapolis, MN 55414 • 612.378.4930

AQUENT

1-877-PARTNER
aquent.com

who we are.
and why we're like no one else.

Aquent Partners is a specialized talent agency that focuses exclusively on providing Design and Production experts for contract, contract-to-hire, and permanent work. Since 1987, we've led the way in making the best specialized matches for more than 35,000 professionals and 30,000 client companies. Today, with 48 offices in 10 countries, we're the world's largest specialized talent agency. The secret to our success is simple. By specializing, we've been able to focus all our energies on providing the best solutions for you.

what we do.

creative and design
Art and Creative Direction   Content Development
Web Architecture   Illustration   Graphic Design
Animation   Project Management   Photography
Copywriting   Technical Writing   Editing/Proofreading

system administration and technical support
System Administration   Webmaster
Desktop Support   Technical Support
Help Desk   Network Administration

production and presentations
Graphics Production   Prepress
HTML and JavaScript
Presentation Graphics

web programming and development
Project Management   Programming
Development

where we are.

Minneapolis MN
43 Main St., SE, Suite 413
Minneapolis, MN 55414-1029
tel 612.378.4930   fax 612.378.2520

Learn how we can help to guarantee your organization's success. Call us at **1-877-PARTNER** and come visit us at aquent.com

Film & Video Support Services / 245

STUDIOCRAFTS

STUDIOCRAFTS, INC.   **612-331-7884**
451 Taft Street NE   **Minneapolis 55413**
FAX: 612-331-2057
CONTACT: Greg Cornell
E-MAIL: studiocr@bitstream.net
SERVICES: Custom design and fabrication of scenery, props, display and tradeshow exhibits.
CAPABILITIES: Full service scenic facility. We have the people, the experience, and the facilities to take your idea to reality on time, and on budget.
CURRENT/RECENT CLIENTS/PROJECTS: Best Buy Television Commercial, 1999; General Mills National Sales Meeting, 1998, 1999, 2000; Guthrie Theater, Feb. 2000.
PRESIDENT/CEO/OWNER: Greg Cornell, Chris Johnson

T

TAG TEAM FILM & VIDEO, INC.   **651-917-0058**
2375 University Avenue West #200   **St. Paul 55114**
FAX: 651-917-0368
CONTACT: Jeff Byers
E-MAIL: jeff@tagteamfilmvideo.com
SERVICES: Digital Betacam and Betacam SP video production, 16 mm film production, off-line and on-line non-linear editing.
EQUIPMENT: Field production - complete crew and equipment packages featuring Sony BVP-570/550 digital cameras with 16 x 9 capability. Sony DVW-250 digital Betacam VTR, BVW-50 and BVV-5 Betacam SP VTRs. Extensive audio, lighting, grip and monitoring equipment. Single camera and live-switched multi-camera configurations. Aaton LTR-7 16mm camera pkg. Post production - SoftImage DS and Avid 1000.
SPECIALTIES: Providing independent, corporate and broadcast producer/directors with comprehensive, professional production and post-production services.
CURRENT/RECENT CLIENTS/PROJECTS: The St. Paul Companies; Corporate Video; ABC; Novartis; The Producers Consortium; Honeywell; Shandwick; Mayo Clinic; General Mills; Falls Agency; ESPN; Fleishman-Hillard; A & E.
PRESIDENT/CEO/OWNER: Thomas G. Krohn, Jeffrey J. Byers

TAKE 1 PRODUCTIONS   **952-831-7757**
9969 Valley View Road   **Eden Prairie 55344**
CONTACT: Rob Hewitt

246 / Film & Video Support Services

SERVICES: Full service video and multimedia production company. Complete scripting, studio and location shooting, digital non-linear editing, computer generated graphics, 3D animation, digital video effects, multimedia authoring, MPEG encoding, video/CD-ROM duplication.
SPECIALTIES: Presentations for sales, training, and product demonstrations.
PRESIDENT/CEO/OWNER: Teri Murphy

TASTY LIGHTING SUPPLY	612-875-5074
3017 46th Avenue South	Minneapolis 55406

FAX: 612-721-2317
CONTACT: Mike Handley
CAPABILITIES: Goffer and lighting director. Lighting and grip equipment rentals.
SPECIALTIES: Corporate grip/lighting packages, to 2 ton equipment packages. 12 years experience. Ability to book crews. One phone call for equipment and crew. Tungsten, HMI, Kino flo, Dedo.

TRAIL MIX INC.	612-332-5331
400 1st Avenue North #510	Minneapolis 55401

FAX: 612-332-7671
CONTACT: Jim May
E-MAIL: trailmix@minn.net
WWW: trailmixrecording.com

JENNIFER TURNER-BRAND	612-922-0700
3308 St. Paul Avenue	Minneapolis 55416

CONTACT: Jennifer Turner-Brand
CAPABILITIES: 17 years experience/licensed cosmetologist.
SPECIALTIES: Makeup and hair styling for print advertisement, film/video productions and TV broadcast. Extensive work/experience in high fashion, corrective and natural makeup techniques.

V

VEE CORPORATION	612-378-2561
504 Malcolm Avenue SE #200	Minneapolis 55414

FAX: 612-378-2635
CONTACT: Bonnie Ehlers
E-MAIL: bonniee@vee.com
WWW: vee.com
SERVICES: Concept, design and construction of special scenic elements and props within an exhibit booth; specialty displays; interactive exhibits. Unusual Items: Design, fabricated set for Northwest Airlines "Airplane Safety Video."
SPECIALTIES: Scenic art, sculpting, aluminum and steel fabrication.
PRESIDENT/CEO/OWNER: Vincent E. Egan, P; Jack Pence, Mrg.

VIDEO ASSIST SUPPORT SERVICES	651-224-5152
432 Summit Avenue	St. Paul 55102

Film & Video Support Services / 247

CONTACT: Judah Hannah
SERVICES: Digital and analog video/photographic support, equipment and systems. Digital image acquisition, transmedia generation support and services. Calibrated motion analysis, photosonics playback, 24 frame playback and transfers, match frame systems, film/video synchronizers, digital video printers, story boards, still store imaging systems, casting and location survey support equipment.
CAPABILITIES: Image acquisition support for the video, motion picture, photographic communities.

W

WINDFLOWER PRODUCTIONS	612-831-7937
201 W. Burnsville Parkway #130	Burnsville 55437

FAX: 612-831-7937
CONTACT: Robert Ozasky
E-MAIL: ozasky@cs.com
SERVICES: Screenwriting/videowriting/copywriting/editing - scripts/manuscripts. Robert - Screen Actors Guild affiliated.
CAPABILITIES: Screenwriting/Screenplay Evaluation - Editing/Acting - Voice over.
CURRENT/RECENT CLIENTS/PROJECTS: "Body Slam" - A look at the underside of professional wrestling - Fiction Feature Screenplay - currently in packaging with Atkins & Associates, Los Angeles. "Hardball" - Play about baseball at the turn of the Century (1900's). Currently to be produced in the 2000 season at the Herberger Theatre in Phoenix, AZ. Danger Canyon - A unique miniature golf course to be built with an annually scheduled Children's Charity tournament.

WOLF MARINE, INC.	651-439-2341
514 East Alder Street	Stillwater 55082

CONTACT: Ken Wolf
SERVICES: Float equipment or personnel on our deck barges, pontoons, work boats. Production site available - St. Croix River.
PRESIDENT/CEO/OWNER: Lynn W. Wolf

WOODLAND PRODUCTIONS	612-929-1087
4449 Xerxes Avenue South	Minneapolis 55410

CONTACT: Wayne Krefting
CAPABILITIES: Puppet design, building and manipulation, all styles, especially hand, body and animatronics; set design and construction for puppetry.
SPECIALTIES: Puppetry for film and video.
CURRENT/RECENT CLIENTS/PROJECTS: AGS Publishers, Best Brains, Inc., Minneapolis Children's Healthcare, Diercks Productions, Video Link-Canada, Tremendous Productions, Peterson Milla Hooks, Viacom, KTCA television.
PRESIDENT/CEO/OWNER: Wayne L. Krefting, President; Robert Lane, Vice President

Film Processing

B

BLACK & WHITE PHOTOLAB, INC.　　　　　　　　612-673-9321
212 3rd Avenue No #105　　　　　　　　　　　　Minneapolis 55401
CONTACT: Mike Daoust
SERVICES: Custom hand processing of black and white film, 35mm to 4 x 5. Custom fine art printing services, toning of prints and special effects printing.
CAPABILITIES: The most knowledgeable printing and film processing people in the five state area, with the most advanced equipment.
CURRENT/RECENT CLIENTS/PROJECTS: We work with mainly commercial, professional photographers, advertising agencies, law firms, museums and other professional labs.
PRESIDENT/CEO/OWNER: Dirah Biermann/Mike Daoust

I

IMAGETECH SOLUTIONS, INC.　　　　　　　　　612-379-0699
958 East Hennepin Avenue　　　　　　　　　　Minneapolis 55414
FAX: 612-379-2229
CONTACT: Terry Nelson
E-MAIL: itsolutions@earthlink.net
SERVICES: Photographic services: E-6 and C-41 and black and white dip and dunk film processing, custom and quantity color and black and white printing, transparency duplicating, trade show prints and transparencies, complete mounting and print finishing services, Rush service available. Digital Imaging services: Scanning low to high resolution, creative image manipulation, film recording 4" x 5" to 8" x 10", direct digital ink-jet outputs, preproofs.
PRESIDENT/CEO/OWNER: David Lundberg, Terry Nelson

P

PHOTOGRAPHIC SPECIALTIES　　　　　　　　612-522-7741
1718 Washington Avenue North　　　　　　　　Minneapolis 55411
FAX: 612-522-1934
CONTACT: Rick Schuenemann
E-MAIL: drewkal@photospec.com
SERVICES: P.S. is a full service custom photo lab and digital imaging service., We specialize in large runs of prints and transparencies for visual merchandising, POP, Trade Show Exhibits and museums. We have in-house graphic designers, a stock photo library and shipping and kitting capabilities.
CAPABILITIES: Two Light Jet 5000 Digital photo images for true photographic images up to 48" x 96" in one piece. Drum and flatbed scanning, LVT 8 x 10 film recorder, and Repri and Ellegro scan/retouch system. Color span inkjet printers (4) and full mounting and laminating capabilities up to 80" wide. 4 traditional mural rooms with wall easels, prints and trans up to 72" x 16' one piece.
CURRENT/RECENT CLIENTS/PROJECTS: Large nationwide retail chains, display and store design firms.
PRESIDENT/CEO/OWNER: Drew Kalman

Film Processing / 249

PROFESSIONAL COLOR SERVICE, INC.　　　　　　　　　612-673-8900
909 Hennepin Avenue South　　　　　　　　　　　　Minneapolis 55403
FAX: 612-673-8988
CONTACT: Tim Doe
E-MAIL: procolor@procolor.com
WWW: procolor.com
CAPABILITIES: Over forty years of processing experience made us the premier color lab in the Midwest. We're the wish of may New York photographers, and have equalled our expertise in the black and white department. Film processing 24 hours a day Monday through Friday and 8:30 to 11:30 on Saturday. Our one-stop-shop line of products and services includes: new 3D lenticular display prints, digital display photographs and transparencies, as well as a complete range of scanning services, including those from our high res drum, Photo CD, and Dicomed digital camera. Fine art IRIS reproduction. Short-run digital 4-color printing on our Heidelberg DI and Docucolor systems. Color laser copies and Bubblejet copies up to 24" x 36". Pick up and delivery.
SPECIALTIES: One-stop shop imaging services.
OFFICE HOURS: Monday through Friday 7:30 am to 8:00 pm; Saturday 8:30 to 2:00 pm.

S

RICH SILHA　　　　　　　　　　　　　　　　　　　612-338-7172
420 North 5th Street　　　　　　　　　　　　　　　Minneapolis 55401
40 Ford Center
CONTACT: Rich Silha
SERVICES: Custom processing of B&W film and prints.
CAPABILITIES: Hand film process, fiber based and RC prints, B&W internegatives, copy negs, alternative process and specialty work.

SUNSHINE PHOTO, INC.　　　　　　　　　　　　　　952-881-2083
9056 Lyndale Avenue South　　　　　　　　　　　　Bloomington 55420
FAX: 952-881-0184
CONTACT: Brian Schrupp
SERVICES: Process and print color film - 1 hr and APS (new); process and print B&W film - 1 Hr; process 35mm E-6 Film - 1 Hr; custom color enlargements; custom B&W enlargements; passport photos; copy slides & duplicate slides; portrait/product studio; event photography.
CAPABILITIES: Photo restoration/enhancement; photo CD's; prints from digital cameras; PowerPoint slides; photo business cards; print to print duplication; rush service available.

Game, Puzzle & Toy Designers

E

EXCEL DEVELOPMENT GROUP, INC.   612-374-3233
1123 Mt. Curve Avenue   Minneapolis 55403
FAX: 612-377-0865
CONTACT: Andrew Berton
E-MAIL: info@exceld.com
WWW: exceld.com
SERVICES: Toy and game design, development. Representation of inventors, designers in toy and game industry.
CAPABILITIES: Domestic and international contacts, engineering, 3D rendering.
CURRENT/RECENT CLIENTS/PROJECTS: Hasbro, Mattel, and 400+ international.

R

RAINY LAKES PUZZLES   612-827-5757
4255 Garfield Avenue South   Minneapolis 55409
CONTACT: Mary Logeland
E-MAIL: goldbooks@rainylakepuzzles.com
WWW: rainylakepuzzles.com
SERVICES: Hand cut, custom designed wood, foam core and syntra jigsaw puzzles (personalized with names, dates, logos, special messages and intricate shapes-silhouettes) to be used for: executive and business gifts, recognition/retirement programs, displays, meetings, conferences and conventions, corporate identity programs, advertising programs, product introductions, frameable art, games.
SPECIALTIES: Original watercolor puzzle art, photograph puzzles, limited edition puzzles, designer paper, puzzles, company logo puzzles, etc. Since Rainy lake jigsaw puzzles are one of a kind they can be designed and cut to meet any specification.
CURRENT/RECENT CLIENTS/PROJECTS: Honeywell; General Mills; Minnesota Historical Society; U of M; Graham Marketing Group; Larsen Design Office; Quattro Creative; Motorola; Digital Equipment; NCS; Spectrum Studio, Inc.; Children's Health Care; T C Industries; BI Performance.
PRESIDENT/CEO/OWNER: Doug and Mary Logeland

Graphic Designers

A

ADVENTURE GRAPHIC DESIGN   952-467-4312
715 West Elm Street   Norwood 55368
FAX: 952-467-4316
CONTACT: Jessica Klaustermeier
E-MAIL: jklaustermeier@sprintmail.com
CAPABILITIES: Complete design services including: packaging, promotion, logos, complete business identities, trade publication advertising, newspaper advertising, newsletters, direct mail postcards and brochures, posters and flyers.

AIRGRAPHICS 1   763-421-1500
13117 Valley Forge Lane   Champlin 55316
E-MAIL: airgraphics1@hotmail.com
SERVICES: Photo restoration of black and white, color photos. Some work on originals in restoration (only in very specific cases.) Oil coloring on photos; corrective brush work. Black and white prints, color prints. Color and black and white corrective retouching and airbrushing.
OTHER CAPABILITIES: Twenty-three years in business servicing both large and small commercial businesses and retail customers as well. Expertise in restoration photographic artwork (airbrushing & retouching); hand colored oils, both transparent and heavy brush on photos as well as custom black and white and color printing. All work is hand done and fully restored--no partial work. Work can be done on customers print or prints can be made.
CONTACT: Sandra Ostendorf

FRANK ARISS DESIGN   612-331-7413
12C Grove Street, Nicollet Island   Minneapolis 55401
FAX: 612-331-2214
CONTACT: Mary Rolph
E-MAIL: frankariss@aol.com
PRESIDENT/CEO/OWNER: Mary Rolph, Corporate Client Support

B

BARTLETT STUDIO, INC.   651-699-5571
2014 Juliet Avenue   St. Paul 55105
FAX: 651-699-6255
CONTACT: Therese Bartlett
E-MAIL: therese@bartlettstudio.com
CAPABILITIES: Complete graphic design services, concept, layout, design, photography, photo art direction, production and print supervision. Macintosh-based design systems.
SPECIALTIES: Corporate communications: brochures, catalogs, direct mail, marketing materials, print ads, identity systems, newsletters and annual reports.
PRESIDENT/CEO/OWNER: Therese Bartlett, Bill Bartlett

252 / Graphic Designers

BAU, INC. **952-912-0191**
5511 Bristol Lane **Minnetonka 55343**
FAX: 952-933-0295
CONTACT: Douglas Johnson
E-MAIL: johns93@bitstream.net
SERVICES: We are the graphics bureau to the Twin Cities. The most capable center for scanning, retouching, photo-manipulation, illustration, and illustration integrated with design. We have years of experience in working seamlessly with business and design schedules. Call for our free, clearly understandable pricing and information booklet.
CAPABILITIES: No better scanning or retouching can be found in the Twin Cities area. We can work with any item from 8mm film to the side of a building. All can be saved in any file format needed, to a variety of convenient storage media. True photographic printing is available also - and always an index print. Our art department brings illustration and design to a higher level of effectiveness by being able to integrate the two into a more communicative whole. We have many styles at our disposal to meet any clients needs.
CURRENT/RECENT CLIENTS/PROJECTS: American Medical Systems; Adult Option in Education; Banc; Campbell Mithun Esty; Carlson Marketing Group; Chez Francoise; La Flame; Photo Quick; VRB Art; Wellington Windows.
PRESIDENT/CEO/OWNER: Douglas Johnson

Advanced Results by Design

THE BENYAS DESIGN GROUP **612-340-9804**
126 North Third Street, Suite 300 **Minneapolis 55401**
FAX: 612-334-5950
CONTACT: Bradley A. Benyas
E-MAIL: benyas@visi.com
CAPABILITIES: Design and development of primary marketing support materials including capabilities brochures, print ads, product graphics and literature, sales training materials, and corporate identity.
SPECIALTIES: The Benyas AD Group is a results-oriented graphic design firm specializing in printed communications that advance our clients, their companies, and their products. From concept through production, we provide the services you need, when you need them. State-of-the-art pre-press resources, expert photo direction and print supervision. We deliver results.

BRW, INC. **612-370-0700**
700 Third Street South **Minneapolis 55415**
FAX: 612-370-1378

Graphic Designers / 253

CONTACT: Paul Tatge
E-MAIL: info@brwmsp.com
WWW: brwinc.com
SERVICES: Full service graphic design including: plan graphics, transportation graphics, proposal graphics, marketing literature, newsletters, posters, publications, trade show exhibits, web site design and development, electronic presentation.
PRESIDENT/CEO/OWNER: Richard Wolsfeld, Gary Ehret

C

PAT CARNEY STUDIO, INC.   612-339-4021
400 1st Avenue North #614   Minneapolis 55401
FAX: 612-339-9432
CONTACT: Patrick Carney
E-MAIL: pat@carney.com
SERVICES: Providing award-winning graphic design (concept to completion) for over 15 years. Retail, educational, industrial and a variety of other clients offering innovative design for all applications. Pat Carney Studio offers complete web site development and design, logos, collateral, catalogs, packaging, direct mail, interactive media, pos/pop.
CAPABILITIES: Design/produce original work from concept to completion. Pat Carney Studio with its award-winning designers handle traditional and new media such as interactive, internet, and branding strategies.
CURRENT/RECENT CLIENTS/PROJECTS: Target, Lominger Limited, Inc., 3M, Public Radio International, Garelick Mfg. Co., General Mills, Inc., Carlson Marketing Group, Lightfaire, Deluxe Corp., Polaris, Victory Motorcycles, Select Comfort, Skore Financial Management, Datamyte, Green Financial.

CHARLIE WALBERG CREATIVE SERVICES   651-213-0012
27421 Quinlan Avenue   Lindstrom 55045
FAX: 651-213-0508
CONTACT: Charlie Walberg
E-MAIL: dobe@fishnet.com
WWW: walberg.net
SERVICES: Design and art direction, concept and photo illustration.
CAPABILITIES: Design and art direction from a professional with over 20 years experience in a wide variety of business categories.

CHURCHWARD BENSON DESIGN, INC.   612-333-4473
119 North 4th Street #307   Minneapolis 55401
FAX: 612-335-3799
CONTACT: Shannon Churchward
E-MAIL: cbdesign@pioneerplanet.infi.net
SERVICES: Complete graphic design services.
CAPABILITIES: Capabilities brochures, annual reports, large format display graphics for trade shows, corporate identities and other collateral materials.

COGSWELL DESIGN COMPANY   952-472-7795
2549 Emerald Drive   Mound 55364

254 / Graphic Designers

FAX: 952-472-1525
CONTACT: Laura Cogswell
E-MAIL: cogsdesign@aol.com
SERVICES: Complete graphic design services.
SPECIALTIES: Corporate communications: logos/identity, annual reports, brochures, newsletters/publications, package design, direct mail, sales and marketing materials.

D

DESIGN COMMUNICATIONS   651-224-2148
829 Lincoln Avenue   St. Paul 55105
FAX: 651-224-9488
SERVICES: 3D Display and Exhibit - Trade Show, Retail, Business Displays.
CAPABILITIES/SPECIALTIES: YoYo Expert; Halloween Display and Props.
CURRENT/RECENT CLIENTS/PROJECTS: Spirit Halloween Superstores.
CONTACT: Dick Cohn

THE DESIGN COMPANY   651-221-1030
26 East Exchange Street #315   St. Paul 55101
FAX: 651-221-0526
CONTACT: Joy Yoshikawa
E-MAIL: joy@thedesigncompany.com
CAPABILITIES: The Design Company is a graphic design firm specializing in print and electronic communications for non-profit arts, education, and human services organizations.
SPECIALTIES: Since 1978, having fun, doing good work, making a profit.

DESIGNABILIA   612-529-2537
4825 Markay Ridge   Golden Valley 55422
FAX: 612-529-1167
CONTACT: Lucy A. Feneis
E-MAIL: designabilia@mn.mediaone.net
SERVICES: I can take a project from concept to finished product or printed piece, or any step in between, whether it be company identity, brochures, flyers, P.O.S. materials, presentation boards, logo clean-up. You name it, I can do it or I'll find someone who can.
CAPABILITIES: I've been in the business since 1981. My expertise is design, project coordination and production. I own a blue and white Macintosh G3 450 Mhz with 512 MB RAM. I have the current versions of Quark, Illustrator and PhotoShop. I have a Epson Photo Stylus 1200 color printer with 13" x 19" paper size capability.
CURRENT/RECENT CLIENTS/PROJECTS: General Mills, The Life Place, Nelson Research Services, State of Minnesota, First Fuel Banks, East Side Oil Company, Pennington and Lies, PA., P & H Graphics Communications.

DIGITAL PEOPLE   952-842-8359
5151 Edina Industrial Boulevard   Edina 55439
FAX: 952-835-7326
CONTACT: Ken Marshall

E-MAIL: ken_marshall@digitalpeople.net
WWW: digitalpeople.net
SERVICES: We represent exceptional freelance graphics and web/Internet talent for on-site or off-site projects, permanent employee recruiting, or project based assignments. Complete background checking, software testing and skills verification of all talent assures you the right talent for that all-important project.
CAPABILITIES: Macintosh or PC/Windows based professionals in the areas of Art Direction, Graphic Design, Illustration, Web Design, Web Coding, Web Productions, Web Content Development, Multimedia Design, Video Production, Copywriting, Editing/Proofreading, Electronic Production Artists, Traffic/Print Productions, Media and much more. Digital People currently have 14 offices in 11 major cities; if we can't find the talent you need locally, we will source them in other markets.
CURRENT/RECENT CLIENTS/PROJECTS: Corporate Communication Departments, Advertising Agencies, Sales Promotion Agencies, Dot.com's, Internet Solution Providers, Internet Based Communication Agencies, Graphic Design Agencies. We provide complete references from a broad base of clients.

E

EATON & ASSOCIATES DESIGN COMPANY   612-338-2266
708 South 3rd Street #420   Minneapolis 55415
FAX: 612-338-2268
CONTACT: Sandra Eaton
E-MAIL: eanda@dgi.net
WWW: eanda.com
SERVICES: Graphic design, marketing communications, web site design, corporate identity programs, branding, annual reports, packaging, signs and displays.
CAPABILITIES: Design concept development, design layout and production, communication strategies, project management, art direction - photography and illustration, copy writing, typesetting, electronic file formatting, production specification and supervision.
CURRENT/RECENT CLIENTS/PROJECTS: Cargill, Blandin Foundation, TCF/Winthrop Resources, Johnstech International, The Wilderness Society, Search Institute, Possis Medical, Lutheran Brotherhood, Lifeworks Services University of Minnesota
PRESIDENT/CEO/OWNER: Timothy Eaton

EDW DESIGN   952-920-7300
3809 Kipling Avenue   Minneapolis 55416
CONTACT: Jo Dougherty
SERVICES: Graphic design - creative concept through printed piece. Complete service - Mac design system, pre-print production, art direction and project management.
CAPABILITIES: Company ID programs, corporate graphic systems, any printed materials and web page applications.

F

45 DEGREES/MINNEAPOLIS   612-349-3790
1645 Hennepin Avenue South #312   Minneapolis 55403
FAX: 612-349-3899
CONTACT: Susan Hopp
E-MAIL: Susan@45minneapolis.com
CAPABILITIES: Graphic design - looking beyond the expected.
SPECIALTIES: Promotional materials, corporate identity and literature, collateral, annual reports, posters, publications, packaging.
OFFICERS: Susan Hopp, Karl Schweikart, Partners

4FRONT PRODUCTIONS   612-824-2508
4927 Bryant Avenue South   Minneapolis 55409
FAX: 612-824-6915
CONTACT: David J. Thompson
E-MAIL: davidjth@winternet.com
SERVICES: Award-winning computer graphic design, electronic media production, interactive multimedia and web development for advertising, graphic design and marketing. Computer graphics for advertising, animation, audio visual, broadcast, graphic design, illustration, interactive multimedia, Internet/www, marketing, packaging, point-of-purchase, print media and speaker support presentations.
EQUIPMENT: State-of-the-art Macintosh color system with all the most current design, illustration, image processing, interactive multimedia, paint, page layout, scanning and web software.
SPECIALTIES: Computer graphic design, flash animation, illustration, electronic media production, interactive multimedia, CD-ROM authoring and web site development. Computer graphic system and software consulting and training.
CURRENT/RECENT CLIENTS/PROJECTS: American Express, Apple Computer, BMW, Buddy Lee, Canon, Creative Resource Center, Duffy Design, Fallon Advertising, Foote, Cone, Belding, Franke + Fiorella, Insight Interactive, IVI Publishing, Larsen Design Office, Macromedia, Magnovox, Nikon, Novellus, Qualcomm, Purina
PRESIDENT/CEO/OWNER: David J. Thompson, President, Computer Graphic Specialist

FAME - A RETAIL IMAGE MANAGEMENT FIRM   612-342-9801
60 South 6th Street #2600   Minneapolis 55402
FAX: 612-342-9750
CONTACT: Tina Wilcox
WWW: fameretail.com
CAPABILITIES: Complete store design, fixture design, retail brand image, product development, packaging, merchandise strategy, point of purchase, visual merchandising, interactive and emerging technologies.
SPECIALTIES: Total retail image management.

Graphic Designers / 257

CURRENT/RECENT CLIENTS/PROJECTS: target Stores, Wrangler Jeans,. Best Buy, multiple divisions of the Limited Inc., Wilson's Leather, Dayton Hudson Department Stores, Mervyn's, 3M, Disney Stores, Footlocker, Software Etc., Gander Mountain Stores, Select Comfort, Wild Oats Markets, US Bank, Bally Total Fitness, Barnes & Noble, Coleman, Polaris, Sorel Boots

FLEMING DESIGN
4515 Zenith Avenue South
CONTACT: Bob Fleming
E-MAIL: fleming@bitstream.net
CAPABILITIES: Graphic design, architectural signage.
SPECIALTIES: Identity design, exhibit and display, product and service publications, signage systems.
PRESIDENT/CEO/OWNER: Bob Fleming

952-926-4515
Minneapolis 55410

FRANEYDESIGN
126 North Third Street #506
FAX: 612-630-2849
CONTACT: Nora Franey
E-MAIL: franey@visi.com
CAPABILITIES: Full service, from initial idea to finished product, working with large and small companies. Emphasis on strong conceptual graphic design. Also: art direction, creative marketing, layout and illustration. Team with writer; direct photo-shoots; production; proofing; printing coordination and supervision. Brochures, collateral, logos, packaging, corporate identity, promotional marketing materials and direct mail.
SPECIALTIES: Known for quality designs that get effective results, clear one-on-one communication; strong listening skills; attention to detail; natural rapport with people; enthusiasm for each project; and the ability to always meet deadlines. Experience in the use of color, type, photography, illustration, marketing, and printing. Expertise in creative concepts, design aesthetics and technical aspects of visual communication.

612-630-2838
Minneapolis 55401

FRETHEIM & FRIENDS
8677 Zinnia Way North
CONTACT: Kristine Fretheim
E-MAIL: kfretheim@earthlink.net
SERVICES: Type of work: Advertising and graphic design, concept to finish. Services include design, copywritng, photography, illustration, production coordination. Macintosh technology is used to create logos, annual reports, brochures, catalogs, sales literature, newsletters, packaging, direct mail, and print advertising.
CAPABILITIES: Creative design and dependable service at moderate rates.

763-494-4564
Maple Grove 55369

BETH FULLER DESIGN
400 Second Avenue NE
FAX: 763-684-0962
CONTACT: Beth Fuller

763-684-0962
Buffalo 55313

258 / Graphic Designers

SERVICES: Graphic design business that personally develops and produces print communications from concept to delivery. Specific projects include: corporate materials from business cards to brochures, sales incentive pieces, direct mail and presentations. Other services include: invitations and other materials for special events, personal monograms for individuals or couples and company logos.
CAPABILITIES: 12 years experience in graphic design and computer illustration using Macintosh based equipment and software.
CURRENT/RECENT CLIENTS/PROJECTS: Lincoln Financial Institutions Group - corporate material; digitalpeople - talent guide and advertising; SimonDelivers.com - customer product materials; Hoe and Marek - wedding invitation, announcement, thank you and monogram.

G

LAURIE GROSS 612-865-1796
1500 Jackson Street #431 Minneapolis 55413
FAX: 612-788-2211
CONTACT: Laurie Gross
CAPABILITIES: Conceptual art direction and design. Experience in all media.
SPECIALTIES: Colorful solutions for creating and building a strong corporate and product identity.

GROUP DESIGN, INC. 612-338-1353
401 North 3rd Street #360 Minneapolis 55401
FAX: 612-338-1660
CONTACT: Bruce Eaton
E-MAIL: bruce@groupdesigninc.com
SERVICES: Providing thoughtful and creative graphic design for strategic marketing and communication projects. Capabilities include corporate identity, brochures, packaging, point-of-purchase materials, direct marketing, annual reports, advertising, exhibit design and name generation services. Our work breaks through visual clutter to help clients develop a distinct place for themselves in the minds of their audience. We do this through design work that is relevant, compelling and effective.
PRESIDENT/CEO/OWNER: Bruce Eaton

H

HAAG DESIGN, INC. 612-376-0333
126 North 3rd Street #209 Minneapolis 55401
FAX: 612-376-0444
CONTACT: Allan Haag, President; Jane Kathryn Kolles, Business Development
E-MAIL: info@haagdesign.com
WWW: haagdesign.com

Graphic Designers / 259

CAPABILITIES: Haag Design is an award-winning firm with over ten years of successful performance meeting clients' needs. The firm offers a variety of services, including conceptual development, design, photo/art direction, conventional and computer-generated illustration, and production. Haag Design has in-depth experience in identity systems and logos, web and interactive, marketing and sales materials, tradeshow and exhibits, direct mail campaigns, product intro materials, advertising campaigns, annual reports, conference and event materials, foyer, atrium and lobby design, IPO materials, oversized posters and banners, packaging, invitations, name generation, apparel design, announcement, newsletters and presentations.

SPECIALTIES: Identity, corporate marketing materials, exhibit design and internet applications for software technology companies, internet start-ups, health care companies, financial companies, and food and grocery retailers. Haag Design's client base includes regional, national and international companies that range in size from start-ups to multi-million Fortune 500 companies.

HALL KELLEY, INC.   651-433-4610
661 Nason Hill Road   Marine on St. Croix 55047
FAX: 651-433-4910
CONTACT: Debra Kelley
WWW: hallkelley.com
SERVICES: Corporate identity and communication design; information design/communication efficiency.
PRESIDENT/CEO/OWNER: Michael Hall/Debra Kelly

HEDSTROM/BLESSING, INC.

HEDSTROM/BLESSING, INC.   763-591-6200
8301 Golden Valley Road #300   Minneapolis 55427
FAX: 763-591-6232
CONTACT: Julie Pearl
E-MAIL: info@hb-inc.com
WWW: www.hb-inc.com
SERVICES: Total creative concepts: planning and strategy; layout and design; copywriting; illustration; keyline and production; typesetting; photo art direction; interactive authoring and programming.
SPECIALTIES: Graphic design for a full range of media including corporate and brand identity, packaging, advertising, sales promotion and collateral, point-of-purchase, direct mail, interactive and website design.
CURRENT/RECENT CLIENTS/PROJECTS: Selected accounts include 3M; Bachman's; Carlson Leisure Group; Fabcon; Intellisol International; Interactive Learning Group; Land O'Lakes; Pillsbury; Target

260 / Graphic Designers

HELLMAN ASSOCIATES 612-375-9598
400 1st Avenue North #218 Minneapolis 55401
FAX: 612-375-0215
CONTACT: Kathy Forslund
E-MAIL: kathyf@winternet.com or info@hellman.com
WWW: hellman.com
SERVICES: We are a total creative resource group specializing in graphic design, copywriting, illustration, electronic media and market research.
CAPABILITIES: We offer a full range of marketing communications and fulfillment services.
CURRENT/RECENT CLIENTS/PROJECTS: National and international client base.
PRESIDENT/CEO/OWNER: Robert Hellman

HENDLER - JOHNSTON, LLC 952-346-9258
9448 Lyndale Avenue South #222 Bloomington 55420
FAX: 952-346-9259
CONTACT: Adam Johnston
SERVICES: Full range of corporate identity including the following: annual reports, direct mail, brochures, advertising, catalogs, packaging, posters, logos, collateral and much more. Web design and implementation of your site including e-business solutions.
CAPABILITIES: Industrial, financial, consumer branding of products or services. Clients retain H & J because they are seeking innovative solutions to their marketing needs.
CURRENT/RECENT CLIENTS/PROJECTS: Thermo King; Gingiss Formalwear; Dolan Media Company; Commerce Financial Group; Café Chateau, Donatelle Plastics, Inc. and Wireless Ronin Technologies, Inc.
PRESIDENT/CEO/OWNER: Adam Johnston, Chris Hendler

I

ImageTrend INC. 952-469-1589
20890 Kenbridge Court Lakeville 55044
FAX: 952-985-5671
WWW: www.ImageTrend.com
E-MAIL: Sales@ImageTrend.com
CAPABILITIES/SPECIALTIES: ImageTrend helps organizations implement Internet strategies with a rapid application development approach using ImageTrend's suite of integrated web applications. ImageTrend uses its web applications and application components to offer organizations cost effective, industry standard web applications. Solutions combine business analysis, creative and cognitive design, and technical design and development.
CURRENT/RECENT CLIENTS/PROJECTS: Ag-Chem Equipment Co. Inc., Cargill, HealthEast Care Systems, Honeywell, Medtronic, Motorola, Russell Athletic , State of Minnesota, Transcape
CAPABILITIES: Our vision is to assist our clients in achieving their goals by applying our knowledge and experience to their environment. At ImageTrend we focus on database driven, web-based application solutions for use on the Internet, Intranet and in Web CD-ROM publishing. Our customers can then maximize their resources more effectively in marketing, promotion, sales, production and order fulfillment, through the use of state-of the art technology.
PRESIDENT/CEO/OWNER: Mike McBrady
SPECIALTIES: Web Development, E-Commerce, CD-ROM Publishing

Graphic Designers / 261

INFINITY DIRECT, INC.   763-559-1111
13220 County Road 6   Plymouth 55441
FAX: 763-553-1852
CONTACT: Mike Boyle
WWW: infinitydirect.com
SPECIALTIES: Full service capabilities. Consumer and business-to-business direct marketing programs.
CREATIVE SERVICES: Collateral development, brand/identity programs, concept design, brochures, promotion development, planning and execution, copywriting, graphic design, interactive--CD ROM/DVD, web page and web response.
PRODUCTION SERVICES: Printing, lettershop, fulfillment. Interactive--CD-ROM/DVD processing and personalization services.
PRESIDENT/CEO/OWNER: Thomas L. Harding, CEO/Owner

IPARES, LTD.   612-215-2300
5000 Union Plaza   Minneapolis 55401
FAX: 612-215-2310
CONTACT: Tom Harold
E-MAIL: info@ipares.com
WWW: ipares.com
FOCUS: Integration of marketing, design and technology.
SERVICES: Internet Professional Services: Providing Fortune 1000 corporations with Internet, Intranet, Extranet, Sales Force Automation, Kiosk and Database Marketing solutions. Multimedia Related Services: Design/concepting, consulting, writing/instructional design and programming. Internet/Intranet: In-house design and programming including secure E-commerce solutions and web-based training.
CAPABILITIES/SPECIALTIES: Graphic design services for brochures, catalogs, ads, display and packaging. Complete prepress production services.
PRESIDENT/CEO/OWNER: Lon Bencini/Tom Harold

J

JODEE KULP DIGITAL DESIGN   763-531-9548
6289 Brunswick Avenue North   Brooklyn Park 55429
FAX: 612-522-3223
CONTACT: Jodee Kulp
E-MAIL: jodee@connetworks.com
WWW: betterendings.org/digital
CREATIVE: Creative & Production: Specializing in complex creative projects from concept through completion utilizing either PC or MAC environments, print or electronic media.
SERVICES: Special Computer Services: Networking of PC and MAC environments, merging of mixed data files, specialized postscript programming, paperless office systems and conversion of designed pieces into work processing for internal corporate use.

K

KNITTIG DESIGN, INC.
322 Groveland Avenue
FAX: 612-870-0059
CONTACT: Denny Knittig, Betsy Nagle
E-MAIL: bjnagle@knittigdesign.com

612-870-3753
Minneapolis 55403

SERVICES: Creative design services with total project management from concept through print production depending on individual client needs.
SPECIALTIES: Creative solutions to marketing communications needs including packaging, brochures, point-of-sale, annual reports, cookbook and editorial publications, photo art direction.
PRESIDENT/CEO/OWNER: Denny Knittig, Betsy Nagle

KRS DESIGN
4233 Zane Avenue North
FAX: 612-536-0179
CONTACT: Kate Sheeley
E-MAIL: kshee56766@aol.com

612-536-0179
Minneapolis 55422

SERVICES: Freelance graphic design and set styling/propping. Project organization and development from creative concept to finished product. Production coordination and client communication. 10 years experience in graphic design, advertising, theatre, television and film. Traditional and electronic design, print and video formats.
CAPABILITIES: Graphic Design: Innovative design; typography, art and photo direction; scanning; copywriting; logos; ads; brochures; newsletters; direct mail; annual reports; promotional pieces; publications; 4-color & B/W identity and collateral campaigns. Complete Macintosh platform. Set Styling/Propping: Set/prop research and buying; set decorating and dressing; numerous sources; in-studio or on-location; commercial, feature, industrial, video, still photography (tabletop & soft goods).
CURRENT/RECENT CLIENTS/PROJECTS: Fingerhut; IATSE 490; KELO-TV; KTCA-TV; Media Loft; New Line; RE/MAX North Central; River Road Entertainment; Saver's Edge; Target; Travel Graphics Intl.; Tundra Films; Vail Place; Voodoo Films; WCCO-TV.
PRESIDENT/CEO/OWNER: Kate Sheeley

KRUEGERWRIGHT
6409 City West Parkway #205
FAX: 952-946-0983
CONTACT: Steve Wallace
E-MAIL: steve@kruegerwright.com
WWW: kruegerwright.com

952-946-1055
Eden Prairie 55344

Graphic Designers / 263

SERVICES: KruegerWright is a digital marketing communications firm that designs and builds technology-based design solutions. Our expertise is in translating traditional concepts of brand in to the Interactive realm and merging them with sound business strategies to create Interactive digital marketing tools that help businesses thrive in the new economy. KruegerWright creates web sites, Interactive Presentations, Kiosks, Screen Savers, Software interface, and Digital adverting. Our business model is Collaborative - working with the best businesses, consultants, back-end developers, and advertising agencies in the country. From the opening take to the final scene, we make sure the user experience is as good as the back-end behind it, and aligned with the marketing activities in front of it.

CAPABILITIES: HTML, DHTML, JavaScript, Perl, Lingo, Cold Fusion, Adobe PhotoShop, Adobe Illustrator, Adobe Dimensions, Macromedia Dreamweaver, Macromedia Director, Macromedia Flash, 3D Studio Max. Experience: Founded 19 years ago as a traditional identity and print collateral agency, KruegerWright made a strategic move to the digital-space to bring a record of strategic thinking, disciplined design, and strong-branding capabilities to the market.

RECENT PROJECTS: Touch Screen Kiosk for Ceridan, Home Depot interactive CD with Rapp Collins, Web application Interface design with BreakAway Solutions. Interactive software demo including video for HighJump Software, Flash Web site for WorldWalk Media. Screen Saver for cMore Medical Solutions. Rich media banner ads for Ipswitch. Touch screen interface for Beckman Coulter.

CURRENT/RECENT CLIENTS/PROJECTS: Corporate Clients: Ceridian, RiverTown Trading, The Pelican Group, Ipswitch, University of Minnesota, HighJump Software, Gelco Information Network, cMore Medical Solutions, WamNeT. Agency Partners: Rapp Collins, Martin Bastian, John Ryan, Maccabee Group, Colle & McVoy. Back-End Partners: Egg Rock Partners, Imaginet, Breakaway Solutions, ImageTrend, Syntegra

L

LARSEN DESIGN + INTERACTIVE 888-590-4405
7101 York Avenue South Minneapolis 55435
FAX: 612-921-3368
CONTACT: Elise Williams, Marketing Specialist - 612-835-227
AFFILIATED OFFICES: 410 South First Street, San Jose, CA 95113
WWW: larsen.com
CAPABILITIES: Creating strategic communication solutions through branding, corporate identity, graphic design and interactive media.
SPECIALTIES: Branding, corporate and product identity, interactive media design and development, motion graphics, marketing communication systems, annual reports. Packaging, sign systems and exhibit design.

LECY DESIGN, INC. 612-722-1626
3018 East 28th Street Minneapolis 55406
FAX: 612-722-1626
CONTACT: Eric Lecy
E-MAIL: eric@lecydesign.com
WWW: lecydesign.com
SERVICES: Graphic design services for book publishing. Corporate, identity, trade ads, packaging, product design, direct mail, catalogs, and presentations.
PRESIDENT/CEO/OWNER: Eric Lecy

M

MACLEAN & TUMINELLY   612-338-2075
400 First Avenue North #626   Minneapolis 55401
FAX: 612-338-4817
E-MAIL: mt@good-design.com
WWW: good-design.com
SERVICES: Graphic design, web design, art direction, concept development, layout, production, illustration and project management.
CAPABILITIES: Trade, library and niche book design, consumer catalog design and production, marketing, promotion, and sales materials, logo and visual identity, and employee communications.
CURRENT/RECENT CLIENTS/PROJECTS: Publishing, corporate, business-to-business, real estate, and non-profit.
PRESIDENT/CEO/OWNER: Nancy Tuminelly/Mike Tuminelly

MAJERES GRAPHIC DESIGN   952-474-8693
6450 Oriole Avenue   Excelsior 55331
FAX: 952-474-6797
CONTACT: Jody Majeres
E-MAIL: mgdesign@earthlink.net
WWW: majeresdesign.com
SERVICES: Promotional and marketing material. Brochures, corporate identity and corporate identity packages, annual reports. Magazine, websites, ads and POP along with booths and displays.

MARTIN ROSS DESIGN   612-377-5138
1125 Xerxes Avenue South   Minneapolis 55405
CONTACT: Ross Rezac
E-MAIL: mrdesign@pclink.com
SERVICES: Creative graphic design solutions for corporate identity, marketing and communications programs, reflecting each client's unique position in the marketplace. Work from concept through completion of printed and electronic materials.
SPECIALTIES: Corporate identities, logos and trademarks, annual reports, books, marketing brochure systems, signage, packaging and web page design.
CURRENT/RECENT CLIENTS/PROJECTS: Fortune 500 to small businesses to non-profit organizations.
PRESIDENT/CEO/OWNER: Ross Rezac, Martin Skoro

MARTIN/WILLIAMS - I GROUP   612-340-0800
520 Marquette Avenue #800   Minneapolis 55402
FAX: 612-342-4375
CONTACT: Gregg Sampson, Managing Director
WWW: martinwilliams.com

Graphic Designers / 265

CAPABILITIES: Interactive design, front-end and back-end development, online advertising, direct marketing, e-mail marketing, graphic design.

SPECIALTIES: Website development and marketing, customer acquisition and retention, graphic design and promotional marketing.

CURRENT/RECENT CLIENTS/PROJECTS: 24k.com, 3M, AIGA Creatives, Allina/Mediva, Avenet, Berkline, Blake Schools, Brueggers, Cargill, Catholic Charities, Churchill, Datalink, Dayton's Downtown Council, Gold 'n Plump, Henredon, Homebytes.com, Homehaven/LFI, iPool, Kozy Hat, Lincoln Financial, The Loft, Marvin Windows, Mervyn's, Novartis, Polaris, Victory, Powertel, R-Tech, rooster.com, Rubbermaid, Scots, Search 401k,.com, target, US Bank, Virtual Ink/Mimio, Zonetrader.

MOMENTUM DESIGN, INC.
2550 University Avenue W #245-N
FAX: 651-646-3621
CONTACT: Maureen M. McIlhargey
E-MAIL: momentum@bitstream.net

651-646-3300
St. Paul 55114

SERVICES: Complete graphic design services that move. Quality with quick turnaround. Marketing solutions from the initial concept through printing.

SPECIALTIES: Corporate identity systems, brochures, direct mail, catalogs, annual reports, newsletters, sales and marketing materials, presentations, packaging, POP, signage. Consumer and corporate clientele.

MULTIMEDIA
1011 First Street South #300
FAX: 952-935-1318
CONTACT: Dianne Thill
WWW: multimedia-inc.com

952-931-2112
Hopkins 55343

SERVICES: Production of video presentations, interactive CD-ROM development, web page design, multi-image and live musical shows.

EQUIPMENT: Betacam video location and studio equipment, edit suite, multi-image programming.

SPECIALTIES: Sales meetings, sales training, marketing presentations.

N

THE NANCEKIVELL GROUP
400 North First Street #100
FAX: 612-340-1833
CONTACT: Jim Nancekivell
E-MAIL: tng@nancekivell.com
WWW: nancekivell.com

612-341-8003
Minneapolis 55401

SERVICES: The Nancekivell Group is a leading full-service marketing communications consulting and design firm assisting national and regional clients in the strategic development, writing and design of a broad range of communication tools. We serve as strategic consultants to our clients, helping them evaluate their current brand equity in existing communications tools and creating new communications. We also help them extend their brand presence to the internet and other interactive mediums. At the Nancekivell Group, we measure our success by the value we create for our clients. We build value into every project with our strategic approach to marketing communications, a process that blends the principles of design excellence with the realities and requirements of business.

266 / Graphic Designers

CAPABILITIES: Special capabilities include: annual report design, investor and financial communications, corporate and brand identity systems, marketing and corporate literature, publication design, interactive and CD-ROM tools, Website design and development and Web interface design, programming and testing.
CURRENT/RECENT CLIENTS/PROJECTS: ADC Telecommunications; American Express Financial Advisors; Arctic Cat; Cargill; Case Corporation; Consolidated Paper; Ecolab; Guidant Corporation; Hutchinson Technology; The St. Paul Companies; SUPERVALU, Inc.; The Toro Company; 3M Corporation; U.S. Bank and U.S. Bancorp Piper Jaffray.

NOCTAGRAPHICS: COMPUTER ILLUSTRATION AND DESIGN STUDIO
4512 Harriet Avenue South

612-827-3431

Minneapolis 55409

CONTACT: Nancy Bacher
CAPABILITIES: Surreal images, logo design, illustration, typography and photo montage, enhancement and manipulation. Cartooning, both freehand and computer styles. Page design including: magazines, brochures, posters and billboards. Package design including T-shirts, labels and creative solution for new and existing products from concept to final separations. Also, Macintosh training and support available.
EQUIPMENT: Macintosh environment: 2 Mac systems, external optical, Syquest and zip drives, color scanner, fax, modem and printer. Fast access to color proofing and separation. Primary software: Adobe Illustrator, PhotoShop and QuarkXPress.
SPECIALTIES: Concern for quality illustration and design, speed and efficiency. Creative solutions and expertise in a variety of styles.
PRESIDENT/CEO/OWNER: Derek Brigham

NYGARD DIMENSIONS
1414 Marshall Street N.E.

612-371-9228

Minneapolis 55413

FAX: 612-371-9232
CONTACT: Ben Wallace, Director of Account Services
E-MAIL: id@brandcommunications.com
WWW: brandcommunications.com
SERVICES: Brand-based marketing communications: brand strategy and identity development, integrated marketing communications planning, creative development, design, production, implementation, measurement and management through all media: Print: literature, stationery, direct mail, advertising, sales tools, packaging, sales kits; Digital: Websites (internet/intranet/extranet), online promotion, sales tools/software, product demos, video presentations, kiosks, online brand identity management; Environmental: themed events, stage sets, exhibits, displays/POP.
CAPABILITIES: Brand identity systems, including naming, logo, brand elements and guidelines. Unique approach to brand identity strategy, design development and management through all points of stakeholder contact to create the "whole brand experience." Sister companies Nygard Set Design and Harmony Box contribute to brand experience creation. Industries: information technology/e-business, healthcare/pharmaceuticals, financial services, manufacturing, retail and more.
CURRENT/RECENT CLIENTS/PROJECTS: 3M Company; Auxilium Software; Compass Productions; Conseco Finance; Larson Manufacturing; Lawson Software; Lutheran Brotherhood; MedIntelligence; nQuire Software; Pharmaceutical Care Network (PCN); Proliant (formerly AMPC, Inc.); Qtech Systems, Inc.; Sales Force 2000 Software; Safe Reflections; Sunrise Community Banks (formerly Franklin Bancorp), U.S. Magnetix; U of M Physicians.
PRESIDENT/CEO/OWNER: Jim Nygard, P

O

ORANGESEED DESIGN   **612-252-9757**
800 Washington Ave. N., Suite 461   **Minneapolis 55401-1196**
FAX: 612-252-9760
CONTACT: Damien Wolf
E-MAIL: info@orangeseed.com
WWW: orangeseed.com
SERVICES: Providing smart, friendly, confident, non ego-based professional design and communications services, to create corporate branding, identity systems, product and company brochures, sales literature, advertising, direct mail, web sites, package design and a whole lot more.
SPECIALTIES: Nurturing healthy minds and bodies to think, create and produce business communications tools for your company.
CURRENT/RECENT CLIENTS/PROJECTS: Andersen Windows, West Group, ReliaStar, NSP/Xcel Energy, Grand Casino Corp., Newcourt Financial/The CIT Group, MI-Assistant Software, LawOffice.com, InsSites.com, Lundgren Brothers Construction.

ORCHESTRATED CREATIVE SERVICES   **763-535-5234**
3443 Yates Avenue North   **Crystal 55422**
FAX: 763-504-0137
E-MAIL: pmorrisey@aol.com
SERVICES: Creation of visual communications from creative concept through printing. Services include: creative concept, graphic design, art direction, photography (traditional and digital), image manipulation, illustration, copywriting, electronic production, project management, electronic pre-press and printing.
CAPABILITIES/SPECIALTIES: Specialties include: logo and identity systems, brochures and catalogs, ads, direct mail, annual reports, and package design.
PRESIDENT/CEO/OWNER: Pamela J. Morrisey-Herzog

P

PARACHUTE DESIGN   612-340-0333
120 South 6th Street #1300   Minneapolis 55402
FAX: 612-359-4390
CONTACT: Marcia Miller
E-MAIL: miller@parachute-design.com
WWW: parachute-design.com
SERVICES: Strategic, non-mass media, brand building tools such as packaging, corporate identities, point-of-sale, sales support systems and collateral.
CURRENT/RECENT CLIENTS/PROJECTS: Toro: Chopin Vodka; Belvedere Vodka; Harmon AutoGlass; Target; DBI/SALA; Lawn-Boy; Childrens Hospitals & Clinic Foundation; Crystal Farms; Galleria Shopping Center; Juut SalonSpa; Michael Foods; Pillsbury Bakeries & Food Service; Redline HealthCare; Altru Health System.

PATRICIA GARDNER DESIGN, INC. (PLEASE SEE SPOT DESIGN)

GEORGE PETERS DESIGN & ILLUSTRATION   612-546-4808
209 Turners Crossroad South   Minneapolis 55416
FAX: 612-595-8093
E-MAIL: zeinkstr@bitstream
SERVICES: Graphic design and illustration.
PRESIDENT/CEO/OWNER: George Peters

PICAS & Points, INC.
PREPRESS SERVICES GRAPHIC DESIGN STUDIO

PICAS AND POINTS, INC.   952-881-2626
8070 Morgan Circle   Bloomington 55431
FAX: 952-881-2737
CONTACT: Barbara J. Pflipsen
E-MAIL: picas@picas-points.com
WWW: picas-points.com

Graphic Designers / 269

SERVICES: Complete range of graphic design, including website design, brochures, ads, catalogs, packaging, corporate identity, etc.; Prepress service, including output to imagesetters, drumscanning, color correction, color proof printers and 3M match prints.
CAPABILITIES: Out graphic designers have a wide range of technical expertise in prepress services to complement their creativity. Also film output, including process film and match prints.
PRESIDENT/CEO/OWNER: Doris Brennan-Webb

PRENTICE CREATIVE, INC.   507-645-6413
10670 Gates Avenue   Northfield 55057
FAX: 800-861-3113
CONTACT: Patricia Edel
E-MAIL: pattie@prcreative.com
WWW: prcreative.com
ALTERNATE PHONE: Cell phone: 651-260-3874
CAPABILITIES: Projects include design for all types of print material, web site design and illustration.
CURRENT/RECENT CLIENTS/PROJECTS: Johnson Brothers Liquor Co., Ramsey County, Deluxe Business Systems, 3M Media Intouch, Joe's Sporting Goods, Plasmon Data. Also a variety of designers and agencies (as support).

R

BARBARA REDMOND DESIGN, INC.   612-339-3861
120 South 6th Street #2025   Minneapolis 55402
FAX: 612-339-5918
CONTACT: Barbara Redmond
E-MAIL: redmonddesign@uswest.net
CAPABILITIES: Graphic design, graphic consultant. Design communications company specializing in design consultation and communications for corporate identity, literature design systems, brochures, annual reports and multi-lingual design systems.
PRESIDENT/CEO/OWNER: Barbara Redmond

SUSAN REED DESIGN   612-724-4440
3549 46th Avenue South   Minneapolis 55406
FAX: 612-724-4441
CONTACT: Susan Reed
E-MAIL: srdesign@visi.com
SERVICES: Award-winning print communications for individuals and businesses at reasonable rates. Comprehensive services, from concept through completion.
CAPABILITIES: Corporate identity and symbol development, publication design, capabilities brochures, special events promotion, packaging. Creative, cost-effective design solutions for new and small businesses.
CURRENT/RECENT CLIENTS/PROJECTS: Clients include environmental, health care, public service, educational, retail and food organizations, and individuals in creative services.
PRESIDENT/CEO/OWNER: Susan Reed

270 / Graphic Designers

REZERVOIR
315 Fifth Avenue NW
FAX: 651-251-6511
CONTACT: Nick Vetter, GM
WWW: rezervoir.com
651-251-6500
St. Paul 55112

CAPABILITIES: Mission Statement: To provide High-Bandwidth data downpour solutions directly to the corporate client, utilizing a central storage "rezervoir." This is a value-added service that will streamline workflow and allow for a managed, customized, collaborative environment at the corporate level. Digital Asset Management Solutions Summary.

DIGITAL ASSET MANAGEMENT SOLUTIONS: Centralized on-line storage, High-bandwidth delivery, Multi-Point access, Secure, Redundant. No Scalability constraints, No Capital investment required, Internet accessible.

DIGITAL ASSET MANAGEMENT: On-line data storage; Analysis/Planning and Integration; DAM Consulting; Workflow Consulting/Organization; Archive Management and Administration; High bandwidth Access and Distribution; Internet Accessible Browsing; Digital Data Fulfillment; Applescript Integration; Archive Data Migration; Disaster Recovery (Data Insurance Policy Options); FTP Site Setup; Management and Administration.

PREPRESS: Hi resolution Drum Scanning; Hi/Low resolution Digital Flatbed Scanning; PDF Creation; Digital Graphic Production; Digital Color Retouch/Correction; Digital Layout/Design; Digital Photography; Remote digital Proofing; Film Output (Scitex Environment); Iris Digital Color Proofing; Analog Color Proofing (Matchprint & Color Art/Key).

NEW MEDIA: Short Run CD Duplication and Face Printing; CD business Cards and Face Printing; Digital Render ON-Demand Services (ROD.)

CAPABILITIES/SPECIALTIES: Our focus is on improving the digital workflow while enabling global collaboration. Rezervior, A Taylor Corporation Communications Group Company is an Authorized mastermind™ Channel Partner of WAM!BASE™ and WAM!NET® and member of International prepress Association.

CURRENT/RECENT CLIENTS/PROJECTS: Rapala USA, LTS Print Systems, Print Craft, Inc., Minnesota Timberwolves

S

SCIDMORE, HERSOM & OTHERS
1115 Vicksburg Lane #18
CONTACT: Linda Hersom
OFFICERS: James Scidmore, Linda Hersom
CREATIVE DIRECTOR: James Scidmore
MEDIA DIRECTOR: Linda Hersom
763-476-4976
Plymouth 55447

SPECIALTIES: International, consumer/industrial and business-to-business advertising, media placement and collateral materials, electronic graphics, internet and www.

GRETA SEBALD CREATIVE, INC.
5241 41st Avenue South
FAX: 612-728-1109
CONTACT: Greta Sebald
E-MAIL: greta@gscreative.com
WWW: gscreative.com
612-728-1170
Minneapolis 55417

Graphic Designers / 271

SERVICES: Our goal is to be effectively creative through graphic design along with a twist of marketing expertise and creative writing services. We manage and design all projects, including company/product names and logos, packaging, direct mail (flat and 3-dimensional), brochures, newsletters, annual reports, catalogs, advertisements, presentations and web sites. In addition to our graphics services, we also offer marketing consulting and creative writing to ensure your complete project reflects a consistent message and feel. We are both PC and Mac based to meet your specific needs.
SPECIALTIES: Complete project management from initial concept to final press check.
PRESIDENT/CEO/OWNER: Greta Sebald

SPOT DESIGN
300 Marshall Avenue #4

651-291-1931
St. Paul 55102

FAX: 651-291-1934
CONTACT: Patricia Gardner
E-MAIL: spotdesign@ix.netcom.com
CAPABILITIES: Full-service design studio offering graphic design, illustration and electronic production at affordable prices.
SPECIALTIES: Print media including brochures, posters, direct mail, ads, logos, catalogs and publications. Professional and dependable service since 1988.
PRESIDENT/CEO/OWNER: Patricia Gardner Voje

STANLEY WAI - GRAPHIC DESIGN OFFICE
4624 Ewing Avenue South

612-925-0546
Minneapolis 55410

FAX: 612-925-5002
CONTACT: Stanley Wai
CAPABILITIES: Graphic design, project consultation and management.
SPECIALTIES: Corporate communication, brochure, poster, annual report, sales literature, educational literature, book and publication.

STRANDESIGN STUDIO
1518 Quince Street

218-828-3404
Brainerd 56401

CONTACT: Cheryl Peterson
E-MAIL: strand@uslink.net
WWW: uslink.net/~strand
SERVICES: Strandesign Studio offers all forms of design services from logo/identity packages to annual reports, advertisements to brochures, animations to web sites. Located in central Minnesota, Strandesign offers personal one-on-one service.
CAPABILITIES: Plus 21 years of design experience on Macintosh equipment. Expert level on Adobe Photoshop, Adobe Illustrator, QuarkXPress, Dreamweaver, Flash, etc.
CURRENT/RECENT CLIENTS/PROJECTS: Mediafest 2000; MN Coalition for Battered Women; D Designs.
PRESIDENT/CEO/OWNER: Cheryl Peterson

STUDE-BECKER ADVERTISING & COMMUNICATIONS
332 Minnesota Street

651-293-1393

St. Paul 55101

272 / Graphic Designers

Suite East 100 First Bank
CONTACT: Michael Dunn
SPECIALTIES: Full service advertising and business communications.
CURRENT/RECENT CLIENTS/PROJECTS: Healthcare, education, manufacturing, insurance, banking.com and e-commerce
PRESIDENT/CEO/OWNER: Michael Dunn, Steve Peterson

STUDIO ONE, INC.   612-831-6313
7300 Metro Blvd. #400   Edina 55439
FAX: 612-831-6529
CONTACT: David Kuettel
E-MAIL: systems@studio1.com
WWW: studio1.com
SERVICES: With over 40 years of servicing clients that demand results, Studio One provides complete creative service for print communications including graphic design and production, copywriting and illustration, as well as web design.
SPECIALTIES: Direct marketing, packaging, corporate communications, marketing communications and illustration.
PRESIDENT/CEO/OWNER: David Kuettel

B SUTER GRAPHICS AND DESIGN, INC.   612-544-0930
7103 Medicine Lake Road   Minneapolis 55427
FAX: 612-544-0094
CONTACT: Bryon Suter
E-MAIL: bsuter@visi.com
SERVICES: Full-service creative and design, illustration, and production studio for over 17 years. Concept through final production through full color art.
CAPABILITIES: Marketing and communications collateral, advertising, corporate image, logo, digital illustration, animation, multimedia and web sites.

T

TANDEM COMMUNICATIONS   651-224-6747
332 Minnesota Street   St. Paul 55101
FAX: 651-224-6926
CONTACT: Peter B. Myers or Steve Weil
E-MAIL: info@tandemcom.com
WWW: tandemcom.com
CAPABILITIES: Full service marketing communications design firm, with strategic and tactical capabilities in print and interactive media. Strategic services include communications audits, marketing plans, writing/editing, and helping clients define their message and audience. Tactical services include graphic design for annual reports, print collateral. Web sites, signage and multimedia, organizational identity systems, brand asset management.
SPECIALTIES: Brand asset management. Communications audits and developing integrated solutions to a client's branding and identity needs. Turnkey project management. Extensive experience working with corporate and non-profit organizations.
CURRENT/RECENT CLIENTS/PROJECTS: 3M, Andersen Windows, District Energy St. Paul, YWCA of St. Paul, Minnesota Landmarks.
OFFICERS: Peter B. Myers or Steve Weil, Principals

Graphic Designers / 273

TEAM CREATIVE 763-425-7007
9101 Nantwick Ridge Brooklyn Park 55443
CONTACT: Robert Jacobs, Creative Director
E-MAIL: rjacobs@teamcreative.com
PRESIDENT/CEO/OWNER: Robert Jacobs, Creative Director

THOMAS DESIGN GROUP 763-546-6097
945 Highway 169 North Plymouth 55441
FAX: 763-546-1021
CONTACT: Thomas McClellan, Owner; Joe Otto, Officer; Nora Boulden, Contact
E-MAIL: tdg@thomasdesign.com
SERVICES: We deliver on-target visual design solutions that help drive our clients' business. How? By listening. By building trusted client relationships thanks to our staff of smart, hardworking, experienced people who know what it takes to ensure our clients' success. And by delivering more than we promise. On budget. On time. Every time. We've done this for our long list of loyal clients for 20 years. We can do it for you.
SPECIALTIES: Our mission is to provide effective visual strategies for business for software/high-tech, pharmaceutical, medical and financial companies, retail and business to business.

TILKA DESIGN 612-664-8994
921 Marquette Avenue #200 Minneapolis 55402
FAX: 612-664-8991
CONTACT: Jane Tilka
E-MAIL: jtilka@tilka.com
WWW: tilka.com
CAPABILITIES: Development of brand character through speciality, visual identity creation. Visual identity systems are then expressed through creation of sales collateral, web design, communication design and environmental design.
SPECIALTIES: Visual identity systems.

U

ULTRA CREATIVE, INC. 612-338-7908
920 Second Avenue South #1200 Minneapolis 55402
FAX: 612-337-8178
CONTACT: Dave Biebighauser
E-MAIL: dave@ultracreative.com
CAPABILITIES: Planning and positioning, creative development, graphic design and production. Project based creative marketing firm for corporate communications; print, direct, packaging, POP, identity and collateral.
SPECIALTIES: Food products, retail, kid marketing, new products, and brand equity maintenance.
CURRENT/RECENT CLIENTS/PROJECTS: General Mills, Inc.; The Pillsbury Company; Campbell's Foods, Inc.; Marigold Foods; Gymamerica.com; Govt.com.
PRESIDENT/CEO/OWNER: Dave Biebighauser, President; Gino Perfetti, Vice President

274 / Graphic Designers

UPFRONT PRODUCTIONS 651-633-5299
2350 County Road C #120 St. Paul 55113
FAX: 651-633-5197
CONTACT: Tricia Nordby Hamrin/Chris Hamrin
WWW: hoopjumping.com
CAPABILITIES: Organizational Communications Solutions Center. A Spectrum. A Synergy. Concept Development, Copywriting, Graphic Design, Illustration, Document Production, Web Site Creation, Scanning, Photo Retouching, Pre-press, Offset Printing, Digital B&W Printing, Color Copies, Posters, Displays, Signs, Custom Assembly, Inventory, Distribution, Corporate Compass® MIS, VantagePoint™, Hoop Jumping™.
SPECIALTIES: Choose your hoop. We'll jump through it™.
OFFICERS: Tricia Nordby Hamrin/Chris Hamrin

W

MORGAN WILLIAMS & ASSOCIATES, INC. 612-339-5000
400 First Avenue North Minneapolis 55401
CONTACT: Starr Morgan
E-MAIL: smorgan@morganwilliamsgrafx.com
SERVICES: All types of graphic design for: corporate identity systems, logos, marketing and sales materials, annual reports magazines, packaging, signage.
CAPABILITIES: In business for 23 years - much experience with a variety of clients from food, health care to retail.

MORGAN WILLIAMS & ASSOCIATES, INC. 612-339-5000
400 1st Avenue North Minneapolis 55401
CONTACT: Jean Falk
SERVICES: Creative design, advertising layout, illustration, and production.
CAPABILITIES: Annual reports, logo design, brochures, corporate identity systems, marketing and sales materials, direct mail, catalogs, advertisements. Packaging, publications, all types of print collateral materials.
PRESIDENT/CEO/OWNER: Starr Morgan; Jean Falk

Z

PEGGY ZETAH, LTD. 612-359-9547
529 South 7th Street #623 Minneapolis 55415
FAX: 612-359-9555
CONTACT: Peggy Zetah
E-MAIL: peggyz@bitstream.net
SERVICES: Art direction and graphic design services.
CAPABILITIES: Corporate identity, annual reports, brochures, package design, sales promotion and direct mail.

Graphics Consultants

B

BARSUHN DESIGN INCORPORATED 612-339-2146
1186 Ford Center Minneapolis 55401
420 North Fifth Street
FAX: 612-339-8760
CONTACT: Rochelle Barsuhn
E-MAIL: shellyb@barsuhndesign.com
WWW: barsuhndesign.com
PRESIDENT/CEO/OWNER: Scott Barsuhn
SERVICES: Strategic marketing planning and design services in three interrelated areas: print communications (company literature, identity development, annual reports, publications), interactive technologies (web sites, CD-ROM, etc.) and corporate gift and product development (client relations, event materials, etc).
CURRENT/RECENT CLIENTS/PROJECTS: Retek; Pentair; Hewitt Associates; HealthPartners; Allianz Life Insurance Company; Musicland; Padilla Speer Beardsley

BRUCE WILLITS DESIGN 952-927-1061
3120 Pennsylvania Avenue South Minneapolis 55426
FAX: 952-927-1062
CONTACT: Bruce Willits
SERVICES: Graphic design, corporate identity, logo design.
PRESIDENT/CEO/OWNER: Bruce Willits

G

GROSSMAN DESIGN ASSOCIATES 612-922-4343
4301 Highway 7 #120 Minneapolis 55416
FAX: 612-922-7576
E-MAIL: steve@usazone.com
WWW: Grossmandesign.com
SERVICES: Graphic design, advertising layout, keyline and production art, illustration, photo retouching, creative copy writing.
CAPABILITIES: Design and production of brochures, catalogs, annual reports, direct mail, websites, packaging, POP, ads, all types of printed collaterals.
PRESIDENT/CEO/OWNER: David Grossman

I

IMAGINALITY, INC. 612-545-4123
6182 Olson Memorial Highway Golden Valley 55422
FAX: 612-545-4266
CONTACT: Myrna Orensten
E-MAIL: myrna@imaginality.inc
WWW: imaginality.com

276 / Graphics Consultants

SERVICES: Corporate identity, graphic design, signage.

J

JOHNSTON DESIGN OFFICE 612-929-3765
5912 Bernard Place Edina 55436
FAX: 612-929-3122
CONTACT: Dale K. Johnston
E-MAIL: dj77@aol.com
SERVICES: Graphic design, corporate identification, packaging design/systems, print.
CAPABILITIES: 35+ years experience in all areas of graphic design.

K

KDG INTERACTIVE 612-861-8890
1720 East 66th Street Richfield 55423
FAX: 612-861-8967
CONTACT: Steven Haas
E-MAIL: shaas@kdg.com
WWW: kdg.com
SERVICES: With over 150 years combined (in-house) experience, KDG InterActive is an e-business and enterprise learning outfitter recognized as a major player in their industry. They combine sophisticated strategies, award-winning design capabilities and cutting-edge technology solutions to assist today's progressive companies in their strategic migration to the e-business edge. They offer: strategic planning, marketing consulting, interactive design and production services, e-commerce site development and software development and have served a variety of global brand leaders such as 3M, Honeywell, US Bancorp, Carlson Marketing Group and Disney Online.

CAPABILITIES: KDG InterActive is fully equipped with a state-of-the-art interactive multimedia development studio and hosts an innovative team of designers, developers and programmers who create online and disk-based programs for: Information Kiosks; CBT (computer-based training); TEST (technology enabled sales tools); EPSS (electronic performance support systems). Their specialties include: Authorware, Director, programming in C++, HTML, CGI, Java, Lotus Notes, Microsoft Office Suite, PhotoShop, Premiere, Painter, Illustrator, After Effects, Infini-D, 3D Studio Max, StrataVision, etc.

CURRENT/RECENT CLIENTS/PROJECTS: American Express, (information kiosks and training presentation); 3M, (software interface design); Business Incentives, (assorted projects); Carlson Marketing Group, (laptop sales presentations); Cray Research, (3D modeling); Disney Online, (assorted online animations); Honeywell, (electronic brochure); US Bancorp, (web based training); US West Communications, (training program); Q Tech Systems, (electronic performance support software); The Saint Paul Companies, (speaker support); Wilson Learning, (consumer self-improvement CD ROM); Minnesota Historical Society, (information kiosks); Ronald Reagan Library, (electronic cabinet room); St. Croix Medical, (computer-based training/online clinical trials); The Great Lakes Aquarium, (information kiosks).

Graphics Consultants / 277

KV GRAPHICS
710 Canterbury Circle
CONTACT: Bob Cavey
E-MAIL: bob@kvgraphics.com
WWW: kvgraphics.com

612-949-2902
Chanhassen 55317

SERVICES: We create custom 2D and 3D graphics for our clients. We create bitmap and vector graphics. Samples of our work can be seen and/or downloaded at our website (see above). We create Mac and PC graphics.
CAPABILITIES: We can create Shockwaved animations for your website. We work in conjunction with a team of programmers who can assist us in customer software and game development. We create 3D graphics on the PC using 3D Studio Max.
CURRENT/RECENT CLIENTS/PROJECTS: Schatz Real Estate Group Website; 3D Graphics for FLW Bass Fishing Software game for Wizardworks.

PROSPERA DESIGN
8400 Normandale Lake Blvd #500
FAX: 952-831-9191
CONTACT: Heidi Libera
E-MAIL: info@prospera.com
WWW: prospera.com

952-832-5588
Minneapolis 55437

SERVICES: Prospera Design offers inventive solutions to help your company thrive and prosper as you invest in new methods of design, marketing and global communications. Prospera is owned by Shandwick International, a leader in public relations, offering clients a global network of resources with over 100 offices worldwide.
SPECIALTIES: Prospera specializes in corporate identity, material audits, graphic standards, publications, marketing collateral, annual reports, video, environmental graphics and print management.
CURRENT/RECENT CLIENTS/PROJECTS: Deluxe Corp.; Greater Minneapolis Chamber of Commerce; Merck-Medco; University of Minnesota; Minnesota State University Mankato; Lawson Software; Lutheran Brotherhood; Novartis; Seagate Technology; SCIMED
PRESIDENT/CEO/OWNER: Heidi Libera, Senior Vice President, Design Director; Todd Spichke, Design Director; Lawrence Sahulka, Design Director

278 / Graphics Consultants

R

BARBARA REDMOND DESIGN, INC.   612-339-3861
120 South 6th Street #2025   Minneapolis 55402
FAX: 612-339-5918
CONTACT: Barbara Redmond
E-MAIL: redmonddesign@uswest.net
CAPABILITIES: Graphic design, graphic consultant. Design communications company specializing in design consultation and communications for corporate identity, literature design systems, brochures, annual reports and multi-lingual design systems.
PRESIDENT/CEO/OWNER: Barbara Redmond

PATRICK REDMOND DESIGN   651-646-4254
PO BOX 75430 - TGB   St. Paul 55175-0430
CONTACT: Patrick M. Redmond
E-MAIL: redmond@patrickredmonddesign.com
WWW: patrickredmonddesign.com
SERVICES: Creative concept, creative direction and design consulting.
CAPABILITIES: Branding, brand identity, corporate identity, logos and trademarks, marketing communication, graphic design (creative), publication design, book cover design, package design, brochures, art direction, photo direction, web site design. State-of-the-art equipment (hardware and software) used as needed, via service bureaus and outside resources. Patrick Redmond Design provides creative concepts and creative direction and is not a production facilities or provider of technical services. Extensive experience providing creative for over 130 clients, from small start-ups to Fortune 500 companies. Former creative art direction at major corporation and former senior art director at one of the world's leading marketing companies.
PRESIDENT/CEO/OWNER: Patrick M. Redmond, M.A.

REZERVOIR   651-251-6500
315 Fifth Avenue NW   St. Paul 55112
FAX: 651-251-6511
CONTACT: Nick Vetter, GM
WWW: rezervoir.com

CAPABILITIES: Mission Statement: To provide high-bandwidth data downpour solutions directly to the corporate client, utilizing a central storage "rezervoir." This is a value-added service that will streamline workflow and allow for a managed, customized, collaborative environment at the corporate level. Digital Asset Management Solutions Summary.

DIGITAL ASSET MANAGEMENT SOLUTIONS: Centralized on-line storage, High-bandwidth delivery, Multi-Point access, Secure, Redundant., No Scalability constraints, No Capital investment required, Internet accessible.

DIGITAL ASSET MANAGEMENT: On-line data storage; Analysis/Planning and Integration; DAM Consulting; Workflow Consulting/Organization; Archive Management and Administration; High bandwidth Access and Distribution; Internet Accessible Browsing; Digital Data Fulfillment; Applescript Integration; Archive Data Migration; Disaster Recovery (Data Insurance Policy Options); FTP Site Setup; Management and Administration.

PREPRESS: Hi resolution Drum Scanning; Hi/Low resolution Digital Flatbed Scanning; PDF Creation; Digital Graphic Production; Digital Color Retouch/Correction; Digital Layout/Design; Digital Photography; Remote digital Proofing; Film Output (Scitex Environment); Iris Digital Color Proofing; Analog Color Proofing (Matchprint & Color Art/Key).

NEW MEDIA: Short Run CD Duplication and Face Printing; CD business Cards and Face Printing; Digital Render ON-Demand Services (ROD.)

CAPABILITIES/SPECIALTIES: Our focus is on improving the digital workflow while enabling global collaboration. Rezervior, A Taylor Corporation Communications Group Company is an Authorized mastermind™ Channel Partner of WAM!BASE™ and WAM!NET® and member of International prepress Association.

CURRENT/RECENT CLIENTS/PROJECTS: Rapala USA, LTS Print Systems, Print Craft, Inc., Minnesota Timberwolves

S

SPANGLER DESIGN TEAM
4850 Park Glen Road
FAX: 952-927-7034
CONTACT: Mark Spangler
E-MAIL: mail@spanglerdesign.com
WWW: spanglerdesign.com

952-927-5425
St. Louis Park 55416

CAPABILITIES: Creative consultation, web sites, corporate identity, annual reports, product design, packaging, and promotional materials.
SPECIALTIES: Simplicity and quality.
PRESIDENT/CEO/OWNER: Mark Spangler

Graphics Temporaries

A

AQUENT PARTNERS 612-378-4930
43 Main Street SE #413 Minneapolis 55414
FAX: 612-378-2520
CONTACT: Craig Seal, Area Manager
E-MAIL: cseal@aquent.com
WWW: aquent.com
SPECIALTIES: Temporary and permanent placement in web, tech and print. Including Graphic design, Print production, Pre-press, Web design, Web development, and Mac Tech Support.
CAPABILITIES: Over 50 offices in 12 countries. Aquent is the world's largest staffing agency for web, tech and print talent. Intensive screening of all freelancer, including interview, portfolio review, reference checks and real world testing. The industry's only unequivocal 110% guarantee on all temporary and permanent placements.
CURRENT/RECENT CLIENTS/PROJECTS: Augsburg Fortress, Blue Cross/Blue Shield, Fallon/Duffy, Lutheran Brotherhood, Martin Williams (I), Reliant Energy, Star Tribune, Ruckus.

C

CREATIVE CADRE, INC. 952-897-3503
PO Box 390007 Edina 55439
FAX: 952-897-1030
CONTACT: Yvette Bosela
SERVICES: Temporary and permanent personnel for creative needs. On-site and off-site.
CAPABILITIES: We provide experienced, talented web designers, graphic designers, production artists, copywriters and other creative types. No rookies, no prima donnas!
CURRENT/RECENT CLIENTS/PROJECTS: Agencies, corporations, professional organizations, anyone who requires creative help.

D

DIGITAL PEOPLE 952-842-8359
5151 Edina Industrial Boulevard Edina 55439
FAX: 952-835-7326
CONTACT: Ken Marshall
E-MAIL: ken_marshall@digitalpeople.net
WWW: digitalpeople.net

Graphics Temporaries / 281

SERVICES: We represent exceptional freelance graphics and web/Internet talent for on-site or off-site projects, permanent employee recruiting, or project based assignments. Complete background checking, software testing and skills verification of all talent assures you the right talent for that all-important project.

CAPABILITIES: Macintosh or PC/Windows based professionals in the areas of Art Direction, Graphic Design, Illustration, Web Design, Web Coding, Web Productions, Web Content Development, Multimedia Design, Video Production, Copywriting, Editing/Proofreading, Electronic Production Artists, Traffic/Print Productions, Media and much more. Digital People currently have 14 offices in 11 major cities; if we can't find the talent you need locally, we will source them in other markets.

CURRENT/RECENT CLIENTS/PROJECTS: Corporate Communication Departments, Advertising Agencies, Sales Promotion Agencies, Dot.com's, Internet Solution Providers, Internet Based Communication Agencies, Graphic Design Agencies. We provide complete references from a broad base of clients.

E

SUSAN ERICKSON 952-474-2675
2198 Baneberry Way West   Chanhassen 55317
CONTACT: Susan Erickson
PAGER: 612-510-7788
CAPABILITIES: Reliable, professional and experienced freelance assistance. Traffic and project management. Graphic and photography studio coordination. Services offered on a part-time, full-time or contract basis.
SPECIALTIES: Large print projects, cookbooks, catalogs, packaging.

F

Twin Cities Best Connection for Creative Staffing

FREELANCE CREATIVE SERVICES   952-941-0022
7835 Telegraph Road   Bloomington 55438
FAX: 952-941-0709
CONTACT: Marlene Phipps
E-MAIL: marlenep@freelancecreative.com
WWW: freelancecreative.com

282 / Graphics Temporaries

FOCUS: Freelance Creative Services, Inc. is the best connection for temporary creative and technical talent in the areas of: art direction, graphic design/production, writing, editing and proofing, web design and maintenance, presentations and multi-media development. We provide quality professional service by upholding the highest industry standards. You can completely rely on our judgement and expertise in quickly finding the talent you need or the perfect assignment to match your unique talent. With over 25 years of experience in the Twin Cities creative community, we are totally committed to your satisfaction.

SERVICES: Why work with an agency? We have the time, knowledge, and resources to evaluate and build relationships with people you need. It's what we do every day. If reviewing resumes, interviewing, testing and checking references is not an efficient use of your time, make Freelance Creative Services your resource. On the other hand, if making sales calls to prospective clients during the day, working all night, invoicing and trying to collect your money in less than 30 days is not your idea of a career, make Freelance Creative Services your connection. Our recruiting staff is constantly recruiting, screening, and testing to build the strongest pool of freelance talent for our clients. Our seasoned sales staff is proactively marketing our talented pool of freelancers. Let us handle all the paperwork involved so you can focus on what you do best.

CAPABILITIES: More than any other factor, success in the outsourcing business is dependent on the strength of our business relationships. We have met clients and freelancers through our involvement with industry organizations, training centers and referrals from satisfied clients and freelancers through 25 years of networking in the Twin Cities creative community. Our focus on working with the most skilled, highly-qualified people and building quality relationships, results in individualized service and solutions for both clients and freelancers.

PRESIDENT/CEO/OWNER: Marlene and Douglas Phipps

G

GRAPHIC RELIEF 612-386-8088
15207 94th Place North Maple Grove 55369
CONTACT: Tony Rubasch
E-MAIL: tonyr@graphicrelief.com
WWW: inet-serv.com/~tonyr

SPECIALTIES: A relief designer with strong emphaiss in retail direct mail catlaogs and web site creation for general consumer merchandise. Along with creative marketing communications for industrial manufacturing, food industry, retail clothing, recreation providers and health care.

CURRENT/RECENT CLIENTS/PROJECTS: Major advertising and marketing communication agencies in the Twin Cities location.

Indoor Advertising & Signage

C

CENTRAL CONTAINER CORP.　　　　　　　　　　612-425-7444
PO Box 43310　　　　　　　　　　　　　　　　　　Minneapolis 55443
FAX: 612-425-7917
CONTACT: Steven Braun
E-MAIL: sbraun@centralcontainer.com
WWW: centralcontainer.com

SERVICES: Designs created by an award winning structural design team. From promotional packaging and point-of-sale shelf cartons, to protective, cushioned shipping containers, we provide complete prototyping and engineered solutions. Point-of-purchase displays and "club pack" designs are turned out in minimal time. Full color mock-ups of proposed art are produced on our 54" H. P. Color Plotter. Sophisticated warehouse and logistics management within our 175,000 square foot state of the art production facility, coupled with our in-house fulfillment group, allow for true "turnkey" project management.

CAPABILITIES: Litho/label mounting on 2 automatic mounters. Substrates from corrugated to foam core. 4 color flexo press capable of process work as well as vibrant, rich solid color and line work. Precision die cutters - 2 flat bed and 2 rotary presses. Standard cartons from our flexo/folder/gluers, and specialty boxes with intricate glue patterns for "crash bottoms," 6 corner trays, and internal parts - all glued on computer automated systems.

PRESIDENT/CEO/OWNER: James E. Haglund

D

DRAWING CARD　　　　　　　　　　　　　　　　612-339-7586
275 Market Street #169　　　　　　　　　　　　Minneapolis 55405
FAX: 612-339-7586
CONTACT: Bernie McNally
E-MAIL: drawincard@aol.com

SERVICES: Signs and graphics (non-electric), Illustration, Custom Art, Storefronts, Murals, Design, Banners, Showcards, Vehicle graphics, Wall graphics, Real Estate signage, Construction site, Pictorials, Logo design, Vinyl lettering, Ink jet vinyl printing, Hand lettering, Sandblasting.

CAPABILITIES: Master of Fine Arts - U of M 1973.

CURRENT/RECENT CLIENTS/PROJECTS: Towle Real Estate (International Market Square); Wm Beson Interior Design; Kravet/Lee Jofa; Makaram.

PRESIDENT/CEO/OWNER: Bernie McNally

Industrial & Product Designers

B

WALTER BIEGER ASSOCIATES   651-636-8500
1689 Lake Valentine Road   Arden Hills 55112
E-MAIL: bieger@wavefront.com
SERVICES: Creative design and development of new products, including prototyping and graphic arts services. Consultation, research, product concept studies, styling illustrations, assembly layouts, CAD production drawings and solid-modeling; mechanical/electronic engineering, styling and working prototype models; sourcing, ergonomics, production quoting/coordination, patent assistance; corporate identification, logos/letterheads, signage, office/home/plant layouts, convention displays, technical illustration.
SPECIALTIES: Wood and plastic office and home accessories, control panels and instrumentation, plastic and metal product housings, medical equipment, computer peripherals and cabinetry, executive gifts and ad specialties, plastic parts design. Serving the Twin Cities business and industry for 35 years.
CONTACT: Walter Bieger

BILITZ DESIGN, INC.   612-922-3735
3546 Dakota Avenue South   St. Louis Park 55416
CONTACT: Mark R. Bilitz
CAPABILITIES: Product design, user studies, engineering and product graphics.
SPECIALTIES: Medical products, industrial controls, and consumer products, product graphics, control panel design. Model and prototyping.

J

JOHANNES GASTON DESIGN, INC.   612-935-5355
5139 Mayview Road   Minnetonka 55345
FAX: 612-935-8567
CONTACT: Doug Van Onnum
E-MAIL: info@jgdesign.com
WWW: jgdesign.com
SERVICES: Cutting edge product design from ideation to production. User research, appearance concepts, and working prototypes. Ergonomic and interface analysis. Design for manufacture. Check out our website.
CAPABILITIES: High tech consumer, medical, commercial and industrial products and equipment. Experience with both low and high volume domestic and foreign production.
CURRENT/RECENT CLIENTS/PROJECTS: 3M Company; Proctor and Gamble and many start-up companies.
PRESIDENT/CEO/OWNER: Johannes Gaston

Industrial & Product Designers / 285

K

KABLOOE DESIGN, INC.   763-785-9595
9162 Davenport Street NE   Minneapolis 55449
FAX: 763-785-9446
CONTACT: Tom Kramer, VP Product Development
E-MAIL: ideas@kablooe.com
WWW: kablooe.com
CAPABILITIES: Ideas and lots of them. Concept Ideations, Product Design, Mock-ups, Prototype models and mechanisms, Engineering, Final design models for pre-production evaluation as well as photo shoots, rapid tooling and casting dept. for pre-production sample support, final part drawings, manufacturing liaison and sourcing.
SPECIALTIES: An exceptionally creative & energetic product design team working in areas of Consumer, Industrial, Fitness, Sporting Goods, Medical, Hardware, Electronics, Housewares, Toys and Licensing. We've done a lot of stuff over the years!
FACILITIES: A fun place to develop your project with all the standard stuff you would expect from a full service facility.
CURRENT/RECENT CLIENTS/PROJECTS: 3M, UltraWheels, Universal Studios, Honeywell, Medtronic. These are just some of our big name accounts to impress you, but most of our work load is with small to medium sized companies needing big time help. So now is the time to call us.
OFFICERS: David Powell, President

Industry Organizations

A

ACADEMY FOR FILM AND TELEVISION AT   952-915-9132
CARYN INTERNATIONAL STUDIOS
6651 Highway 7   Minneapolis 55426
FAX: 952-915-9181
CONTACT: Kathleen Bloom, Chad Raukar, Tom Payne, Theresa Namie, Imee Abdelwahed, Angela McRoy
SERVICES: Professional actor training program affiliated with Three of Us Studios in New York City (NAST college-accredited). The Academy seeking accreditation, proposed completion by National PONSI in 2001. The Academy for Film and Television has conservatory-level curriculum for foundational to advanced training for stage and film for ages 7 and up. The Academy is located in a working film studio; students learn in the professional environment. Industry-oriented training for Television, Industrial, Commercial, Film and Voiceover. 4 - 6 week classes on trimester schedule and short-term master classes, workshops and seminars offered. Resource and support for working and new actors in the Midwest.
SPECIALTIES: Prepares actors for a career in the commercial electronic media.
HOURS: Monday - Thursday 9:00 AM - 9:00 PM, Friday and Saturday 9:00 AM - 5:00 PM.
OFFICERS: Caryn Rosenberg, Chuck Rosenberg, Kathleen Bloom, Lance Rosenberg

ADVERTISING FEDERATION OF MINNESOTA   651-917-6251
1821 University Avenue West #S156   St. Paul 55104
FAX: 651-917-1835
E-MAIL: office@adfed.org
WWW: adfed.org
SERVICES: Non-profit, professional trade association bringing together representatives from ad agencies, corporate advertising departments, the media, and supplier firms. Meetings: one luncheon meeting monthly, one breakfast professional development seminar each month, other special activities through the year.
CAPABILITIES/SPECIALTIES: Membership requirements, dues: those with an interest in the advertising industry, including: students, professionals in ad agencies, corporate advertising/marketing departments, media, supplier, firms. Dues are $135.00 per year, per individual. Discounts are available for companies with five or more members.
CURRENT/RECENT CLIENTS/PROJECTS: Number of members: 500
CONTACT: Kris Finger

AFTRA/SAG TWIN CITIES LOCAL   612-371-9120
708 First Street North #333   Minneapolis 55401
FAX: 612-371-9119
CONTACT: Colleen A. Aho
SERVICES: Unions representing broadcast station staff and performing talent in Minnesota. Also regulation of talent agencies franchised by union.
SPECIALTIES: Provides servicing and enforcement of AFTRA and SAG collective bargaining agreements in Minnesota; membership services and outreach to local broadcast, film industry.
PRESIDENT/CEO/OWNER: Colleen A. Aho

Industry Organizations / 287

ALLIANCE FRANCAISE OF THE TWIN CITIES   612-332-0436
113 North First Street   Minneapolis 55401
FAX: 612-332-0438
CONTACT: Abdon Berthelot
SERVICES: French language classes, translation and interpretation. Advanced business and commercial French. 25 years of experience, supported by French Foreign Ministry.

AMERICAN MARKETING ASSOCIATION   651-917-6241
1821 University Avenue West #156   St. Paul 55104
FAX: 651-917-1835
CONTACT: Kris Finger
E-MAIL: amamn@nonprofitsolutions.com
WWW: mnama.org
SERVICES: American Marketing Association is a professional not-for-profit organization for marketers. The purpose of the AMA is to promote education and assist in the personal and professional career development among marketing professionals, and to advance the science and ethical practice of marketing disciplines.
CAPABILITIES: Organization that provides direct benefits to marketing professionals in both business and education, and serves all levels of marketing practitioners, educators and students.

I

INTERNATIONAL ASSOCIATION OF BUSINESS COMMUNICATORS   612-333-4222
1821 University Avenue W #5156   St. Paul 55104
FAX: 651-917-1835
CONTACT: Kris Finger
E-MAIL: iabcmn@nonprofitsolutions.com
WWW: iabcmn.com
SERVICES: Field of Service: Non-profit association of professional business communicators providing ongoing professional development, networking and career development opportunities. Meetings: One dialogue session monthly, other local, district and international conferences and seminars throughout the year.
CAPABILITIES: Membership Requirements, Dues: Professionals and students who specialize in the communications industry, including: marketing and employee communications, investor and public relations and graphic design. Dues are $225 per year, per individual ($45 for students), plus a one-time enrollment fee of $40.
CURRENT/RECENT CLIENTS/PROJECTS: Number of members: 500.

INTERNATIONAL TELEVISION ASSOC. (ITVA)   612-927-8747
P.O. Box 582862   Minneapolis 55458

288 / Industry Organizations

CONTACT: Mary Jo Allen
WWW: itvatwincities.org
SERVICES: ITVA is a professional organization for anyone interested or involved in the field of visual communication, including video, film and multimedia production. The local chapter offers networking and career services including: workshops, monthly meetings, newsletters, special interest groups, and an annual Twin Cities video festival. Monthly meetings held the last Wednesday of the month at various production and related facilities.
PRESIDENT/CEO/OWNER: Rebecca Bryden

M

MIDWEST INDEPENDENT PUBLISHERS ASSN.   651-917-0021
PO Box 581432   Minneapolis 55458
CONTACT: Doug Shidell
SERVICES: Trade association, publishers. Membership Requirements: Publisher; field related to book production aspects. Meetings: Monthly; generally at Women Venture at 2324 University Avenue West, St. Paul.

MINNESOTA SCHOOL OF COMPUTER IMAGING   612-861-2000
1401 West 76th Street   Richfield 55423
FAX: 612-861-5548
CONTACT: Admissions Department, MN School of Business, Richfield 861-2000. Brooklyn Center 566-7777; Globe College 651-730-5100; or Oakdale 730-5100
WWW: msbcollege.com or globecollege.com
SERVICES: Minnesota School of Computer Imaging, a division of the Minnesota School of Business and Globe College is comprised of a team of specialists in the computer imaging field. Students have the opportunity to master interrelated skill sets, including CD-ROM Production, Graphic Design, Multimedia broadcast animation and Website Development. Graduates are qualified to interview for positions in traditional print graphics, multimedia production animation and website development. Classes are available in three Twin Cities location. Degrees: Associate in Applied Science (AAS) in Animation Design; Associate in Applied Science (AAS) in Multimedia/Computer Graphics production, Associate in Applied Science E-Commerce Design.
CAPABILITIES: G3 and G4 workstations - SGI workstations - NT workstations. Software: PhotoShop - Illustrator - QuarkXPress - Director - Dreamweaver - Flash - HTML - Cold Fusion - Final Cut - After Affects - Softimage - Maya.
PRESIDENT/CEO/OWNER: Terry Myhre

N

NATIONAL ASSOCIATION OF GOVERNMENT COMMUNICATORS - VOYAGEUR CHAPTER   651-297-7363
395 John Ireland Blvd   St. Paul 55155
G-60 Transportation Building
FAX: 651-297-8260
CONTACT: Robin Panlener. 651-297-7963; email: robin.panlener@state.mn.us

Industry Organizations / 289

SERVICES: Communications professionals working in government as information officers, public affairs and public service officers, managers and directors. Specific work assignments; editors, writers, graphic artists, photographers, technical writers, video and audio producers. Members receive local and national notices of program. Awards competitions, directories, publications.

MEMBERSHIP DUES: Perform communication, education and information activities for federal, state, county and local units of government. $85 a year.

MEETINGS: Professional development training, speakers, seminars, workshops, awards, networking opportunities, annual fall conferences both locally and nationally.

MEMBERS: Active - 100; Government Communicators on statewide mailing list = 850.

Legal Services

G

BARBARA J. GISLASON & ASSOCIATES 612-331-8033
219 SE Main Street #506 Minneapolis 55414
FAX: 612-331-8115
CONTACT: Barbara J. Gislason
E-MAIL: gislasonbj@aol.com
CAPABILITIES: A fourth-generation attorney, Ms. Gislason was chosen by her peers as a Law & Leading Attorney in the practice of Art & Entertainment Law.
SPECIALTIES: Expertise in literary publishing and the visual arts. Represent a broad spectrum of art and entertainment clients, including educational, developers, media personalities, galleries, small presses, musicians, fashion designers, photographers, software developers, fine artists and playwrights. Recognized as Top Lawyer in Mpls/St. Paul Magazine, Minnesota Law & Politics and Minnesota Monthly. Listed in Who's Who. Lectures at a variety of educational institutions. Literary agent representing nationally acclaimed authors.

K

DAVID W. KOEHSER 612-204-4567
700 Lumber Exchange Minneapolis 55402
10 South Fifth Street
FAX: 612-204-4568
CONTACT: David W. Koehser
CAPABILITIES: Legal counsel for individuals and businesses in the publishing, graphic design, entertainment and creative arts industries: book contracts, merchandise, character and design licensing; copyright registrations; collaboration/project agreements; theatre/performing arts agreements; business formations; and office/studio leases.
SPECIALTIES: Copyright, publishing and licensing law, business law.
PRESIDENT/CEO/OWNER: David W. Koehser

KENNETH L KUNKLE, ATTORNEY AT LAW 612-414-3113
1769 Lexington Avenue North #182 St. Paul 55113
FAX: 651-917-0422
CONTACT: Kenneth L Kunkle
E-MAIL: kenneth@kunklelaw.com
WWW: kunklelaw.com
SERVICES: Serving the legal needs of creative professionals. Services include: assisting with all areas affected by the sale, use, or creation of copyrighted or trademarked works; drafting, reviewing, and negotiation contracts; and providing assistance and counsel regarding the formation and development of small to mid-size businesses.
CURRENT/RECENT CLIENTS/PROJECTS: Clients include a broad range of creative professionals, including designers, photographers, musicians, web developers, film/video professionals, and other artisans working in assorted mediums.

DAVID W. KOEHSER
Attorney at Law

Copyright Law
Publishing Law
Artwork & Character Licensing
New Business Formations
Office/Studio Leases

700 Lumber Exchange
10 South Fifth Street
Minneapolis, MN 55402

Phone (612) 204-4567 Fax (612) 204-4568
E-Mail dklaw@cognisinc.com

YOUR IMAGE IS OUR BUSINESS.

In today's complex and changing business environment, your company's image is your brand. Managing that brand aggressively and effectively can fire imaginations. Open doors. Launch relationships. Raise capital. Catalyze markets. And *sell* your product or service.

BUSCH+ PARTNERS INC.

612.872.7700

Managing the Images of Emerging and Established Businesses

M

MERCHANT & GOULD®

MERCHANT & GOULD 612-332-5300
3200 IDS Center **Minneapolis 55402-2215**
80 South 8th Street
FAX: 612-332-9081
CONTACT: Jane Boers, Director of Marketing & Client Services
E-MAIL: info@merchant-gould.com
AFFILIATED OFFICES: Denver, Seattle, Atlanta.
CAPABILITIES: With more than 110 lawyers, it is the largest intellectual property law firm in Minnesota, and one of the largest in the United States; practice exclusively in intellectual property law including: copyright, trademark, advertising, arts and entertainment, patent, unfair competition, trade secrets, computer law and litigation; nationally and internationally.
OFFICERS: D. Randall King, Managing Director

Libraries: Film, Music, Photo, Slide Video

A

ANTARCTIC RESOURCES   763-536-8483
5536 Xenia Avenue North   Crystal 55428
FAX: 763-536-8483
CONTACT: Tom Jungroth
E-MAIL: tjungroth@earthlink.net
SERVICES: 8,000 color 35 mm slides and B/W images updated yearly. Subject Matter: Antarctica (1987) Wildlife, USA, South Pacific Aerials, children life styles, will shoot special requests. New underwater stock and Germany. Usage fee, usage dependant.
CAPABILITIES: Can do digital retouching and creative. Will shoot for web design custom.

C

CONUS PRODUCTIONS & SATELLITE SERVICES   651-642-4477
3415 University Avenue   Minneapolis 55414
FAX: 651-642-4551
CONTACT: Brian Tuttle
CAPABILITIES: Single and multi-camera video production service. Mobile and fixed satellite uplinks, and full production crews available for event broadcast.
EQUIPMENT: Sony CCD cameras, modular control rooms. Chyron graphics. Support Beta SP video tape format 4 uplink trucks, tape playback.
SPECIALTIES: Mobile uplink and multi-camera video production.
PRESIDENT/CEO/OWNER: Terry O'Reilly, GM

F

*Your **First** Source for the past 13 Years!*

FAST FOOTAGE   612-789-6000
PO Box 8176   Minneapolis 55408
FAX: 612-788-0088

Libraries: Film, Music, Photo, Slide Video / 293

CONTACT: John P. Eisner
E-MAIL: info@fastfootage.com
WWW: fastfootage.com
SIZE OF COLLECTION: Fast Footage continues to expand our offerings to a diverse client base. We represent footage from a large number of contacts developed over the past decade along with material generated in-house. Most is film original. We license content for all types of video productions, from corporate non-broadcast to International TV commercials.
SUBJECT MATTER: Contemporary to archival. Aerials throughout the US. Agriculture, Airports, Americana, Balloons, Business, Children, Cityscapes, Clouds, Communications, Computers, Construction, Eagles, Flowers, Globes, Graphics and Effects, High Tech., Historical, Humor, Industry, International Cities and Landmarks, Lifestyles, Medical, Moon, Nature, National Parks. News Occupations, Ocean, Outdoors, People, Scenics, Seasons, Seniors, Space, Sports, Stars, Sunsets, Time Lapse, Transportation, Travel, 20th Century Events, Waterfalls, Weather, Wildlife. This is just a sample of some general categories to give an idea of scope. Please call to discuss further. If you need multiple shots to illustrate your concept or a single shot to fill a hole, we can help. Preview tapes can usually be assembled and delivered in a day or two. Most often selects can be delivered as fast, in the format you require. Do you have quality transferred film or video that may be of value for other projects? Give us a call about possible representation.
SERVICES: Reproduction/Usage Fee: Depends on use. Conditions for Use: Usually one-time rights.
PRESIDENT/CEO/OWNER: John P. Eisner

G

JEFFREY GROSSCUP, PHOTOGRAPHER   612-825-3587
4801 Portland Avenue South   Minneapolis 55417
CONTACT: Jeffrey Grosscup
E-MAIL: jgrosscup@aol.com
WWW: grosscup.com
SERVICES: Size of Collection: extensive black and white and color from 1973 to present; Journalistic photos suitable for editorial. Textbook and advertising use. Subject Matter: Broad, but with special concentration in health care, sociology, children, elderly, schools, business and high technology. Reproduction/Usage Fee: Negotiated according to usage. Open to Public: Yes.

H

HUSOM & ROSE PHOTOGRAPHICS   651-699-1858
1988 Stanford Avenue   St. Paul 55105
CONTACT: David Husom
E-MAIL: david@husomandrose.com
WWW: husomandrose.com
SERVICES: Collection: Royalty Free photography, Single images and CD-ROM collections from 72 dpi thumbnails to 8 x 12 300 dpi. RGB and CMYK professionally scanned and converted.

294 / Libraries: Film, Music, Photo, Slide Video

CAPABILITIES: Subject Matter: Midwest Heartland - nature, rural, scenic and landscapes. PhotoMonet TM - Impressionistic art landscapes. Backgrounds - studio and natural. Fees: Royalty free- lifelong usage for a single fixed fee as low as $3.00 each. No negotiations, no hassle. Buy on our website above.
SPECIALTIES: Usage: For print, media or web. Used by national publications including "Time" and "Red Herring", design firms, companies, schools, non-profits and individuals.

I

INFORM RESEARCH SERVICES	612-630-6020
300 Nicollet Mall	Minneapolis 55401

FAX: 612-630-6030
CONTACT: Ted Hathaway, Manager
E-MAIL: inform@mpls.lib.mn.us
WWW: mpls.lib.mn.us/inform.asp
SERVICES: Research using online (Internet) resources, published information, library resources, and professional organizations. Document delivery using library resources and online services.
CAPABILITIES: Online (Internet) searching of information resources.

J

JUNTUNEN MEDIA GROUP	612-341-3348
708 North First Street	Minneapolis 55401

FAX: 612-341-0242
CONTACT: John Gorski
ALTERNATE PHONE: 800-535-4366
E-MAIL: mjuntunen@juntunen.com
WWW: juntunen.com
SERVICES: Our library gives you a collection of extremely powerful library, search, and ordering tools that were developed for large media-rich companies like ABC News, the Discovery Channel, and CNN. You can access your library of media assets, including video and stills, from any computer with a standard web browser, quickly search using plain English, and place orders for exactly what you need from anywhere in the world! Web-based - access from anywhere in the world; secure interface - user name and password required for access; simple search - using plain English queries; On-line ordering - place delivery or duplication orders to multiple addresses; instant verification of order.
CAPABILITIES: Juntunen Media 2000: Broadband services. DVD authoring. Full digital video support. Webcasting. Our web-based library is the place to catalog, store, retrieve and reuse your brand assets - all your marketing and communicaiotn visuals - from anywhere in the world.
CURRENT/RECENT CLIENTS/PROJECTS: Major national and international corporations and organizations; sports and entertainment organizations; government organizations.
PRESIDENT/CEO/OWNER: Bill Juntunen

K

TIMOTHY D. KEHR ADVERTISING 952-935-7347
6008 Saxony Road Edina 55436
CONTACT: Timothy D. Kehr
SPECIALTIES: Available for outside use - film clip service from thousands of public domain films, fee per clip.
BILLINGS: $1 million
PRESIDENT/CEO/OWNER: Timothy D. Kehr

M

MANUSCRIPTS DIVISION 612-625-3550
213 Andersen Library Minneapolis 55455
222 21st Avenue South
FAX: 612-626-7953
CONTACT: Barb Bezat; Al Lathrop
E-MAIL: mssref@tc.umn.edu
WWW: lib.umn.edu/special/manuscripts/index.html
CAPABILITIES: Repository for architectural plans, photos, other types of records from architects, engineers, contractors, landscape architects and interior designers; records of performing arts groups and individuals (music, theatre ad dance); papers or poets, novelists, and playwrights World Wars I & II posters and photographs. Provider of reference service in these collections by phone, e-mail, fax and in-person. No loans or borrowing privileges to individuals or organizations except museums. Open by appointment Monday - Friday 9:00 AM to 4:30 PM.
SPECIALTIES: Same-size photocopying; digitization capabilities for photos and other document types; database searches.
CURRENT/RECENT CLIENTS/PROJECTS: Trade and professions related to subject areas of the Manuscripts Division, building owners, realtors, attorneys, and general public.
PRESIDENT/CEO/OWNER: University of Minnesota

MINNEAPOLIS PUBLIC LIBRARY 612-630-6350
300 Nicollet Mall Minneapolis 55401
FAX: 612-630-6210
CONTACT: Edward R. Kukla
SIZE OF COLLECTION: About 10,000 B&W glossies on Minneapolis, Minnesota and local area from 1857 to date, with emphasis on period before 1950.
SUBJECT MATTER: A comprehensive resource on Minneapolis including city directories, maps, books, PHONE books, news clips, pamphlets, high school yearbooks, trade catalogs, menus, postcards, playbills, calendars, etc.

296 / Libraries: Film, Music, Photo, Slide Video

MINNESOTA HISTORICAL SOCIETY   651-296-2143
RESEARCH CENTER
345 Kellogg Boulevard West   St. Paul 55102
CONTACT: Tracey Baker
E-MAIL: reference@mnhs.org
WWW: mnhs.org
SIZE OF COLLECTION: 10,000 color slides; 250,000 B&W photos; 200 motion pictures.
SUBJECT MATTER: Minnesota people, places and activities 1850 to present.
REPRODUCTION/USAGE FEE: $25 - 100
OPEN TO PUBLIC: Yes
CONDITIONS FOR USE: Purchase print (no loans); 1 - 2 week waiting period for orders; credit required; commercial users pay use fee.

R

GREG RYAN/SALLY BEYER   651-426-6994
855 Village Center Drive #379   North Oaks 55127
CONTACT: Sally Beyer
E-MAIL: ryanandbeyer@aol.com
SERVICES: Size of Collection: 60,000 + 4 x 5 and 35mm color transparencies. Subject Matter: Diverse library with emphasis on Minneapolis - St. Paul travel, lifestyle, architecture, gardens; Minnesota Landscape, travel and agriculture; Minnesota and western U.S. fly fishing and historical recreations. Other U.S. travel. All images completely captioned. Files constantly updated. Call for samples and national clients/credits list. Images also available at www.tonystone.com.
CAPABILITIES: 20 years experience shooting assignments on location for advertising and editorial clients. References available upon request.

S

SCENIC PHOTO!   612-810-0797
9208 32nd Avenue North   New Hope 55427
FAX: 763-542-8740
CONTACT: Conrad Bloomquist
E-MAIL: manager@scenicphoto.com
WWW: scenicphoto.com
SERVICES: Size of Collection: 40,000 4 x 5 transparencies and 35mm slides. Subject matter: North America, London, Paris, French Riviera - pristine scenics, landscapes, cityscapes, and macro nature. Hot air balloons, cityscapes, clouds/skyscapes, coastlines, crops, desert scenes, flora-all types, forest/trees in all seasons, gardens, lakes, lighthouses, mountains, National/State Parks, rivers/streams. Shorelines, sunrise/sunset, transportation, waterfalls, and winter scenes. Reproduction/usage fee: Negotiated, based on usage type, reproduction size, duration, and circulation. No research fees.

Libraries: Film, Music, Photo, Slide Video / 297

CURRENT/RECENT CLIENTS/PROJECTS: Fallon McElligott Advertising; Carmichael Lynch Advertising; Microsoft Corp.; Seltzer Studio; Readers Digests Books; Holt Rinehart Winston Pub.; Browntrout Pub; Terrill Pub; Towery Pub; Guest Informant Pub; MN/DOT and many more.

STUDIO STOCK   612-798-0349
5900 S. Chicago   Minneapolis 55417
CONTACT: Roxanne Kjarum
SERVICES: Size of Collection: 10,000 color slides, color prints, B&W prints. Catalog available. Subject Matter: Seasonal images for projected backgrounds in studio room sets. Model released, vintage, (1950's) and multi-racial people/family shots for picture frames. Designed to enhance the commercial studio shot. Reproduction/Usage Fee: Reasonable rates.

T

TOBYS TUNES, INC.   612-377-0690
2325 Girard Avenue South   Minneapolis 55405
FAX: 612-377-2744
CONTACT: Chris Doane
E-MAIL: toby@tobystunes.com
WWW: tobystunes.com
SERVICES: We will find the best music cuts from over 70 production music libraries in-house. Complete sound design locked to picture with ProTools 24/mix. Superior sound conversions to any file format for CD-ROM or websites. Vocal booth for voice over recordings. AFTRA signature services.
CAPABILITIES: 27 years of quality and creative soundtracks. Location recording.
EQUIPMENT: ProTools 24/mix, 16 track 1", 2 track with center track time code, DAT time code, 1/4" 4 track. Largest supplier of production music in the area. Over 70 music libraries and 15 sound effect libraries.
CURRENT/RECENT CLIENTS/PROJECTS: We work for all the ad agencies and video/multi-media producers. Too many jobs to mention, many awards.
PRESIDENT/CEO/OWNER: Harley Toberman

Licensing Agents

U

U. S. LICENSING GROUP 952-949-1102
14808 Cherry Lane Minnetonka 55345
CONTACT: Chip Walters
E-MAIL: walters5@uswest.net
SERVICES: Full-service licensing company specializing in professional sports (PGA/LPGA Tour); artists (juvenile and wildlife art); Christian products; and brands.

Literary Agents

G

THE GISLASON AGENCY   612-331-8033
219 SE Main Street #506   Minneapolis 55414
FAX: 612-331-8115
CONTACT: Patti Anderson, Deborah Sweney, Jocelyn Pihlaja, Sally Morem
E-MAIL: gislasonbj@aol.com
CAPABILITIES: Published and unpublished mystery, science fiction, fantasy, romantic and law related works.
SPECIALTIES: We are looking for a great writer with a poetic, lyrical or quirky writing style who can create intriguing ambiguities. We expect a well-researched imaginative and fresh plot that reflects a familiarity with the applicable genre. Do not send a work with ordinary writing, a worn-out plot of copycat characters. Scenes with sex and violence must be intrinsic to the plot. Remember to proofread. If the work was written with a specific publisher in mind, this should be communicated. In addition to owning an agency, Ms. Gislason practices law in the area of Art and Entertainment and has a broad spectrum of entertainment and industry contacts.
CURRENT/RECENT CLIENTS/PROJECTS: Deborah Woodworth; Linda Cook; Robert Kline; Marjorie DeBoer; Paul Luke; Joan Verba; Candace Kohl.
PRESIDENT/CEO/OWNER: Barbara J. Gislason

Location Scouting

J

SUSAN JORGENSEN 952-470-0275
6510 Yosemite Avenue Excelsior 55331
FAX: 952-470-0275
CONTACT: Susan Jorgensen
PAGER: 612-534-7257
CAPABILITIES: Still photography, commercial and video. Complete knowledge of Metro area and Southwest Minnesota.

L

WADE C. LUNEBURG 612-824-1931
3535 Pillsbury Avenue South Minneapolis 55408
CONTACT: Wade C. Luneburg
ALTERNATE PHONE: 612-281-9954 Cell
CAPABILITIES: Expertise in beginning to end "location" service.
SPECIALTIES: Working with non-profit corporations, communications/planning staffs, film companies.

Marketing Consultants

A

ALLOUT MARKETING, INC.   952-404-0800
742 Twelve Oaks Center   Wayzata 55391
15500 Wayzata Blvd.
FAX: 952-404-0900
CONTACT: Christine Mignogna, Director of First Impressions/Cheryl Schwanke, Marketing Guru
E-MAIL: marketing@alloutmarketinginc.com
CAPABILITIES: Full-service strategic marketing firm which identifies, develops, plans and implements effective, revenue-generating global marketing visions for technology-based, high-tech, and biotechnology/medical companies. AOM offers a comprehensive portfolio of services including Marketing Consulting, Market Research, Internet Marketing, Graphic Design, Event Management and Public Relations. This wide range of offerings, backed by extensive experience in business development, provides a powerful combination for AllOut Marketing clients. AOM clients benefit from a focused analysis of their current business environment that leads to clear cut global strategies for revenue growth.
SPECIALTIES: Business-to-Business; Technology-based; High-tech; Biotechnology/Medical
PRESIDENT/CEO/OWNER: Ruth R. Lane

JAN APPLE AGENCY RELATIONS CONSULTANT   612-933-3995
3634 Oakton Ridge   Minnetonka 55305
FAX: 612-930-1589
E-MAIL: japple21@aol.com
SERVICES: Focus exclusively on agency searches and client-agency performance reviews. In case of an agency search, I custom design, guide and administer the resource review process whether the client company is in need of advertising, direct marketing, marketing communications, media only, promotional marketing, public relations, employee communications, design, etc. Regional and national. Performance reviews are custom designed and administered according to the client's circumstances. Some are more quantitative, some more qualitative-depending on the state of client-agency relationship and objectives of the review.
CURRENT/RECENT CLIENTS/PROJECTS: B. Dalton Software Etc.; Braun's Fashions; Celebrity Cruises; Ceridian Crop.; College of St. Scholastica; Cub Foods; DBI/SALA; Dalberg Electronics; Dyneon; First Bank Systems; Malt-O-Meal; Royal Carribean International; Target Stores; 3M; Vision World.
PRESIDENT/CEO/OWNER: Jan Apple

302 / Marketing Agencies

B

THE
BENYAS
AD GROUP
INC

Advanced Results by Design

THE BENYAS AD GROUP, INC.   **612-340-9804**
126 North Third Street, Suite 300   **Minneapolis 55401**
FAX: 612-334-5950
CONTACT: Bradley A. Benyas
E-MAIL: benyas@visi.com
CAPABILITIES: Strategic planning, design and development of primary marketing support materials including capabilities brochures, print ads, direct mail, product graphics and literature, sales training materials, point-of-sale materials, internet (www) marketing and corporate identity.
SPECIALTIES: The Benyas AD Group is a results-oriented marketing agency specializing in printed communications that advance our clients, their companies, and their products. From concept through production, we provide the services you need, when you need them. State-of-the-art pre-press resources, expert photo direction and print supervision. We deliver results.

BLACK CAR MARKETING   **612-339-8445**
400 1st Avenue North #306   **Minneapolis 55401**
FAX: 612-339-5690
CONTACT: Kathleen Novak
E-MAIL: krnovak@blcar.com
CAPABILITIES: Focused, integrated marketing services. Professional team with 20 years experience.
CURRENT/RECENT CLIENTS/PROJECTS: Oracle Corporation; Simon & Schuster Education Technologies; City of New Richmond; Mansfield; Tanick & Cohen; learningbits.com; facultynet.com

BLACK DIAMOND MARKETING   **612-927-7415**
4212 Lynn Avenue   **Edina 55416**
CONTACT: Eric Flach
SERVICES: Market analysis, evaluation, research to support marketing plan development for both products and services. Design and development of all marketing support materials including brochures and packaging materials.

Marketing Agencies / 303

CAPABILITIES/SPECIALTIES: Private label and specialty manufacturers in consumer package goods, recreation, sports and leisure products. The secondary focus is on business-to-business marketing for light manufacturers' in the metals, and value-added machining operations.
PRESIDENT/CEO/OWNER: Eric Flach/Beverly Pieracci

THE BOB PETERSON GROUP   952-473-1501
15500 Wayzata Blvd, #911   Wayzata 55391
FAX: 952-475-1756
CONTACT: Mike Peterson
E-MAIL: mikebpg@2z.net
SPECIALTIES: Assisting the corporate marketing effort by providing creative support for all phases of product promotion and company identification. Agency role varies from developing total market strategies to specific project involvement, all within a personal and highly responsive agency environment. Specialized fields include: forestry, industrial, construction equipment and building materials, chemicals, dairy, food, agriculture, automotive, and recreational/fitness products.
CURRENT/RECENT CLIENTS/PROJECTS: Accessory Research Engineering, Allied Equipment, Brush Technology, Carlson Tractor & Equipment, Cimline, Inc., Easy Auger, FEC/Food Engineering Corporation, Gamet Manufacturing, Garlock Equipment Company, Govesan, Jacobson LLC, Native American Tubcraft, Nu-Con Equipment, Tioga Inc., Vendtronics LLC, Waconia Manufacturing.
PRESIDENT/CEO/OWNER: Michael Peterson, P; Kristi Johnson, VP

BOERNER, INC.   612-473-7322
15500 Wayzata Boulevard #1007   Wayzata 55391
FAX: 612-473-7123
CONTACT: Kurt Boerner

THE BUSINESS EDGE   612-927-9014
2820 Chowen Avenue South   Minneapolis 55416
FAX: 612-546-2297
CONTACT: Joseph Baron
E-MAIL: jcbaron@usinternet.com
SERVICES: Business consulting services in the areas of marketing, business planning, e-commerce, telemarketing and strategy.
PRESIDENT/CEO/OWNER: Joseph Baron

C

CITY'S BEST MARKETING, INC.   952-888-1174
10740 Lyndale Avenue S #15E   Minneapolis 55420
FAX: 952-888-2764
CONTACT: Linda E. Kelley, Lynn Adler
WWW: c-b-m.com
SERVICES: Full service marketing communications and design firm. Creative/Design/Print Services, Marketing Strategy development. Corporate identity development. Target/Direct Marketing (business-to-business and consumer), Website Design, Media Negotiation/Placement, Package Design.

304 / Marketing Agencies

CURRENT/RECENT CLIENTS/PROJECTS: Firstel Federal Credit Union; 3M; Karastan Floor Design Gallery; Southview Design & Landscaping; Packnet; Tecnifoam Manufacturing; Minneapolis Convention Center; Minnesota Department of Transportation; Minnesota Wire and Cable; ECI Corp.; Construction Services; Newman Financial; Uptime Computer Service; Coit
PRESIDENT/CEO/OWNER: Linda E. Kelly, P; Lynn Adler, VP Sales

RAPP COLLINS WORLDWIDE   **612-373-3000**
901 Marquette Avenue - 17th Floor   **Minneapolis 55402**
FAX: 612-373-3063
CONTACT: George Benson
E-MAIL: gbenson@rcwmpls.com
WWW: rappcollins.com
SERVICES: RCW operates five full-service agencies and six "centers of excellence" in North America that are committed to helping clients build and manage more profitable relationships with their customers. RCW's Customer Value Management strategies enable clients to develop one-to-one communications for individual customers via multiple points of contact. RCW's world-class capabilities include brand planning (for direct print, broadcast and interactive), direct mail, teleservices, interactive marketing, media planning and buying (online and offline), database development and management, data warehousing, decision sciences (including data mining, analytics and customer modeling), enabling technology, employee relationship management and consumer/retail promotions.
CURRENT/RECENT CLIENTS/PROJECTS: A sampling of RCW clients includes Mercedes Benz, Pfizer, Dell Computer, 3M, Target Corporation, US Navy, and Schwan's. RCW is a division of Omnicom.
PRESIDENT/CEO/OWNER: Patrick Furey, President - Mpls Office

1128 harmon place, suite 304
minneapolis, mn 55403
AN INTEGRATED MARKETING AGENCY

THE CULLINAN GROUP   **612-338-7636**
1128 Harmon Place, #304   **Minneapolis 55403**
FAX: 612-338-8173
CONTACT: Wayne Cullinan, Carol Miletti
E-MAIL: amenzel@cullinangroup.com; Wayne Cullinan - wcullinan@cullinangroup.com; Carol Miletti - cmiletti@cullinangroup.com
WWW: cullinangroup.com
SERVICES: Full service integrated marketing communications agency practicing strategic marketing in the disciplines of advertising, sales promotion and direct response. Additional services include retail marketing, point-of-purchase, merchandising, multi-media and event production. Billings: 20 million

CURRENT/RECENT CLIENTS/PROJECTS: GreenMountain.com; Orion Food Systems/Hot Stuff Pizza; Smash Hit Subs; Thinsulate/3M; Georgia Pacific/Vinyl Siding Divisions; Hearth Technologies/Heat-N-Glo Fireplaces; Pillsbury Foodservice/Bakery Division; General Mills/Yoplait Division
PRESIDENT/CEO/OWNER: Wayne A. Cullinan, P/CEO; Lynne Cullinan, COO; Jerry Little, VP/CD; Gary Scott, VP; Julie Bain, VP Account Planning & Interactive; Ron Signorelli, Gary A. Scott, Management Supervisors; Dana Misner, Shari Bell, Account Supervisor; Barb Shelstad, Nate Koepsell, Cheryl Turk, Gina Parker, Acct. Executives; Lori Haugesag, Manager of Production; Jerry Little, Lisa Proctor, Terri Wykle, Jim Davis, Matt Howd, Willie Ford, Wendy Lukaszewski, Creative.

D

D.W. ET AL.   612-339-7848
400 First Avenue North #316   Minneapolis 55401
CONTACT: Dan Wallace
WWW: dwetal.com
CAPABILITIES: D.W. et al. Ltd. works with B2B firms to build businesses and brands. As consultants, we craft strategies and write plans. As marketing agents, we implement plans through a network we've cultivated since 1986. Core deliverables: strategic Marketing plans, positioning and brand plans, company brochures, web sites and advertising campaigns. Extended capabilities are available through allied advisors and specialists.
SPECIALTIES: Business-to-business firms.
CURRENT/RECENT CLIENTS/PROJECTS: Alliant Consulting; The Bureau Electronics Division; Carlson School of Management IRC; City of Minneapolis ITS; e-fortunecookie.com; Fredrickson & Byron; GTE; hrtomorrow.com; Honeywell; IBM; KruegerWright; Norberg Management; NRG; personallitigation.com; PDI; Palamino Euro Bistro; Pro Group; Research Resources; Serving Software; The Collaborative; Wilson Learning; and Winona Research

TODD DANIELS MARKETING & ADVERTISING   651-291-8074
26 East Exchange Street #610   St. Paul 55101
FAX: 651-297-6548
CONTACT: Dan Foote
E-MAIL: danf@todd-daniels.com
WWW: todd-daniels.com
SERVICES: Full-service marketing and advertising agency. Specialties include: strategic planning, corporate identities, point-of-purchase, literature development, public relations, ad design, media placement, event planning, direct mail, website design. Product positioning, tradeshow execution, and merchandising.
PRESIDENT/CEO/OWNER: Dan Foote, Todd Butzer

F

FOUR STAR PARTNERS   763-780-3600
8060 University Avenue NE   Minneapolis 55432
FAX: 763-786-9656
CONTACT: Linda Greve
E-MAIL: linda@4starpartners.com

306 / Marketing Agencies

WWW: 4starpartners.com
SERVICES: Management/Marketing Services: market plan development, promotional materials, advertising, publicity, competitive intelligence, web site development. Training, Meetings, Events: themes and logo design, curriculum development. Speaker support materials, site selection, hotel negotiation, registration service.
CURRENT/RECENT CLIENTS/PROJECTS: International Associate of Professional Security Consultants, Midwest Systems, Inc., Embers America, The Centre for Operational Business Intelligence, Grow Biz International, Gesundheit Institute (Dr. Patch Adams), 3M Pharmaceuticals, University of Minnesota.

G

GAGE MARKETING GROUP 763-595-3800
10000 Highway 55 Minneapolis 55441
FAX: 763-595-3871
CONTACT: Tony Thomas
E-MAIL: info@gage.com
WWW: gage.com
SERVICES: Gage Marketing Group is a marketing agency whose sole purpose is to increase its clients' sales and market share by influencing and motivating behavior, through delivering superior strategic, creative and executional marketing solutions in the areas of Creative Concepting and Development, Sales Promotion, In-store Display, Direct Marketing, Internet Marketing and Performance Improvement and Incentive. Gage Marketing Group also partners with AHL Services, Inc. to provide executional services including Trade and Consumer Fulfillment, Teleservices, and Lettership through Gage Marketing Services. Gage Marketing Group is headquartered in Minneapolis with offices in Newport Beach, CA; New Hope, MN; and Wayzata, MN.
CURRENT/RECENT CLIENTS/PROJECTS: 3M; Alcoa; Anheuser Busch; Banquet; Butterball; Buena Vista Home Video; ConAgra; General Mills; General Motors; Goodyear; Healthy Choice; Hunts; Kimberly Clark; Kraft; Lawry's Foods; Manwich; Mattel; Meredith Publishing; Miller Brewing; Nabisco; Nissan; Orville Redenbacher; Pillsbury; Proctor & Gamble; Snack Pack Pudding; Swiss Miss Cocoa; Quaker; Van Camps; etc.
PRESIDENT/CEO/OWNER: Edwin C. "Skip" Gage

J

JAMCO MARKETING GROUP 952-368-4600
1234 Lakeview Drive Chaska 55318
P.O. Box 66
FAX: 952-368-4601
SERVICES: Service awards and recognition programs. Safety award recognition programs. Retirement gift systems and services. Promotional merchandise programs.
CAPABILITIES/SPECIALTIES: Creative directing and design.
PRESIDENT/CEO/OWNER: James A. Machen
CONTACT: Wayne K. Crump, Jr.

M

MARKETING SOURCE USA
5038 29th Avenue South
612-722-3020
Minneapolis 55417
FAX: 612-722-3081
CONTACT: Anne Hunter
CAPABILITIES: Founded in 1994, Marketing Source USA is a twin cities-based marketing resource for businesses and non-profit organizations throughout the Midwest. It specializes in strategic planning, copywriting, branding and positioning, advertising and public relations.
SPECIALTIES: Detroit native Anne Hunter (formerly Anne Hittler Grover) is the strategist, writer and creative force behind Marketing Source USA. She brings to the firm 19 years of marketing/PR experience and an MBA in marketing. A journalist, published author, and college marketing professor, she has consulted with more than 100 clients on a project or on-going basis.
CURRENT/RECENT CLIENTS/PROJECTS: More than 100 clients in the fields of arts and entertainment, community development, education, real estate and construction, media, health care, professional services, technology, manufacturing, hospitality and tourism.

MARKETRAIN
26 East Exchange Street #610
651-297-6000
St. Paul 55101
FAX: 651-297-6548
CONTACT: Todd Butzer
E-MAIL: toddb@marketrain.com
WWW: marketrain.com
SERVICES: Customized marketing and advertising for small businesses, real estate agents, and quick projects -- on a budget. All work is project-based, and prices include all creative, copywriting and design. Specialties include: logos, direct mail, ID packages, flyers, brochures, websites, and ad campaigns.
PRESIDENT/CEO/OWNER: Todd Butzer, Dan Foote

MCNAUGHTON INCORPORATED
236 Girard Avenue North
612-381-0020
Minneapolis 55405
FAX: 612-381-0021
CONTACT: Lisa Logan
E-MAIL: xquez@aol.com
CAPABILITIES: Start to finish - work openly with customers to develop specific areas of need and/or work together from inception through design, development, packaging, and distribution.
SPECIALTIES: Family owned, quality affordable service through all levels of marketing channels. Vertically integrated to perform the following services in-house; product and market evaluation, package design and production, ad copy and press releases, sales and distribution.
PRESIDENT/CEO/OWNER: Patrick McNaughton

MESH CORPORATION
545 Summit Avenue
651-224-7534
St. Paul 55102
FAX: 651-224-7671
CONTACT: Mark Hulsey

308 / Marketing Agencies

E-MAIL: hulsey@meshcorp.com
WWW: meshcorp.com
CAPABILITIES: MESH provides their clients a marketing roadmap for new business growth. We develop "living" marketing, positioning and communications plans, including tactical recommendations for an integrated (online & traditional) strategic approach. We marshal the business development process by defining, prioritizing and implementing each set of "critical steps" in order to achieve substantial, measurable growth for the near and long term.
SPECIALTIES: New business development consulting. High-level marketing and communication planning. Oversee development of communication tools.
CURRENT/RECENT CLIENTS/PROJECTS: Our successful and collaborative relationships include: corporate clients, advertising agencies, marketing firms, Internet developers and specialized consultants.

MONJA MARKETING
6121 York Avenue South
952-927-7964
Edina 55410
FAX: 952-927-0142
CONTACT: Bob Andersen, MBA
E-MAIL: bmonja@aol.com
SERVICES: Full service agency: Marketing plans, marketing research, advertising, promotion, merchandising, web site development, Power Point presentations, labels and packaging.
CAPABILITIES: New product introductions and roll-outs. E-commerce. Brand and product positioning. New business programs.
CURRENT/RECENT CLIENTS/PROJECTS: Arden International Kitchens, AH Bennett Company, Odenberg Engineering (Ireland), Negril Resort Association (Jamaica), ProSumer Corp., Green Burrito Restaurants (Los Angeles), Mitten Software, Main Event Restaurants, Ratwik, Roszak & Maloney, PA, Sullivan Dental, and William J. Company.

MWA DIRECT, INC.
6465 Wayzata Blvd #330
763-591-1007
Minneapolis 55426
FAX: 763-591-1447
CONTACT: Michael R. Wikman
E-MAIL: mwadirect@aol.com
WWW: mwadirect.com
SERVICES: Channel marketing service employing direct marketing strategies.
CURRENT/RECENT CLIENTS/PROJECTS: Sage Software, Irvine, CA; Bruce Hardwood Floors, Dallas, TX; Rheem Air Conditioning, Ft. Smith, AK; Oticon Hearing Aids, Somerset, NJ.

N

NORTH WOODS ADVERTISING
200 Textile Building
119 North Fourth Street
612-340-9999
Minneapolis 55401

Marketing Agencies / 309

FAX: 612-340-0857
CONTACT: Bill Hillsman, Greta Unowsky, John Blackshaw
WWW: northwoodsadvertising.com
SERVICES: Integrated marketing communications, advertising, and public relations; marketing strategy and research; media strategy, planning and buying; creative direction, copywriting, design and art direction; interactive media/website design; broadcast and print production; brand valuation, brand extension and strategic planning; political strategy and communications.
CAPABILITIES: Retail, sports marketing, enthusiast products, politics, law and government, public service, non-profits, publishing, higher education, food (organic and health), professional services, book and motion picture promotion, emerging technology, turnaround situations and crisis communications.
CURRENT/RECENT CLIENTS/PROJECTS: Mall of America; Harper Collins; American Oats; Jesse Ventura for Governor (MN); Ciresi for US Senate (MN); Christabella, Inc.; Airline Pilots Assn.; Wellstone for US Senate; Center for a Sustainable Economy; American Iron & Supply; Earth Day 2000; Canterbury Park; Robins Kaplan Miller & Ciresi LLP; Mahoney Ulbrich Christiansen Russ; Carleton College; Minnesota State Colleges & Universities; Logan for US Senate (FL); Minnesota Outdoor Heritage Assn.; Boyd for Governor (OK); International Assn. of Machinists & Aerospace Workers; Jacob Wetterling Foundation; Ventura for Minnesota, Inc.; SpeakOut.com.
PRESIDENT/CEO/OWNER: Bill Hillsman, Owner/Chief Creative Officer; John Blackshaw, President

NYGARD DIMENSIONS   **612-371-9228**
1414 Marshall Street N.E.   **Minneapolis 55413**
FAX: 612-371-9232
CONTACT: Ben Wallace, Director of Account Services
E-MAIL: id@brandcommunications.com
WWW: brandcommunications.com
SERVICES: Brand-based marketing communications: brand strategy and identity development, integrated marketing communications planning, creative development, design, production, implementation, measurement and management through all media: Print: literature, stationery, direct mail, advertising, sales tools, packaging, sales kits; Digital: Websites (internet/intranet/extranet), online promotion, sales tools/software, product demos, video presentations, kiosks, online brand identity management; Environmental: themed events, stage sets, exhibits, displays/POP.
CAPABILITIES: Brand identity systems, including naming, logo, brand elements and guidelines. Unique approach to brand identity strategy, design development and management through all points of stakeholder contact to create the "whole brand experience." Sister companies Nygard Set Design and Harmony Box contribute to brand experience creation. Industries: information technology/e-business, healthcare/pharmaceuticals, financial services, manufacturing, retail and more.
CURRENT/RECENT CLIENTS/PROJECTS: 3M Company; Auxilium Software; Compass Productions; Conseco Finance; Larson Manufacturing; Lawson Software; Lutheran Brotherhood; MedIntelligence; nQuire Software; Pharmaceutical Care Network (PCN); Proliant (formerly AMPC, Inc.); Qtech Systems, Inc.; Sales Force 2000 Software; Safe Reflections; Sunrise Community Banks (formerly Franklin Bancorp), U.S. Magnetix; U of M Physicians.
PRESIDENT/CEO/OWNER: Jim Nygard, P

310 / Marketing Agencies

P

THE POLL GROUP   612-338-7664
126 North Third Street #100   Minneapolis 55401
FAX: 612-338-5423
CONTACT: Roger Hegeman
E-MAIL: pollgroup@pollgroup.com
WWW: pollgroup.com
SERVICES: Extensive experience in developing customized web and print for growth-oriented companies. Complete strategic and creative services, corporate identity, lead generation programs, media/public relations, multimedia/web pages. CD-ROM, collateral and sales support materials, trade shows, special events and sales training.
CURRENT/RECENT CLIENTS/PROJECTS: Medtronic; 3M; Blue Cross and Blue Shield of Minnesota; Lutheran Brotherhood; Met Council; Multifoods; Minnesota Opera; United Health Group.
PRESIDENT/CEO/OWNER: Donn Poll, Roger Hegeman, Camille Holthaus

R

RISDALL LINNIHAN ADVERTISING   651-286-6700
2475 15th Street NW   New Brighton 55112
FAX: 651-631-2561
CONTACT: John Risdall, Chairman
E-MAIL: getwired@risdall.com
WWW: risdall.com
SERVICES: Full service advertising agency offering marketing strategy and planning, marketing research, advertising, direct response, promotion, collateral, publicity/PR and business strategy and planning in the traditional and interactive arenas.
CAPABILITIES: Specializing in the educational, medical, institutional, retail, computer and environmental industries. Internet expertise from site design to site development to marketing planning and implementation.

Marketing Agencies / 311

CURRENT/RECENT CLIENTS/PROJECTS: Aeration Industries; Agribank; Allegheny Power; Alliance Water Resources; American Guidance Service; Applied Technology Consultants; ATG Laboratories, Inc.; Bang Printing; Birchwood Casey; Blanks USA; Brown Wilbert Vault Company; City of New Brighton; Clinch-On Products; Clique Capital; Cocola Palm; cranespharmacy.com; Curative; Decker Publications; Digital River; Diversity Village; EBP HealthPlans, Inc.; Electrosonic; EMPI; E. W. Blanch; Paragon; UniSure; Finnleo Sauna; Fox River; Funeral.com; Galyans; GunVault; Highland Banks; HomeRight; Honeywell; House of Hope, Hubler Family Business Consultants; Innsbruck Jewelers; Isaksen Promotional Specialties; Kinney & Lange; Learning Outfitters; Lease Point.com; Lemna Corporation; Liquid Dynamics; 3M Industrial Mineral Products Division; 3M Traffic Control Materials; 3M Dental Products; 3M Healthcare; 3M Industrial Tapes and Specialties; Magnum Research; Medtronic (Neurological Division); Micom Circuits, Inc.; Morries Automotive Group; Mounds View School District; Normark Rapala; Northern States Power; Norwest Equity Partners, Novartis, Onan Corporation; Photos, Inc.; Pillsbury; Premier Mounts; Printing Industry of MN; Progressive Marketing; Pur (Recovery Engineering); Purus, Inc.; Rainforest Café; RSR Wholesale Guns; Ramsey County Library; Rottlund Homes; SafeWater Anywhere LLC; Schoolbell.com; Schoonover Bodyworks, Inc.; Smith Foundry Company; Smith System Manufacturing, Inc.; Summit Envirosolutions; Target; Tertronics, Inc.; The TPA; Time Savers; Uni-Hydro, Inc.; Upsher-Smith Laboratories; US Filter-Autocon; USFilter-Consolidated Electric; USFilter-Control Systems; USFilter Corporate; USFilter-CPC; USFilter-General Filter; USFilter-Filterite; USFilter-Recovery Services; USFilte- Seitz; USF Johnson (France); USF Johnson Screens; Verdant Brands; VerticalNet; Vista Technologies; WalMart; Water Pollution Control Corp.; Waterworld; Western Bank.

T

TARTAN MARKETING
15500 Wayzata Blvd, Suite 1000
Twelve Oaks Center

952-473-7575
Wayzata 55391

CONTACT: James J. MacLachlan
E-MAIL: jim@tartanmarketing.com
WWW: tartanmarketing.com

FOCUS: Tartan Marketing helps business-to-business clients form long-term strategies for creating, revitalizing and leveraging strong brands. Core competency in multi-tactical program development, carried out with strong creative articulation. Media-neutral approach, with tactical recommendations based on most effective strategies for addressing clients' unique needs, issues and opportunities.

312 / Marketing Agencies

CAPABILITIES: Quantitative/qualitative research & discovery, market and brand planning, naming and identity development, communications planning. Integrated execution (collateral, advertising, interactive, custom publications, direct response, promotions, sales programs.) Market Segment Expertise: Food marketing: foodservice/bakery/deli/distribution. High tech: e-business/Intellectual properties. Financial: banking/insurance.
OFFICERS: James J. MacLachlan, CEO/Margie D. MacLachlan, VP Creative
ACCOUNT SUPERVISORS: Account Services: Terri Juranek, AE; Gina Wifler, AE; Justin Erickson, AE
BILLINGS: $7 million
YEARS IN BUSINESS: 14

W

WATERS MOLITOR
1000 Shelard Parkway #600
952-797-5000
Minneapolis 55426
FAX: 952-797-5001
CONTACT: Dori Molitor
E-MAIL: dmolitor@watersmolitor.com
WWW: watersmolitor.com
SERVICES: Brand positioning, communications platform and go-to-market strategies, Strategy development, brand events, co-marketing. Promotion planning and execution., Creative development, interactive communications, post-event analysis.
CAPABILITIES: Marketing brands to women. Strengthening the bond between brand and consumer to create Brand Enthusiasm™. Building an emotional connection between brand and consumer leading to competitive differentiation and long-term loyalty, Winner of 5 best in the World PRO Awards of Excellence, unprecedented in the industry.
CURRENT/RECENT CLIENTS/PROJECTS: Dunkin/ Donuts, Gerber, Innuity.com, Malt-O-Meal, Nabisco, Respond.com, Sargenton, SuperValu, Tone Brothers Spices, US Bank, WomenVenture.

WORDS AT WORK
126 North Third Street #309
612-334-5960
Minneapolis 55401
FAX: 612-334-3170
CONTACT: Carol Cooksley, Dave Levi
E-MAIL: carol.cooksley@wordsatwork.com
WWW: wordsatwork.com
SERVICES: Strategic consulting, writing, and design services for marketing communications (product launches, sales collateral, channel communications, sales training, direct marketing, video, CD-ROM, Internet); financial communications (annual reports, investor relations, sales collateral); and organizational communications (information design, identity systems, employee communications, intranet, executive speechwriting).
SPECIALTIES: Creative executions based on your business strategies.
CURRENT/RECENT CLIENTS/PROJECTS: American Express Financial Advisors; Best Buy; Datacard; Ecolab; Ellerbe Becket; EW Blanch, Fair, Isaac; GMAC-RFC; Honeywell; IBM; Imation; ITT Industries; Lanier Worldwide; Kodak; Osmonics; Polaris; Price Waterhouse Coopers; Red Wing Shoe Company; US Bank; Wells Fargo.

Marketing Communications

AVA GROUP INC.
480 W. Highway 96, #100
FAX: 651-766-9800
CONTACT: Jennifer Pedalty
E-MAIL: jpedalty@avagroup.com

651-766-9500
St. Paul 55126

CAPABILITIES: Full-service marketing communications firm devoted to medial, health care and wellness businesses. We offer a full spectrum of services from consultation through produced materials in many mediums including the web.
SPECIALTIES: Help medical and health care businesses position their companies and their products, develop strategies and messages that reach and motivate the target audience. We bring clients decades of experience in the medical device, HMO, hospital home health care and wellness industries.
CURRENT/RECENT CLIENTS/PROJECTS: Medtronic, Pfizer, Allina, Comprehensive Reimbursement Consultants, Kinesis medical, First Circle Medial,. Hypertension Diagnostics, Inc., Cardinal Health, CORDLogistics, and others.
PRESIDENT/CEO/OWNER: Jennifer Pedalty, O

AVA GROUP, INC.
4287 Colleen Circle
FAX: 651-785-1497
CONTACT: Mary Strom
E-MAIL: mstrom@avagroup.com

651-785-1498
St. Paul 55112

CAPABILITIES: Full-service marketing communications firm devoted to medical, health care and wellness businesses. We offer a full spectrum of services from consultation through produced materials in many mediums including the web.
SPECIALTIES: Help medical and health care businesses position their companies and their products, develop strategies and messages that reach and motivate the target audience. We bring clients decades of experience in the medical device, HMO, hospital home health care and wellness industries.
CURRENT/RECENT CLIENTS/PROJECTS: Medtronic, Pfizer, Allina, Comprehensive Reimbursement Consultants, Kinesis Medical, First Circle Medical, Hypertension Diagnostics, Inc., Cardinal Health, CORDLogistics, and others
PRESIDENT/CEO/OWNER: Mary Strom, Owner; Jennifer Pedalty, Owner

314 / Marketing Communications

B

THE BENYAS AD GROUP INC

Advertising + Design

THE BENYAS AD GROUP, INC.   **612-340-9804**
126 North Third Street, Suite 300   **Minneapolis 55401**
FAX: 612-334-5950
CONTACT: Bradley A. Benyas
E-MAIL: benyas@visi.com
CAPABILITIES: Strategic planning, design and development of primary marketing support materials including capabilities brochures, print ads, direct mail, product graphics and literature, sales training materials, point-of-sale materials, Internet (www) marketing and corporate identity.
SPECIALTIES: The Benyas AD Group is a results-oriented marketing agency specializing in printed communications that advance our clients, their companies, and their products. From concept through production, we provide the services you need, when you need them. State-of-the-art pre-press resources, expert photo direction and print supervision. We deliver results.

C

CARR CREATIVES   **651-222-3691**
1000 Portland Avenue   **St. Paul 55104**
FAX: 651-222-3387
CONTACT: Joan Nitz
E-MAIL: sacarr@mn.uswest.net
SERVICES: Creative communications for small to medium sized organizations in business, nonprofit, and educational markets. We write, design, and print a wide range of brochures, viewbooks, logs and icons, catalogs, direct mail campaigns, fundraising materials. etc. Strategic marketing consultation, publications planning and audits. Fifteen years in business. Exceptional personal service. Great teamwork.
PRESIDENT/CEO/OWNER: Susan Robbins Carr

CELSKI COMMUNICATIONS   **651-766-9298**
5835 Oxford Street North   **Shoreview 55126**
FAX: 651-766-9299

Marketing Communications / 315

CONTACT: Vicki Celski
E-MAIL: celskicomm@aol.com
SERVICES: Types of writing/editing/project management: employee publications, corporate capabilities brochures and other marketing materials, annual reports, video scripts, speeches and presentations, ads and other promotional copy.
SPECIALTIES: All types of business writing, editing, rewriting, proofreading, communication project management working with designers, photographers, printers, video producers, communication planning, evaluation (surveys, focus groups.)
CURRENT/RECENT CLIENTS/PROJECTS: 3M; Allina Health Systems; HealthSystem Minnesota; Ecolab.

CITY'S BEST MARKETING, INC.   952-888-1174
10740 Lyndale Avenue S #15E   Minneapolis 55420

FAX: 952-888-2764
CONTACT: Linda E. Kelley, Lynn Adler
WWW: c-b-m.com
SERVICES: Full service marketing communications and design firm. Creative/Design/Print Services, Marketing Strategy development. Corporate Identity development. Target/Direct Marketing (business-to-business and consumer), Website Design, Media Negotiation/Placement, Package Design.
CURRENT/RECENT CLIENTS/PROJECTS: Firstel Federal Credit Union; 3M; Karastan Floor Design Gallery; Southview Design & Landscaping; Packnet; Tecnifoam Manufacturing; Minneapolis Convention Center; Minnesota Department of Transportation; Minnesota Wire and Cable; ECI Corp.; Construction Services; Newman Financial; Uptime Computer Service; Coit
PRESIDENT/CEO/OWNER: Linda E. Kelly, P; Lynn Adler, VP Sales

CLICK COMMUNICATIONS CORP.   612-332-0719
233 Park Avenue, Third Floor   Minneapolis 55415

FAX: 612-332-5637
CONTACT: Naomi Teske
E-MAIL: clk-clk@isd.net
WWW: clk-clk.com
CAPABILITIES: Project management of effective print communications from concept through production. Strategic planning, brand development and marketing consulting.

COCHRAN COMMUNICATIONS NETWORK   763-420-9589
16783 80th Place North   Maple Grove 55311

FAX: 763-920-9531
CONTACT: Deborah Cochran
E-MAIL: debccn@hotmail.com
SERVICES: Marketing communications strategy and implementation; writing; design; promotion; web pages; client loyalty programs, etc.
CAPABILITIES: Image development, creative concepting and execution, project management, copy and design that boosts the bottom line.
CURRENT/RECENT CLIENTS/PROJECTS: Newsletters, web sites, brochures, PR programs, client appreciation programs - especially for financial planners, other marketing agencies, insurance companies and health care agencies.
PRESIDENT/CEO/OWNER: Deborah Cochran

316 / Marketing Communications

RAPP COLLINS WORLDWIDE
901 Marquette Avenue - 17th Floor
FAX: 612-373-3063
CONTACT: George Benson
E-MAIL: gbenson@rcwmpls.com
WWW: rappcollins.com

612-373-3000
Minneapolis 55402

SERVICES: RCW operates five full-service agencies and six "centers of excellence" in North America that are committed to helping clients build and manage more profitable relationships with their customers. RCW's Customer Value Management strategies enable clients to develop one-to-one communications for individual customers via multiple points of contact. RCW's world-class capabilities include brand planning (for direct print, broadcast and interactive), direct mail, teleservices, interactive marketing, media planning and buying (online and offline), database development and management, data warehousing, decision sciences (including data mining, analytics and customer modeling), enabling technology, employee relationship management and consumer/retail promotions.

CURRENT/RECENT CLIENTS/PROJECTS: A sampling of RCW clients includes Mercedes Benz, Pfizer, Dell Computer, 3M, Target Corporation, US Navy, and Schwan's. RCW is a division of Omnicom.

PRESIDENT/CEO/OWNER: Patrick Furey, President - Mpls Office

CONCEPT GROUP INC.
192 West Ninth Street
FAX: 651-227-4591
CONTACT: Brad Moore
E-MAIL: info@conceptgroup.com
WWW: conceptgroup.com

651-221-9710
St. Paul 55102

SERVICES: Full-service marketing communications; strategic communications planning; account management; concept and creative development; design; computer illustration; copywriting; production; post production coordination and implementation; photography studio.

CAPABILITIES: Print advertising; collateral; direct marketing; brand and identity development; sales promotion and incentive programs; public relations; video concepting and scripting; interactive and electronic media; including web site planning, design, development and implementation; CD-ROM development

CURRENT/RECENT CLIENTS/PROJECTS: High tech, low tech and "no tech" clients - B to B and B to C.

PRESIDENT/CEO/OWNER: John Ruddy, P, Brad Moore, EVP, Jay Troe, VP/AD; Mike Davis, CD; Vicki Giefer, Director of Account Services; Mike Brunner, Director of Strategic Planning and Marketing; George Ramsay, Director of New Business Development; Paul Larson, Interactive Services Manager.

Marketing Communications / 317

COTTAGE COMMUNICATIONS, INC.
5519 Butternut Circle
FAX: 952-931-0061
E-MAIL: cottcom@aol.com
952-931-9752
Minnetonka 55343

SERVICES: Full-service public relations, advertising and design, publication layout, design and writing, web site design and copy, brochure and direct mail design.
CAPABILITIES: Integrated public relations and advertising programs. Mac based electronic design and publishing.
CURRENT/RECENT CLIENTS/PROJECTS: Daystar U.S., Valley Green Business Park and Corporate Center, Lloyd's Barbecue Company (Div. of General Mills), The Maguire Agency, Burnsville Business Action Council, Fresh Strategies, Heartmates, Inc.
PRESIDENT/CEO/OWNER: Bonnie S. Barland

CRC, INC.
6321 Bury Drive #10
FAX: 952-937-5155
CONTACT: Cindy Owens, New Business Specialist
WWW: crc-inc.com
952-937-6000
Eden Prairie 55346

CREATIVE RESOURCE CENTER/CRC, INC.
6321 Bury Drive #10
FAX: 952-937-5155
CONTACT: Cindy Owens, New Business Specialist
WWW: crc-inc.com
952-937-6000
Eden Prairie 55346

SERVICES: A full-service integrated marketing communications agency with 20 years experience in strategic communications planning across a range of delivery forms. Services include planning and implementation of strategic marketing communications, internet presence, sales promotion, relationship marketing, internet list development and maintenance, and development of full-scale e-commerce web stores. Full in-house planning and creative teams for both print and internet development include experts in planning, design, copy, content management, database design and development, website development, management, hosting and serving. In-house photography studio.
SPECIALTIES: Integrated marketing communications planning and implementation, internet business strategy, sales promotion including sales materials, collateral, POS, full integration of promotion on the internet including interactive relationship marketing. Corporate and brand identity programs, package design, business-to-business and consumer advertising, and direct mail.
CURRENT/RECENT CLIENTS/PROJECTS: CNS Interactive; FSMC; Graco; Haagen-Dazs Interactive, Interactive Learning Group (Video Buddy); Loffler Business Systems; McGlynn's Retail Bakeries; Multifoods Bakery Products; NK Lawn & Garden; Old Dutch; Pillsbury Interactive; Primera Technology; Rosemount Office Systems Interactive; Sargento Foods, Inc.; 3M Intranet.
PRESIDENT/CEO/OWNER: Michael Lundeby, CEO; Elizabeth Petrangelo, EVP; Joe Andrews, VP; Troy Braun, Creative Director

CREATIVE VENTURES, INC.
2950 Dean Parkway
FAX: 612-925-0425
CONTACT: Helene Burton
612-925-3297
Minneapolis 55416

318 / Marketing Communications

SERVICES: Trend reports and trade show coverage on a project basis. New product development, including naming, positioning and concept writing; strategic planning, promotions.
CAPABILITIES: Every aspect of food marketing from R & D to store shelf. Considerable experience in housewares, health and beauty products, travel/resort services.
CURRENT/RECENT CLIENTS/PROJECTS: 3M (scotchgard, scotch-brite); Green Giant; Lifesavers; Healthy Choice; Universal Travel Clubs; Rescue Solutions; Write Expressions; Nordic Ware; New Product News; Mattel

D

DEEG PRODUCTIONS
2450 Bridgeview Court
FAX: 651-454-7734
CONTACT: Chuck Deeg
E-MAIL: deegcm@hotmail.com

651-454-7734
Mendota Heights 55120

SERVICES: Full service marketing communications for both business-to-business and consumer products and services. Capabilities include: creative art direction, copywriting, graphic design, media planning and placement, public relations, tradeshow exhibit design and production, retail environment design and production, market research and branding.

F

FRANKE + FIORELLA
401 North 3rd Street, Suite 380
FAX: 612-338-2300
CONTACT: Deb Fiorella
E-MAIL: deb@frankefiorella.com
WWW: frankefiorella.com

612-338-1700
Minneapolis 55401

CAPABILITIES: Corporate identity, brochures and literature system development, corporate publications, website development, brand identity and exhibit design. Services include: strategic planning, market analysis, competitive audit, copywriting and complete production capabilities.
SPECIALTIES: Developing brand identity systems for new and existing products, services and companies.
PRESIDENT/CEO/OWNER: Craig Franke, Deborah Fiorella

G

GOLD FISH COMMUNICATIONS
420 N. Fifth Street #855
FAX: 952-920-0449
CONTACT: Debra Fisher Goldstein
E-MAIL: dfgold19@idt.net

612-371-4501
Minneapolis 55401

Marketing Communications / 319

SERVICES: Positioning, Brand Identity, then Complete Creative through three distinct programs that maximize your advertising dollar. 1) Dive into the "Gold Fish Think Tank", a personalized process that ask key questions of your target audience and then creates your company's personality, marketing messages, and creative concepts based on what's important to your audience. The results strengthen every area of your marketing. 2) Eyeball your advertising through the "Gold Fish Bowl"; a per-piece review and edit of your existing marketing materials designed to increase their impact and effectiveness. 3) Hatch new marketing pieces with "Gold Fish Creative"; a start-to-finish process for brochures, advertising, sales letters, direct mail, websites and videos that move your potential customer up the purchase-decision-making ladder.
SPECIALTIES: Conversational-style writing. Warmth and Wit. Graphic design that strengthens your message. A process you will enjoy. No budget surprises.
CURRENT/RECENT CLIENTS/PROJECTS: KTCA/KTCI, Twin Cities Public Television; Abbott Northwestern Hospital; Multi-Ad Services, Inc. - automotive, retail, and medical marketing divisions; Hennepin County, Department of Environmental Services; YWCA and Urban Sports Center, Minneapolis; Neighborhood Health Care Network; MedCenters Health Insurance; UCARE Minnesota; Minnesota Chiropractic Association, statewide lobbying/education; Advanced Medical; Clean Green Packing Biodegradable Packaging Material; Loften Label; Financial Management Leasing; Pope Investment Economics; Edina Realty; Coldwell Banker Burnet Realty; Steven Scott Real Estate Management; Nesbit Insurance Agencies; Lerhke Reinsurance, Inc.; Access Insurance Agency; Cartier Insurance Agency; Interactive Personalities; Learning Ware, Inc.; On-Hold Marketing; Guidance Computer Systems; Writing Assistance, Inc.; Sweetman Communications Inc.; Wilder Image Development; A+ Training; Applause, Inc.; Goldfarb and Associates - legal practice; Austin and Abrams - legal practice; Southwest Family Room & Northeast Strong Together - Way To Grow organizations; United Way of Minneapolis and St. Paul, MN; and many more great clients.

GRAPHXPOINT
4249 Edgemont Street
FAX: 651-762-1471
CONTACT: Mark Dawson
E-MAIL: imd@graphxpoint.com
WWW: graphxpoint.com

651-762-1470
Vadnais Heights 55127

CAPABILITIES: Marketing/sales brochures, direct mail, promotional literature, print media advertising. Marketing strategy development. Design and product collateral from strategy phase to final printed piece. Market research, campaign strategy, graphic design, copywriting, full production.
SPECIALTIES: Business-to-business. Represent all major industrial sectors.
CURRENT/RECENT CLIENTS/PROJECTS: 3M, Imation, GT Global, Benhama Capital Mng, Restoration Technologies
PRESIDENT/CEO/OWNER: Mark Dawson

H

HEDSTROM/BLESSING, INC.
8301 Golden Valley Road #300
FAX: 763-591-6232
CONTACT: Julie Pearl
E-MAIL: info@hb-inc.com
WWW: www.hb-inc.com

763-591-6200
Minneapolis 55427

320 / Marketing Communications

SERVICES: Strategic marketing communications and graphic design for business-to-business and consumer products including corporate and product brand stewardship, new product launches, identity development, packaging, advertising, sales promotion and collateral, point-of-purchase, direct mail, interactive and website design.
CURRENT/RECENT CLIENTS/PROJECTS: Selected accounts include 3M; Bachman's; Carlson Leisure Group; Fabcon; Intellisol International; Interactive Learning Group; Land O'Lakes; Pillsbury; Target

HIEBEL & ASSOCIATES
3300 Bass Lake Road, #120
763-566-5999
Minneapolis 55429
FAX: 763-566-5780
CONTACT: Colleen LesSard
E-MAIL: colleen@hiebel.com
SERVICES: Full service marketing communications firm providing consulting, design, development. Production implementation and program administration to destinations and travel products and services providers.
CAPABILITIES: Destination marketing and promotions, education and training of travel agents and trade sales force.
CURRENT/RECENT CLIENTS/PROJECTS: Barbados Tourism Authority, Aruba Tourism Authority, Travel Professionals, ASTA Training, Air Jamaica Vacations
PRESIDENT/CEO/OWNER: JoAnn Hiebel

HIGH POINT CREATIVE, LLC
4583 Shady Lane
651-426-4012
St. Paul 55110
FAX: 651-426-6699
CONTACT: Kate Huebsch
E-MAIL: kate@highpointcreative.com
WWW: highpointcreative.com
SERVICES: Copywriting and full project management for business-to-business and consumer brochures, catalogs, direct mail, websites, newsletters, speeches and presentations, PowerPoint shows, special events, marketing and internal communication pieces. A special interest in "translating" high-tech products and services into compelling and effective copy for non-technical readers.
CAPABILITIES: Marketing communications with an emphasis on strategic development and effective writing.
CURRENT/RECENT CLIENTS/PROJECTS: 12 years in business serving financial services companies, industrial manufacturers, health care organizations and community not-for-profit organizations.
PRESIDENT/CEO/OWNER: Kate Huebsch, President/Owner; Maiya Willits, Creative Director

HOFFMAN COMMUNICATIONS INC
160 Glenwood Avenue North
612-673-9630
Minneapolis 55405
FAX: 612-673-9634
CONTACT: Heather Chapdelaine
E-MAIL: hoffman@isd.net
WWW: hoffmancom.com
SERVICES: Hoffman Communications is a full-service marketing communications agency/production studio, fluent in a variety of media for many corporate applications. We offer full service capabilities for: event planning and staging, script writing, creative development., audio production, video/film production, DVD production, multi-media system design and equipment installation, equipment sales and rental.

Marketing Communications / 321

CAPABILITIES: Discreet edit* non-linear editing, BetaSP online editing, Pro-tools digital audio suite, VHS duplication, TVL workstations, Mac/IBM graphic workstations, a complete line of staging rental equipment, multi-image equipment, conference facility, shooting studio and set construction facility.
PRESIDENT/CEO/OWNER: Mark Hoffman

I

world-class ebusiness results

IPARES, LTD. 612-215-2300
5000 Union Plaza **Minneapolis 55401**
FAX: 612-215-2310
CONTACT: Tom Harold
E-MAIL: info@ipares.com
WWW: ipares.com
FOCUS: Integration of marketing, design and technology.
SERVICES: Internet Professional Services: Providing Fortune 1000 corporations with Internet, Intranet, Extranet, Sales Force Automation, Kiosk and Database Marketing solutions. Multimedia Related Services: Design/concepting, consulting, writing/instructional design and programming. Internet/Intranet: In-house design and programming including secure E-commerce solutions and web-based training.
CAPABILITIES/SPECIALTIES: Graphic design services for brochures, catalogs, ads, display and packaging. Complete prepress production services.
PRESIDENT/CEO/OWNER: Lon Bencini/Tom Harold

K

K· M· T COMMUNICATIONS 952-472-7155
5450 Ridgewood Cove Mound 55364
FAX: 952-472-4648
E-MAIL: kmtcomm@aol.com
SERVICES: News releases, corporate publications, employee communications, special event planning, newsletter, brochures, promotional materials, business communications, public relations.

322 / Marketing Communications

CAPABILITIES/SPECIALTIES: Media buying, production and placement. Coordination of special events including press conferences. Project management from start to finish: concept, writing, editing, photography, design and layout, and coordination of printing and delivery. In business since 1985.
CURRENT/RECENT CLIENTS/PROJECTS: Plymouth Metrolink - ongoing marketing projects. Fingerhut - copywriting for catalogs. The Brimeyer Group - ongoing newsletter.
PRESIDENT/CEO/OWNER: Jane Norling

KDG INTERACTIVE
1720 East 66th Street
FAX: 612-861-8967
CONTACT: Steven Haas
E-MAIL: shaas@kdg.com
WWW: kdg.com

612-861-8890
Richfield 55423

SERVICES: With over 150 years combined (in-house) experience, KDG InterActive is an e-business and enterprise learning outfitter recognized as a major player in their industry. They combine sophisticated strategies, award-winning design capabilities and cutting-edge technology solutions to assist today's progressive companies in their strategic migration to the e-business edge. They offer: strategic planning, marketing consulting, interactive design and production services, e-commerce site development and software development and have served a variety of global brand leaders such as 3M, Honeywell, US Bancorp, Carlson Marketing Group and Disney Online.
CAPABILITIES: KDG InterActive is fully equipped with a state-of-the-art interactive multimedia development studio and hosts an innovative team of designers, developers and programmers who create online and disk-based programs for: Information Kiosks; CBT (computer-based training); TEST (technology enabled sales tools); EPSS (electronic performance support systems). Their specialties include: Authorware, Director, programming in C++, HTML, CGI, Java, Lotus Notes, Microsoft Office Suite, PhotoShop, Premiere, Painter, Illustrator, After Effects, Infini-D, 3D Studio Max, StrataVision, etc.
CURRENT/RECENT CLIENTS/PROJECTS: American Express, (information kiosks and training presentation); 3M, (software interface design); Business Incentives, (assorted projects); Carlson Marketing Group, (laptop sales presentations); Cray Research, (3D modeling); Disney Online, (assorted online animations); Honeywell, (electronic brochure); US Bancorp, (web based training); US West Communications, (training program); Q Tech Systems, (electronic performance support software); The Saint Paul Companies, (speaker support); Wilson Learning, (consumer self-improvement CD ROM); Minnesota Historical Society, (information kiosks); Ronald Reagan Library, (electronic cabinet room); St. Croix Medical, (computer-based training/online clinical trials); The Great Lakes Aquarium, (information kiosks.)

THE KYDD GROUP (TKG)
400 First Avenue North #640
FAX: 612-630-2151
CONTACT: Karen Kydd, President

612-630-9000
Minneapolis 55401

CAPABILITIES: Strategic marketing, marketing communications, public relations and publicity, consumer promotions, event marketing and sponsorships.

Marketing Communications / 323

SPECIALTIES: TKG is a nationally recognized African-American, female-owned company offering exceptional value and flawless service. Our vision is to create a world-class marketing services agency that applies its expertise and knowledge to understanding our clients needs and delivering valuable business solutions to address those needs. TKG uses its front-line management structure to establish and grow a strong client-agency relationship. Because our organizational structure allows for immediate and excellent client responsiveness, our team delivers the promise of flawless service. Prominent among our clients are those who expect the highest levels of service and require accountability. It also includes those who actively seek to reach diverse communities. Ultimately, it is our objective to manage our business efficiently and profitability.
PRESIDENT/CEO/OWNER: Karen Kydd, President

L

L A, INC.   612-424-9433
8818 Telford Crossing   Minneapolis 55443
CONTACT: Laurie Janu
WWW: lauriejanu@yahoo.com
CAPABILITIES: Concept-to-completion producing for broadcast and non-broadcast. Marketing and advertising copywriting, web content, corporate video, television, radio, direct response, infomercials, news release, and corporate programming.
SPECIALTIES: Cost-effective and customized marketing and communications solutions.

M

MASTER COMMUNICATIONS GROUP, INC.   952-835-6164
7805 Telegraph Road #100   Bloomington 55438
CONTACT: Christine Dean
WWW: mastcom.com
CAPABILITIES: Full service electronic communications. Complete video production services from concept and scripting through post production. BetacamSp. Media 100, non-linear editing (Boris Effects, Adobe After Effects, Commotion) 2D and 3D animation, lightWave. Audio production. Web development (adobe Go Live, Dream Weaver, Flash/Live Motion) and interactive multimedia authoring and development (authorware, Director, iShell and others.)
SPECIALTIES: Education, training and marketing for medical, technical, foreign language translations and voiceovers, and ESL/EFL.
CURRENT/RECENT CLIENTS/PROJECTS: ADP Hollander, Augustine Medical, Cambridge University Press, Evangelical Lutheran Church in America, Lutheran Church--Missouri Synod, Seagate, RSM McGladrey, Syracuse Language Systems.

MAX STUDIO   612-362-8477
618 Second Avenue SE   Minneapolis 55414
FAX: 612-362-8469
CONTACT: Max Allers
E-MAIL: max@maxdesign.com

324 / Marketing Communications

SERVICES: Full service Marketing Communications firm. Turnkey services, from advertising, packaging, publication design and production, catalogs, corporate identity and brochures to web presence.

MEDIA PRODUCTIONS, INC.
125 SE Main Street #100
FAX: 612-379-7988
CONTACT: Judy Kessel

612-379-4678
Minneapolis 55414

SERVICES: Award-winning full service marketing communications company, offering project consulting, strategic planning and production services for film, video, print and computer-based materials.
SPECIALTIES: Medical device industry, occupational health and safety.
PRESIDENT/CEO/OWNER: Judy Kessel, P; Jerrold Gershone, EVP; Jerry Kolb, VP.

MEDVEC-EPPERS ADVERTISING, LTD.
4441 Lake Avenue South
FAX: 651-429-3812
CONTACT: Jason Medvec
E-MAIL: jason-m@medvec-eppers.com
WWW: medvec-eppers.com

651-429-1001
St. Paul 55110

SERVICES: Fresh, intrusive and memorable communications. Strategic planning for consumer, retail and e-business clients; concept development and production of advertising; comprehensive web site development, implementation and marketing; broadcast concept and production; collateral, direct mail and promotional programs.
CAPABILITIES: Offering recommendations regarding all aspects of the marketing communications process; web(in)Site, our strategic system for optimizing internet communications; impatience with communications that don't communicate; elimination (yes, elimination) of mark-ups on all outside charges including media, printing and production.
CURRENT/RECENT CLIENTS/PROJECTS: Old Home Foods, Northern States Power Company (NSP), Bruegger's Bagels, Slumberland Stores, Hardware Hank/Trustworthy Hardware Stores, Uptown Art Fair, Banc Midwest Corp, Aerosim Technologies, Air-Serve, Auto Glass Plus, Caribou Highlands Lodge, County Banks, Digisource, Mammoth Outfitters, Outdoor Viewing Systems, Oxboro Medical, Shavlik Technologies, Southview Banks, Twin Cities Marathon, White Rock Banks, Zaud Squad (Edina Realty.)
OFFICERS: Jason T. Medvec, P; Shawn Lee Eppers, VP; Randy Phillips, CFO
ACCOUNT SUPERVISORS: Alex Heiser
CREATIVE DIRECTOR: Christine Howey

MESH CORPORATION
545 Summit Avenue
FAX: 651-224-7671
CONTACT: Mark Hulsey
E-MAIL: hulsey@meshcorp.com
WWW: meshcorp.com

651-224-7534
St. Paul 55102

CAPABILITIES: MESH provides their clients a marketing roadmap for new business growth. We develop "living" marketing, positioning and communications plans, including tactical recommendations for an integrated (online & traditional) strategic approach. We marshal the business development process by defining, prioritizing and implementing each set of "critical steps" in order to achieve substantial, measurable growth for the near and long term.
SPECIALTIES: New business development consulting. High-level marketing and communication planning. Oversee development of communication tools.

Marketing Communications / 325

CURRENT/RECENT CLIENTS/PROJECTS: Our successful and collaborative relationships include: corporate clients, advertising agencies, marketing firms, Internet developers and specialized consultants.

MULTIMEDIA 952-931-2112
1011 First Street South #300 Hopkins 55343
FAX: 952-935-1318
CONTACT: Dianne Thill
WWW: multimedia-inc.com
SERVICES: Production of video presentations, interactive CD-ROM development, web page design, multi-image and live musical shows.
EQUIPMENT: Betacam video location and studio equipment, edit suite, multi-image programming.
SPECIALTIES: Sales meetings, sales training, marketing presentations.

N

NYGARD DIMENSIONS 612-371-9228
1414 Marshall Street N.E. Minneapolis 55413
FAX: 612-371-9232
CONTACT: Ben Wallace, Director of Account Services
E-MAIL: id@brandcommunications.com
WWW: brandcommunications.com
SERVICES: Brand-based marketing communications: brand strategy and identity development, integrated marketing communications planning, creative development, design, production, implementation, measurement and management through all media: Print: literature, stationery, direct mail, advertising, sales tools, packaging, sales kits; Digital: Websites (internet/intranet/extranet), online promotion, sales tools/software, product demos, video presentations, kiosks, online brand identity management; Environmental: themed events, stage sets, exhibits, displays/POP.
CAPABILITIES: Brand identity systems, including naming, logo, brand elements and guidelines. Unique approach to brand identity strategy, design development and management through all points of stakeholder contact to create the "whole brand experience." Sister companies Nygard Set Design and Harmony Box contribute to brand experience creation. Industries: information technology/e-business, healthcare/pharmaceuticals, financial services, manufacturing, retail and more.

326 / Marketing Communications

CURRENT/RECENT CLIENTS/PROJECTS: 3M Company; Auxilium Software; Compass Productions; Conseco Finance; Larson Manufacturing; Lawson Software; Lutheran Brotherhood; MedIntelligence; nQuire Software; Pharmaceutical Care Network (PCN); Proliant (formerly AMPC, Inc.); Qtech Systems, Inc.; Sales Force 2000 Software; Safe Reflections; Sunrise Community Banks (formerly Franklin Bancorp), U.S. Magnetix; U of M Physicians.
PRESIDENT/CEO/OWNER: Jim Nygard, P

O

O'CONNOR & WALTER 612-338-7859
420 N 5th Street #1080 Minneapolis 55401
FAX: 612-338-7859
CONTACT: Jay Walter
SERVICES: Marketing Communications. Print and electronic graphics for corporate communications; advertising, publishing, web sites and packaging.
CAPABILITIES: Strong design background combined with complete range of electronic digital production and prepress capabilities.
CURRENT/RECENT CLIENTS/PROJECTS: Metropolitan Airports Commission; American Diabetes Association; Capstone Publishing; Marcus Dental Supply Company; Fairview Hospitals.
PRESIDENT/CEO/OWNER: Jay Walter

P

MARGERY PETERSON, FREELANCE WRITER 651-731-0591
625 Hillwood Court St. Paul 55119
CONTACT: Margery Peterson
E-MAIL: interplay@uswest.net
SERVICES: Types of Writing: Brochures, newsletters, press releases, holiday cards, web pages and other marketing and promotional materials. Journalism, articles.
SPECIALTIES: Creative concepts using humor and unique angles.
CURRENT/RECENT CLIENTS/PROJECTS: Written For: Architecture and construction, health, fitness and medical, consumer products, education, the arts, environment, government, and service industries.

PRECISION POWERHOUSE 612-333-9111
911 Second Street South Minneapolis 55415
FAX: 612-332-9200
CONTACT: Dan Piepho, Paul Sunberg, Gene Gunderson
E-MAIL: dan@power-house.com; pauls@power-house.com or geneg@power-house.com
WWW: precisionpowerhouse.com
SERVICES: Full service communications company specializing in award-winning sales, marketing and training videos, audio and Interactive media production and post-production. Video sales presentation, product marketing presentations, video news releases, video/floppy disk/CD-ROM/DVD, annual reports, Interactive media training programs, video/audio/CD-ROM, catalogs, etc. Web site construction and design for business, data-base configuration, e-business, web publishing, hosting.

Marketing Communications / 327

EQUIPMENT: Sony DME 3000, Silicon Graphics Maximum Impact Indigo 2 with Alias/Wavefront 2D and 3D software, Maya ACCOM 5 minute digital disk recorder, Pinnacle Aladdin digital effects, DVE and CG. Audio sound featuring Sonic Solutions, High resolution 96/24 DVD/Surround Sound ready digital/audio workstation, Interactive media video digitizing workstation, Autodesk Animator workstation. Silicon Graphics maximum impact indigo 2, Accom 5 minute digital disk recorder. Pinnacle Aladdin digital effects, DVE and CG, Autodesk Animator workstation, Macromedia's Director, Flo and Morph Software, Adobe PhotoShop, Adobe Illustrator, DeBabelizer, Macromodel CorelDraw5, Barco Paint. Maximum Impact, 40 x 60 production soundstage, full-scale complete digital audio post production suite, full-scale complete digital/video post production suite, digital/analog video post production suite, SFI 3D animation suite, Interactive media workstations, DVD surround sound authoring suite, complete internet services, class five thousand clean-room, large scale audio/video duplication, CD and DVD replication, package designers on staff, worldwide shipping services, producer/director services, writers, technicians.

SPECIALTIES: Sales presentations, Interactive Training, Catalogs, e-business web sites, Intranet, Extranet, consumer products, radio, television, and web commercials, lap-top presentations, Interactive kiosks, video and interactive direct mail marketing, DVD authoring.

BARB PRIBYL COMMUNICATIONS 952-882-8809
13420 Knox Drive Burnsville 55337
FAX: 952-882-8897
CONTACT: Barb Pribyl
E-MAIL: bpribyl@spacestar.net
SERVICES: Copywriting, editing, Macintosh desktop publishing design, project management, public relations planning, writing and media relations, brochures, newsletters, news releases/media kits, news and feature articles, promotional materials and direct mail.
CAPABILITIES: Expertise in writing and publication management for health care and health and fitness companies; publicity for consumer products; employee communications.
CURRENT/RECENT CLIENTS/PROJECTS: Target Corporation (internal communications projects); First Nationwide Mortgage Corporation; Shandwick; Healthpartners; LifeFit Health; International Aerobic Education.

R

ROSSOW COMMUNICAITONS 612-831-3280
4200 Parklawn #103 Edina 55435
FAX: 612-831-3260
CONTACT: Dustin J. Rossow
E-MAIL: djrossow@aol.com
SERVICES: Development of advertising sales and promotions.
CURRENT/RECENT CLIENTS/PROJECTS: Publications: Travelhost Twin Cities Magazine; MetroDoctors Magazine; The Hennepin Lawyer Magazine.

S

THE SAGE GROUP, INC.   612-321-9897
10 South Fifth Street #435   Minneapolis 55403
FAX: 612-321-9896
CONTACT: Elin Raymond
E-MAIL: eraymond@sagegrp.com
WWW: sagegrp.com
SERVICES: Strategic corporate and marketing communications; investor relations. Marketing planning, brand development and advertising.
CAPABILITIES: Full service public relations, marketing communications, and financial communications services. Web-based communications, including newsletters. Annual reports, investor presentations and speeches.
CURRENT/RECENT CLIENTS/PROJECTS: Digital Visions/Netzee; Merrill Corporation FDS; Northern States Power; Affinity Plus Federal Credit Union; Medamicus; Vida Healthcare; Rocketchips; Krones, Inc.; LTG Technologies; Check Technology Corp; NAPFA; Fleming Companies; Research Inc.; Northstar Computer Forms, Rural Cellular Corporation.
PRESIDENT/CEO/OWNER: Elin Raymond

VICKI L SCHUMAN   763-541-0711
235 North Nathan Lane #324   Minneapolis 55441
FAX: 763-541-1032
CONTACT: Vicki L Schuman
E-MAIL: vlschuman@uswest.net
SERVICES: Biomedical and technical marketing communications and public relations, particularly technical writing and editing.
CAPABILITIES: Experience in both laboratory research and communications enables me to write at the level at which a technical audience expects to read.
CURRENT/RECENT CLIENTS/PROJECTS: 3M; various biomedical companies.

TIMOTHY SHOLINE HEDGES   612-378-1464
725 7th Street SE   Minneapolis 55414
CONTACT: Timothy Hedges
E-MAIL: timhedges@earthlink.net
SPECIALTIES: Creative consulting. Providing liason, insight and inside contacts to regional media, book selling and arts markets. Conception and rendering of original ideas. Copywriting and editing.
Affiliation: Around Town Agency, Media Guides.
PRESIDENT/CEO/OWNER: Timothy Hedges

SMITH COMMUNICATIONS   952-473-7658
30 Orono Orchard Road   Wayzata 55391
FAX: 952-475-0968
CONTACT: Sandra Smith
E-MAIL: smithcom@mail.goldengate.net

Marketing Communications / 329

SERVICES: Strategic marketing communications and public relations plans and programs to support an organization's business and marketing goals and objective. Recent client projects include: qualitative research and focus groups, internal organizational audits, strategic marketing and communications plans, brand positioning, corporate identity make-overs, employee communications, community outreach, customer communication programs, benchmarking and merger/acquisition communications.

SPECIALTIES: Senior level expertise in marketing communications and public relations for companies in transition or facing increased competition. Strategic plans, research and internal due diligence, program implementation, writing and producing marketing and communication materials. Audits include determining the brandabilty of an organization, increasing the effectiveness of internal staffs and improving relationships with key stakeholders.

CURRENT/RECENT CLIENTS/PROJECTS: National and international utility and energy service companies, manufacturers, telecommunications, healthcare organizations, professional service firms, local government, professional/trade associations.

PRESIDENT/CEO/OWNER: Sandra Smith

U

UPFRONT PRODUCTIONS 651-633-5299
2350 County Road C #120 St. Paul 55113
FAX: 651-633-5197
CONTACT: Tricia Nordby Hamrin/Chris Hamrin
WWW: hoopjumping.com
CAPABILITIES: Organizational Communications Solutions Center. A Spectrum. A Synergy. Concept Development, Copywriting, Graphic Design, Illustration, Document Production, Web Site Creation, Scanning, Photo Retouching, Pre-press, Offset Printing, Digital B&W Printing, Color Copies, Posters, Displays, Signs, Custom Assembly, Inventory, Distribution, Corporate Compass® MIS, VantagePoint™, Hoop Jumping™.
SPECIALTIES: Choose your hoop. We'll jump through it™.
OFFICERS: Tricia Nordby Hamrin/Chris Hamrin

V

VAVRICKA JUNTTI & COMPANY 612-335-8865
10 South 5th Street #100 Minneapolis 55402
FAX: 612-335-8866
CONTACT: Anita Juntti
E-MAIL: anita@vavrickajuntti.com
WWW: vavrickajuntti.com
SERVICES: Strategy development and creative execution of wide variety of marketing communication materials including sales collateral, direct mail and point-of-sale.
CAPABILITIES: Specialize in business-to-business marketing, with extensive experience in food industry.
CURRENT/RECENT CLIENTS/PROJECTS: Pillsbury Foodservice (Bakery and Old El Paso); Dawn Food Products; Land O' Lakes Food Service; Rexam Flexible Packaging; Burger King; Subway; Hyvee, Kemps/Marigold Foods.
PRESIDENT/CEO/OWNER: Anita Juntti/Cheryl Vavricka

W

WINNERS MARKETING COMMUNICATIONS
3425 Oakton Drive
FAX: 612-945-0955
CONTACT: Karen Winner
E-MAIL: winners@rconnect.com

612-945-0955
Minnetonka 55305

SERVICES: Freelance copywriting and project management for advertising, public relations, direct mail, sales literature, speeches, video, websites, shareholder communications, newsletters.
CAPABILITIES: Computer and medical technologies.
CURRENT/RECENT CLIENTS/PROJECTS: American Medical Systems; ACT Networks; H.B. Fuller; Applications Developer (AppDev); OneLink; Profit Solutions; PROSAR; Perceptual Engineering.

Marketing Agencies

A

ALLOUT MARKETING, INC. 952-404-0800
742 Twelve Oaks Center Wayzata 55391
15500 Wayzata Blvd.
FAX: 952-404-0900
CONTACT: Christine Mignogna, Director of First Impressions/Cheryl Schwanke, Marketing Guru
E-MAIL: marketing@alloutmarketinginc.com
CAPABILITIES: Full-service strategic marketing firm which identifies, develops, plans and implements effective, revenue-generating global marketing visions for technology-based, high-tech, and biotechnology/medical companies. AOM offers a comprehensive portfolio of services including Marketing Consulting, Market Research, Internet Marketing, Graphic Design, Event Management and Public Relations. This wide range of offerings, backed by extensive experience in business development, provides a powerful combination for AllOut Marketing clients. AOM clients benefit from a focused analysis of their current business environment that leads to clear cut global strategies for revenue growth.
SPECIALTIES: Business-to-Business; Technology-based; High-tech; Biotechnology/Medical
PRESIDENT/CEO/OWNER: Ruth R. Lane

AMUNDSON MARKETING 612-333-7700
10 South Fifth Street #580 Minneapolis 55402
FAX: 612-333-7701
CONTACT: Kathleen J. Amundson
CAPABILITIES: Amundson Marketing is a strategically-driven marketing agency focused on building the value of our clients' organizations through the development of valuable relationships with their customers. Our expertise encompasses the full array of marketing disciplines including strategic planning, positioning and branding, relationship marketing, direct and database marketing, frequency and loyalty marketing and promotional marketing. Our team is experienced in developing solutions based on the needs of clients and their customers, doing so in a manner that helps our clients stay ahead of their business while delivering a powerful return on investment.
SERVICES: Strategic and tactical planning, primary and secondary research, program design, management and fulfillment, creative services, production management, economic modeling, customer segmentation, modeling and profiling, partner negotiations, measurement and analysis.
CURRENT/RECENT CLIENTS/PROJECTS: National and international clients in the telecommunications, utility, high-tech, business-to-business, consumer products and service industries.

B

THE
BENYAS
AD GROUP
INC

Advertising + Design

THE BENYAS AD GROUP, INC.   **612-340-9804**
126 North Third Street, Suite 300   **Minneapolis 55401**
FAX: 612-334-5950
CONTACT: Bradley A. Benyas
E-MAIL: benyas@visi.com
CAPABILITIES: Strategic planning, design and development of primary marketing support materials including capabilities brochures, print ads, direct mail, product graphics and literature, sales training materials, point-of-sale materials, Internet (www) marketing and corporate identity.
SPECIALTIES: The Benyas AD Group is a results-oriented marketing agency specializing in printed communications that advance our clients, their companies, and their products. From concept through production, we provide the services you need, when you need them. State-of-the-art pre-press resources, expert photo direction and print supervision. We deliver results.

BEYOND MARKETING THOUGHT   **612-338-5009**
510 First Avenue North #605   **Minneapolis 55403**
FAX: 612-338-4714
CONTACT: Becky Ewert
E-MAIL: info@brandnetwork.com
WWW: beyondmarketingthought.com
CAPABILITIES: Brand management consulting, research, and training to build brand equity. Proprietary process used with clients of all sizes and industries includes 3 core steps: gaining the commitment of the executive team on focusing on brand as a strategic business asset; injecting a consistent brand-building discipline throughout the entire marketing process; and engaging the entire organization in reinforcing the brand's promise.
SPECIALTIES: Brand management consulting, brand assessment research, and brand-based training is woven into every part of our brand-building process.
CURRENT/RECENT CLIENTS/PROJECTS: Target Stores, Incyte Genomics, Lutheran Brotherhood, 3M, University of Minnesota, Allina Health System, Honeywell, Cargill, Star Tribune, CNT
PRESIDENT/CEO/OWNER: Karl D. Speak

Marketing Consultants / 333

BOLIN MARKETING AND ADVERTISING 612-374-1200
2523 Wayzata Blvd, #300 Minneapolis 55405
FAX: 612-377-4226
CONTACT: Todd Bolin
WWW: bolinideas.com
SERVICES: Bolin is a full-service advertising and marketing resource. From strategic planning development through creative execution. Bolin works with its clients to develop integrated campaigns that work. Media planning and buying (both on and off-line, broadcast, print, out of home and direct); promotion, graphic design, public relations and creative brand building advertising campaigns.

C

C J OLSON MARKET RESEARCH, INC. 612-378-5040
2125 East Hennepin Avenue #100 Minneapolis 55413
FAX: 612-378-5401
CONTACT: Gayle Belkengren
CAPABILITIES: Full service design, sampling, data collection, data processing, statistical analysis, multivariate analysis, full reports with color charts and graphs and follow through recommendations.
SPECIALTIES: Strategic planning, marketing communications plans, market and marketing research, concept testing, feasibility studies, taste testing, advertising pre/post testing for business-to-business and consumer products and services.
RESEARCH & TESTING METHODS: Focus groups, in-depth telephone interviews, one-on-one executive interviews, mail questionnaires, mall intercept interviews, secret shopper. Local, regional, national and international.
FACILITIES: Focus group room with client viewing area, kitchen, 14 line monitored telephone center, data processing using SPSS and custom designed software.
PRESIDENT/CEO/OWNER: Carolyn J. Olson, P

CLICK COMMUNICATIONS CORP. 612-332-0719
233 Park Avenue, Third Floor Minneapolis 55415
FAX: 612-332-5637
CONTACT: Naomi Teske
E-MAIL: clk-clk@isd.net
WWW: clk-clk.com
CAPABILITIES: Project management of effective print communications from concept through production. Strategic planning, brand development and marketing consulting.

D

D.W. ET AL. 612-339-7848
400 First Avenue North #316 Minneapolis 55401
CONTACT: Dan Wallace
WWW: dwetal.com

334 / Marketing Consultants

CAPABILITIES: D.W. et al. Ltd. works with B2B firms to build businesses and brands. As consultants, we craft strategies and write plans. As marketing agents, we implement plans through a network we've cultivated since 1986. Core deliverables: strategic Marketing plans, positioning and brand plans, company brochures, web sites and advertising campaigns. Extended capabilities are available through allied advisors and specialists.
SPECIALTIES: Business-to-business firms.
CURRENT/RECENT CLIENTS/PROJECTS: Alliant Consulting; The Bureau Electronics Division; Carlson School of Management IRC; City of Minneapolis ITS; e-fortunecookie.com; Fredrickson & Byron; GTE; hrtomorrow.com; Honeywell; IBM; KruegerWright; Norberg Management; NRG; personallitigation.com; PDI; Palamino Euro Bistro; Pro Group; Research Resources; Serving Software; The Collaborative; Wilson Learning; and Winona Research

E

E. LIVINGSTON & ASSOCIATES
3305 Shepherd Hills Drive
CONTACT: Edward Livingston
952-835-4080
Bloomington 55431
CAPABILITIES: Business-to-business advertising, public relations and sales promotion.
CURRENT/RECENT CLIENTS/PROJECTS: National manufacturers and marketers of industrial and technical products.

EMERGE MARKETING
4315 Aldrich Avenue South
CONTACT: Jay Lipe
E-MAIL: lipe@uswest.net
WWW: emergemarketing.com
612-824-4833
Minneapolis 55409
SERVICES: Strategic marketing consulting; act as a virtual marketing director for growing companies (1 million - 50 million in sales)
CAPABILITIES: Proven marketing planning process that includes templates, tools, and worksheets. Specialize in working with growing companies ($1 million - $50 million.) Over 14 years experience in writing and implementing marketing plans.
CURRENT/RECENT CLIENTS/PROJECTS: Over 60 clients including Mainline Cruise and Travel; IWP Components; Brookdale Plastics; Daytons Travel; First Security Bank; Ehlers & Associates; City of Richfield.

G

GILLIES GROUP, INC.
5942 Fairwood Lane
FAX: 612-934-6711
CONTACT: Donald Gillies
E-MAIL: gilliesgroup@usa.net
612-934-1922
Minnetonka 55345
SERVICES: Marketing and management consulting services to advertisers and advertising agencies. Efficient agency searches and strategic planning for advertisers. Valuable assistance in positioning, strategic planning and new business development for small and mid-sized advertising agencies.

Marketing Consultants / 335

CAPABILITIES: Expert in efficient, confidential agency searches. Uniquely experienced in strategic planning for profitable agency growth. Also available for presentation skills training.

GROUP ONE RESPONSE MARKETING 612-334-8100
1221 Nicollet Mall #218 Minneapolis 55403
FAX: 612-334-8102
CONTACT: John Marinovich
SERVICES: Full service strategic marketing partner. Specializing in integrated, brand development, marketing services including: positioning, research marketing communications, sales promotion, response marketing, graphic design and execution.

H

HAUCK MARKETING 952-470-0121
4831 Vine Hill Road Minneapolis 55331
FAX: 952-470-0156
CONTACT: James Hauck
CAPABILITIES: Strategic planning from idea through execution. Target identification, situation analysis, strategy development, positioning for new and existing businesses, both niche and mass market.
SPECIALTIES: Medical, banking/financial, computers, food and beverage, and automotive.
CURRENT/RECENT CLIENTS/PROJECTS: Automotive Tier 1 Supplier; Internet/MP3 Product.

MICHAEL A HOHMANN AND COMPANY 612-922-1490
4100 Ewing Avenue South Minneapolis 55410
FAX: 612-922-1490
CONTACT: Michael Hohmann
E-MAIL: mhohm@aol.com
SERVICES: Market research, analysis and planning (primary and secondary research capability); financial analysis and profit planning; competitive analysis and strategic planning; operational audits and writings; business planning seminars and training sessions.

336 / Marketing Consultants

CAPABILITIES: Design and develop complete custom business plans, including marketing plan and complete pro forma financial statements. Qualitative and quantitative research and analysis experience. Publications: Business Notes - News and Information, Tips and Trends for Small Business.

KATHY HORWATH, MARKETING SERVICES   651-481-9734
4486 Timberline Court   Vadnais Heights 55127
FAX: 651-481-0278
CONTACT: Kathy Horwath
E-MAIL: khorwath@attglobal.net
SERVICES: Over 25 years of experience in medical marketing, providing comprehensive, integrated and effective marketing programs. Plan development and program execution that satisfy strategic business goals.
CAPABILITIES: Primary focus: Medical technology, Biotechnology.
CURRENT/RECENT CLIENTS/PROJECTS: Princeton Reimbursement Group, Cellex Biosciences, National Cell Culture Center.

I

INDEX GROUP   952-934-6922
6393 Ginger Drive   Eden Prairie 55346
FAX: 952-934-7193
CONTACT: Gregory N. Fern
E-MAIL: gfern@indexgroup.com
WWW: indexgroup.com
SERVICES: Strategic marketing consulting, audits and assessments; strategic business planning and management counsel; market analysis; marketing and sales plan development; visual communications systems including name development, image audits and evaluation, identity planning, capability and literature systems and web design; proposal and presentation development; sales process engineering; and marketing program management.
CAPABILITIES: Specialized marketing and strategic business planning for public and private organizations. Unique expertise in long-cycled marketing and sales systems based on relationship driven business models. Representative client segments: accounting; architecture; city, county, and state agencies; construction; engineering; environmental; graphic and industrial design; information and technology; interiors; legal; landscape architecture; manufacturing; planning and; real estate and development companies.
PRESIDENT/CEO/OWNER: Gregory N. Fern. FSMPS

J

JALIVAY & ASSOCIATES   651-322-1405
4821 Weston Hills Drive   Eagan 55123
FAX: 651-322-4813
CONTACT: Kathy Jalivay
E-MAIL: kathy@jalivay.com
WWW: jalivay.com

Marketing Consultants / 337

CAPABILITIES: Event production, planning, coordinating, writing and distribution press releases, advertising placement and creative consulting, marketing communication planning and executing.
SPECIALTIES: Marketing communications including press releases, direct mail pieces, brochures, sales materials, event and trade show planning.
CURRENT/RECENT CLIENTS/PROJECTS: USTA, Mall of America, D.E.A.F., Gourmet Express, Fresh Paint, Inc., Clubkid, Learning Curve Toys, ATT Broadband, MAEF.

CLIFF JOHNSON MARKETING 612-466-2288
12820 Laurie Lane Chaska 55318
FAX: 612-466-2277
CONTACT: Cliff Johnson
E-MAIL: cliffmg@aol.com
SERVICES: I help leaders clarify their vision and develop innovative strategies for transforming their vision into reality.
CAPABILITIES: Gardening/horticulture, agriculture, non-profit organizations. Book, self-publishing.
CURRENT/RECENT CLIENTS/PROJECTS: Self-published gardening book in 1999: "Putting Down Roots."

L

LYNCH JARVIS JONES, INC. 612-371-0014
119 North Fourth Street #301 Minneapolis 55401
FAX: 612-371-0459
CONTACT: Kevin Lynch
E-MAIL: kevinlynch@ljj.com
WWW: ljj.com
SERVICES: Business analysis, marketing research, strategic planning, mass communications and public education, for growing, ethical organizations which offer products, services, ideas and issues fundamental to the fulfillment, happiness and wellness of the human race and the planet earth.
CURRENT/RECENT CLIENTS/PROJECTS: Fairview Health Service; Minnesota Department of Health; Minnesota Department of Public Safety; Minnesota Department of Children, Families and Learning; The Minneapolis Foundation; Minnesota Center for Health Promotion; Minneapolis Public Schools; Loantech; Centers for the Application of Prevention Technologies; Minnesota State Colleges, and Universities; Wedge Community Co-op.
PRESIDENT/CEO/OWNER: Kevin Lynch, CEO; Gregg Byers, CD; Paul Engebretson, Director of Operations

M

MARKETING WORKS 763-745-0226
815 Brockton Lane North Plymouth 55447
FAX: 763-449-9674
CONTACT: Ed Cerier
E-MAIL: mktgwrks@visi.com

338 / Marketing Consultants

SERVICES: Analyses and ideas that power business growth. Specific services: marketing plans, communications plans, advertising and design strategies, brand and advertising positioning, advertising execution, employee development.
CAPABILITIES: Manufacturers, service companies, advertising agencies and design firms of all sizes; companies with established and new products and services; businesses that want to grow using the power of marketing.
CURRENT/RECENT CLIENTS/PROJECTS: Ad Café, Minnesota Chapter of the American Academy of Pediatrics, Art Packs, Beshoar Nicolo Studios, Richard Byrd Management Consultants, Campbell Mithun Advertising, (for their clients: Andersen Windows, Commerce Bank, H&R Block), Colle & McVoy Advertising, for their Pfizer client; Hedstrom/Blessing, ImagiNETive Computing, Osborn Medical, Palco Marketing, West Group. Also run seminars on marketing, teach marketing management at the University of St. Thomas Graduate School of Business, and lecture at the University of Minnesota Graduate School of Business.

MARKGRAF & WELLS ADVERTISING & MARKETING
430 Oak Grove Street #308

612-870-8550

Minneapolis 55403

CONTACT: Richard Markgraf
SERVICES: Sophisticated marketing and communications skills for small and medium sized organizations. Marketing consultation for large organizations. Market audits, project management, competitive analysis, custom problem solving and program development, program development from Research and Data Mining results, research findings interpreted into application programs. Advertising agency program and creative materials development.
CAPABILITIES: Extensive experience in marketing consultation for commercial, government and non-profit sectors. Client rosters and project information available upon request. Consultation areas: market definition, competitive analysis, prospect profiling, strategy formation.
CURRENT/RECENT CLIENTS/PROJECTS: In addition to continuity clients selected project work: RDO Equipment Company - Dealer/Customer analysis. Lexus Automobiles - pilot program for satellite dealer opening/Dayton's' Department partnership promotion. Fisher Rosemount - competitive companies market analysis. Allen-Bradley - Data-Mining results analysis and strategy. Mangen Research Associates, Inc. - market analyst services for selected clients.

MESH CORPORATION
545 Summit Avenue

651-224-7534

St. Paul 55102

FAX: 651-224-7671
CONTACT: Mark Hulsey
E-MAIL: hulsey@meshcorp.com
WWW: meshcorp.com
CAPABILITIES: MESH provides their clients a marketing roadmap for new business growth. We develop "living" marketing, positioning and communications plans, including tactical recommendations for an integrated (online & traditional) strategic approach. We marshal the business development process by defining, prioritizing and implementing each set of "critical steps" in order to achieve substantial, measurable growth for the near and long term.
SPECIALTIES: New business development consulting. High-level marketing and communication planning. Oversee development of communication tools.
CURRENT/RECENT CLIENTS/PROJECTS: Our successful and collaborative relationships include: corporate clients, advertising agencies, marketing firms, Internet developers and specialized consultants.

We are a superb **Custom Photo Lab and Digital Imaging** service. We are committed to providing the finest possible imagery, and service beyond our customers' expectations. If you haven't worked with ProColor lately, you should take a look at us today.

ProColor has the widest array of photographic imaging capabilities in the Upper Midwest, including the following:

SCANNING
- High resolution drum scanning
- Artwork up to 48" X 72"
- Up to 450 MB file size
- Kodak Photo CD, Master & Pro

TRADESHOW/DISPLAY GRAPHICS
- Large-format digital photographic prints and transparencies
- Backlit display transparencies
- Lambda and LightJet technology
- Highest quality mounting and finishing services
- Lenticular imaging (3-D, Flip and Motion)
- Display One brand trade show display units
- Light boxes for backlit display

SHORT-RUN/ON-DEMAND PRINTING
- Heidelberg Quickmaster DI 4CP Press
- Xerox DocuColor 2060 4CP Digital Press
- Xerox DocuPrint 65 B & W Digital Press
- Canon Bubble Jet 2436 Large-Format (24" X 36") Color Copier
- Canon Color Copiers (standard page sizes)
- Color copies directly from 35mm, 2-1/4, or 4 X 5 transparencies

FINE ART REPRODUCTION
- IRIS prints up to 30" X 47"
- B&W Inkjet prints up to 24" X 72"
- Scanning, color matching, and manipulation for artists

FILM PROCESSING
- Committed to serving photographers for the long-term
- E-6, C-41, Kodachrome, Agfa Scala, and B&W
- Multiple proofing options for professionals
- Our third E-6 machine is on the way

TRADITIONAL FILM SERVICES
- Small and large dupes, internegs
- Computer and copy slides
- Commercial and custom prints

MINILAB SERVICES
- Fuji Frontier Digital Minilab, laser imaged prints up to 10" X 15"
- Prints from transparencies, negatives or digital camera files
- Guaranteed quality for all minilab services

COLOR AND IMAGE MANIPULATION
- Expert color correction and color management
- Creative retouching services

FREE PICKUP AND DELIVERY

PROCOLOR

909 Hennepin Avenue South
Minneapolis, MN 55403
t 612.673.8900 800.332.7753
f 612.673.8991
e www.procolor.com

P

J M PETERSON & ASSOCIATES
370 Selby Avenue #303
FAX: 651-222-1177
CONTACT: Jan Peterson
E-MAIL: janmpete@aol.com

651-222-3377
St. Paul 55102

CAPABILITIES: Wanted: high tech, original equipment manufacturers (OEMs) and maintenance/repair/operations (MRO) companies who want to increase market share. Your objectives met through strategic thinking and sound tactics delivered on-time and on-budget.
SPECIALTIES: Marketing communications planning and execution for businesses that sell products or services to other businesses a specialty. Tactics include print and electronic vehicles that work together.
CURRENT/RECENT CLIENTS/PROJECTS: 3M; H. B. Fuller Company; West Group; KAPAK Corporation; Lee Communications, Inc.
PRESIDENT/CEO/OWNER: Jan Peterson

PROFESSIONAL SERVICES MARKETING
806 12th Avenue NW
FAX: 651-636-0422
CONTACT: Terrie S. Wheeler
E-MAIL: twheeler@proservmarketing.com
WWW: proservmarketing.com

651-633-2711
New Brighton 55112

SERVICES: Professional Services Marketing works with leading professional services firms and corporations to develop creative, cost-effective, and results-oriented marketing and communications strategies. We help clients develop targeted, strategies for business growth by working strategically at various levels in our clients organizations. These levels include the development of firm-wide marketing strategies, practice or industry group marketing initiatives, regional office initiatives, and individual professional development planning.
CAPABILITIES: Strategic marketing planning which may lead to advertising campaign development; Association marketing strategy development; change and corporate transition communications; client communications; client satisfaction and service program development; cross-marketing program development; desktop publishing and corporation presentations; Employee/Internal communications; focus group planning and facilitation; individual business development planning, consulting, and career coaching; Internet website planning, development, content creation and marketing; marketing database and client information management; marketing materials development; marketing skills training and development - professional and staff levels; market research and competitive market assessments; marketing to trade and professional associations; merger and acquisition communications strategy; practice and industry group marketing; presentation skills coaching; public and media relations; local and national; request for proposal (RFP) and proposal response tools; seminar and event planning.
PRESIDENT/CEO/OWNER: Terrie S. Wheeler, President

340 / Marketing Consultants

R

RDO MARKETING   952-925-9785
3948 West 50th Street #208   Minneapolis 55424
FAX: 952-925-9784
CONTACT: Doug O'Leary
E-MAIL: rdomarketing@worldnet.att.net
SERVICES: Marketing consulting and strategic services including market planning, market research, brand development, advertising, direct/database marketing, loyalty marketing, sales promotion, performance improvement and direct sales (products and services).
CAPABILITIES: Providing Balanced Marketing Solutions(*!) for growth-insistent ventures. We focus on building relevant relationships between our clients and their preferred prospects, customers, employees and stakeholders in order to accelerate and sustain business success.
CURRENT/RECENT CLIENTS/PROJECTS: Bracknell Corporation; Call Center Concepts; Edina Realty; General Mills; Grand Teton National Park; Great Universal; i-Purpose; Nybo Manufacturing; Onvoy; Oviation Communications; Serengeti Software; Stirtz Bernards Boyden Surdel & Larter, Ty.

RISDALL LINNIHAN ADVERTISING   651-286-6700
2475 15th Street NW   New Brighton 55112
FAX: 651-631-2561
CONTACT: John Risdall, Chairman
E-MAIL: getwired@risdall.com
WWW: risdall.com
SERVICES: Full service advertising agency offering marketing strategy and planning, marketing research, advertising, direct response, promotion, collateral, publicity/PR and business strategy and planning in the traditional and interactive arenas.
CAPABILITIES: Specializing in the educational, medical, institutional, retail, computer and environmental industries. Internet expertise from site design to site development to marketing planning and implementation.

Marketing Consultants / 341

CURRENT/RECENT CLIENTS/PROJECTS: Aeration Industries; Agribank; Allegheny Power; Alliance Water Resources; American Guidance Service; Applied Technology Consultants; ATG Laboratories, Inc.; Bang Printing; Birchwood Casey; Blanks USA; Brown Wilbert Vault Company; City of New Brighton; Clinch-On Products; Clique Capital; Cocola Palm; cranespharmacy.com; Curative; Decker Publications; Digital River; Diversity Village; EBP HealthPlans, Inc.; Electrosonic; EMPI; E. W. Blanch; Paragon; UniSure; Finnleo Sauna; Fox River; Funeral.com; Galyans; GunVault; Highland Banks; HomeRight; Honeywell; House of Hope; Hubler Family Business Consultants; Innsbruck Jewelers; Isaksen Promotional Specialties; Kinney & Lange; Learning Outfitters; Lease Point.com; Lemna Corporation; Liquid Dynamics; 3M Industrial Mineral Products Division; 3M Traffic Control Materials; 3M Dental Products; 3M Healthcare; 3M Industrial Tapes and Specialties; Magnum Research; Medtronic (Neurological Division); Micom Circuits, Inc.; Morries Automotive Group; Mounds View School District; Normark Rapala; Northern States Power; Norwest Equity Partners, Novartis, Onan Corporation; Photos, Inc.; Pillsbury; Premier Mounts; Printing Industry of MN; Progressive Marketing; Pur (Recovery Engineering); Purus, Inc.; Rainforest Café; RSR Wholesale Guns; Ramsey County Library; Rottlund Homes; SafeWater Anywhere LLC; Schoolbell.com; Schoonover Bodyworks, Inc.; Smith Foundry Company; Smith System Manufacturing, Inc.; Summit Envirosolutions; Target; Tertronics, Inc.; The TPA; Time Savers; Uni-Hydro, Inc.; Upsher-Smith Laboratories; US Filter-Autocon; USFilter-Consolidated Electric; USFilter-Control Systems; USFilter Corporate; USFilter-CPC; USFilter-General Filter; USFilter-Filterite; USFilter-Recovery Services; USFilte- Seitz; USF Johnson (France); USF Johnson Screens; Verdant Brands; VerticalNet; Vista Technologies; WalMart; Water Pollution Control Corp.; Waterworld; Western Bank.

RUSTEN MARKETING GROUP, INC.   612-870-9044
310 Clifton Avenue   Minneapolis 55403
FAX: 612-870-1016
CONTACT: Pamela Rusten
E-MAIL: pam@rusten.com
WWW: rusten.com
SERVICES: Competitive strategic positioning®; market evaluation, marketing development and strategic communications for markets including consumer packaged goods, consumer durables, financial, health care, retail and industrial/manufacturing.
OFFICERS: Pamela Rusten, P; Robert Jones, CFO; Dave Bradley, VP/Creative

R-W & ASSOCIATES - MANAGEMENT CONSULTANTS   612-938-0739
4615 Ellerdale Road   Minnetonka 55345
FAX: 612-522-7372
CONTACT: R. Donavan Riley
CAPABILITIES: Full service marketing resource. Marketing feasibility studies, demographic studies, strategic and tactical planning, management information systems. Legal audits, opportunity assessment, new product development and introduction, pre-acquisition evaluations, logistics and distribution retail and restaurant evaluations. Executive conferences, focus groups, secret shoppers.
SPECIALTIES: Dog and horse racing, pre-food manufacturing and distribution, transportation, retailing, food service, legal and management information services. Training, ADA consultation.
PRESIDENT/CEO/OWNER: R. Donavan Riley, Managing Partner

S

SATISFACTION MANAGEMENT SYSTEMS   952-939-4307
5959 Baker Road, #300   Minnetonka 55345
FAX: 952-935-7815
CONTACT: Wayne Serie
E-MAIL: sales@satmansys.com
WWW: satmansys.com
CAPABILITIES: A consulting and market research firm focused on helping organizations bring critical market data into their strategic planning process to improve customer, employee and market performance, and to increase competitive advantage. Since 1989, we have helped clients understand their markets and make positive business changes through our consulting processes and research tools.
SPECIALTIES: Customer Satisfaction/Loyalty Measurement, Customer Value Management, Market Develop/Assessment, Employee Organizational Assessment, Call Center Management, Key Account Assessment and Win/Loss Assessment.
PRESIDENT/CEO/OWNER: Vince Farace, CEO/Wayne Serie, President

Shandwick USA

SHANDWICK INTERNATIONAL   952-832-5000
8400 Normandale Lake Blvd #500   Minneapolis 55437
FAX: 952-831-8241
CONTACT: Jeanne Carpenter, Senior VP of Marketing and Business Development
E-MAIL: jcarpenter@shandwick.com
WWW: shandwick.com
CAPABILITIES: In addition to the capabilities outlined under Public Relations, Shandwick International offers its clients full-service marketing communications solutions, including strategic marketing plans, new product launches, channel marketing, cause-related marketing, collateral and sales support materials and special events. We provide our clients with objectivity and broad points of view. We conduct focus groups, analyze and help frame the client's marketing mission and make recommendations for marketing group staff structures. Shandwick International focuses on the client's goals and offers the added marketing resources to help the client reach them.

MYLES SPICER & ASSOCIATES   612-544-0159
1660 South Hwy 100 #568   Minneapolis 55416
E-MAIL: admin@opendoors.com

Marketing Consultants / 343

CAPABILITIES: Advertising and marketing consultation to business; also provide consulting to advertising agencies for staffing, financial planning, new business. 42 years of agency experience.
SPECIALTIES: For businesses: we will audit your agency relationship. Can assist in selection process of new agency. Evaluate current advertising and marketing strategy, creative product and budgeting. For agencies we can arrange merger, sale or purchase of agency.
PRESIDENT/CEO/OWNER: Myles Spicer

T

TECMARK, INC. 651-452-9551
2060 Centre Pointe Blvd, Suite 7 St. Paul 55120
FAX: 651-452-9196
CONTACT: Karen Drost
E-MAIL: sales@loyaltymarketing.com
WWW: www.loyaltymarketing.com
SERVICES: Tecmark is a leader in loyalty marketing solutions for traditional and e-business organizations. Tecmark provides a comprehensive range of services and technology to design, develop, administer, and analyze customer loyalty, frequency, and employee incentive programs. Whether such programs are new for your company or your existing program requires administrative assistance. Tecmark can help. Strategic planning and concept development. Program development. Implementation and training. Program administration and support. Database management and segmentation. Internet integration. Theme and collateral development. Fulfillment, distribution, and mailing service. ROI analysis and management reporting. Tecmark has been recognized among the nation's fastest-growing companies by the Inc Magazine 500 - an exclusive report on the country's top business innovators - and ranked among the 50 fastest-growing companies by City Business Magazine.
PRESIDENT/CEO/OWNER: Brent Harms

U

UPFRONT PRODUCTIONS 651-633-5299
2350 County Road C #120 St. Paul 55113
FAX: 651-633-5197
CONTACT: Tricia Nordby Hamrin/Chris Hamrin
WWW: hoopjumping.com
CAPABILITIES: Organizational Communications Solutions Center. A Spectrum. A Synergy. Concept Development, Copywriting, Graphic Design, Illustration, Document Production, Web Site Creation, Scanning, Photo Retouching, Pre-press, Offset Printing, Digital B&W Printing, Color Copies, Posters, Displays, Signs, Custom Assembly, Inventory, Distribution, Corporate Compass®, MIS, VantagePoint™, Hoop Jumping™.
SPECIALTIES: Choose your hoop. We'll jump through it™.
OFFICERS: Tricia Nordby Hamrin/Chris Hamrin

Marketing Research

A

ANDERSON MARKETING RESEARCH 612-822-1822
3412 Irving Avenue South #200 Minneapolis 55408
FAX: 612-822-1422
E-MAIL: amrsurvey@aol.com
WWW: amrsurvey.usdex.com
SERVICES: Overnight "Mini-surveys": we specialize in getting survey information fast. Telephone surveys conducted overnight with data tables to you the next day. Order a "mini-survey" of fifty two or three minute interviews for just over $1,000. (This can be an alternative to a slower, higher cost focus group project.) Fast Response on Large National Surveys: a national RDD telephone sample of 1,000 US adults 18+ interviewed weekly (500 men, 500 women). Projectable to US adults. Questionnaire due 11 am Thursday, results back to you on Monday with demographics. 24-hour National Survey: fast, custom 24-hr telephone survey any day.
CONSUMER MALL STUDIES: Faster Consumer Mall Intercept Studies: we conduct your study in any of 125+ US shopping malls with quicker results. Shopping malls provide face-to-face interviewing. Use this technique when consumers must see your product, touch it, taste it, or rank multiple designs. Valuable when consumers must shop competitive products to react to advertising ideas, packaging alternatives, names or labels. We can conduct your study in several US cities at once for a wider range of consumer opinion and faster results. Almost the same cost as using one location.
FOCUS GROUP STUDIES: A focus group study is appropriate to explore a subject in depth (for up to 2 hours) with a group of customers, non-customers, prospects, employees, etc. Focus groups are used effectively to study how customers and competitors' customers perceive, buy and use products. And to evaluate advertising ideas, concepts and copy. Use them to study attitudes, practices, packaging designs, readership of publications. And other issues. A focus group project consists of study design, respondent recruiting, incentives, a meeting room, a group of moderators/analyst, audio and/or video taping, analysis, printed reports and a meeting on the results and recommendations. We provide it all or individual services. Research may be conducted at any US location. Depending on the facility, the recruiting required, and the size of the respondent incentive, the cost of a focus group study conducted locally will run from $2,400 up to $3,900 per group. We recommend three groups per project for best results, but will work with fewer.
OTHER CAPABILITIES: Internet surveys, lead qualification, high 90% return mail surveys, in-store interviewing. Individual offerings: name lists, quick demographic trade area and site reports, consulting, questionnaire design, data processing, group moderating, respondent recruiting. Project quotes are free.
PRESIDENT/CEO/OWNER: Al Anderson

ANDERSON, NIEBUHR & ASSOCIATES, INC. 651-486-8712
6 Pine Tree Drive #200 Arden Hills 55112
FAX: 651-486-0536
CONTACT: John Anderson
E-MAIL: info@ana-inc.com
WWW: ana-inc.com
SERVICES: Survey research using mail, telephone (CAT1), and in-person data collection methods, focus groups and training workshops in conducting market research. Study design and implementation are tailored to fit the client's specific needs, as are data analysis and reporting of results.

Marketing Research / 345

CAPABILITIES: Market research; customer satisfaction; health care research; Inpatient Parent's Satisfaction®; NCQA certified for HEDIS®/CAHPS® surveys; industrial market research; consumer research; ad-tracking; education, association, and non-profit research. Mail and telephone surveys routinely achieve 90% response rates.
CURRENT/RECENT CLIENTS/PROJECTS: NCQA HEDIS®/CAHPS® surveys; Inpatient Parent's Satisfaction® Programs; Clients include Hewlett-Packard; 3M; FSI International; Weyerhauser Paper Company; Kaiser Permanente; Mayo Clinic; Children's Hospitals and Clinics of Minneapolis and St. Paul; United Health Group.

B

NANCY S. BROWN 952-922-5947
2625 Salem Avenue South Minneapolis 55416
FAX: 952-929-8866
CONTACT: Nancy Brown
SERVICES: Qualitative research: focus groups, one-on-ones, triads. Moderating, research design, project supervision, report writing, presentations, meeting facilitation, creative problem-solving.
CAPABILITIES: Work with children, communications.
CURRENT/RECENT CLIENTS/PROJECTS: Non-profits, Star Tribune, 3M, General Mills

C

CJOlson

C J OLSON MARKET RESEARCH, INC. 612-378-5040
2125 East Hennepin Avenue #100 Minneapolis 55413
FAX: 612-378-5401
CONTACT: Gayle Belkengren
CAPABILITIES: Full service design, sampling, data collection, data processing, statistical analysis, multivariate analysis, full reports with color charts and graphs and follow through recommendations.
SPECIALTIES: Strategic planning, marketing communications plans, market and marketing research, concept testing, feasibility studies, taste testing, advertising pre/post testing for business-to-business and consumer products and services.

346 / Marketing Research

RESEARCH & TESTING METHODS: Focus groups, in-depth telephone interviews, one-on-one executive interviews, mail questionnaires, mall intercept interviews, secret shopper. Local, regional, national and international.
FACILITIES: Focus group room with client viewing area, kitchen, 14 line monitored telephone center, data processing using SPSS and custom designed software.
PRESIDENT/CEO/OWNER: Carolyn J. Olson, P

CML MARKETING SERVICES, INC.   952-933-3453
350 Highwood Office Center   Minnetonka 55345
15612 Highway 7

FAX: 952-933-6245
CONTACT: Francis J. Cook
E-MAIL: cml.frankc@worldnet.att.net
SERVICES: Full-service product/market research facility specializing in consumer, trade and business-to-business research and strategic planning.
TYPES OF RESEARCH: On-going or special project research custom-designed to meet individual objectives; extensive secondary research capability backed with computerized databases.
RESEARCH & TESTING METHODS: Local, regional and national surveying and fact-fathering employing mail, telephone and personal methodologies; maintains a 22-city network of professional data gatherers and field reporters.
SPECIALTIES: Consumer and commercial products including home products, hospitality industry, automotive, personal service, association member surveys and industrial products.
PRESIDENT/CEO/OWNER: Francis J. Cook, Managing Director

COMPASS INTERNATIONAL RESEARCH & INFORMATION SERVICE   651-905-8400
1365 Corporate Center Curve   Eagan 55121

FAX: 651-905-8487
CONTACT: Peggy Davies
SERVICES: Compass International is a full service market research firm. Capabilities include data analysis and consulting; primary and secondary research; complete focus group facilities; and specialized power industry databases. Our office in St. Paul, Brussels, Detroit, Los Angeles and Tokyo are ready to serve you.
CURRENT/RECENT CLIENTS/PROJECTS: Clients such as Manufacturing, Health Care, Government, Consumer Products/Services, Financial, MIS, and Utilities
PRESIDENT/CEO/OWNER: George Zirnhelt

CONSUMER RESEARCH CORPORATION   612-332-8741
445 Butler Square   Minneapolis 55403
100 North 6th Street

FAX: 612-332-8617
CONTACT: David Frey
E-MAIL: crc@conresco.com

SERVICES: Full-service consumer and marketing research firm providing both quantitative and qualitative studies. Offers complete research services with expertise in consumer survey design, administration, and interpretation. Typical projects include the areas of: shopping habits, patterns, and attitudes; product, service and store concept evaluation; customer satisfaction; merchandising research; performance audits; and communications analysis.
CAPABILITIES: Specialty areas: retail and shopping centers, communications, financial services, customer satisfaction, consumer products.
PRESIDENT/CEO/OWNER: David L. Frey. Ph.D.

COOK RESEARCH & CONSULTING, INC. 952-920-6251
6600 France Avenue So #214 Edina 55435
FAX: 952-920-1230
CONTACT: Bobbi Schribman
E-MAIL: cookresearch@att.net
SERVICES: Full-service quantitative and qualitative research with consumers, business industry and professionals; top quality recruiting; experienced moderators/in-depth interviewers on staff; spacious comfortable focus group/viewing rooms with one-way mirror; fully-equipped test kitchen; client lounge; audio/video capabilities.
CAPABILITIES: Consumer products; health care industry; foodservice; business-to-business.
PRESIDENT/CEO/OWNER: Harold Cook

D

JEANNE DREW SURVEYS 612-729-2306
5005 1/2 34th Avenue South Minneapolis 55417
FAX: 612-729-7645
CONTACT: Jeanne Drew
SERVICES: A data collection facility specializing in local and watts telephone interviewing, store audits, and distribution checks.
CAPABILITIES: Consumer and industrial data collection nationally and locally by telephone, store audits and distribution checks and group session recruiting.

E

ESK MARKETING RESEARCH 763-577-1961
3155 Sycamore Lane Plymouth 55441
FAX: 763-577-1962
CONTACT: Eileen Kohn or Sheri Yarosh
E-MAIL: ekohn1@aol.com or shyar@pconline.com
SERVICES: Types of Research: Consumer and industrial research, new product development, new concepts, customer satisfaction and advertising research.
CAPABILITIES: Market research design and analysis; qualitative and quantitative. Focus group moderating.
PRESIDENT/CEO/OWNER: Eileen Kohn

348 / Marketing Research

I

INFORMATION SPECIALISTS GROUP, INC.   952-941-1600
9905 Hamilton Road   Eden Prairie 55344
FAX: 952-942-0747
CONTACT: Robert T. McGarry, Jr. or Kaarina Meyer
E-MAIL: isg@isgmn.com
CAPABILITIES: Provide telephone interviewing and focus group recruiting in consumer, business-to-business and medical fields. Experienced data processing including coding, typing and table production. Data delivered in multiple formats including SPSS, database spreadsheet and ASCII.
SPECIALTIES: Consumer and business-to-business telephone interviewing, focus group recruiting including executive and medical. Data processing from programming to quality table production.

J

JEDD, MARCIA/MJ & ASSOCIATES   612-861-4855
5716 Pillsbury Avenue   Minneapolis 55419
FAX: 612-861-3863
CONTACT: Marcia Jedd
E-MAIL: marciajedd@cs.com
TYPES OF RESEARCH: Secondary research (library and online); primary or qualitative research (telephone surveys, in-person interviews, etc).
CAPABILITIES: Strategic planning, account planning, communications planning. Access to industry experts, online databases and referrals to all types of research functions. Excellent marketing research skills combined with marketing savvy means you get research results. Access to propriety internet databases, including business information and trade/business publications. Ten years plus experience in online searches and report writing. Call or e-mail for research tip sheet, client list or rate information.
SPECIALTIES: Comprehensive market analysis; market niche or competitive analysis, quick questions or searches on a market or topic.
PRESIDENT/CEO/OWNER: Marcia Jedd

L

LYNCH JARVIS JONES, INC.   612-371-0014
119 North Fourth Street #301   Minneapolis 55401
FAX: 612-371-0459
CONTACT: Kevin Lynch
E-MAIL: kevinlynch@ljj.com
WWW: ljj.com
SERVICES: Business analysis, marketing research, strategic planing, mass communications and public education, for growing, ethical organizations which offer products, services, ideas and issues fundamental to the fulfillment, happiness and wellness of the human race and the planet earth.
SPECIALTIES: Marketing that matters.

CURRENT/RECENT CLIENTS/PROJECTS: Fairview Health Service; Minnesota Department of Health; Minnesota Department of Public Safety; Minnesota Department of Children, Families and Learning; The Minneapolis Foundation; Minnesota Center for Health Promotion; Minneapolis Public Schools; Loantech; Centers for the Application of Prevention Technologies; Minnesota State Colleges, and Universities; Wedge Community Co-op.

PRESIDENT/CEO/OWNER: Kevin Lynch, CEO; Gregg Byers, CD; Paul Engebretson, Director of Operations

*Venture investments in digital media assets,
information technology, software, internet and new media
content development and publishing*

612.872.7700
FAX 612.872.0121

Your Market Research Goals: Faster, Better, Cheaper!

MRA has developed new methods to achieve your goals:

The pioneer and leader in delivering focus groups and in-depth interviews live and on-demand over the Internet directly to your computer. You can watch from anywhere you have Internet access, be it an office, a hotel room or your very own home.

Quantitative –
- Totally automated toll-free inbound telephone interviewing
- Out-bound telephone interviewing
- Business-to-business
- Consumer

Or – We'll custom design a solution to achieve your goals!

Call or visit us at *www.mraonline.com*, (800) 795-3056 or (612) 334-3056.
See our listing in this section for more capabilities.

When Attention To Detail Matters

MARKET RESOURCE ASSOCIATES, INC.
800 Marquette Avenue, Suite 990E ■ Minneapolis, MN 55402
(612) 334-3056 ■ Fax: (612) 334-3121 ■ e-mail: johnmra@aol.com

352 / Marketing Research

MARKET RESOURCE ASSOCIATES, INC.
800 Marquette Avenue #990E
612-334-3056
Minneapolis 55402
FAX: 612-334-3121
CONTACT: John Cashmore, Ryan Frazee
E-MAIL: johnmra@aol.com
WWW: mraonline.com
TOLL FREE: 1-800-795-3056
SERVICES: A Twin Cities, full-service, custom research and consulting company based in downtown Minneapolis. Newer, centrally located focus group facilities complete with ActiveGroup® focus group internet broadcast capability, tiered viewing, full audio and video, on-site recruiting, in-house moderators available, free parking. Qualitative and quantitative studies, including customer satisfaction, new product introduction/feature determination, competitive assessment, market size quantification, and OpinionQuest™ inbound automated, tol- free telephone interviewing.
SPECIALTIES: Consumer products, business-to-business, industrial products, building materials, forest products, lawn and garden/agricultural products, kitchen and bath, hardware and related industries.

MARKET VISION
4324 43 1/2 Street West
952-922-1689
St. Louis Park 55424
FAX: 952-925-4706
CONTACT: Bill Jordan
E-MAIL: marketvision1@aol.com
SERVICES: Market Vision provides experienced, professional planning and execution of marketing programs, with an emphasis in: marketing and strategic planning; program and project execution management; and market research for both consumer and business-to-business channels.
CAPABILITIES: Internet marketing, customer acquisition, activation and retention; development of marketing and business plans; facilitation of planning discussions and brainstorming sessions. Hands-on management of product or service marketing programs; management of qualitative and quantitative interviews and surveys and focus groups; infomercials, direct mail and other forms of direct marketing.

MOLGREN RESEARCH ASSOCIATES, INC.
2656 Pioneer Trail
612-478-3099
Medina 55340
CONTACT: Doug Dickerson, President
CAPABILITIES: Full service consumer research, site analysis, and retail locational planning. Company founded in 1950.
TYPES OF RESEARCH: Site selection, consumer research, trouble store analysis, demographic analysis GIS mapping, gravity modeling, regression modeling, and normalization modeling.

MRA GROUP
16355 36th Avenue North #400
763-509-0005
Minneapolis 55446
FAX: 763-509-0010
CONTACT: Gregory Tommerdahl
E-MAIL: info@mrainc.com
WWW: mrainc.com

Marketing Research / 353

CAPABILITIES: Full-service market research firm specializing in state-of-the-art statistical analysis. Special capabilities in new product design, pricing analysis, sales forecasting, segmentation, and data mining.
SPECIALTIES: Health-related issues, financial services, web surveys.
PRESIDENT/CEO/OWNER: David J. Mangen

N

NAMETAG INTERNATIONAL, INC.
7701 France Avenue South #105
FAX: 952-841-2242
CONTACT: Mollie Young
E-MAIL: info@nametagintl.com
WWW: nametagintl.com

952-841-2244
Edina 55435

SERVICES: Brand strategy, naming, research.
CAPABILITIES: Global capabilities in brand strategy and name development. Proprietary ideation process which generates strategic, unique and market advantageous results. Types of Research: Consumer and business-to-business. Research and Testing Methods: Focus groups, one-on-ones, panels.
CURRENT/RECENT CLIENTS/PROJECTS: Pfizer; Pepsi Cola Company; 3M; McDonald's Corporation; Frito Lay; Dow; Revlon; Motorola, Chevrolet, General Electric.
PRESIDENT/CEO/OWNER: Mollie Young & Bridget Levin

O

ORMAN GUIDANCE RESEARCH®, INC.
5001 West 80th Street
FAX: 612-831-4913
CONTACT: Allan D. Orman
E-MAIL: aorman@ormanguidance.com
WWW: ormanguidance.com

612-831-4911
Minneapolis 55437

SERVICES: Marketing Research. Focus Groups. Moderating, Analysis, Videoconferencing. Spacious facility designed especially for conducting focus groups and sensory evaluations. Four discussion studios, one large kitchen. View through 4' x 10' mirrors and/or CCTV. Computer assisted recruiting conducted on-site from monitored telephone center. Audio-video taping. Member of AMA, MRA, ORCA. Focus Vision network video conferencing member.
CAPABILITIES: Videoconferencing (FocusVision); Recruiting; Sensory Evaluation
PRESIDENT/CEO/OWNER: Allan D. Orman

OUTSMART MARKETING
2840 Xenwood Avenue
FAX: 612-924-0920

612-924-0053
Minneapolis 55416

SERVICES: Qualitative research: focus groups, individual interviews. Full-service including: facility rental, recruiting, moderating report. Experience in all major markets nationwide.
CAPABILITIES/SPECIALTIES: 10 years of service to Fortune 500 companies, advertising agencies, packaging design firms.
CURRENT/RECENT CLIENTS/PROJECTS: Food products, website design, new product development, positioning, advertising, packaging.

354 / Marketing Research

PRESIDENT/CEO/OWNER: Paul Tuchman

R

READEX 651-439-1554
2251 Tower Drive West Stillwater 55082
FAX: 651-439-1564
CONTACT: Steve Blom
E-MAIL: sales@readexresearch.com
WWW: readexresearch.com
SERVICES: Mail survey Research for publishers for over 50 years. Ad Readership Studies: a variety of programs are available, varying in both price and type/depth of data gathered.
CURRENT/RECENT CLIENTS/PROJECTS: Custom Research Studies: projects are designed and priced to meet your specific needs. High response rates (50 - 70%) allow you to project results with confidence. Study types include reader profiles, editorial audit, brand awareness, buyer's guide studies and trade show conferences.
PRESIDENT/CEO/OWNER: Jack Semler

S

SATISFACTION MANAGEMENT SYSTEMS 952-939-4307
5959 Baker Road, #300 Minnetonka 55345
FAX: 952-935-7815
CONTACT: Wayne Serie
E-MAIL: sales@satmansys.com
WWW: satmansys.com
CAPABILITIES: A consulting and market research firm focused on helping organizations bring critical market data into their strategic planning process to improve customer, employee and market performance, and to increase competitive advantage. Since 1989, we have helped clients understand their markets and make positive business changes through our consulting processes and research tools.
SPECIALTIES: Customer Satisfaction/Loyalty Measurement, Customer Value Management, Market Develop/Assessment, Employee Organizational Assessment, Call Center Management, Key Account Assessment and Win/Loss Assessment.
PRESIDENT/CEO/OWNER: Vince Farace, CEO/Wayne Serie, President

DIANE SIMS PAGE 612-377-4048
1732 Knox Avenue South Minneapolis 55403
FAX: 612-377-4058
SERVICES: Market research - focus groups and other qualitative techniques. Ideation/brainstorming services for new product ideas, new names, promotions, etc. Database of articulate consumers.
PRESIDENT/CEO/OWNER: Diane Sims Page

Marketing Research / 355

T

THE TCI GROUP 612-823-6214
3225 Hennepin Avenue So Minneapolis 55408
FAX: 612-823-6215
CONTACT: Beth Fischer
E-MAIL: bethfischer@theTCIgroup.com
WWW: theTCIgroup.com
SERVICES: A 44 year old, Minneapolis based company providing a fusion of solid, systematic research and the imaginative art of creative thinking processes resulting in a client's REAL TIME experience. Reputable approach to be Telling, Elemental tools to be Innovative, a 360% perspective to be Mindful, Learns, the insight to be Enlightening. Knowledge for being innovative in what you do.
CAPABILITIES: Marketing Research, Innovative Marketing, Creative, Strategic thinking.

W

WHITNEY WORLDWIDE, INC. 651-749-5000
1845 Buerkle Road White Bear Lake 55110
FAX: 651-748-4000
CONTACT: Les Layton
E-MAIL: 1layton@whitneyworld.com
WWW: whitneyworld.com
SERVICES: 17-year old Direct Response and Marketing Research company that has worked for many Fortune 500 and other leading companies in Minnesota. We offer experienced writers, designers and strategists who have obtained superior response rates and beaten many companies controls. We also can handle many projects completely in-house. Having acquired 3M's Direct Response Marketing business unit 14 years ago, we also "practice what we preach". Our MarketMaster® lead-generation survey system produce higher response rates and better-quality leads than many companies have ever experienced before.
CAPABILITIES: Lead generation of higher-quality leads via direct mail or the Internet and super research surveys done via the same media--not on the phone. Staff has held top corporate marketing jobs, been department heads at largest agencies, been Pulitzer Prize finalist and run their own graphic design agency.
CURRENT/RECENT CLIENTS/PROJECTS: 3M, Lawson Software, Pioneer Press, Firstar, St. Paul Companies, Cargill, Minnesota Twins, Tousley Ford, Community Credit, United Way

Z

SALLY E. ZORICH & ASSOCIATES 651-290-2564
819 Ashland Avenue St. Paul 55104
FAX: 651-290-2564
CONTACT: Sally Zorich
E-MAIL: salzorich@aol.com

SERVICES: Data collection field service specializing in on-site interview projects at locations around the Twin Cities. Sites include banks, stores, offices, zoos, museums, convention centers, theatres, restaurants, the airport, etc. In addition, we conduct mystery shops, on-site focus group recruits, in-depth interview and telephone interviews. We are known for quality work done by highly professional interviewers.

PRESIDENT/CEO/OWNER: Sally Zorich

Media Planning & Buying

E

ELLER MEDIA COMPANY
3225 Spring Street NE
FAX: 612-869-7082
CONTACT: Dave Sturzl
E-MAIL: ellermedia.com
SIZES HANDLED: Painted bulletins and poster panels. Creative/art department: Full service art department and paint studio.
CAPABILITIES/SPECIALTIES: Complete billboard coverage throughout the 11-county metro area.
PRESIDENT/CEO/OWNER: Lee Ann Muller

612-869-1900
Minneapolis 55413

F

FUTUREPAGES, INC.
817 N Vandalia Street, #200
FAX: 651-644-9379
CONTACT: Tom Borgerding
E-MAIL: tom@futurepages.com
WWW: futurepages.com
SERVICES: FuturePages - College Media Gurus takes care of the pains of media research, planning, placement/buying and management. We focus exclusively on the 18 - 24 demographic group. Our media expertise is in print media, online media, ooh, events, and sampling with four years of exclusive experience in the college market. We handle and perform media campaigns on budget and need, both nationally and locally.
CAPABILITIES: Strategic media planning and placement, negotiations with media channels including online, print, ooh and more. FuturePages was the first to place advertising on college newspaper web sites and continues to manage advertising buys on over 250 college focused web sites. FuturePages negotiates and places advertising on over 1500 college print newspapers nationally - all digitally and through the internet. With over four years of internet advertising buying and planning we know what to do and where to buy advertising on the web.
CURRENT/RECENT CLIENTS/PROJECTS: Clients include: Student Advantage, Inc.; BigWords.com; iBetcha.com; College Club; Sprint Communications; US West; Monster.com; Food.com; Phonehog.com; Memolink; Coca-Cola; Microsoft; Nabisco; Apple Computer; MADD: Paramount Pictures; University of Pennsylvania; Versity.com; Planetalumni.com; Varsitybooks.com; TMP Worldwide, R.A.D.A.
PRESIDENT/CEO/OWNER: Lance Stendal, President/CEO

651-644-4191
St. Paul 55114

G

GALLAGHER MEDIA, INC.
2626 East 82nd Street #201
FAX: 952-853-2262
CONTACT: Anne Gallagher, Carrie DeNet
E-MAIL: anne.gmi@manleygroup.com

952-853-2266
Minneapolis 55425

358 / Media Planning & Buying

SERVICES: Since 1972, a flexible and collaborative approach to clients' needs, especially budgeting, media planning and placement, negotiation, marketing, political planning and placement.
CURRENT/RECENT CLIENTS/PROJECTS: Bachman's; Home Valu; Drexel; Taco John's; Mail Boxes Etc.; Kawasaki; Minnesota Department of Agriculture; Minnesota Business Partnership; Minnesota Beef Council; Parts Plus, and political candidates and issues nationwide.

K

KENNEDY & COMPANY	612-447-0188
16677 Duluth Avenue SE #202	Prior Lake 55372

FAX: 612-447-0190
CONTACT: Patricia Kennedy
E-MAIL: pkennedy@pioneerplanet.infi.net
SERVICES: Media planning, and buying; marketing, retail, direct response, internet, political.
CURRENT/RECENT CLIENTS/PROJECTS: State of Minnesota, Office of Tourism, Scenic Byway's, Papa Johns Pizza, Pet Junction.

M

MARKETING MIDWEST, INC.	952-351-0607
5666 Lincoln Drive #215	Edina 55436

FAX: 952-351-0608
CONTACT: Steve Karolewski, Barbara Epstein
E-MAIL: steve@marketingmidwest.com
WWW: marketingmidwest.com
SERVICES: Complete turn-key media placement service for broadcast, print, outdoor, new media and direct response on a local, regional or national level. Services include media research, analysis and recommendations; determining goals, establishing budgets and designing value-added promotions.
CURRENT/RECENT CLIENTS/PROJECTS: M.A. Gedney Company; Old Home Foods; HealthPartners; City Business; Precision Tune; 2nd Wind Exercise Equipment; Erik's Bike Shop; Simek's Carpenters' Union; Electricians' Union; MN Department of Transportation; Minnesota Safety Council; Metropolitan Airports Commission; Metropolitan Council; AVCAM (Anti Vehicle-Crime Association of MN); Schuler Shoes; Scheherazade Jewelers; RoadRunner Transportation; AutoFun; Wedding Guide Bridal Spectacular; Table for Two; TurnStyle Consignment Shops; Padilla Speer Beardsley; John Pope Company; Broadview Media.
PRESIDENT/CEO/OWNER: Barbara Epstein, P/Med Dir.; Steve Karolewski, EVP

MEDIATECH	651-646-0166
2003 Ashland Avenue #2	St. Paul 55104

FAX: 612-397-8662
CONTACT: Thomas Malone
SERVICES: Strategic planning, media buying and negotiations for television, radio, print and outdoor advertising, market research, promotion planning and implementation.

SPECIALTIES: Developing effective Media plans for a wide variety of retail, national and business-to-business accounts. Specialties include casino advertising and promotions for regional casinos, building product accounts and hospitality.
CURRENT/RECENT CLIENTS/PROJECTS: Shooting Star Casino & Hotel; Dairyland Power Cooperatives; EnPower, Touchstone; Medical Institute of Minnesota; JPMP; Wallace Marx & Associates; Miller Marketing.

R

KRISTI K. RAZINK 612-722-8156
4609 30th Avenue South Minneapolis 55406
FAX: 612-722-1101
CONTACT: Kristi K. Razink
E-MAIL: razink@aol.com
SERVICES: Advertising and media planning, buying, negotiation, and presentation. Expertise with all media including print, TV, radio, out-of-home, direct mail and advertising online. Assistance in all media efforts including competitive research, new business pitches, new product introductions, sales promotions, co-op, ethnic, international, PR and special events. Industries: Automotive, building, education, financial, food, health care, health and beauty, high tech, hospitality, manufacturing, medical, packaged goods, retail and travel.

T

THE THIRD EYE 952-974-2832
6121 Creek Ridge Court Minnetonka 55345
FAX: 952-974-2830
CONTACT: Patty Persons
E-MAIL: patriciapersons@hotmail.com
CAPABILITIES: Representing cable station advertising insertion.

TOTAL MARKET COVERAGE, INC. 612-825-9205
3225 Lyndale Avenue South Minneapolis 55408
FAX: 612-825-0929
CONTACT: Terry Gahan
E-MAIL: swjournal@uswest.net
SERVICES: Media planning and buying services to access broad list of Twin Cities community newspapers - weeklies, monthlies, minority publications- a list of over 60 publications. Comprehensive ad production support (please call with details for a specific price quote) for both ROP ads and inserts. Specialty publication services - printing, ad/editorial production, distribution.
CAPABILITIES: In newspaper production business for 10 years through experience on Southwest Journal - a sister company.
CURRENT/RECENT CLIENTS/PROJECTS: Call for our list of current clients and references.
PRESIDENT/CEO/OWNER: Terry Gahan, President

Mergers & Acquisitions

K

K2 ASSETS   651-221-0702
420 Summit Avenue   St. Paul 55102
FAX: 651-222-3490
CONTACT: Dennis Kelly, Eric Kercheval
E-MAIL: dennis@k2assets.com
WWW: k2assets.com

CAPABILITIES: K2 Assets is a strategic advisory firm focused on mergers, acquisitions and strategic alliances within the Marketing Services industry. We represent the "seller" to qualified, screened buyers. We consult with "buyers" to help formulate a "growth through acquisition strategy" and represent their interest to appropriate sellers. We facilitate strategic alliances; assist companies in the valuation of their assets and facilitate capital funding. Our domain expertise and experience is with companies representing; advertising, media, promotion creative, direct marketing, direct marketing support, interactive and internet related services, software development and operations and other related niche marketing businesses. K2 Assets has a well defined network of contacts within our industry niche. We have perfected research and investigative data gathering techniques that enable us to keep track of and beware of small to medium size merger/acquisition opportunities in the marketing service industry. We are in regular contact with key decision makers of hundreds of marketing services companies.

Models & Talent

A

ACTORS PLUS/VOICE PLUS
1564 5th Street
CONTACT: Debbie Klemmer Rush
TOLL FREE: 877-426-9500
E-MAIL: agency@voiceplustalent.com
WWW: voiceplustalent.com

651-426-9400
St. Paul 55110

SERVICES: Since 1972, providing professional voice and on-camera actors and narrators; men, women, children, ethnic and earprompted talent; foreign language translators and narrators. Photos, audio clips, resumes, resources and other topics of interest are available on our website. CD's and audition arrangements available.
CAPABILITIES: We represent highly qualified Voice talent and on-camera actors for broadcast commercials, industrials, educational videos, documentaries, IVR systems, voicemail, CD-ROM's, actors and spokespersons for live training programs, trade shows, conventions, sales meetings and award dinners, real people models for print.
CURRENT/RECENT CLIENTS/PROJECTS: Honda (1986 - present) Commercial; Mayo Clinic (1990 - present) Industrial; Best Buy (1985 - present) Industrial and Commercial; Many advertising agencies, A/V production studios, Independent producers, Broadcast stations and Corporate media departments.
PRESIDENT/CEO/OWNER: Linda Klemmer

AKERLIND & ASSOCIATES CASTING
212 3rd Avenue North #250
FAX: 612-339-6507
CONTACT: Kat Rapheal, Michelle Masera, Curt Akerlind

612-339-6141
Minneapolis 55401

SERVICES: Casting for features, industrials, commercials, voiceovers, and print ads. On set baby wrangling and youth talent coaching. Wrangling for large extra scenes. Coaching for live talent bookings.
EQUIPMENT: 2,200 square foot studio space, two casting rooms, 3/4" & 1/2" decks. Space rental available.
CURRENT/RECENT CLIENTS/PROJECTS: Films: Sugar & Spice, Drop Dead Gorgeous, Sixth Sense, Stepmom, Ed TV, Jingle All the Way, Mighty Ducks, Mighty Ducks II, Mighty Ducks D3, and Equinox. Commercial and/or Print: Walt Disney World, Coca Cola, Marie Callender's, Midol, Huggies, Leap Frog, Target, Pampers, Pillsbury, National Egg Board, Miller Light, MCI, Timex and Centrum.
PRESIDENT/CEO/OWNER: Curt Akerlind

THE ANIMAL CONNECTION
233 Poplar Street West
CONTACT: Barbara Obrien
E-MAIL: barbara@animal-connection.com
WWW: animal-connection.com

651-552-8622
South St. Paul 55075

SERVICES: Suppliers of trained animal actors for all uses including print, TV, features and commercials since 1984. "Animal actors that really work." Minnesota's only full-time full service animal actors agency.
CAPABILITIES: Largest selection of photo ready, studio steady animal actors in the Midwest.
CURRENT/RECENT CLIENTS/PROJECTS: See web site for full credit list.

362 / Models & Talent

ANIMAL TALENT POOL 612-479-2281
3205 Lake Sarah Road Maple Plain 55359
FAX: 520-441-3883
CONTACT: Debi Pool
E-MAIL: animaltalentpool@mail.com
SERVICES: Animals of all types, for print, broadcast.

F

KIMBERLY FRANSON MODEL/ACTOR 612-386-5588
AGENCY
1300 Nicollet Mall #220C Minneapolis 55403
Hyatt Regency Complex
FAX: 612-338-1411
CONTACT: Kimberly Franson
E-MAIL: kfa@kimberlyfranson.com
WWW: kimberlyfranson.com
TYPES OF TALENT: Actors, on and off camera; voice; specialty; men, women, children of all ages and sizes; hair and make-up artists.
TYPES OF MODELS: Fashion, character, real people, celebrity, men, women, and children of all ages and sizes.
SPECIALTIES: Providing models and actors for all types of industry work. Preparing and conducting castings for clients.
CURRENT/RECENT CLIENTS/PROJECTS: Farouk Systems, Toni & Guy, Shandwick International, Spiderman Movie Casting, Wella Corporation, Maxim Magazine, Target, Ford Motor Company, Hoyle, Regis Corporation, Scruples, Procter & Gamble.

H

THE HOLLYWOOD-MADISON GROUP 818-762-8008
11684 Ventura Blvd #258 Studio City 91604
FAX: 818-762-8089
CONTACT: Jonathan Holiff, President
E-MAIL: info@hollywood-madison.com
WWW: hollywood-madison.com
SERVICES: The Hollywood-Madison Group is the nation's leading procurer of celebrities. The Hollywood-Madison Group (HMG) is the only full-service agency specializing in celebrity endorsements and Hollywood tie-ins. With our exclusive Fame Index™, we can help you search over 10,000 celebrities - from actors to athletes - to find every performer who matches your unique requirements. And, we can rank them by their fees and popularity too! Simply the best access to celebrities!
CAPABILITIES: Talent Casting, Celebrity Endorsements, Personal Appearances, Hollywood Tie-Ins; Celebrity P.S.A.S/Celebrity "Seeding", Research, Licensing, Video News Releases (VNRs), Satellite Media Tours (SMTs), Special Events, Television Production, Parties, Premieres, Merchandising, Focus Groups/Consumer Testing, Event Management, Marketing and Consulting.

Models & Talent / 363

CURRENT/RECENT CLIENTS/PROJECTS: Aspen Club; Bal Harbour Shops, Florida; Cinemax; Disney (Disney Online); Drugstore.com; Eli-Lilly & Co. (Humalog); Fetzer Wines; General Motors Corporate; The Gillette Company; Hanes Hosiery; Hewlett-Packard, Inc.; Johnson & Johnson (Motrin, Concerta); Kellogg USA, Inc.; Mattel, Inc. (Cabbage Patch Kids); Pharmacia/Upjohn; Phillips Consumer Electronics; Pizza hut; Pontiac (Axtek); Proctor & Gamble (Pringles, ThermaCare; Fixodent; Charmin; Bounty; Swiffer); Prudential Insurance Corporation.

J

JOHMAR FARMS 651-433-5312
14330 Ostrum Trail North Marine on St. Croix 55047
FAX: Same - call first
CONTACT: John or Mary Block
E-MAIL: johmar@onvoymail.com
SERVICES: Types of Talent: Animals that can work in studio or on location.
CAPABILITIES: Types of Models: Animals: domestics and exotics.
CURRENT/RECENT CLIENTS/PROJECTS: Feature film, ad agencies, production companies, corporate in-house, film studios, photographers, TV, festivals, corporate events, plays and productions.

K

JOE KATZ MODELS 612-377-7630
3033 Excelsior Blvd. #300 Minneapolis 55416
FAX: 612-253-6100
CONTACT: Joe Katz
SERVICES: Types of models: Women, men, children (all types) AFTRA SAG franchised.
CAPABILITIES: Represent men and women and children locally and throughout the United States of print, on camera advertising, fashion shows, conventions and feature films.
CURRENT/RECENT CLIENTS/PROJECTS: Photographers, advertising agencies, film studios, department stores, corporations.

L

LA TERESA IMAGE CONSULTING & 320-743-4200
MODELING SCHOOL/AGENCY
9811 54th Street Clear Lake 55319
FAX: 320-743-3257
CONTACT: Teresa Koshiol
E-MAIL: LaTerese@earthlink.net
WWW: laterese.com
SERVICES: Modeling school: image, modeling and self-improvement courses. Image consulting, seminars and workshops. Types of Models: men, women, children. Types of Talent: fashion, character, commercial, real people, actors, voice.

Models & Talent

CAPABILITIES: Established: 1991 Central and Northern Minnesota's oldest, most successful and #1 rated education and training. Capabilities: fashion shows, conventions, sales meetings, mannequin modeling, bridal fashion shows, speaking, seminars, education, training customized seminars and training in 50 different topics.

SPECIALTIES: Specialties: professional modeling and self-improvement education and training, model photo shoots and photo services, image and wardrobe seminars/workshops, image consulting, bridal and image makeovers from head-to-toe; pageant training, summer camps, self-improvement courses, color and skin analysis, skin care and cosmetic sales, non-union talent.

CURRENT/RECENT CLIENTS/PROJECTS: Advertising agencies; photographers; cable & TV productions; print media; cable TV; video production companies; direct corporate companies; conventions seminars/workshops; industrial and educational films/videos; promotions; talent and extras for feature films; fashion shows, malls; model searches. Main client base of St. Cloud - Central and Northern Minnesota. Local and out of town models and talent.

LIPSERVICE, INC.
400 First Avenue North #514
FAX: 612-338-1847
CONTACT: Erika V. Way or Joanne M. Kaufman
E-MAIL: lipservice@mcg.net
WWW: mcg.net/lipservice/liptease.html

612-338-5477
Minneapolis 55401

SERVICES: A talent guild representing 30 on-camera and voice talent. Our members perform locally and nationally in film, television, radio, theatre, industrials, live industrials and video. Lipservice members have helped create and win dozens of awards. Compilation CD, demos, talent book and digital qualty auditions are all available. A union talent guild - AFTRA/SAG.

CAPABILITIES: Types of Clients: Advertising agencies, film studios, casting agents, audio and video production studios, independent producers, commercial photographers, corporate in-house, and companies directly related.

PRESIDENT/CEO/OWNER: Erika V. Way or Joanne M. Kaufman, Talent Coordinators

M

MEREDITH MODEL & TALENT AGENCY
800 Washington Avenue N #511
FAX: 612-340-9533
CONTACT: Stacy Meredith
E-MAIL: meredithagency@earthlink.com
WWW: meredithagency.com

612-340-9555
Minneapolis 55401

SERVICES: Experienced in services provided for film, TV, voice-overs, industrials and print advertising. Represent SAG, AFTRA, AEA actors, actresses, children, print models, make-up and hair stylists, and prop stylists. We work with advertings agencies, commercial photographers, film studios, video production companies and in-house corporate customers.

CAPABILITIES: Established in 1978, Meredith Model and Talent is the only local agency with a NY and NJ office. Full commercial talent agency representing models for print advertising, runway, conventions, trade shows and sales meetings. Talent for TV, radio commercials, industrial, educational and feature films. Full color agency book.

Models & Talent / 365

CURRENT/RECENT CLIENTS/PROJECTS: National and International TV commercials; Coca-Cola (Powerade); Mervyns California; Funcoland National Basketball Association; American Cynamid; Best Buy; Northwest Airlines; Honeywell; Land O' Lakes; Dayton's; Target; Novartis; Artic Cat; Computer Renaissance; Home Depot, etc.; Radio/Industrial: K-Market; Lloyds' Barbeque; Borders Pasta; Jeane Thorne, etc.; Print Advertising: Target; Dayton Hudson; General Mills; 3M; Pillsbury; Best Buy; Fingerhut; American Express; Dairy Queen; Jostens; Mervyns California; Hormel; Musicland; Bachmans; US Bank, etc.

MOORE CREATIVE TALENT, INC.   612-827-3823
1610 West Lake Street   Minneapolis 55408
CONTACT: Julie Polander, Alycya Cardwell, Print; Heidi Heintz, Carol McCormick, On-Camera; Jessica Brewin, Victoria Eide, Voiceover
WWW: mooretalent.com
SERVICES: Casting AFTRA/SAG/AEA actors and actresses and children for feature film, TV, voiceovers, on-camera and live industrials. Providing models, make-up and hair stylists for print media, fashion shows, conventions, sales meetings and promotions.
CAPABILITIES: Experienced agents since 1958. Facilities for video and audio auditions.
CURRENT/RECENT CLIENTS/PROJECTS: K-Mart; General Mills; US West; 3M; United Airlines; BMW; Purina; Miller; Lee Jeans; Target; McDonald's; Sears; Leinenkugel; Coca-Cola; Pillsbury; Dekalb; Ciba-Geigy.

N

NED KANTAR PRODUCTIONS, INC.   612-926-5655
3430 St. Paul Avenue   Minneapolis 55416
FAX: 912-920-8482
CONTACT: Ned Kantar
E-MAIL: ned@nedkantar.com
WWW: nedkantar.com
SERVICES: Live music, celebrity talent.
SPECIALTIES: Entertainment and show production, specialty contracting. Customized service for companies and individuals. Partnering of talent with corporate marketing projects. Call or fax for information. 25 years experience.
CURRENT/RECENT CLIENTS/PROJECTS: Corporate, convention, private individuals, concert presenters.
PRESIDENT/CEO/OWNER: Ned Kantar

NUTS, ltd   763-529-0330
810 N. Lilac Drive #101   Golden Valley 55422
FAX: 763-529-0353
CONTACT: Peta Barrett or Jan Hilton
E-MAIL: nuts@usinternet.com
WWW: nutsltd.com
SERVICES: Types of Talent: Hundreds of experienced actors, actresses, and narrators, ethnic range, all ages, many exclusive to Nuts, ltd. Voice, on-camera and live events.

366 / Models & Talent

SPECIALTIES: We represent professional non-union talent for TV and radio commercials, industrial and educational video and film, web projects, voicemail, and live events such as trade shows, conventions, sales meetings, etc. Many narrators and spokespersons are skilled with ear-prompter and teleprompter.
CURRENT/RECENT CLIENTS/PROJECTS: Advertising agencies, audio/video production companies, independent producers, in-house corporate producers, many companies from the smallest to the largest.
PRESIDENT/CEO/OWNER: Jan Hilton, CEO

P

PREMIERE SCHOOL OF SELF-IMPROVEMENT AND PROFESSIONAL MODELING, INC.   612-920-0681
3455 Dakota Avenue South   Minneapolis 55416
CONTACT: Faith Schway
E-MAIL: faithschway@premieremodeling.com
WWW: premieremodeling.com
SERVICES: 20 week/60 hour course for male and female teens (ages 11 & up) and adults in self-improvement and professional modeling. 18 hour course for male and female children (ages 4 - 10). The school was established in 1982, approved by the Minnesota Department of Education. Both programs are taught by experts. The students graduate at the Mall of America once a year in front of all the top Minnesota modeling agencies.
CAPABILITIES: We specialize in modeling training, etiquette, pageants, television commercials. We produce the Mrs. Minnesota-America Pageant and the Miss Minnesota Teen All American Pageant.
CURRENT/RECENT CLIENTS/PROJECTS: We have had thousands of graduates.

R

R RANDOLPH STUDIO   612-823-9224
3929 Lyndale Avenue South   Minneapolis 55409
CONTACT: Bob Grassel
E-MAIL: gbobg@aol.com
SERVICES: Glamour, Fashion, Model Photography - on location or in-studio.
CAPABILITIES: All formats, color or black and white.

RICHTER CASTING   952-975-9305
701 Fourth Avenue South #500   Minneapolis 55415
CONTACT: Raulla Mitchell
TYPES OF TALENT: Actors, models, dancers, voice talent. Men, women and children of all ages (from babies to great grandparents), and character types. Many are ear-prompter and teleprompter spokespersons.
CURRENT/RECENT CLIENTS/PROJECTS: Film/video producers, production companies, advertising agencies, corporate in-house, industrial/educational producers, p.s.a.'s, voice over and electronic/new media producers.

Models & Talent / 367

T

TALENT POOLE TALENT AGENCY 612-843-4294
1828 Jefferson Street NE Minneapolis 55418
FAX: 612-843-4293
CONTACT: Geanette Poole
WWW: talentpoole.com
SERVICES: Talent Poole represents on-camera and voice talent for film, television, radio, live industrials, print and video, We also represent a select number of writers, and wardrobe and make-up personnel.
CAPABILITIES: Many of our talent are ear-prompter and teleprompter proficient. We have space available to hold on-camera auditions and a sound studio to record voice auditions.
CURRENT/RECENT CLIENTS/PROJECTS: "Here On Earth", "Sugar and Spice" "The Well", "Winter Shorts", Lifetime Fitness, Medtronic, US Banks, Target Corporation, Voice Mail Broadcasting Corporation (VMBC), Whirlpool Corporation, 3M/Imation, University of Minnesota, Toys R Us, Carlson Custom Learning, Mayo Clinic.
PRESIDENT/CEO/OWNER: Geanette Poole

U

UNFORGETTABLE MODEL 952-842-8222
PO Box 24029 Edina 55424
FAX: 952-842-8288
CONTACT: Easter Hailey
SERVICES: Models, actors, non-union. Men, women, children for print, runway, television conventions and trade shows. Types of Clients: ad agencies, production companies, corporation, special events and meeting planners.
CAPABILITIES: 20 years managing models, producing 2 - 4 fashion events a year.
CURRENT/RECENT CLIENTS/PROJECTS: Teen People Magazine, Target, Dayton's, Aveda.

V

VOICE PLUS/ACTORS PLUS 651-426-9400
1564 5th Street St. Paul 55110
CONTACT: Debbie Klemmer Rush
TOLL FREE: 877-426-9500
E-MAIL: agency@voiceplustalent.com
WWW: voiceplustalent.com
SERVICES: Since 1972, providing professional voice and on-camera actors and narrators; men, women, children, ethnic and earprompted talent; foreign language translators and narrators. Photos, audio clips, resumes, resources and other topics of interest are available on our website. CD's and audition arrangements available.

368 / Models & Talent

CAPABILITIES: We represent highly qualified Voice talent and on-camera actors for broadcast commercials, industrials, educational videos, documentaries, IVR systems, voicemail, CD-ROM's, actors and spokespersons for live training programs, trade shows, conventions, sales meetings and award dinners. Real people models for print.

CURRENT/RECENT CLIENTS/PROJECTS: Honda (1986 - present) Commercial; Mayo Clinic (1990 - present) Industrial; Best Buy (1985 - present) Industrial and Commercial; Many advertising agencies, A/V production studios, Independent producers, Broadcast stations and Corporate media departments.

PRESIDENT/CEO/OWNER: Linda Klemmer

W

WEHMANN MODELS/TALENT, INC.
1128 Harmon Place #205
CONTACT: Susan Wehmann
E-MAIL: agents@wehmann.com
WWW: wehmann.com

612-333-6393
Minneapolis 55403

Music & Jingles

A

AARON-STOKES MUSIC, LTD.　　　　　　　　　　612-373-2220
708 North First Street #135　　　　　　　　　　Minneapolis 55401
CONTACT: Phil Aaron, Brad Stokes
E-MAIL: brads@visualmusicandsound.com
WWW: visualmusicandsound.com
SERVICES: Original music post-scoring and sound-design for film, video and new media.
CAPABILITIES: Cinematic film scoring in a broad spectrum of musical styles. Also specialize in cross-stylization where widely varying styles from jazz to rock to multi-cultural to orchestral and blended or juxtaposed for dramatic impact.
CURRENT/RECENT CLIENTS/PROJECTS: ATX; American Cancer Society; Andersen Windows; Arctic Cat; Best Buy; Cadillac; Carlson Companies; Campbell-Mithun-Esty; Citrix; Cray Research; Dayton-Hudson; Fresh Pictures; Frigidaire; General Mills; Grant Tornton; Hazelden; Honeywell; Horst/Aveda; Information Advantage; Interactive Personalities; Jack Morton Productions; James Production; Johnson Institute; Juntunen Media Group; Lee Pictures; Lunds; Lutheran Brotherhood; Martin/Bastian Communications; Mayo Clinic; Media Loft; Medtronic; Minnesota Vikings; Minnesota Timberwolves; MR Bolin; Nelson Henry; Northwest Airlines; Northwest Teleproduction; Periscope; Pillsbury; Renewal by Andersen; St. Paul Companies; Sandoz Nutrition; Science Museum of Minnesota Omni Theatre; Super Valu; 3M; U of M; US Air Force; US Satellite Broadcasting; Wilson-Griak; World Wide Pictures.

ABSOLUTE MUSIC　　　　　　　　　　　　　　612-339-6758
12 South 6th Street #1226　　　　　　　　　　Minneapolis 55402
FAX: 612-339-9492
CONTACT: Jennifer Downham
CAPABILITIES: Compose and arrange all styles of music. Recording studio with complete audio post facilities. Newly installed DIGI-patch and duplication services.
SPECIALTIES: Original music and sound design/mix for television commercials. Radio and film. Radio design and voice recording.
CURRENT/RECENT CLIENTS/PROJECTS: Miller Lite, Nike, US Banks, Toyota, Suncoast, Fujitsu, K-Mart, Northwest, Target, Pizza Hut, Gateway.
PRESIDENT/CEO/OWNER: Johnny Hagen, Officer

B

RAYMOND BERG'S MUSIC WORKS　　　　　　612-810-1400
212 Third Avenue North #545　　　　　　　　　Minneapolis 55401
FAX: 612-375-0244
E-MAIL: raymond@visi.com
SERVICES: Original music composition, adaptations and arrangements of existing music. Musical direction for live corporate and industrial events.
CAPABILITIES: Providing musical services (live and/or pre-produced) for corporate meetings and events. Music and entertainment integrated into corporate themes and presentations. 15 years of experience with industry and production clients as a musician, composer and musical director.

370 / Music & Jingles

CURRENT/RECENT CLIENTS/PROJECTS: Deluxe Corp., MLT Vacations, Guidant, Toro, Reliastar, Great Clips, Jack Morton Company, Watkins, Schwan's, Medtronic, Cenex Harvest States, NFL Alumni.
PRESIDENT/CEO/OWNER: Raymond Berg

BRADLEY JOSEPH　　　　　　　　　　　　　　　　　　　651-762-8123
PO Box 3452　　　　　　　　　　　　　　　　　　　　Minneapolis 55403
FAX: 651-762-8140
CONTACT: Bradley Joseph
E-MAIL: bjoseph@bradleyjoseph.com
WWW: bradleyjoseph.com
SERVICES: Original music, scoring with full orchestrations; music designed with low budgets, but high results. Full electronic scores as well.
CAPABILITIES: Bradley Joseph performed and worked with Yanni for 5 years. As co-musical director for Sheena Easton for 5 years. Is a virgin recording artists with 3 solo original CDs in the market place. Main instrument is the keyboards, but can compose in all areas.
CURRENT/RECENT CLIENTS/PROJECTS: Yanni: "Live at the Acropolis"; ABC World News Theme; Super Valu; PRI's "Lives of the Children"; Randillium Interactive CD ROM's; "the Human Touch" video; WCCO; Cortless Radio Themes.

C

THE COAST　　　　　　　　　　　　　　　　　　　　　612-476-2204
1844 W. Wayzata Blvd.　　　　　　　　　　　　　　　Long Lake 55356
FAX: 612-476-4198
CONTACT: Terry Esau
E-MAIL: puddlehill@aol.com
SERVICES: Composition, arrangement and production of original music for radio and TV commercials, videos, industrial and corporate, feature films and sound design.
SPECIALTIES: State-of-the art equipment for recording, editing and dubbing. AFM, AFTRA and SAF signatory.
CURRENT/RECENT CLIENTS/PROJECTS: Pepsi-Cola; Phillips 66; McDonalds; Dayton-Hudson; Kemps; MS State Lottery; Start Tribune; General Mills; Ciatti's; Target; 3M; KARE-TV; Fox 29.

E

ECHO BOYS, INC.　　　　　　　　　　　　　　　　　　612-338-7947
510 Marquette Suite #600　　　　　　　　　　　　　Minneapolis 55402
FAX: 612-338-4601
CONTACT: Kathy Yanko
E-MAIL: kathy.yanko@echoboys.com
WWW: echoboys.com
SERVICES: Original music and sound design for television, film and radio at a full service post-production facility.

Music & Jingles / 371

EIII PRODUCTIONS, INC.   612-925-2442
5606 Concord Avenue   Edina 55424
FAX: 612-925-3898
CONTACT: Eddy Nelson
CAPABILITIES: Original music composition, arrangement and production.
SPECIALTIES: Television commercials, radio jingles, and corporate programs.
PRESIDENT/CEO/OWNER: Eddy Nelson

F

FLOATING HEAD   612-823-6645
4849 Aldrich Avenue South   Minneapolis 55409
FAX: 612-823-6572
CONTACT: Jeff Mueller
SPECIALTIES: The words (that make the young girls cry).

G

JON GARON CREATIVE, INC.   952-474-7000
208 Central Avenue South   Wayzata 55391
FAX: 952-404-2277
CONTACT: Jon Garon
E-MAIL: jgaron@uswest.net
SERVICES: Creative & production of: Radio, television, print, video and original music for a variety of advertising agencies, public relations firms and in-house advertising and marketing departments. Since 1975, Jon Garon Creative has created and produced broadcast, corporate and print communications for clients nationwide.
SPECIALTIES: Corporate image video, original music, humorous radio and television spots. Good dancer. Has own car. Limited felony convictions.
CURRENT/RECENT CLIENTS/PROJECTS: Dayton-Hudson; Fleishman-Hillard Public Relations; Lifetouch; Hey City Theatre; Craig Wiese & Company; Zimmerman Group; Department of Defense; Slumberland; Sable Advertising; John Miles Company; McCracken Brooks; Lutsen Mountains; Bill Smith Adv.(Portland); Respond 2 Adv; 3M; Pillsbury; Golden Valley Microwave Foods; The Hadley Companies.
PRESIDENT/CEO/OWNER: Jon Garon

H

HARTWIG MUSIC AND SOUND   612-375-9578
123 North 3rd Street #201   Minneapolis 55401
FAX: 612-334-5929
CONTACT: Paul Hartwig
E-MAIL: brgwigg@earthlink.net
WWW: hartwigmusic.com
SERVICES: Music composition - film, commercial broadcast.

372 / Music & Jingles

RALPH HEPOLA
1298 Folsom Street
651-488-1144
St. Paul 55117
CONTACT: Ralph Hepola
CAPABILITIES: Plays, jazz, popular and classical music on brass instruments, leads two musical groups; Route 3 an American musical journey; 3 musicians take you on a trip through time and around the country. Hear and Now: jazz and an eclectic variety of contemporary music. Numerous recordings; music degree from Northwestern University; The US Army Band of Washington DC; five years with a major European symphony orchestra in Switzerland.
SPECIALTIES: Route 3 performs 150 years of popular American music - hundreds of songs. Hear and Now performs jazz, ballads, blues, fusion, latin and original compositions.
CURRENT/RECENT CLIENTS/PROJECTS: Highland Fest,. St. Paul, Hormel Nature Center in Austin, Mall of America, Minnesota Splash in Edina, Northland Senior Games in Duluth, Queen of Excelsior on Lake Minnetonka, St. Croix Sailing Club, St. Paul Winter Carnival, Numerous national and regional television and radio commercials. Since 1983 has been with Minnesota Opera at the Ordway Center for the Performing Arts, and Plymouth Music Series of Minnesota.

I

IN THE GROOVE MUSIC
625 2nd Avenue South #102
612-305-1229
Minneapolis 55402
FAX: 612-305-0704
CONTACT: Darren Drew, Brian Reidinger
E-MAIL: itgmusic@uswest.net
WWW: planetpoint.com/inthegroovemusic.com
SERVICES: Composing producing and mixing music and sound design for TV, radio, multimedia and Surround Sound.
CAPABILITIES: Original composition of music and sound design.
CURRENT/RECENT CLIENTS/PROJECTS: Martin Williams; McCann Erickson; BBDO; Momentum; Initio; Odney, Initio, Meyocks and Priebe; ABC; CBS; MSC; Fox; Star Tribune; MN Twins; Lynch Jarvis Jones.

L

LOUD NEIGHBORS
3712 Garfield Avenue South
612-825-2900
Minneapolis 55409
FAX: 612-825-4171
CONTACT: Dick Hedlund
E-MAIL: loudnabrz@aol.com
WWW: loudneighborsrecords.com
SERVICES: Music composition (pre/post scoring), production, sound design, ADR, Foley, Digital recording/editing, conforming, voice/music recording, post-production mixing for film/video/radio/TV.
CAPABILITIES: Full-service music and audio production.
PRESIDENT/CEO/OWNER: John Calder, P

M

MAJOR GROOVE MUSIC COMPANY
160 Glenwood Avenue North #300
FAX: 763-535-8989
CONTACT: Aimee Fischer
E-MAIL: contact@majorgroovemusic.com
WWW: majorgroovemusic.com

763-537-8900
Minneapolis 55405

SERVICES: A broad range of original music, lyrics and musical adaptations. We do audio production and sound design for film, video, business theater, commercials and jingles, live events and entertainment. We use the top vocal, voice-over and instrumental talent available, and have professional producers, engineers, writers and talent on staff. On-site musical direction and project coordination available, especially for business theater and live entertainment events.
CAPABILITIES: Corporate music doesn't have to sound corporate! We produce music that will move you and your audience, with powerful arrangements and lyrics that aren't trite. Synclavier digital workstation, ProTools system. Yamaha O2R console and more.
CURRENT/RECENT CLIENTS/PROJECTS: ITM; United Airlines; Citibank; Grand Casino; ICONOS; World International Records; Travelers; Design Group; Golden Rule Productions; EcoQuest International; West Group Publishing; Genius Products; Baby Music Boom, Inc.; Hoffman Communications; Alpine Industries; Unkommon Productions; Troupe America; Page Music; B J Productions; Michael Whalen Music; Marianne Richmond Studios, Inc.; F. Whitley Music; Macromedia; DoReMedia; and Internet Florist
PRESIDENT/CEO/OWNER: Aimee Fischer, David Jacobi, Owners

MUSICAL MARKETING
9400 Clinton Avenue South
CONTACT: Anita Cracauer
E-MAIL: jinglez@uswest.net
WWW: musicalmarketing.com

952-414-9535
Bloomington 55420

SERVICES: Phenomenal jingles and original music in a wide variety of styles for commercials, film, theatre, and multimedia applications. Digital recording, editing and mastering. Telephone on-hold marketing music. Voice talent available. Quick turnaround - demo available. Live solo piano for corporate and other events.
CAPABILITIES: Memorable melodies, vocal arrangements, and piano and guitar talent. State of the art production software. Fast, quality music for any budget.
CURRENT/RECENT CLIENTS/PROJECTS: Ontrack Data International; USA Financial Inc.; Crisis Point Theater.

N

NATURAL SOUND RECORDING STUDIO
1604 Frost Avenue
FAX: 651-770-3270
CONTACT: Martha Kluth
E-MAIL: mkluth@mkluth.com
WWW: naturalsoundstudio.com

651-770-3270
St. Paul 55109

374 / Music & Jingles

SERVICES: State-of-the-art fully digital recording in a comfortable environment; 24 track, 20 bit recording; professional mastering; complete mix automation and recall; CD one-offs; MP3 encoding; jingle, theme and incidental music composition; educational resources; location recording; very reasonable rates.

CAPABILITIES: Featuring the RAMSA WR-DA7 digital recording console, 3 20-bit ADAT recorders, Alesis MasterLink mastering, CD recorder, Sony DAT, Mackie HR824 monitors, Lexicon digital FX, Kawai Grand Piano, Boss GT-3 Guitar synthesizer/FX, Alesis Nano Synth, Alesis D4, Roland U20, other sound modules, Windows PC, Cubasis sequencing software, large selection of microphones; professional engineering and production staff with over 30 years experience.

Q

Q SOUND PRODUCTIONS, INC.
2107 Ericon Drive
FAX: 763-585-0506
CONTACT: Rob Solberg
E-MAIL: rob@qsoundinc.com
WWW: qsoundinc.com

763-503-2400
Minneapolis 55430

SERVICES: Strikingly original music composition for film, video, TV, radio, internet and new media. We also provide sound design and have a roster of professional voice talent available to our clientele. Audio editing and sweetening.

CAPABILITIES: We have experience creating and recording music tracks in a wide variety of musical styles from classical to big band swing to techno. We also have extensive experience preparing audio for delivery over the internet and via CD-ROM and other new media formats.

CURRENT/RECENT CLIENTS/PROJECTS: "Kid's Dance Party" - Nationally released music CD for Metacom Music, "Ranger Rex" - Nationally released children's audio adventure for RNR, Corp., other clients include: Target, General Mills, Seward Learning, Integrated Advertising Network, Young America Corp., Gerten Greenhouses, Select Comfort Corp., Rent-A-Wreck; Ghost Productions, Triad Communications.

R

ROUTE 3
1298 Folsom Street
CONTACT: Ralph Hepola

651-488-1144
St. Paul 55117

SERVICES: Popular American Music from the 1850s to the present. Three musicians take you on a trip through time and around the country. Our compact disc, "An American Musical Journey", is available. Concerts, conventions, festivals, trade shows, trips, tours, strolling music. Classic Jazz, Broadway Show Tunes, the Swing Era, Waltzes, the Roaring Twenties, Contemporary, Americana, Minstrel Tunes, Turn-of-the-Century and more.

CAPABILITIES: We provide a sound system. We are very portable and flexible; can move easily from one location at a venue to another. Founded in 1988.

CURRENT/RECENT CLIENTS/PROJECTS: 35 to 55 performances a year in the Upper Midwest. Our compact disc, "An American Musical Journey", is available as a demo recording. Ralph Hepola is with the Minnesota Opera at the Ordway, also with Plymouth Music Series of Minnesota and has performed at the Guthrie Theater, with the Minnesota Orchestra, and the St. Paul Chamber Orchestra. Heard on recordings; commercials.

PRESIDENT/CEO/OWNER: Ralph Hepola

S

SLIPSTREAM MUSIC 612-940-2573
1568 Eustis Street St. Paul 55108
FAX: 651-645-3515
CONTACT: Erik Nilsen, Pat Phillips
E-MAIL: erik@slipstream-music.com
WWW: slipstream-music.com
SERVICES: Original music for spots, video production, multimedia and web. Scores, jingles, underscore, theme songs, sound design and arrangement.
CAPABILITIES: We offer solutions to your needs and preferences that improve your production and keep you on budget. Full Smpte Sync for frame accurate scoring. Complete 32 track digital facility including: Yamaha O2R console, Apple G3, ADAT, TC Electronics, Lexicon, UREI, JoeMEEK, Sohmer 6'4" grand piano, DBX.
CURRENT/RECENT CLIENTS/PROJECTS: Fox Movie Network; Discovery Channel; Musicland Group, Inc; Best Buy; Lutheran Brotherhood; AICP; 3M; Pillsbury Corp.; PBS "Newton's Apple"; DMPML Music Library (London).
PRESIDENT/CEO/OWNER: Erik Nilsen

T

TANGLETOWN RECORDING STUDIOS 651-335-5083
PO Box 8496 Minneapolis 55408
CONTACT: William Winfield
ALTERNATE PHONE: 612-824-8844
E-MAIL: williamwinfield@aol.com
WWW: ttwn.com
SERVICES: Music production, provide singers, jingles, mastering house, CD one-offs, commercial production, Dance music, R&B, Hiphop, pop, and house music.
CURRENT/RECENT CLIENTS/PROJECTS: Campbell Mithun Esty, MN Anti-Smoking Radio Campaign, Olson & Company, Riverfront Corp - "The Bridge" Video; Minneapolis Convention and Visitors Bureau (music and jingle for radio campaign); James Grier & Co.; Mayor Norm Coleman; David & Latonia Hughes of MGS and many more local and national credits.
PRESIDENT/CEO/OWNER: William Winfield

THIS BOYS FREE 651-482-0194
23 Nord Circle Road North Oaks 55127
FAX: 651-490-5993
CONTACT: Peter N. Holste
CAPABILITIES: Voice talent (male) for audio or video production; telephone for live audition.
SPECIALTIES: Advertising scripting and public relations.
CURRENT/RECENT CLIENTS/PROJECTS: Cherbo Publishing, Encino, CA; The Boone Society, Atlanta, GA.
PRESIDENT/CEO/OWNER: Peter N. Holste

376 / Music & Jingles

THOUGHTS UNSEEN
5123 Third Street NE
CONTACT: Nicole Smith
E-MAIL: thoughtsunseen@hotmail.com
WWW: thoughtsunseen.bigstep.com

763-571-5512
Fridley 55421

SERVICES: Musical trio consisting of two vocalists and a pianist. The esteemed trio will perform your favorite music at your next dinner/cocktail party, reception or corporate function. Performances can be customized for your themed event, or include a variety of musical styles, such as Jazz, Broadway, Big Band, Pop or Contemporary.
CAPABILITIES: Each featured musician brings a diverse musical background to the group, ranging from intense jazz to classical training, Jeff, Linda and Nicole are all dedicated professionals who thrive on performing quality music, while adding elegance to the room.

3SCORE MUSIC/ETC.
510 First Avenue North #404
FAX: 612-333-2232
CONTACT: Mark Henderson, Dave Karr, Adi Yeshaya
E-MAIL: mark@3scoremusic.com
WWW: 3scoremusic.com

612-333-2233
Minneapolis 55403

SERVICES: Original music composition/production and sound design for television, radio, film. Voiceover recording/editing./ Composing/scoring/arranging for "live" ensembles and recording (from trios to full orchestra and big bands.)
CAPABILITIES/SPECIALTIES: Compose, orchestrate and arrange for live musicians. 32 track Pro Tools systems; DA88 Tascam recorder; Panasonic digital mixer; Lock to picture capability; Variety of microphones, synthesizers, sound effects.
CURRENT/RECENT CLIENTS/PROJECTS: 3M; Disney; Target; Best Buy; Houlihan's; Perkins; The Goodman Group; MN Credit Unions; Northwest Airlines; Mall of America; Mystic Lake Casino; Pfizer; Minnesota Orchestra; Whitney Houston; Aretha Franklin; Lena Horne; Doc Severinsen; Wal-Mart; Star Tribune; Minnesota Zoo.

U

UNDERTONE MUSIC, INC.
600 Washington Avenue No. #305
FAX: 612-339-0470
CONTACT: Scott Reddington
E-MAIL: undertone@bitstream.net

612-339-8911
Minneapolis 55401

CAPABILITIES: Original music and sound design for TV, radio, film, industrial video, and new media.
SPECIALTIES: Unique music composition tailored to programs, including pre and post-scoring, underscoring, sound-alikes, parody, and songs.

Music & Jingles / 377

CURRENT/RECENT CLIENTS/PROJECTS: Aurora Pictures; M & H Advertising; Greer & Associates; Kitchener Productions; The Falls Agency; Crosspurpose Productions; Imageworks Inc.; Miller Meester Advertising; Cascade Communications; The Cortland Group; Old Dutch Potato Chips; IBM; Rollerblade; Kemps; Glenwood Inglewood; Packard Bell; Kawasaki; Homecrest Patio Furniture; Dong Bu Insurance (Korea); The Learning Channel; Discovery Channel; KTCA TV (PBS); Home & Gardens TV; Comedy Central; Land O' Lakes; HB Fuller; Prince Tennis Racquets; Redmond; General Mills; Reliastar; Egodyne; Featherlite Corp.; Federated Insurance; Praxair; Wheels, Inc.; Dain Rauscher; Caterpillar; Tower Automotive; America Cyanamid; Arsenal, Inc.; Lockheed/Martin; Northrup King; Novartis Seeds; United Way; The Smithsonian Institute; Hazelden/Stone Circle Productions; Department of Natural Resources; Prairie Fish Pictures; Minneapolis Institute of Arts; The Minnesota Children's Museum; Stone Circle Productions; The Weissman Museum; The Bell Museum of Natural History; Red Eye Theatre; Walker Art Center; Tom Schroeder Animation; Canopy Games.

PRESIDENT/CEO/OWNER: Scott Reddington, Tom Hambelton

Naming Services

N
NAMETAG INTERNATIONAL, INC.   952-841-2244
7701 France Avenue So #105   Edina 55435
FAX: 952-841-2242
CONTACT: Mollie Young
E-MAIL: info@nametagintl.com
WWW: nametagintl.com
SERVICES: Brand strategy, naming, research.
CAPABILITIES: Actionable naming work. Proprietary ideation process which generates strategic, unique and market advantageous results. Strategic marketing emphasis. Types of Research: Consumer and professional. Research and Testing Methods: Focus groups, one-on-ones, panels.
CURRENT/RECENT CLIENTS/PROJECTS: Pfizer; Target; Pepsi Cola Company; 3M; McDonald's Corporation; Frito Lay; Dow; Revlon; Motorola.
PRESIDENT/CEO/OWNER: Mollie Young & Bridget Levin

Outdoor Advertising & Signage

A

ADTRACK, INC.
383 W 60th Street
FAX: 612-866-9896
CONTACT: Robert J. Pigozzi
E-MAIL: adtrack@bpsi.net

612-866-9620
Minneapolis 55419

SERVICES: Adtrack is a full-service vehicle graphics and advertising company. If your commercial vehicle needs a make-over, we can help with the creative development, production, application and ongoing maintenance. Adtrack can apply your creative ideas using traditional decal or adhesive-backed vinyl materials or our changeable graphics system. Our changeable system allows you to quickly and systematically change the images on your box trucks just like a billboard. Don't have your own Vehicles? Adtrack Media Services can still put your message on commercial delivery trucks in your target market. Instead of billboards or buses, we use trucks!

CAPABILITIES: Adtrack is the only company in the US that provides a high quality non-adhesive, changeable mobile billboard system for box trucks. When you consider that the typical commercial delivery vehicle is seen by 20,000 - 60,000 consumers per day, you realize that these vehicles are also a very powerful advertising medium. Just as you would change billboards to keep your message fresh, Adtrack's quick-change system allows you to change your vehicle images as your advertising needs change.

CURRENT/RECENT CLIENTS/PROJECTS: Target Corporation, Department Store Division uses Adtrack and our changeable graphics system as it's "Fleet Advertising Manager" for its Dayton's, Marshall Field's and Hudson's delivery trucks. Ultimate Electronics, Denver, CO uses Adtrack to make-over 60 installation vans, for 3 divisions in over 30 locations. In addition, this client also uses Adtrack's quick-change system on its home delivery vehicles.

PRESIDENT/CEO/OWNER: Robert J. Pigozzi

ASI SIGN SYSTEMS
1301 Washington Avenue North
CONTACT: Steven Pajor

612-332-1223
Minneapolis 55411

SERVICES: Full service architectural sign company.
SPECIALTIES: Services include sign system planning, design, manufacturing, installation and maintenance. Products include interior plaque signs, illuminated and non-illuminated building directories, dimensional letters, custom logos, etched metal signs, porcelain enamel signs, exterior monument signs and employee identification systems.
PRESIDENT/CEO/OWNER: Steven Pajor, P

B

BALLOON ASCENSIONS UNLIMITED
4776 East 220th Street
CONTACT: Ed Chapman

952-447-5677
Prior Lake 55372

SERVICES: Outdoor advertising; production and placement; outdoor. Banner or artwork carried on hot air balloons or blimps.
SIZE OF COLLECTION: Up to 40 feet high and 100 feet long.
CREATIVE: Artwork by Sky High Art.

380 / Outdoor Advertising & Signage

SPECIALTIES: Utilization of hot air balloons to maximize product identity and trademark visibility; complete range of services from a single flight to multiple year campaign. Chief pilot has over 18,000 hours of flight experience.

C

CENTRAL CONTAINER CORP.   612-425-7444
PO Box 43310   Minneapolis 55443
FAX: 612-425-7917
CONTACT: Steven Braun
E-MAIL: sbraun@centralcontainer.com
WWW: centralcontainer.com
SERVICES: Designs created by an award winning structural design team. From promotional packaging and point-of-sale shelf cartons, to protective, cushioned shipping containers, we provide complete prototyping and engineered solutions. Point-of-purchase displays and "club pack" designs are turned out in minimal time. Full color mock-ups of proposed art are produced on our 54" H. P. Color Plotter. Sophisticated warehousing and logistics management within our 175,000 square foot state of the art production facility, coupled with our in-house fulfillment group, allow for true "turnkey" project management.
CAPABILITIES: Litho/label mounting on 2 automatic mounters. Substrates from corrugated to foam core. 4 color flexo press capable of process work as well as vibrant, rich solid color and line work. Precision die cutters - 2 flat bed and 2 rotary presses. Standard cartons from our flexo/folder/gluers, and specialty boxes with intricate glue patterns for "crash bottoms," 6 corner trays, and internal parts - all glued on computer automated systems.
PRESIDENT/CEO/OWNER: James E. Haglund

CITYLITES USA, INC.   612-339-6875
12 South 6th Street   Minneapolis 55402
FAX: 320-693-8631
CONTACT: Mark Lease
E-MAIL: citylites@usa.com
SIZES HANDLED: 22 7/8" x 35" and larger. Types: Lit Displays, Duratrans, Animation, 3D.
SPECIALTIES: Back lighted advertising displays located in downtown skyway systems of Minneapolis, St. Paul and Rochester, MN and Des Moines, Iowa.
CREATIVE: Creative Department: Yes.
PRESIDENT/CEO/OWNER: Joel Shanahan, Mark Lease

D

DELITE OUTDOOR ADVERTISING, INC.   651-686-9295
1380 Corporate Center Curve   Eagan 55121
FAX: 651-454-7995
CONTACT: Tim Scott
E-MAIL: info@deliteoutdoor.com
WWW: deliteoutdoor.com
CONTACT: Chris Ballis, Sales Manager

Outdoor Advertising & Signage / 381

SERVICES: Full-service national outdoor advertising company with inventory in 24 states. 1,200 billboard faces in Minnesota and Western Wisconsin. Complete coverage of the state of Minnesota including Twin Cities metro and out-state markets. Bulletins, 30-sheet posters, premier panels, 8-sheet posters. In-house art department, complete commercial sign shop.
PRESIDENT/CEO/OWNER: Jeff Evrard, CEO; Lon Binder, CFO

E

E J SIGNS
9011 Portland Avenue South
FAX: 952-888-8041
CONTACT: Joyce Aspenwall
E-MAIL: ejsigns@isd.net

952-888-8041
Bloomington 55420

SERVICES: Custom hand lettering; Computerized vinyl lettering: Truck, boats, banners, yard signs magnetics; Interior and exterior signs; subsurface and top surface signs.

G

GOPHER SIGN COMPANY
1310 Randolph Avenue
FAX: 651-699-3727
CONTACT: Greg Smith
E-MAIL: gophersign@aol.com
SERVICES: Screenprinted and embossed metal signs.
CAPABILITIES: Embossing signs.
PRESIDENT/CEO/OWNER: B. Smith

651-698-5095
St. Paul 55105

L

LAMAR ADVERTISING COMPANY
PO Box 865
2625 Clearwater Road
FAX: 320-253-3746
ALTERNATE PHONE: 320-253-3000
CONTACT: Emil Radaich

1-800-777-4896
St. Cloud 56302

AFFILIATED OFFICES: 9331 Westgate Blvd, PO Box 16030, Duluth, MN 55816; 1-800-234-7293. 2209 Birch Street, PO Box 1242, Eau Claire, WI 54702, 715-832-2313.
SERVICES: Sizes Handled: all standard sizes
SPECIALTIES: Outdoor advertising coverage throughout Central Minnesota and Eastern North Dakota.
PRESIDENT/CEO/OWNER: Kevin Reilly

382 / Outdoor Advertising & Signage

LASER GRAPHICS, INC.   612-835-8346
5100 Edina Industrial Blvd.   Minneapolis 55349
FAX: 612-835-8347
CONTACT: Peter Linstroth
E-MAIL: lgi@gipromotions.com
WWW: lgipromtions.com
SERVICES: A full-service production and fulfillment house. Products include: banner and signage; personalized merchandise; screen printed and embroidered apparel awards; fulfillment; incentive awards; special event planning.
CAPABILITIES: In-house creative; large format banner reproduction; warehouse fulfillment; Internet accessible; banner installation.
CURRENT/RECENT CLIENTS/PROJECTS: Target; Dayton's' Blue Cross/Blue Shield; Minnesota Timberwolves; Minnesota Twins; Minnesota Vikings; Jostens; US West
PRESIDENT/CEO/OWNER: Peter Linstroth

S

SCHUBERT & HOEY OUTDOOR ADVERTISING   612-722-1090
2747 26th Avenue South   Minneapolis 55406
FAX: 612-722-8775
CONTACT: Mary Teske
SERVICES: Classification: Outdoor advertising Sizes handled: All sizes, bulletins and posters. Creative/Art Department: Full service art department.
SPECIALTIES: High quality, custom-designed bulletins located in Minnesota and Wisconsin.
CURRENT/RECENT CLIENTS/PROJECTS: National advertisers to local businesses.
PRESIDENT/CEO/OWNER: Diane Hoey

SIGNS & GRAPHICS   612-890-2011
1161 East Cliff Road   Burnsville 55337
FAX: 612-890-8324
CONTACT: John Hansen
E-MAIL: johndahl@pconline.com
SERVICES: Classification: Sign company; production and placement; indoor and outdoor. Types of Printing: Painted wood, vinyl letters and graphics, sandblasted redwood, monuments, plaques, vehicle graphics, magnets. Creative/Art Department: Signs designed and produced in conjunction with advertising/promotional programs primarily for the construction industry.
SPECIALTIES: Logo designs and architectural illustrations/displays.
PRESIDENT/CEO/OWNER: John Hansen, Mary Dahl

T

TDI   612-920-1657
6950 France Avenue South   Minneapolis 55435
FAX: 612-920-6298
CONTACT: William Regis
E-MAIL: tdiminn@uswest.net

Outdoor Advertising & Signage / 383

WWW: tdiworldwide.com
SERVICES: Classification: Outdoor advertising placement. Sizes handled: 21" x 72"; 15" x 48"; 30" x 144".
SPECIALTIES: Transportation advertising on Twin City buses; 37 major cities nationwide.

TRANSTOP MINNESOTA, INC.   952-854-1900
8009 34th Avenue South   Minneapolis 55425
Riverview Office Tower #1520
FAX: 952-854-8303
CONTACT: Connie Barry
SPECIALTIES: 670 backlit bus shelter advertising panels in Minneapolis and St. Paul.
PRESIDENT/CEO/OWNER: Connie Barry, President/CEO; Joyce Kucera, Account Executive

Package Designers

B

THE BENYAS DESIGN GROUP   612-340-9804
Advanced Results by Design
126 North Third Street, Suite 300   Minneapolis 55401
FAX: 612-334-5950
CONTACT: Bradley A. Benyas
E-MAIL: benyas@visi.com
CAPABILITIES: The Benyas AD Group is a results-oriented graphic design firm specializing in printed communications that advance our clients, their companies, and their products. From concept through production, we provide the services you need, when you need them. Market analysis/positioning, name generation and branding...design and comping using state-of-the-art pre-press resources...expert photo direction and print supervision. We deliver results.

C

CENTRAL CONTAINER CORP.   612-425-7444
PO Box 43310   Minneapolis 55443
FAX: 612-425-7917
CONTACT: Steven Braun
E-MAIL: sbraun@centralcontainer.com
WWW: centralcontainer.com
SERVICES: Designs created by an award winning structural design team. From promotional packaging and point-of-sale shelf cartons, to protective, cushioned shipping containers, we provide complete prototyping and engineered solutions. Point-of-purchase displays and "club pack" designs are turned out in minimal time. Full color mock-ups of proposed art are produced on our 54" H. P. Color Plotter. Sophisticated warehousing and logistics management within our 175,000 square foot state of the art production facility, coupled with our in-house fulfillment group, allow for true "turnkey" project management.
CAPABILITIES: Litho/label mounting on 2 automatic mounters. Substrates from corrugated to foam core. 4 color flexo press capable of process work as well as vibrant, rich solid color and line work. Precision die cutters - 2 flat bed and 2 rotary presses. Standard cartons from our flexo/folder/gluers, and specialty boxes with intricate glue patterns for "crash bottoms," 6 corner trays, and internal parts - all glued on computer automated systems.
PRESIDENT/CEO/OWNER: James E. Haglund

CRC, INC.   952-937-6000
6321 Bury Drive #10   Eden Prairie 55346
FAX: 952-937-5155
CONTACT: Cindy Owens, New Business Specialist
WWW: crc-inc.com

CREATIVE RESOURCE CENTER/CRC, INC.   952-937-6000
6321 Bury Drive #10   Eden Prairie 55346
FAX: 952-937-5155
CONTACT: Cindy Owens, New Business Specialist
WWW: crc-inc.com

Package Designers / 385

SERVICES: A full-service integrated marketing communications agency with 20 years experience in strategic communications planning across a range of delivery forms. Services include planning and implementation of strategic marketing communications, internet presence, sales promotion, relationship marketing, internet list development and maintenance, and development of full-scale e-commerce web stores. Full in-house planning and creative teams for both print and internet development include experts in planning, design, copy, content management, database design and development, website development, management, hosting and serving. In-house photography studio.

SPECIALTIES: Integrated marketing communications planning and implementation, internet business strategy, sales promotion including sales materials, collateral, POS, full integration of promotion on the internet including interactive relationship marketing. Corporate and brand identity programs, package design, business-to-business and consumer advertising, and direct mail.

CURRENT/RECENT CLIENTS/PROJECTS: CNS Interactive; FSMC; Graco; Haagen-Dazs Interactive, Interactive Learning Group (Video Buddy); Loffler Business Systems; McGlynn's Retail Bakeries; Multifoods Bakery Products; NK Lawn & Garden; Old Dutch; Pillsbury Interactive; Primera Technology; Rosemount Office Systems Interactive; Sargento Foods, Inc.; 3M Intranet.

PRESIDENT/CEO/OWNER: Michael Lundeby, CEO; Elizabeth Petrangelo, EVP; Joe Andrews, VP; Troy Braun, Creative Director

F

FRANKE + FIORELLA
401 North 3rd Street, Suite 380
FAX: 612-338-2300
CONTACT: Deb Fiorella
E-MAIL: deb@frankefiorella.com
WWW: frankefiorella.com

612-338-1700
Minneapolis 55401

CAPABILITIES: Comprehensive single and multi-lingual package design development including: market analysis and strategic planning, brand identity, competitive audits, positioning and naming, concept/design exploration and refinement through production of final electronic files.

SPECIALTIES: Commercial and consumer package design (single and multi-lingual), brand identity development.

PRESIDENT/CEO/OWNER: Craig Franke, Deborah Fiorella

H

HEDSTROM/BLESSING, INC.

HEDSTROM/BLESSING, INC.　　　　　　　　**763-591-6200**
8301 Golden Valley Road #300　　　　　**Minneapolis 55427**
FAX: 763-591-6232
CONTACT: Julie Pearl
E-MAIL: info@hb-inc.com
WWW: www.hb-inc.com
CAPABILITIES: Complete package design services including: market analysis, positioning, naming/branding/identity, concepting, packaging graphics design and production, photo art direction.
SPECIALTIES: Consumer and commercial package design and production; brand identity and logo development.
CURRENT/RECENT CLIENTS/PROJECTS: Selected accounts include 3M; Bachman's; Carlson Leisure Group; Fabcon; Intellisol International; Interactive Learning Group; Land O'Lakes; Pillsbury; Target

J

JEDLICKA DESIGN　　　　　　　　　　　　**651-636-0964**
2164 Rosewood Lane North　　　　　　　**Roseville 55113**
FAX: 651-636-0964
CONTACT: Wendy Jedlicka
E-MAIL: wendy@jedlicka.com
WWW: jedlicka.com
SERVICES: Eco-friendly packaging design and marketing for the world economy. Packaging design, packaging graphics, product placement, and multilingual packaging.
CAPABILITIES: Member of IOPP, O2, O2-USA/UMN. Founding Member of Independent Designers Network (indes.net).

Package Designers / 387

M

MCSMITH PACKAGE & DISPLAY, INC.   952-808-1227
PO Box 1907   Burnsville 55337
FAX: 952-808-7705
CONTACT: Diane M. McConnell
WWW: mcsmith.com
CAPABILITIES: Sales of virtually all types of standard packaging supplies, plus selected custom categories.
SPECIALTIES: Retail, promotional, and consumer-product packaging. Decorative stock and custom boxes, bags, wrapping/packing accessories and merchandising displays, shipping boxes and specialty mailers; customer product packaging.
PRESIDENT/CEO/OWNER: Diane M. McConnell

S

SPANGLER DESIGN TEAM   952-927-5425
4850 Park Glen Road   St. Louis Park 55416
FAX: 952-927-7034
CONTACT: Mark Spangler
E-MAIL: mail@spanglerdesign.com
WWW: spanglerdesign.com
CAPABILITIES: Creative consultation, web sites, corporate identity, annual reports, product design, packaging, and promotional materials.
SPECIALTIES: Simplicity and quality.
PRESIDENT/CEO/OWNER: Mark Spangler

U

ULTRA CREATIVE, INC.   612-338-7908
920 Second Avenue South #1200   Minneapolis 55402
FAX: 612-337-8178
CONTACT: Dave Biebighauser
E-MAIL: dave@ultracreative.com
CAPABILITIES: Planning and positioning, creative development, graphic design and production. Project based creative marketing firm for corporate communications; print, direct, packaging, POP, identity and collateral.
SPECIALTIES: Food products, retail, kid marketing, new products, and brand equity maintenance.
CURRENT/RECENT CLIENTS/PROJECTS: General Mills, Inc.; The Pillsbury Company; Campbell's Foods, Inc.; Marigold Foods; Gymamerica.com; Govt.com.
PRESIDENT/CEO/OWNER: Dave Biebighauser, President; Gino Perfetti, Vice President

V

VOLTAGGIO JOHNSON 612-338-2920
401 North Third Street **Minneapolis 55401**
FAX: 612-338-2997
CONTACT: Jerry Johnson
E-MAIL: design@voltaggiojohnson.com
CAPABILITIES: Voltaggio Johnson Design is a full-service brand consultancy and graphic design firm specializing in branding, identity development, market analysis, positioning and product concepting. Our focus is on consumer and commercial packaging and retail point-of-sale collateral from creative concept through production.
SPECIALTIES: We take an active approach by listening and understanding our clients' problems, then developing a strategic solution to meet their needs.
CURRENT/RECENT CLIENTS/PROJECTS: We enjoy long-term successful relationships with Fortune 100 Corporations as well as local entrepreneurial companies.
PRESIDENT/CEO/OWNER: Jerry Johnson

Photo Stylists

B

PATRICIA BILCIK   612-441-8680
14684 221st Avenue NW   Elk River 55330
CONTACT: Pat Bilcik
SERVICES: Complete range of product styling for catalog advertising.
SPECIALTIES: Studio life-style roomset, tabletop and location. Trends, art and propping inclusive.

C

BRENT CASEY, INC. PHOTO/FILM STYLING   612-822-7676
4312 First Avenue South   Minneapolis 55409
FAX: 612-822-7673
CONTACT: Brent Casey
PAGER: 651-229-5625
SERVICES: Styling, production, project coordination, set design/set dressing, props, wardrobe, and creative direction. Clothing and accessories; both on and off figure. 15+ years' photo styling and adjunct experience. Accomplished at styling in studio or on location (multiple room sets through small sets.)
CAPABILITIES: Creative approach with nearly all aspects of project including stretching budgets. Discounts for portfolio building photo/film/video. Portfolio and references available.

COMPLIMENTS, INC.   651-275-1115
11080 Arcola Trail North   Stillwater 55082
FAX: 651-275-1116
CONTACT: Ronald Johnson
E-MAIL: compliments@visi.com
SERVICES: Food styling, cookbook and recipe development.
CAPABILITIES: Photography, print, television and video

E

FAYE ELLISON   952-929-9323
5712 Melody Lane   Edina 55436
FAX: 612-836-1367
CONTACT: Faye Ellison
PAGER: 612-530-9995
CAPABILITIES: Photo stylists, propping and wardrobe. Fashion laydown/on figure, wardrobing, softgoods, interiors/room sets, tabletop propping. In-studio or location. BFA/Design - Minneapolis College of Art & Design. 19 years experience as stylist.
CURRENT/RECENT CLIENTS/PROJECTS: Editorial/commercial/lifestyle/fashion. Fashion on figure & laydown. Softgoods.

F

FIELD DRESSING   612-545-1541
7417 Franklin Avenue West   St. Louis Park 55426
CONTACT: Joey Beattie
E-MAIL: joeybeattie@hotmail.com
SERVICES: Wardrobe and prop styling, location scouting, casting and project management.
SPECIALTIES: Camping, hunting and fishing location shooting for product photography. Military uniforms and custom sewing.
CURRENT/RECENT CLIENTS/PROJECTS: The Sportsman's Guide - a catalog and internet company. Model and location coordinator for clothing and outdoor gear. Gold 'n Plump chicken - custom costumes for live chickens.

G

HEIDI GRAYDEN   651-643-5904
4940 3rd Avenue South   Minneapolis 55401
CONTACT: Heidi Grayden
SERVICES: Wardrobe, prop and room set stylist for print advertising.

J

SUSAN JORGENSEN   952-470-0275
6510 Yosemite Avenue   Excelsior 55331
FAX: 952-470-0275
CONTACT: Susan Jorgensen
PAGER: 612-534-7257
CAPABILITIES: Still photo stylist and prop stylist with experience in tabletop, softgoods, wardrobe and room sets.

K

KIM HORECKA, MAKE-UP ARTIST   612-377-6877
2200 Aldrich Avenue South, Suite 4   Minneapolis 55405
CONTACT: Kim Horecka
PAGER: 612-622-7229
CAPABILITIES: Freelance make-up artist, wardrobe and hair maintenance.
SPECIALTIES: Personable & professional, make-up artist for film, video, television and still photography. Experience in corporate, corrective, fashion, subtle "real" looks, cuts and bruises. References available.

Photo Stylists / 391

CURRENT/RECENT CLIENTS/PROJECTS: Dayton's, US West, NordicTrack, Mystic Lake, West Publishing, IBM, AT&T, Carlson Companies, British Airways, US Bank, Fallon McElligot, 3M, Northwest Airlines, Nemer, Fieger, Honda, Toyota, Oldsmobile, Bristol Myers, Pillsbury, Motorola, Funari Advertising, Campbell-Mithun Esty, HBO, Fox, Turner, Radio City Music Hall, BBC, ESPN. Resume available upon request.

M

CHRISTINE MARTIN CONSULTANTS   612-544-3232
5219 Wayzata Blvd   St. Louis Park 55416
FAX: 612-823-2629
E-MAIL: cam1@cpinternet
CAPABILITIES/SPECIALTIES: Nailcare, skincare, makeup.
PRESIDENT/CEO/OWNER: Christine Martin

LOIS MEISCHPHOTO/FILM STYLIST   651-698-2381
811 South Cleveland   St. Paul 55116
CONTACT: Lois Meisch
CAPABILITIES: Styling; propping; set design.
SPECIALTIES: Propping for food, interiors (studio sets and location.)

R

RAJTAR PRODUCTIONS   612-827-1974
1520 East 46th Street   Minneapolis 55407
FAX: 612-827-1979
CONTACT: John Rajtar
E-MAIL: rajtarprod@worldnet.att.net
SERVICES: Propping, styling, design.
CAPABILITIES: Creative propping, styling internationally, nationally, regionally in your back yard.

Photographers

B

ROGER BLOOM PHOTOGRAPHY   763-535-7171
4324 Adair Avenue North   Minneapolis 55422
FAX: 763-533-3168
CONTACT: Roger Bloom
E-MAIL: rbphoto@hutman.net

C

CABLE PHOTO SYSTEMS   952-888-6642
9201 E. Bloomington Freeway   Bloomington 55420
FAX: 952-888-6711
CONTACT: Gary Cable
E-MAIL: garycable8@aol.com
WWW: cablephoto.com
SERVICES: Studio - 3 staff photographers, 3 digital cameras, large studio with cove and kitchen, specialized in food, product and catalogs. Lab - lightjet, 72" mounting, full service lab, ink jet, outdoor graphics, lenticular images, banners, E-6, C41.

F

AARON FAHRMANN   612-823-1155
5531 Chicago Avenue South   Minneapolis 55417
CONTACT: Aaron Fahrmann

FRANCISCO PHOTOGRAPHY   612-924-9485
4200 Zenith Avenue South   Minneapolis 55410
CONTACT: Tim Francisco
CAPABILITIES: Studio or location, 35mm to 5 x 7.
SPECIALTIES: People, lighting, fine B&W printing.

S

SARA JORDE PHOTOGRAPHY   612-338-3923
529 South 7th Street #637   Minneapolis 55415
FAX: 612-344-1259
CONTACT: Sara Jorde
E-MAIL: sjorde@hutman.net
CAPABILITIES: Studio and location, all formats, color and black & white.
SPECIALTIES: People, environment portraits for advertising and corporate.

R. MYLES SIEGEL PHOTOGRAPHY
7601 Knox Avenue South
FAX: 612-861-4204
CONTACT: Dick Siegel
E-MAIL: mylessiegelphoto@earthlink.net
CAPABILITIES: 4 x 5, 2 - 1/4 and 35mm. Studio or on location. Color transparencies of B&W.
SPECIALTIES: Tabletop, industrial and on location.

612-934-0682
Minneapolis 55413

STEVEN WEWERKA PHOTOGRAPHY
2242 University Avenue #311
FAX: 651-645-8263
CONTACT: Lynn Mersch
E-MAIL: wewerkaphoto@uswest.net
CAPABILITIES: Photography of people, sports, adventure and editorial.
SPECIALTIES: 35mm & 2 1/4 color, black and white.
PRESIDENT/CEO/OWNER: Steven Wewerka

651-917-7927
St. Paul 55114

T

TRELEVEN PHOTOGRAPHY, INC.
3338 University Avenue SE #240
FAX: 612-331-5241
CONTACT: Joe Treleven
CAPABILITIES: Conceptual portrait or lifestyle photographs of people in studio or on location. Studio capabilities including: 6,000 square feet space, full-equipped oversized kitchen, separate client conference room and dedicate makeup, dressing and prop preparation room. Experienced staff producer. Stock available.
SPECIALTIES: Color photography, plus B&W photography hand-printed. Skilled in print manipulation and toning.
PRESIDENT/CEO/OWNER: Joe or Lisa Treleven

612-331-5305
Minneapolis 55414

Photographers - Advertising

A

AARON & MCCANN ADVERTISING PHOTOGRAPHY
15416 Village Woods Drive
FAX: 952-949-2407
CONTACT: Mike McCann
WWW: mccannphoto.com
SERVICES: Studio: 1600 sq. ft. with kitchen, workshop, darkroom, dressing room and reception area with view of Red Rock Lake.
CAPABILITIES: Experience: in business since 1979. Photography of people, products and architecture. Stock photography available.
PRESIDENT/CEO/OWNER: Jack Aaron, Mike McCann

952-949-2407

Eden Prairie 55347

AMOS/SMITH PHOTOGRAPHY
7662 Golden Triangle Drive
FAX: 952-942-6228
CONTACT: Steve or David Amos
E-MAIL: fotogs@amossmith.com
WWW: amossmith.com

952-942-6252

Eden Prairie 55344

GREG R. ANDERSON COMMERCIAL PHOTOGRAPHY
3004 27th Avenue South
PO BOX 6076
CONTACT: Greg R. Anderson
CAPABILITIES: Product/Catalog, PR, Architectural, Full-studio and location, Digital output, Photoshop ready.
SPECIALTIES: Small product photography, industrial, in-plant photography.

612-722-3848

Minneapolis 55406

TERRY ANDERSON PHOTOGRAPHY
5249 W 73rd Street
FAX: 952-835-5531
CONTACT: Terry Anderson
E-MAIL: tkaphoto@visi.com
WWW: visi.com/~tkaphoto
SERVICES: Location and studio photography, 8 x 10, 4 x 4, 1 - 1/4 35mm and full digital capabilities including digital photography, scanning, color correction, retouching and proofing, 10,000 square foot studio with 9 shooting bays, full kitchen, 35' foot cove with both dock and drive-in access.
SPECIALTIES: Large project and large product photography. We have a full-service studio with three full-time photographers and complete support staff to accommodate all levels of projects and time constraints. We shoot people and products in large constructed sets, sweeps, tabletop and on location.
CURRENT/RECENT CLIENTS/PROJECTS: Local, regional and national clients.

952-835-1811

Edina 55439

Photographers - Advertising / 395

ARMSTRONG PHOTOGRAPHY 612-522-7139
2655 Upton Avenue North Minneapolis 55411
CONTACT: Rick Armstrong
SERVICES: Still photography, video production
SPECIALTIES: Photography and oil phases of video production

JIM ARNDT PHOTOGRAPHY, INC. 612-332-5050
400 1st Avenue North #650 Minneapolis 55401
FAX: 612-332-8614
CONTACT: Jim Arndt
SERVICES: Location, studio, advertising, editorial photography.
CAPABILITIES: People, large and small productions on location and in studio.

AURORA PHOTOGRAPHY, LTD. 763-535-7171
4324 Adair Avenue North Minneapolis 55422
FAX: 763-535-7171
CONTACT: Brian Meier
E-MAIL: aurora@auroraphoto.co
WWW: auroraphoto.com
SERVICES: Platinum and Alternative Process Printing, all formats photography, color, b/w and digital imaging.
CAPABILITIES: Studio, location, tabletop, product, advertising and people photography with a fine art background.
PRESIDENT/CEO/OWNER: Roger Bloom, Brian Meier

B

BEASLEY PHOTOGRAPHY 651-644-1400
2370 Hendon Avenue St. Paul 55108
FAX: 651-644-8777
CONTACT: Doug Beasley
E-MAIL: beasley@bitstream.net
WWW: vqphoto.com

PETER BECK PHOTOGRAPHY 612-822-6115
4349 Fremont Avenue South Minneapolis 55409
FAX: 612-822-7117
CONTACT: Peter Beck
E-MAIL: peter@peterbeck.com
WWW: peterbeck.com
CAPABILITIES: People on location and stock photography.
CURRENT/RECENT CLIENTS/PROJECTS: Ford Motor Company, IBM, Microsoft, Apple Computer, Cargill, Unum, Pennzoil, Phillips Petroleum, Prudential, First Bank, American Express, Prentice Hall, Honeywell, Deluxe Check, CNA Insurance, Houghton-Mifflin, McGraw-Hill, Groiler, Encyclopedia Britannica, Linso Private Ledger, Target, Bell Atlantic Creative, ITT Hartford, Toyota, Eastman Kodak, Qualex, Merrill Lynch, Dain Bosworth, Reliastar, MCI, Locheed Martin, Providian, Time Life Books, Chase Manhattan Bank, Unicef and others.

396 / Photographers - Advertising

RAOUL BENAVIDES 612-341-6585
310 North 2nd Street Minneapolis 55401
FAX: 612-333-0609
CONTACT: Raoul Benavides
SERVICES: People on location: emotionally moving black and white portraits of people of color and people with interesting, endangered and/or strange occupations.
SPECIALTIES: All formats: black and white, color.
CURRENT/RECENT CLIENTS/PROJECTS: Photography for editorials, designers, and social service agencies.
PRESIDENT/CEO/OWNER: Raoul Benavides

BERKLEY PHOTOGRAPHY 612-476-4910
2411 Sheridan Hills Curve Minneapolis 55391
CONTACT: Berkley G. Fogelsonger
ALTERNATE PHONE: 612-578-1212
CAPABILITIES: Location, studio, color and B&W. Corporate, advertising, industrial, editorial, annual/quarterly reports high technology photography; medical/surgical/health care; photojournalism; AV productions, interior/exterior architectural. Public relations/event documentation. Able to piggyback expenses on travel assignments. Digital imaging available.
SPECIALTIES: Placing people in the proper light/setting - evoking the appropriate response - capturing the moment on film. People/lifestyles and product portraiture - photography on location or in the studio using natural and created lighting with various formats. Flexibility and problem solving also a specialty. Extensive stock library. Founded 1983.

PER BREIEHAGEN PHOTOGRAPHY 612-338-2581
708 North First Street #314 Minneapolis 55401
FAX: 612-338-2596
CONTACT: Per Breiehagen or Karyn Kopecko
PAGER: 612-621-6974
E-MAIL: pbreiehagen@uswest.net
WWW: breiehagen.com
SPECIALTIES: Location, action, lifestyle and people. Stock available.
PRESIDENT/CEO/OWNER: Per Breiehagen

MIKE BURIAN PHOTOGRAPHY 651-635-9942
1418 Belmont Lane West Roseville 55113
CONTACT: Mike Burian
E-MAIL: mike.burian@worldnet.att.net
WWW: mikeburian.com
SERVICES: Photography people on location for corporate, editorial and advertising clients.
CAPABILITIES: Capturing the decisive moment as a photograph.
CURRENT/RECENT CLIENTS/PROJECTS: 3M Company, Blue Cross/Blue Shield of Minnesota, Computer Network Technology Corporation, Corporate Report Minnesota, Digital River, Forbes, Inc. Magazine, Medtronic, Mpls/St. Paul Magazine, Minnesota Monthly, Southern Minnesota Municipal Power Agency, Strong Funds, Twin Cities Business Monthly, UPS, Ventures.

C

CALLAHAN & COMPANY PHOTO, INC. 612-333-0133
600 Washington Avenue North #205 Minneapolis 55401
FAX: 612-333-0498
CONTACT: Carrie Cleveland
E-MAIL: callahan@winternet.com
SERVICES: Full photographic services, all formats and film types.
CAPABILITIES: Illustrate advertising and editorial assignments in studio or on location. Tabletop, food, fashion, advertising product and editorial illustration.
PRESIDENT/CEO/OWNER: Lawrence Callahan

LEAH CAMPBELL PHOTOGRAPHY 612-872-1102
2445 Lyndale Avenue South Minneapolis 55405
FAX: 612-872-1106
CONTACT: Leah Campbell
SERVICES: Documentary style photography for special events, weddings, engagement photos, family and children photography.
SPECIALTIES: Photographers using medium format, Nikon 35mm, filters, background lighting, black and white, color and infared film.
CURRENT/RECENT CLIENTS/PROJECTS: Mostly local bride and grooms.
PRESIDENT/CEO/OWNER: Leah Campbell

CASWELL PHOTOGRAPHY 612-332-2729
700 Washington Avenue North #308 Minneapolis 55401
FAX: 612-340-1538
CONTACT: George or Karin
E-MAIL: george@caswellphoto.com
WWW: caswellphoto.com
SERVICES: Photo illustrator creating dynamic visual images utilizing traditional and digital techniques for the advertising, corporate and graphic design communities. Color, humor and whimsy are combined with exceptional technical skills resulting in strong visuals that sell products and services.
PRESIDENT/CEO/OWNER: George Caswell

LAUREL CAZIN PHOTOGRAPHY 651-290-9681
300 Broadway Street #604 St. Paul 55101-1475
FAX: 651-665-0343
CONTACT: Laurel Cazin
WWW: lcazinphoto.com
SERVICES: Editorial, documentary, stock, non-profit digital black and white and color photography. In-house lab specializing in black and white prints with optimal quality.

398 / Photographers - Advertising

CAPABILITIES: Editorial, stock, digital, non-profit, black and white and color photograph, specialties. Portraiture, black and white and digital. High resolution negative and flatbed scanning, image manipulation, retouching ad output to film. Prints, CD or disk. 35mm - 6 x 7 cm, digital capture, BFA in photography from MCAD (1978) with numerous awards, grants, and fellowships.

JOANN CHERRY 952-898-2895
14513 Chateau Lane Burnsville 55306
CONTACT: JoAnn Cherry
SERVICES: Photography and film food styling.
CAPABILITIES: Editorial food styling (cookbooks, magazines.)
CURRENT/RECENT CLIENTS/PROJECTS: Pillsbury; Hormel; General Mills; Target; Watkins

CHERYL WALSH BELLVILLE PHOTOGRAPHY 651-291-8483
308 Prince Street, Studio 214 St. Paul 55101
FAX: 651-684-5291
CONTACT: Cheryl Walsh Bellville
E-MAIL: cherylhastings@hotmail.com
WWW: artcrawl.org/artistsites/cwb
SERVICES: Studio and location photography. Specializing in people and portraits. Corporate, industrial, entertainment. Stock photography.
CAPABILITIES: Thousands of stock photography images.
CURRENT/RECENT CLIENTS/PROJECTS: Primary photographer for the 25th anniversary book for Prairie Home Companion Radio Show (Garrison Keillor).
PRESIDENT/CEO/OWNER: Cheryl Walsh Bellville

CITY VISIONS 612-331-7377
20 Second Street NE #2005 Minneapolis 55413
FAX: 612-623-3162
CONTACT: Patrick Siegrist
E-MAIL: siegrist@ekquehl.com
SERVICES: Employing digital and conventional photography in a variety of formats. Affiliated with e.k. Quehl Company a full service advertising agency providing computer enhancement, Internet and design services.
SPECIALTIES: 25 years of experience in architectural, commercial and industrial photography. Design and digital construction of high-resolution digital imagery for advertising, corporate and print applications.
PRESIDENT/CEO/OWNER: Patrick Siegrist

BOB COLE PHOTOGRAPHER 952-492-3686
208 Maple Lane Jordan 55352
CONTACT: Bob Cole

TOM CONNORS PHOTOGRAPHY 612-339-9838
400 First Avenue No #600 Minneapolis 55401
FAX: 612-339-9830
CONTACT: Angi Milchesky
E-MAIL: tomconnors@uswest.net

SERVICES: Full service in studio photographic illustration for advertising and corporate community; all formats 35mm to 8 x 10.
SPECIALTIES: Still life, product illustration and alternative processes.
PRESIDENT/CEO/OWNER: Tom Connors

CRAIG PERMAN PICTURES   612-338-7727
1645 Hennepin Avenue #311   Minneapolis 55403
FAX: 612-338-7731
CONTACT: Craig Perman
E-MAIL: pictures@perman.com
WWW: perman.com
SERVICES: Advertising photography.
CAPABILITIES: People, location, b&w and color.

D

DOZZI PHOTOGRAPHY, INC.   612-338-6727
1201 Currie Avenue   Minneapolis 55403
FAX: 612-338-6383
CONTACT: Kevin Dozzi
E-MAIL: skunkhat@winternet.com
CAPABILITIES: Studio and location, all formats, kitchen, cove.
SPECIALTIES: Product and food photography for advertising, catalog and editorial use.
PRESIDENT/CEO/OWNER: Kevin Dozzi

E

DAVID ELLIS PHOTOGRAPHY, INC.   651-642-9873
1395 Grantham Street   St. Paul 55108
FAX: 651-642-9917
E-MAIL: ellis041@tc.umn.edu
SERVICES: Commercial photography, people and product in studio and on location. Specialize in environmental portraits.
CAPABILITIES/SPECIALTIES: All formats and digital imaging.
PRESIDENT/CEO/OWNER: David Ellis

ELLIS PHOTOGRAPHY INC.   651-644-0121
637 North Snelling Avenue   St. Paul 55104
FAX: 651-647-5688
CONTACT: Stephen E. Ellis
E-MAIL: sellis@ellisphoto.com
SERVICES: On location and in-studio executive portraiture.
CAPABILITIES: 35mm to medium format.

400 / Photographers - Advertising

JAMES ERICKSON PHOTOGRAPHY/DIGITAL   612-332-5112
IMAGING
700 Washington Avenue North #401   Minneapolis 55401
FAX: 612-332-5112
CONTACT: James Erickson
E-MAIL: jim@thestudio-mpls.com
WWW: thestudio-mpls.com
SERVICES: A full-service commercial studio specializing in table top to location for advertising and industry since 1980.
SPECIALTIES: Architecture, food and product illustration. Digital Imaging: manipulate, retouch and composite images. Digital capture or high-end Flextight film scanner, Fujix Pictography printer/proofer. Output on CD, Zip or photographic quality Fujix print.

TONY EVANS, PHOTOGRAPHER   612-759-1733
3951 West 49th Street   Edina 55424
FAX: 612-926-0295
CONTACT: Tony Evans
E-MAIL: tonephoto@aol.com
SERVICES: Photography in all formats in studio or on location for: advertising, industrial, annual reports, public relations, editorial, product, illustration, catalog and portraiture. Complete custom black and white and color lab. Digital still and digital video.
CAPABILITIES: Advertising, commercial industrial on location, in-studio or on location. 20 years experience in photography and 10 years experience in digital imaging and digital video services.

F

TOM FOLEY PHOTOGRAPHY   612-922-8151
4100 Washburn Avenue South   Minneapolis 55410
FAX: 612-624-6369
CONTACT: Tom Foley
E-MAIL: tfoley@mailbox.mail.umn.edu
WWW: fotogod.com
SERVICES: Headshots of models, actors, musicians, writers, authors, business people. Portraits of individuals or groups seeking to promote themselves. "Promotional portraiture."

LIZA FOURRE PHOTOGRAHICS   612-825-0747
4758 Lyndale Avenue   Minneapolis 55409
FAX: 612-825-6637
CONTACT: Liza Fourre
E-MAIL: fourre@artguat.org
WWW: artguat.org
CAPABILITIES: Corporate collateral and editorial illustration.
SPECIALTIES: Environmental portraiture. On location half year in Guatemala.

Photographers - Advertising / 401

FOX STUDIO LTD   612-340-0254
420 North Fifth Street #860   Minneapolis 55401
FAX: 612-340-1576
CONTACT: Patrick Fox, Rod Komis, Andrew Kamin
E-MAIL: info@foxstudio.com
WWW: foxstudio.com
SERVICES: Location, studio, color and B&W. All formats and digital photography.
CAPABILITIES: Advertising, product photography. Large sets and annual report photography.

JANA FREIBAND PHOTOGRAPHY   612-928-9104
4916 Newton Avenue South   Minneapolis 55409
PAGER: 612-680-0153
E-MAIL: jmtband@bitstream.net
CAPABILITIES: Location and studio, lifestyle, people, landscape.
SPECIALTIES: Handcoloring of black and white imagery, fine arts application of illustrative photography for advertising, corporate and editorial: still photography for video, film, events and commercial. Fine arts stock imagery available.
CONTACT: Jana Freiband

G

GEHLHAR PHOTOGRAPHY   612-808-9695
11204 19th Avenue South   Minneapolis 55337
FAX: 612-808-9655
CONTACT: Glenn Gehlhar
E-MAIL: ggehlhar@aol.com
SERVICES: We do gorgeous still-life and product photography with beautiful lighting for advertisements and catalogs.
CAPABILITIES: We use all formats in cameras and digital photography available.

GRAHAM BROWN PHOTOGRAPHY   612-332-3905
420 North 5th Street #100   Minneapolis 55401
FAX: 612-332-2247
CONTACT: Emily Kosokar
E-MAIL: graham@photograham.com
WWW: photograham.com
SERVICES: 3,500 sq. ft. studio, fully equipped kitchen, large prop room, full digital capabilities, 35mm to 8 x 10.
SPECIALTIES: Food, product, still life.
PRESIDENT/CEO/OWNER: Graham Brown

CHRIS GRAJCZYK PHOTOGRAPHY   612-378-0078
77 13th Avenue NE #202   Minneapolis 55413
FAX: 612-378-2168
CONTACT: Chris Grajczyk
E-MAIL: cgreyart@mm.com

402 / Photographers - Advertising

SERVICES: Full service studio, all formats. Specialties include people, fashion, health and beauty, portrait, product and special effects. Experienced digital retoucher and film prep. Traditional darkroom technician on staff. Stock represented by age Fotostock, Barcelona. Complimentary food and beverages for all clients.

H

MIKE HABERMANN PHOTOGRAPHY, INC.   612-338-4696
700 Washington Avenue North   Minneapolis 55401
FAX: 612-332-7416
CONTACT: Mike Habermann
E-MAIL: mike@thestudio-mpls.com
WWW: thestudio-mpls.com
SERVICES: Studio and location photography, all formats.
CAPABILITIES: People, kids, advertising, corporate and editorial.

TODD HAFERMANN PHOTOGRAPHY   612-332-5112
700 Washington Avenue North #401   Minneapolis 55401
FAX: 612-332-7416
E-MAIL: todd@thestudio-mpls.com
WWW: thestudio-mpls.com
SERVICES: Product photography with beautifully detailed lighting.
PRESIDENT/CEO/OWNER: Todd Hafermann

HALSEY CREATIVE SERVICES, INC.   952-898-4564
213 Crestridge Drive   Burnsville 55337
FAX: 952-898-4564
CONTACT: Daniel Halsey
E-MAIL: dan@halsey1.com
WWW: halsey1.com
SERVICES: Full service photography and imaging. Film scanning, retouching and CD-ROM delivery. Long term corporate and industrial resource for concepts, design, photography, formatting and distribution archiving.
CAPABILITIES: Food photography for print, packaging, outdoor board, and tradeshow exhibits. Location studio equipment trailer. Prototype rendering and retouching. Corporate style and image continuity. 20 years experience. 75% of our client base have been using our services for 5 - 16 years.
CURRENT/RECENT CLIENTS/PROJECTS: National and International Food packaging clients; Exhibit murals 11 x 16 feet; on site product shoots, application shoots, and market targeted visuals.
PRESIDENT/CEO/OWNER: Daniel Halsey

LARS HANSEN PHOTOGRAPHY   612-332-5112
700 North Washington Avenue #401   Minneapolis 55401
CONTACT: Lars Hansen
E-MAIL: lars@thestudio-mpls.com
WWW: thestudio-mpls.com
SERVICES: Advertising photography and product illustration; studio and location.

Photographers - Advertising / 403

CAPABILITIES: Product portraiture; large format in studio.
PRESIDENT/CEO/OWNER: Lars Hansen

GRETCHEN HARRIS & ASSOCIATES
5230 13th Avenue South
612-822-0650
Minneapolis 55417
FAX: 612-822-0358
CONTACT: Gretchen Harris
E-MAIL: gretchenharris@gretchenharris-assoc.com
WWW: gretchenharris-assoc.com
SERVICES: Representation for photography & illustration services for commercial, editorial, advertising, design, food and packaging. Photographers: Graham Brown & Russell Brannon. Illustrators: Matthew Coffin - handlettering; Ken Jacobsen - pen and ink, digital; John Kleber - mixed media, pen and ink, digital; Eric Mueller - digital; Jody Winger - Pen and ink, digital; Jane Mjolsness - pastel; Mary Worcester - oil and watercolor.

SUE HARTLEY PHOTO
8832 7th Avenue North
763-546-9190
Golden Valley 55427
FAX: 763-546-9464
SERVICES: 35mm to 8 x 10 color and B/W, kitchen facilities. Studio and location photography creatively lit using daylight, stroke and/or tungsten lighting.
CAPABILITIES/SPECIALTIES: Photo illustration; catalogs; brochures; still life; garden scapes and Christmas (any time of the year).
PRESIDENT/CEO/OWNER: Sue Hartley
CONTACT: Sue or Bob

BRIAN SCOTT HOLMAN
420 North 5th Street #460
612-337-0300
Minneapolis 55401
FAX: 612-337-0696
CONTACT: Brian Holman
E-MAIL: bshphotog@holman.net
SERVICES: Lifestyles/portrait/location photography. B & W and color.
CURRENT/RECENT CLIENTS/PROJECTS: Northwest Airlines; EMB; Dayton Hudson; Target Stores; Aveda; Mpls/St. Paul Magazine; ADC Telecommunications.

LINDA HUHN & RICHARD JOHNSON PHOTOGRAPHY
2553 Dupont Avenue South
612-374-1435
Minneapolis 55405
CONTACT: Linda Huhn or Richard Johnson
E-MAIL: rjohnsonphoto@uswest.net
ALTERNATE PHONE: 612-599-0293
SERVICES: Corporate and event photography, including annual report, newsletter, and brochure photos as well as full coverage of conventions, trade shows and company celebrations. Environmental portraiture, large group shots, golf tournaments.
CAPABILITIES: We are both experienced in photojournalistic/documentary style, 35mm and medium format capability.
CURRENT/RECENT CLIENTS/PROJECTS: Cover of Minnesota Meetings & Events, Fall 1999.
PRESIDENT/CEO/OWNER: Linda Huhn or Richard Johnson

404 / Photographers - Advertising

HUMMEL PHOTOGRAPHY 507-645-0148
10625 First Timberlane Drive Northfield 55057
E-MAIL: hummel@rconnect.com
SERVICES: People/location for corporate and advertising clients.
CAPABILITIES/SPECIALTIES: 2 1/4, color, location.
PRESIDENT/CEO/OWNER: Danny Hummel

I

IMAGE GROUP 612-672-9181
529 South 7th Street #550 Minneapolis 55415
FAX: 612-672-9464
CONTACT: Gary Cook
E-MAIL: imagegc@bitstream.net
CAPABILITIES: Advertising illustration, product, fashion, editorial, travel, unique views of people and things.
SPECIALTIES: 35mm - 4 x 5 studio and location

IMAGE ONE STUDIOS 612-551-1067
12896 Highway 55 Minneapolis 55441
FAX: 612-551-1068
CONTACT: Becky Kocemba
E-MAIL: becky@imageonestudios.com
WWW: imageonestudios.com
SERVICES: Full-service commercial photography. 7,500 sq. ft. drive-in studio, 25' x 30' infinity cove, 10' x 20' light bank, fully equipped kitchen, dressing room, client lounge, conference room, set construction, large inventory of backgrounds, sets and props. Conventional as well as state-of-the-art digital photography.

J

SCOTT JACOBSON STUDIO, INC. 763-533-1413
9411 Science Center Drive Minneapolis 55428
FAX: 763-533-1630
CONTACT: Jennifer Dissell
E-MAIL: scott@scottjacobsonstudio.com
WWW: scottjacobsonstudio.com
SERVICES: Studio and location photography and video production. All formats and digital imaging. 5,000 square feet of space with infinity cove, drive-in door, conference room, full kitchen and dressing room.
CAPABILITIES: Product photography for advertising illustration, catalog, brochures; table top to room set. Production for videos.
PRESIDENT/CEO/OWNER: Scott Jacobson

Photographers - Advertising / 405

JG STUDIOS
1500 Jackson Street NE #431
FAX: 612-788-2211
CONTACT: James Gross or Photo Rep, Matt Krieger, Optic Nirvana, 612-827-5539
E-MAIL: jgstudios@mindspring.com
WWW: jgstudios.com
CAPABILITIES: Digital and conventional commercial photography, concept through completion for any size project.
SPECIALTIES: Digital shooting and creative lighting using quartz lights and "painting with light" techniques.

612-788-8830
Minneapolis 55413

CURTIS JOHNSON & ASSOCIATES
400 First Avenue North #752
FAX: 612-630-1035
CONTACT: Curtis Johnson
E-MAIL: cjphoto@bitstream.net
WWW: curtisjohnsonphoto.com
CAPABILITIES: Advertising, photography, still life, people, sets and product.

612-630-1032
Minneapolis 55401

JEFF JOHNSON PHOTOGRAPHY
529 South Seventh Street #698
FAX: 612-339-6717
CONTACT: Jeff Johnson or Robin Ogden, 612-925-4174
E-MAIL: jjphoto2mninter.net
WWW: mninter.net/jjphoto/index.html
SERVICES: Advertising and editorial photography. Covering all aspects of assignment photography.
CAPABILITIES: Managing all photography formats. 8 x 10, 4 x 5, medium and 35mm. 2000 sq. ft., studio with available light in downtown Minneapolis. Location and on site availabilities. Extensive experience in fashion, people, portraiture and artistic imagery. Black and white, color. Polaroid manipulations, and alternative processes for advertising, corporate and editorial assignments, national and international travel experience.
CURRENT/RECENT CLIENTS/PROJECTS: Nordstrom; Target; Musicland; Lifetime Fitness; Shades Optical; Sampo Pensions Finland; Campbell Mithun Esty; MSP Communications; Northwest Airlines; Carmichael Lynch; Olson & Company; Tiger Oak Publications; Select Comfort.
PRESIDENT/CEO/OWNER: Jeff Johnson

612-339-7929
Minneapolis 55415

K

KEELER PHOTOGRAPHY
5339 Beachside Drive
FAX: 952-912-0976
CONTACT: Chuck Keeler
E-MAIL: chuck@chuckkeelerphoto.com
WWW: chuckkeelerphoto.com
CAPABILITIES: Location photography.
SPECIALTIES: People.

952-804-3919
Minnetonka 55343

406 / Photographers - Advertising

KENDALL PHOTOGRAPHS 612-321-0575
616 S. Third Street, Second Floor Minneapolis 55415
CONTACT: Earl at 612-321-0575 or KLP at 612-332-5635
E-MAIL: earl@kendallphotographs.com
WWW: kendallphotographs.com
SPECIALTIES: Advertising photography.

KINGSBURY STUDIOS 505-425-3800
1803 Plaza Las Vegas 87701
FAX: 505-425-1700
CONTACT: Andrew Kingsbury
E-MAIL: kingcong@usurf.com
SERVICES: Advertising photography to the trade - all formats - studio my specialty. Also location, prop building, E-6 processing in-house.
CAPABILITIES: 25 years studio, prop building.
CURRENT/RECENT CLIENTS/PROJECTS: Dow Elanco, Pumitol, Labor Ready, Uniroyal, Bandag, Optimum, First Rate, Scorpion, Spintor, Hornet, Ericcson, New Mexico Film Board

BRUCE KLUCKHOHN 612-929-6010
4125 Chowen Avenue South Minneapolis 55410
FAX: 612-929-4230
CONTACT: Bruce Kluckhohn
E-MAIL: bruce@bruceckphoto.com
WWW: brucekphoto.com
SERVICES: People on location photography. Environmental portraits, events, creative portraits, places, corporate, editorial color and B/W.
CAPABILITIES: Location, creating lighting, using mixed lighting, 35mm, 2 1/4 formats.
CURRENT/RECENT CLIENTS/PROJECTS: Martin Williams; Dayton's; Sports Illustrated; Business Week; MN Wild; St. Paul Chamber Orchestra; Tim Magazine; Design Guys; People Magazine.

KNUTSON PHOTOGRAPHY, INC. 612-870-7376
1807 Elliot Avenue South Minneapolis 55404
FAX: 612-871-6614
CONTACT: Doug Knutson
E-MAIL: knutsonphoto@uswest.net
SERVICES: Photographic illustration of people for articles, ads, and annuals.
CAPABILITIES: Children, black & white, location, executives and international.
CURRENT/RECENT CLIENTS/PROJECTS: Bozell Kamstra; Carmichael Lynch; Eaton Design; Think Design; Fortune; Forbes; Business Week.

ROD KOMIS PHOTOGRAPHY 612-340-0254
420 North Fifth Street #860 Minneapolis 55401
FAX: 612-340-1576
CONTACT: Rod Komis, Andrew Kamin
E-MAIL: info@rodkomis.com
WWW: rodkomis.com
SERVICES: Location and studio still life photography in all formats.

Photographers - Advertising / 407

CAPABILITIES: Specialize in food and product photography. Large natural light studio with full kitchen, conference room, and full-time producer.
PRESIDENT/CEO/OWNER: Rod Komis

KRIVIT PHOTOGRAPHY   651-646-2021
2412 Valentine Avenue   St. Paul 55108
CONTACT: Sue Krivit
CAPABILITIES: Studio photography for advertising, editorial and corporate clients. Comfortable 6,000 square foot studio with drive-in access and many extras. Close to both downtown and freeways. Easy parking. All camera formats, color and B&W.
PRESIDENT/CEO/OWNER: Mike Krivit, Photographer; Sue Krivit, Studio Manager

L

L A STUDIOS, INC.   612-944-6152
7625 Golden Triangle Drive   Eden Prairie 55344
FAX: 612-829-1728
CONTACT: Allen Brown, Studio Manager
E-MAIL: lastudio@isd.net
WWW: lastudio.com
SERVICES: Full service commercial photography. Digital and conventional in studio or on location. 8,000 sq. ft., 35 ft. cove, set building and design, kitchen.
CAPABILITIES: Product, industrial, e-commerce, food and special effects. Digital location, watercraft/recreation.
PRESIDENT/CEO/OWNER: Phil Leisenheimer, Patti Alt

ART LARSON PHOTOGRAPHY   612-789-8691
3307 Benjamin Street NE   Minneapolis 55418
CONTACT: Artie Larson
SERVICES: Photography all formats. Location and studio.

LBF, INC.   952-922-9522
3625 Hampshire Avenue South   Minneapolis 55426
FAX: 952-922-1024
CONTACT: Valeri Lennon
E-MAIL: lbf@lbfphoto.com
CAPABILITIES: Advertising photography - 35mm to 8 x 10; large kitchen facility, drive-in and dock doors, in-house color and B&W processing.
SPECIALTIES: Photography advertising illustration, food, products, people and location.
PHOTOGRAPHERS: Dave Bausman, Sean Fitzgerald, Phil Bode

LIGHTNING IN A JAR STUDIOS   952-942-7842
6840 Washington Avenue South   Eden Prairie 55344
CONTACT: Howard Lambert
CAPABILITIES: Full-service advertising studio.

408 / Photographers - Advertising

SPECIALTIES: Classic sporting still life for books, calendars and magazines.

JOHN LINN PHOTOGRAPHY   612-533-2724
3812 Regent Avenue North   Minneapolis 55422
FAX: 612-533-2725
CONTACT: John Linn
E-MAIL: john@johnlinnphotography.com
WWW: johnlinnphotography.com
SERVICES: Advertising, editorial and corporate photography projects.
SPECIALTIES: Sports and adventure photography, products in use or in motion, environmental portraiture and lifestyle, and alternative techniques and processor including tilt focus, infrared, x-process, hand coloring and digital manipulation.

STUART LORENZ PHOTOGRAPHIC DESIGN STUDIO   612-789-6099
2931 Central Avenue NE   Minneapolis 55418
FAX: 612-789-6098
CONTACT: Stuart Lorenz
E-MAIL: info@lightshadows.com
WWW: lightshadows.com
TOLL FREE: 1-800-728-5113
SERVICES: Established in 1984. A full-service advertising photography studio providing small and large project support. Technically flawless photography in all formats for interior, exterior, product, image manipulation, documentation and digital post production services. Comprehensive multi-vendor estimates for projects.
CAPABILITIES: Full-service on location support with production trucks and 18KW Generator. Digital capture formats 35mm through 4x5. In-house cross platform CD-ROM mastering and Web Publishing.
PRESIDENT/CEO/OWNER: Stuart Lorenz

PAUL LUNDQUIST PHOTOGRAPHY   612-379-2844
616 SE 6th Street   Minneapolis 55414
FAX: 612-379-2845
CONTACT: Paul Lundquist
SERVICES: Advertising and Editorial Photography. 35 mm to 8 x 10 and Mac based digital. Delivering digital files, web images, film and silver prints. B/W & Color. Full kitchen. Creating and collaborating in-studio and location.
CAPABILITIES: Food, people, and product. Creative lighting and composition for effective photographic communication.
PRESIDENT/CEO/OWNER: Paul Lundquist

M

MARKERT PHOTOGRAPHY   612-338-6727
1201 Currie Avenue   Minneapolis 55403
FAX: 612-338-6383
CONTACT: Jeanette Moss

Photographers - Advertising / 409

E-MAIL: markertphoto.com
WWW: markertphoto.com
SERVICES: 12,000 square foot studio in a great downtown location, with two client rooms, free off-street parking and a full-time studio manager.
CAPABILITIES: Specializing in people and product in environmental settings.

JOHN MARKOVICH PHOTOGRAPHY — 612-938-6716
3325 Utah Avenue South — Minneapolis 55426
FAX: 612-933-5726
CONTACT: John Markovich
E-MAIL: john@jmphoto.com
WWW: jmphoto.com
SERVICES: Photography with 35mm, 120mm, 4 x 5 and digital event imaging.
SPECIALTIES: Meetings and special events.
CURRENT/RECENT CLIENTS/PROJECTS: Martin Bastian; Jack Morton; Media Loft; Carlson Company; Nordstroms.

MARVY! — 952-474-1923
5810 Salisbury Avenue — Minnetonka 55345
FAX: 952-474-0552
CAPABILITIES: Photographic illustration, advertising and food.
PRESIDENT/CEO/OWNER: Jim Marvy

ALAN MATHIOWETZ PHOTOGRAPHY — 952-945-0150
219 North Second Street — Minneapolis 55401
FAX: 612-288-0630
CONTACT: Alan Mathiowetz
E-MAIL: ampfotog@aol.com
WWW: alanmathiowetz.com
SERVICES: Advertising, photo illustration, people, product, annual reports and corporate work.
CAPABILITIES: Studio or location, all formats.

SANDY MAY PHOTOGRAPHY — 612-379-3318
201 North Second Street — Minneapolis 55401
FAX: 612-377-8916
CONTACT: Sandy May
CAPABILITIES: Location or studio, all formats.
SPECIALTIES: Illustrative photography for advertising and editorial, specializing in people, fashion, annual reports. Corporate image, portraiture, travel.

MCMAHON STUDIO PHOTOGRAPHY — 612-339-9709
900 Third Street South — Minneapolis 55415
FAX: 612-339-1774
CONTACT: David McMahon
E-MAIL: dmcmahon@bitstream.net
CAPABILITIES: We shoot both still life and real life in the studio or on location. 8 x 10 to 35mm. Digital capture and digital retouching. Newly renovated studio in the historic Bingham Roller Building across the street from the Metrodome.

410 / Photographers - Advertising

SPECIALTIES: Food and beverage for advertising and restaurants. Product and still life illustrations for advertising catalog. People, portraits and children for retail and advertising use.
CURRENT/RECENT CLIENTS/PROJECTS: Minneapolis Community Development Agency, Famous Dave's of America, Ali Mac! Children's Clothing, Rainforest Café, MN Monthly Magazine, Harvest Ventures, Arctic Air Refrigerators, Schwebel Goetz and Sieben Attorneys, Target Stores, Malt-O-Meal

N

PAUL NELSON PHOTOGRAPHY 612-623-7696
3338 University Avenue SE #370 Minneapolis 55414
FAX: 612-623-9204
CONTACT: Paul Nelson
E-MAIL: pauln@visi.com
WWW: paulnelsonphoto.com
CAPABILITIES: Product and people photography.
CURRENT/RECENT CLIENTS/PROJECTS: Drugstore.com, Target Stores, Wilson's Leather Outlet, Select Comfort

JOHN NOLTNER PHOTOGRAPHY 651-966-9904
10425 Washburn Avenue South Minneapolis 55431
FAX: 612-887-0670
E-MAIL: john@noltner.com
WWW: noltner.com
SERVICES: Specializing in images of people for editorial, corporate and advertising clients, working in studio or on location around the world.
PRESIDENT/CEO/OWNER: John Noltner

PAUL NYLIS PHOTOGRAPHY 612-333-2747
529 South Seventh Street #498 Minneapolis 55415
FAX: 612-333-4055
CONTACT: Paul Nylis
E-MAIL: najlis@hutman.net
SERVICES: All formats, studio and location.
CAPABILITIES: Table top, food, people, location

O

OLAUSEN PHOTOGRAPHY 612-332-5009
213 North Washington Avenue Minneapolis 55401
FAX: 612-342-0000
CONTACT: Judy Olausen
SERVICES: People and corporate.

P

PARKER PHOTOGRAPHIC
1500 Jackson Street NE
612-788-2633
Minneapolis 55413
FAX: 612-788-2456
CONTACT: Laura Justus
E-MAIL: parkphoto@earthlink.net
SERVICES: Shooting all film formats, studio or location. Large 6,000 sq. ft. studio accommodates room sets or multiple bays. Studio also features roomy stylist's kitchen, prop and merchandise storage.
CAPABILITIES: Food, tabletop, produce as well as architectural, room sets and locations, Appetite appeal and product ambience a specialty. Photography for advertising, catalogs, consumer packaging, cookbooks, recipe booklets, editorial.
PRESIDENT/CEO/OWNER: Mike Parker

REBECCA PAVLENKO PHOTOGRAPHY
500 North Robert Street #306
651-222-0436
St. Paul 55101
CONTACT: Rebecca Pavlenko
E-MAIL: pavlenko@bitstream.net
WWW: rebeccapavlenko.com
SERVICES: Portraits, headshots, PR photos, CD covers, theater, publicity creative product and concept and editorial. Japanese gardens a personal specialty.
CURRENT/RECENT CLIENTS/PROJECTS: Black and white, handcoloring, color, polaroid tranfers and Chinese tea ceremonies.
PRESIDENT/CEO/OWNER: Relocation Today, Guthrie Theatre; Card line of Japanese Gardens for Artists to watch card company, Book jacket for sign language poetry guide, CD covers, exhibitions for theater productions.

GLENN PETERSON, INC.
401 North Third Street
612-332-2595
Minneapolis 55401
CONTACT: Assunta (Susan) Bagnoli
SERVICES: 35mm to 8 x 10. 3,000 sq. ft. studio. Fully equipped photo kitchen adjacent to but separate from studio. Client office.
SPECIALTIES: Photographic illustration with food or product; tabletop to large sets. Food stylist, food props, prop styling and set building available. Stock library available.
PRESIDENT/CEO/OWNER: Assunta (Susan) Bagnoli

PETTERS LEWMAN STUDIO
701 North Third Street
612-338-0886
Minneapolis 55401
FAX: 612-338-0769
CONTACT: Fred Petters, Photographer/Dana Lewman, Studio Manager/Producer
E-MAIL: fpetters@visi.com or dlewman@visi.com
SERVICES: Photo illustration for advertising and editorial purposes. Both studio and location.
CAPABILITIES: Experienced, efficient and personable photography and production team.
PRESIDENT/CEO/OWNER: Fred Petters/Dana Lewman

412 / Photographers - Advertising

POPULAR FRONT STUDIO, INC.   612-362-0900
605 Central Avenue NE   Minneapolis 55414
FAX: 612-362-0999
CONTACT: Sarah Bratnober
E-MAIL: studio@popularfront.com
WWW: popularfront.com
SERVICES: 6500 sq. ft. facility. 3500 sq. ft. ground level studio with drive-in photo bay, full kitchen, dressing room and natural light. With 10 years of experience in digital production and 5 years of experience in digital photography. Offering both film and filmless photography. Print capabilities include: photography, photo illustration, retouching; visual special effects and prepress. Motion capabilities include website design and programming, multimedia; video production and post, and motion special effects.
CURRENT/RECENT CLIENTS/PROJECTS: Amerimark, Beautopia International Haircare, Blu Dot Design & Manufacturing, Conwed Plastics, Fallon McElligott, Imation Corporation, Jasc Software, KTCA Television, Life Time Fitness, Malt-O-Meal Company, Microsoft Sidewalk, PBS, Starkey Laboratories, TriSense Software, Ltd., WAM!NET, William Mitchell College of Law.
PRESIDENT/CEO/OWNER: Michael Keefe, Laurence Bricker

POSL PHOTOGRAPHY, INC.   612-338-0257
2601 East Franklin Avenue   Minneapolis 55406
FAX: 612-338-6102
CONTACT: John Posl
E-MAIL: poslphoto@aol.com
CAPABILITIES: Cameras in all formats. 6,000 square foot studio with drive-in dock. Free easy parking. Conference and work areas for clients with fax, phone and computer. Advertising and corporate photography, studio and location. People illustration and product photography. A lot of experience with medical products and jewelry projects.

R

REACTION STUDIOS   612-337-0242
219 North 2nd Street #306   Minneapolis 55401
FAX: 612-337-0840
CONTACT: Tom J. Kanthak
E-MAIL: reaction@usinternet.com
SERVICES: Commercial photography, innovative thinking and creative solutions for people, product and interiors.
CAPABILITIES: All formats, traditional, digital, color and black & white, studio and location.

RICH RYAN PHOTOGRAPHY   612-251-6561
4928 York Avenue South   Minneapolis 55410
FAX: 952-915-1530
CONTACT: Rich Ryan
E-MAIL: richryan@worldnet.att.net
WWW: home.att.net/~richryan

Photographers - Advertising / 413

SERVICES: Panoramas, editorial, people, portrait, action. I can put people at ease and make them look great. I do this both on location and in the studio with extreme professionalism.
CAPABILITIES: I photograph 360 degrees panoramas. This way of seeing works as a web product, but have found it equally intriguing in print form. On the web Virtual Reality (VR) puts you in a 360 degree photographic environment. You can interact with each scene by panning 360 degrees as well as zooming in and out. VR's can be linked together with "hotspots" or linked to a floor plan giving one the ability to "walk" through an environment and feel what it will be like to be there. Examples are available at my website: http://home.att.net/~qtvr. I create in many formats both vertically and horizontally including 35mm, medium format, swing lens, digital.
CURRENT/RECENT CLIENTS/PROJECTS: Minnesota Historical Society, Ventures Magazine, Minneapolis St. Paul Magazine, City Pages, Compass, Kodak, Sala Architects, MCDA, NRP, OneBigTable.com and my big sister.

S

PETER SCHMIDT PHOTOGRAPHY 612-378-9454
411 East Hennepin Minneapolis 55414
FAX: 612-623-7654
CONTACT: Peter Schmidt
SERVICES: Commercial photography, studio and location.
CAPABILITIES: Table top, people, food, and location.

STEVE SCHNEIDER/PHOTOGRAPHY 651-644-6588
2242 University Avenue #333 St. Paul 55114
FAX: 651-645-8263
CONTACT: Steve Schneider
SERVICES: 35mm plus 2 - 1/4 photography in color and black and white. Location and studio settings. Editorial and commercial applications.
CAPABILITIES: Photographs of real people in real settings, the office, the factory, the classroom, the boardroom; on the street, or in the woods. I make photographs; I do not take them!
CURRENT/RECENT CLIENTS/PROJECTS: Columbia University; University of Minnesota Dental School; Children's Cancer Research Fund; Famous Dave's of America, Luther Seminary; VOA (Volunteers of America).
PRESIDENT/CEO/OWNER: Steve Schneider

JOEL SCHNELL PHOTOGRAPHER 612-930-0018
1310 Oxford Street Hopkins 55343
FAX: 612-930-3136
CONTACT: Joel Schnell
E-MAIL: joel@schnellphoto.com
WWW: schnellphoto.com

PAUL SHAMBROOM, PHOTOGRAPHER 612-922-3224
3825 Washburn Avenue Minneapolis 55410
CONTACT: Paul Shambroom
E-MAIL: shambroom@aol.com

414 / Photographers - Advertising

SERVICES: People, technology, challenging locations. Distinctive image making for advertising, corporate, and editorial clients. Fine art photographs exhibited and collected by major museums.
CURRENT/RECENT CLIENTS/PROJECTS: Apple Computer; Silicon Graphics; Cray Research; New York Times Magazine; 3M; Medtronic; General Mills; Northwest Airlines; Time; Newsweek; Forbes.

JOEL SHEAGREN PHOTOGRAPHY — 888-945-3474
2303 NE Kennedy Street #400 — Minneapolis 55413
FAX: 612-623-4637
CONTACT: Kim Sheagren
E-MAIL: joel@ejoel.com or kim@ejoel.com
SERVICES: Specializes in photography for advertising, on location of people and products. Provide production services for large and small productions. In-house producer available.
CAPABILITIES: Areas of expertise include lifestyle, recreation, labor/industry and marine/transportation.
CURRENT/RECENT CLIENTS/PROJECTS: Bombardier (Skidoo), DELKALB, Allstate Motorcycle Insurance, Hurd Windows, Landscape Structures, Inc., Minnesota Zoo, Miracle Ear, Red Wing Shoe Co. (Irish Setter, Red Wing and Worxbrands), Voyager Outward Bound, Winnebago Industries, Mercruiser, Hogar de Ninos Emmanuel
PRESIDENT/CEO/OWNER: Joel Sheagren

KELLY SHIELDS PHOTOGRAPHY — 612-378-9454
411 East Hennepin — Minneapolis 55414
FAX: 612-623-7654
CONTACT: Kelly Shields
SERVICES: Commercial photography, studio and location.
CAPABILITIES: Table top, people, food, and location.

SINKLER PHOTOGRAPHY — 612-343-0325
420 North 5th Street #516 — Minneapolis 55401
FAX: 612-373-0908
CONTACT: Paul Sinkler
E-MAIL: paul@sinklerphoto.com
WWW: sinklerphoto.com
SERVICES: Creative photography for ad agencies, design firms and corporations. Products and people. Digital and conventional photography.
CAPABILITIES: Digital capture: Leaf contare. Extensive photoshop experience.

SAL SKOG PHOTOGRAPHY — 612-332-3502
420 North 5th Street #707 — Minneapolis 55401
FAX: 612-332-0352
CONTACT: Sally Skog
E-MAIL: sal@northwired.com
SERVICES: Outstanding environmental portraiture and photojournalism for annual reports, advertising and editorial.
CAPABILITIES: 2 - 1/4 and 35 mm, B & W and color. Studio or location.
CURRENT/RECENT CLIENTS/PROJECTS: US Bank; Medtronic; Northwest Airlines; Health Partners; Children's Theatre Co.; MSI; Ceridan; Regions Hospital; Carleton College; Entrepreneur; ComputerWorld; Woman's Day, Inc.; Smithsonian.

Photographers - Advertising / 415

RICHARD HAMILTON SMITH PHOTOGRAPHY 218-732-2600
17456 Half Moon Road Park Rapids 56470
FAX: 218-732-2626
CONTACT: Richard Smith
E-MAIL: studio@richardhamiltonsmith.com
WWW: richardhamiltonsmith.com
SERVICES: Advertising, corporate and editorial location photography - all formats including panoramic.
CAPABILITIES: Aerial, agriculture, landscape, nature, conceptual, outdoor recreation, extensive stock library.
PRESIDENT/CEO/OWNER: Richard Hamilton Smith

STAFFORD PHOTOGRAPHY 612-333-2122
1018 N 5th Street Minneapolis 55411
CONTACT: Mary Danna
E-MAIL: joe@staffordphoto.com
WWW: staffordphoto.com
SERVICES: Photo illustration from table top to large sets. All formats. B&W and color.
CAPABILITIES: Digital photography and hi-end composites specializing in food and product.
PRESIDENT/CEO/OWNER: Joe Stafford

STANISLAW PHOTOGRAPHY 612-370-1363
510 First Avenue North #311 Minneapolis 55403
FAX: 612-370-9004
CONTACT: James Stanislaw
E-MAIL: stanis@bitstream.net
SERVICES: Full service studio.
CAPABILITIES: Studio and location, all formats.
SPECIALTIES: Retail advertising photography.
PRESIDENT/CEO/OWNER: James Stanislaw

STEVEN LINDER PHOTO 952-884-8134
10824 River Terrace Drive Bloomington 55431
FAX: 952-884-9876
CONTACT: Steven Linder
E-MAIL: slinder@pioneerplanet.infi.net
WWW: linderphoto.com
CAPABILITIES: Stock photography, Aeriel photography, Commercial photography.

THOMAS STRAND STUDIO 612-333-4155
701 N. Third Street #208 Minneapolis 55401
FAX: 612-333-5444
CONTACT: Rebecca Strand
E-MAIL: rebecca@thomasstrand.com
WWW: thomasstrand.com
SERVICES: People, location work, annual reports, advertising.

CURRENT/RECENT CLIENTS/PROJECTS: The Nancekivell Group; Martin Williams; Colle & McVoy; Amgen; Yamamoto Moss; 3M; American Crystal Sugar; Larsen Design; National Dairy Council.
PRESIDENT/CEO/OWNER: Thomas Strand

MAKI STRUNC PHOTOGRAPHY, INC.   612-541-4722
6156 Olson Memorial Highway   Golden Valley 55422
FAX: 612-541-0958
CONTACT: Christine Reese
E-MAIL: makistrunc@aol.com
SERVICES: 11,000 sq. ft. of studio space comprised of three extensively equipped shooting areas, computer facilities, scanners, modems. State of the art kitchen, dressing rooms, conference facilities, 20 x 20 infinity cove, construction area with full shop, huge inventory of sets, walls, surfaces, flooring, props and unusual items from years of challenging projects. Production, casting, scouting, propping, styling and location services also available. Complete studio and location capabilities in all formats conventional and digital.

STUDIO   612-332-5009
213 N. Washington Avenue   Minneapolis 55401
FAX: 612-342-0000
CONTACT: Judy Olausen
SERVICES: Photo studio specializing in corporate/advertising people photography.

THE STUDIO CENTRAL, INC.   612-378-2511
309 Central Avenue SE   Minneapolis 55414
FAX: 612-378-1648
CONTACT: Bruce Nimmer
E-MAIL: info@studiocentral.com
SERVICES: Commercial photography; studio and location. Film formats 35mm, 2 1/4, 4 x 5, 8 x 10, and complete digital services. Two separate studio boys, each with its own adjacent, full-equipped kitchen; complete security for new product work; 6,700 sq. ft. facility; four full time photographers.
CAPABILITIES: Table top food and product; people, location and small sets. Photography for packaging, sales promotion, cookbooks and other publications, advertising, and corporate communications.
PRESIDENT/CEO/OWNER: Bruce Nimmer

STUDIO X   612-414-4645
2710 NE Sumner Street   Minneapolis 55413
FAX: 612-623-4810
CONTACT: Jon Morris
E-MAIL: jon@bigideas.com
SERVICES: Comprehensive commercial photography studio including traditional and digital photography and complete image manipulation capabilities.
CAPABILITIES: 2,500 sq. ft. studio; 4 x 5, 2 - 1/4 and 35 mm capability; Full dock access.

Photographers - Advertising / 417

T

THOEN & ASSOCIATES ADVERTISING PHOTOGRAPHY, INC. 952-938-2433
14940 Minnetonka Industrial Road Minnetonka 55345
FAX: 952-938-4157
CONTACT: Greg Thoen
SERVICES: Specializing in large and medium format photography. Extensive knowledge of electronic enhancement. 11,000 sq. ft. of clean and organized space. Full kitchen, 25' x 30' cove, and a 1,500 sq. ft. prop room. Deadlines and budgets are met with ease!
CAPABILITIES: Aerial, digital enhancement, food, illustrative, large sets.

U

ALVIS UPITIS PHOTOGRAPHY 612-374-9375
620 Morgan Avenue South Minneapolis 55415
FAX: 612-374-9389
CONTACT: Alvis
E-MAIL: auphoto@aol.com
WWW: irtualsourcebook.procolor.com
SERVICES: Shooting the people and places of industry for corporate and advertising clients. On location anywhere. Experience in medical, agriculture, clean rooms, heavy industry, editorial, environmental portraits, aerial, travel and Panoramas. Master black and white printer.

V

RON VAN ZEE PHOTOGRAPHY 651-439-2508
470 South 5th Street Bayport 55003
CONTACT: Ron Van Zee
SERVICES: "On location" industry, commercial, specialized, editorial, agriculture, country, rural, midwest, people, places, things, machines, magazine and book illustration, and brochure illustration.
CAPABILITIES: "On location" production truck with 25 foot high shooting platform, full lighting gear, studio equipment on wheels.

VISIONQUEST PHOTOGRAPHIC ARTS CENTER 651-644-1400
2370 Hendon Avenue St. Paul 55108
FAX: 651-644-8777
CONTACT: Doug or Janell
E-MAIL: beasley@bitstream.net
WWW: VQphoto.com

W

TAD WARE PHOTOGRAPHY   612-338-4686
716 North First Street   Minneapolis 55401
FAX: 612-337-5502
CONTACT: Rhonda Vicknair
CAPABILITIES: Medium and large format cameras providing digital and traditional photography. Four completely equipped kitchens, extensive prop room, studio space 8,000 square feet.
SPECIALTIES: Food, location, product.

WEBER PHOTOGRAPHY   612-581-2782
4431 Newton Avenue N   Minneapolis 55412
CONTACT: Paul Weber
SERVICES: Studio and location photography, product to people, table top to room size sets in small, medium and large formats, including digital.
CAPABILITIES: Table top, catalog.
PRESIDENT/CEO/OWNER: Paul Weber

WENTINK PHOTOGRAPHY   612-252-6797
718 Washington Avenue North #600   Minneapolis 55401
FAX: 612-252-6799
CONTACT: Ted Wentink
E-MAIL: wentinkphoto@uswest.net
SERVICES: Established studio and location photography for commercial usages.
CAPABILITIES: New 4500' studio, freight elevator, conference room.

WILLETTE MPLS PHOTOGRAPHY   612-338-6727
1201 Currie Avenue   Minneapolis 55403
FAX: 612-338-6383
CONTACT: Brady Willette
E-MAIL: willettempls.com
WWW: willettempls.com
SERVICES: Commercial photography. People and locations.

STEVE WOIT PHOTOGRAPHY   612-822-8619
6028 Kaymar Drive   Minneapolis 55436
FAX: 612-822-1013
CONTACT: Steve Woit
E-MAIL: steve@stevewoit.com
WWW: stevewoit.com
SERVICES: Creative location photography of people for corporate, advertising or editorial purposes.

WOLD PHOTOGRAPHY   612-813-1304
1009 Nicollet Avenue South, 3rd   Minneapolis 55403
1009 Nicollet Avenue South, 3rd Floor

CONTACT: Jayson Wold
E-MAIL: info@woldphoto.com
WWW: woldphoto.com
SERVICES: Specializing in people and products on location and in the studio.
CAPABILITIES: 35mm to 8 x 10. Studio location in the heart of downtown. Walking distance from most downtown agencies.

Z

ZEBRA PHOTOGRAPHY
406 East 48th Street Minneapolis 55409
FAX: 612-825-9243
CONTACT: Jerry O'Connor
E-MAIL: oconlib@usinternet.com
SERVICES: Conventional and digital photography; studio or location; all formats, industrial location and plant photography, Studio product photography, corporate portraiture. Computer color correction, retouching, montage, efx.
CAPABILITIES: High end digital photography. Design, layout, file formatting for print reproduction.
CURRENT/RECENT CLIENTS/PROJECTS: Manufacturing, medical, and catalogers.

BILL ZUEHLKE PHOTOGRAPHY 612-729-8998
1832 East 38th Street Minneapolis 55407
FAX: 612-729-9392
CONTACT: Bill Zuehlke
CAPABILITIES: 19 years experience

Photographers - Architectural

A

GREG. R ANDERSON 612-722-3848
3004 27th Avenue South Minneapolis 55406
CONTACT: Greg Anderson
CAPABILITIES: Product/Catalog, PR, Architectural. Full studio and location, digital ouput, Photoshop ready.
SPECIALTIES: Small product photography, industrial, in-plant photography.

D

STEVEN DAHLMAN PHOTOGRAPHY 612-627-9174
20 Second Street NE #803 Minneapolis 55413
FAX: 612-331-3676
CONTACT: Steven Dahlman
E-MAIL: steved@dcmsoft.com
WWW: dcmsoft.com/photo
SERVICES: Architectural, advertising, and industrial photography. Digital photo enhancement and restoration.
CAPABILITIES: Medium format and 35mm.

DROEGE PHOTOGRPAHY 612-276-0151
5030 Nokomis Avenue South Minneapolis 55417
CONTACT: Brian Droege
CAPABILITIES: 4 x 5, 2 - 1/4 and 35mm formats on location. Color and Black & White. In-house black & white lab for quick, custom turnaround.
SPECIALTIES: Architectural photography; interiors, exteriors and models.

G

SUSAN GILMORE PHOTOGRAPHER 763-545-4608
8415 Wesley Drive Minneapolis 55427
FAX: 763-545-2693
CONTACT: Rep/Jennifer Frost - 651-690-9631 or myself
E-MAIL: sqphoto@mninter.net
WWW: susangilmorephoto.com
SERVICES: Interior and architectural photography.

M

PETER MARCUS PHOTOGRAPHY 763-545-0051
7031 Glenwood Avenue Minneapolis 55427
CONTACT: Peter Marcus

Photographers - Architectural / 421

SERVICES: Commercial photography, brochures, annual reports, photojournalism, portraits, architectural, special events, advertising.
CAPABILITIES: 50 years of photographic experience including news and magazine work. All formats 35mm, 120 and 4 x 5 color and black & white. Location assignments and travel.

PAT MILLER PHOTOGRAPHY   651-426-5920
1645 Ridgewood Avenue   **White Bear Lake 55110**
FAX: 651-426-4087
CONTACT: Pat Miller
SERVICES: Photography.
CAPABILITIES: 35mm to 8 x 10. Studio and location, industrial, people, annual reports, product, architectural (interiors - exterior).

P

PARKER PHOTOGRAPHIC   612-788-2633
1500 Jackson Street NE   **Minneapolis 55413**
FAX: 612-788-2456
CONTACT: Laura Justus
E-MAIL: parkphoto@earthlink.net
SERVICES: Shooting all film formats, studio or location. Large 6,000 sq. ft. studio accommodates room sets or multiple bays. Studio also features roomy stylist's kitchen, prop and merchandise storage.
CAPABILITIES: Food, tabletop, produce as well as architectural, room sets and locations, Appetite appeal and product ambience a specialty. Photography for advertising, catalogs, consumer packaging, cookbooks, recipe booklets, editorial.
PRESIDENT/CEO/OWNER: Mike Parker

R

STEVE ROUCH PHOTO   651-644-2184
2184 Marshall Avenue   **St. Paul 55104**
CONTACT: Steve Rouch
E-MAIL: choicephoto.com
SERVICES: People photography, creative "art" photo.
CAPABILITIES: Master photographer, work chosen for display at Epcot Center Disney World.
CURRENT/RECENT CLIENTS/PROJECTS: Personal art photographs of Santa Fe, New York, New Orleans, Savannah. Infrared photos of ghost towns in Arizona. Work is about capturing color and texture of old walls, doorways and buildings.

S

SAARI & FORRAI PHOTOGRAPHY 763-780-3255
9752 Quincy Avenue NE Minneapolis 55434
FAX: 763-784-4588
CONTACT: Denes Saari
WWW: saariphoto.com
CAPABILITIES: On location, commercial photography. Art direction, in-house printing. 35mm, 4 x 5" format. Will travel. Since 1974.
SPECIALTIES: Architectural, interior, industrial, architectural product and aerial photography.
CURRENT/RECENT CLIENTS/PROJECTS: LHB Engineer and Architects, Inc., Walsh Bishop Facility Development and Consulting, Station Nineteen Architects, Inc., Benson Orth Associates Inc., Sawhill Custom Kitchens and Design, Inc., Wausau Window and Wall System, Una-Clad - Cooper Sales, Inc., HMS Host, Bethesda, MD. Landscape Architecture Magazine, Washington, DC, Smiley, Glotter, Nyberg Architects, Inc., Canac Kitchens, Ontario, CA. Recent Projects: American Express Bldg., Minneapolis, MN; LA Municipal Courthouse, Los Angeles, CA; Airport Stores, Dallas, TX; Children's Hospital, Minneapolis, MN; Life Fitness, Ramsey, MN; Several custom built kitchens and custom built homes; senior housing, churches and schools in MN, MI, OH, SD, NE, WI

RICH SILHA PHOTOGRAPHER 612-338-7172
420 North 5th Street #600 Minneapolis 55401
CONTACT: Rich Silha
SERVICES: Black and white, 20 x 24 large format photography. 6 x 17 panoramic photography, architecture, group events, portraits.
CAPABILITIES: Black and white. Contact printed 20 x 24, film originals on RC or fiber silver based materials. Custom black and white service with over 30 years experience in photography.

ALEX STEINBERG PHOTOGRAPHY 612-384-3404
5701 James Avenue South Minneapolis 55419
FAX: 612-928-9821
CONTACT: Alex Steinberg
SERVICES: Location photography. Architectural interiors and exteriors. People, product, fine art, editorial.
CAPABILITIES: 35mm - 4 x 5 formats. Color and B & W architectural interiors and exteriors. Creative imagery. Polaroid transfers. Fine art.
CURRENT/RECENT CLIENTS/PROJECTS: Aveda Institute; Midwest Home and Garden; Mark Kawell Architects; Thomas Whitcomb Architect; The Walsh Design Group; Cheryl Gardner Interior Design; MN Monthly; Minneapolis College of Art and Design; Design Works.
PRESIDENT/CEO/OWNER: Alex Steinberg

JERRY SWANSON PHOTOGRAPHY 800-985-1595
1490 McCarthy Road Eagan 55121
FAX: 651-452-4854
CONTACT: Jerry Swanson
WWW: swansonphoto.com

Photographers - Architectural / 423

SERVICES: Specializing in photography of architecture and interior spaces. Published locally and nationally. Professional service and excellent images. Photography includes: corporate interiors, education, health care, hospitality, industrial, landscape, residential, retail and aerial.
SPECIALTIES: 35mm, 2 1/4, 4 x 5 format, over 20 years experience.
CURRENT/RECENT CLIENTS/PROJECTS: Cartier, WA, Fitzgerald Hotel, Tunica, MS, Hubbard Broadcast Center, Mall of America, Winona State Library, Winona, MN, Homestead, Boulder City, NV, Midwest Wireless, Mankato, MN.

W

WIESE PHOTOGRAPHY AND DESIGN   **612-247-3346**
21176 Sawmill Road   **Jordan 55352**
FAX: 612-492-3839
CONTACT: John Wiese
E-MAIL: johnwmn@earthlink.net
WWW: wiesephoto.com
SERVICES: Full service studio and design capabilities that include desktop publishing, digital retouching and web design.
CAPABILITIES: Two decades experience in architectural and location assignments providing affordable persuasive multi-use images.
CURRENT/RECENT CLIENTS/PROJECTS: Wells Fargo; Scherer Brothers Lumber Company.

Photographers - Industrial

B

BANBURY STUDIOS   763-785-7944
717 97th Avenue NE   Minneapolis 55434
FAX: 763-785-7944
CONTACT: Dale Banbury
E-MAIL: jdban88@uswest.net
SERVICES: B&W, color negative and color transparency photography. Any format up to 8x10 size.
SPECIALTIES: Industrial-illustrative advertising in studio or on location.

BLUE MOON PRODUCTIONS, INC.   612-339-7175
212 3rd Avenue No. #390   Minneapolis 55401
FAX: 612-339-4272
CONTACT: Will Hommeyer
E-MAIL: mail@bluemoonpro.com
CAPABILITIES: 2 1/4" and 35mm photography formats for commercial, industrial and fine art applications. Studio/locations, color, B&W, and multi-image productions.
SPECIALTIES: International travel, annual reports, portraits and location photography.

GERALD BRIMACOMBE   952-941-5860
7112 Mark Terrace Drive   Edina 55439
E-MAIL: gbrim@usinternet.com
SERVICES: Travel and Scenic Photography.
CAPABILITIES/SPECIALTIES: Special world-wide assignments for major Cruise lines. Have extensive library of travel photographs for stock use.
CURRENT/RECENT CLIENTS/PROJECTS: Two book projects in progress, self publishing GicLee prints for fine art market.
CONTACT: Gerald Brimacombe

M

MAGOFFIN ASSOCIATES   952-941-0609
6340 Warren Avenue   Edina 55439
CONTACT: James "Jay" Magoffin
CAPABILITIES: Commercial, industrial location. Photo macrography. Color and black and white, 35 mm and 2 1/4. 20 years experience.
SPECIALTIES: Photography for corporate/industrial applications, legal books/publications, and fiber artists.

MITCHELL PHOTOGRAPHY   952-831-6917
7346 Ohms Lane   Edina 55439
SERVICES: Commercial - Industrial photography for catalogs and brochures. Advertising and public relations, studio or location.
PRESIDENT/CEO/OWNER: Guy R. Astell

CONTACT: Mark Ehlen

R

KELLY E. ROGERS PHOTOGRAPHY
1843 Monroe NE
PO Box 18637

612-310-6576
Minneapolis 55418

FAX: 612-781-4701
CONTACT: Kelly E. Rogers
E-MAIL: kellyr@ker-photos.com
SERVICES: I produce industrial photography with an editorial twist. This particular style is very applicable to corporate needs. I also offer "intriguing" portrait work - especially in black and white. Being used to "moving targets", I can provide unique model composites and interesting sports action that is very documentary.
CAPABILITIES: With eleven years experience, I am able to work with minimal art direction or supervision. I am very compliant with time and budgets. By specializing in mobile lighting, I am able to take drab or boring situations and make them appear very interesting on film or disc.
CURRENT/RECENT CLIENTS/PROJECTS: MSP Communications; 3M; US West
PRESIDENT/CEO/OWNER: Kelly E. Rogers

Photographers - News & PR

A

ABSOLUTE PHOTOGRAPHY   612-906-7626
15550 Michele Lane   Eden Prairie 55346
FAX: 612-906-1720
E-MAIL: airstar@uswest.net
SERVICES: Professional photography including: individual/group portraits, architectural, product, PR/event/location, corporate reports.
CAPABILITIES: 2 1/4", 35mm, 15 years experience, color B/W, slide, etc.
PRESIDENT/CEO/OWNER: Mark Kuller

H

SANDEE HORK PHOTOGRAPHY   952-922-6020
6400 York Avenue South, #309   Edina 55435
CONTACT: Sandee Hork
CAPABILITIES: Art documentary and editorial style photography in color or black and white. Event coverage and location shooting. Stock photos. Everything from galley quality prints and framed photos to hand made photographic products such as notecards, magnets and jewelry. Other art products available, such as candles. Custom orders welcome.
SPECIALTIES: Skyscapes, cityscapes and landscapes. Non-studio portraits. The moon. Written text.

W

DIANA WATTERS PHOTOGRAPHY   612-729-6079
3017 16th Avenue South   Minneapolis 55407
FAX: 612-729-6079
CONTACT: Diana Watters
CAPABILITIES: Editorial location portrait photography.

Photomechanical Services

T

TECHNICAL REPRODUCTIONS 612-331-3955
2101 Broadway Street NE Minneapolis 55413
FAX: 612-331-3958
CONTACT: Robert Kemmet
E-MAIL: triminn@aol.com
CAPABILITIES: Line negs, halftone negs, digital negs, large film positives, stats, diazo prints, inkjet display prints, print mounting and laminating.
SPECIALTIES: Services for printers, silk screeners, architects, engineers, land surveyors, trade show exhibitors and POP displayers.
PRESIDENT/CEO/OWNER: Robert L. Kemmet, P; Wallace Cornelius, Plant Manager

Point of Purchase

A

THE ART FARM ADVERTISING, INC. 651-293-0162
310 Sherman Street St. Paul 55102
FAX: 651-293-0204
CONTACT: Pat Salkowicz
E-MAIL: artfarm@bitstream.net
SERVICES: Full-service promotional marketing agency. Complete research and creative concepts, layout and design, copywriting, production, full execution and fulfillment. Design and production of display fixtures.
SPECIALTIES: Retail, trade and consumer promotions, Point-of-purchase signing and fixtures. Sales promotion and collateral materials, direct mail, corporate design, packaging and catalogs.

ART-TECH PRODUCTIONS, INC. 612-379-4840
1331 Water Street NE Minneapolis 55413
FAX: 612-379-1447
CONTACT: Nancy Teel
E-MAIL: fab@art-tech.net
WWW: art-tech.net
SERVICES: A design/production company that specializes in themed retail environments. Retail display fixtures, tradeshow booths, 3D signage and sculpture, theatrical props, theme painting, kiosks and showroom design.
CAPABILITIES: 20,000 sq. ft workshop area filled with the best crafts people in town. Will work with any client to design and produce a unique and distinctive product. All work is done on-site. We work on jobs both locally and nationally.
CURRENT/RECENT CLIENTS/PROJECTS: Manhattan Toy - trade show booth and display fixtures; Knotts Camp Snoopy - 3D signage, retail fixtures, props, sculpture; Wirsbo - trade show display unit; Howie G's Steakhouse - 3 D statues, caricature paintings; Cleveland MetroParks Zoo - Theme painting of Australian Outback, Creative Kidstuff Toystores - retail display fixtures and storage design/production.
PRESIDENT/CEO/OWNER: Carey W. Thornton

B

GRUGGEN BUCKLEY 612-321-0744
430 1st Avenue N. Suite 470 Minneapolis 55401
FAX: 612-321-0646
CONTACT: Terry Gruggen
E-MAIL: terry@gruggen.com or gordy@gruggen.com
WWW: gruggen.com
SERVICES: The agency specializes in the design and production of collateral materials. These include point-of-sale displays, in-store graphics, signage, brochures, newsletters, flyers, custom display pieces and retail maps. We are especially strong in retail applications that require fast turnaround and low costs.

Point of Purchase / 429

CURRENT/RECENT CLIENTS/PROJECTS: AT&T Corporate; AT&T Wireless Services; Best Buy; CellularOne; Cincinnati Bell; Cincinnati Bell Wireless; Circuit City; Corporate Learning Center; Dobson Communications; Greene Holcomb & Fisher; Giant Eagle; iwireless; Lucent Technologies; McDonald's; Metrocall; Minnesota Timberwolves; Polaris; Office Depot; Red Cross; Rollerblade; Ronald McDonald House Charities; SFX Entertainment; SunCom; Target; Triton PCS; Valvoline Oil Company

C

CENTRAL CONTAINER CORP.   612-425-7444
PO Box 43310   Minneapolis 55443
FAX: 612-425-7917
CONTACT: Steven Braun
E-MAIL: sbraun@centralcontainer.com
WWW: centralcontainer.com
SERVICES: Designs created by an award winning structural design team. From promotional packaging and point-of-sale shelf cartons, to protective, cushioned shipping containers, we provide complete prototyping and engineered solutions. Point-of-purchase displays and "club pack" designs are turned out in minimal time. Full color mock-ups of proposed art are produced on our 54" H. P. Color Plotter. Sophisticated warehousing and logistics management within our 175,000 square foot state of the art production facility, coupled with our in-house fulfillment group, allow for true "turnkey" project management.
CAPABILITIES: Litho/label mounting on 2 automatic mounters. Substrates from corrugated to foam core. 4 color flexo press capable of process work as well as vibrant, rich solid color and line work. Precision die cutters - 2 flat bed and 2 rotary presses. Standard cartons from our flexo/folder/gluers, and specialty boxes with intricate glue patterns for "crash bottoms," 6 corner trays, and internal parts - all glued on computer automated systems.
PRESIDENT/CEO/OWNER: James E. Haglund

M

MIKE MEEHAN COMPANY   612-475-1449
13805 First Avenue North   Minneapolis 55441
FAX: 612-475-1671
CONTACT: Thomas P. Meehan
E-MAIL: meehan@minn.net
SERVICES: Creative concepts, design and engineering of both semi-permanent and permanent point-of-purchase displays for consumer products. All preparations, production, distribution and warehousing.
CURRENT/RECENT CLIENTS/PROJECTS: Anagram International; Cargill; The Chinet Company; Johnson Worldwide; Michael Foods; 3M; Pillsbury Green Giant; Onen Corporation; Ore-Ida Foods; Singleton Seafood; Sta-Rite; Target; United Sugars Recovery Engineering; Kraft Foods; Land O' Lakes.
PRESIDENT/CEO/OWNER: Thomas P. Meehan

MODERNISTIC, INC.   651-291-7650
169 Jenks Avenue   St. Paul 55117
FAX: 651-291-2571

430 / Point of Purchase

CONTACT: Deb Olson
E-MAIL: info@modernisticinc.com
WWW: modernisticinc.com
SERVICES: Full service screenprinter and print finisher. Services offered; Foil stamping, embossing, die cutting, mounting, finishing, UV coating, strip taping, die making and specialty screen printing including glow-in-the-dark printing, scratch off printing, scented ink printing, and glitter printing.
CAPABILITIES: Products we offer: Point-of-purchase signage, floor graphics, window graphics, clip strips, temporary displays, fleet graphics, prototyping, banners.
PRESIDENT/CEO/OWNER: Keith Wilson

N

NYGARD DIMENSIONS	**612-623-8150**
1414 Marshall Street N.E.	**Minneapolis 55413**

FAX: 612-623-8147
CONTACT: Luis Ferreiro, General Manager
E-MAIL: events@stagesets.com
WWW: stagesets.com
SERVICES: Custom design, fabrication, installation of themed environments including special events; trade show exhibits; stage sets for meetings, film, video and photography; corporate and point-of-purchase displays and more. Creative development and design, computer renderings and 3D modeling, site inspection, on-site management and other event planning/management capabilities.
CAPABILITIES: Specializes in dimensional environments that create the "whole brand experience", integrating brand and creative theme through all media. Brand identity and design available through sister company, Nygard & Associates. State-of-the-art 60' x 80' x 31' sound stage on-location (Harmony Box).
CURRENT/RECENT CLIENTS/PROJECTS: 3M, ADC Telecommunications, American Express Financial Advisors, Larson Manufacturing, Lawson Software, Lutheran Brotherhood, Minnesota Department of Agriculture, Minnesota Mutual Insurance, Musicland, nQuire Software, and Target Stores.

P

PHOTOGRAPHIC SPECIALTIES	**612-522-7741**
1718 Washington Avenue North	**Minneapolis 55411**

FAX: 612-522-1934
CONTACT: Rick Schuenemann
E-MAIL: drewkal@photospec.com
SERVICES: P.S. is a full service custom photo lab and digital imaging service., We specialize in large runs of prints and transparencies for visual merchandising, POP, Trade Show Exhibits and museums. We have in-house graphic designers, a stock photo library and shipping and kitting capabilities.
CAPABILITIES: Two Light Jet 5000 Digital photo images for true photographic images up to 48" x 96" in one piece. Drum and flatbed scanning, LVT 8 x 10 film recorder, and Repri and Ellegro scan/retouch system. Color span Inkjet printers (4) and full mounting and laminating capabilities up to 80" wide. 4 traditional mural rooms with wall easels, prints and trans up to 72" x 16' one piece.
CURRENT/RECENT CLIENTS/PROJECTS: Large nationwide retail chains, display and store design firms.
PRESIDENT/CEO/OWNER: Drew Kalman

Premium & Specialty Advertising

A

ADVON INCORPORATED
8804 Seventh Avenue North
FAX: 763-545-8045
CONTACT: P.J. Conroy
E-MAIL: yupoong@advon.com
WWW: advon.com

763-545-0074
Minneapolis 55427

CAPABILITIES: Supplier to the specialty advertising marketplace of Yupoong headwear - blank and/or embroidered/screen printed.
SPECIALTIES: One-stop shop for digitization of logos, embroidered headwear, screen printed headwear with ten working day lead times.
PRESIDENT/CEO/OWNER: Charles J. Schaefer

AMERICAN BUSINESS FORMS AND PROMOTIONS
4308 Eton Place
FAX: 952-927-0678
CONTACT: La Verne Kintop
E-MAIL: lkintop@uswest.net
WWW: americanbus.com

952-927-5233
Edina 55424

SERVICES: Full service printing and promotions since 1979.
SPECIALTIES: Your source for high-quality premiums including Victorinox © Swiss Army products, Godiva Chocolates, Waterman writing instruments and many other fine products.
RUSH SERVICE: Most of the companies I represent offer rush service.
LINES HANDLED: Sourcing through ASI and PPAI including magnets, calendars, wearables, writing instruments and much, much more.

B

BUTTONS ON BRISTOL/ADAMS PROMOTIONAL GROUP
7122 Bunker Court
FAX: 952-470-0798
CONTACT: Julie Grube, Sales Manager, Lynn Wright, AD
E-MAIL: buttons@isd.net

952-470-5786
Eden Prairie 55346

CAPABILITIES: Lines Produced: buttons (five sizes: round, squares, ovals and rectangles), bumper strips, ribbons, T-shirts, hats, banners, mugs and cloisonné pins. Complete line of ad specialties.
CREATIVE: Creative Department: full art department, including layout, typesetting and keylining. Imprinting: complete service - hot stamping, silk screening, offset and four color process printing.
SPECIALTIES: Rush service, factory direct prices, professional treatment, quality products.

432 / Premium & Specialty Advertising

C

CENTRAL PRINTING COMPANY   612-980-4040
PO 50494   Minneapolis 55403
FAX: 612-951-4640
CONTACT: G. Wayne Wilcox
WWW: bicyclebrandblankbooks.com
SERVICES: Custom imprinted blank books, portfolios, and albums. Made of acid free materials. These books are called "Bicycle Brand Blank Books." And I would prefer the brand name at head of listing. These books are bound with inventive methods using materials recycled from Metro Bicycle shops. Book sizes from 1.75 x 2.75 to 26 x 40" Blueprints bound.
CAPABILITIES: 10 x 15 letterpress, custom equipment; 12 x 18 letterpress used in the manufacturer. 12 x 18 2-color offset of my products. 26 1/2 paper cutter. Drilling machines. Engraving, imprinting. 25 bin collator, Embossing dies, Staplers. Camera platemakers. Computer typesetting.
CURRENT/RECENT CLIENTS/PROJECTS: Distributed to over 400 retail stores. Custom printed books for Cyberx Coffee Shop, Damon Farber Architects, Louise Syretto, Attorney.

CONSUMER MARKETING & PROMOTIONS, INC.   651-430-2600
202 N. Martha Street   Stillwater 55082
FAX: 651-430-1726
CONTACT: Kyle Weed
E-MAIL: kweedcmp@att.net
LINES HANDLED: All top quality advertising specialty manufacturers, recognition awards, locally produced wearables, pottery, food/coffee and wood premiums. In-house manufacturing of custom Yukon Fleece outdoor apparel for corporate logo embroidering. We manufacture or source every type of item, including in-pack and mail-in custom merchandise.
SERVICES: No charge rush service or minor artwork development. Competitive pricing. Collating and drop shipping of premiums. Develop custom wearables. Three-day to two-week turnaround on many items. Imprinting: Embroidery, silk screening, die sublimation, pad printing, engraving, laser engraving, etching, debossing on any promotional product. One color to four color process. Corporate logos, personalized names, etc.
SPECIALTIES: Development and sourcing of custom premium merchandise. 25 to 25,000,000 quantities .01 to $100/item. Specializing in custom premiums; wearables; corporate gifts, in-packs, on-packs, near packs, container packs, food premiums, mail-in offers, integrated point-of-purchase, new product introductions, dealer/sales premiums. Equity reinforcing, brand building and value-added promotions. Strategic promotion planning and marketing integration. Domestic and worldwide sourcing and manufacturing. Packaging, collating, drop shipping. Email presentations.

CORPORATE INCENTIVES OF AMERCIA   612-822-2222
3416 Nicollet Avenue South   Minneapolis 55408
FAX: 612-822-9719
CONTACT: Linda Cobb
E-MAIL: sales@cipromo.com

Premium & Specialty Advertising / 433

WWW: cipromo.com
SERVICES: Internet hosting of customer's corporate identity products (golfballs, corporate casual wear, business folders, pens, etc.). Our company designs layouts, assists in selecting merchandise (golfballs, etc.) puts customer logo on products and displays products on a customer exclusive website. Corporate incentives stocks this customized inventory and ships within 24 hours.
CAPABILITIES: Website catalog design and service for customer imprinted promotional clothing and products. Warehouse storage plus individual fulfillment services. 24 hour turnaround time for orders. Realtime proprietary shipping and tracking software.
CURRENT/RECENT CLIENTS/PROJECTS: Online promotions catalog for the medical, electronic and financial industries.
PRESIDENT/CEO/OWNER: Jerry A. Finnerty

G

G & J PATCH AND PIN 651-459-1271
PO Box 2046 Cottage Grove 55016
8974 Jasmine Lane South
FAX: 651-459-9348
CONTACT: Gary Golusky
E-MAIL: g-j@mediaone.net
WWW: patchandpin.com
SERVICES: Custom lapel pins, badges, embroidered emblems and laser engraved items. Full service art department to assist customers with selection of product which will best convey their message.
CAPABILITIES: Over 30 years experience in design. Service oriented. Advertising incentives. Custom designed lapel pins, badges, embroidered emblems, laser engraved items, lucite embedments. And other items.
CURRENT/RECENT CLIENTS/PROJECTS: Law Enforcement Departments; Boy Scout and Girl Scout Councils; Advertising Agencies; Professional Sports Teams

GRAPHIC IMPRINTS, INC. 612-828-9835
6523 Cecilia Circle Bloomington 55439
CONTACT: Dennis Steck
WWW: gimprints.com
SERVICES: All promotional products for specialty advertising (ASI Distribution). Screen printed and embroidered apparel.
CAPABILITIES: 8 color automatic screen printing press, (2) 6 color manual presses.
CURRENT/RECENT CLIENTS/PROJECTS: SW Bell, Hormel, BI Performance Services.

GREAT GARMENTS 763-428-3702
14372 Heather Ridge Drive Rogers 55374
FAX: 763-428-3826
E-MAIL: sharp4cp@aol.com
SERVICES: Fashionable corporate garments for employees, customers, tradeshows, incentives, promotions teams, presents, etc. Unsurpassed product quality, finishing and service...second to none. In-office sample showing of the latest sportswear. Most favorable pricing--fast turn-around.
PRESIDENT/CEO/OWNER: Al Smith

434 / Premium & Specialty Advertising

I

ISA PROMOTIONS, INC.
206 Mariner Way
FAX: 651-439-4512
CONTACT: Maralee Meissner
E-MAIL: isapromo@ix.netcom.com
WWW: isapromo.com
PRESIDENT/CEO/OWNER: Susan J. Larimer

651-439-1339
Bayport 55003

L

LASER GRAPHICS, INC.
5100 Edina Industrial Blvd.
FAX: 612-835-8347
CONTACT: Peter Linstroth
E-MAIL: lgi@gipromotions.com
WWW: lgipromtions.com
SERVICES: A full-service production and fulfillment house. Products include: banner and signage; personalized merchandise; screen printed and embroidered apparel awards; fulfillment; incentive awards; special event planning.
CAPABILITIES: In-house creative; large format banner reproduction; warehouse fulfillment; Internet accessible; banner installation.
CURRENT/RECENT CLIENTS/PROJECTS: Target; Dayton's' Blue Cross/Blue Shield; Minnesota Timberwolves; Minnesota Twins; Minnesota Vikings; Jostens; US West
PRESIDENT/CEO/OWNER: Peter Linstroth

612-835-8346
Minneapolis 55349

M

METRO PROMOTIONS
935 Washington Avenue SE #319
FAX: 612-623-3162
CONTACT: Liz Siegrist
E-MAIL: lsiegrist@earthlink.net
SERVICES: All top quality lines of advertising specialties. Products including: wearables, business accessories, sales incentives and recognition items. Imprinting: Silkscreen, embroidery, pad print, etching, debossing, laser engraving and more for any promotional product.
CAPABILITIES: Research and sourcing of stock and custom premium merchandise. Convention and trade show support. Co-op and safety program development. Complete graphic design, printing, special packaging, and fulfillment services.

612-331-7180
Minneapolis 55414

Standards.

A degree or level of requirement for excellence.

 Experienced

 Service Orientated

 Professional

 Flaire Print Communications, Inc.

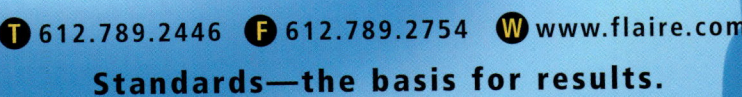

T 612.789.2446 **F** 612.789.2754 **W** www.flaire.com

Standards—the basis for results.

Standards—
the basis for results.

At Flaire, we focus on standards. We combine old-fashioned craftsmanship and advanced technology to achieve award-winning quality. We employ professionals who are authorities in the field. We listen to your expectations, develop innovative solutions to meet your budget, and deliver your work in a timely manner. Customers have come to rely on our project management skills for over 22 years. Count on us to bring your next project to life.

Services

Full-service project management

Complete desktop department including typesetting, scanning, production support, image manipulation, and film output

1 to 5 color sheet-fed printing

Complete finishing services

Custom printed 3M Post-it™ Notes; Authorized distributor

2110 Washington **STREET** Northeast • Minneapolis, MN 55418

T 612.789.2446   **F** 612.789.2754   **W** www.flaire.com

Premium & Specialty Advertising

MIDWEST BADGE & NOVELTY COMPANY, INC.　　612-927-9901
3337 Republic Avenue　　Minneapolis 55426
FAX: 612-927-9903
CONTACT: Mark Saba, Jacqueline Chouinard
SERVICES: Manufacturer. Lines Handled: Buttons, badges, ribbons, etc. Imprinting: Ribbons, inserts for badges, and advertising buttons. Creative: Art.
SPECIALTIES: Advertising.
PRESIDENT/CEO/OWNER: Mark J. Saba, President

P

PINS DIRECT　　763-476-0602
2500 Louisiana Avenue North　　Golden Valley 55427
FAX: 763-545-7353
CONTACT: Dawn Dahlsten
CAPABILITIES: Manufacturer, importer and designer of custom made lapel pins, badges, buttons, metal pins and key chains. Employee recognition and client appreciation gifts. Custom designed and custom-made to create a pin with the designed name, logo recognition, date or special message.
SPECIALTIES: Graphics department available. Cloisonné, photo-etched, die struck, soft enamel, key chains, celluloid, metal litho buttons and scale-sized log props. Full-service art department; stock lapel pins available. Call for samples.

PROMOTIONAL SYSTEMS GROUP, INC.　　1-800-726-8396
2020 O'Neil Road　　Hudson 54016
PO Box 226
FAX: 715-381-3123
CONTACT: Craig Beemer
E-MAIL: cbeemer@promotionalsystems.com
WWW: promotionalsystems.com
SERVICES: A promotional products and fulfillment company that is focused on providing cost-effective marketing solutions to the consumer packaged goods industry. Services include promotional product design and production, warehousing and inventory management, product inquiry response fulfillment, telemarketing, inbound 800 service, sample fulfillment, and sales material fulfillment.
CAPABILITIES: Systems: Microsoft BackOffice Small Business Server, MAS90 Inventory Management Software, Norstar-PLUS Prelude ACD Phone System, Norstar Voice Mail Model 2 and 11,276 square feet Office/Warehouse.
CURRENT/RECENT CLIENTS/PROJECTS: General Mills; Procter & Gamble; Old Home Foods; Land O'Lakes; PUR Drinking Water Products

436 / Premium & Specialty Advertising

R

RUTABAGA RAGS   952-938-4841
8700 W 36th Street Ste 3-E   Minneapolis 55426
FAX: 952-938-5412
CONTACT: Fern Meshbesher
E-MAIL: rutarags@aol.com
WWW: rutabagarags.com
SERVICES: We offer a broad range of promotional products, clothing, premiums, business gifts and awards. We can provide unique items for any special promotion.
CAPABILITIES: Meetings and conventions, trade shows, civic events, golf outings and picnics, new product introductions, new store openings.
CURRENT/RECENT CLIENTS/PROJECTS: Chubb Insurance; Highland Industries; International Prepress Association; Metropolitan Public Airport Foundation; MidAmerica Festivals; Park Jeep; Race for the Cure; See's Candies; Twin City Federal; among others.
PRESIDENT/CEO/OWNER: Julie Miller

S

SA ADVERTISING   763-428-1477
18850 North Diamond Lake Road   Rogers 55374
FAX: 763-428-5092
CONTACT: Scott Auld
SERVICES: Broker, manufacturer
LINES HANDLED: All ASI-listed manufacturers, many custom products and unique gifts/promotional items. Premiums - incentives. Imprinting: Yes. Screen printing, hot stamp, pad printing, engraving, silk screening, and many more. Also available without. Warehousing: Yes, and fulfillment
SPECIALTIES: Creative generation of ideas, products and promotions; service-oriented.
OFFICERS: Scott Auld, Cindy Auld

T

W J THOM COMPANY   612-870-8100
211 Varner Street   Jordan 55352
CONTACT: Mary Kaye Doerr
SERVICES: Imprinted promotional advertising items.
CAPABILITIES: Embroidery, silkscreen on apparel, bus. Cards, greeting cards, calendars, trade show give-away-items, golf balls and accessories, brand name pens: Pilot, BIC, Mont Blanc, Schaefer.

TRILOGY MARKETING GROUP   651-482-8270
944 Cobb Road   Shoreview 55126-3804

Premium & Specialty Advertising / 437

FAX: 651-482-8270
CONTACT: James D. Lemke
E-MAIL: trilogymktg@aol.com
SERVICES: Great ideas to meet your needs. Premium and promotional merchandise Broker, Distributor, Jobber. Lines Handled: "Anything except cars and people." Top-quality, brand name ad specialties, premiums, incentives, business gifts, wearables and recognition awards. Imprinting: Any merchandise item can be imprinted, engraved, lasered, silk screened and/or embroidered with a logo, name or message.
SPECIALTIES: Copywriting, art and print production. Warehousing and complete fulfillment services available. Stock and custom product resourcing. Extensive program experience includes: safety and awareness campaigns, cost reduction, dealer incentives, target market direct mail, open house, trade show, anniversary and sales meetings, as well as employee motivation, performance and service awards.
PRESIDENT/CEO/OWNER: James D. Lemke

WHITNEY WORLDWIDE, INC.
1845 Buerkle Road
FAX: 651-748-4000
CONTACT: Les Layton
E-MAIL: 1layton@whitneyworld.com
WWW: whitneyworld.com

651-749-5000
White Bear Lake 55110

SERVICES: 17-year old Direct Response and Marketing Research company that has worked for many Fortune 500 and other leading companies in Minnesota. We offer experienced writers, designers and strategists who have obtained superior response rates and beaten many companies controls. We also can handle many projects completely in-house. Having acquired 3M's Direct Response Marketing business unit 14 years ago, we also "practice what we preach". Our MarketMaster® lead-generation survey system produce higher response rates and better-quality leads than many companies have ever experienced before.
CAPABILITIES: Lead generation of higher-quality leads via direct mail or the Internet and super research surveys done via the same media--not on the phone. Staff has held top corporate marketing jobs, been department heads at largest agencies, been Pulitzer Prize finalist and run their own graphic design agency.
CURRENT/RECENT CLIENTS/PROJECTS: 3M, Lawson Software, Pioneer Press, Firstar, St. Paul Companies, Cargill, Minnesota Twins, Tousley Ford, Community Credit, United Way

Presentation Services

F

FREESTYLE PRODUCTIONS, INC.   **763-417-9575**
6112 Olson Memorial Highway   **Minneapolis 55422**
FAX: 763-417-9576
CONTACT: Dale Kivimaki, Mark Hulsey
E-MAIL: dale@freestyle-productions.com
WWW: freestyle-productions.com

CAPABILITIES: Freestyle Productions provides video and multimedia communication services with a specialized focus on high-profile, live-event productions including corporate meetings, trade shows, conventions and concerts. Complete array of broadcast equipment: multi-camera field packages, post production/mobile, non-linear edit suites, switcher/effects & graphic systems, large-format video and data projection, front & rear screens and videowalls.

SPECIALTIES: Over 10 years of national and international experience producing all types of live and special events shows. Freestyle provides an intuitive understanding of how to best communicate their client's message to impact large and small audiences.

CURRENT/RECENT CLIENTS/PROJECTS: Fox Sports Net, Coca-Cola, Lucent Technologies, Apple Computer, Northwest Airlines, Promise Keepers, Carlson Companies, Lutheran Brotherhood, US West, Minnesota State Fair, Universal Studios Hollywood.

H

HIGH POINT CREATIVE, LLC   **651-426-4012**
4583 Shady Lane   **St. Paul 55110**
FAX: 651-426-6699
CONTACT: Kate Huebsch
E-MAIL: kate@highpointcreative.com
WWW: highpointcreative.com

SERVICES: Copywriting and full project management for business-to-business and consumer brochures, catalogs, direct mail, websites, newsletters, speeches and presentations, PowerPoint shows, special events, marketing and internal communication pieces. A special interest in "translating" high-tech products and services into compelling and effective copy for non-technical readers.

CAPABILITIES: Marketing communications with an emphasis on strategic development and effective writing.

CURRENT/RECENT CLIENTS/PROJECTS: 12 years in business serving financial services companies, industrial manufacturers, health care organizations and community not-for-profit organizations.

PRESIDENT/CEO/OWNER: Kate Huebsch, President/Owner; Maiya Willits, Creative Director

P

PRECISION POWERHOUSE   **612-333-9111**
911 Second Street South   **Minneapolis 55415**
FAX: 612-332-9200
CONTACT: Dan Piepho, Paul Sunberg, Gene Gunderson

E-MAIL: dan@power-house.com; pauls@power-house.com or geneg@power-house.com
WWW: precisionpowerhouse.com
SERVICES: Full service communications company specializing in award-winning sales, marketing and training videos, audio and Interactive media production and post-production. Video sales presentation, product marketing presentations, video news releases, video/floppy disk/CD-ROM/DVD, annual reports, Interactive media training programs, video/audio/CD-ROM, catalogs, etc. Web site construction and design for business, data-base configuration, e-business, web publishing, hosting.

EQUIPMENT: Sony DME 3000, Silicon Graphics Maximum Impact Indigo 2 with Alias/Wavefront 2D and 3D software, Maya ACCOM 5 minute digital disk recorder, Pinnacle Aladdin digital effects, DVE and CG, Audio sound featuring Sonic Solutions, High Resolution 96/24 DVD/SurroundSound ready digital/audio workstation, Interactive media video digitizing workstation, Autodesk Animator workstation. Silicon Graphics maximum impact indigo 2, Accom 5 minute digital disk recorder. Pinnacle Aladdin digital effects, DVE and CG, Autodesk Animator workstation, Macromedia's Director, Flo and Morph Software, Adobe PhotoShop, Adobe Illustrator, DeBabelizer, Macromedel CorelDraw5, Barco Paint, Maximum Impact, 40 x 60 production soundstage, full-scale complete digital audio post production suite, full-scale complete digital/video post production suite, digital/analog video post production suite, SFI 3D animation suite, Interactive media workstations, DVD surround sound authoring suite, complete internet services, class five thousand clean-room, large scale audio/video duplication, CD and DVD replication, package designers on staff, worldwide shipping services, producer/director services, writers, technicians.

SPECIALTIES: Sales presentations, Interactive Training, Catalogs, e-business web sites, Intranet, Extranet, consumer products, radio, television, and web commercials, lap-top presentations, Interactive kiosks, video and interactive direct mail marketing, DVD authoring.

R

R.E.M. VIDEO & EVENT COMPANY
1828 NE Jefferson Street
FAX: 612-788-7712
CONTACT: Roger Miller
E-MAIL: info@remvideoevent.com
WWW: remvideoevent.com

612-788-9221
Minneapolis 55418

SERVICES: Full service production house for video, events/presentations, audio, multimedia. Our focus is in business to business communications delivered live or on media. We have in-house presentation expertise and equipment for TVL, Powerpoint (advanced), Astound and SCALA. Video productions on Betacam and DV formats. Non-linear broadcast and non-broadcast editing. Non-linear audio production for audio CD., video and film sweetening and music production scoring.

SPECIALTIES: Historical productions commemorating companies and places. Business to business marketing and training. Original music.

PRESIDENT/CEO/OWNER: Roger Miller, Presentations & Video; Michael Loonan, Audio & Multimedia; Pat Miller, Production Management.

Printing Services

A

A-1 PRINTERS, INC.   952-933-3852
4545 West 77th Street   Edina 55435
FAX: 952-893-1650
CONTACT: Don Kellett
E-MAIL: a1printers@sprynet.com
WWW: a1printers.com
CAPABILITIES: Desktop publishing, design/layout, color separations, imaging with direct-to-plate capabilities, 1-6 color high quality commercial printing, quick printing, high-speed copying, full bindery including diecutting, thermography. Professional and knowledgeable print consultants.
SPECIALTIES: Brochures, catalogues, sales collateral, pocket folders, manuals/booklets, newsletters, business cards, letterhead, envelopes.

AMBASSADOR PRESS   612-521-0123
1400 Washington Avenue North   Minneapolis 55411
FAX: 612-521-4587
E-MAIL: prepress@ambpress.com
WWW: ambpress.com
SERVICES: Printing, lithography 40" 6 color with in-line coating. 40' 2 color, 18" 1 color. Docutech Booklet maker, prep work. Computer to plate (no negatives - no stripping.) Mac desk top. Scitex Dolex PS imagesetter. Kodak approval color proofs, Bindex: complete.
CAPABILITIES: Computer to plate (no negatives - no stripping) 40th year. Perfecting on presses.
PRESIDENT/CEO/OWNER: Barry Engle
CONTACT: Edward Engle

AMERICAN SPIRIT GRAPHICS CORPORATION   612-623-3333
801 SE 9th Street   Minneapolis 55414
FAX: 612-623-9314
CONTACT: Lauren Drevlow

Printing Services / 441

SERVICES: Sheetfed Offset Presses: 28" x 40" 6-unit plus aqueous Mitsubishi, 20" x 28" 6-unit plus aqueous Mitsubishi, 28" x 40" 2-unit perfector Heidelberg. Web Offset Presses: 5-color 22 3/4 x 36" & 4-color 22 3/4 x 38" Baker-Perkins G-14's with high speed VITS sheeters and pattern perf units; 4-color 22 3/4 x 38" Baker-Pekins G-14 with high speed VITS sheeter, double former folder, pattern perf unit, in-line glue; (2) 4-color 35 " x 49" Toshibas with ribbon folders, in-line pasting and trimming, pattern perf unit; 6-color 17 3/4 x 26" Zircon Supra with pattern perf unit, pattern remoist gluer, in-line folding and trimming, sheeter, plate scanner, micro-trac registration system; 4-color 17 3/4 x 26" Zircon 6611 with in-line folding and trimming, sheeter, plate scanner, micro-trac registration system.
PREPRESS: Digital and conventional pre-press capabilities, including digital proofing and image setting. Computer-to-plate capabilities on sheeetfed presses.
BINDERY: 20", 23" and 30" MBO folders; (6) 26" Stahl folders; (3) 22" Stahl folders; 26" Baum folder; 6-pocket Mueller-Martini saddle stit10 x 15" Heidelberg Windmill die cutter; 14" x 20" Miehle Vertical die cutter; (2) 41" Miller Major die cutters; 40" Itoh cutter; 45" Prism cutter; (2) Polar cutters; 47" Lawson cutter; (27) 6" x 9" Bell & Howell inserter/mailers with up to 20 pockets; 9 x 11" Buhrs Enveloper System with 12 pockets; (4) 9" x 12" Mailcraft inserter/mailers with 12 pockets; (2) Domino ink jet; Avery tabber; Profold tabber.
PRESIDENT/CEO/OWNER: A. Oscar Carlson, CH & CEO; Suzanne L. Miller, VP-Fin & Admin.; Myron D. Angel, Exec. VP; Lauren E. Drevlow, VP-Sales; Timothy Franzen, VP-Operations

B

BRAEMAR PRINTING, INC. 612-941-1857
7111 Amundson Avenue South Edina 55439
FAX: 612-941-7826

SERVICES: Full-service printing company since 1979 specializing in newsletters, brochures, product sheets, booklets, manuals, all types of business forms. Letterhead, envelopes, business cards, and labels. Full-service 4-color process printing. Free pickup and delivery seven county metro area.
SPECIALTIES: Complete prepress, design, desktop publishing, camera department, typesetting, keylining and complete bindery services.
EQUIPMENT: Processes: Sheetfed offset
PRESIDENT/CEO/OWNER: Thomas J. Hildman

442 / Printing Services

C

THE
CARLSON
P R I N T
G R O U P

THE CARLSON PRINT GROUP   **952-886-3400**
9201 Penn Avenue South #40   **Bloomington 55431**
FAX: 952-888-2997
CONTACT: Jason Carlson
WWW: asgc.com
SERVICES: Commercial printer -- electronic prepress: imagesetting, direct to plate, Mac workstations, CREO/SCITEX equipment. Conventional Prepress: full color systems. Offset Lithography - 6 color 40" Mitsubishi press. 1 - 6 color, 28" Mitsubishi press and 1 newly installed 2 color 40" Heidelberg perfector - all sheetfed presses. 1 Muller Martini sadle sticher - diecutting, scoring, perforating, drilling, sheetcounting. Shrinkwrapping wet score attachment.
CURRENT/RECENT CLIENTS/PROJECTS: Eco Lab, Gage Marketing, Pillsbury, Canterbury Park.

COLOR PRINTING   **612-835-4441**
7326 Ohms Lane   **Minneapolis 55439**
FAX: 612-835-2613
CONTACT: Karen Walhof
SERVICES: Graphic design, pre-press, printing, bindery.
CAPABILITIES: Marketing mailers, catalogs, books, flyers, brochures, business forms, art prints.
PRESIDENT/CEO/OWNER: Leonard Flachman

COMMERS PRINTING, INC.   **763-792-0109**
8560 Cottonwood Street NW   **Coon Rapids 55433**
FAX: 763-792-3227
CONTACT: Steven Commers
E-MAIL: sales@commersprinting.com
WWW: commersprinting.com
SERVICES: Commers Printing provides sheet feed printing for your business needs - letterhead, envelopes, and carbonless forms. Marketing needs - brochures, pocket folders, product sheets. Production needs - product inserts, manuals, and booklets including their bindings. A complete single source provider.

Printing Services / 443

PREPRESS: Full electronic prepress capabilities including typesetting, punched film output, pre and post negative proofing from both Mac and IBM platforms. Offset Presses: 6 Heidelberg presses from 12 x 18 to 19 x 25.5 sheet size 1 to 5 colors.
BINDERY: Full bindery featuring Polar cutters, Stahl folders, Heidelberg letterpress and Horizon collating-stitching. Complete with large shrink-wrapping packaging department.
PRESIDENT/CEO/OWNER: Steven Commers

D

DANNER PRESS CORPORATION
5200 West 73rd Street
FAX: 612-897-6553
CONTACT: David Lamphere
E-MAIL: dlamph1410@aol.com
WWW: dannerpress.com

612-835-5411
Minneapolis 55439

SERVICES: Quality color printing for the catalog and magazine markets. Processes: Offset - web and sheetfed; UV coating; maximum sheet size: 22 - 3/4 x 38.
CAPABILITIES: Complete conventional and digital prepress including direct to plate, saddle and perfect binding, ink jet imaging and mailing, demographics, polybag, mailing, cheshire label, list services processing, BMC mail drop, newsstand distribution, spiral binding.
PRESIDENT/CEO/OWNER: Roy Mayers, CEO

DOCUMENT RESOURCES
11011 Smetana Road
FAX: 952-912-0300

952-912-0200
Minnetonka 55343

SERVICES: Brochures; Labels; Invoices; Envelopes; Print Management & Inventory; Mailing Services; Design; Distribution; Letterheads; Mailers; Imprinted Ad Specialty Items; Business Cards; Laser Security Checks; Thermal Labels & Supplies; Stock Paper; Computer Forms; Booklets; Binders; Folders; Posters; Digital Printing; Variable Imaging.
CONTACT: Wally Piroyan

DORN PRODUCTION MANAGEMENT SERVICE, INC.
4405 Polaris Lane North
FAX: 612-553-0566
CONTACT: Stasia Dorn
E-MAIL: stasia@dorninc.com

612-640-5156

Plymouth 55446

SERVICES: 16 years print production and color management. Specializing in project management, estimating, competitive bidding, color review and presschecks.
CAPABILITIES: Collateral, brochures, annual reports, catalogs, print ad and billboard campaigns, direct mail, POP, gamecards/sweepstakes, signs and banners.

DYNOPRESS, INC.

763-541-0966
Golden Valley

FAX: 763-541-3128

444 / Printing Services

CONTACT: Todd Amar
E-MAIL: info@dynopress.com
WWW: dynopress.com
SERVICES: A one-stop, full service print finishing company specializing in CAD design and sample making, laser steel rule dies, diecutting, foil stamping, embossing, thermal cutting, mounting, laminating, automated folding and gluing, shrink wrapping and hand assembly services.
PRESIDENT/CEO/OWNER: Tom Mumford

G

GENERAL LITHO SERVICES, INC. 763-535-7277
6845 Winnetka Circle **Minneapolis 55428**
FAX: 763-535-7322
CONTACT: Gary Garner
TOLL FREE & WWW: 888-646-7277; www.genlitho.com
SERVICES: It is the dedication to details that make the difference between acceptable and exceptional project management. From the first creative idea to arriving in the hands of your customers, GLS has the expertise to make it happen. Call today and discover all of the services that provide Integrated Communication Solutions(*!).
CREATIVE: Our award winning designs cover a wide range of projects from logos, brochures, ads and web pages, to complete corporate identities.
PREPRESS: We offer full electronic prepress capabilities such as punched film output, in-house scanning, and digital proofing. In addition to film output, we provide image enhancement, color correction and file manipulation services.
DIGITAL & CONVENTIONAL PRESSES: We operate state-of-the-art presses; Docutech NP-135 digital printer, 14 x 20 2 - color Heidelberg, 25 1/4 x 36 2-color Heidelberg, 20 x 28 5-color Heidelberg with coater, 20 x 28 6-color Heidelberg with coater, 28 x 40 5-color Heidelberg Perfector, 28 x 40 6-color Heidelberg CD with coater, 12 x 18 Halm Superjet 2-color perfecting envelope press.
BINDERY: Complete bindery featuring Stahl folders with in-line gluing. Muller Martini and ITOH saddle stitchers with cover feeders, 12 x 18, 20 x 26, and 28 x 40 diecutting presses, automated collating, binding, gluing and converting, along with miscellaneous machinery for special finishing applications.
DATA PROCESSING: We have highly-skilled programmers and a powerful PC-based network to handle the most complex data processing and mailing projects with ease. We have a 9-track reel tape system - 1650 or 6250 BPI. From inkjet to laser personalized components, to address standardization and postal presort optimization, merge/purge, database management and file manipulation, GLS has the direct response capabilities to maximize your results.

Printing Services / 445

LETTERSHOP: Phillipsburg 6 x 9 and 9 x 12 inserters, GBR smart folder feeder for intelligent document processing. Getting your project into the mail is the goal. With a fully equipped lettership and an on-site United States Post Office. GLS can move your project out the door in rapid time.

GOPHER STATE LITHO CORPORATION
3232 East 40th Street

612-724-3600
Minneapolis 55406

FAX: 1-800-451-9195
CONTACT: Orton Tofte
E-MAIL: gopher@gopherstatelitho.com
WWW: gopherstatelitho.com.
ALTERNATE PHONE: 888-351-3600
SERVICES: Commercial printer, 1 - 6 color sheetfed and heat set web (5 overs) full bindery.
CAPABILITIES: Full function mailing department. Variable data laser printing (High speed). Computer file archiving.
PRESIDENT/CEO/OWNER: William Ketz

GV GRAPHICS, INC.
2730 Nevada Avenue North

763-542-8330
Minneapolis 55427

FAX: 763-542-8309
CONTACT: John Hagenstein
E-MAIL: sjh@gvgraphics.com
WWW: gvgraphics.com
SERVICES: Prepress, production management and printing services featuring the best in today's equipment and staffing. Utilizing the Heidelberg Quickmaster digital press and Kodak approval in its workflow. Come to us for all your print needs.
CAPABILITIES: Heidelberg Quickmaster Digital Imaging Press Kodak approval.
CURRENT/RECENT CLIENTS/PROJECTS: MSP Publications, General Mills, Zomax, Bachman's, Tiger Oak Publications, Northrup King, International Home Foods and Navarre.
PRESIDENT/CEO/OWNER: S. John Hagenstein

H

HOLDEN GRAPHIC SERVICES
607 North Washington Avenue

612-339-0241
Minneapolis 55401

CONTACT: George T. Holden
SERVICES: Lithography: 15 high-speed rotary offset multi-color business form presses; Ultra Violet ink 4-color process on coated stock, polyfilm; foil, on press folding, pattern perforating. Preparatory Work: Complete art and design, totally integrated, in-house litho prep. Full service, in-house production capabilities from rough art to finished product, full complement of forms, press cuttoff sizes up to five colors plus double numbering, maximum flexibility in collating equipment, experienced warehousing/distribution/traffic control services. Plus full service direct mail, data processing, lettershop, fulfillment and telemarketing.
SPECIALTIES: Continuous data-processing, snap-a-part forms with specialties in 4-color process forms product using ultraviolet drying, magnetic recognition (MICR-checks) forms, optical character recognition (OCR) forms, the use of invisible (latent) ink, mini-computer forms and word processing forms.

446 / Printing Services

HOPF & HOPF PRINTING, INC.   612-338-4800
2711 East Franklin Avenue   Minneapolis 55406
FAX: 612-338-5986
CONTACT: Pam Hopf
E-MAIL: hopf@hopfprinting.com
SERVICES: Production of top quality stationery, business forms, mailers, design and production of full color brochures and catalogs, mailing services. 50 years of service to the metropolitan business community.
CAPABILITIES: Distribution, fulfillment, stock management, imprint shell programs. We accept Mac or IBM discs or e-mail copy.
PRESIDENT/CEO/OWNER: Leo J. Hopf

I

IDEAL PRINTERS, INC.   651-855-1100
645 Olive Street   St. Paul 55101
FAX: 651-855-1055
CONTACT: Lana Siewert Olson
SPECIALTIES: All types of commercial printing.
PROCESSES: Offset, sheetfed, lithography: 1-, 2-, 4-, and 6- color.
MAXIMUM SHEET SIZE: 28 x 40.
SERVICES: Art, desktop, film prep, printing, binding.
OFFICERS: Howard Siewert, P; Rhoda Siewert, VP/T

IMPRESSIONS INCORPORATED   651-646-1050
1050 Westgate Drive   St. Paul 55114
FAX: 651-646-7228
CONTACT: Timothy Hewitt
E-MAIL: i-i.com
SERVICES: Impressions, Inc. is a multi-color printer specializing in the complete production of: packaging, commercial printing, labels and inserts, manuals. Other services we offer: digital asset management, inventory management, complete in-house pre-press capabilities including: digital proofing and computers to plate (CTP) technology, color management.
PRESIDENT/CEO/OWNER: Mark A. Jorgensen

INFINITY DIRECT, INC.   763-559-1111
13220 County Road 6   Plymouth 55441
FAX: 763-553-1852
CONTACT: Mike Boyle
WWW: infinitydirect.com
SPECIALTIES: Full service capabilities. Consumer and business-to-business direct marketing programs.
CREATIVE SERVICES: Collateral development, brand/identity programs, concept design, brochures, promotion development, planning and execution, copywriting, graphic design, interactive--CD ROM/DVD, web page and web response.
PRODUCTION SERVICES: Printing, lettershop, fulfillment. Interactive--CD-ROM/DVD processing and personalization services.
PRESIDENT/CEO/OWNER: Thomas L. Harding, CEO/Owner

Printing Services / 447

J

JAPS OLSON COMPANY   952-932-9393
7500 Excelsior Blvd   St. Louis Park 55426
FAX: 952-912-1900
CONTACT: Michael Beddor
WWW: japsolson.com
SERVICES: Commercial printing and direct mail production for clients nationwide who seek total production under one roof.
CAPABILITIES: Sheetfed, web, flexo and forms printing, laser and ink jet personalization, complete lettershop, and mail center.
PRESIDENT/CEO/OWNER: Robert Murphy

JOHNSON PRINTING & PACKAGING   612-571-2000
40 - 77th Avenue NE   Minneapolis 55432
FAX: 612-574-0191
CONTACT: Stuart Weitzman
E-MAIL: sweitz1835@aol.com
SERVICES: Manufacturing of folding cartons, point of purchase displays and commercial printing. In-house structural and graphic design, printing, UV, blister and skin pack coating, diecutting and gluing.
EQUIPMENT: 38 x 50 five color with coater, 28 x 40 seven color with coater, 28 x 40 five color with coater, 14 x 20 four color, and 28 x 40 one color. Bindery: 2 computerized cutters, 6 pocket stitcher/trimmer, shrink wrapper, PMC die cutter, 28 x 40 diecutter blanker, 28 x 40 die cutter, 38 x 50 die cutter, 4 computerized folder/gluers, 38 x 50 coater.
PRESIDENT/CEO/OWNER: Stuart Weitzman, Charles Silverman

K

MARY ANN KNOX   612-822-8533
3300 Bryant Avenue South   Minneapolis 55408
FAX: 612-822-5058
CONTACT: Mary Ann Knox
E-MAIL: maknox@earthlink.com
SERVICES: Print consultant/project management - manage and produce print projects: advertising, collateral, direct mail, packaging. Training, set up systems, traffic, internet.
CAPABILITIES: 20 years experience.

L

LABEL PRODUCTS, INC.   952-996-0909
10525 Hampshire Avenue #300   Bloomington 55438
FAX: 952-996-0202

448 / Printing Services

CONTACT: Donald J. Burke
WWW: labelproducts.com
SERVICES: Special services: art department, typesetting, embossing, plate making, design work.
CAPABILITIES: Printing processes available: hot stamping, Flexographics, plateless digital to print, consecutive and random serializing, re-registration capabilities.
SPECIALTIES: Foil stamping, embossing, consecutive and random serializing, re-registration capabilities, high quality 4-color process labels, UV varnish, UL approved.
PRESIDENT/CEO/OWNER: Ed Christenson

LARKIN INDUSTRIES   651-645-6000
2020 Energy Park Drive   St. Paul 55108
FAX: 651-645-6082
E-MAIL: larkin@bpsi.net
SERVICES: Foil stamping, embossing/debossing, die cutting, folding, gluing, holograms, shrink wrapping, strip taping, packaging, spot taping, hand assembly steel rule die making, kiss cutting, industrial parts fabrication.
CAPABILITIES: In business since 1975, state-of-the-art equipment, experienced, professional technical staff. Convenient location in St. Paul's Energy Park district.
PRESIDENT/CEO/OWNER: Mike Larkin

M

MARACOM CORPORATION   763-593-1529
320 Trenton Lane North   Plymouth 55441
FAX: 763-593-1623
CONTACT: Mark Peterson
E-MAIL: sales@maracom.com
WWW: maracom.com
SERVICES: Full-service, 4-color prep and printing through fulfillment. Pre-priced for quick phone estimates.
SPECIALTIES: National specialty printer of beautiful full-color postcards, rack cards, greeting cards, business cards.

MERIT PRINTING   612-339-8193
117 North 2nd Street   Minneapolis 55401
FAX: 612-338-1444
CONTACT: Ron Boerboom
E-MAIL: ron@meritprinting.com
CAPABILITIES: Offset sheetfed up to 6 colors with aqueous coating. Electronic prepress, diecutting and complete Lettershop including inkjet. Docutech and jumbo inserters.

MODERN PRESS   651-633-4000
808 First Street SW   New Brighton 55113
FAX: 651-633-3234
CONTACT: Kelley Frain

Printing Services / 449

E-MAIL: modern@superprinter.com
WWW: superprinter.com
SERVICES: High quality 1, 2, 4 and 5 color sheetfed printing with Aqueous coating as well as non-heatset web presses. Complete electronic prepress services. Full service bindery. Courteous, knowledgeable and professional staff.
CAPABILITIES: Annual reports, brochures, catalogs, corporate identity packages, newsletters, pocket folders and posters, or almost anything else you need printed.
PRESIDENT/CEO/OWNER: Gerald Frain

MODERNISTIC, INC.   **651-291-7650**
169 Jenks Avenue   **St. Paul 55117**
FAX: 651-291-2571
CONTACT: Deb Olson
E-MAIL: info@modernisticinc.com
WWW: modernisticinc.com
SERVICES: Full service screenprinter and print finisher. Services offered; Foil stamping, embossing, die cutting, mounting, finishing, UV coating, strip taping, die making and specialty screen printing including glow-in-the-dark printing, scratch off printing, scented ink printing, and glitter printing.
CAPABILITIES: Products we offer: Point-of-purchase signage, floor graphics, window graphics, clip strips, temporary displays, fleet graphics, prototyping, banners.
PRESIDENT/CEO/OWNER: Keith Wilson

P

PAR CONSULTING, INC.   **952-835-5155**
4444 West 76th Street #700   **Edina 55435**
FAX: 952-835-5122
CONTACT: Mary West
E-MAIL: mary@parplus.com
WWW: parplus.com
SERVICES: Printing broker; professional printing management; production planning and coordination. Promotional products. Complete digital capabilities to get job from idea to print. MAC computer consulting, configuration and planning.
CAPABILITIES: Apple VAR Reseller, Apple Solutions Network Professional
CURRENT/RECENT CLIENTS/PROJECTS: Industrial and commercial accounts; catalogs, direct mail, posters, and books.
PRESIDENT/CEO/OWNER: Phyllis Rivard

PRECISION GRAPHICS, INC.   **763-476-4100**
2525 Fernbrook Lane North   **Plymouth 55447**
FAX: 763-476-2738
CONTACT: Sales Dept.
E-MAIL: jay.n@pgiprint.com
SERVICES: Specialize in greeting cards, brochures, pocket folders and catalogs, High quality 2, 4, 6 color commercial sheetfed printing with aqua coating and film lamination. Mac and PC desktop. Scitex brisque work station.
PRESIDENT/CEO/OWNER: Jay Nelson

450 / Printing Services

PRINTER PROS	**651-778-1324**
1412 Arcade Street	St. Paul 55106

FAX: 651-776-2651
CONTACT: John Tolo
E-MAIL: jtolo@uswest.net
WWW: printerservicepros.com
SERVICES: Color printer service, sales and supplies, Provider of the highest quality graphics printers on the market. Repair services for these products. Printouts for color proofs and other small runs of color documents. Current Models of the highest quality color and monochrome printers on display. Demonstrations available.
CAPABILITIES: Able to print out color proofs up to full-bleed tabloid sizes. 1 to 1000 with great prices. Photo quality. Flyers, postcards, brochures, etc.

PROFESSIONAL COLOR SERVICE, INC.	**612-673-8900**
909 Hennepin Avenue South	**Minneapolis 55403**

FAX: 612-673-8988
CONTACT: Tim Doe
E-MAIL: procolor@procolor.com
WWW: procolor.com
CAPABILITIES: Digital printing that's hard to believe it's digital. Over forty years of making color judgements gives us an edge on color accuracy. That's why you'll want to give us your prepress file prep. If it's short run you're looking for, look to ProColor's Heidelberg DI. For quantities of 250 or less, we can accommodate you with Docucolor printouts. Great for low run, low cost posters, the Bubblejet delivers color printouts up to 24" x 36". Color laser copies are also available. Our one-stop-shop line of products and services includes: new 3D lenticular display prints, digital display photographs and transparencies, as well as a complete range of scanning services, including those from our high res drum, Photo CD, and Dicomed digital camera. Fine art IRIS reproduction. Short-run digital 4-color printing on our Heidelberg DI and Docucolor systems. Film processing 24 hours a day Monday through Friday and 8:30 to 11:30 on Saturday. Pick up and delivery.
SPECIALTIES: One-stop shop imaging services.
OFFICE HOURS: Monday through Friday 7:30 am to 8:00 pm; Saturday 8:30 to 2:00 pm.

R

REPRO PRINTING, INC.	612-861-2245
7701 Morgan Avenue South	Richfield 55423

FAX: 612-861-2247
SERVICES: Printing services.
PRESIDENT/CEO/OWNER: May Lund

"Brilliant, precise color at a price that is affordable."

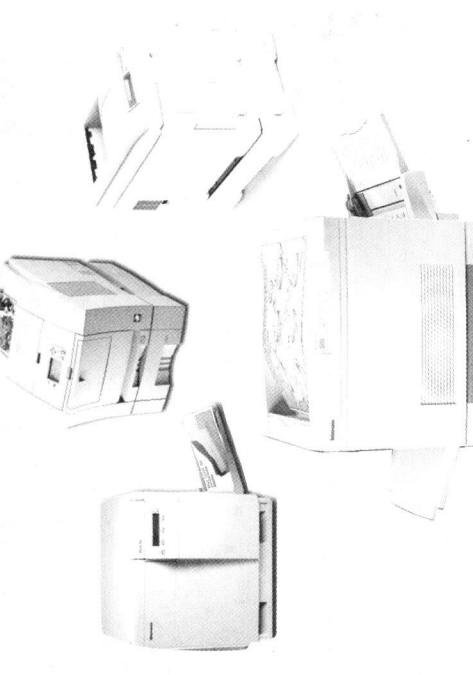

COLOR PRINTER SPECIALISTS

We sell a wide variety of Color Printer to meet every need.
Hi-Speed color, up to 20 pages per minute
Photo quality with paper sizes up to 13" x 19"
Leases as low as $65 per month

Call Now To Try Out Our Awesome Printers!

PRINTER SERVICE PROFESSIONALS

SERVICE • SALES • SUPPLIES

We are the local Color and Network Printer & Copier Specialists!
When you need quality Service, Sales or Supplies support,
Call us to see why Printer Pros is the best in town!.

OUR CUSTOMERS SAY WE'RE THE BEST IN TOWN! CALL NOW TO SEE WHY

Printer Pros offers provides specialized support on all types of printers andt we are authorized by the following Companies.

- Xerox
- QMS
- Minolta
- Lexmark
- Zebra
- Kyocera
- Okidata
- Hewlett Packard
- Canon
- Ricoh
- Printek
- and more.....

www.printerservicepros.com

1412 Arcade St. • St. Paul, MN 55106 • Phone: (651) 778-1324 • Fax: (651) 776-2651

ON THE WEB AT

gogoldbook.com

Printing Services / 451

S

SHAFER & FELD, INC.
2933 N 2nd Street
FAX: 612-521-2289
CONTACT: Dick Newman
SERVICES: Commercial printing - sheet fed one through four colors, quality printer with art and design, offset letterpress and bindery - union shop.

612-521-2286
Minneapolis 55411

SIR SPEEDY PRINTING & COPYING
1254 Hennepin Avenue
FAX: 612-376-7677
CONTACT: Karen Murray
E-MAIL: info@srspeedy.com
WWW: srspeedy.com
SERVICES: Full printing services, including four-color process. High-speed color copying and output from disk. High-speed B&W copying. Full service bindery, including mailing services. Graphic design. Wide-format color. Free pick-up and delivery. Send your files over the internet.
CAPABILITIES: We run the best equipment from Heidelberg, Canon, Xerox, and Kodak.
PRESIDENT/CEO/OWNER: Ed Stych

612-376-0888
Minneapolis 55403

T

THOELE PRINTING COMPANY
253 State Street
CONTACT: G. Thoele
SPECIALTIES: Four color, up to 25 x 38.
PROCESSES: Letterpress, offset, sheetfed.
SERVICES: Typesetting, binding, embossing, foil embossing. Printing - Newsletter, stationery, books, brochures, etc. Maximum Sheet Size: 25 1/4 x 38 1/2.
PRESIDENT/CEO/OWNER: G. Thoele, P; Pam Zeidler, VP

651-224-9631
St. Paul 55107

TRIANGLE PRINTING COMPANY
710 West 40th Street
FAX: 612-822-1424
CONTACT: Bruce Thomson
E-MAIL: brucetig22@aol.com

612-822-7871
Minneapolis 55409

452 / Printing Services

U

UPFRONT PRODUCTIONS   651-633-5299
2350 County Road C #120   St. Paul 55113
FAX: 651-633-5197
CONTACT: Tricia Nordby Hamrin/Chris Hamrin
WWW: hoopjumping.com
CAPABILITIES: Organizational Communications Solutions Center. A Spectrum. A Synergy. Concept Development, Copywriting, Graphic Design, Illustration, Document Production, Web Site Creation, Scanning, Photo Retouching, Pre-press, Offset Printing, Digital B&W Printing, Color Copies, Posters, Displays, Signs, Custom Assembly, Inventory, Distribution, Corporate Compass® MIS, VantagePoint™, Hoop Jumping™.
SPECIALTIES: Choose your hoop. We'll jump through it™.
OFFICERS: Tricia Nordby Hamrin/Chris Hamrin

Production Management

G

GV GRAPHICS, INC.
2730 Nevada Avenue North
FAX: 763-542-8309
CONTACT: John Hagenstein
E-MAIL: sjh@gvgraphics.com
WWW: gvgraphics.com

763-542-8330
Minneapolis 55427

SERVICES: Prepress, production management and printing services featuring the best in today's equipment and staffing. Utilizing the Heidelberg Quickmaster digital press and Kodak approval in its workflow. Come to us for all your print needs.

CAPABILITIES: Heidelberg Quickmaster Digital Imaging Press Kodak approval.

CURRENT/RECENT CLIENTS/PROJECTS: MSP Publications, General Mills, Zomax, Bachman's, Tiger Oak Publications, Northrup King, International Home Foods and Navarre.

PRESIDENT/CEO/OWNER: S. John Hagenstein

Props, Costumes & Wardrobe

A

BRUCE S. ALLEN, INC.   **612-341-0660**
1018 North Fifth Street   **Minneapolis 55411**
FAX: 612-333-2278
CONTACT: Bruce S. Allen
CAPABILITIES: Complete scenic studio.
SPECIALTIES: Custom design and fabrication in all media, miniature to giant size sets and props for still, video, film, displays and exhibits.

ART-TECH PRODUCTIONS, INC.   **612-379-4840**
1331 Water Street NE   **Minneapolis 55413**
FAX: 612-379-1447
CONTACT: Nancy Teel
E-MAIL: fab@art-tech.net
WWW: art-tech.net
SERVICES: A design/production company that specializes in themed retail environments. Retail display fixtures, tradeshow booths, 3D signage and sculpture, theatrical props, small theme painting, kiosks and showroom design.
CAPABILITIES: 20,000 sq. ft workshop area filled with the best crafts people in town. Will work with any client to design and produce a unique and distinctive product. All work is done on-site. We work on jobs both locally and nationally.
CURRENT/RECENT CLIENTS/PROJECTS: Manhattan Toy - trade show booth and display fixtures; Knotts Camp Snoopy - 3D signage, retail fixtures, props, sculpture; Wirsbo - trade show display unit; Howie G's Steakhouse - 3 D statues, caricature paintings; Cleveland MetroParks Zoo - Theme painting of Australian Outback, Creative Kidstuff Toystores - retail display fixtures and storage design/production.
PRESIDENT/CEO/OWNER: Carey W. Thornton

B

THE BEAUDRY GROUP   612-940-3244
3402 Hennepin Avenue South   Minneapolis 55408
FAX: 612-338-2732
CONTACT: Steve Beaudry
E-MAIL: bg@2z.net
SERVICES: 3- dimensional illustration, miniature sets, ad props.

C

COLLECTOR CAR PROPS   612-472-4435
5641 Bartlett Boulevard   Mound 55364
FAX: 612-472-4435
CONTACT: Tom Reese
E-MAIL: twrcars@winternet.com
WWW: carprops.com
SERVICES: Car props, provides all manner of automobiles for photo shoots, filming and other events requiring older cars from 1900 through the 1980's. Also provide consulting and costumes for historical accuracy, pertaining to the settings for the cars provided.
CAPABILITIES: Experienced historical writer on automotive topics. Project management for sites.
CURRENT/RECENT CLIENTS/PROJECTS: Make -Strunc Photography, MW Telephoto Productions, Media Productions, Minneapolis Institute of Art.

COSTUMES & CREATURES   612-333-2223
420 North Fifth Street #350   Minneapolis 55401
FAX: 612-333-2317
CONTACT: Bonnie Ehlers
E-MAIL: bonniee@vee.com
WWW: vee.com
SERVICES: Types of Props/Costumes Available: full-body character costumes, team and corporate mascots, animal costumes, soft sculpture, and puppets.

456 / Props, Costumes & Wardrobe

SPECIALTIES: Design and construction; staff of talented professionals with experience in creating costumes for advertising, theater, film, television, displays, business promotions and sports teams. Rent/Sell: sell commissioned work only. No rentals.
PRESIDENT/CEO/OWNER: Vincent E. Egan, P; Chris Vesper, Costume Shop Manager

D

DR. OF PROPTOLOGY   651-642-1628
1716 Blair Avenue   St. Paul 55104
CONTACT: Paul Berglund
CAPABILITIES: I find the props, transport the props, dress the set and work the props.
SPECIALTIES: I have worked in the film and TV commercial (art department) for 12 years now. Most of those as a Propmaster. I have a van and many wonderful tools.

DREAMSTITCHER CUSTOM COSTUME   612-722-8868
5340 47th Avenue South   Minneapolis 55417
CONTACT: Rae Lundquist
E-MAIL: dreamstch@foxinternet.net
SERVICES: Costumes: For sale - Rush orders. Off the rack or mass produced items not available. Our motto "historical to hysterical, fantasy to science fiction," covers our range and capabilities. Our customers cover the spectrum from historical reenactors to ad agencies, from science fiction fans to dance groups. We offer our clients 25 years of costume research and sewing experience, with research documentation available upon request. All work is backed with a 30-day guarantee of quality construction. We offer each client a free consultation session, and shipping is free if garment not delivered by due date. Clients' fitting sessions are free.
CAPABILITIES: Historical reproductions are our specialty. We can take a sketch or photo of a historical garment (or comic book hero) and reproduce it as close to original, as modern materials will allow, right down to the proper type of cloth and appropriate buttons and trims. Research notes and historical documentation available upon request. Historical reproductions are constructed as clothing, not costume, and are guaranteed to be wearable under conditions suitable to the item. Liberal repairs/return policy. Customers' own original designs can be translated into reality. 3 price levels of construction available: machine stitched; hand finished; or completely hand stitched (most expensive).
CURRENT/RECENT CLIENTS/PROJECTS: "Wolf in Sheep's Clothing"/Sheehan Photography. Minnesota Historical Society/Fort Snelling, NW Co. Fur Post, etc. 1840 Gentleman's Outfit/Tailcoat, Vest, Trousers, Pleated Front shirt, Cuffed Boots. 1760's Pirate's Frockcoat and Pantaloons, with Shirt, Vest and Tri-Corn. Xmas Bow for Snowmobile/Periscope Advertising.

G

GUTHRIE THEATER COSTUME RENTALS   612-375-8722
3100 California Street NE   Minneapolis 55418
FAX: 612-375-8733

Props, Costumes & Wardrobe / 457

CONTACT: Deb Murphy
E-MAIL: costumes@guthrietheater.org
WWW: guthrietheater.org/act-II/costume-rental.htm
CAPABILITIES: Rental of classical theatrical period costumes ranging from Gothic to contemporary, including hats, shoes, and accessories, designed for the Guthrie stage.
PRESIDENT/CEO/OWNER: Joe Dowling, Artistic Director

H

HARRIS WAREHOUSE & CANVAS SALES 612-331-1829
501 30th Avenue SE Minneapolis 55414
FAX: 612-331-6651
CONTACT: Marc or Sigmund Harris
E-MAIL: harrismchy501@aol.com
SERVICES: Sewing facilities for fabrication to order repairs - many materials in stock - art work for banners.
CAPABILITIES: We do work in our workrooms and have experienced sewers.
PRESIDENT/CEO/OWNER: Marc Harris

J

JOHMAR FARMS 651-433-5312
14330 Ostrum Trail North Marine on St. Croix 55047
FAX: Same - call first
CONTACT: John or Mary Block
E-MAIL: johmar@onvoymail.com
SERVICES: Types of Props/Costumes: buggies, carriages, sleighs, western prop.. Cars, trucks or any hard to find items Unusual Items: 100 plus carriages, wagons, and sleighs of various sizes and styles.
SPECIALTIES: Can't find it? Call us! Rent/Sell: Rent
CURRENT/RECENT CLIENTS/PROJECTS: Feature film, ad agencies, production companies, corporate in-house, film studios, photographers, TV, festivals, corporate events, plays and productions.

K

KILROY'S 612-339-5848
219 N 2nd Street, Suite B-100 Minneapolis 55401
FAX: 612-275-2244
CONTACT: Kevin Hammerbeck
E-MAIL: kilroys@pclink.com

458 / Props, Costumes & Wardrobe

SERVICES: Prop rental. Types of props/costumes available: Antique and modern slot machines, jukeboxes, diner and malt shop furniture and memorabilia. Unusual Items: Soda fountains, neon clocks. Gas pumps, 500 old advertising signs and neons, gambling wheels and memorabilia, old coin-operated machines, arcade, scales, soda machines, vending barber poles, many unusual antiques. Special Services: Will modify machines for special effects, mechanical prop building and prop hunting. 25 years experience. Rent/Sell: Both.
CURRENT/RECENT CLIENTS/PROJECTS: Many - in business since 1975

CYNTHIA KURKOWSKI   320-274-2939
11675 County Road 37 NW   **Annandale 55302**
CONTACT: Cynthia Kurkowski
SERVICES: Complete wardrobe services, design, construction, styling of anything in Funk.
CAPABILITIES: Worked in the business for 15 years. Favorite - to help create "characters" with wardrobe.
CURRENT/RECENT CLIENTS/PROJECTS: Currently printing and constructing clothing with Targets for Peterson, Milla, Hooks for Target Stores.

P

PROP RENTAL SERVICE   612-881-6160
9039 Dupont Avenue South   **Bloomington 55420**
FAX: 612-888-5464
CONTACT: Mark Cameron
E-MAIL: mcameron@pclink.com
SERVICES: Specializing in antique microphones, automobiles, and auto-related antiques. Period clothing and accessories 1880 - 1930. Model T Ford cars available as well as 1940's - 1950's cars. Antique radios and furniture - 1925 - 1935.
CAPABILITIES: Restoration services for early brass automobiles and period clothing. Consulting services on authenticity for period items: 1885 - 1930.
CURRENT/RECENT CLIENTS/PROJECTS: Numerous ad stills and film shots during 1999.

PROPAGANDA   612-341-0660
1018 North Fifth Street   **Minneapolis 55411**
FAX: 612-333-2278
CONTACT: Bruce S. Allen
CAPABILITIES: Complete scenic studio.
SPECIALTIES: Custom design and fabrication in all media. Minature to giant-size sets and props for still, video, film, displays and exhibits.

R

RADARMS   612-334-5900
420 North 5th Street #300   **Minneapolis 55401**
FAX: 612-334-5907
CONTACT: Richard Diercks
E-MAIL: radarms@diercks.com

Props, Costumes & Wardrobe / 459

SERVICES: Movie weapons and firearms for blank fire. Set weapons master. Semi-automatic, full-auto military, law enforcement. Firearms and tactical training.
CAPABILITIES: M16; UZ1; AK-47; MAC; SIG: Beretta; S&W; Calico; MP5; M-16 and more. Blank fire; semi-automatic; full-automatic; weapons for film and training.
CURRENT/RECENT CLIENTS/PROJECTS: Caswell International; Detroit Armor; US Marine Corps; LAPD SWAT; Orange County Sheriff; Minnnetonka Police.
PRESIDENT/CEO/OWNER: Richard Diercks

S

SCROUNGERS, INC.　　　　　　　　　　　　　　612-823-2346
3541 Lyndale Avenue South　　　　　　　　　　Minneapolis 55408
CONTACT: Diane McGrath
SERVICES: Prop House - Rental items for print, film and video.

STAGES THEATRE COMPANY, INC.　　　　　　952-979-1115
1111 Main Street　　　　　　　　　　　　　　　　Hopkins 55343
FAX: 952-979-1124
CONTACT: Laura Kalgren
SUBJECT MATTER: Types of Props/Costumes available: costumes, props from past productions.
RENT/SELL: $5 - $40 per piece for costumes; $2 - $30 per piece for props.

T

TEENER'S THEATRICAL DEPARTMENT　　　　612-339-2793
STORE
729 Hennepin Avenue　　　　　　　　　　　　　Minneapolis 55403
FAX: 612-339-9116
CONTACT: Steve Teener
E-MAIL: teeners@mninter.net
WWW: teenerstheatricals.com
SERVICES: Fabrics from around the world, full line of dance wear and ballet, tap, and jazz dance shoes, suppliers of theatrical make-up (Ben Nye, Kroyolan, Mehron). Customer costume designing plus the Midwest's' largest costume rental department with over 3,000 costumes wigs and accessories. We are celebrating 50 years in the theatrical industry.
CAPABILITIES: Fog machines rentals, mannequins for sale and rental, fun house mirrors, artificial snow, disco balls, our number 1 priority is customer service and satisfaction. We search worldwide to fill customer requests! We carry an exquisite array of loose rhinestones, rhinestone tiaras, and rhinestones by the yard.
CURRENT/RECENT CLIENTS/PROJECTS: Norwest/Wells Fargo Bank; US Bank; Maki-Struc; Carmichael Lynch; Anderson Consulting; Star Tribune; Faegre & Benson; Best Buy; Buca Restaurant; Dayton Marshall Fields; Target Stores; Minnesota Timberwolves; SpookyWorld; Ripsaw; Miss Richfield; Patrick's Cabaret; Children's Theatre; Vee Corp; Ballet of the Dolls; APROPO; BRAVO; Radisson Hotels.
PRESIDENT/CEO/OWNER: Steven Teener, Sophie Teener, Susan Teener

460 / Props, Costumes & Wardrobe

TRADITIONS CLASSIC HOME FURNISHINGS 651-222-5253
1039 Grand Avenue St. Paul 55105
CONTACT: Suzanne Schumann
CAPABILITIES: Rental of home furnishings and accessories for use as props in the film and graphic arts industries.
PRESIDENT/CEO/OWNER: Suzanne Schumann, President

V

VEE CORPORATION 612-378-2561
504 Malcolm Avenue SE #200 Minneapolis 55414
FAX: 612-378-2635
CONTACT: Bonnie Ehlers
E-MAIL: bonniee@vee.com
WWW: vee.com
SERVICES: Concept, design and construction of properties and scenic elements; electronics and special effects available Unusual Items: Production house for Sesame Street Live for 20 years.
SPECIALTIES: Carpentry, welding, sculpting, mold making, steel , aluminum, foam, plastics, fabrics, laminates, pneumatics and kevlar. Rent/Sell: Sell only.
PRESIDENT/CEO/OWNER: Vincent E. Egan, P; Jack Pence, Mrg.

Public Relations

A

MELISSA A. ABRAMS, INC.   763-377-2266
4720 Circle Down   Golden Valley 55416
FAX: 763-377-2378
CONTACT: Melissa A. Abrams
E-MAIL: mabrams@sprintmail.com
SERVICES: Public relations strategy and implementation, media relations. Writing - newsletters, brochures, media materials, speeches, internal communications, bylined articles, communication plans, crisis communication plans, case histories. Editing - newsletters, other communication materials.
CAPABILITIES: 17 years of experience in many industries including, but not limited to, health care, agriculture/agribusiness, manufacturing, technology, commercial real estate, food, service industries.

B

BOZELL KAMSTRA   612-371-7500
100 North 6th Street #800A   Minneapolis 55403
FAX: 612-371-7540
CONTACT: Bill Coontz
WWW: bozellkamstra.com
SERVICES: Consumer packaged goods, consumer products and services, business branding.
CAPABILITIES: Full service public relations, advertising (print and broadcast), yellow page advertising, business and technical, interactive.
SALES CONTACT: Officers: Dean Buresh, President; Bill Coontz, Partner, General Manager; Claire Canavan, Chief Financial Officer; Ron Anderson, VC & Exe. Creative Director; David Dasenbrock, Partner in Charge, Media; Katherine Johnson, Partner, Director of Client Services; Jack Stanton, Partner, Director of Strategic Planning. Bob Kay, Partner, Creative Director. Connie McCaffrey, Partner, Director of Public Relations.
CURRENT/RECENT CLIENTS/PROJECTS: Billy Graham Evangelical Association; Cargill Foods; Ceridian Employer Services; Deluxe Corp; eFunds; General Mills, Inc.'; GOVT.com; Hurd Millwork Company; North Star Steel; Schwan's Grocery Products Division; Wagner Spray Tech.
AFFILIATED OFFICES: Austin, TX; Boston, MA; Cleveland, OH; Dallas, TX; New York, NY; Pittsburgh, PA

ROB BROWN COMMUNICATIONS   612-386-0509
2835 James Avenue South   Minneapolis 55408
FAX: 612-872-0062
E-MAIL: rbcpr@gateway.net
SERVICES: In-house focus facilitation; PR plan writing; hands-on media coordination; events planning. Fees by hour, project, or not-to-exceed retainer. No Mark up on expenses.
CURRENT/RECENT CLIENTS/PROJECTS: 3M High Performance Cloth; Hom Furniture; Simek's Foods; Magnetic Technologies; ABRA; Minneapolis Ski Club; North Shore Commercial Fishing Museum.
PRESIDENT/CEO/OWNER: Rob Brown

462 / Public Relations

BRUCATO & HALLIDAY, LTD.   952-925-2892
6109 Sherman Circle   Edina 55436
FAX: 952-925-2953
CONTACT: Brian Halliday
E-MAIL: bph@brucato.com
WWW: brucato.com
SERVICES: Public relations/strategic communications consulting. Graphic integration, logos, web design, print ad design.
CAPABILITIES: Highest level experience in public affairs, media and politics.
CURRENT/RECENT CLIENTS/PROJECTS: Ordway Theatre for the Performing Arts; Minnesota Chamber of Commerce; American Iron and Steel
PRESIDENT/CEO/OWNER: Cyndy Brucato

BUSCH & PARTNERS, INC.   612-872-7700
318 Groveland Avenue   Minneapolis 55403
CONTACT: Merrill Busch
E-MAIL: buschptnr@aol.com
ACCOUNT EXECUTIVES: Jennifer Busch, Theresa Anderson
SPECIALTIES: Public relations, marketing planning and consulting, government relations, and legislative information services, corporate and marketing communications, direct response/direct mail; strategic communications planning.
CURRENT/RECENT CLIENTS/PROJECTS: Building Owners & Managers Association of Minneapolis; BOR-SON Construction; Marifield Belgarde Yaffe Companies; Lowertown Redevelopment Corporation; Awsumb & Associates; Marquette Advisors; National Association of Industrial & Office Properties (NAIOP); Northco Realtors; Pfeffer Company; SB Commercial; Five Star Realty & Development; Schwieters Group; Sibley House Condominiums; Essex on the Park; Upland Farm; Sherman/Lander Group; City of Brooklyn Park; TSP Architects; NewBridge; Commercial Investment Real Estate Institute (CIREI).

C

CARLISANO COMMUNICATIONS   952-882-1547
12730 Portland Circle   Burnsville 55337
FAX: 952-890-2330
CONTACT: Marta Carlisano
E-MAIL: marta.carlisano@prodigy.net
CAPABILITIES: Producing quality public relations and marketing materials within budget and on deadline. Former newspaper reporter whose passion is writing and providing clients with a product they are proud of.
SPECIALTIES: Helath care marketing and public relations, which includes newsletters, print ads, press releases, brochures, magazine articles. PR and direct mail campaigns and feature articles. Expertise includes writing physician newsletters, health care employee newsletters and direct mail to consumers.
CURRENT/RECENT CLIENTS/PROJECTS: Allina, Children's Health Care, VHA Upper Midwest, Fairview, Health East, MPG, Minnesota Sun Publications, Arthritis Today Magazine.
PRESIDENT/CEO/OWNER: Marta Carlisano

Public Relations / 463

D

DESIGN WRITE COMMUNICATIONS
9308 Rich Road

612-835-7746
Bloomington 55437

E-MAIL: maryjoexley@earthlink.net
SERVICES: Public Relations Planning and Implementation; Media Events; Press Releases; Company Profiles; Trade Show Planning.
CAPABILITIES/SPECIALTIES: Planning; Writing; Design; Production; Event Execution; Recap and Evaluation.
CURRENT/RECENT CLIENTS/PROJECTS: Innovative Cooking Enterprises, Inc.; American Harvest; Nordic Ware; Eye Physicians and Surgeons, P.A.; Edina Laser Eye Center; Foley Martins
CONTACT: Mary Jo Exley

E

ERNSTER PUBLIC RELATIONS
5225 Lincoln Street NE

763-502-0792
Minneapolis 55421

FAX: 763-502-0797
CONTACT: Barb Ernster
SERVICES: Founded in 1995, Ernster Public Relations serves a variety of industries, including apparel, high-tech, manufacturing, performing arts, environment, service and non-profit groups.
CAPABILITIES: Trade and consumer media relations, media tours, trade shows and press conferences, new product introductions and business-to-business communications; press kit development, feature articles, newsletters and marketing materials.
CURRENT/RECENT CLIENTS/PROJECTS: Devold Norwegian Woolens; St. Anthony Performing Arts Group; Honeywell; Digital· Net; Alliance Health Products; Nightmare At Trout Air celebrity appearances.

G

GOFF & HOWARD
255 E. Kellogg Blvd #102

651-292-8062
St. Paul 55101

FAX: 651-292-8091
CONTACT: Paula Howard
E-MAIL: goff.howard@bpsi.net
WWW: goffhoward.com
SERVICES: Strategic services, project management, media relations, media training, lobbying/government relations, grassroots organization, community relations, research, writing and editing, design/production of communication material, communication technology.
CURRENT/RECENT CLIENTS/PROJECTS: Aetna Retirement Services; Andersen Consulting; BlueCross BlueShield of MN; CB Richard Ellis; Center for Policy Studies; Davisco Foods Intl; Fibrowatt; BOMA; Griggs Cooper & Co.; Hamline University; Insurance Federation of MN; Mille Lacs Band of Ojibwe Indians; Polaris Industries; Pueblo Laguna; Smoke-Free Coalition; US West; Wells Fargo

464 / Public Relations

PRESIDENT/CEO/OWNER: Robert E. Goff

H

HABERLE COMMUNICATIONS 763-550-0101
14910 47th Avenue North Plymouth 55446
FAX: 763-550-0721
CONTACT: Susan E. Haberle
E-MAIL: habcom@usinternet.com
CAPABILITIES: Full capabilities in communications planning and implementation.
SPECIALTIES: Corporate communications, marketing communications, speechwriting, publication development and production, employee communications, scriptwriting, community relations, media relations.
CURRENT/RECENT CLIENTS/PROJECTS: Allina Health System; Blue Cross Blue Shield of N.D.; Fairview Health Services; Carlson Companies; HealthEast Care System; McGraw-Hill Companies; National Institute of Health Policy; Vanco Services; Medtronic; Wayzata Public Schools
PRESIDENT/CEO/OWNER: Susan E. Haberle

K

KARWOSKI & COURAGE - PUBLIC RELATIONS 612-342-9898
520 Marquette Avenue #750 Minneapolis 55402
FAX: 612-372-4340
CONTACT: Glenn Karwoski
WWW: creativepr.com
SPECIALTIES: Reputation creation, Marketing PR, Crisis Communications.
CURRENT/RECENT CLIENTS/PROJECTS: Best-Lock, City of Burnsville, GN ReSound, Gateway Computers, First American Funds, Gold 'n Plump, Hazelden Foundation, Hubert W. White, Innuity, KB Gear, Kozy Heat, Lexington Home Furnishings, Liberty Diversified Industries (LDI), Martin/Williams Advertising, McCormick & Schmick's, Polaris, Powertel, 3M, US Bank

FRED KELLER COMMUNICATIONS 612-929-4477
4829 Minnetonka Blvd #202 Minneapolis 55416
FAX: 612-929-4488
CONTACT: Fred Keller
SERVICES: Special events, general publicity. Clients include: McDonalds Restaurants of Minnesota; Disetronic Medical Systems; Source Food Technology.

Public Relations / 465

KERKER MARKETING COMMUNICATIONS
7701 France Avenue South #600
FAX: 952-835-2232
CONTACT: Charles H. Kelly
E-MAIL: results@kerker.com
WWW: kerker.com
OFFICERS: Charles H. Kelly, President; Gary Young, VP/PR Dir.
FOCUS: Kerker is in the business of creating customers by igniting passion for clients' brands. The firm specializes in creative public relations strategies aggressively delivered to achieve maximum results.
SPECIALTIES: Product publicity; media relations; targeted publications; special events; employee relations; counseling; and trade show relations for consumer, retail, high tech and business-to-business clients.
CURRENT/RECENT CLIENTS/PROJECTS: 3M Adhesives; Bonding Systems; Packaging Systems; Industrial Tapes; Industrial Markets Group; Protective Materials (Scotchgard™ Protection); American Medical Systems; Baldwin Hardware; Central Research Laboratories; Eco Water Systems; Health Care Minneapolis Grand Hotel; North Memorial Health Care; Race for the Cure; Sico; Stratasys; Sub-Zero Freezer Company; Thermo King; United Sugars; Wolf Gourmet; Target Stores; Zonetrader.com

952-835-7922
Minneapolis 55435

KETCHUM METZ, INC.
PO Box 874
FAX: 763-479-6828
CONTACT: Perry Ketchum
WWW: pketchum@ketchummetz.com
SPECIALTIES: Communication, marketing and business development firm. Specializing in strategic counsel, image/identity and other areas of public relations and marketing for multiple sectors, including biotech, technology, medical/health care, international and non-profit. Most of our business comes by referral, based on our firm's 14-year reputation for highly skilled counsel.
CURRENT/RECENT CLIENTS/PROJECTS: Fortune 100's to young, growing companies and non-profits. Our networks are regional, national and international.

763-479-0145
Long Lake 55359

KOHNSTAMM COMMUNICATIONS
213 E Fourth Street #202
FAX: 651-298-0628
CONTACT: Josh Kohnstamm, Ricka Robb Kohnstamm
E-MAIL: media@kohnstamm.com
WWW: kohnstamm.com

651-228-9141
St. Paul 55101

SERVICES: Media relations, generating non-paid regional and national newspaper, magazine, television, radio and online publicity.
SPECIALTIES: Fast growth companies, new product introductions, higher education, food and beverage, housewares, outdoor products, toys and youth marketing, technology, architecture.
CURRENT/RECENT CLIENTS/PROJECTS: Carlson School of Management; Potlach Paper; General Mills; Creative Kidstuff; Honest Tea (Bethesda); Present Tense (Virginia); Devine Foods (Philadelphia.)
PRESIDENT/CEO/OWNER: Josh Kohnstamm, Ricka Kohnstamm

L

PAT LINDQUIST & ASSOCIATES, LTD.
7515 Wayzata Blvd, #215
FAX: 952-544-3081
CONTACT: Pat Lindquist or Lisa Zelickson
E-MAIL: lindquistpat@earthlink.net
WWW: patlindquist.com

952-544-3080
Minneapolis 55426

CAPABILITIES: Full public relations practice with advertising support. Special events and benefits, media relations, corporate publications, restaurant consultations, graphic layout and design for collateral material, copywriting, web site copy, direct mail, broadcast production, product development and marketing.
SPECIALTIES: Strong hospitality, restaurant industry, Support coordinate and program special events.
CURRENT/RECENT CLIENTS/PROJECTS: Aquavit Restaurant; Trepper Group; Famous Dave's; La Toscana; Asia Grille; Lord Fletcher's; Marquette Hotel; St. Francis Medical Center; Minnesota Zephyr; Creative Light Worldwide; Pickled Parrot; Vine Park Brewing Company; Flat Land Gallery.
PRESIDENT/CEO/OWNER: Pat Lindquist

THE LINK
406 Stevens Street
P.O. Box 640
FAX: 515-648-4765
CONTACT: Donnie Myers
E-MAIL: link@iafalls.com

800-373-1719
Iowa Falls 50126

SERVICES: The Link is an electronic news release distribution service transmitting news and information. Free of charge to the media of the Midwest.
CAPABILITIES: Mass broadcasting via fax, email, and modem.
PRESIDENT/CEO/OWNER: Mark Hamilton

M

MACCABEE GROUP, INC.
211 North First Street #425
FAX: 612-337-0054
CONTACT: Paul Maccabee
E-MAIL: paul@maccabee.com

612-337-0087
Minneapolis 55401

Public Relations / 467

SERVICES: Full-service PR agency offering consumer and trade media relations, crisis communications, sales promotion, event marketing, new product publicity, community relations and cause marketing, speechwriting and media training, and strategic market planning.
CAPABILITIES: Called "PR Firm of the Year" by Twin Cities Business Monthly Online, Maccabee Group offers special expertise in counseling entrepreneurial companies during times of transition i.e. name changes, mergers, new product launches, and corporate crisis. Trade show support, creative PR events and media relations.
CURRENT/RECENT CLIENTS/PROJECTS: General Mills; Cirque du Soleil; Coldwell Banker Burnet; Nextel; Restaurants Unlimited; Miracle-Ear; Kemps Ice Cream; Wellbridge/Northwest Athletic Club; InH; Buffalo Wild Wings; Visi.com/Nector Internet; MegaMags, Inc.; Metropolitan State University; Johnson Institute Foundation; Better Business Bureau; St. Anthony Park Bank; The Thymes Limited; SweatShop; Upsher-Smith Laboratories.

MCCARTHY-KERN PUBLIC RELATIONS
2720 Garfield Avenue
FAX: 612-879-0625
CONTACT: Pamela McCarthy-Kern
E-MAIL: pmacpr@juno.com

612-879-9349
Minneapolis 55408

SERVICES: Marketing communications, media relations, writing/editing, event planning.
CAPABILITIES: Developing and implementing publicity campaigns for organizations, products and events. Planning events for openings, launches, celebrity appearances and benefits. More than 15 years experience.
CURRENT/RECENT CLIENTS/PROJECTS: Consumer products; retail; performing arts; non-profits.

MINNESOTA CLIPPING SERVICE
12 South 6th Street #1237
FAX: 612-672-9174
CONTACT: Debbie Friez
E-MAIL: mnclip@visi.com
WWW: burrelles.com

612-672-9141
Minneapolis 55402

SERVICES: Providing complete local, regional, national, and international media monitoring including newspapers, magazines, broadcast media, wire services and the Internet. Additional services include electronic clipping, media directory, PR evaluation, clip mounting, fax service and advertising analysis services.
CAPABILITIES: Burrelle's Information Office (BIO), our complete software package, efficiently manages all types of media clips. Receive, store, display, organize, search, share and report on all monitored media quickly and digitally. Clip book presentations can be prepared in minutes.

MINNESOTA LINK
PO Box 640
406 Stevens
FAX: 641-648-4765
CONTACT: Donnie Myers, Marketing Director
E-MAIL: link@iafalls.com
WWW: iafalls.com

800-373-1719
Iowa Falls 50126

CAPABILITIES: News distribution to media via e-mail, modem and fax.

468 / Public Relations

SPECIALTIES: Electronic delivery service for press releases that transmits news and information from government agencies, businesses, organizations and individuals to news media sites among the state of Iowa, Minnesota, Missouri, Kansas, Nebraska and Wisconsin.
CURRENT/RECENT CLIENTS/PROJECTS: Network consists of over 1,300 media outlets in the Midwest (290 in Minnesota) and approximately 500 senders of news.
OFFICERS: Mark Hamilton, Owner; Jo Martin, GM; Donnie Myers, Marketing Director

MINNESOTA NEWSPAPER ASSOCIATION   612-332-8844
12 South 6th Street #1120   Minneapolis 55402
CONTACT: Linda Falkman
E-MAIL: mnaadv@visi.com or mna@mna.org
WWW: mnnewspapmet.org
SERVICES: Information resource for newspapers and the public. Services include advertising, one-order, one-bill newspaper advertising placement; mailing press releases to Minnesota newspapers along with weekly newsletter; legislative, representing newspapers' interests in the legislature. Complete newspaper; member directory is printed annually.
PRESIDENT/CEO/OWNER: Linda Falkman, Executive Director

MRC PUBLIC RELATIONS, INC.   612-377-0272
120 North Westwood Drive   Minneapolis 55422
FAX: 612-377-0274
E-MAIL: meliss1221@aol.com
SERVICES: National, regional and local media relations and coordination including campaign strategy and execution, print and electronic news and feature coverage arrangements, news conferences, writing and editing (news releases, media advisories, media kits, newsletters), public relations, special events consulting, and media coaching.
CURRENT/RECENT CLIENTS/PROJECTS: Bachman's; Hey City Theater, KTCA TV/Twin Cities Public Television; Minneapolis Actors' Theater; Como Park Conservatory; Jujamcyn Productions.
PRESIDENT/CEO/OWNER: Melissa R. Cohen

N

NEMER, FIEGER & ASSOCIATES, INC.   952-925-4848
6250 Excelsior Blvd #203   Minneapolis 55416
CONTACT: James Fieger
SERVICES: Full-service advertising, marketing, public relations, publicity, promotions and special events with heavy emphasis on hospitality, entertainment, leisure and fast food industries plus various local retail products and services.
CAPABILITIES/SPECIALTIES: Account Managers: Kenna Conway, Amy Frantti, Joe Kvam, Molly Mulvehill, Chad Olson, Gina Paz.

Public Relations / 469

CURRENT/RECENT CLIENTS/PROJECTS: Artisan Entertainment; Championship Auto Shows; Dangerfield's Restaurant; Fine Line Features; Goodfellow's Restaurant; Gramercy Films; Health & Fitness Experience; Hollywood Pictures; Ivories Restaurant; Justus Lumber; Metro-Goldwyn-Mayer; Minneapolis Shrine Circus; Minnesota Street Rod Association; Nascar Silicon Motor Speedway; New Line Cinema; Paramount Pictures; Southdale Center; Subway Sandwich & Salad Shops; Tejas - Cuisine of the American Southwest; Touchstone Pictures; Walt Disney Pictures; Whole Life Expo.
PRESIDENT/CEO/OWNER: Officers: James Fieger, CEO; June Fieger, EVP; Tony Harris, EVP; Jon Woestehoff, COO; J. Marie Fieger, Sr. VP Pub. Relations; Chad Olson, Director Film Pub & Promo.

NEW SCHOOL, INC./E-STRATEGY
748 Grand Avenue, #200
FAX: 651-221-4440
CONTACT: Blois Olson

651-221-1999
St. Paul 55105

SPECIALTIES: Public affairs, media relations, community relations, crisis communications, media training, and online communications strategies for small to medium size businesses and organizations.
CURRENT/RECENT CLIENTS/PROJECTS: Soccerdocs, Dominium, SSESCO, Great North Alliance, Minnesota Academy of Ophthalmology, Pritzker and Associates, Meyer & Nuts, Lockridge Grindal Nauen, Kennedy & Graven, Schoolbell, Inc., Ramsey County, University of Minnesota - Humphrey Institute, University of Minnesota - CLA, Ramsey County Regional Rail Authority.
OFFICERS: Blois R. Olson, Ted Davis, David Erickson, Bob Meek

P

PADILLA · SPEER · BEARDSLEY
PUBLIC RELATIONS

PADILLA SPEER BEARDSLEY
224 Franklin Avenue West
FAX: 612-871-7792
CONTACT: John Beardsley
WWW: psbpr.com

612-871-8877
Minneapolis 55404

SPECIALTIES: Full-service, multi-specialty public relations counseling firm; corporate relations, investor relations, marketing public relations, public affairs, employee communications, community relations, executive coaching, media relations, crisis communications, publicity, communications audits and special events marketing. Allied with leading independent public relations firms throughout the world through Worldcom Public Relations Group, An ESOP Company.

470 / Public Relations

OFFICERS: John Beardsley, CH & CEO; Lynn Casey, SVP & COO; Gerald L. Erickson, SVP & CFO; Tom Bartikoski, David Kistle, John Mackay, Marian Briggs, David Hakensen, Tom Jollie, Tony Carideo, SVP's; Paul Batz, Kathy Burnham, Steve Sterling, Sandra Swanson, Brian James, Kerri Safian, Bob Brin, Malkie Bernheim, Mike Greece, Matt Kucharski, Kevin O'Connor, Diane Rose, Larry Spiett, Gordon Leighton, VP's.
AFFILIATED OFFICES: 1460 World Trade Center, 30 East Seventh Street, St. Paul. 651-297-6500; Third Avenue, New York, 10022. 212-752-8338.

THE POLL GROUP
126 North Third Street #100

612-338-7664
Minneapolis 55401

FAX: 612-338-5423
CONTACT: Roger Hegeman
E-MAIL: pollgroup@pollgroup.com
WWW: pollgroup.com
SERVICES: Extensive experience in developing customized web and print for growth-oriented companies. Complete strategic and creative services, corporate identity, lead generation programs, media/public relations, multimedia/web pages. CD-ROM, collateral and sales support materials, trade shows, special events and sales training.
CURRENT/RECENT CLIENTS/PROJECTS: Medtronic; 3M; Blue Cross and Blue Shield of Minnesota; Lutheran Brotherhood; Met Council; Multifoods; Minnesota Opera; United Health Group.
PRESIDENT/CEO/OWNER: Donn Poll, Roger Hegeman, Camille Holthaus

PR NEWSWIRE
970 East Hennepin Avenue

612-331-7800
Minneapolis 55077

FAX: 612-331-3700
CONTACT: Debbie Smith
E-MAIL: debbie-smith@prnewswire.com
WWW: prnewswire.com
SERVICES: PR Newswire is the world leader in the electronic delivery of information directly from companies, institutions and agencies to the media, financial community and consumers through its vast wire, fax, satellite, e-mail and Internet network. PR Newswire provides a broad complement of traditional and new media public relations and investor relations services, including: the delivery of news releases and photos to a broad or targeted audience; the creation of online investor information; the production of video news releases; and the interactive connection between experts and the media. Also provides video and audio clips of local and national news programs.

PUBLIC ISSUE MANAGEMENT, LLP
386 N. Wabasha Street #1180

651-225-8449
St. Paul 55102

FAX: 651-225-8355
CONTACT: Steve Knuth
SERVICES: Governmental relations, grass roots lobbying, media production, campaign management.
CAPABILITIES: 20 years political/issue experience in 15 midwestern and western states. Office in Madison, WI.
CURRENT/RECENT CLIENTS/PROJECTS: U of MN; US West; Oracle
PRESIDENT/CEO/OWNER: Steve Knuth, Managing Partner

Public Relations / 471

PUBLIC RELATIONS SOCIETY OF AMERICA,   **651-917-6248**
MINNESOTA CHAPTER
1821 University Avenue West #S156   **St. Paul 55104**
FAX: 651-917-1835
CONTACT: Jennifer Dark
E-MAIL: prsa@nonprofitsolutions.com
WWW: mnprsa.com
SERVICES: Professional association of public relations practitioners. Education, career development and networking opportunities through chapter meetings and volunteer positions. Membership: Contact office for information packet.

R

RISDALL LINNIHAN ADVERTISING   **651-286-6700**
2475 15th Street NW   **New Brighton 55112**
FAX: 651-631-2561
CONTACT: John Risdall, Chairman
E-MAIL: getwired@risdall.com
WWW: risdall.com
SERVICES: Full service advertising agency offering marketing strategy and planning, marketing research, advertising, direct response, promotion, collateral, publicity/PR and business strategy and planning in the traditional and interactive arenas.
CAPABILITIES: Specializing in the educational, medical, institutional, retail, computer and environmental industries. Internet expertise from site design to site development to marketing planning and implementation.
CURRENT/RECENT CLIENTS/PROJECTS: Aeration Industries; Agribank; Allegheny Power; Alliance Water Resources; American Guidance Service; Applied Technology Consultants; ATG Laboratories, Inc.; Bang Printing; Birchwood Casey; Blanks USA; Brown Wilbert Vault Company; City of New Brighton; Clinch-On Products; Clique Capital; Cocola Palm; cranespharmacy.com; Curative; Decker Publications; Digital River; Diversity Village; EBP HealthPlans, Inc.; Electrosonic; EMPI; E. W. Blanch; Paragon; UniSure; Finnleo Sauna; Fox River; Funeral.com; Galyans; GunVault; Highland Banks; HomeRight; Honeywell; House of Hope, Hubler Family Business Consultants; Innsbruck Jewelers; Isaksen Promotional Specialties; Kinney & Lange; Learning Outfitters; Lease Point.com; Lemna Corporation; Liquid Dynamics; 3M Industrial Mineral Products Division; 3M Traffic Control Materials; 3M Dental Products; 3M Healthcare; 3M Industrial Tapes and Specialties; Magnum Research; Medtronic (Neurological Division); Micom Circuits, Inc.; Morries Automotive Group; Mounds View School District; Normark Rapala; Northern States Power; Norwest Equity Partners, Novartis, Onan Corporation; Photos, Inc.; Pillsbury; Premier Mounts; Printing Industry of MN; Progressive Marketing; Pur (Recovery Engineering); Purus, Inc.; Rainforest Café; RSR Wholesale Guns; Ramsey County Library; Rottlund Homes; SafeWater Anywhere LLC; Schoolbell.com; Schoonover Bodyworks, Inc.; Smith Foundry Company; Smith System Manufacturing, Inc.; Summit Envirosolutions; Target; Tertronics, Inc.; The TPA; Time Savers; Uni-Hydro, Inc.; Upsher-Smith Laboratories; US Filter-Autocon; USFilter-Consolidated Electric; USFilter-Control Systems; USFilter Corporate; USFilter-CPC; USFilter-General Filter; USFilter-Filterite; USFilter-Recovery Services; USFilte-Seitz; USF Johnson (France); USF Johnson Screens; Verdant Brands; VerticalNet; Vista Technologies; WalMart; Water Pollution Control Corp.; Waterworld; Western Bank.

472 / Public Relations

RMS PUBLIC RELATIONS
1038 Quebec Avenue North
FAX: 763-525-8766
CONTACT: Robin Smothers

763-525-8750
Golden Valley 55427

S

THE SAGE GROUP, INC.
10 South Fifth Street #435
FAX: 612-321-9896
CONTACT: Elin Raymond
E-MAIL: eraymond@sagegrp.com
WWW: sagegrp.com

612-321-9897
Minneapolis 55403

SERVICES: Strategic corporate and marketing communications; investor relations. Marketing planning, brand development and advertising.
CAPABILITIES: Full service public relations, marketing communications, and financial communications services. Web-based communications, including newsletters. Annual reports., investor presentations and speeches.
CURRENT/RECENT CLIENTS/PROJECTS: Digital Visions/Netzee; Merrill Corporation FDS; Northern States Power; Affinity Plus Federal Credit Union; Medamicus; Vida Healthcare; Rocketchips; Krones, Inc.; LTG Technologies; Check Technology Corp; NAPFA; Fleming Companies; Research Inc.; Northstar Computer Forms, Rural Cellular Corporation.
PRESIDENT/CEO/OWNER: Elin Raymond

Shandwick International

SHANDWICK INTERNATIONAL
8400 Normandale Lake Blvd #500
FAX: 952-831-8241

952-832-5000
Minneapolis 55437

CONTACT: Sara H, Gavin, Managing Director; David L. Mona, Chairman; Jeanne Carpenter, Senior VP of Marketing and Business Development.
E-MAIL: jcarpenter@shandwick.com
WWW: shandwick.com
CAPABILITIES: Shandwick is a leader in global reputation management and is known for developing innovative and creative solutions to complex communications issues. We work closely with other Shandwick International offices located in major markets across the country and around the world.

Public Relations / 473

SPECIALTIES: Shandwick International specializes in reputation management services including; business-to-business marketing; media training; crisis communications; investor relations; public affairs; event management; internal communications; design, interactive PR and Web marketing services. Strong national expertise in consumer brands, health care, financial and professional services, technology, investor relations, home products, environment and agribusiness. Our Corporate Relations group specializes in government affairs; Minnesota issues and serves Minnesota-based clients. Prospera is Shandwick's print design and video services firm specializing in graphic standards, publications, retail graphics and video.

SHORE TO SHORE COMMUNICATIONS
4209 Branson Street

612-925-6102
Edina 55424

FAX: 612-925-4709
E-MAIL: gshore@winternet.com
SERVICES: Public relations management and consulting to large and small businesses and organizations.
SPECIALTIES: Specialties include strategic planning and implementation of media relations and communications programs, news conferences, awareness campaigns and special events.
CURRENT/RECENT CLIENTS/PROJECTS: Robins, Kaplan, Miller & Ciresi (law firm); AT&T Wireless Service; Sun Country Airlines; Braun Intertec Corp; Cabela's; American Women's Expedition (AWE); Minnesota Senior Federation; Periscope; The Minneapolis Foundation; Bloomington Convention & Visitors Bureau; The Jack Morton Company; Artstone Corp.; Mosaic Marketing; Advants; Walksport America; Dance Partners; Minnesota Women's Press.
PRESIDENT/CEO/OWNER: Gail D. Shore

LINDSAY STRAND ASSOCIATES, INC.
4840 Kingsberry Lane

952-936-7596
Minnetonka 55345

FAX: 952-936-7696
CONTACT: Lindsay Strand
E-MAIL: lsa@ix.netcom.com
SERVICES: Strategic communications including media relations consulting and executive coaching to master media interviews and persuasive presentations. Media emphasis on crisis communications, special events and public affairs issues.
CURRENT/RECENT CLIENTS/PROJECTS: Cenex Harvest States; Children's Defense Fund-MN; Hamline University School of Law; Minnesota Chiropractic Association; Minnesota Dental Association.

474 / Public Relations

STROTHER **SG**
COMMUNICATIONS
GROUP
*Creating Masterpieces
In Integrated
Communication*

STROTHER COMMUNICATIONS GROUP   **612-288-2401**
2700 Foshay Tower   **Minneapolis 55402**
FAX: 612-288-0504
CONTACT: Patrick Strother
E-MAIL: pats@strothercom.com
WWW: strothercom.com
SERVICES: Strother Communications Group (SCG) was founded in 1992 with a mission of providing value to clients by offering strategic, well-executed, cost-effective, exceptionally creative marketing communications services. This is still the mission of SCG and we have now shared it with more than 90 clients. The agency works with high quality clients from a wide variety of categories including consumer/retail, high-tech, professional services, apparel, manufacturing, sports, and event marketing.
CAPABILITIES: Publicity, marketing communications and integrated strategy and research. Also offer graphic design, new media, event marketing and telemarketing services.
CURRENT/RECENT CLIENTS/PROJECTS: Target Stores; NSP; Ryan Companies; Riedell Skates; Smead Manufacturing; GE Capital; United HealthCare; SuperValu.

T
SUSAN THOMPSON, PR   612-416-3705
PO Box 2076   Maple Grove 55311
FAX: 612-416-3762
CONTACT: Susan Thompson
E-MAIL: skt_2k@yahoo.com
SERVICES: Full public relation and writing services, news and product releases, feature articles, media kits, promotion, consultation and media placement.
CAPABILITIES: Authors, books, publishing, small and home-based companies, non-profits and health care.
CURRENT/RECENT CLIENTS/PROJECTS: Client placements with KARE 11, WCCO, WLTE, Star Tribune, Minneapolis- St. Paul Magazine.

W

WEICHERT FINANCIAL RELATIONS, INC.
922 Douglas
FAX: 651-686-9752
CONTACT: Jennifer A. Weichert
E-MAIL: weichertfr@aol.com

651-686-9751
Mendota Heights 55118

SERVICES: Strategic investor relations program development and analysis. Capital formation strategies. Natural and local business media relations. Business plan development. Crisis communications and planning. Experienced in disclosure issues. Hostile takeover defense and offense. Speechwriting.
CAPABILITIES: Nearly 25 years experience raising capital through initial public offerings. Secondaries, private placement. Specializing in crisis communications, particularly with Wall Street constituents (analysts, portfolio managers and shareholders), strategic planning, communications audits and development of integrated investor relations programs; speech writing; creative annual reports; speakers, training.
CURRENT/RECENT CLIENTS/PROJECTS: Sheldahl Investor Relations and Crisis Communications; Anadarko Petroleum; Media Relations; Hawkins Chemical, Inc.; Areadia Financial Crisis Communications.

WELLAND LAIKE COMMUNICATION
255 E Kellogg Blvd #103
FAX: 651-224-9566
CONTACT: Steve Miller
E-MAIL: slm@welland-laike.com

651-224-9554
St. Paul 55101

SERVICES: Strategic development of marketing & advertising campaigns, design and production of promotional material, media buying, internet marketing and web site design, public relations.
CAPABILITIES: Corporate identities, logos, public relations and advertising for regulated industries; legal, financial and health care.
CURRENT/RECENT CLIENTS/PROJECTS: Sieben, Grose & Von Holtum; Brovillette Greater Metro Insurance; Nile Healthcare; Nichols Financial Services Company; Beverly Healthcare; United Bankers Bank; Oasis Markets.
PRESIDENT/CEO/OWNER: Steven L. Miller, APR

HEATHER WEST PUBLIC RELATIONS
4110 39th Avenue South
FAX: 612-724-8760
CONTACT: Heather West
E-MAIL: heatherwest@earthlink.net

612-724-8760
Minneapolis 55406

SERVICES: Heather West specializes in organizations that combine aesthetics and performance for the benefit of their customers, their employees and their community. For eight years she has managed and implemented public relations programs for clients including the American Institute of Graphic Arts/Minnesota; Colonial Craft wood components; Compass Design; Harmon, Inc. glass services; Thomas Design Group, the United Way of the Saint Paul Area; and Wausau Window and Walls Systems. Although she enjoys all aspects of public relations, trade media relations are her specialty. For more information on starting a public relations program, e-mail her at heatherwest@earthlink.net.

Publications

A

AMERICAN HOW-TO   **612-988-7117**
12301 Whitewater Drive, #260   **Minnetonka 55343**
FAX: 612-936-9169
E-MAIL: addept@naoginc.com
WWW: handymanclub.com
SERVICES: American How-To is a special interest magazine published for members of the Handyman Club of America. The magazine is edited to provide the know-how to design, build, install, maintain, repair and purchase products and services to preserve and improve homes and yards. It emphasizes craftsmanship innovation, safety and value. Regular topics include home repair, maintenance and remodeling, woodworking, yard/garden care and landscaping. How-To information includes how to understand, how to plan and how to buy as well as how to do. Regular departments include modern methods, expert answers, tool techniques and workshop.
CONTACT: Sheila Riley Becker, Publisher

AMERICAN JEWISH WORLD   **612-920-7000**
4509 Minnetonka Blvd.   **Minneapolis 55416**
FAX: 612-920-6205
E-MAIL: amjewish@isd.net
SERVICES: Weekly newspaper providing information for the Jewish Community of Minnesota and upper Midwest.
PRESIDENT/CEO/OWNER: Rabbi Marc Liebhaber

AMERICAN SNOWMOBILER   **651-738-1953**
PO Box 25127   **St. Paul 55125**
7582 Currell Boulevard #212
FAX: 651-738-2302
CONTACT: Jerry Bassett
PUBLISHING COMPANY: Recreational Publications, Inc.
EDITORS: Jerry Bassett; Pam Bailey, VP Advertising
CIRCULATION: 90,000 paid
FOCUS: Includes new machine comparisons, technical/mechanical, high-performance and how-to information with a special focus on the people, places and aftermarket products of interest to American snowmobile enthusiasts.
FREQUENCY: 6 times from September to March, along with Sourcebook annual issue published in October.

ASIAN PAGES   **612-884-3265**
PO Box 11932   **St. Paul 55111**
FAX: 612-888-9373
E-MAIL: asianpages@att.net
WWW: asianpages.com
PRESIDENT/CEO/OWNER: Kita Associates, Inc.
CONTACT: Cheryl Weiberg

B

BABY TIMES
PO Box 16422
CONTACT: Marci Mannis
PUBLISHING COMPANY: Family Times, Inc.; Marci Mannis, Publisher
CIRCULATION: 65,000
FOCUS: This Minnesota resource book has been approved by hospitals to be distributed to all expectant mothers in their take homes kits, prenatal classes and OB/GYN offices, corporations, Bylerly's grocery store chain and Caribou Coffee. We will also be distributing Baby Times to the Twin Cities largest diaper services to include in their customer diaper bundles. In addition, Baby Times will be inserted into a large portion of the June/July 2001 issue of Family Times.

952-922-6186
St. Louis Park 55416

BENCH & BAR OF MINNESOTA
600 Nicollet Avenue #380
CONTACT: Judson Haverkamp
E-MAIL: jhaver@statebar.gen.mn.us
PUBLISHING COMPANY: Minnesota State Bar Association
EDITORS: Judson Haverkamp
ACCOUNT SUPERVISORS: Ad Manager: Julie Schaefer
CIRCULATION: Regional; statewide
FOCUS: Law, legal practice and the legal profession in Minnesota
FREQUENCY: 11 times/year; May/June combined

612-333-1183
Minneapolis 55402

BIRD DOG & RETRIEVER NEWS
563 17th Avenue NW
FAX: 651-636-8045
CONTACT: Dennis Guldan
E-MAIL: publisher@bird-dog-news.com
WWW: bdarn.com
SERVICES: Publish Magazine Bird Dog & Retriever News bi-monthly February - December. We host the largest hunting and dog site on the net. We develop print and internet advertising programs.
CAPABILITIES: Web design, ad layout.

651-636-8045
St. Paul 55112

THE BOOK
4601 Excelsior Blvd #337
FAX: 952-924-2371
CONTACT: Rick Christiansen
CAPABILITIES: Minnesota's Advertising Creative Resource. Annually in print and on the web at mnadbook.com

952-924-2322
Minneapolis 55416

478 / Publications

NOT LISTED?

IF YOU'RE ACTIVE IN THE CREATIVE WORLD OF THE TWIN CITIES, E-MAIL YOUR PROFILE INFORMATION TO

listings@primepub.com

TO BE INCLUDED IN THE NEXT EDITION.

OR VISIT US ON THE WEB

gogoldbook.com

C

CITY PAGES, INC.   612-375-1015
401 North 3rd Street #550   Minneapolis 55401
FAX: 612-372-3737
CONTACT: Sara Hartley
E-MAIL: adinfo@citypages.com
WWW: citypages.com
PUBLICATIONS: Publication: City Pages.
PUBLISHING COMPANY: Publishing Company: City Pages, Inc.
EDITORS: Editor: Tom Finkel; Advertising Director: Jerry Gloe
CIRCULATION: Circulation: Local, 120,000, VAC audited.
FOCUS: Focus: Alternative news and arts weekly for the Twin Cities. Editorial content consists of news stories, arts features, sports commentary, reviews, previews and entertainment listings.
FREQUENCY: Frequency: Weekly, on Wednesdays.

CITYBUSINESS, THE BUSINESS JOURNAL   612-288-2100
BOOK OF LISTS
527 Marquette Avenue S #300   Minneapolis 55402

Publications / 479

FAX: 612-288-2121
CONTACT: Kris Lilienthal
WWW: amcity.com
SERVICES: The Book of Lists is the one market reference that the Twin Cities executives turn to time and again throughout the year. A compilation of CityBusinsss: The Business Journal's weekly Top 25 lists for the entire year. The Book of Lists is the most trusted, definitive and indispensable source of information about Twin Cities companies. More than 90 lists ranking companies in selected industries appear in this annual publication.
PRESIDENT/CEO/OWNER: Publisher: Lisa Bormaster

CITYBUSINESS: THE BUSINESS JOURNAL
527 Marquette Avenue S #300

612-288-2100
Minneapolis 55402

FAX: 612-288-2121
CONTACT: Kris Lilienthal
WWW: amcity.com
SERVICES: CityBusiness is the Twin Cities' only weekly source of breaking business news. In addition, CityBusiness provides a must read record section that includes listings of people on the move, new corporations, real estate transactions, bankruptcies, judgements, lawsuits, as well as a weekly business event calendar and other company notes.
PRESIDENT/CEO/OWNER: Publisher: Lisa Bormaster

COMMON LAW PUBLISHING, INC.
5101 Olson Memorial Highway #4000

612-525-0393
Minneapolis 55422

FAX: 612-525-0266
CONTACT: Clarence E. Hagglund
PUBLISHING COMPANY: Publishing Company: Common Law Publishing, Inc.
EDITORS: Editor: Clarence E. Hagglund.
FREQUENCY: Frequency: Periodic

COMPUTER USER
220 South Sixth Street #500
Pillsbury Center, South Tower

612-339-7571
Minneapolis 55402

FAX: 612-339-5806
CONTACT: Christy Mulligan
E-MAIL: edit@computeruser.com
WWW: computeruser.com
PUBLISHING COMPANY: MSP Communications, Inc.
EDITORS: James Matthewson; Assistant Editor: Christy Mulligan
CIRCULATION: Local; 50,000, National 1.75 million.
FOCUS: Monthly print and daily online publication covering the latest developments in office technology and computers for home and business.
FREQUENCY: Monthly.

COOKING PLEASURES
12301 Whitewater Drive, #260

612-988-7117
Minnetonka 55343

FAX: 612-936-9169
CONTACT: Cari Wolf
E-MAIL: addept@naoginc.com

480 / Publications

SERVICES: Cooking Pleasures is edited for people who are passionate about food and cooking. It provides new recipes and ingredients, and new techniques. Topics range from ethnic foods to every day meals, with an emphasis on scratch cooking using readily available ingredients. It also features member recipes, tips, questions, profiles and member testing of new food and cooking related products.
PRESIDENT/CEO/OWNER: Nancy Benedict, Publisher

D

DRAGON DOOR PUBLICATIONS 651-645-0517
PO Box 4381 St. Paul 55104
FAX: 651-644-5676
CONTACT: John Du Cane
PUBLISHING COMPANY: Dragon Door Publications
EDITORS: John Du Cane
FOCUS: Books on videos, audios, T'ai Chi, martial arts, fitness, catalogs of related products.

DUERR & TIERNEY, LTD, ART OF THE WEST 612-935-5850
15612 Hwy 7, #235 Minnetonka 55345
FAX: 612-935-6546
CONTACT: Tom Tierney
E-MAIL: aotw@aotw.com
PUBLICATIONS: Art of the West
CAPABILITIES: A representational western art magazine devoted to lovers of fine western art. New and established artists bring the beauty and the deep roots of our heritage to life through a wide variety of western subject matter. ART OF THE WEST offers landscape and seascapes. Native American art. Mountain man art and "cowboy" art, both from the old wild west days to the working cowboys of today.
FREQUENCY: 7 times annually.
CIRCULATION: 30,000.
PRESIDENT/CEO/OWNER: Tom Tierney, Allan Duerr

F

FAMILY TIMES, INC. 952-922-6186
PO Box 16422 St. Louis Park 55416
CONTACT: Marci Mannis
PUBLISHING COMPANY: Family Times, Inc.
CIRCULATION: 65,000
FOCUS: Family Times are distributed in major retail and restaurant areas, public libraries, childcare centers, grocery stores, coffee shops, health clubs, area hospitals, clinics and doctor's office. The magazines are continually restocked at locations year round.
FREQUENCY: 6 times per year (February/March, April/May, June/July, August/September, October/November, December/January).

Publications / 481

FFI MAGAZINE 651-293-1544
4215 White Bear Parkway #100 St. Paul 55110
FAX: 651-653-4308
CONTACT: Christine Tomlinson
E-MAIL: ffiedit@gwmcnamara.com
WWW: finefurnitureintl.com
PUBLISHING COMPANY: G & W McNamara Publishing, Inc. Publisher: Grace McNamara
EDITORS: Christine Tomlinson
CIRCULATION: 21,000
FOCUS: Bi-monthly professional magazine for international home and garden furnishings. It's purpose is to provide interior design professionals with information they can use to find and merchandise quality furnishings to their customers and clients.

FORMAT MAGAZINE 952-924-2322
4601 Excelsior Blvd #337 Minneapolis 55416
FAX: 952-924-2371
CONTACT: Dale Decker
E-MAIL: format2@aol.com
CAPABILITIES: Minnesota's Advertising and Communications monthly magazine.
PRESIDENT/CEO/OWNER: Deb Gustafson

FROGTOWN TIMES 651-489-2318
843 Van Buren Avenue St. Paul 55104
FAX: 651-488-9052
CONTACT: Anthony Schmitz
E-MAIL: frogtimes@aol.com
SERVICES: Monthly newspaper, 8000 circulation, delivered door-to-door to every household in the Frogtown neighborhood of St. Paul.

FTL PUBLICATIONS 612-938-4275
PO Box 1363 Minnetonka 55345
CONTACT: Joan Marie Verba
E-MAIL: ftl_publications@compuserve.com
WWW: ourworld.compuserve.com/homepages/ftl_publications
SERVICES: Writing and editing of short stories, novels, nonfiction, articles, user guides, technical materials. Proofreading, copyediting, and critiquing services also. Experience: 9 years.
SPECIALTIES: Technical, nonfiction, science fiction and fantasy, children's.
CURRENT/RECENT CLIENTS/PROJECTS: Written for: Lerner Publications, Mpls/St. Paul Magazine, ComputerUser Magazine.

G

GARDENING HOW-TO 612-988-7117
12301 Whitewater Drive, #260 Minnetonka 55343
FAX: 612-936-9169

482 / Publications

E-MAIL: addept@naoginc.com
WWW: gardeningclub.com
SERVICES: Gardening How-To is published for members of the National Home Gardening Club. The Magazine is edited for the avid home gardner providing timely information. The editorial content provides practical answers to questions. How-to information includes how to plan and how to buy, as well as how to do. Regular departments include Good News!, Show and Tell, Questions and Answers, Member Tested, Great Garden Giveaway, Seeds of Change, and Swap Meet.
CONTACT: Jim Bryant, Publisher

THE GOLD BOOK
318 Groveland Avenue South
612-872-7700
Minneapolis 55403
FAX: 612-872-0121
CONTACT: Jennifer Busch, Associate Publisher/VP
E-MAIL: info@primepub.com
WWW: gogoldbook.com
PUBLISHING COMPANY: Prime Publications, Inc.
CIRCULATION: Regional.
FOCUS: Directory of the advertising, publishing, public relations, film, radio and TV, communications and all other creative services industries and professionals in the Twin Cities and Greater Minnesota.
FREQUENCY: Annual.

THE GOLD BOOK/ARIZONA
318 Groveland Avenue South
612-872-7700
Minneapolis 55403
FAX: 612-872-0121
CONTACT: Jennifer Busch, Associate Publisher/VP
E-MAIL: info@primepub.com
WWW: gogoldbook.com
PUBLISHING COMPANY: Prime Publications, Inc.
CIRCULATION: Regional.
FOCUS: Directory of the advertising, publishing, public relations, film, radio and TV, communications and all other creative services industries and professionals in the Phoenix-Scottsdale-Tucson metropolitan areas.
FREQUENCY: Annual.

GOOD AGE
570 Asbury, Suite 305
651-917-1212
St. Paul 55104
FAX: 651-917-1827
CONTACT: William Kosfeld
E-MAIL: wfk@wilder.org
WWW: wilder.org
SERVICES: Free distribution monthly newspaper for senior citizens, available at more than 1,000 locations metro-wide. Advertising available in east or west metro splits. Generally run news/ad ratio of 50/50.
CIRCULATION: 70,000 copies
CAPABILITIES: Put on senior expo events quarterly at Mall of America.
CURRENT/RECENT CLIENTS/PROJECTS: Special State Fair issue in conjunction with Minnesota Board. Senior Expos on Aging and Talent Show at Mall of America.
PRESIDENT/CEO/OWNER: Amherst H. Wilder Foundation

GRANDPARENT TIMES
PO Box 16422
CONTACT: Marci Mannis
PUBLISHING COMPANY: Family Times, Inc.; Marci Mannis, Publisher
CIRCULATION: 65,000
FOCUS: Grandparent Times is a special quarterly publication within a publication that appears in the two-month combined issues of Family Times (April/May, June/July, August/September, and October/November). It will focus on many issues, aspects and important lifestyle topics that concern today's grandparents.

952-922-6186
St. Louis Park 55416

I

IRISH GAZETTE
PO Box 65782
FAX: 651-695-0886
CONTACT: James Brooks
E-MAIL: irish@mn.state.net
SERVICES: The Irish Gazette is a publication devoted to Irish culture, current events, and the Irish-American experience.
PRESIDENT/CEO/OWNER: James Brooks

651-698-3083
St. Paul 55165

J

JOLA PUBLICATIONS
2933 North 2nd Street
FAX: 612-521-2289
E-MAIL: jolapub@aol.com
WWW: jolapub.com
SERVICES: Medical directories for Minnesota, Wisconsin, Iowa, Nebraska, Kansas and Dakotas-Montana. Publications on Montessori education.
PRESIDENT/CEO/OWNER: Dennis Schapiro

612-529-5001
Minneapolis 55411

K

K L PUBLICATIONS, INC.
2001 Killebrew Drive #105
FAX: 612-854-9440
CONTACT: Karel A Laing
E-MAIL: klpub@aol.com
SERVICES: Custom magazine publishers providing all creative services -- management, editorial, design, fulfillment, mailing.

612-854-0155
Bloomington 55425

L

LA VOZ
PO Box 19206
Diamond Lake Station
612-825-1490
Minneapolis 55419
FAX: 612-825-1490
CONTACT: Joan E. Ramirez
E-MAIL: lavoznewsmag@aol.com
SERVICES: La Voz brings you local and national news of interest in Spanish as well as English. Also, features on health, employment, housing, immigration, food, arts and entertainment as well as personalities. Accept advertising in black and white as well as color. Rates available on request. La Voz Newsmagazine is a commercial publication rather than a non-profit. La Voz has been in continuous publication since 1970.
CAPABILITIES/SPECIALTIES: La Voz publishes small run specialty books, current books include: "El Tesoro de la Sierra Madre, "Legends Myths and History of Mexico," and "From the Family Tree, a Century of Pickle Recipes."

LAKESHORE WEEKLY NEWS
10001 Wayzata Blvd.
612-843-4612
Minnetonka 55305
CONTACT: Mark Beckstrom
EDITORS: Amy Cicchese
PUBLISHING COMPANY: Skyway Publications
ACCOUNT SUPERVISORS: Ad Manager: Mark Beckstrom

LANGUAGEPOWER PUBLICATIONS
1402 N. Albert Street
651-487-3189
St. Paul 55108
FAX: 651-487-3189
CONTACT: Edward Voeller
SERVICES: Publishers of language teaching and learning material; consultants to publishers in the US and overseas.
CAPABILITIES: Complete publishing facilities; expertise in languages.
CURRENT/RECENT CLIENTS/PROJECTS: NTC/Contemporary; Capstone Press; KTCA Public TV; other publishers of language teaching and learning material.
PRESIDENT/CEO/OWNER: Edward Voeller

LAVENDER™

LAVENDER MAGAZINE
2344 Nicollet Avenue South #300
FAX: 612-871-2650
CONTACT: Pierre Tardif, Vice President & COO
E-MAIL: advertising@lavendermagazine.com
WWW: lavendermagazine.com
PUBLISHING COMPANY: Lavender Media, Inc.
PRESIDENT/CEO/OWNER: Stephen J. Rocheford, President & CEO
EDITORS: Rudy Renaud
ADVERTISING DIRECTOR: David Skillings
CIRCULATION: 30,377 verified by Audit Bureau of Circulation. Distribution: Twin Cities with additional limited distribution in greater Minnesota, Wisconsin, Illinois, North/South Dakota, Nebraska and Iowa. Frequency: Biweekly (every other Friday.)
FOCUS: Gay-lesbian-bisexual-transgender readers and progressive and A&E straight readership; local to international news and politics, arts and entertainment, leisure and travel, nightlife. Readership 58% male/41% female, highly educated, average household income $69,708. Highly awarded by Minnesota Magazine & Publications Association and Q Syndicate Vice Versa Awards for Excellence in the Gay and Lesbian Press. Free.

612-871-2237
Minneapolis 55404

LERNER PUBLICATIONS
241 First Avenue North
FAX: 612-332-7615
CONTACT: Adam Lerner
WWW: lernerbooks.com
PUBLICATIONS: Juvenile: nature, biographies, fiction, geography, history, science, picture books.
OFFICERS: Harry J. Lerner, Chairman & CEO; Adam Lerner, Publisher; Mary Rodgers, VP, Editor in Chief; David Wexler, VP, Director of Sales & Marketing; Gary Hansen, VP, Production Director; Gar Willets, Director of Contracts & Author Relations; Margaret Wunderlich, VP, Chief Financial Officer; Jim Laib, VP, Director of Technology; Deborah Hilden, VP, Director of Human Resources; David Lamberger, VP, General Manager; Beth Heiss, Marketing Manager; Zach Marell, Art Director

612-332-3344
Minneapolis 55401

LETS PLAY, INC.
2721 East 42nd Street
FAX: 612-729-0259
CONTACT: Doug Johnson

612-729-0023
Minneapolis 55406

486 / Publications

E-MAIL: letsplay@letsplayhockey.com
WWW: letsplayhockey.com
CAPABILITIES: We've published Let's Play Hockey newspaper for 29 years and Let's Play Softball for 15 years. For the past 10 years the Let's Play Hockey TV Magazine has aired on Midwest Sports Channel. We also produce three trade shows; the 10th Annual Let's Play Hockey Expo held in conjunction with the Minnesota Boy's State Hockey Tournament. The Third Annual Let's play Hockey international Expo in Las Vegas for the hockey trade plus the American Hockey Coaches Association Trade Show is organized by Let's Play Hockey.
SPECIALTIES: Publishing game programs association newsletters, sports marketing and trade show coordination.

LET'S PLAY, INC.   **612-729-0023**
2721 East 42nd Street   **Minneapolis 55406**
FAX: 612-729-0259
CONTACT: Doug Johnson
E-MAIL: letsplay@letsplayhockey.com
WWW: letsplayhockey.com
SERVICES: Publications: Let's Play Softball, Let's Play Hockey.

LLEWELLYN PUBLICATIONS   **800-THE-MOON**
PO Box 64383   **St. Paul 55164**
FAX: 651-291-1908
CONTACT: Lisa Braun
CAPABILITIES: Llewellyn Worldwide, Ltd., is the nation's oldest and largest new age publisher. With over 550 books, tarot kits, and decks, we are dedicated to the spiritual advancement of the individual. Our publishing goals is to provide options and tools for exploring new worlds of mind and spirit, thereby aiding the quest for expanded human potential, spiritual consciousness, and awareness of the earth.
PRESIDENT/CEO/OWNER: Carl Llewellyn Wescheke

LOW AND INSIDE   **612-701-2799**
PO Box 290228   **Minneapolis 55429**
FAX: 763-767-5510
CONTACT: Nick Vetter
E-MAIL: have-a-ball@lowandinside.com
WWW: lowandinside.com
FOCUS: Have a ball! A non-statistical look into and around the Great American Pastime where history is respected and the baseball fan has a voice. Based 1988.
EDITORS: Nick Vetter, Scott Mahlmann, Rads E. Publishing Company: Low and Inside Creative
CIRCULATION: Subscription based, Internet community users.
FREQUENCY: Regular web site-based updates and additions.
PRESIDENT/CEO/OWNER: Nick Vetter

M

MACHALEK COMMUNICATIONS, INC. 952-736-8000
432 Gateway Boulevard Burnsville 55337
FAX: 952-736-0234
CONTACT: Tammy Earley
E-MAIL: jon@machalek.com
WWW: machalek.com
PUBLICATIONS: Bars & Clubs-Dek, Dental-Dek, Foodservice Marketplace, Grounds, Parks & Playgrounds-Dek, Police & Security Action Cards, Vet-Dek.
PRESIDENT/CEO/OWNER: Jonathan Machalek

MARLOR PRESS, INC. 651-484-4600
4304 Brigadoon Drive St. Paul 55126
CONTACT: Marlin Bree
E-MAIL: marlor@minn.net
SERVICES: Marlor Press publishes nonfiction trade paperback books for boaters, children and travelers.
CURRENT/RECENT CLIENTS/PROJECTS: Recent books are: Kid's Book to Welcome a New Baby and the Kid's Trip Diary; Heavy Weather Boating Emergencies, and London for the Independent Traveler.

G & W MCNAMARA PUBLISHING, INC. 651-293-1544
4215 White Bear Parkway, #100 St. Paul 55110
CONTACT: Grace W. McNamara
SERVICES: Window Fashions Magazine, Fine Furniture International (FFI) Magazine, The Wall Paper, Idea Book.
PRESIDENT/CEO/OWNER: Grace W. McNamara, President

MERRIAM PARK POST 651-645-6887
1573 Selby Avenue #311 St. Paul 55104
CONTACT: Matt Hollinshead
SALES CONTACT: Editorial: Mat Hollinshead, 651-645-4267
SERVICES: Publishing Company: Merriam Park Post; Focus: Community Issues; Frequency: Monthly.

MIDWEST INDEPENDENT PUBLISHERS ASSN. 651-917-0021
PO Box 581432 Minneapolis 55458
CONTACT: Doug Shidell
SERVICES: Publishing Company: Midwest Independent Publishers Assn. Circulation: 200 Focus: Independent Publishing. Frequency: Monthly.

MINNESOTA BRIDE MAGAZINE 612-338-4125
251 First Avenue North #401 Minneapolis 55401
CONTACT: R. Craig Bednar
PUBLISHING COMPANY: Tiger Oak Publications

488 / Publications

EDITORS: Diane Richard
ACCOUNT SUPERVISORS: Dena Alspach, Dave Ritsgma
CIRCULATION: 15,000 per issue
FOCUS: Regional guide for fashion, wedding planning and the newly married lifestyle.
FREQUENCY: Semi-annual (January and July)

MINNESOTA GUIDEBOOK TO STATE AGENCY SERVICES
651-297-7963

117 University Avenue   St. Paul 55155
FAX: 651-297-8260
CONTACT: Robin PanLener
PUBLISHING COMPANY: Minnesota State Department of Administration; Communications, Media Division.
EDITORS: Robin PanLener
CIRCULATION: Regional; 10,000
FOCUS: Minnesota state government, agency services, history, data, statistics, information, resources.
FREQUENCY: Quadrennial 2000-2003

MINNESOTA LAW & POLITICS
612-335-8808
220 South 6th Street #500   Minneapolis 55402
FAX: 612-335-8809
CONTACT: William White
E-MAIL: kaplan@lawandpolitics.com
WWW: lawandpolitics.com
SERVICES: Publisher of Minnesota Law & Politics Magazine, Washington Law & Politics Magazine.

MINNESOTA MEDICINE
612-378-1875
3433 Broadway Street NE #300   Minneapolis 55413
FAX: 612-378-3875
CONTACT: Meredith McNab
E-MAIL: mm@mmmed.org
SERVICES: Publishing Company: Minnesota Medical Association; Editor: Meredith McNab; Ad Manager: Michele Holzwarth; Circulation: 10,000; Focus: State medical journal covering scientific, socioeconomic, public health, medical, legal, and bio-medical ethnic issues of interest to physicians. Frequency: Monthly.

MINNESOTA WOMENS PRESS
651-646-3968
771 Raymond Avenue   St. Paul 55114
FAX: 651-646-2186
CONTACT: Kathy Magnuson
E-MAIL: women@womenspress.com
WWW: womenspress.com

SERVICES: Minnesota Women's Press is a biweekly newspaper. The Minnesota Women's Press is distributed free of charge at over 450 metro locations and 60 greater Minnesota locations. Circulation is 40,000 with 2,000 of those distributed in greater Minnesota. The newspaper offers a fresh perspective on women's ideas and issues and is proud to celebrate its 15th year of Minnesota's only women's newspaper. Directory - this annual publication is the area's most comprehensive listing of women in business and resources for women. It is distributed free of charge as an insert to the newspaper. Now in its 13th year, the directory is over 150 pages, and provides information on the vast network of resources available to women. BookWomen - this bimonthly book celebrates women's words and the women who read/write them. Our subscribers make connections with each other through this publication, sharing thoughts, feelings and ideas concerning women writers.

MINNESOTA'S BOOKSTORE
117 University Avenue #110A
FAX: 651-297-8260
CONTACT: Susan Culligan
ALTERNATE PHONE: 1-800-657-3706
E-MAIL: mnbook.list@state.mn.us
WWW: comm.media.state.mn.us

800-657-3757
St. Paul 55155

SERVICES: Publications: Minnesota's Guidebook to State Agency Services, State Register (weekly magazine), Minnesota Laws and Rules, wide variety of business, professional and educational manuals, directories, federal government publications, over 7000 maps, natural resource and recreation guides, mailing lists.
CURRENT/RECENT CLIENTS/PROJECTS: Department of Natural Resources publications.
PRESIDENT/CEO/OWNER: Mary Mikes, Director

N

NEW RESIDENTS GUIDE
10001 Wayzata Blvd.
FAX: 612-375-9208
CONTACT: Char Delaney
EDITORS: Pam Mellskog
PUBLISHING COMPANY: Skyway Publications
ACCOUNT SUPERVISORS: Ad Manager: Char Delaney

612-375-9222
Minnetonka 55305

NORTH AMERICAN FISHERMAN
12301 Whitewater Drive, #260
FAX: 612-936-9169
E-MAIL: addept@naoginc.com
WWW: fishingclub.com

612-988-7117
Minnetonka 55343

SERVICES: North American Fisherman is edited for the fishing enthusiast. Editorial features both freshwater and saltwater species and related techniques on how to better fish for those species. Also covered are new products and equipment as well as regular fishing destination articles.
CONTACT: Todd Siebell

490 / Publications

NORTH AMERICAN HUNTER
12301 Whitewater Drive, #260
FAX: 612-936-9169
E-MAIL: addept@naoginc.com
WWW: huntingclub.com

612-988-7117
Minnetonka 55343

SERVICES: North American Hunter is edited for members nationwide of the North American Hunting Club. Editorial content consists of how-to features by outdoor writers and club members. Emphasis on hunting with bow, black powder, shot gun, rifle and handgun for big game, small game, upland birds and waterfowl. Also emphasizes how to plan out-of-state hunts. Includes hunting tips, outdoor equipment ratings.
CONTACT: Tom Perrier, Publisher

NYSTROM PUBLISHING COMPANY, INC.
9100 Cottonwood Lane
FAX: 763-425-0898
E-MAIL: nystrm@minn.net

763-425-7900
Maple Grove 55369

SERVICES: Printing and mailing.
CAPABILITIES/SPECIALTIES: Full service from desktop to printing, binding, mailing. Specialize in publications: newsletters, magazines, manuals, catalogs, booklets, directories, and books. Processes: Offset, sheetfed. Maximum sheet size: 25 x 38.
PRESIDENT/CEO/OWNER: Gerry Nystrom

P

PGA TOUR PARTNERS
12301 Whitewater Drive, #260
FAX: 612-936-9169
E-MAIL: addept@naoginc.com
WWW: pgatour.com

612-988-7117
Minnetonka 55343

SERVICES: PGA Tour Partners Magazine is edited for members of the PGA Tour Partners Club. It focuses on how to increase the golfing skill, knowledge and enjoyment of the club members. It promotes golf sportsmanship, courtesy and respect for the rules of the game, and provides how-to information designed to improve every player's game. Regular topics include instruction--from the fundamentals to the fine points--tour coverage, equipment reviews, health and fitness, course reviews, travel and personalities. Included are player human interest/instructional features.
CONTACT: Scot Ramm, Publisher

S

SAN FRANCISCO BRIDE
1067 Valencia, #8
FAX: 415-647-2421
CONTACT: R. Craig Bednar
PUBLISHING COMPANY: Tiger Oak Publications

415-786-9231
San Francisco 94110

EDITORS: Chiori Santiago
ACCOUNT SUPERVISORS: Ad Manager: Antra Picard
CIRCULATION: 18,000 per issue
FOCUS: Regional guide for fashion, wedding planning and the newly married lifestyle.
FREQUENCY: Semi-annual (January and July)

SEATTLE BRIDE   206-284-1750
423 Third Avenue West   Seattle 98119
FAX: 206-284-2550
CONTACT: R. Craig Bednar
PUBLISHING COMPANY: Tiger Oak Publications
EDITORS: Rachel Hart
ACCOUNT SUPERVISORS: Ad Manager: Melissa Coffman
CIRCULATION: 13,000 per issue
FOCUS: Regional guide for fashion, wedding planning and the newly married lifestyle.
FREQUENCY: Semi-annual (January and July)

SEATTLE MAGAZINE   206-284-1750
423 Third Avenue West   Seattle 98119
FAX: 206-284-2550
CONTACT: R. Craig Bednar
PUBLISHING COMPANY: Tiger Oak Publications
EDITORS: Rachel Hart
ACCOUNT SUPERVISORS: Ad Manager: Melissa Coffman
CIRCULATION: 45,000 per issue
FOCUS: Seattle's city magazine with resources for dining, entertainment, the arts, homes, and the people who make Seattle.
FREQUENCY: Monthly (except February and August)

SENIOR TIMES   952-922-6186
PO Box 16422   St. Louis Park 55416
CONTACT: Marci Mannis
PUBLISHING COMPANY: Family Times, Inc.; Marci Mannis, Publisher
CIRCULATION: 55,000
FOCUS: Senior Times is a free quarterly publication that is produced in February, May, August and November. However, it is distributed continuously throughout the year. In essence, an advertiser receives 3 months of advertising with each issue. This allows us to offer our advertisers one of the best media values reaching the fastest growing segment of our population. Senior Times is strategically distributed to the seven county metropolitan area, conservatively reaching in excess of 1 million interested readers each year. We are continually expanding our exciting distribution network to reach over 850 of the most important and exclusive venues in this market such as the Byerly's grocery store chain and Caribou Coffees.

THE SILVER BOOK   612-872-7700
318 Groveland Avenue South   Minneapolis 55403
FAX: 612-872-0121
CONTACT: Jennifer Busch, Associate Publisher/VP
E-MAIL: info@primepub.com

492 / Publications

WWW: gosilverbook.com
PUBLISHING COMPANY: Prime Publications, Inc.
CIRCULATION: Regional.
FOCUS: Guide to the information technology and digital creative world of the Twin Cities and Greater Minnesota.
FREQUENCY: Annual.

SKYWAY NEWS
15 South 5th Street #1060
612-843-5226
Minneapolis 55402
CONTACT: Gary L'Herault
EDITORS: Gary L'Herault
PUBLISHING COMPANY: Skyway Publications
ACCOUNT SUPERVISORS: Ad Manager: Gary L'Herault

SONS OF NORWAY
1455 West Lake Street
612-827-3611
Minneapolis 55408
FAX: 612-827-0658
CONTACT: Vicki Stumpf
E-MAIL: fraternal@sofn.com
WWW: sofn.com
PUBLISHING COMPANY: MSP Communications
EDITORS: Karen Anway
ACCOUNT SUPERVISORS: Ad Manager: Bonnie Oslund
CIRCULATION: 55,000
FOCUS: Norwegian and Norwegian-American current events, history and culture. Life insurance products, membership to start, develop or intensify an interest in Nordic heritage. Supports a variety of humanitarian outreach programs. Provide monthly magazine, Viking. Helps you stay in touch with your Nordic heritage.
FREQUENCY: Monthly

SOUTHWEST JOURNAL
3225 Lyndale Avenue South
612-825-9205
Minneapolis 55408
FAX: 612-825-0929
CONTACT: Terry Gahan, Advertising Sales Manager
E-MAIL: swjournal@uswest.net
WWW: swjournal.com
SERVICES: Publish an award-winning bi-weekly newspaper which is distributed to 100% of households in Southwest Minneapolis area - including recently expanded coverage to downtown Minneapolis. Circulation, both home-delivered and newsstand, is 50,000. Advertising rates available upon request. Editorial offers a comprehensive news source for residents and business owners in our community, from issues of city wide concern to local and community news on schools, parks, churches, businesses and neighborhoods.
CAPABILITIES: Southwest Journal has a full-time editor, four full-time reporters and a staff photographer. We recently won the Frank Premack Public Affairs award for a series of articles on affordable housing. We offer comprehensive ad production services (please call with specifics to get a price quote) and specialty publication services. See the listing under Total Market Coverage, Inc, - a sister company - for media planning and buying services.
PRESIDENT/CEO/OWNER: Janis Hall, Publisher; Terry Gahan, VP

Publications / 493

STAGES THEATRE COMPANY, INC.
1111 Main Street
952-979-1121
Hopkins 55343
FAX: 952-979-1124
CONTACT: Jill Booher
SPECIALTIES: Playbill advertising. Place advertisement in the playbills at one of the largest youth theater organizations in the state. Stages Theatre Company plays to about 86,000 people annually, living primarily in the Twin Cities metro area. Call for specifics.

STATE REGISTER
117 University Avenue Room 110A
651-297-7963
St. Paul 55155
FAX: 651-297-8260
CONTACT: Subscriptions: 297-8774; Editorial 297-7963
WWW: comm.media.state.mn.us
PUBLISHING COMPANY: Minnesota Department of Administration: Communications Media Division.
EDITORS: Robin Panlener
CIRCULATION: 500 print, 5,000 (via Internet)
FOCUS: Official notices, state contracts and advertised bids, rulemaking of state agencies, executive orders of governor, revenue notices, commissioner's orders, state grants and loans; non-state public contracts. Audience includes corporations and businesses providing professional, technical and consulting services; all regulated professions: real estate, insurance, law, securities, medicine and health care, human service providers, libraries, schools and colleges.
FREQUENCY: Published every Monday, Tuesday when Monday is a holiday.

SUN NEWSPAPERS
10917 Valley View Road
612-829-0797
Eden Prairie 55344
FAX: 612-392-6802
CONTACT: Kevin True
E-MAIL: ktrue@mnsunpub.com
WWW: mnsun.com
SERVICES: Circulation: 375,000. CAC-Audited. Frequently: Weekly on Wednesday. Focus: Local and community news in the areas of school, sports, city meetings, school board meetings, etc. Local and national advertising and inserts.
CAPABILITIES: Sun Newspapers is the largest weekly community newspaper group in the state. With a weekly home delivered circulation of over 375,000 households, Sun Newspapers is able to deliver strong metropolitan numbers as well as targeting individual communities. Its Twin cities' suburban coverage is divided into five major geographical areas. These areas include the Sun-Sailor in the western suburbs, the Sun-Post in the northern suburbs, the Sun-Press and News in the northwest suburbs, the Sun Current Central in the central suburbs, the Sun-Current South in the suburbs south of the Minnesota River, the Sun-Patriot reaching to the far southwestern suburbs and the Sun-Gazette in the Stillwater area along the St. Croix River. Sun publishes 37 titles and serves 129 communities in the greater metropolitan area. Advertisers have the choice of running their ads full circulation or by individual communities. Display ads for Sun papers are in a convenient modular format and are published every Wednesday. In addition to the normal products offered through the print industry, Sun also offers Post-It Note advertising, Web printing, internet advertising and commercial printing.
PRESIDENT/CEO/OWNER: Frank Chilinski, Publisher

494 / Publications

T

TPT MAGAZINE   612-375-9222
10001 Wayzata Blvd.   Minnetonka 55305
FAX: 612-375-9208
CONTACT: Scott Briggs
PUBLISHING COMPANY: Skyway Publications, Inc.
EDITORS: Scott Briggs
ACCOUNT SUPERVISORS: Ad Manager: Todd Hyde
CIRCULATION: Local 106,000
FOCUS: Services the membership of KTCA Twin Cities Public TV.
FREQUENCY: 7 times a year.

TWIN CITIES EMPLOYMENT WEEKLY   612-359-2100
527 Marquette Avenue S #150   Minneapolis 55402
FAX: 612-359-2110
CONTACT: Jo Nelson
WWW: getwork.com
SERVICES: Twin Cities Employment Weekly, the Twin Cities original employment newspaper, assist job seekers, recruiters and HR personnel with the career goals and objectives. TCEW provides an opportunity for employers to advertise its job openings and editorial content that educates, informs and alerts readers about the Twin Cities job market. TCEW also features the area's most comprehensive career calendar informing readers of job fairs and career-related classes and seminars.
PRESIDENT/CEO/OWNER: Publisher: Jo Nelson

TWIN CITIES PARENT   612-338-4125
251 First Avenue North #401   Minneapolis 55401
CONTACT: R. Craig Bednar
PUBLISHING COMPANY: Tiger Oak Publications
EDITORS: Barbara Knox
ACCOUNT SUPERVISORS: Ad Manager: Dave Ritsema, Dena Alspach
CIRCULATION: 22,000 per issue
FOCUS: Regional parenting resource for activities, physicians, events and education. Focuses primarily on children from 0 - 12.
FREQUENCY: Bi-monthly (Jan, March, May, July, Sept., Nov).

U

UPFRONT PRODUCTIONS   651-633-5299
2350 County Road C #120   St. Paul 55113
FAX: 651-633-5197
CONTACT: Tricia Nordby Hamrin/Chris Hamrin
WWW: hoopjumping.com

CAPABILITIES: Organizational Communications Solutions Center. A Spectrum. A Synergy. Concept Development, Copywriting, Graphic Design, Illustration, Document Production, Web Site Creation, Scanning, Photo Retouching, Pre-press, Offset Printing, Digital B&W Printing, Color Copies, Posters, Displays, Signs, Custom Assembly, Inventory, Distribution, Corporate Compass® MIS, VantagePoint™, Hoop Jumping™.
SPECIALTIES: Choose your hoop. We'll jump through it™.
OFFICERS: Tricia Nordby Hamrin/Chris Hamrin

W

WINDOW FASHIONS MAGAZINE
4215 White Bear Pkwy #100
FAX: 651-653-4308
CONTACT: Suzanne Worthly
E-MAIL: bcarlson@gwmcnamara.com
WWW: window-fashions.com

651-293-1544
St. Paul 55110

SERVICES: To the trade only magazine for window coverings professionals; international trade show producer.
CAPABILITIES: Publishing.
PRESIDENT/CEO/OWNER: Grace McNamara

Publishers - Books

B

BEAVERS POND PRESS, INC.   952-829-8818
5125 Danen's Drive   Edina 55439
FAX: 952-944-4065
CONTACT: Milton E. Adams, Publisher
E-MAIL: adamsppo@aol.com
WWW: beaverspondpress.com
SERVICES: Full Service General Publisher
SPECIALTIES: Established in 1965. Specializing in books (soft cover and case bound), manuals, price books, 4/c product catalogs and on-demand litho and Docutech printing. Printing brokerage, sheetfed, web and specialty printing.
PRESIDENT/CEO/OWNER: Milton E. Adams

BETHANY HOUSE PUBLISHERS   952-829-2500
11400 Hampshire Avenue So   Minneapolis 55438
FAX: 952-829-2768
E-MAIL: cs@bethanyhouse.com
WWW: bethanyhouse.com
CONTACT: Gary Johnson, Publisher
SALES CONTACT: Rowen Wipf, Customer Service Manager

C

CAROLRHODA BOOKS, INC.   612-332-3344
241 First Avenue North   Minneapolis 55401
FAX: 612-332-7615
CONTACT: Alison Grey
WWW: lernerbooks.com
PUBLICATIONS: Juvenile picture books, biographies, early-readers, history, geography, culture studies, fiction, science.
PRESIDENT/CEO/OWNER: Harry J. Lerner, Chairman & CEO; Adam Lerner, Publisher; Mary Rodgers, VP, Editor in Chief; David Wexler, VP, Director of Sales & Marketing; Gary Hansen, VP, Production Director; Gar Willets, Director of Contracts & Author Relations; Margaret Wunderlich, VP, Chief Financial Offer; Jim Laib, VP, Director of Technology; Debra Hilden, VP, Director of Human Resources; David Lamberger, VP, General Manager; Beth Heiss, Marketing Manager; Zach Marell, Art Director

COMMON LAW PUBLISHING, INC.   612-525-0393
5101 Olson Memorial Highway #4000   Minneapolis 55422
FAX: 612-525-0266
CONTACT: Clarance E. Hagglund
PUBLICATIONS: Publications: Insurance Producer Liability in Plain Language, Real Estate Agency & Appraiser Liability in Plain Language, Minnesota Insurance Law, Stay Out of Court and Stay in Business.

Publishers - Books / 497

CORPORATE REPORT FACT BOOK   612-338-4288
527 Marquette Avenue S #300   Minneapolis 55402
FAX: 612-573-6300
CONTACT: Kris Lilienthal
WWW: corpreport.com
SERVICES: The Corporate Report Fact Book is the definitive resource of statistical and contact research on Minnesota business published annually. The Fact Book has comprehensive listing of thousands of companies including company descriptions, earnings, histories and recent events. Also contains over 10,000 names, addresses, phone and fax numbers of key executives. The Fact Book is a complete who's who guide to the companies of the upper Midwest.
PRESIDENT/CEO/OWNER: Publisher: Lisa Bormaster

D

DUERR & TIERNEY, LTD, ART OF THE WEST   612-935-5850
15612 Hwy 7, #235   Minnetonka 55345
FAX: 612-935-6546
CONTACT: Tom Tierney
E-MAIL: aotw@aotw.com
PUBLICATIONS: Art of the West
PRESIDENT/CEO/OWNER: Tom Tierney, Allan Duerr

F

FINNEY COMPANY   952-938-9330
3943 Meadowbrook Road   Minneapolis 55426
FAX: 952-938-7353
CONTACT: Janet A. Zahn
E-MAIL: feedback@finney-hobar.com
WWW: finney-hobar.com
SERVICES: Publisher of Career, Education, and Life Planning Materials--for the K-12 education market.
SPECIALTIES: Specializing in Career Development and Exploration, School-to-Work, Tech Prep, Placement and On the Job. Textbooks, Workbooks and Software.
PRESIDENT/CEO/OWNER: Janet A. Zahn

FINS PUBLICATIONS   651-490-9408
2700 Rice Street   Roseville 55113
FAX: 651-490-1450
CONTACT: Sybil Smith
E-MAIL: smithse@aol.com
SPECIALTIES: Fishing-Guide books.
PUBLICATIONS: Twin Cities Fishing Guide, Brainerd-Whitefish Fishing Guide, also Plastic Lake Maps showing where fish can be caught on each lake.
PRESIDENT/CEO/OWNER: Sybil Smith

498 / Publishers - Books

H

HOBAR PUBLICATIONS　　　　　　　　　　952-938-9330
3943 Meadowbrook Road　　　　　　　　　　Minneapolis 55426
FAX: 952-938-7353
CONTACT: Alan E. Krysan
E-MAIL: feedback@finney-hobar.com
WWW: finney-hobar.com
SERVICES: Publishers of Agricultural, Career, and Industrial Technology Education Materials.
SPECIALTIES: Specializing in Textbooks, workbooks, software and other classroom instructional materials.

K

KIMM PUBLISHING　　　　　　　　　　　 763-572-9194
PO Box 32927　　　　　　　　　　　　　　　 Fridley 55432
FAX: 763-572-9194
CONTACT: Lora Oberle
E-MAIL: jgoberle@aol.com
PRESIDENT/CEO/OWNER: Leo Polack

M

MIDWEST INDEPENDENT PUBLISHERS　　　 651-917-0021
ASSN.
PO Box 581432　　　　　　　　　　　　　　　Minneapolis 55458
CONTACT: Doug Shidell
SERVICES: Publications: Midwest Publishers News (monthly).

P

PATHWAY BOOKS　　　　　　　　　　　　 612-694-9434
PO Box 27790　　　　　　　　　　　　　　　 Golden Valley 55427
CONTACT: James R. Sherman, Ph.D.
WWW: caregiver911.com
SERVICES: Publications: Stop Procrastinating - Do It!, Patience Pays Off, No More Mistakes, Plan For Success, Farewell To Fear, Be A Winner, Rejection, Middle Age Is Not A Disease, Escape To The Gunflint, Preventing Caregiver Burnout, Creative Caregiving, Positive Caregiver Attitudes, The Magic of Humor in Caregiving, Coping with Caregiver Worries.

THE PLACE IN THE WOODS
3900 Glenwood Avenue
612-374-2120
Golden Valley 55422

CONTACT: Roger Hammer
SERVICES: Edits and publishes books that are non-fiction on American minorities and fiction for children, plus adult fiction in essay, poetry. Fiction titles are published under the imprint "different" books. We research and write articles for large and small companies for trade magazines, and offer public relations consulting by accredited professionals. We also publish "Read, America!", a national quarterly for reading/literacy program leaders.
CAPABILITIES: News and story writing, PR program planning based on 20 years in the corporate/business environment. Publishing company specializes in using first time authors and illustrators, and is interested in helping unpublished writers and minority talent get started.
CURRENT/RECENT CLIENTS/PROJECTS: Newest books featured children's stories where main characters with disabilities are heroes and heroines. Most recent title "Through Kathryn's Eyes" by a special education/autism teacher has been nominated for a book of the year award in poetry by the Library of Virginia.

POGO PRESS, INC.
4 Cardinal Lane
651-483-4692
St. Paul 55127

FAX: 651-483-4692
CONTACT: Leo J. Harris
E-MAIL: pogopres@minn.net
WWW: pogopress.com
CAPABILITIES: Small press which publishes three books each year, alternating regional titles with books on the arts, history, music, breweriana and popular culture.
SPECIALTIES: Custom-write and produce books for non-profit organizations and cultural institutions.
PRESIDENT/CEO/OWNER: Leo J. Harris, President

R

RESOURCES AND COUNSELING FOR THE ARTS
308 Prince Street #270
651-292-4381
St. Paul 55101

CONTACT: Fred Schmalz
E-MAIL: info@rc4arts.org
WWW: rc4arts.org
CAPABILITIES: Resources and Counseling for the Arts (RCA) is an arts service organization that provides affordable business and management training for independent artists and cultural organizations. RCA is a rich, diverse resource center offering consulting and referrals. RCA publishes a quarterly newsletter with information about upcoming workshops and events designed to help artists and to put artists in touch with artist-friendly services.
PUBLICATIONS: Handbook for Minnesota Artists: a Guide to Minnesota Resources, opportunities and other useful information for self-employed creative people. Grants: a Basic guide to grants for Minnesota artists. exhibit: a basic guide to gallery and exhibition spaces in Minnesota. Space: a basic guide to performance and rehearsal spaces in Minnesota.

500 / Publishers - Books

CURRENT/RECENT CLIENTS/PROJECTS: Dayton Hudson Artists Loan Fund - RCA's quarterly loan from 1,000 - 5,000 for Minnesota artists - informational meetings listed in RCA news quarterly newsletter. Job Book - check out recent job opportunities on our web site or come into RCA.
PRESIDENT/CEO/OWNER: Joan Wells

S

SCHMIDT COMMUNICATIONS 651-501-9260
643 Hale Avenue North Oakdale 55128
FAX: 651-501-9230
CONTACT: Pamela Roemer
E-MAIL: schmidt@bitstream.net
SERVICES: We publish and sell "Schmidt's Minnesota Media Directory" and "Schmidt's Wisconsin Media Directory" each representing total statewide media coverage with daily and weekly newspapers, college and neighborhood press, specialty publications, TV and radio stations, TV and radio programs (locally produced), news services and cable stations.
PRESIDENT/CEO/OWNER: Gary E. Schmidt

SMITH HOUSE PRESS 651-490-9408
2700 Rice Street Roseville 55113
FAX: 651-490-1450
CONTACT: Sybil Smith
E-MAIL: smithse@aol.com
SPECIALTIES: Specializes in Fibromyalgia and chronic illness books. Publications: Fibromyalgia help book.
PRESIDENT/CEO/OWNER: Sybil Smith

ST. JOHNS PUBLISHING, INC. 612-920-9044
6824 Oaklawn Avenue Edina 55435
CONTACT: Donna L. Montgomery
PUBLICATIONS: We publish: Parenting books, Kids + Modeling = Money, Surviving Motherhood, Parenting A Business, Bury Me With Balloons, Invisible Fences, The Polluters, Perfect Just The Way I Am, Love, Life & Chocolate Chip Cookies, Coffee Talk, Tea Party, Bread & Wine, Business Briefs Aged Wine.

V

VOYAGEUR PRESS 651-430-2210
123 North 2nd Street Stillwater 55082
FAX: 651-430-2211
CONTACT: Tricia Theurer
E-MAIL: books@voyageurpress.com
WWW: voyageurpress.com
SERVICES: Publisher of special interest books and calendars. Categories include pets, outdoors, nature, Americana transportation, travel, regional - interest, cookbooks.
PRESIDENT/CEO/OWNER: Tom Lebovsky, Publisher; Bob Dubois, President

Publishers - Custom

B

BENSON COMMUNICATIONS, INC.   612-974-0014
17554 Bearpath Trail   Eden Prairie 55347
FAX: 612-974-0015
CONTACT: Tom Benson
E-MAIL: bensoncom@uswest.net

SERVICES: Benson Communications, Inc. is a full-service, turnkey provider of custom publishing and media services, specializing in publications for marketers of travel, but experienced in many industries. Specialties are magazines, newsletters, and promotional materials, as well as consulting in these areas.

CAPABILITIES: Tom E. Benson, president, is a 40-year publishing veteran who spent 24 years at the Webb Company, St. Paul. 15 years at Meredith in Des Moines, IA, and also was group publisher at MSP Communications in Minneapolis. He was group publisher responsible for The Family Handyman Magazine, and founding publisher of Farm Industry News and Midwest Living Magazines and has custom-published magazines for such organizations as Northwest, TWA, and Frontier Airlines, Farmers Insurance Group, Kampgrounds of America, Michigan and Nebraska Tourism Departments. The staff of BC, Inc. includes experienced professionals in all aspects of publishing, including editorial, design, production, marketing, circulation development, public relations and the internet--all currently self-employed as specialists. Most have worked closely with Benson for many years.

CURRENT/RECENT CLIENTS/PROJECTS: In the past year, BC has published two International Travel Guides for America's Heartland (group of 5 Midwestern states), an International visitors' guide to Sweden, and a map of the Great River Road along the Mississippi from Canada to New Orleans--all for Carlson Destination Marketing Services. BC also purchased and currently publishes Travelhost Twin Cities Magazine.

C

CREATIVE PUBLISHING INTERNATIONAL   952-988-0264
5900 Green Oak Drive   Minnetonka 55343
FAX: 952-988-0245
CONTACT: Hugh Kennedy
E-MAIL: hkennedy@creativepub.com
WWW: how-tobookstore.com

SERVICES: Creative Publishing International was founded in 1969 to fill a need within the Food industry for highly, visual creative publishing materials. Over the past 3 decades, CPI has become a recognized authority and the nation's leading source for "How-to" published materials. Today, CPI has a dedicated custom publishing unit developing books, magazines, newsletters, brochures, catalogs, photography for many of America's leading brands and products. The CPI custom publishing unit is staffed to provide our client-partners with a comprehensive turnkey publishing resource - including account management, editorial, art direction, art production, photography publication/production management and support services.

502 / Publishers - Custom

CAPABILITIES: Concept/product development; Complete editorial services; Design concepts/production artwork; Account/process management; Photography (digital, as well); On-site test kitchens/photo kitchens; Recipe library; Photo library (stock); Production/print management; Fulfillment management; Retail distribution; Ad sales management; Data base management; Core editorial competencies; Home improvement; Home Décor/crafts; Outdoor/nature; Cooking/parenting; Gardening/travel.
CURRENT/RECENT CLIENTS/PROJECTS: Pillsbury Co.; Hearst Corporation; Target Stores, Inc.; Black & Decker, Co.; Carlson Companies; Land O' Lakes; Wal-Mart Stores; Healthy Choice; Hormel Foods; Gander Mountain; Singer; General Mills; Mason Shoe; Business Incentives; Briggs & Stratton
PRESIDENT/CEO/OWNER: David Murphy

Q

QUIRK PUBLISHING 612-854-5101
PO Box 23536 Minneapolis 55423
FAX: 612-854-8191
CONTACT: Tom Quirk
E-MAIL: info@quirks.com
WWW: quirks.com
SERVICES: Publisher of Quirk's Marketing Research Review, a monthly magazine for the marketing research industry. The magazine emphasizes practical applications of marketing research techniques.
PRESIDENT/CEO/OWNER: Tom Quirk

Publishers - Periodical

B

BEARD COMMUNICATIONS, INC. 952-562-1234
7317 Cahill Road #201 Edina 55439
FAX: 952-941-3010
CONTACT: Michael Beard
CAPABILITIES: Advertising and specialty publishing to a Christian-faith audience in the larger Twin Cities area. Write, edit, design, sell and circulate.
SPECIALTIES: Publishers of The Lutheran Journal Magazine. The Minnesota Christian Chronicle newspaper. McAlester Park Publishing Books. The Twin City Church Guide and several specialty publications.
OFFICERS: Michael Beard, P; Doug Trouten, Editor

C

COMMON LAW PUBLISHING, INC. 612-525-0393
5101 Olson Memorial Highway #4000 Minneapolis 55422
FAX: 612-525-0266
CONTACT: Clarance E. Hagglund
PUBLICATIONS: Publications: Insurance Producer Liability in Plain Language, Real Estate Agency & Appraiser Liability in Plain Language, Minnesota Insurance Law, Stay Out of Court and Stay in Business.

CORPORATE REPORT MAGAZINE 612-338-4288
527 Marquette Avenue S #300 Minneapolis 55402
FAX: 612-573-6300
CONTACT: Kris Lilenthal
WWW: corpreport.com
SERVICES: Delivered the first of every month with CityBusiness, Corporate Report is the magazine of record for corporate Minnesota, covering major Minnesota companies and the top level people who make them work. In addition, Corporate Report delivers exclusive research on vital business rankings, including Top 100 CEO salaries; great places to work; top 200 public companies; largest non-profits and wealthiest Minnesotan's and others.
PRESIDENT/CEO/OWNER: Publisher: Lisa Bormaster

D

DECKER PUBLICATIONS 952-924-2322
4601 Excelsior Blvd #337 Minneapolis 55416
FAX: 952-924-2371
SERVICES: Publishers of Format Magazine, Minnesota's monthly advertising and communications magazine. Publisher of The Book, Minnesota's annual advertising creative resource in print and on the web at mnadbook.com.
CONTACT: Deb Gustafson

504 / Publishers - Periodical

DUERR & TIERNEY, LTD, ART OF THE WEST 612-935-5850
15612 Hwy 7, #235 Minnetonka 55345
FAX: 612-935-6546
CONTACT: Tom Tierney
E-MAIL: aotw@aotw.com
PUBLICATIONS: Art of the West
PRESIDENT/CEO/OWNER: Tom Tierney, Allan Duerr

F

FAMILY TIMES, INC. 952-922-6186
PO Box 16422 St. Louis Park 55416
CONTACT: Marci Mannis
PUBLICATIONS: Family Times, Baby Times, Senior Times, Grandparent Times

I

INDUSTRIAL EQUIPMENT NEWS 763-571-5518
6230 Highway 65 NE #106 Minneapolis 55432
FAX: 763-571-1569
CONTACT: Albert J. Loushin
SERVICES: Publishing Company: Thomas Publishing Company; Editor: Joe Rosta, Editor-In-Chief; Ad Manager: Ciro Buttacavoli, Publisher. Circulation: 205,000 industrial buyers, 102,400 plants. Focus: Manufacturing plants, mines, utilities, industrial builders, transportation industry, divisions of the government and military. Audience: Administrative, production, plant operations, design, engineering & purchasing personnel. Frequency: Monthly.
CURRENT/RECENT CLIENTS/PROJECTS: Publications: Industrial Equipment News-Canada; IEN; IEN Latin America; IEN Mexico; IEN Europe; Technische Revue-Germany; Produits Equipment Industriales, France; Equipos Productos Industriales, Spain; IEN Eastern Europe; IEN Japan; IEN Korea; Postcards and Lit. Reviews.

K

KITA ASSOCIATES, INC. 952-884-3265
PO Box 11932 St. Paul 55111
FAX: 952-888-9373
CONTACT: Cheryl Weiberg, Editor-In-Chief
E-MAIL: asianpages@att.net
WWW: asianpages.com
CAPABILITIES: Display and classified advertising.
SPECIALTIES: The Midwest Asian market
PUBLICATIONS: Asian pages. Publisher: C. Ting Insixiengmay

Publishers – Periodical / 505

L

LET'S PLAY, INC.   612-729-0023
2721 East 42nd Street   Minneapolis 55406
FAX: 612-729-0259
CONTACT: Doug Johnson
E-MAIL: letsplay@letsplayhockey.com
WWW: letsplayhockey.com
SERVICES: Publications: Let's Play Softball, Let's Play Hockey.

M

MCGRAW-HILL HEALTHCARE INFORMATION GROUP   952-835-3222
4530 West 77th Street 3rd Floor   Minneapolis 55435
FAX: 952-935-3460
CONTACT: Gretchen Drasner, Director of Marketing
WWW: postgrdmed.com; physsportsmed.com; hospprat.com; edotmd.com; healthcare-informatics.com
CAPABILITIES: Publisher of five healthcare magazines. Four are monthly, one is bi-monthly. Also produce special reports, collected readings, and other custom publishing products related to healthcare.
CURRENT/RECENT CLIENTS/PROJECTS: Advertisers include all major pharmaceutical, nutrition, allied health, managed care, medical technology, and medial products organizations/manufacturers.
PUBLICATIONS: Postgraduate Medicine; The Physician and Sportsmedicine; Hospital Practice; Healthcare Informatics; e.MD
OFFICERS: M. James Dougherty, Group Vice President

G & W MCNAMARA PUBLISHING, INC.   651-293-1544
4215 White Bear Parkway, #100   St. Paul 55110
CONTACT: Grace W. McNamara
SERVICES: Window Fashions Magazine, Fine Furniture International (FFI) Magazine, The Wall Paper, Idea Book.
PRESIDENT/CEO/OWNER: Grace W. McNamara, Publisher; Kathleen Stoehr, Editor-in-Chief of Window Fashions; Peggy Yung, General Manager; Michelle Larson, Associate Publisher; Christine Tomlinson, Editor-in-Chief of The Wall Paper.

MERRIAM PARK POST   651-645-6887
A1573 Selby Avenue #311   St. Paul 55104
CONTACT: Matt Hollinshead
SERVICES: Advertising & Editorial: 651-645-4267; Publications: Merriam Park Post.

506 / Publishers - Periodical

MEUSEY COMMUNICATIONS   612-448-8816
1107 Hazeltine Blvd #539   Chaska 55318
FAX: 612-448-7850
CONTACT: Jim Meusey
SERVICES: Publish three magazines: Engineering Contacts, Minnesota Insurance and Minnesota Claims. Publish two directories: Minnesota Directory of Engineering, and Minnesota Property-Casualty Directory.
CAPABILITIES: Firm started in 1973.

MINNESOTA MEETINGS & EVENTS   763-544-5941
2525 Nevada Avenue North #203   Golden Valley 55427
FAX: 763-544-5316
CONTACT: Judith Swatosh
E-MAIL: info@meetings-and-events.com
WWW: meetings-and-events.com
CAPABILITIES: We publish several magazines relative to the meetings and events industry including Minnesota Meetings and Events, Missouri Meetings and Events, and New England Meetings and Events. Circulation is 20,000 to industry professionals nationally. Also within Minnesota we publish Minnesota Group Tour Planner and Minnesota Destinations. Magazines are distributed via direct mail, trade shows, and conferences.
PRESIDENT/CEO/OWNER: Thomas Swatosh

MINNESOTA PARENT   651-454-5145
1750 Yankee Doodle Road, #108   Eagan 55121
FAX: 651-454-6577
CONTACT: Colleen Drum
E-MAIL: cdrum@unitedad.com
WWW: parenthoodweb.com
PUBLISHING COMPANY: United Advertising Publications, Inc.
CAPABILITIES: Free monthly resource for Twin Cities families. Covers family news and issues such as health, education, product reviews and family dynamics. Offers parents and kids calendar of family entertainment and events. Published 12 times a year, distributed at over 625 locations throughout the metro area.
CIRCULATION: 58,500
CURRENT/RECENT CLIENTS/PROJECTS: Nordstrom, Mervyns California, Radio Disney, Mall of America, Room & Board, Beyond Conception, Minnesota Children's Museum, Minnesota Science Museum, Minnesota Zoo
PRESIDENT/CEO/OWNER: Richard Davey, Vice President

MINNESOTA STATE BAR ASSOCIATION   612-333-1183
600 Nicollet Avenue Suite 380   Minneapolis 55402
FAX: 612-333-4927
CONTACT: Judson Haverkamp
WWW: mnbar.org
PUBLICATIONS: Bench & Bar of Minnesota
SERVICES: Association services, including periodical publications, books, continuing education, legislative representation, etc.
CURRENT/RECENT CLIENTS/PROJECTS: Monthly Periodical: Bench & Bar of Minnesota; History of Law of Lawyers in Minnesota: For The Record
PRESIDENT/CEO/OWNER: Tim Groshens, Executive Director

Publishers — Periodical / 507

THE MISSISSIPPI RAG, INC.
9448 Lyndale Avenue #120
FAX: 952-885-9943
CONTACT: Leslie Johnson
E-MAIL: editor@mississippirag.com
WWW: mississippirag.com
CIRCULATION: Paid circulation of 4,200.
FOCUS: Traditional jazz and ragtime. Articles on past and present performers, festival coverage, record and book reviews, current news.
FREQUENCY: Monthly.

952-885-9918
Bloomington 55420

Q

QUIRK'S MARKETING RESEARCH REVIEW
8030 Cedar Avenue South #229
FAX: 952-854-8191
E-MAIL: tomqmrr@uswest.net
WWW: quirks.com
SERVICES: A business periodical directed toward individuals involved in marketing research.
PRESIDENT/CEO/OWNER: Tom Quirk
CONTACT: Evan Tweed

952-854-5101
Bloomington 55425

R

RECREATIONAL PUBLICATIONS INC
7582 Currell Boulevard #212
FAX: 651-738-2302
CONTACT: Pamela Bailey
WWW: amsnow.com
SERVICES: Publisher of: American Snowmobiler Magazine; American Snowmobiler Online (amsnow.com)

651-738-1953
St. Paul 55125

S

SKYWAY PUBLICATIONS, INC.
10001 Wayzata Blvd.
CONTACT: Todd Hyde
PUBLICATIONS: Lakeshore Weekly News, New Residents and Relocation Guide, Minnesota Orchestra Showcase Magazine, Children's Theatre Company program, Guthrie Theater Magazine, The Minnesota Opera Program, Ordway Center for the Performing Arts Program, The Saint Paul Chamber Orchestra Prelude Magazine, Twin Cities Public Television (TPT) Program Magazine, Minnesota Dance Theatre Nutcracker Fantasy, Twin West chamber of Commerce Membership Directory, Bloomington Chamber of Commerce Member Directory, Minneapolis Aquatennial Official Festival Events Guide

612-843-4601
Minnetonka 55305

508 / Publishers – Periodical

T

TWIN CITIES LUTHERAN NEWSPAPER, INC. 612-872-8653
122 West Franklin Avenue #214 Minneapolis 55404
FAX: 612-872-1724
CONTACT: Michael L. Sherer
E-MAIL: metrolutheran@usa.com
CAPABILITIES: 40,000 copies to 700 Lutheran churches in 20 counties monthly.
SPECIALTIES: Niche newspaper publishing to Lutheran Readers.
PUBLICATIONS: Metro Lutheran
OFFICERS: Michael L. Sherer, Editor; Jean Johansson, Ad Sales

V

VENTURES MAGAZINE 612-338-4288
527 Marquette Avenue S #300 Minneapolis 55402
FAX: 612-573-6300
CONTACT: Janice Meyer
WWW: corpreport.com
SERVICES: Ventures is the Magazine for growing Twin Cities Companies. Published monthly, Ventures offers strategies for the Twin Cities fast-growing entrepreneurial companies. The magazine reports on trends affecting small business, and provides advice from experts on ways to manager company growth, focusing on a practical approach for busy entrepreneurs.
PRESIDENT/CEO/OWNER: Publisher: Lisa Bormaster

Radio

K

KASM AM/FM
PO Box 390
FAX: 320-845-2187
CONTACT: Robert Ingstad
SALES CONTACT: Steve Gretsch

320-845-2184
Albany 56307

KATE AM/KCPO FM
305 South First Avenue
FAX: 507-373-4736
CONTACT: Phil Kelly
SALES CONTACT: Vern Rasmussen

507-373-2338
Albert Lea 56007

KAUS AM/FM
Po Box 159
FAX: 507-437-7669
CONTACT: Phil Nolan
SALES CONTACT: Ken Soderberg

507-437-1480
Austin 55912

KBEW AM/FM
Box 278
FAX: 507-526-3320
CONTACT: Wanda Nichols

507-526-2181
Blue Earth 56013

KBMW
PO Box 286
FAX: 701-642-9501
CONTACT: Dean Aamodt

701-642-8747
Breckenridge 56520

KBPR FM
501 W College Drive #402
CONTACT: Tim Walstrom

218-829-1072
Brainerd 56401

KBSB FM
215 Deputy Hall
CONTACT: Roger Paskvan

218-755-2912
Bemidji 56601

KBUN
PO Box 1656
FAX: 218-751-8091
CONTACT: Lou H. Buron
SALES CONTACT: Peggy Hanson

218-751-4120
Bemidji 56619

510 / Radio

KCRB FM
PO Box 578
CONTACT: Marilyn Helzer

218-751-8864
Bemidji 56601

KGWB
Box 127
FAX: 701-642-9501
CONTACT: Dean Aamodt

701-642-8747
Wahpeton 58074

KIKV FM
604 3rd Avenue West
FAX: 320-762-2156
CONTACT: Lou H, Buron, Mary Campbell
SALES CONTACT: Trudy Blanshan

320-762-2154
Alexandria 56308

KJLY FM
PO Box 72
FAX: 507-526-3236
CONTACT: Paul Schneider

507-526-3233
Blue Earth 56013

KKBJ AM/FM
2115 Washington Avenue
FAX: 218-759-0658
CONTACT: Roger Paskvan

218-754-7777
Bemidji 56601

KKIN/KEZZ
PO Box 930
FAX: 218-927-4090
CONTACT: Jim Birkemeyer
SALES CONTACT: Boyd Bremner

218-927-2344
Aitkin 56431

KLIZ AM/FM
Box 980, 602 Laurel Street
FAX: 218-829-6983
CONTACT: Mike Overton

218-829-2853
Brainerd 56401

KLKS FM
PO Box 300
FAX: 218-562-4058
CONTACT: Robert Bundgaard

218-562-4884
Breezy Point 56472

Radio / 511

KLLZ FM
Box 1312
FAX: 218-751-2533
CONTACT: Jim Ingstad
SALES CONTACT: Brad Walhof

218-751-3421
Bemidji 56601

KMSK FM
Box 153
FAX: 507-389-1705
CONTACT: Richard Rush

800-456-7810
Mankato 56001

KNFX AM
29 7th Street NE
FAX: 507-288-7815
CONTACT: Robert Ingstad
SALES CONTACT: Mary Anne Nonn

507-288-3888
Rochester 55906

KQPR FM
Box 1106
FAX: 507-373-9045
CONTACT: Kymn Anderson

507-373-9600
Albert Lea 56007

KRJB FM
312 W Main Street
FAX: 218-784-3749
CONTACT: Jim Birkemeyer/Richard Haraldson
SALES CONTACT: Jim Birkemeyer

218-784-2844
Ada 56510

KRWC AM
PO Box 267
FAX: 800-380-1360
CONTACT: Kurt Weiche

612-682-4444
Buffalo 55313

KSCR AM/FM
105 13th Street North
FAX: 320-843-3955
CONTACT: Paul Estenson

320-843-3290
Benson 56215

KSTQ FM
312 Spruce Street
FAX: 320-763-7779
CONTACT: Steve R. Nestor
SALES CONTACT: John Messenger

320-763-6515
Alexandria 56308

512 / Radio

KVBR AM/FM
602 Laurel Street
FAX: 218-829-6983
CONTACT: Mike Overton

218-829-2853
Brainerd 56401

KXDL FM
PO Box 187
FAX: 320-732-2284
CONTACT: Donald Schermerhorn

320-732-2164
Long Prairie 56347

KXRA AM/FM
1312 Broadway Avenue
FAX: 320-763-5641
CONTACT: Mel Paradis
SALES CONTACT: Bill Franzen

320-763-3131
Alexandria 56308

KYRS FM
PO Box 30
FAX: 320-974-8095
CONTACT: Al & Linda Quarnstrom
SALES CONTACT: Dean Randall

320-974-3694
Atwater 56209

R

RADIO K/KUOM-AM
330 21st Avenue South
FAX: 612-625-2112
CONTACT: David Lee Olson
WWW: radiok.org
GEOGRAPHICAL AREA COVERED: Southern two-thirds of Minnesota and west central Wisconsin.
HOURS: Broadcasting hours: Daytime. Radio Band Location: 770 AM
RATE INFORMATION: Underwriting available at variable rates.
FORMAT: Alternative rock.
STATION MANAGER: Andy Marlow
NEWS DIRECTOR: David Lee Olson

612-625-3500
Minneapolis 55455

W

WBJI FM
2115 Washington Avenue South
FAX: 218-759-0658
CONTACT: Roger Paskvan

218-751-7777
Bemidji 56601

WDGY RADIO
PO Box 25130
FAX: 651-436-5018
CONTACT: Greg Borgen
SERVICES: AM 630, 24 7 sportstalk; live sports broadcast.
CAPABILITIES: Full service production room.

651-436-4000
St. Paul 55125

WJJY FM
410 Front Street
FAX: 218-828-1119
CONTACT: Mike Boen

218-828-1244
Brainerd 56401

WWWI AM
PO Box 783
FAX: 218-828-8327
CONTACT: James Pryor

218-828-9994
Brainerd 56401

Recording & Sound Services

B

B R PRODUCTIONS, INC. 612-421-2606
11989 Utah Avenue North Champlin 55316
FAX: 612-421-2606
E-MAIL: tamasling@uswest.net
WWW: users.uswest.net/~tamasling/index.html
SERVICES: Drummer/Keyboardist/Arranger/Sound Engineer Bruce Rudolph offers complete audio production for all applications. CD and demo projects for singer/songwriters, including full arrangement and charting (for copyright) of your originals. Final mix and master to CD-R pre-master for duplication, and complete artwork layout and design (CD inserts and trays.) Radio commercial production from concept to airplay, including script writing, voice talent, original music bed creation, all recording, editing, final mix and master to any format, all digital stereo. Also work with established media buying company for best airtime packages. Complete audio for visual applications as well (film, TV, business presentations, etc.)
CAPABILITIES/SPECIALTIES: Singer/Songwriters! Bruce Rudolph has over 25 years experience as a drummer/keyboardist and can bring your originals to life! Will create any style you desire. All parts are played in real time - no "programming" of instrumental parts or "drum machines"...EVER! Companies looking to advertise: BR Productions works up-close and personally with you to create the kind of radio spot or on-hold messaging that you want your customers (both present and future) to hear.
CURRENT/RECENT CLIENTS/PROJECTS: Arrangement and/or live performance clients include: King Errisson (25+ years as percussionist with the Neil Diamond band) Williams and Ree (The Indian and White Guy), Clark Terry (Legendary jazz flugelhornist formely with the "Tonight Show" orchestra), and many other performers at all levels of the music industry. Commercial/Industrial audio production for: Road Runner Transportation, AM Express, Consan, Inc., The Sheldon Theatre (Red Wing, MN), AutoFun, Inc., Mall of America, WCCO Radio, and more.
PRESIDENT/CEO/OWNER: Bruce Rudolph/Jim Nienaber

BLUE MOON PRODUCTIONS, INC. 612-339-7175
212 3rd Avenue No. #390 Minneapolis 55401
FAX: 612-339-4272
CONTACT: Jeff Sylvestre
E-MAIL: mail@bluemoonpro.com
CAPABILITIES: A comprehensive blend of engineering talent with the latest in audio production tools. Original composition in a wide variety of styles with digital based recording alongside acoustic session players. Services include: sync to picture, sound sweetening, SFX library, narration, and field audio recording.

BRYTE SPOT STUDIO 612-722-2508
4501 34th Avenue South Minneapolis 55417
CONTACT: Robert Hilstrom
E-MAIL: brytespot@hotmail.com
SERVICES: Recording and sound, audio for video, music creation and production, jingles, internet audio.
CAPABILITIES: Protools - computer editing. Mackie D8B - Digital Automated Mixing. ADAT - Digital recording.

Recording & Sound Services / 515

CURRENT/RECENT CLIENTS/PROJECTS: Craig Anderton; Michael Kac & Linda Cohen; Waking Virginia

C

CINE SOUND 2   **612-866-5049**
6461 Lyndale Avenue South   **Richfield 55423**
CONTACT: Dennis O'Rourke
CAPABILITIES: Two full-service audio studios for commercial, industrial, television programs and feature films. Features: AMS/NEVE Logic 3 Digital Console with moving fader automation & surround sound for mixing. Re-recording, ADR, foley and narration.
SERVICES: All digital audio mixing/recording/editing from any combination of source material from all video formats listed 35mm, RDAT, DA88 and timecode 1/4". Sound design, complete ADR/Looping stage. Lay-up/lay-back from /to all formats listed. Online interformat video editing. We have an extensive music and sound effects library.
FORMAT: Video: Digital Betacam, D2, 1", Beta SP, 3/4", SVHS, Hi8, Audio: RDAT, DA88, timecode 1/4", 35mm, 16mm optical and 16mm mag.
SPECIALTIES: Over 25 years experience in film and video sound design (editing and mixing for feature film, commercial, industrial, documentary and network television programs).
PRESIDENT/CEO/OWNER: Dennis O'Rourke

COOKHOUSE RECORDING STUDIOS, INC.   **612-333-2067**
10 South 5th Street #440   **Minneapolis 55402**
FAX: 612-333-2961
CONTACT: Mona Almsted
E-MAIL: info@cookhouse.net
WWW: cookhouse.net
SERVICES: Since 1972, four fully fortified totally digital audio studios configured for voice over and music recording. Radio production, sound design, audio sweetening, original music recording, television voice over, video lock-up and phone patch. Digitally linkable worldwide with most major studios through Land Patch (Mpge128) or 3D2 (APTx). Digital Generation Systems for digital transmission of radio spots directly to stations via ISDN lines. Select from 20 music and sound effects libraries. CD, DAT, reel and cassette duplication.
EQUIPMENT: The latest ProTools digital work-stations and automated mixing in all studios.
CURRENT/RECENT CLIENTS/PROJECTS: Various local and national clients..call for specifics.
PRESIDENT/CEO/OWNER: Doug Dixon; Mohsen Sadeghi; Jerry Stenstadvold

CRASH & SUES   **612-338-7947**
510 Marquette Avenue #600   **Minneapolis 55402**
FAX: 612-338-4601
CONTACT: Crash Medin

516 / Recording & Sound Services

E-MAIL: crash@crash-sues.com
WWW: crash-sues.com
SERVICES: C-Reality Film to tape transfer system with Da Vinci 2K color correction system; fire HD and D1 online edit; Inferno HD graphics and compositing; 2D/3D CGI; closed captioning; videoboards, and duplication/traffic; NTSC/PAL; various multi-media capabilities; Echoboys original music, sound design and mix.
CAPABILITIES: Expertise in television commercials, music videos.

CUSTOM CASSETTE, INC. — 763-789-2660
3809 Third Street NE — Minneapolis 55421
CONTACT: Timothy DeVilbiss, Kelly Chyrklund
CAPABILITIES: Whisper Room Recording booth for voice recording sessions. Sonic Solutions. No Noise digital editing and audio restoration equipment for audio cleanup. Quality cassette duplication services via digital bin loop process. In-house graphics, design and printing services for audio related materials. Short and large run compact disc replication and packaging services. Cassette and compact disc production capacity of 100,000/week. 23 years of experience in the cassette manufacturing business.
SPECIALTIES: 3 - 5 day turnaround on cassette orders, 7 - 10 day turnaround on compact discs. High quality on-cassette or on-disc imprinting in single or multiple colors including photographs. 2 day digital printing or color graphics for cassettes and compact discs.
PRESIDENT/CEO/OWNER: Timothy DeVilbiss

CUSTOM RECORDING STUDIOS — 612-521-2950
4800 Drake Road — Golden Valley 55422
FAX: 612-521-9165
CONTACT: Jim Reynolds
SERVICES: A full service digital & analog 16 track studio specializing in music and voice recording. Real time cassette duplicating and CD duplication. In business since 1965.
CAPABILITIES: Musical instruments include Yamaha conservatory grand piano, Hammond B-3 with RV-122 Leslie and Synths. Over 25 of the finest microphones available, including Neumann U-87's, U 67, M-147's, KM-84's, RCA 77 DX's, AKG-414 EB's Shure SM-81's, 330's & B&O Ribbons. Tape machines include 2 Tascam D-38's 16 track HI-8 digital, 1 Alesis LX-20 Adat II. Fostex 16 track, and 4 reel to reel tape machines, crown, Otari, Technics, Pioneer.
CURRENT/RECENT CLIENTS/PROJECTS: Over 500 Albums and CD's recorded and produced. Specializing in Jazz, Classical, Country, Gospel, and Ethnic type music. No hard acid rock or rap and hip hop.

D

DIGITAL EXCELLENCE, INC. — 651-772-5100
300 York Avenue — St. Paul 55101
FAX: 651-771-5629
CONTACT: Tracy Reider, Cheryl Miller
E-MAIL: sales@digx.com
WWW: digx.com

Recording & Sound Services / 517

SERVICES: We provide cassette, video, and 3.5" diskette duplication CD/CD-ROM replication, sound effects, voice-overs, multi language services, post production, packaging and fulfillment. We also replicate and silkscreen CD one-offs in one or more ink colors.
CAPABILITIES: Avid video edit suite, DVC, PRO-Tools 24, Sonic Solutions.

G

GREATAPES CORPORATION   612-872-8284
1523 Nicollet Avenue   Minneapolis 55403
FAX: 612-872-0635
CONTACT: Robert M. McCarthy
TOLL FREE: 1-800-879-8273
CAPABILITIES: Full-service video and audio production/duplication services.

H

HARMONY BOX   612-331-2699
1414 Marshall Street N.E.   Minneapolis 55413
FAX: 612-623-8147
CONTACT: Kathy Nygard
E-MAIL: stage@harmonybox.com
WWW: harmonybox.com
SERVICES: Sound stage for film, video and photography.
CAPABILITIES: 60' x 80' x 31' clear, state-of-the-art facility designed specifically for film and commercial video production industry needs. 25' x 60' cover wall, 10' x 20' x 8' special effects pit and 50' x 35' loading/staging area. Drive-in loading and stage access, 2 dressing rooms. Makeup area, 2 production offices with dedicated phones with fax and copy capabilities, bathroom with showers, and foodservice staging area. Scissors lift, 3000 amp service. Off-street parking for up to 70 vehicles. On-site set design, fabrication and installation for film, video, photography, and meetings available through Nygard Set Design.
CURRENT/RECENT CLIENTS/PROJECTS: Film and video production including commercial television advertising, corporate video and music video production. Best Buy Company, Inc. commercial featuring Alanis Morissette and Tori Amos, Columbia Records/DNA Inc. Aerosmith music video, Gold'n Plump Chicken commercial, Sears Roebuck & Company commercial. Production Companies/Agencies: A Band Apart/Harder-Fuller Films, Area 51, Hallau Shoots & Company, Buck Holzemer Productions, Juntunen Media Group Inc., Twist Production, Two Popes, Voodoo Films and Young & Company.

I

INTUITIVE   612-872-0444
2544 Pillsbury Avenue   Minneapolis 55404
FAX: 612-872-8317
E-MAIL: mike@intuaudio.com

518 / Recording & Sound Services

WWW: intuaudio.com
SERVICES: Turnkey media subcontracting for interactive multimedia specializing in all aspects of audio production.
CAPABILITIES/SPECIALTIES: Full in-house audio production capabilities. Many years of experience producing voice overs, sound effects and music for corporate and retail projects.
CURRENT/RECENT CLIENTS/PROJECTS: Allen Interactions: Chrysler, Target; Connecting Images: American Express, Anchor Wall; Jack Morton Company: Yamaha, Suzuki; Logic Bay: Lucent Technologies, Cyrus Intersoft.
PRESIDENT/CEO/OWNER: Mike Olson

L

LOUD NEIGHBORS   612-825-2900
3712 Garfield Avenue South   **Minneapolis 55409**
FAX: 612-825-4171
CONTACT: Dick Hedlund
E-MAIL: loudnabrz@aol.com
WWW: loudneighborsrecords.com
SERVICES: Music composition (pre/post scoring), production, sound design, ADR, Foley, Digital recording/editing, conforming, voice/music recording, post-production mixing for film/video/radio/TV.
CAPABILITIES: Full-service music and audio production.
PRESIDENT/CEO/OWNER: John Calder, P

M

MAJOR GROOVE MUSIC COMPANY   **763-537-8900**
160 Glenwood Avenue North #300   **Minneapolis 55405**
FAX: 763-535-8989
CONTACT: Aimee Fischer
E-MAIL: contact@majorgroovemusic.com
WWW: majorgroovemusic.com
SERVICES: A broad range of original music, lyrics and musical adaptations. We do audio production and sound design for film, video, business theater, commercials and jingles, live events and entertainment. We use the top vocal, voice-over and instrumental talent available, and have professional producers, engineers, writers and talent on staff. On-site musical direction and project coordination available, especially for business theater and live entertainment events.
CAPABILITIES: Corporate music doesn't have to sound corporate! We produce music that will move you and your audience, with powerful arrangements and lyrics that aren't trite. Synclavier digital workstation, ProTools system. Yamaha O2R console and more.
CURRENT/RECENT CLIENTS/PROJECTS: ITM; United Airlines; Citibank; Grand Casino; ICONOS; World International Records; Travelers; Design Group; Golden Rule Productions; EcoQuest International; West Group Publishing; Genius Products; Baby Music Boom, Inc.; Hoffman Communications; Alpine Industries; Uncommon Productions; Troupe America; Page Music; B J Productions; Michael Whalen Music; Marianne Richmond Studios, Inc.; F. Whitley Music; Macromedia; DoReMedia; and Internet Florist
PRESIDENT/CEO/OWNER: Aimee Fischer, David Jacobi, Owners

Recording & Sound Services / 519

MODERN MUSIC
42 South 12th Street
FAX: 612-332-4910
CONTACT: Jess Ford
E-MAIL: info@modern-music.com
WWW: modern-music.com
SERVICES: Music composition, arrangement and sound design for TV, radio, film and new media.
CAPABILITIES: State-of-the-art pro-tools studio. Creative atmosphere, downtown location.

612-332-6299
Minneapolis 55403

N

24 Track Digital Recording Studio

NATURAL SOUND RECORDING STUDIO
1604 Frost Avenue
FAX: 651-770-3270
CONTACT: Martha Kluth
E-MAIL: mkluth@mkluth.com
WWW: naturalsoundstudio.com
SERVICES: State-of-the-art fully digital recording in a comfortable environment; 24 track, 20 bit recording; professional mastering; complete mix automation and recall; CD one-offs; MP3 encoding; jingle, theme and incidental music composition; educational resources; location recording; very reasonable rates.
CAPABILITIES: Featuring the RAMSA WR-DA7 digital recording console, 3 20-bit ADAT recorders, Alesis MasterLink mastering, CD recorder, Sony DAT, Mackie HR824 monitors, Lexicon digital FX, Kawai Grand Piano, Boss GT-3 Guitar synthesizer/FX, Alesis Nano Synth, Alesis D4, Roland U20, other sound modules, Windows PC, Cubasis sequencing software, large selection of microphones; professional engineering and production staff with over 30 years experience.

651-770-3270
St. Paul 55109

O

ORFIELD LABS, INC.
2709 E. 25th Street
FAX: 612-721-2457

612-721-2455
Minneapolis 55406

520 / Recording & Sound Services

E-MAIL: orfieldlabs.com
SERVICES: Consultants, lighting, audio/video and acoustic.
SPECIALTIES: Acoustic, lighting, audio/visual system design and testing.
PRESIDENT/CEO/OWNER: Steve Orfield

P

PRECISION POWERHOUSE 612-333-9111
911 Second Street South Minneapolis 55415
FAX: 612-332-9200
CONTACT: Dan Piepho, Paul Sunberg, Gene Gunderson
E-MAIL: dan@power-house.com; pauls@power-house.com or geneg@power-house.com
WWW: precisionpowerhouse.com
SERVICES: Sonic Solutions, high resolution 96/24 DVD/Surround Sound ready digital audio workstations featuring non-destructive digital multi-track recording and editing, digital equalization, compress/expansion, mixing desk automation with NoNoise Sonic restorations, CD pre-mastering, and DVD production.
SPECIALTIES: Commercials (TV and Radio) corporate DVD video, websites, and Intreactive Media marketing and sales presentations, CD pre-mastering, complete music and sound effects libraries.

R

R.E.M. VIDEO & EVENT COMPANY 612-788-9221
1828 NE Jefferson Street Minneapolis 55418
FAX: 612-788-7712
CONTACT: Roger Miller
E-MAIL: info@remvideoevent.com
WWW: remvideoevent.com
SERVICES: Full service production house for video, events/presentations, audio, multimedia. Our focus is in business to business communications delivered live or on media. We have in-house presentation expertise and equipment for TVL, Powerpoint (advanced), Astound and SCALA. Video productions on Betacam and DV formats. Non-linear broadcast and non-broadcast editing. Non-linear audio production for audio CD., video and film sweetening and music production scoring.
SPECIALTIES: Historical productions commemorating companies and places. Business to business marketing and training. Original music.
PRESIDENT/CEO/OWNER: Roger Miller, Presentations & Video; Michael Loonan, Audio & Multimedia; Pat Miller, Production Management.

S

SLIPSTREAM MUSIC
1568 Eustis Street
FAX: 651-645-3515
CONTACT: Erik Nilsen, Pat Phillips
E-MAIL: erik@slipstream-music.com
WWW: slipstream-music.com

612-940-2573
St. Paul 55108

SERVICES: 32 track digital recording, voice overs, on hold messaging, audio sweetening, audio post, web audio preparation, audio for multi-media. See our listing under "Music and Jingles" for your music and sound design needs.
CAPABILITIES: We offer solutions to your needs and preferences that improve your production and keep you on budget. Full SMPTE Sync for frame accurate scoring. Complete 32 track digital facility including: Yamaha O2R console, Apple G3, ADAT, TC Electronics, Lexicon, UREI, JoeMEEK, Sohmer 6'4" grand piano, DBX.
CURRENT/RECENT CLIENTS/PROJECTS: Fox Movie Network; Discovery Channel; Musicland Group, Inc; Best Buy; Lutheran Brotherhood; AICP; 3M; Pillsbury Corp.; PBS "Newton's Apple"; DMPML Music Library (London).
PRESIDENT/CEO/OWNER: Erik Nilsen

SOUND80
IDS Tower Suite 4027
FAX: 612-339-1277
CONTACT: Clay Nicles
WWW: sound80.com

612-339-9313
Minneapolis 55402

CAPABILITIES: Audio: 3 Studios, full stereo land patch, phone patch, e-mail/internet spot download, surround, spot ADR, sound design, 12 music, 8 sound effects libraries, video: spot assemble, tagging, slating, close captioning, non-linear video/graphics edit, CD ROM/Internet compression, CD ROM interactive. On-line file import. Duplication: radio spot to high-speed magnetic and digital. TV spot to all formats. Shipping: online trafficking with major freight couriers, radio spots shipped via courier or high speed ISDN, TV spots shipped via courier or satellite. Talent: AFTRA/SAG/AFM/ACTRA signatory services, crew payroll service. Equipment: ProTools (4) + digital and analog mastering, media 100, DigiBeta, BetaSP, 1" 3/4" 1/2".
PRESIDENT/CEO/OWNER: Jan Erickson

T

TANGLETOWN RECORDING STUDIOS
PO Box 8496
CONTACT: William Winfield
ALTERNATE PHONE: 612-824-8844
E-MAIL: williamwinfield@aol.com
WWW: ttwn.com

651-335-5083
Minneapolis 55408

SERVICES: Music production, provide singers, jingles, mastering house, CD one-offs, commercial production, Dance music, R&B, Hiphop, pop, and house music.

522 / Recording & Sound Services

CURRENT/RECENT CLIENTS/PROJECTS: Campbell Mithun Esty, MN Anti-Smoking Radio Campaign, Olson & Company, Riverfront Corp - "The Bridge" Video; Minneapolis Convention and Visitors Bureau (music and jingle for radio campaign); James Grier & Co.; Mayor Norm Coleman; David & Latonia Hughes of MGS and many more local and national credits.
PRESIDENT/CEO/OWNER: William Winfield

TOBY'S TUNES, INC.   612-377-0690
2325 Girard Avenue South   Minneapolis 55405
FAX: 612-377-2744
CONTACT: Chris Doane
E-MAIL: toby@tobystunes.com
WWW: tobystunes.com
SERVICES: We will find the best music cuts from over 70 production music libraries in-house. Complete sound design locked to picture with ProTools 24/mix. Superior sound conversions to any file format for CD-ROM or websites. Vocal booth for voice over recordings. AFTRA signature services.
CAPABILITIES: 27 years of quality and creative soundtracks. Location recording.
EQUIPMENT: ProTools 24/mix, 16 track 1", 2 track with center track time code, DAT time code, 1/4" 4 track. Largest supplier of production music in the area. Over 70 music libraries and 15 sound effect libraries.
CURRENT/RECENT CLIENTS/PROJECTS: We work for all the ad agencies and video/multi-media producers. Too many jobs to mention, many awards.
PRESIDENT/CEO/OWNER: Harley Toberman

TRACK RECORD STUDIOS   651-645-9281
1561 Sherburne Avenue   St. Paul 55104
FAX: 651-645-6983
CONTACT: Norton Lawellin
CAPABILITIES: Narration and VO Recording, Jingles.

TRACK SEVENTEEN PRODUCTIONS, INC.   763-391-8060
2724 Edinbrook Terrace North   Brooklyn Park 55443
FAX: 612-904-0118
CONTACT: Curt Olson
E-MAIL: cro@trackseventeen.com
WWW: trackseventeen.com
SERVICES: Audio production.
CAPABILITIES: Syndicated programming and specialty items for radio. Books on tape. Audio magazines and newsletters. Cassettes and CDs packaged for retail sale and promotion. Web audio.
EQUIPMENT: ProTools TDM, high-end peripherals.
PRESIDENT/CEO/OWNER: Curt Olson

V

VISUAL MUSIC & SOUND, LTD.   612-373-2220
708 North First Street #135   Minneapolis 55401
FAX: 612-341-0242
CONTACT: Tom Lindquist

Recording & Sound Services / 523

E-MAIL: toml@visualmusicandsound.com
WWW: visualmusicandsound.com
SERVICES: Music, SFX, and voice recording for film, video, television, and new media. Extensive music and SFX capabilities. All-digital, state of the art facility with 3 audio suites.
SPECIALTIES: Audio Production, sweetening and editing. Surround sound mixing. Music and sound-design for picture. Original music post-scoring. Surround Hybrid Scoring.™
EQUIPMENT: Avid AudioVision/Yamaha O2R digital audio workstations, ProTools, Dolby SEU4 ProLogic surround encoder, Dolby DP562 5.1 surround decoder, Sony 7050 DAT, Panasonic DAT, Tascam DAT, Tascam DA98, AKG 414 Microphones, ISDN digital land patch. Full integration with Juntunen Media Group machine room, satellite uplink, and fiber optic network.
CURRENT/RECENT CLIENTS/PROJECTS: American Express; Aveda Corporation; Bankers Systems; Best Buy Company; Billy Graham Evangelical Association; Carlson Companies; Carmichael Lynch; Campbell-Mithun-Esty; Charthouse International; Colle & McVoy; Compass Media; Dayton's; Dublin Productions; Edelman Productions; Fleishman-Hillard; Flying Colors; Foley Sackett; General Growth; General Mills; Hallau Shoots & Co.; Hearst Broadcasting; Home Value; Honeywell; Hunt Adkins; IBM; Imation; Interactive Learning Group; Interactive Personalities; Jack Morton Companies; James Productions; John Ryan Co; Juntunen Media Group; LaPalm & Sons Productions; Lawson Software; Lee Pictures; Lund Food Holdings; Lutheran Brotherhood; MA Mortenson Company; Mayo Clinic; Media Loft; Media Productions; Medtronic; Metris Companies; Minnesota Timberwolves; Minnesota Vikings; Minnesota Wild; Nelson Henry; New Line Cinema Productions; North Woods Advertising; Northwest Airlines; Northwest Teleproductions; NSP; Periscope Marketing; Peterson Milla Hooks; Science Museum of Minnesota; Setterholm Productions; Shandwick USA; Slumberland; SUPERVALU; The St. Paul Companies; Tremendous Entertainment; Tripp & Associates; Tunheim Santrizos Company; US Bancorp; Wilson-Griak; Wilsons Leather; World Wide Pictures. wwwrrr.
PRESIDENT/CEO/OWNER: Brad Stokes

W

WILD SOUND   612-706-0815
2400 2nd Street NE   Minneapolis 55418
FAX: 612-706-0815
CONTACT: Matthew Zimmerman
E-MAIL: wild-sound.com or wildsound@visi.com
WWW: wild-sound.com
SERVICES: Complete digital audio and music production studio.
CAPABILITIES: Tracking, mixing, CD mastering and sound editing for music. Theater, and corporate clients. World class studio and equipment in a private freestanding facility.

WOW AND FLUTTER MUSIC AND SOUND   612-333-0502
110 North 5th Street - 11th Floor   Minneapolis 55403
FAX: 612-338-3449
CONTACT: Dale Goulett/Jerry Brunskill
E-MAIL: info@wowandflutter.com
WWW: wowandflutter.com

SERVICES: Full-service music and audio post facility providing composition, arrangement, orchestration, sound design and audio finish services for feature film, TV and radio, Three production studios with Avid AudioVision and ProTools systems. Four discrete live rooms. Experienced ADR engineer on staff.

CURRENT/RECENT CLIENTS/PROJECTS: Fallon McElligott; Martin Williams; Hunt Adkins; Carmichael Lynch; CME; CBS; NBC; ABC; PBS; NBA; Miller Meester; BBDO; DDB Needham; Bozell; most major film studios, et cetera.

PRESIDENT/CEO/OWNER: Dale Goulett/Jerry Brunskill

Retail Promotion

B

GRUGGEN BUCKLEY
430 1st Avenue N. Suite 470
FAX: 612-321-0646
CONTACT: Terry Gruggen
E-MAIL: terry@gruggen.com or gordy@gruggen.com
WWW: gruggen.com

612-321-0744
Minneapolis 55401

SERVICES: The agency specializes in the design and production of collateral materials. These include point-of-sale displays, in-store graphics, signage, brochures, newsletters, flyers, custom display pieces and retail maps. We are especially strong in retail applications that require fast turnaround and low costs.
CURRENT/RECENT CLIENTS/PROJECTS: AT&T Corporate; AT&T Wireless Services; Best Buy; CellularOne; Cincinnati Bell; Cincinnati Bell Wireless; Circuit City; Corporate Learning Center; Dobson Communications; Greene Holcomb & Fisher; Giant Eagle; iwireless; Lucent Technologies; McDonald's; Metrocall; Minnesota Timberwolves; Polaris; Office Depot; Red Cross; Rollerblade; Ronald McDonald House Charities; SFX Entertainment; SunCom; Target; Triton PCS; Valvoline Oil Company

M

MIKE MEEHAN COMPANY
13805 First Avenue North
FAX: 612-475-1671
CONTACT: Thomas P. Meehan
E-MAIL: meehan@minn.net

612-475-1449
Minneapolis 55441

SERVICES: Creative concepts, design and engineering of both semi-permanent and permanent point-of-purchase displays for consumer products. All preparations, production, distribution and warehousing.
CURRENT/RECENT CLIENTS/PROJECTS: Anagram International; Cargill; The Chinet Company; Johnson Worldwide; Michael Foods; 3M; Pillsbury Green Giant; Onen Corporation; Ore-Ida Foods; Singleton Seafood; Sta-Rite; Target; United Sugars Recovery Engineering; Kraft Foods; Land O' Lakes.
PRESIDENT/CEO/OWNER: Thomas P. Meehan

U

UPFRONT PRODUCTIONS
2350 County Road C #120
FAX: 651-633-5197
CONTACT: Tricia Nordby Hamrin/Chris Hamrin
WWW: hoopjumping.com

651-633-5299
St. Paul 55113

CAPABILITIES: Organizational Communications Solutions Center. A Spectrum. A Synergy. Concept Development, Copywriting, Graphic Design, Illustration, Document Production, Web Site Creation, Scanning, Photo Retouching, Pre-press, Offset Printing, Digital B&W Printing, Color Copies, Posters, Displays, Signs, Custom Assembly, Inventory, Distribution, Corporate Compass® MIS, VantagePoint™, Hoop Jumping™.
SPECIALTIES: Choose your hoop. We'll jump through it™.

OFFICERS: Tricia Nordby Hamrin/Chris Hamrin

V

VEE CORPORATION
504 Malcolm Avenue SE #200
FAX: 612-378-2635
CONTACT: Bonnie Ehlers
E-MAIL: bonniee@vee.com
WWW: vee.com

612-378-2561
Minneapolis 55414

SERVICES: Concept, design and construction of themed retail storefronts and interiors including special effects. Single-source provider from development of the original concept through education and installation. Unusual Items: Designed, fabricated and installed The Florida Vacation Store in Minnesota and Illinois.
SPECIALTIES: Scenic art, sculpting, aluminum and steel fabrication.
PRESIDENT/CEO/OWNER: Vincent E. Egan, P; Jack Pence, Mrg.

Retouching

B

BAU, INC.
5511 Bristol Lane
FAX: 952-933-0295
CONTACT: Douglas Johnson
E-MAIL: johns93@bitstream.net
952-912-0191
Minnetonka 55343

SERVICES: We are the graphics bureau to the Twin Cities. The most capable center for scanning, retouching, photo-manipulation, illustration, and illustration integrated with design. We have years of experience in working seamlessly with business and design schedules. Call for our free, clearly understandable pricing and information booklet.
CAPABILITIES: No better scanning or retouching can be found in the Twin Cities area. We can work with any item from 8mm film to the side of a building. All can be saved in any file format needed, to a variety of convenient storage media. True photographic printing is available also - and always an Index print. Our art department brings illustration and design to a higher level of effectiveness by being able to integrate the two into a more communicative whole. We have many styles at our disposal to meet any clients needs.
CURRENT/RECENT CLIENTS/PROJECTS: American Medical Systems; Adult Option in Education; Banc; Campbell Mithun Esty; Carlson Marketing Group; Chez Francoise; La Flame; Photo Quick; VRB Art; Wellington Windows.
PRESIDENT/CEO/OWNER: Douglas Johnson

C

CANNON CREATIVE RETOUCHING
1049 Thomas Avenue South
FAX: 612-381-0453
CONTACT: Michael Cannon
E-MAIL: mcannon@visi.com
612-381-0452
Minneapolis 55405

SERVICES: Hi-end digital retouching, color, and compositing.
CAPABILITIES: Creative image manipulation (warping, cloning, special effects). Print ready CMYK color correction. Expert compositing skills for large or complex multi-layered files. 11 Graphics Barco Creator, and Mac G4 workstations.

CATHERINE CARLSON ARTIST
529 South 7th Street #400
CONTACT: Catherine Carlson
612-332-4606
Minneapolis 55415

SERVICES: Photo retouching - airbrush and PhotoShop. Graphic design using Quark, PhotoShop, Illustrator. Also, traditional keylining.
CAPABILITIES: Over 25 years of photo retouching and graphics experience.

528 / Retouching

CASWELL PHOTOGRAPHY
700 Washington Avenue North #308
FAX: 612-340-1538
CONTACT: George Caswell
E-MAIL: george@caswellphoto.com
WWW: caswellphoto.com
SERVICES: Photo illustrator creating dynamic visual images utilizing traditional and digital techniques for the advertising, corporate and graphic design communities. Color, humor and whimsy are combined with exceptional technical skills resulting in strong visuals that sell products and services.
PRESIDENT/CEO/OWNER: George Caswell

612-332-2729
Minneapolis 55401

COLORHOUSE
13010 County Road 6
FAX: 763-550-3600
CONTACT: William Klocke
SERVICES: If you need an image that couldn't possibly exist in the real world, come to Colorhouse's Creative Imaging Studio. Out talented artists are adept at manipulating color and form. They can gently retouch existing images or use technical wizardry to create believable reality from the most outlandish ideas you can concoot. Anything you can possibly imagine, they can create.
SPECIALTIES: Performing miracles. Our creative artists have an average of 15 years experience in color and retouching. Using cutting-edge equipment and software, they can execute the most difficult and subtle changes with remarkable accuracy.

763-553-0100
Minneapolis 55441

D

DIGITAL MANN
958 East Hennepin Avenue
CONTACT: Sue Mann
E-MAIL: sue@digitalmann.com
WWW: digitalmann.com
SERVICES: Creating the perfect image or the crazy composite utilizing PhotoShop. I'm all Mac, with lots of bells and whistles. High resolution scan to the final film record done in-house. I love what I do.

612-617-9828
Minneapolis 55414

J

JKL STUDIOS
3810 Edmund Boulevard
FAX: 612-729-0133
CONTACT: Jerry or Marietta Mason; Kurt Lang
ALTERNATE PHONE: 651-653-0811
E-MAIL: jklstudios@tcinternet.net
SERVICES: High-end digital imaging; includes scanning, retouching, compositing and photo restoration. Mac or Windows platforms, various output services provided.

612-729-1774
Minneapolis 55406

CAPABILITIES: 16 plus years experience photo/digital manipulation working with large files, photo composition and assembly on high-end equipment in the print industry. Complete understanding of reproduction capabilities of CMYK process on press.
CURRENT/RECENT CLIENTS/PROJECTS: Produced and continues to produce digital "magic" for all major agencies in the Twin Cities.
PRESIDENT/CEO/OWNER: Kurt Lang

P

PROFESSIONAL COLOR SERVICE, INC.
909 Hennepin Avenue South

612-673-8900
Minneapolis 55403

FAX: 612-673-8988
CONTACT: Tim Doe
E-MAIL: procolor@procolor.com
WWW: procolor.com
CAPABILITIES: First you see it, then you don't, or first you don't see it, then you do. Try our switch-hitter digital retouchers. They'll even let you look over their shoulder, so you can better command the magic. Our one-stop-shop line of products and services includes: new 3D lenticular display prints and transparencies, digital display photographs and transparencies, as well as a complete range of scanning services, including those from our high res drum, Photo CD, and Dicomed digital camera. Fine art IRIS reproduction. Short-run digital 4-color printing on our Heidelberg DI and Docucolor systems. Color laser copies and Bubblejet copies up to 24" x 36". Film processing 24 hours a day Monday through Friday and 8:30 to 11:30 on Saturday. Pick up and delivery.
SPECIALTIES: One-stop shop imaging services.
OFFICE HOURS: Monday through Friday 7:30 am to 8:00 pm; Saturday 8:30 to 2:00 pm.

S

LEE STOKES ADVERTISING ARTIST, INC.
121 South 8th Street
TCF Tower #825

612-339-5770
Minneapolis 55402

FAX: 612-338-2080
CONTACT: Lee Stokes
E-MAIL: lstokes@intxxnet.com
WWW: retoucher.com
SERVICES: High end digital retouching and compositing, realistic special effects to simple cast shadows. Provides new transparency and digital files.
CAPABILITIES: 25 years conventional retouching with air brush, dyes. 10 years with DiComed and Mac work stations.
CURRENT/RECENT CLIENTS/PROJECTS: Hormel; 3M; Target; Anderson Windows; National Presto Industries; National Car; US Bank; MN Orchestra.

Sales Promotion & Incentives

A

AMUNDSON MARKETING   612-333-7700
10 South Fifth Street #580   Minneapolis 55402
FAX: 612-333-7701
CONTACT: Kathleen J. Amundson
CAPABILITIES: Amundson Marketing is a strategically-driven marketing agency focused on building the value of our clients' organizations through the development of valuable relationships with their customers. Our expertise encompasses the full array of marketing disciplines including strategic planning, positioning and branding, relationship marketing, direct and database marketing, frequency and loyalty marketing and promotional marketing. Our team is experienced in developing solutions based on the needs of clients and their customers, doing so in a manner that helps our clients stay ahead of their business while delivering a powerful return on investment.
SERVICES: Strategic and tactical planning, primary and secondary research, program design, management and fulfillment, creative services, production management, economic modeling, customer segmentation, modeling and profiling, partner negotiations, measurement and analysis.
CURRENT/RECENT CLIENTS/PROJECTS: National and international clients in the telecommunications, utility, high-tech, business-to-business, consumer products and service industries.

B

B & B PROMOTIONAL ADV. INC.   952-258-0440
15500 Wayzata Blvd. #803B   Wayzata 55391
FAX: 952-258-0550
CONTACT: David W. Brown
SERVICES: Custom printing long run, short run, typesetting, copywriting, binding, creative services.
SPECIALTIES: Complete ad specialties, premiums. Incentive programs. Business gifts.

C

CRC, INC.   952-937-6000
6321 Bury Drive #10   Eden Prairie 55346
FAX: 952-937-5155
CONTACT: Cindy Owens, New Business Specialist
WWW: crc-inc.com

CREATIVE RESOURCE CENTER/CRC, INC.   952-937-6000
6321 Bury Drive #10   Eden Prairie 55346
FAX: 952-937-5155
CONTACT: Cindy Owens, New Business Specialist
WWW: crc-inc.com

Sales Promotion & Incentives / 531

SERVICES: A full-service integrated marketing communications agency with 20 years experience in strategic communications planning across a range of delivery forms. Services include planning and implementation of strategic marketing communications, internet presence, sales promotion, relationship marketing, internet list development and maintenance, and development of full-scale e-commerce web stores. Full in-house planning and creative teams for both print and internet development include experts in planning, design, copy, content management, database design and development, website development, management, hosting and serving. In-house photography studio.

SPECIALTIES: Integrated marketing communications planning and implementation, internet business strategy, sales promotion including sales materials, collateral, POS, full integration of promotion on the internet including interactive relationship marketing. Corporate and brand identity programs, package design, business-to-business and consumer advertising, and direct mail.

CURRENT/RECENT CLIENTS/PROJECTS: CNS Interactive; FSMC; Graco; Haagen-Dazs Interactive, Interactive Learning Group (Video Buddy); Loffler Business Systems; McGlynn's Retail Bakeries; Multifoods Bakery Products; NK Lawn & Garden; Old Dutch; Pillsbury Interactive; Primera Technology; Rosemount Office Systems Interactive; Sargento Foods, Inc.; 3M Intranet.

PRESIDENT/CEO/OWNER: Michael Lundeby, CEO; Elizabeth Petrangelo, EVP; Joe Andrews, VP; Troy Braun, Creative Director

1128 harmon place, suite 304
minneapolis, mn 55403

AN INTEGRATED MARKETING AGENCY

THE CULLINAN GROUP
1128 Harmon Place, #304
612-338-7636
Minneapolis 55403
FAX: 612-338-8173
CONTACT: Wayne Cullinan, Carol Miletti
E-MAIL: amenzel@cullinangroup.com; Wayne Cullinan - wcullinan@cullinangroup.com; Carol Miletti - cmiletti@cullinangroup.com
WWW: cullinangroup.com
SERVICES: Full service integrated marketing communications agency practicing strategic marketing in the disciplines of advertising, sales promotion and direct response. Additional services include retail marketing, point-of-purchase, merchandising, multi-media and event production. Billings: 20 million
CURRENT/RECENT CLIENTS/PROJECTS: GreenMountain.com; Orion Food Systems/Hot Stuff Pizza; Smash Hit Subs; Thinsulate/3M; Georgia Pacific/Vinyl Siding Divisions; Hearth Technologies/Heat-N-Glo Fireplaces; Pillsbury Foodservice/Bakery Division; General Mills/Yoplait Division
PRESIDENT/CEO/OWNER: Wayne A. Cullinan, P/CEO; Lynne Cullinan, COO; Jerry Little, VP/CD; Gary Scott, VP; Julie Bain, VP Account Planning & Interactive; Ron Signorelli, Gary A. Scott, Management Supervisors; Dana Misner, Shari Bell, Account Supervisor; Barb Shelstad, Nate Koepsell, Cheryl Turk, Gina Parker, Acct. Executives; Lori Haugesag, Manager of Production; Jerry Little, Lisa Proctor, Terri Wykle, Jim Davis, Matt Howd, Willie Ford, Wendy Lukaszewski, Creative.

532 / Sales Promotion & Incentives

H

HEDSTROM/BLESSING, INC. 763-591-6200
8301 Golden Valley Road #300 **Minneapolis 55427**
FAX: 763-591-6232
CONTACT: Julie Pearl
E-MAIL: info@hb-inc.com
WWW: www.hb-inc.com
SERVICES: Total creative concepts: planning and strategy; layout and design; copywriting; illustration; keyline and production; typesetting; photo art direction; interactive authoring and programming.
SPECIALTIES: Broad range of sales promotion and advertising services including direct mail, print ads, FSI's, collateral materials, packaging graphics, point-of-purchase, and trade show/event display graphics and promotion, incentive and award programs.
CURRENT/RECENT CLIENTS/PROJECTS: Selected accounts include 3M; Bachman's; Carlson Leisure Group; Fabcon; Intellisol International; Interactive Learning Group; Land O'Lakes; Pillsbury; Target

I

ISA PROMOTIONS, INC. 651-439-1339
206 Mariner Way **Bayport 55003**
FAX: 651-439-4512
CONTACT: Maralee Meissner
E-MAIL: isapromo@ix.netcom.com
WWW: isapromo.com
PRESIDENT/CEO/OWNER: Susan J. Larimer

J

JOHNSON GROSSFIELD, 612-341-0814
INC./PROMOTIONAL MARKETING
275 Market Street #541 **Minneapolis 55405**
FAX: 612-341-0965
CONTACT: Thom Johnson
E-MAIL: thom@jpic.com
CURRENT/RECENT CLIENTS/PROJECTS: Subway Sandwich and Salad Shop; Hormel Food Corp.; Anheuser Busch; Ralston Purina; S.C. Johnson; Dayton's Department Stores; Marvin Windows; Disney Productions; Kroger Foods; TriSense Inc; Hunt Wesson; Promotional Marketing Association; Target Stores.
PRESIDENT/CEO/OWNER: Thom Johnson, Co-P; Mark Grossfield, CO-P; Neil Domeyer, Controller

Sales Promotion & Incentives / 533

P

PAR CONSULTING, INC.   952-835-5155
4444 West 76th Street #700   Edina 55435
FAX: 952-835-5122
CONTACT: Mary West
E-MAIL: mary@parplus.com
WWW: parplus.com
SERVICES: Printing broker; professional printing management; production planning and coordination. Promotional products. Complete digital capabilities to get job from idea to print. MAC computer consulting, configuration and planning.
CAPABILITIES: Apple VAR Reseller, Apple Solutions Network Professional.
CURRENT/RECENT CLIENTS/PROJECTS: Industrial and commercial accounts; catalogs, direct mail, posters, and books.
PRESIDENT/CEO/OWNER: Phyllis Rivard

PROMOTIONAL SYSTEMS GROUP, INC.   1-800-726-8396
2020 O'Neil Road   Hudson 54016
PO Box 226
FAX: 715-381-3123
CONTACT: Craig Beemer
E-MAIL: cbeemer@promotionalsystems.com
WWW: promotionalsystems.com
SERVICES: A promotional products and fulfillment company that is focused on providing cost-effective marketing solutions to the consumer packaged goods industry. Services include promotional product design and production, warehousing and inventory management, product inquiry response fulfillment, telemarketing, inbound 800 service, sample fulfillment, and sales material fulfillment.
CAPABILITIES: Systems: Microsoft BackOffice Small Business Server, MAS90 Inventory Management Software, Norstar-PLUS Prelude ACD Phone System, Norstar Voice Mail Model 2 and 11,276 square feet Office/Warehouse.
CURRENT/RECENT CLIENTS/PROJECTS: General Mills; Procter & Gamble; Old Home Foods; Land O'Lakes; PUR Drinking Water Products

T

W J THOM COMPANY   612-870-8100
211 Varner Street   Jordan 55352
CONTACT: Mary Kaye Doerr
SERVICES: Imprinted promotional advertising items.
CAPABILITIES: Embroidery, silkscreen on apparel, bus. Cards, greeting cards, calendars, trade show give-away-items, golf balls and accessories, brand name pens: Pilot, BIC, Mont Blanc, Schaefer.

TRAVEL GRAPHICS INTERNATIONAL   612-377-1080
1118 South Cedar Lake Road   Minneapolis 55405
CONTACT: Wayne Dunifon

534 / Sales Promotion & Incentives

E-MAIL: trip@tgimaps.com
WWW: virtualtravelmaps.com
CAPABILITIES: Design, develop and produce advertising and promotional materials such as illustrated maps, posters and cards.
SPECIALTIES: Specialized graphics for maps and posters, for travel industry.
PRESIDENT/CEO/OWNER: Stuart Sellars, President; Paula Hylle, Vice President; Wayne Dunifon, Art Director

TRILOGY MARKETING GROUP
944 Cobb Road
FAX: 651-482-8270
CONTACT: James D. Lemke
E-MAIL: trilogymktg@aol.com

651-482-8270
Shoreview 55126-3804

SERVICES: Great ideas to meet your needs. Promotion and incentive merchandise Broker, Distribution, Jobber. Copywriting, art and print production.
SPECIALTIES: Promotional programs using ad specialties, premiums, incentives, business gifts, wearables and recognition awards. Extensive program experience includes: safety and awareness campaigns, cost reduction, dealer incentives, point-of-purchase, new product introduction, premium incentive, target market direct mail, open house, trade show, anniversary and sales meetings, as well as employee motivation, performance, and service awards. Stock and custom product resourcing; warehousing and complete fulfillment services available.
PRESIDENT/CEO/OWNER: James D. Lemke

U

ULTRA CREATIVE, INC.
920 Second Avenue South #1200
FAX: 612-337-8178
CONTACT: Dave Biebighauser
E-MAIL: dave@ultracreative.com

612-338-7908
Minneapolis 55402

CAPABILITIES: Planning and positioning, creative development, graphic design and production. Project based creative marketing firm for corporate communications; print, direct, packaging, POP, identity and collateral.
SPECIALTIES: Food products, retail, kid marketing, new products, and brand equity maintenance.
CURRENT/RECENT CLIENTS/PROJECTS: General Mills, Inc.; The Pillsbury Company; Campbell's Foods, Inc.; Marigold Foods; Gymamerica.com; Govt.com.
PRESIDENT/CEO/OWNER: Dave Biebighauser, President; Gino Perfetti, Vice President

Schools

B

the minneapolis
school of advertising

BRAINCO: THE MINNEAPOLIS SCHOOL OF ADVERTISING 612-822-1313
2922 Bryant Avenue South   Minneapolis 55408
FAX: 612-827-3185
CONTACT: Ryan O'Hara Thiesen
E-MAIL: braincomsa.com
SERVICES: Brainco is the first school to integrate creative, strategy and technology across so many different communication disciplines. We're a haven for folks who are looking for a curriculum that will not only allow them to hit the ground running, but to have long successful careers and eventually be the innovators in our industry. We've worked with current industry leaders to create a whole new kind of school. A creative school. A practical school.
CAPABILITIES: Programs offered: Art Direction, Graphic Design, Promotional Designs, Interactive Design, Copywriting, Interactive Writing, Promotional Writing, Interactive Account Management, Account Management. Account Planning, Media Planning and Branding.
PRESIDENT/CEO/OWNER: Edward Prentiss

Screen Printers

C

COLOR ARTS   612-377-0656
56 Russell Avenue South   Minneapolis 55405
FAX: 612-377-0656
E-MAIL: mktg@colorarts.com
WWW: colorarts.com
SERVICES: Bus wraps, fleet graphics, retail décor, graphic programs and product graphics. Office in: Minneapolis, Racine, Dallas, Atlanta, Pasadena and Chicago.
CAPABILITIES: Large format screenprinting 48" x 132"; 5 color inline screen printing 46" x 66"; 3M scotchprint graphic system; Ink jet printing.
CURRENT/RECENT CLIENTS/PROJECTS: Target, Harley Davidson, Super Valu, Disney, Warner Brothers, Fleming Foods, Coca Cola, Grey Hound, Polaris, Arctic Cat.
PRESIDENT/CEO/OWNER: Robert Nordin

M

MODERNISTIC, INC.   651-291-7650
169 Jenks Avenue   St. Paul 55117
FAX: 651-291-2571
CONTACT: Deb Olson
E-MAIL: info@modernisticinc.com
WWW: modernisticinc.com
SERVICES: Full service screenprinter and print finisher. Services offered; Foil stamping, embossing, die cutting, mounting, finishing, UV coating, strip taping, die making and specialty screen printing including glow-in-the-dark printing, scratch off printing, scented ink printing, and glitter printing.
CAPABILITIES: Products we offer: Point-of-purchase signage, floor graphics, window graphics, clip strips, temporary displays, fleet graphics, prototyping, banners.
PRESIDENT/CEO/OWNER: Keith Wilson

P

PRINTS CHARMING (DBA BUTTONS ON BRISTOL)   952-470-5786
7122 Bunker Court   Eden Prairie 55346
FAX: 952-470-0798
CONTACT: Julie Grube
E-MAIL: buttons@isd.net
CREATIVE: Creative Department: full in-house art department, including layout, typesetting, keylining, and stat camera. Materials: all types of textiles - T's, sweats, hats tote bags. Also imprinting of signs.
SPECIALTIES: Large selection of in-stock clothing, automatic presses, large run capacity, rush service.

Set Design & Styling

C

MAGGIE BELLE CALIN   612-522-1973
1821 York Avenue North   Minneapolis 55422
CONTACT: Maggie Belle Calin
SERVICES: Design with renderings and elevations to scale also props, costumes, painted backdrops. Set and prop stylings.
CAPABILITIES: Concept illustration. Realistic large scale painting. Sculpting.
CURRENT/RECENT CLIENTS/PROJECTS: Dayton Hudson; Target; Marshall Field; Cunningham Group; Full Effect; Wilson Griak

BRENT CASEY, INC. PHOTO/FILM STYLING   612-822-7676
4312 First Avenue South   Minneapolis 55409
FAX: 612-822-7673
CONTACT: Brent Casey
PAGER: 651-229-5625
SERVICES: Set design, styling, production, project coordination, props, wardrobe, and creative direction. Clothing and accessories; both on and off figure. 15+ years' photo styling and adjunct experience. Accomplished at styling in studio or on location (multiple room sets through small sets.)
CAPABILITIES: Creative approach with nearly all aspects of project including stretching budgets. Discounts for portfolio building photo/film/video. Portfolio and references available.

K

KRS DESIGN   612-536-0179
4233 Zane Avenue North   Minneapolis 55422
FAX: 612-536-0179
CONTACT: Kate Sheeley
E-MAIL: kshee56766@aol.com
SERVICES: Freelance graphic design and set styling/propping. Project organization and development from creative concept to finished product. Production coordination and client communication. 10 years experience in graphic design, advertising, theatre, television and film. Traditional and electronic design, print and video formats.
CAPABILITIES: Graphic Design: Innovative design; typography, art and photo direction; scanning; copywriting; logos; ads; brochures; newsletters; direct mail; annual reports; promotional pieces; publications; 4-color & B/W identity and collateral campaigns. Complete Macintosh platform. Set Styling/Propping: Set/prop research and buying; set decorating and dressing; numerous sources; in-studio or on-location; commercial, feature, industrial, video, still photography (tabletop & soft goods).
CURRENT/RECENT CLIENTS/PROJECTS: Fingerhut; IATSE 490; KELO-TV; KTCA-TV; Media Loft; New Line; RE/MAX North Central; River Road Entertainment; Saver's Edge; Target; Travel Graphics Intl.; Tundra Films; Vail Place; Voodoo Films; WCCO-TV.
PRESIDENT/CEO/OWNER: Kate Sheeley

538 / Set Design & Styling

N

NYGARD  DIMENSIONS

NYGARD DIMENSIONS
1414 Marshall Street N.E.
FAX: 612-623-8147
CONTACT: Luis Ferreiro, General Manager
E-MAIL: events@stagesets.com
WWW: stagesets.com

612-623-8150
Minneapolis 55413

SERVICES: Custom design, fabrication, installation of themed environments including special events; trade show exhibits; stage sets for meetings, film, video and photography; corporate and point-of-purchase displays and more. Creative development and design, computer renderings and 3D modeling, site inspection, on-site management and other event planning/management capabilities.

CAPABILITIES: Specializes in dimensional environments that create the "whole brand experience", integrating brand and creative theme through all media. Brand identity and design available through sister company, Nygard & Associates. State-of-the-art 60' x 80' x 31' sound stage on-location (Harmony Box).

CURRENT/RECENT CLIENTS/PROJECTS: 3M, ADC Telecommunications, American Express Financial Advisors, Larson Manufacturing, Lawson Software, Lutheran Brotherhood, Minnesota Department of Agriculture, Minnesota Mutual Insurance, Musicland, nQuire Software, and Target Stores.

S

STUDIOCRAFTS, INC.
451 Taft Street NE
FAX: 612-331-2057
CONTACT: Greg Cornell
E-MAIL: studiocr@bitstream.net

612-331-7884
Minneapolis 55413

SERVICES: Custom design and fabrication of scenery, props, display and tradeshow exhibits.

CAPABILITIES: Full service scenic facility. We have the people, the experience, and the facilities to take your idea to reality on time, and on budget.

CURRENT/RECENT CLIENTS/PROJECTS: Best Buy Television Commercial, 1999; General Mills National Sales Meeting, 1998, 1999, 2000; Guthrie Theater, Feb. 2000.

PRESIDENT/CEO/OWNER: Greg Cornell, Chris Johnson

Set Design & Styling / 539

V

VEE CORPORATION   612-378-2561
504 Malcolm Avenue SE #200   Minneapolis 55414
FAX: 612-378-2635
CONTACT: Bonnie Ehlers
E-MAIL: bonniee@vee.com
WWW: vee.com
SERVICES: Concept, design and construction of special scenic elements and props within an exhibit booth; specialty displays; interactive exhibits. Unusual Items: Design, fabricated set for Northwest Airlines "Airplane Safety Video."
SPECIALTIES: Scenic art, sculpting, aluminum and steel fabrication.
PRESIDENT/CEO/OWNER: Vincent E. Egan, P; Jack Pence, Mrg.

Slides

P

PROFESSIONAL COLOR SERVICE, INC. **612-673-8900**
909 Hennepin Avenue South **Minneapolis 55403**
FAX: 612-673-8988
CONTACT: Tim Doe
E-MAIL: procolor@procolor.com
WWW: procolor.com
CAPABILITIES: We've been mounting slides since Ozzie and Harriet were around. Dupes? No problem. Our one-stop-shop line of products and services includes: new 3D lenticular display prints, digital display photographs and transparencies, as well as a complete range of scanning services, including those from our high res drum, Photo CD, and Dicomed digital camera. Fine art IRIS reproduction. Short-run digital 4-color printing on our Heidelberg DI and Docucolor systems. Color laser copies and Bubblejet copies up to 24" x 36". Film processing 24 hours a day Monday through Friday and 8:30 to 11:30 on Saturday. Pick up and delivery.
SPECIALTIES: One-stop shop imaging services.
OFFICE HOURS: Monday through Friday 7:30 am to 8:00 pm; Saturday 8:30 to 2:00 pm.

Sound Stages

H

Harmony Box

HARMONY BOX 612-331-2699
1414 Marshall Street N.E. **Minneapolis 55413**
FAX: 612-623-8147
CONTACT: Kathy Nygard
E-MAIL: stage@harmonybox.com
WWW: harmonybox.com
SERVICES: Sound stage for film, video and photography.
CAPABILITIES: 60' x 80' x 31' clear, state-of-the-art facility designed specifically for film and commercial video production industry needs. 25' x 60' cover wall, 10' x 20' x 8' special effects pit and 50' x 35' loading/staging area. Drive-in loading and stage access, 2 dressing rooms. Makeup area, 2 production offices with dedicated phones with fax and copy capabilities, bathroom with showers, and foodservice staging area. Scissors lift, 3000 amp service. Off-street parking for up to 70 vehicles. On-site set design, fabrication and installation for film, video, photography, and meetings available through Nygard Set Design.
CURRENT/RECENT CLIENTS/PROJECTS: Film and video production including commercial television advertising, corporate video and music video production. Best Buy Company, Inc. commercial featuring Alanis Morissette and Tori Amos, Columbia Records/DNA Inc. Aerosmith music video, Gold'n Plump Chicken commercial, Sears Roebuck & Company commercial. Production Companies/Agencies: A Band Apart/Harder-Fuller Films, Area 51, Hallau Shoots & Company, Buck Holzemer Productions, Juntunen Media Group Inc., Twist Production, Two Popes, Voodoo Films and Young & Company.

P

PRECISION POWERHOUSE 612-333-9111
911 Second Street South **Minneapolis 55415**
FAX: 612-332-9200
CONTACT: Dan Piepho, Paul Sunberg, Gene Gunderson
E-MAIL: dan@power-house.com; pauls@power-house.com or geneg@power-house.com
WWW: precisionpowerhouse.com

542 / Sound Stages

SERVICES: Studio 40 x 60 x 20 ft. H Cyc Wall L shaped cove swept to floor 20 x 32 x 15 ft. H High-jacker lift that raises to a working height of 30 ft. Capacity is 300 lbs. with a 2 x 2 ft. enclosed platform with a 115v AC power outlet. Precision also offers as additional features; a viewing room with a large screen monitor and studio observation window. A conference room with a second floor studio observation window. Two dressing rooms and a make-up room that includes a full sink. Air conditioning, and an on-site studio manager. A street level rolling-door loading dock, 10 x 15 ft., is located on Second Street and is convenient for pickups and deliveries of all types. Double doors to stage 7' 7" wide x 8' high.

EQUIPMENT: The studio design features a floating slab constructed of 8 inches of concrete, one layer of 3/4 inch plywood, 3 inches of compressed rubber and 4 inches of concrete slab for the floor. The tar roof has 12 inches of cement ceiling (planking), metal isolation bars and three layers of 3/4 inch sheetrock. 2,400 amp three phase, 95 - 20 amp circuits, (72 on grid, 23 on floor), 600 amp three phase disconnect box with Camlock and Mole Pin adapters, separately metered. A 40 x 60 ft. fixed grid 20' 6" high with six lights per 12 ft. section load capacity. 1800 amps of power on grid, wired through a distribution panel. Grid includes ten 2k fresnels, and twelve 1k scoop lights, one 750w Ellipsoidal, three 750w Fresnels w/o Barndoors, and three 500w Fresnels with Barndoors.

SPECIALTIES: Sales presentations, Interactive Training, Catalogs, e-business web sites, Intranet, Extranet, consumer products, radio, television, and web commercials, lap top presentations, interactive kiosks, video and interactive direct mail marketing, DVD authoring.

Speakers & Speakers Bureaus

I

INTERNATIONAL EDUCATION SYSTEMS   651-227-2052
26 East Exchange Street #313   St. Paul 55101
CONTACT: Mary Bosrock
WWW: marybosrock.com
SERVICES: Keynote speeches, half and full day seminars, and break-out sessions on global communication. Mary Bosrock is a popular speaker, radio and television guest, and the author of the award-winning "Put Your Best Foot Forward" books. She is an internationally-known expert in this field. Sample speaking topics: P-Commerce-"People Commerce." Selling in a Multi-cultural world. The Multicultural service industry. Understanding Europeans. Understanding Asians.
CAPABILITIES: We have an exclusive relationship with the Brave New Workshop to offer a unique program "Grin and Globalize" A side-splitting study of a serious subject." Learn how to communicate across cultures in this very funny, very entertaining seminar.

J

J MILLER ASSOCIATES   952-890-2071
12319 Oak Leaf Court #4   Burnsville 55337
FAX: 952-890-2072
CONTACT: Jacqueline Miller
E-MAIL: jm@jmillerassociates.com
WWW: jmillerassociates.com
CAPABILITIES: Speeches, Workshops, Written Materials. American Indian Stories, Small Business Consultations.
SPECIALTIES: Humor in the Workplace - Effective Leadership and Followership - Diversity - disc Behavioral Styles - Quantum Learning - Couples playshops - Enjoy your life. Small Business development and consulting.
CURRENT/RECENT CLIENTS/PROJECTS: Cargill; AISES (American Indian Science & Engineering Society); Woods Quality Center; Medtronic; HSC Scenic Services, Ltd.; MN Landscape Arboretum; State of MN; DOR & DRA (Department of Revenue and Department of Retirement Assoc); St. Joseph Hospital; MCDC (MN Cultural Diversity Cente); Inroads, Inc.

M

MARTIN/BASTIAN PRODUCTIONS   612-375-0055
105 Fifth Avenue So #150   Minneapolis 55401
FAX: 612-342-2348
CONTACT: Amy Oriani
E-MAIL: amyo@martinbastian.com
WWW: martinbastian.com

SERVICES: Martin/Bastian Productions offers creative development, execution and project management for corporate meetings and events, including staging services, business theater, speaker support, film and video production, and speakers and entertainment. We create integrated events from concept through execution, as well as offer individual meeting elements in an a la carte fashion, such as sourcing and booking speakers and entertainment.
CAPABILITIES: Martin/Bastian has been in business for nearly 20 years, and we have 18 employees on staff, including meeting and event producers, video producers, graphic designers, writers, and account management. We're housed in the renovated, turn-of-the century, Crown Roller Mill in downtown Minneapolis, complete with a video facility (including on-line Media 100 post-production), a digital sound recording studio, theater, computer graphic workstations, speaker and entertainment video library, and other technical, creative and account services.
CURRENT/RECENT CLIENTS/PROJECTS: We currently produce meetings, events, videos, and book speakers and entertainment for some of the top companies in the Midwest, and have won numerous awards for our film and video work. Recent entertainment acts we've produced for corporate clients include Bill Cosby, Bruce Hornsby, Kenny Loggins, The Neville Brothers, and Lyle Lovett and His Large Band.
PRESIDENT/CEO/OWNER: Al Soukup

S

STOCKHAUSEN INK 763-755-4966
14314 Thrush Street NW Andover 55304
FAX: 763-757-8202
CONTACT: Sharron Stockhausen
E-MAIL: mailroom@stockink.com
WWW: stockink.com
CAPABILITIES: Keynotes, full-day and half-day seminars, workshops and breakout sessions. Most popular topics are stress management, negotiation, the human side of management, and writing for fun and profit. Representative titles include "Living Between Pushy and Pushover," "Get What You Negotiate In Life and Work," "Managing Time--Our Most Finite Resource," and "It's Your Life, Take Charge Of It!" The human side of management series includes "Coaching Day-to-Day," "Delegation and Assertiveness," "Systematic Organization For Success," and "Project Management For People." The writing for fun and profit series includes "Become A Writer While Keeping Your Day Job," "Journaling As Creative Expression," "Freelance Writing for Money," "How To Publish Your Book," and "Editing Your Writing."
SPECIALTIES: We work with individuals to achieve their personal success and with businesses to improve their position in the marketplace through consultation and training programs. We founded Attitudes for Success™, a program for those who want to manage their careers and businesses successfully. Products include audio tapes, books, and booklets. Owner Sharron Stockhausen holds a masters degree in management and administration; teaches business, speech, and marketing at three colleges; and writes a weekly newspaper column and a monthly magazine column. Memberships include the National Speakers Association, the Minnesota Speakers Association, and the International Speakers Network.
CURRENT/RECENT CLIENTS/PROJECTS: Honeywell, Inc.; Allina Health Systems; 3M; St. Paul Convention and Visitors Bureau; Creative Memories; Open U, Inc.; and State of Minnesota.
PRESIDENT/CEO/OWNER: Sharron Stockhausen

Sports and Entertainment Marketing

L
LOW AND INSIDE
PO Box 290228
FAX: 763-767-5510
CONTACT: Nick Vetter
E-MAIL: creative@lowandinside.com
WWW: lowandinside.com

612-701-2799
Minneapolis 55429

SERVICES: Baseball marketing concepts, historical insight and copywriting, graphic design for print and web, logo creation/makeover, illustration, special event promotional materials, book or catalog publishing. Strong print production experience from concept through distribution.

CAPABILITIES: Low and Inside Creative offers a teamwork approach in creating interest in your baseball product, event, idea or dream. Based in 1988, SABR Member, active in the global baseball community.

CURRENT/RECENT CLIENTS/PROJECTS: Field of Dreams Movie Site, variety of other clients.

PRESIDENT/CEO/OWNER: Nick Vetter

Sweepstakes & Contest Designers

I

INTERACTIVE GAMES 651-221-0702
420 Summit Avenue St. Paul 55102
FAX: 651-222-3490
CONTACT: Dennis Kelly
E-MAIL: dk@gamesdesign.com
WWW: gamesdesign.com

CAPABILITIES: Design and implementation of all aspects of promotional game management. Inclusive of sweepstakes, contest and special events. Services include creative development, legal review and registration, bonding, judging, administration, game security and prize fulfillment. Applications include print, internet, telephony and game cards.

SPECIALTIES: Prize insurance, which eliminates the risk of major prize pay-outs for all types of sweepstakes and contest including events i.e. hole-in one; half court shots. Insure up to 10 million dollars per promotion.

CURRENT/RECENT CLIENTS/PROJECTS: Wal-Mart, National Car Rental, Larry King Productions, Walt Disney World, IBM Rayovac, Campbell's Soup Company, US Olympics, Mondo, Home Depot, Signature Group, SNET, AT&T, Chemical Bank plus many others.

Telemarketing Consultants & Services Bureaus

M

MONTAGE
2200 W County Road C
FAX: 651-633-2072
CONTACT: Dick Moberg
E-MAIL: ramoberg@montagenet.com
WWW: montagenet.com
651-633-1955
Roseville 55113

SERVICES: Montage provides customer relationship management services: A customer care center to handle 1-800 calls, e-mails, web visitors, faxes and mail received by our clients; Sales lead management; E-commerce; Outbound telemarketing; Assembly, fulfillment and mailing; Sales seminar administration; Rebate processing; Database marketing.

CAPABILITIES: Montage has been providing marketing services to the business community since 1972. We specialize in programs that build customer relationships with professional, technical and managerial audiences. We specialize in turn-key systems that are tailored to client needs.

CURRENT/RECENT CLIENTS/PROJECTS: 3M Company; Allied Signal; BASF; Carpet One; Century Mfg.; Colder Products Co.; Cuddle Ewe Co.; Dyneon, Inc.; Fujitsu; Horton, Inc.; Medtronic, Inc.; Nexen Group; Norwest Corp; Rockwell Automation; Prometric, Inc.

PRESIDENT/CEO/OWNER: Ken Ehling

T

TELEDIRECT
2790 Autumnwood Lane
CONTACT: Kolette Stevenson
E-MAIL: chakolette@aol.com
952-546-2225
Minnetonka 55305

SPECIALTIES: Teleservices consulting and strategic program planning, recommendations on qualified service providers. TELEDirect has years of experience and the knowledge you need to build successful telemarketing programs.

TELEPHONE SALES ASSOCIATES
7515 Wayzata Boulevard #129
FAX: 612-545-7020
CONTACT: Max Fallek
E-MAIL: aisbofmn@aol.com
612-545-7001
Minneapolis 55426

SERVICES: Provides marketing consulting services for Telephone Marketing. Provides both outgoing and inbound telemarketing specializing in sales, surveys and appointment setting.

PRESIDENT/CEO/OWNER: Max Fallek

Teleprompters

V

Trabajamos tambien en Español!

☞ Director of Photography
☞ Documentaries
☞ BTV Design & Production
☞ Computerized Teleprompting Services

VENUS DIRECTIONS   **651-636-0838**
1519 McClung Drive   **Arden Hills 55112**
FAX: 651-636-0958
CONTACT: Andres A. Parra
E-MAIL: andresdp@aol.com
CAPABILITIES: Bilingual Director (Spanish/English). Director of photography specializing in documentaries, corporate image and human interest pieces; full BetaCam-SP package available 16:9 capabilities. Offer state-of-the-art multi-language Computerized Teleprompting Service for video, film and presidential-style live presentations. Executive speech coaching available. All products and services are custom-designed to meet your specific goals and objectives. Voice-over and on-camera talent in Spanish.
SPECIALTIES: Creating images that move your message. International expertise.
PRESIDENT/CEO/OWNER: Andres A. Parra, President/Owner

Television - Broadcast

M

MEDIAONE 651-312-5000
10 River Park Plaza #400 St. Paul 55107
FAX: 651-312-5317
CONTACT: Gary Houston
E-MAIL: msolac@mediaone.com
SERVICES: Geographic Areas covered: Serving 306,200 households with six advertising zones in Anoka, Ramsey, Hennepin, Washington, and Dakota counties. Offering advertising on 36 cable networks. Half hour time is available on Local Origination Channel 13.
SPECIALTIES: Local e-commerce shopping mall available "shoptwincities.com." Digital insertion equipment. Next day start to your advertising schedule is available.

Television - Cable Access

G
GOVERNMENT TELEVISION NETWORK
7245 Stillwater Boulevard North
FAX: 651-779-8990
CONTACT: Joseph Frazier
E-MAIL: gtn@visi.com
WWW: gtn.org
CAPABILITIES: Government Access Cable Production.

651-779-0230
Oakdale 55128

Temporary Staffing

D

DIGITAL PEOPLE   952-842-8359
5151 Edina Industrial Boulevard   **Edina 55439**
FAX: 952-835-7326
CONTACT: Ken Marshall
E-MAIL: ken_marshall@digitalpeople.net
WWW: digitalpeople.net

SERVICES: We represent exceptional freelance graphics and web/Internet talent for on-site or off-site projects, permanent employee recruiting, or project based assignments. Complete background checking, software testing and skills verification of all talent assures you the right talent for that all-important project.

CAPABILITIES: Macintosh or PC/Windows based professionals in the areas of Art Direction, Graphic Design, Illustration, Web Design, Web Coding, Web Productions, Web Content Development, Multimedia Design, Video Production, Copywriting, Editing/Proofreading, Electronic Production Artists, Traffic/Print Productions, Media and much more. Digital People currently have 14 offices in 11 major cities; if we can't find the talent you need locally, we will source them in other markets.

CURRENT/RECENT CLIENTS/PROJECTS: Corporate Communication Departments, Advertising Agencies, Sales Promotion Agencies, Dot.com's, Internet Solution Providers, Internet Based Communication Agencies, Graphic Design Agencies. We provide complete references from a broad base of clients.

F

FREELANCE CREATIVE SERVICES   952-941-0022
7835 Telegraph Road   **Bloomington 55438**
FAX: 952-941-0709
CONTACT: Marlene Phipps
E-MAIL: marlenep@freelancecreative.com
WWW: freelancecreative.com

552 / Temporary Staffing

FOCUS: Freelance Creative Services, Inc. is the best connection for temporary creative and technical talent in the areas of: art direction, graphic design/production, writing, editing and proofing, web design and maintenance, presentations and multi-media development. We provide quality professional service by upholding the highest industry standards. You can completely rely on our judgement and expertise in quickly finding the talent you need or the perfect assignment to match your unique talent. With over 25 years of experience in the Twin Cities creative community, we are totally committed to your satisfaction.

SERVICES: Why work with an agency? We have the time, knowledge, and resources to evaluate and build relationships with people you need. It's what we do every day. If reviewing resumes, interviewing, testing and checking references is not an efficient use of your time, make Freelance Creative Services your business. On the other hand, if making sales calls to prospective clients during the day, working all night, invoicing and trying to collect your money in less than 30 days is not your idea of a career, make Freelance Creative Services your connection. Our recruiting staff is constantly recruiting, screening, and testing to build the strongest pool of freelance talent for our clients. Our seasoned sales staff is proactively marketing our talented pool of freelancers. Let us handle all the paperwork involved so you can focus on what you do best.

CAPABILITIES: More than any other factor, success in the outsourcing business is dependent on the strength of our business relationships. We have met clients and freelancers through our involvement with industry organizations, training centers and referrals from satisfied clients and freelancers through 25 years of networking in the Twin Cities creative community. Our focus on working with the most skilled, highly-qualified people and building quality relationships, results in individualized service and solutions for both clients and freelancers.

PRESIDENT/CEO/OWNER: Marlene and Douglas Phipps

L

LYNN TEMPORARY 651-645-9233
1821 University Avenue St. Paul 55104
FAX: 651-641-8986
CONTACT: Carl Glewwe
CAPABILITIES: All types of office temporary help including: word processing, desktop publishers, graphics specialists, writers, and editors.

M

MIDWEST STAFFING GROUP, INC. 612-677-0899
730 2nd Avenue South #299 Minneapolis 55402
FAX: 612-677-0225
CONTACT: Brian Thoemke/Cheryl Crawford
E-MAIL: ccrawford@midweststaffing.com; bthoemke@midweststaffing.com
WWW: midweststaffing.com
SERVICES: Midwest Staffing Group specializes in placement of light industrial and clerical employees for the purpose of supporting or supplementing our client's workforce.
CAPABILITIES: Midwest Staffing Group offers unique solutions to solve clients' recruiting and staffing needs. We thoroughly interview and test all applicants to determine an accurate skills assessment. We offer five convenient locations to cover the seven county metro area.

Temporary Staffing / 553

PRESIDENT/CEO/OWNER: Joseph Thoemke

N

THE NYCOR GROUP   **952-831-6444**
4930 W 77th Street #300   **Minneapolis 55435**
FAX: 952-835-2883
CONTACT: Lynn M. Florell
E-MAIL: info@nycor.com
WWW: nycor.com
CAPABILITIES: Nycor Consulting candidates posses Information Technology, Web Design, Animation, E-Commerce, Multimedia, Software Design, Documentation, Implementation and Deployment, ASP, Java, Object-Oriented Platforms, and Order Fulfillment expertise.
NYCOR SEARCH, INC.: Nycor Search, Inc. is a Technical Search Firm specializing in Information Technology, Engineering, Telecommunications, Architecture, Product Development, Technical Management, and Executive-level positions.
NYCOR CONTRACT SERVICES, INC.: Nycor Contract Services, Inc. provides contract services for Information Technology, Engineering, Telecommunications, Architecture, Drafting & Design, and Technical Writing.
NYCOR TECHNICAL, INC.: Nycor Technical, Inc. provides contract services for skilled labor areas including CNC, drafting, biomedical, and technical specialties.
SPECIALTIES: Extensive database of over 45,000 experienced and pre-screened technical professionals. Established and financially sound business for 43 years.
PRESIDENT/CEO/OWNER: John F. Nymark

T

TALENT TEMPS, INC.   **651-426-9909**
1564 5th Street   **St. Paul 55110**
CONTACT: Linda Klemmer
SERVICES: We specialize in employing qualified professional voice and on-camera talent for the broadcast commercial and industrial video industry. Solve your short term talent needs and leave the burden of employment to us.
CAPABILITIES: We employ highly qualified Voice talent and on-camera actors for broadcast commercials, industrials, educational videos, documentaries, IVR systems, voicemail, CD-ROMs and actors and spokespersons for live training programs, trade shows, conventions, sales meetings and award dinners, real people models for print.
CURRENT/RECENT CLIENTS/PROJECTS: Honeywell (1995 - present) Industrial; Northwest Airlines (1995 - present) Commercial and Industrial; Medtronic (1995 - present) Industrial.
PRESIDENT/CEO/OWNER: Linda Klemmer

Translators

A

ACTORS PLUS/VOICE PLUS   651-426-9400
1564 5th Street   St. Paul 55110
CONTACT: Debbie Klemmer Rush
TOLL FREE: 877-426-9500
E-MAIL: agency@voiceplustalent.com
WWW: voiceplustalent.com
SERVICES: Since 1972, providing professional voice and on-camera actors and narrators; men, women, children, ethnic and earprompted talent; foreign language translators and narrators. Photos, audio clips, resumes, resources and other topics of interest are available on our website. CD's and audition arrangements available.
CAPABILITIES: We represent highly qualified Voice talent and on-camera actors for broadcast commercials, industrials, educational videos, documentaries, IVR systems, voicemail, CD-ROM's, actors and spokespersons for live training programs, trade shows, conventions, sales meetings and award dinners. Real people models for print.
CURRENT/RECENT CLIENTS/PROJECTS: Honda (1986 - present) Commercial; Mayo Clinic (1990 - present) Industrial; Best Buy (1985 - present) Industrial and Commercial; Many advertising agencies, A/V production studios, Independent producers, Broadcast stations and Corporate media departments.
PRESIDENT/CEO/OWNER: Linda Klemmer

ALLIANCE FRANCAISE OF THE TWIN CITIES   612-332-0436
113 North First Street   Minneapolis 55401
FAX: 612-332-0438
CONTACT: Abdon Berthelot
SERVICES: French language classes, translation and interpretation. Advanced business and commercial French.
CAPABILITIES: 25 years, non-profit, supported by French Foreign Ministry.
SPECIALTIES: French language and culture.

Translators / 555

B

P.H. Brink
INTERNATIONAL

P. H. BRINK INTERNATIONAL **763-591-1977**
6100 Golden Valley Road **Golden Valley 55442**
FAX: 763-542-9138
CONTACT: Greg Brink or Bob Dungan
E-MAIL: gregb@phbrink.com
CAPABILITIES: Full service language management company offering in-house on-site language adaptations, electronic publishing, audio visual services, interpretation services.
EQUIPMENT: Over 21 years experience. 150 full time (in-house) translators, typesetters and graphic artists. Delivering world class language solutions for over 21 years.
SPECIALTIES: Technical documents, manuals, catalogs, brochures, web sites, services, specification sheets, software localization, packaging, video tapes (voice overs) and graphic replacement, on-camera shooting and post production conversions, and much more. Call today for more information.
CURRENT/RECENT CLIENTS/PROJECTS: Fortune 100 companies worldwide.
PRESIDENT/CEO/OWNER: Paul H. Brink, CEO

C

CREO INTERNATIONAL - INTERNATIONAL **612-342-9800**
AND CROSS CULTURAL COMMUNICATIONS
520 Marquette Avenue #700 **Minneapolis 55402**
FAX: 612-342-9750
CONTACT: Christa Tiefenbacher-Hudson, Managing Director
WWW: creo-works.com

556 / Translators

SPECIALTIES: Marketing and advertising communications for global and US ethnic markets.
CURRENT/RECENT CLIENTS/PROJECTS: American Express, American Medical Systems, Fingerhut, Hormel, Marvin Windows, Northwest Airlines, Target Stores, US Bank.

E

EURUS INC.   612-920-1651
125 Main Street SE #341   Minneapolis 55414
FAX: 612-920-2462
CONTACT: Dora O'Malley
E-MAIL: dora@eurusinc.com
SERVICES: English/Spanish translation and multilingual project management. Translation, editing, foreign language adaptation, copyediting and localization.
CAPABILITIES: Over 16 years of experience in translation and multilingual project management for major US companies. Member of the American Translators Association. Licensed by the Buenos Aires Certified Public Translators Association, Argentina.
SPECIALTIES: Technical manuals, users guides, employee ad customer surveys. Corporate policies, health insurance, 401 (k) plans. Marketing packaging, advertising, catalogs, brochures, videos, newsletters. Legal documents, immigration, contracts, warranties, patents. K-12 school texts and children's books. Hardware and software, medical devices. On-line manuals and web site translation.
CURRENT/RECENT CLIENTS/PROJECTS: International companies, publishers, translation and advertising agencies marketing products for the US or global markets.

G

GERMAN LANGUAGE SERVICE   612-926-9348
6209 Crest Lane   Minneapolis 55436
CONTACT: Hans J. Koenig
CAPABILITIES: Translation: English to German, German to English, German sound recording (voice over.)
SPECIALTIES: Experience: Since 1969. Accredited with American Translators Association. Technical, scientific, patents, legal, promotional.
CURRENT/RECENT CLIENTS/PROJECTS: Major corporations throughout the US and Germany.

Translators / 557

INTERNATIONAL
AND ETHNIC
COMMUNICATIONS

INTERNATIONAL & ETHNIC   **612-359-8390**
COMMUNICATIONS, INC.
4215 Winnetka Avenue North #255   **Minneapolis 55428**
FAX: 763-535-9574
CONTACT: Ricardo Paul Vallejos
E-MAIL: info@intl-ethnic.com
WWW: intl-ethnic.com
TYPES OF WRITING: Multicultural concepting and foreign-language copywriting for consumer and business-to-business print, packaging, collateral, direct response, broadcast, web sites, video, press releases, corporate communications. Also copy translation/adaptation and transcreation. Interview, feature stories for US Hispanic Market.
SPECIALTIES: Collateral, packaging, video.
WRITTEN FOR: US companies and agencies marketing products and services to international and US ethnic markets.

Typesetting & Typographers

A

AS SOON AS POSSIBLE, INC.   952-564-2727
3000 France Avenue South   St. Louis Park 55416
FAX: 952-564-2720
CONTACT: George West, 952-564-2621
E-MAIL: gwest@asap.net
WWW: asap.net
CAPABILITIES: A.S.A.P. is a Marketing Communications Production Company that offers prepress Services (Mac & PC), Printing (digital, offset, and direct-to-plate), Large Trade Show/Display Prints, and Internet & Interactive Multimedia. For more information, call George West today at 952-564-2621 or visit our web site at www.asap.net.
EQUIPMENT: Imagesetters, Canons, Agfa Chromapress, Heidelberg Quickmaster DI's, Xerox Doc 40, Micropress, Offset Presses, Iris, Rainbow, Scanners, and Ink Jet and Electrostatic Large Format Printers. Pick-up and delivery available.

ATLANTIC PRESS   612-824-7322
3457 Chicago Avenue   Minneapolis 55407
FAX: 612-824-0255
CONTACT: Phillip N. Anderson
CAPABILITIES: Typesetting and typography. Pickup and delivery.

B

THE BENYAS GROUP   612-340-9804
126 North Third Street, Suite 300   Minneapolis 55401
FAX: 612-334-5950
CONTACT: Bradley A. Benyas
E-MAIL: benyas@visi.com
CAPABILITIES: From simple to complex, expertly typeset & composed. Typesetting, electronic pre-press, color proofing, mock-ups, proofreading, data archiving, bar code creation, foreign language typography. High quality and fast turnaround.

INTERNATIONAL

P. H. BRINK INTERNATIONAL **763-591-1977**
6100 Golden Valley Road **Golden Valley 55442**
FAX: 763-542-9138
CONTACT: Greg Brink or Bob Dungan
E-MAIL: gregb@phbrink.com
CAPABILITIES: Full service language management company providing on-site language adaptations, electronic publishing/typesetting, audio visual services, interpretation services in any major language.
SPECIALTIES: Technical documents, manuals, IFUS, brochures, web sites, specification sheets, software localization, packaging, and much more. We deliver world class language solutions.

F

FORM & CONTENT **612-788-4252**
340 23rd Avenue NE **Minneapolis 55418**
FAX: 612-788-4252
CONTACT: Virginia Sutton
E-MAIL: riverannex@earthlink.net
SERVICES: Graphic design, typesetting, page layout, project management. Image scanning of photos (FPO) and artwork (1200 dpi). Proofreading for copy and typographic consistency. Quality control.
CAPABILITIES: 18 years experience in graphics industry; 12 in Twin Cities type shops (pre-and post Macintosh). Specializing in typographic solutions to design problems. Output capability: 11 x 17 B & W lasers, 11 x 17 color inkjet.
CURRENT/RECENT CLIENTS/PROJECTS: American Guidance Service (textbook design), Children's Theatre Company (program design/production), Minnesota Orchestra (4 color brochure), Llewellyn Publications (book interiors). Books, booklets, catalogs, annual reports.
PRESIDENT/CEO/OWNER: Virginia Sutton

Voice Talent

A

ACTORS PLUS/VOICE PLUS   651-426-9400
1564 5th Street   St. Paul 55110
CONTACT: Debbie Klemmer Rush
TOLL FREE: 877-426-9500
E-MAIL: agency@voiceplustalent.com
WWW: voiceplustalent.com
SERVICES: Since 1972, providing professional voice and on-camera actors and narrators; men, women, children, ethnic and earprompted talent; foreign language translators and narrators. Photos, audio clips, resumes, resources and other topics of interest are available on our website. CD's and audition arrangements available.
CAPABILITIES: We represent highly qualified Voice talent and on-camera actors for broadcast commercials, industrials, educational videos, documentaries, IVR systems, voicemail, CD-ROM's, actors and spokespersons for live training programs, trade shows, conventions, sales meetings and award dinners. Real people models for print.
CURRENT/RECENT CLIENTS/PROJECTS: Honda (1986 - present) Commercial; Mayo Clinic (1990 - present) Industrial; Best Buy (1985 - present) Industrial and Commercial; Many advertising agencies, A/V production studios, Independent producers, Broadcast stations and Corporate media departments.
PRESIDENT/CEO/OWNER: Linda Klemmer

I

INTERNATIONAL & ETHNIC   612-359-8390
COMMUNICATIONS, INC.
4215 Winnetka Avenue North #255   Minneapolis 55428
FAX: 763-535-9574
CONTACT: Ricardo Paul Vallejos
E-MAIL: Info@intl-ethnic.com
WWW: intl-ethnic.com

Voice Talent / 561

TYPES OF WRITING: Multicultural concepting and foreign-language copywriting for consumer and business-to-business print, packaging, collateral, direct response, broadcast, web sites, video, press releases, corporate communications. Also copy translation/adaptation and transcreation. Interview, feature stories for US Hispanic Market.
SPECIALTIES: Hispanic marketing, Latino advertising, print, radio, collateral, print, video.
WRITTEN FOR: GTE/Verizon; The Gap; Fingerhut; Amoco; Radisson; Toro; 3M; Pillbury; The Olive Garden; Great Clips; Coca Cola; Red Lobster; Regis; Cargill; National Computer Systems; and others.

T

THE TALENT CENTER 651-306-9670
67 Imperial Drive East West St. Paul 55118
FAX: 651-698-7141
CONTACT: Don Cosgrove
E-MAIL: talentdc@visi.com
CAPABILITIES: Full creative range from humorous characters to non-broadcast industrial training and sales, extensive and varied experience on both sides of the mic, broadcast voiceovers, narration, radio drama, industrials, spokesperson, national and international theater, motion pictures and television experience.
SPECIALTIES: Dialogue, comic timing, quick grasp of talent styles needed for any script situation, including friendly, upscales, sensuous, caring, cartoon and real people.
CURRENT/RECENT CLIENTS/PROJECTS: Virtually all major Twin City area - plus many national - companies and products, including 3M, Coca Cola, IDS American Express, Ford Motors, The Guthrie Theater, Dayton Hudson, Purina, Northwest Airlines, Norwest Banks, Star Trek, Science Museum, US Armed Forces, General Mills, General Motors, Lutheran Brotherhood, Cadillac, Bachman's etc.

TRILOGY MARKETING GROUP 651-482-8270
944 Cobb Road Shoreview 55126-3804
FAX: 651-482-8270
CONTACT: James D. Lemke
PAGER: 612-601-0356
E-MAIL: trilogymktg@aol.com
SERVICES: Creative vocal range includes experience in: on-camera commercials, broadcast voiceovers, industrial sales and training films, motion pictures, live and improv theater, comedy, singing venues and celebrity look-alike events.
SPECIALTIES: Quick study of vocal delivery needed - from authoritative to "warm fuzzy" - to match script and meet client communication goals; credible spokes person; dialect characters; Humphrey Bogart sound/look alike; trained actor, improv artist and singer/acoustic guitar player.
CURRENT/RECENT CLIENTS/PROJECTS: A variety of Twin City based companies including: General Mills; The Ordway; Dayton's; E. W. Blanch; and Northwest Athletic Club.
PRESIDENT/CEO/OWNER: James D. Lemke

V

VOICE MATTERS 612-781-6489
1402 Jefferson Street NE Minneapolis 55413
FAX: 612-781-6478
CONTACT: Ellen Petty
E-MAIL: evox@spacestar.net
SERVICES: All applications of voiceover; coaching for communication and presentation.
CAPABILITIES: Material for training in technical, medical and corporate markets.
CURRENT/RECENT CLIENTS/PROJECTS: American Express; ANC Rental Corporation; AT &T; ATX Telecommunications; Carlson Wagonlit; Continental Airlines; Dell Computer; Fox 29; Harvard University Medical School; Kronos, Inc.; Macromedia; Mall of America; Minnesota State Lottery; National Car Rental; Northwest Airlines; Novartis; UPN 9/KMSP - TV; WCCO Radio/TV.

VOICE PLUS/ACTORS PLUS 651-426-9400
1564 5th Street St. Paul 55110
CONTACT: Debbie Klemmer Rush
TOLL FREE: 877-426-9500
E-MAIL: agency@voiceplustalent.com
WWW: voiceplustalent.com
SERVICES: Since 1972, providing professional voice and on-camera actors and narrators; men, women, children, ethnic and earprompted talent; foreign language translators and narrators. Photos, audio clips, resumes, resources and other topics of interest are available on our website. CD's and audition arrangements available.
CAPABILITIES: We represent highly qualified Voice talent and on-camera actors for broadcast commercials, industrials, educational videos, documentaries, IVR systems, voicemail, CD-ROM's, actors and spokespersons for live training programs, trade shows, conventions, sales meetings and award dinners, real people models for print.
CURRENT/RECENT CLIENTS/PROJECTS: Honda (1986 - present) Commercial; Mayo Clinic (1990 - present) Industrial; Best Buy (1985 - present) Industrial and Commercial; Many advertising agencies, A/V production studios, Independent producers, Broadcast stations and Corporate media departments.
PRESIDENT/CEO/OWNER: Linda Klemmer

Writers & Advertising Copywriters

A

AMT COMMUNICATIONS/ANN M. THOMPSON   651-430-0908
PO Box 267   Stillwater 55082
FAX: 651-430-0908
CONTACT: Ann M. Thompson
E-MAIL: amt_communications@compuserve.com
TYPES OF WRITING: Video scripts, speeches, brochures, publications, employee handbooks.
SPECIALTIES: Corporate communications, marketing communications, employee communications (benefits, recruitment, orientation, video news for employees), medical communications.
CURRENT/RECENT CLIENTS/PROJECTS: General Mills, Inc.; Dayton Hudson; Mayo Clinic; McCoy & Associates; CME Video & Film; Rapp Collins Communications; Edina Realty; Media Loft; Metro State University; Shandwick USA; University of Minnesota; United Way of Minneapolis Area; Catholic Charities.
PRESIDENT/CEO/OWNER: Ann M. Thompson

B

BACK MCKAY   612-722-6236
5034 30th Avenue South   Minneapolis 55417
CONTACT: Linda Back McKay
E-MAIL: lbmckay@visi.com
SERVICES: Copywriting and creative direction services to all types of companies, organizations and agencies. Consumer and trade advertising, business-to-business, direct mail, promotions, collateral, radio, packaging, greeting cards, identity materials.
CAPABILITIES: 20 years experience in advertising and marketing communications, with several honors and awards.
CURRENT/RECENT CLIENTS/PROJECTS: Federal Express - Caribbean, Pillsbury, MN/DOT, Como Park Conservatory, Science Museum of Minnesota, US Bancorp, Hennepin County Library Foundation, KFAI Radio, Bakers Square, Medicare/Health Span, Realiastar, Northwest Airlines, ourhouse.com

MICHAEL FRANCIS BEMIS, FREELANCE WRITER   651-778-8282
651 Gotzian Street   St. Paul 55106
CONTACT: Michael Francis Bemis
E-MAIL: mbemis@mn.uswest.net
SERVICES: Types of writing: investigative journalism, news release, personal essay, profiles and biography, magazine feature articles, annotated bibliography, research and analysis.
CAPABILITIES: Humor and human interest.
CURRENT/RECENT CLIENTS/PROJECTS: CFG Insurance Services, Inc., Boy Scouts of America, University of St. Thomas, Minnesota Association of Volunteer Directors, St. Paul Pioneer Press, Metropolitan State University, Minnesota Department of Transportation.

564 / Writers & Advertising Copywriters

RUTH A. BERGENE, WRITER 612-925-2111
2825 Louisiana Avenue South St. Louis Park 55426
FAX: 612-922-2264
CONTACT: Ruth Bergene
E-MAIL: rabe@spacestar.net
SERVICES: Print oriented copy and editorial writer in business since 1978. Newsletters a specialty. Also written sales promotion, direct mail, motivational brochures and other collateral pieces, plus some public relations materials and newspaper and magazine articles. 35 plus years communications background.
CURRENT/RECENT CLIENTS/PROJECTS: Edina Realty; Prosource Educational Services; NCS; Star Tribune; Sun Newspapers; Coldwell Banker Burnet; Animal Humane Society; Minnesota Tourism; Gold n' Plump; ISKA; Jostens; Land O' Lakes, Inc.; Pillsbury; Green Giant and American Beauty; General Mills; Hellman Design; H.B. Fuller; National Car Rental; CPT Corporation and many more.

BOHEN COMMUNICATIONS 651-646-4833
1960 Ashland Avenue St. Paul 55104
FAX: 651-646-5010
CONTACT: James Bohen
E-MAIL: bohe0002@tc.umn.edu
TYPES OF WRITING: Newsletters, brochures, articles, sales promotion, releases, direct mail, employee communications for over 20 years.
CURRENT/RECENT CLIENTS/PROJECTS: Star Tribune, 3M; Carlson Companies; West Group; Guthrie Theater; Shandwick USA; Ecolab; University of St. Thomas; Macalester; University of Minnesota; H B Fuller; Hamline; ADC Telecommunications; Frontier Communications; Minnesota Telephone Assn.; Minnesota Grocers Assn.; Science Museum of Minnesota; GEICO; Minnesota Medical Assn.; Medica; Minnesota PCA; Minnesota Dept. of Children; Families & Learning; United Healthcare; SEH; National Insurance Crime Bureau; Pentair; MSP Communications; various magazines.
PRESIDENT/CEO/OWNER: James Bohen

C

CARL FRANZEN IS A WRITER 612-825-0149
4804 Harriet Avenue South Minneapolis 55409
CONTACT: Carl Franzen
E-MAIL: cfran@mninter.net
WWW: mninternet/~site
SERVICES: New and emerging business development tools: writing, positioning, product naming; desktop design and production of logos, ads, brochures, packaging and websites.
CAPABILITIES: Electronic newsletters

Writers & Advertising Copywriters / 565

COLLEEN SZOT WONDERFUL WRITER, INC.   **763-557-7116**
13615 61st Avenue North   **Minneapolis 55446**
FAX: 763-551-4831
CONTACT: Colleen Szot
TOLL FREE: 888-557-7116
E-MAIL: colleenszot@aol.com
WWW: colleenszot.com
TYPES OF WRITING: Clio award-winning writer of more than 100 direct response/infomercials (CNN's Cold War, George Foreman, Orlimar Trimental, Tony Little, Select Comfort, David Dikeman Command Performance) plus TV commercials (Wendy's, Walt Disney, Kraft, Nutri-Grain cereal), Corporate and Training Videos (Dayton-Hudson Corporation, 3M), and all print (ads, brochure, direct mail collateral). Author of best-selling book (Christian Wives), writer for cable television, 22 years experience with J. Walter Thompson, Foote, Cone & Belding, and Campbell-Mithun-Esty.
WRITTEN FOR: CNN, George Foreman, Target, Walt Disney Pictures, Troy-Bilt, HomeRight (PaintStick), 3M, Select Comfort, Tony Little and more.
SPECIALTIES: All broadcast, plus corporate videos/film, cable television.

CREATIVE BUSINESS INK   **651-436-5315**
14193 70th Street South   **Hastings 55033**
FAX: 651-436-5618
CONTACT: Christine Roen
E-MAIL: cbusink@aol.com
SERVICES: Right writing for business-to-business communications and employee communications including newsletters, brochures, feature stories, press releases, sales letters, web copy, manuals, annual reports and more. Services including electronic publishing and production coordination.
CAPABILITIES: Celebrating 15 years in business - more as a writer. Offers a handy blend of writing and print communications development. Concise, precise, quick. Strong research and interviewing skills. Ability to translate complex issues into understandable messages.
CURRENT/RECENT CLIENTS/PROJECTS: Tom Thumb Food Markets, Inc.; Faribault Foods, Inc.; Imation; Gross-Given Manufacturing; Ecolab; Century College; Lutheran Brotherhood; Cenex Harvest States; MHC Associates; Graphic Design, Inc.

F

FLOATING HEAD   612-823-6645
4849 Aldrich Avenue South   Minneapolis 55409
FAX: 612-823-6572
CONTACT: Jeff Mueller
SPECIALTIES: Concepts and copy as refreshing as complimentary refills for the rest of your dang life.

G

STAN M. GOLDSTEIN   952-927-5186
4000 Forest Road   Minneapolis 55416
CONTACT: Stan Goldstein
TYPES OF WRITING: Advertising, creative, print, brochures, direct mail, public relations, marketing consultations. Film, videotape, audiovisual shows, treatments, instructional materials, script doctoring.
SPECIALTIES: Consumer products, corporate promotional, industrial, computers, electronics.
CURRENT/RECENT CLIENTS/PROJECTS: General Mills, General Foods, Alberto Culver, Cellular One, Contac, Dayton's, Fingerhut, Northwest Airlines, Pillsbury, Practical Computer Applications, Weight Watchers, West Bend, 3M, United Airlines, Aequitron Medical, Control Data, Honeywell, Lee Data, Northern Telecom, SPEED-S Electronic Delivery, Aeration Industries, Sears, American Nurses Assn.; AT&T Long Lines, Bell System. Business Incentives, Cargill, Disney World, Dyco Petroleum, Farmland Industries, First Banks, ITT Life Insurance, Land O' Lakes, Litton Industries, Lutheran Brotherhood, McNeil Labs (Tylenol), Merrill Lynch Realty, Minnetonka, Inc., Phillips, Scientific Computers, 7 Up - National, Toro, United Way, Xerox Corp., Laser Systems. HSB Reliability Technologies, Glasrock, ADP Hollander.

INDIGO INK COMMUNICATIONS
2195 Bayard Avenue
FAX: 651-698-5189
CONTACT: Mary Kate Boylan
E-MAIL: mkboylan@indigoink.com

651-698-4547
St. Paul 55116

TYPES OF WRITING: Organizational communications including newsletters and annual reports, development/fund-raising materials, brochures, promotional materials, direct mail, press releases, advertising copy writing, magazine feature stories and other material. Editing of newsletters, annual reports, position papers, policy documents, oral transcripts, books, employee communications, grant proposals, promotional material, brochures and other material.
SPECIALTIES: Writing, rewriting, substantive editing and copy editing for health care, nonprofits, environmental concerns and technology.
WRITTEN FOR: University of Minnesota School of Dentistry, University of Minnesota, General Colleges, Allina, Actual Software, Minneapolis Institute of Arts, Science Museum of Minnesota, Minnesota International Center, Saint Paul Neighborhood Energy Consortium, MCC Behavioral Care, First Banks System, Infinite Technologies, Technical Strategies Group, 3M, Career Pilot Magazine, Rummell, Dubs & Hill, MetroEast Program for Health, Red Cross, Catholic Charities, United Hospital, Redleaf Press, and others.

INTERNATIONAL & ETHNIC COMMUNICATIONS, INC.
4215 Winnetka Avenue North #255
FAX: 763-535-9574
CONTACT: Ricardo Paul Vallejos
E-MAIL: info@intl-ethnic.com
WWW: intl-ethnic.com

612-359-8390

Minneapolis 55428

TYPES OF WRITING: Multicultural concepting and foreign-language copywriting for consumer and business-to-business print, packaging, collateral, direct response, broadcast, web sites, video, press releases, corporate communications. Also copy translation/adaptation and transcreation. Interview, feature stories for US Hispanic Market.
SPECIALTIES: Hispanic marketing, Latino advertising, print, radio, collateral, print, video.

568 / Writers & Advertising Copywriters

WRITTEN FOR: GTE/Verizon; The Gap; Fingerhut; Amoco; Radisson; Toro; 3M; Pillbury; The Olive Garden; Great Clips; Coca Cola; Red Lobster; Regis; Cargill; National Computer Systems; and others.

J

JIM STOKES COMMUNICATIONS   612-381-9353
453 South Cedar Lake Road   Minneapolis 55405
CONTACT: Jim Stokes
TYPES OF WRITING: Feature writing for magazines, screenwriting, writing for radio programs, commercials and PSA's.
SPECIALTIES: Feature writing for magazines. Medical: respiratory health, public health. Broadcast writing, environmental health. Broadcast (radio) interviewer and producer.

L

LIGHTHOUSE CREATIVE   612-869-6433
6704 Oakland Avenue   Richfield 55423
FAX: 612-866-8017
CONTACT: John C. Moon
SERVICES: Web sites, brochures, sales letters, catalogs, manuals, newsletters, business-to-business ads, sell sheet, sales binder presentations and product bulletins.
WRITTEN FOR: High-tech clients like 3M, low-tech companies like Andersen Windows and no-tech clients such as AAA Minnesota.

M

MESSAGE IN MOTION   218-226-3500
6456 Highway 61   Little Marais 55614
FAX: 218-226-3535
CONTACT: David Klassen
ALTERNATE PHONE: 800-681-6161
E-MAIL: dklassen@mimotion.com
SERVICES: The Whole Show. Full-service video and interactive media production for national and international clients. Award-winning writer, producer, director specialized in clear, compelling communication for marketing, public relations, training and broadcast. 25 years experience completing complex projects from script, through production, to translation and international distribution on critical deadlines.
CAPABILITIES: Script & creative services. Producer/director for studio and field locations. Digital, non-linear, no-compression video editing. Interactive media production. Transcription. Translation services and international distribution.
CURRENT/RECENT CLIENTS/PROJECTS: Technology, manufacturing, automotive, finance, agriculture, mining, government, utilities and health.

Writers & Advertising Copywriters / 569

MGRAPHICS   612-404-0052
3627 Druid Lane   Minnetonka 55345
CONTACT: Mary Brandenburg
E-MAIL: mgraph99@aol.com
SERVICES: Proofreading and editing.
CAPABILITIES: Careful review of content and style (verbal and visual, if desired.) Work from hard copy of rile. Mac G3, Quark 4.1, IBM, Word.
CURRENT/RECENT CLIENTS/PROJECTS: Editorial, industrial, advertising. Annual reports, newsletters, brochures, handbooks.

R

THE RESUME SPECIALIST   612-525-2023
5831 Cedar Lake Road   St. Louis Park 55416
Sunset Ridge Office Park
CONTACT: Vicki Bacal
E-MAIL: bacal003@tc.umn.edu
SERVICES: Resume writing, cover letters, biography writing, job search strategy, interview preparation, seminars (on all of above), public relations writing and seminars.
CAPABILITIES: 15 + years as a resume writer, career consultant and publicist.
CURRENT/RECENT CLIENTS/PROJECTS: AT&T Cellular; Robert Half & Acountemps; United Health Care; Star Tribune Career Expo; Do Afgan Restaurant; Control Data; Medtronic.

RYBAK & ASSOCIATES   612-929-1365
4605 Zenith Avenue South   Minneapolis 55410
FAX: 612-929-6863
CONTACT: Michael J. Rybak
E-MAIL: mrybak@pro-ns.net or michaelr@broadviewmedia.com
SERVICES: Types of Writing: Award winning writer/producer with 20 years experience. Independent since 1991. Extensive experience in both media advertising and sales promotion. Consumer newspaper, magazine, television and radio campaigns from concept through production. Trade and business-to-business advertising and marketing communications: brochures, direct mail, video shows, sales materials. In-depth knowledge of sales promotion and broadcast production.
SPECIALTIES: Innovative print campaigns, brochures, and sales materials. Radio, television, video scripts and broadcast production. Sales promotion concepts. Big idea concepts that translate into high awareness and sales.

570 / Writers & Advertising Copywriters

CURRENT/RECENT CLIENTS/PROJECTS: Written For: ADC Telecommunications, American Cancer Society, Arby's Restaurants, Blue Cross/Blue Shield of Minnesota and Illinois, Byerlys Gallery, Coors Brewing, Crystal Light, Dairy Queen, Dial Corporation, DPRA Environmental., EarthWatch 3D Weather Imaging, Eckrich, First Banks, General Mills (Big G Cereals, Gold Medal Flour, Foodservice), Wm. J Wrigley, Bell Telephone, Jackpot Junction Casino, Jennie-O Turkey, Katun Corp., Kemper Insurance, Kohler Co., Land O' Lakes, Long John Silvers Restaurants, McDonalds Corp., McDonnell Douglas, Minnesota State Fair, Monsanto, Network Systems Corporation, Northern Trust Bank, Chicago, Ovaltine, Peak Antifreeze, Pepsi-Cola Bottlers, Pillsbury, Play It Again Sports, Polaris Snowmobiles, Rosarita Mexican Food, Ruffles Trash Bags, Sealy Mattresses, St. Paul Hotel, Target Stores/Food Avenue Restaurants, Telex Communications, True Value Hardware, WGN Radio, Chicago, 3M Company, 7-Up Corp., Perkins, Marriott, Minnesota Timberwolves, Chuck & Don's Pet Food Outlet.

S

BETHANNE M. SCULLY 612-557-1188
4775 Yorktown Lane Plymouth 55442
FAX: 612-557-8973
CONTACT: Bethanne Scully
SERVICES: Medical, health care, biotechnology award-winning advertising, magazine articles, scriptwriting, marketing communications, public relations, corporate communications, brochures, direct mail, proposals, reports.
CAPABILITIES: Medical writing for physicians and patients, creative advertising concepts, marketing communications, research skills, translation of technical information into articulate, understandable English, adapt to diverse businesses, and industries.
CURRENT/RECENT CLIENTS/PROJECTS: Medtronic, Inc.; Intra-therapeutics; North Memorial Medial Center; Allina Health Care; Gray, Plant, Mooty Law Firm; various small businesses

---

Paul Schersten – Writer
"Wit as needed. Substance and style guaranteed."

→ Emmy-nominated writer for *Mystery Science Theater 3000* with an M.A. in Public Affairs
→ Advertising and corporate writing – print and broadcast – major clients include Schwan's, AAA, Land O' Lakes
→ Magazine journalism – books – television and screenplays

From frozen food to politics...
"I can write that."

Ph. 612-925-3205   pscherst@ix.netcom.com

Writers - Advertising

A

A LA CARTE MARKETING COMMUNICATIONS 651-698-8011
1019 Fairview Avenue South St. Paul 55116
FAX: 651-690-3253
CONTACT: Murray C. Appelbaum
E-MAIL: murray.alacarte@uswestmail.net
SERVICES: Types of writing; print advertising campaigns, direct mail programs. Incentive marketing, sales promotion, collateral materials, press releases, feature articles, sales contests, custom newsletters, presentation materials, sales letters, testimonials, corporate and meeting theme development, marketing and business plans, "How-to" books, proposals, annual reports, catalog copy, sales/product manuals.
CAPABILITIES: Media analysis, media contact, public relations, ad placement, "business-to-business" marketing, financial services, insurance, new business and new product introductions, corporate identity programs, public awareness programs, seminar and special event planning and promotion, media promotion, "ghost-writing books and magazine articles", marketing plans.
CURRENT/RECENT CLIENTS/PROJECTS: Miller & Schroeder Financial, Inc.; Advantus Capital Management; North Central Life Insurance Company; Government Training Service; Perfetti and Oberg, Ltd.; Twin Cities Wedding Pages Bride and Home Magazine; Positive ID Systems, Inc; Interstate Reporting Company; Protec Environmental Consultants, Inc.; Akrosoft, Inc.; Laser Mailing Technologies, Inc.; Paladin Marketing Group; Du All Services, Inc.; CDI, Inc.; Sholom Foundation; Minneapolis Jewish Federation; St. Paul United Jewish Fund and Council; Exclusive Computer Services; H.J. Neon, Inc.; Neon R. Chase Financial, Inc.

AFTERWORDS WITH MIKE KAPEL 952-942-9747
9745 Mill Creek Drive Eden Prairie 55347
FAX: 520-447-7800
CONTACT: Mike Kapel
E-MAIL: actorkap@aol.com
SERVICES: Business-to-business copy, script, editorial and internet content writing and creative direction.
CAPABILITIES: Article writing; trade show management; DOT COM Creative Development and strategic planning; media relations; one to one marketing.
CURRENT/RECENT CLIENTS/PROJECTS: Ask for resume.
PRESIDENT/CEO/OWNER: Mike Kapel

AMUNDSON COMMUNICATIONS 952-835-4613
7310 York Avenue South #106 Edina 55435
FAX: 952-835-5847
CONTACT: Wendy Amundson
E-MAIL: wramundson@aol.com
SERVICES: Amundson Communications is a 12-year old firm that specializes in creative, professional writing for business, government and non-profit clients. Principal, Wendy Amundson pairs nationally award-winning writing with strong client service, resulting in on-time, on-budget and on-target marketing and communication materials.
CAPABILITIES: Annual reports and corporate marketing materials. Business-to-business marketing. Financial writing. Fundraising materials. Healthcare writing. Speeches. Translating complicated information into interesting, understandable language.

572 / Writers - Advertising

CURRENT/RECENT CLIENTS/PROJECTS: Allina; AXIS Healthcare; Cargill; Courage Center; Eldercare Partners; Minnesota Technology; Wilder Foundation; Wells Fargo. Recent projects include annual reports, capabilities brochures, marketing brochures, newsletters, and fundraising materials.

ART OF COPY   952-925-4839
PO Box 24382   Edina 55424
FAX: 952-925-2159
SERVICES: Art Novak
E-MAIL: artofcopy@aol.com
SERVICES: Advertising concepts and copy (all media and collateral), video scripts, speeches, jingles/coporate songs, product name generation, proposals, event theming, and any related production supervision.
CAPABILITIES/SPECIALTIES: Award-winning copywriter with 16 years experience (including three as creative director) at ad agencies in Minneapolis, Chicago, and Boston. Four years as Creative Director of full-service communications agency specializing in meetings, events, and video production. Versatility runs the gamut from distilling simple, on-target ad concepts out of complex technical product information to composing motivational anthems tied to specific meeting themes and corporate cultures. M.A. in Advertising (Michigan State University); B.S. in Journalism (Northwestern University). Member of Communications Faculty (Teaching Advertising Copywriting) at Metropolitan State University.
CURRENT/RECENT CLIENTS/PROJECTS: 3M; Cargill; Tennant; Minneapolis Institute of Arts; Wells Fargo Bank; Target; Novartis; Fingerhut; University of Minnesota.
PRESIDENT/CEO/OWNER: Art Novak

ART WRITE COMMUNICAITONS   651-649-0972
1562 Hague Avenue   St. Paul 55104
CONTACT: Susanne Rohland
E-MAIL: scrohland@aol.com
SERVICES: Creative and promotional writing. Newsletters including conception, design, layout, graphics, writing, editing. Promotional brochures, employee communications, advertising, direct mail, press releases, feature stories, book reviews, sales literature, editing and copy editing. Grant writing including finding the right foundations for your financial needs.
CAPABILITIES: Proven background working with government agencies and non-profit organizations. Excellent grant writer and grant seeker. Providing the very best in internal and external publications and communications tools. Able to create excellent public relations and communications programs on a shoe string budget.
CURRENT/RECENT CLIENTS/PROJECTS: Written for regional and statewide agencies, local and national non-profit organizations, newspapers, and magazines. Client list available.

C

CARLSON - VOHS COMMUNICATIONS   952-975-9317
15900 N Hillcrest Court   Eden Prairie 55346
FAX: 952-975-9316
CONTACT: Lauren Carlson-Vohs
E-MAIL: carlsonvohs@uswest.net

Writers – Advertising / 573

SERVICES: Ad copy, brochures, product literature, catalog copy, direct mail, video scripts, multimedia, newsletters, training materials, educational materials, public relations, news releases and annual reports.
CAPABILITIES: International business and cross-cultural communications background. Extensive research experience.
CURRENT/RECENT CLIENTS/PROJECTS: Carlson Companies; Holiday Inn; Lakewood Publications; Badiyan Productions; Banta; Webber Advertising; Illusion Graphics; University of Minnesota; State of Minnesota; plus numerous small companies; non-profit organizations and individuals.
PRESIDENT/CEO/OWNER: Lauren Carlson-Vohs

CAROL CLAY   612-925-0253
4362 Browndale Avenue So   St. Louis Park 55424
SERVICES: Copywriter.
CAPABILITIES/SPECIALTIES: Specializing in business-to-business, direct market and catalog.
CONTACT: Carol Clay

CREATIVE CONSULTANTS   612-941-4086
7125 Schey Drive   Minneapolis 55439
FAX: 612-996-0773
CONTACT: Bill Greer
E-MAIL: wfgreer@aol.com
SERVICES: Creating concepts and campaigns that clearly communicate client-defined strategies. Involved in concept development, writing and production supervision of capabilities brochures, sales-producing materials, booklets, folders, catalogs.
CAPABILITIES: Sixteen years as a creative ad director for a major national corporation provided myriad opportunities to contribute to financial growth while advancing a contemporary image.
CURRENT/RECENT CLIENTS/PROJECTS: Have been serving selected regional, national and international clients based in the Upper Midwest.

D

JOHN DU CANE   651-645-0517
PO Box 4381   St. Paul 55104
FAX: 651-644-5676
CONTACT: John Du Cane
TYPES OF WRITING: Marketing communications, copy including brochures, catalogs, flyers, newsletters, promotions, print ads and collateral material, press releases, newspaper and magazine articles.
WRITTEN FOR: Institute for Chemical Dependency Professionals, Minnesota Center for Shiatsu Study, Dragon Door Publications, Institute of Internal Arts, Compcare Publishers, Hazelden.
SPECIALTIES: Catalogs, sales letters, space ads, promotional newspaper articles in health, wellness, nutrition, exercise, motivational and marketing.
PRESIDENT/CEO/OWNER: John Du Cane

574 / Writers - Advertising

F

STEVEN V. FITCH & ASSOCIATES　　　　　651-483-0961
4103 Brigadoon Drive　　　　　　　　　　　Shoreview 55126
CONTACT: Steven V. Fitch
E-MAIL: fitch006@tc.umn.edu
SERVICES: Types of Writings: Business to business technical marketing communications and training materials include brochures, datasheets, newsletters, direct mail, trade journal advertising and trade magazine features. QuarkXPress, and FrameMaker, desktop publishing on PC. Technical writing include on-line help screens, software user guides, operating manuals and maintenance manuals. Written for: Healthcare, education, mental health, refrigeration, financial and computer hardware and software.

PAT FUNK COPYWRITER　　　　　　　　952-898-1767
2301 W 150th Street　　　　　　　　　　　Burnsville 55306
FAX: 952-898-1767
CONTACT: Pat Funk
E-MAIL: pfunkcopy@aol.com
SERVICES: Types of Writing: Words and ideas that work for advertising, product brochures, corporate brochures, catalogs, product sheets, direct mail programs, sales letters and executive speeches.
WRITTEN FOR: 3M; Honeywell; Wenger Corporation; Centex Homes; Control Data Corporate; Golden Valley Microwave Foods; Fidelity Products; American Hardware Insurance Company and various other companies large and small. Also work regularly with advertising agencies and graphic designers.
SPECIALTIES: Business-to-business advertising and marketing-based communications of all kinds.
PRESIDENT/CEO/OWNER: Pat Funk

G

JON GARON CREATIVE, INC.　　　　　　952-474-7000
208 Central Avenue South　　　　　　　　Wayzata 55391
FAX: 952-404-2277
CONTACT: Jon Garon
E-MAIL: jgaron@uswest.net
SERVICES: Creative & production of: Radio, television, print, video and original music for a variety of advertising agencies, public relations firms and in-house advertising and marketing departments. Since 1975, Jon Garon Creative has created and produced broadcast, corporate and print communications for clients nationwide.
SPECIALTIES: Corporate image video, original music, humorous radio and television spots. Good dancer. Has own car. Limited felony convictions.
CURRENT/RECENT CLIENTS/PROJECTS: Dayton-Hudson; Fleishman-Hillard Public Relations; Lifetouch; Hey City Theatre; Craig Wiese & Company; Zimmerman Group; Department of Defense; Slumberland; Sable Advertising; John Miles Company; McCracken Brooks; Lutsen Mountains; Bill Smith Adv.(Portland); Respond 2 Adv; 3M; Pillsbury; Golden Valley Microwave Foods; The Hadley Companies.
PRESIDENT/CEO/OWNER: Jon Garon

Writers – Advertising / 575

GILLIES CREATIVE
3848 Lyndale Avenue South

612-824-8114
Minneapolis 55409

FAX: 612-824-4695
CONTACT: Dawn Gillies
E-MAIL: gilliescre@aol.com
SERVICES: Intelligent copywriting--from on-target concepts through carefully chosen words. Each project is completed on time and within budget. I offer a full range of consumer and business-to-business advertising and collateral writing including: print ads, web sites, radio and television spots, brochures, direct mail, promotion, POP, name generation, and new business pitches.
CAPABILITIES: Since 1983, I've had the pleasure of learning about a wide variety of exciting industries, then skillfully selling their goods and services. My industry experience includes: packaged goods, retail, sports and fitness, dot-coms, aviation, nutrition, travel and hospitality, industrial, financial, lawn and garden, health care, legal services, food service, real estate and non-profits. I've also worked with local ad agencies, graphic design firms and marketing consultants. My equipment, naturally, is a Mac computer. (Or, between winter projects, a pair of Volkl Snow Rangers or Olin Super Radius K skis.)
CURRENT/RECENT CLIENTS/PROJECTS: Please call for updated information.

GOLD FISH COMMUNICATIONS
420 N. Fifth Street #855

612-371-4501
Minneapolis 55401

FAX: 952-920-0449
CONTACT: Debra Fisher Goldstein
E-MAIL: dfgold19@idt.net
SERVICES: Positioning, Brand Identity, then Complete Creative through three distinct programs that maximize your advertising dollar. 1) Dive into the "Gold Fish Think Tank", a personalized process that ask key questions of your target audience and then creates your company's personality, marketing messages, and creative concepts based on what's important to your audience. The results strengthen every area of your marketing. 2) Eyeball your advertising through the "Gold Fish Bowl"; a per-piece review and edit of your existing marketing materials designed to increase their impact and effectiveness. 3) Hatch new marketing pieces with "Gold Fish Creative"; a start-to-finish process for brochures, advertising, sales letters, direct mail, websites and videos that move your potential customer up the purchase-decision-making ladder.
SPECIALTIES: Conversational-style writing. Warmth and Wit. Graphic design that strengthens your message. A process you will enjoy. No budget surprises.
CURRENT/RECENT CLIENTS/PROJECTS: KTCA/KTCI, Twin Cities Public Television; Abbott Northwestern Hospital; Multi-Ad Services, Inc. - automotive, retail, and medical marketing division; Hennepin County, Department of Environmental Services; YWCA and Urban Sports Center, Minneapolis; Neighborhood Health Care Network; MedCenters Health Insurance; UCARE Minnesota; Minnesota Chiropractic Association, statewide lobbying/education; Advanced Medical; Clean Green Packing Biodegradable Packaging Material; Loften Label; Financial Management Leasing; Pope Investment Economics; Edina Realty; Coldwell Banker Burnet Realty; Steven Scott Real Estate Management; Nesbit Insurance Agencies; Lerhke Reinsurance, Inc.; Access Insurance Agency; Cartier Insurance Agency; Interactive Personalities; Learning Ware, Inc.; On-Hold Marketing; Guidance Computer Systems; Writing Assistance, Inc.; Sweetnam Communications Inc.; Wilder Image Development; A+ Training; Applause, Inc.; Goldfarb and Associates - legal practice; Austin and Abrams - legal practice; Southwest Family Room & Northeast Strong Together - Way To Grow organizations; United Way of Minneapolis and St. Paul, MN; and many more great clients.

H

DAVID HALSEY   612-550-1987
14848 64th Place North   Maple Grove 55311
FAX: 612-550-1937
CONTACT: David Halsey
E-MAIL: dvhalsey@dhalsey.com
WWW: dhalsey.com
SERVICES: Advertising copywriting; print, outdoor, TV, radio, video, websites., Collateral; brochures, direct mail, promotions, point-of-purchase. Stock photography also available.
CURRENT/RECENT CLIENTS/PROJECTS: Written for: Harley-Davidson, Polaris, Ski-Doo, Yamaha, Victory, Kawasaki; Rollerblade; Toro; Federal Cartridge; Mercury Marine; 3M; Pillsbury, General Mills; Glastron; Tracker; Nitro; Coleman and many more.

HIGH POINT CREATIVE, LLC   651-426-4012
4583 Shady Lane   St. Paul 55110
FAX: 651-426-6699
CONTACT: Kate Huebsch
E-MAIL: kate@highpointcreative.com
WWW: highpointcreative.com
SERVICES: Copywriting and full project management for business-to-business and consumer brochures, catalogs, direct mail, websites, newsletters, speeches and presentations, PowerPoint shows, special events, marketing and internal communication pieces. A special interest in "translating" high-tech products and services into compelling and effective copy for non-technical readers.
CAPABILITIES: Marketing communications with an emphasis on strategic development and effective writing.
CURRENT/RECENT CLIENTS/PROJECTS: 12 years in business serving financial services companies, industrial manufacturers, health care organizations and community not-for-profit organizations.
PRESIDENT/CEO/OWNER: Kate Huebsch, President/Owner; Maiya Willits, Creative Director

JOHN HOLDEN   952-938-0357
5041 Birch Road   Minnetonka 55345
FAX: 952-938-0357
CONTACT: John Holden
E-MAIL: holdenon@bitstream.net
SERVICES: Creative strategies, concept development, copywriting and production management. Call me in just for brainstorming or to take a project from idea to completion.
CAPABILITIES: Nearly three decades' experience creating award-winning and highly effective broadcast, print, collateral, point-of-sale, multimedia, film and video, advertising, promotion, motivation, training, editorial, entertainment, meetings. This includes consumer, business-to-business, packaged goods, food and foodservice, industrial, financial, technology, agriculture, government and non-profit.

Writers – Advertising / 577

CURRENT/RECENT CLIENTS/PROJECTS: Teaming up with agencies and design firms for new business efforts as well as existing clients. Working direct with client companies in conjunction with top creative and production talent. Recent work has included 3M, American Medical Systems, Basilica of Saint Mary, Burger King, Cub Foods, Custom Food Processors, Durkees, Ecolab, Intellisol, Jerneen Mfg., LaSalle Management Group, Pillsbury, Primera, Schuler Shoes, Target, Toro, US Bank.

PRESIDENT/CEO/OWNER: John Holden

THE HOLTON GROUP
2 Greenway Gables
612-338-6984
Minneapolis 55403
CONTACT: Rick Holton
E-MAIL: fsholton@mn.uswest.net

SERVICES: Provide communications consulting, writing, and training services to agencies, industry, and government. Write marketing and sales materials, including marketing brochures, product descriptions, sales proposals, trade journal articles, and conference papers. Also write business plans, industry analyses, speeches, and technical reports. Provide training in business and technical writing, proposal writing, and oral presentation skills.

SPECIALTIES: Business plans, sales proposals, marketing materials, and training. Have specialist industry knowledge in financial services and energy.

CURRENT/RECENT CLIENTS/PROJECTS: Alliant Industrial Services, DPRA Environmental, James J. Hill Group, NSP, Karwoski & Courage, Tunheim Group, US Bank, Wells Fargo & Company.

DAVID HOUSEWRIGHT
2014 N. Cleveland Avenue
651-631-0499
Roseville 55113
FAX: 651-631-0499
CONTACT: David Housewright
E-MAIL: housewright.valois@prodigy.net

SERVICES: Comprehensive copywriting and creative direction for both consumer and trade advertising accounts, as well as editorial writing for consumer and trade publications.

CAPABILITIES: Advertising experience includes award-winning print, direct mail, brochures and catalogues, TV, radio and corporate communications,. Editorial writing includes news stories, features, human interest, sports, essays, biographies, and historical. Macintosh and IBM compatible.

CURRENT/RECENT CLIENTS/PROJECTS: Federal Express; Hormel; Miller Beer; Tony's Pizza; Famous Dave's; Green Tree Financial Services; 3M; McGlynn Bakeries; ECOLAB; Neenah Paper; United HelathCare; Healtheast ; Pharmacia Deltec; Automatic Products Company (vending machines); DAHL & Associates (environmental); Orion Consulting (computers); Staveley Weighing & Systems Group; SUPERAMERICA; Treasure Island Casino; Kawasaki; Como Zoo; Dial LAWYERS; National City Bank; America National Bank; Starkey Hearing Aids; Applebee's Grill & Bar; Jim Beam; Guthrie Theatre; WMIN-AM; Goldiggers; Northland Insurance Companies; Schneiderman's Furniture; Chilly Willee Frozen Soft Drink; Minneapolis StarTribune; Albert Lea Evening Tribune; Grand Forks Herald; Owatonna People's Press.

578 / Writers - Advertising

I

INFORMATION AGE COMMUNICATIONS   952-835-1290
9001 Poplar Bridge Road   Bloomington 55437
CONTACT: Karen M. Hess, Ph.D.
SERVICES: We offer customized, on-site business writing workshops.
CAPABILITIES: 30 years experience in the field. Specializing in workshops for law enforcement, engineering and business.
CURRENT/RECENT CLIENTS/PROJECTS: Ulteig Engineers, Inc.; Integrity Plus; Anoka Sheriff's Department.

K

STEVE KAHN CREATIVE   612-925-4411
4317 Cornelia Circle   Edina 55435
FAX: 612-925-1066
E-MAIL: kahntext@aol.com
SERVICES: Concepts, copy for print and broadcast. TV & Radio production, scripts, collateral pieces, point-of-purchase, web site copy.
CAPABILITIES: Major Agency experience at freelance rates.
CURRENT/RECENT CLIENTS/PROJECTS: Reliastar; Anchor Bank; General Mills; Glastron Boats; RTW (Insurance); Precise Pet Products; Scimed Life Systems; Hormel; 3M; US West Cellular.
PRESIDENT/CEO/OWNER: Steve Kahn

KUEHN CREATIVE   612-926-0988
5325 Ewing Avenue South   Minneapolis 55410
FAX: 612-926-0437
CONTACT: Debbie Kuehn
E-MAIL: dkuehn1@uswest.net
WWW: kuehncreative.com
SERVICES: With more than 20 years of experience, Kuehn Creative is well versed in all types of copywriting and editing, including ads, brochures, books, catalogs, CD-ROMs, direct mail, magazine articles, newsletters, press releases, video scripts and web sites.
SPECIALTIES: If your project needs that special creative touch, if you need help on overflow writing projects, or if you don't have a writer on staff but wish you had one on call, call Kuehn Creative for projects that are on time, on target, on budget.
CURRENT/RECENT CLIENTS/PROJECTS: Ad agencies, construction firms, educational institutions, financial services, graphic design firms, high tech, home improvement, incentive firms, magazines, manufacturing and industrial, printing companies, professional services, realtors, retail, telecommunications, and video production companies, among others.

TIMOTHY KUHLMANN   612-721-3728
4441 33rd Avenue South   Minneapolis 55406
FAX: 612-721-7146

CONTACT: Timothy Kuhlmann
E-MAIL: timothy@pclink.com
TYPES OF WRITING: Advertising, marketing and PR copy for print, internet, video, radio, television, CD-ROM, outdoor and live presentations. Products include: brochures, collateral, sales letters, sell sheets, direct mail, annual reports, newsletters, employee communications, training materials, posters, press releases, speeches, custom sales pitches and presentations, marketing initiatives, and copy editing.
SPECIALTIES: Business-to-business writing for health care, food, financial services and industrial clients. Expertise includes top-drawer concepting and creative, total project management capacity, strong collaborative and diplomatic abilities, excellent presentation skills.
CURRENT/RECENT CLIENTS/PROJECTS: Allina Health System, American Express Financial Advisors, Blue Cross of California, Bozell Kamstra, Carlson Wagonlit Travel, Dayton Hudson, Deluxe, Dillon New Media, Empi, Fairview Healthcare, Group One Communications, Haagen-Dazs, H&R Block, Hedstrom/Blessing, Inc., JGI Communications, KTCA Channel 2, Lawson Software, Little & Company, Maier Marketing, MCDA, Medtronic, Multifoods, Northwest Teleproductions, Nygard & Associates, Pillsbury, Point2Point/PBS, Public Radio International, St. Paul Companies, 3M, Target, Tennant.

L

JIM LARSON
4941 Fremont Avenue South
FAX: 612-825-2318
CONTACT: Jim Larson
E-MAIL: blythejim@aol.com

612-825-4667
Minneapolis 55409

SERVICES: Concepts and copy; sales brochures; capabilities brochures; consumer and business-to-business ads; direct mail; annual reports; letters; histories; name generation; newsletters.
CAPABILITIES: Researched and wrote a 238-page hard cover corporate history; regularly create names for products and product lines; possess a knack for humor; edit books; corporate identity; considerable experience in financial.
CURRENT/RECENT CLIENTS/PROJECTS: Target; Exe & Associates; Pielert & Associates; Braemer Mailing; Quality House.

M

CYNTHIA MILLER CREATIVE CONCEPTS & COPY
5337 Knox Avenue South
FAX: 612-922-7261
CONTACT: Cynthia Miller
E-MAIL: millercopy@isd.net

612-925-6270
Minneapolis 55419

SERVICES: Creative, conceptual advertising copywriting and other communications. Background includes print, outdoor, collateral, speeches, TV, radio, video, promotions, press releases. Currently writing for retailers, corporations, agencies, production houses and design firms. Strategic and presentation skills.

580 / Writers - Advertising

CAPABILITIES: Have won recognition for consumer and business-to-business advertising from the CLIO's Annual, The One Show, New York Art Directors Club, the Show, Print Annual and Regional, the International Film and Television Festival, the OBIE's, the International Radio Festival, and others.

N

MARGARET NELSON & ASSOCIATES
201 Valleyview Place
FAX: 612-827-2822
E-MAIL: mgrtn@aol.com

612-825-8475
Minneapolis 55419

CAPABILITIES: Marketing communications and planning consultant, specializing in commercial construction field, architects, engineers, contractors, and building materials producers.

SPECIALTIES: Photography, research including construction technology, project case histories, guide specifications, technical brochures, news releases. Education, medical, and general interest topics.

CURRENT/RECENT CLIENTS/PROJECTS: Area correspondent for People Magazine, Newsweek, USA Today, past articles for Business Week, Chicago Tribune, Chicago Sun-Times, LA Times Syndicate, Womans Day, Corporate Report, Minneapolis/St. Paul, editing for US News and World Report Books, New York Times Books, projects for Tennant Company, Breck School, Norwest Bank, Quest Learning Systems, among others; editor, Basilica Magazine, Basilica of St. Mary.

PRESIDENT/CEO/OWNER: Margaret Nelson

JOHN NEVILLE
4975 Sleepy Hollow Road #100
FAX: 612-470-4063
CONTACT: John Neville
E-MAIL: jneville@sea-group.com
WWW: sea-group.com

612-470-4407
Excelsior 55331

SERVICES: Communications consulting: determining messages, objectives, audiences and media.

CAPABILITIES: Writing: Internet and Intranet training content; scripts (video, film, AV, audio); corporate communications (newsletters, brochures, capabilities statements, advertising); training/technical (intranet, manuals, workbooks, video); proposals/marketing (environmental impact statements, government agency applications). Production Supervision: design and management of internet, intranet, video, and print production.

SPECIALTIES: Extensive experience and training environmental, health, safety and regulatory affairs; corporate culture; sales and management training; technical messages. Comedy background. Unique ability to understand your audience and how to make them respond positively to what they see, hear and read. Specialize in a creative problem-solving approach to meeting your communication objectives within schedule and budget while providing the creativity twist that makes your presentation truly memorable.

Writers – Advertising / 581

CURRENT/RECENT CLIENTS/PROJECTS: Most major Twin Cities firms, production companies, agencies and clients nationwide. Intranet employee EHS training series for 3M corporatewide; Intranet Employee EHS training series for Honeywell corporatewide; Internet customer service training series for Toro; Leadership development training for 3M; New product technical bulletins for government agencies for 3M Filtration Products; Health care product introduction video for NaviCare; Printing industry capabilities video for World Color; In-service training videos for 3M Health Care; Worldwide convention video for DRUPA 2000; Marketing video for Lowertown Redevelopment; Investment products web site information for Lutheran Brotherhood; Marketing video for Upland Farms Development.

S

STRINZ CREATIVE, INC.   651-686-0041
4769 Hauge Circle   Eagan 55122
CONTACT: J Charles Strinz
E-MAIL: chuck_strinz@tcilink.com
SERVICES: Advertising copywritng, concept development and promotion in all media, with emphasis on radio and internet.
CAPABILITIES: Wrote and produced ads and commercials in all media for hundreds of clients since 1970. Researched and wrote initial content for Microsoft's Twin Cities Sidewalk web site. Creative MPR Online for Minnesota Public Radio. Oversaw design and installation of Interact4, the beta test versions of Channel 4000. Coordinated beta test software distribution for startribune.com. Established North America service bureau for GPT Videotex, P.L.C. Conducted market research and developed services for US West Community Link (pre-Internet product). Provided data communications consultation for numerous individuals, businesses and other organizations since 1983. See our web site at www.strinz.com/creative for samples.
CURRENT/RECENT CLIENTS/PROJECTS: American Academy of Neurology; Baker Group; CBS (WCCO TV); Computer User Magazine; Friends of Rice Lake State Park; Geriatric Research Education and Clinic Center (GRECC); Hirshfield's; Healing Journeys; Integrity Communications; Jazziz Magazine; Just Truffles; Keroff & Rosenberg; Lease-A-Lodge; Majestic Software; Mentor; Microsoft; M.O.R.E., Inc.; MultiTech Systems; Nametag; Periscope; Telident; US West !nterprise Network Services; Windfall Auction Service.
PRESIDENT/CEO/OWNER: J Charles Strinz

T

BETH TORGERSON COPYWRITING AND   651-462-3999
PROJECT MANAGEMENT
34495 Forest Blvd   Stacy 55079
FAX: 651-462-4402
CONTACT: Beth Torgerson
E-MAIL: betht@gciweb.com
SERVICES: Copywriting for marketing communications including sales collateral, catalogs, brochures, advertising, newsletters, training manuals and websites. Brainstorming themes and concepts. Managing projects from concept to print, using a network of designers, artists, photographers, prepress and printers.

582 / Writers - Advertising

CAPABILITIES: Creating a unique selling promise that helps sell more products and services.
SPECIALTIES: Knowledge of digital printing and variable data printing.
CURRENT/RECENT CLIENTS/PROJECTS: General Mills; Burns Engineering; Cenex; Lyle Signs; Utility Chemicals; API Group; Graco; Graphic Consultants.

2 HEADS COMMUNICATION
3240 Owasso Hts Road
FAX: 651-486-7182
CONTACT: Kyia Downing
E-MAIL: kyia@2hc.com

651-486-2922
Shoreview 55126

SERVICES: Copywriting, brand positioning. Naming taglines. Big idea.
CAPABILITIES: Financial services. Health and wellness. Hospitality. Education. Web sites.
CURRENT/RECENT CLIENTS/PROJECTS: Dain Rauscher; D'Amico Restaurants; CIGNA; American Express; wwwrrr.net
PRESIDENT/CEO/OWNER: Kirk Horsted

W

WORKING WORDS
2900 Yosemite Avenue South
FAX: 763-422-0204
CONTACT: Karin B. Miller
E-MAIL: workwords@aol.com

763-422-0648
Minneapolis 55416

SERVICES: Corporate communications and marketing communications, internal and external publications, brochures and special projects. Magazine writing for consumer, corporate and trade publications. Editing, copyediting.
CURRENT/RECENT CLIENTS/PROJECTS: Ecolab; Midwest Living; Star Thrower Distribution; Target Corporation; and the University of Minnesota.

WRITING ON POINT, INC.
4260 Lawndale Lane North
FAX: 763-557-8954
CONTACT: Rita L. Schmidt
E-MAIL: writingpt@aol.com

763-557-8956
Plymouth 55446

CAPABILITIES: Direct mail, sales letters, RFP's, video scripts, presentations, ghostwriting, rewrites, ad copy, feature articles, project management.

Writers - Editorial

A

MELISSA A. ABRAMS, INC.   763-377-2266
4720 Circle Down   Golden Valley 55416
FAX: 763-377-2378
CONTACT: Melissa A. Abrams
E-MAIL: mabrams@sprintmail.com
SERVICES: Writing - newsletters, brochures, media materials, speeches, internal communications, bylined articles, communication plans, crisis communication plans, case histories. Editing - newsletters, other communication materials.
CAPABILITIES: 17 years of experience in many industries including, but not limited to, health care, agriculture/agribusiness, manufacturing, technology, commercial real estate, food, service industries.

B

MARK BRADLEY   651-636-1127
1851 West Shryer Avenue   Roseville 55113
CONTACT: Mark Bradley
SERVICES: Types of Writing: business training; scripts for live or video presentation, leader guides, collaterals. Brochures, press releases, newsletters, profiles, transcribing and editing speeches, interviews, and comedy sketches. Written For: Wilson Learning Corporation; KTCA-TV; U of Minn. Labor Education Service; International TV Association; Healthcare Campaign of Minnesota.; Twin Cities AFTRA newsletter; Career Directions, Inc. Fifteen years experience.
SPECIALTIES: Saving failing projects; re-working, re-thinking and revising projects from concept to final product, focusing ideas without destroying client's individual style.

G

GREEN LIGHT CONSULTING, INC.   651-221-0046
614 Portland Avenue #114   St. Paul 55102
FAX: 651-224-1458
E-MAIL: klgreen@uswest.net
SERVICES: Writing for video and print; writing internet website content; video production; desktop publishing; editing for print; AV services (Power Point).
CAPABILITIES/SPECIALTIES: Extensive experience in training, human resources, financial, investments. Also technical subjects (manufacturing, computers, etc.) Also psychology (MA in counseling psychology). Page Maker, Power Point.
CURRENT/RECENT CLIENTS/PROJECTS: 3M; Precision Powerhouse; St. Paul Port Authority; Associate for Psychological Type; The Witness (Episcopal Church Magazine); AXXIS Petroleum; iPool.com; efunds; Fortis Financial.
PRESIDENT/CEO/OWNER: Ken Green

584 / Writers - Editorial

H

HAKALA COMMUNICATIONS INC   651-436-1161
4111 Penfield Court   Afton 55001
PO Box 250
FAX: 651-436-1131
CONTACT: William Hakala
E-MAIL: bhakala@hakala.com
SERVICES: Types of Writing: complete services for producing book-length history of business or institution. Services include research, interviewing, writing, design and production.
SPECIALTIES: Organizational histories.
CURRENT/RECENT CLIENTS/PROJECTS: Aid Association for Lutherans (AAL); American Crystal Sugar Company; American Family Insurance; Bachmans; Bethesda Lutheran Medical Center; CUNA Mutual Insurance Society; Fairview Health System; Federated Investors; Group Health; Lutheran Brotherhood; Macalester College; Manitowoc Company; Minikahda Club; MSI Insurance; Saint Mary's Hospital of Rochester; Sperry Corporation.

THE HOLTON GROUP   612-338-6984
2 Greenway Gables   Minneapolis 55403
CONTACT: Rick Holton
E-MAIL: fsholton@mn.uswest.net
SERVICES: Provide communications consulting, writing, and training services to agencies, industry, and government. Write marketing and sales materials, including marketing brochures, product descriptions, sales proposals, trade journal articles, and conference papers. Also write business plans, industry analyses, speeches, and technical reports. Provide training in business and technical writing, proposal writing, and oral presentation skills.
SPECIALTIES: Business plans, sales proposals, marketing materials, and training. Have specialist industry knowledge in financial services and energy.
CURRENT/RECENT CLIENTS/PROJECTS: Alliant Industrial Services, DPRA Environmental, James J. Hill Group, NSP, Karwoski & Courage, Tunheim Group, US Bank, Wells Fargo & Company.

J

JEDD, MARCIA/MJ & ASSOCIATES   612-861-4855
5716 Pillsbury Avenue   Minneapolis 55419
FAX: 612-861-3863
CONTACT: Marcia Jedd
E-MAIL: marciajedd@cs.com
SERVICES: Press releases and other promotional pieces, news and feature articles, marketing/business plans, technical writing, case studies and reports.

Writers – Editorial / 585

CAPABILITIES: Written For: Marketing and incentive companies, manufacturers, national and international media, including trade and consumer publications, transportation/logistics. Full-service capabilities from research to writing in the development and execution of marketing/public relations strategies, including publicity and collateral. Expertise in travel, transportation/logistics and various consumer markets.
SPECIALTIES: Feature articles, case studies.
PRESIDENT/CEO/OWNER: Marcia Jedd. Call for e-mail for writing samples, client list or rate information.

BEVERLY JOVANOVICH FREELANCE WRITER   612-427-4122
3402 135th Avenue NW   Andover 55304
CONTACT: Beverly Jovanovich
SERVICES: Types of work: Illustrated children's books, newspaper and magazine reporting, essays and autobiographies.
CAPABILITIES: Interviews and autobiographies. Award wining writer.
CURRENT/RECENT CLIENTS/PROJECTS: Recently published autobiography of celebrity artist Otto Henry Pfeiffer, daily and weekly newspapers.

K

HEATHER RANDALL KING   612-920-1680
2310 West 53rd Street   Minneapolis 55410
FAX: 612-920-8567
CONTACT: Heather Randall King
TYPES OF WRITING: News releases, press kits, brochures, hard and soft-cover books, corporate communications, manuals, feature and news articles, speeches, product introductions, histories, interview, personal profiles columns, editing and ad copy. Also public relations, marketing and fundraising.
SPECIALTIES: Experienced freelance consulting, reader-friendly, award-winning copy. Professional approach with accurate, on-time results.
WRITTEN FOR: General Mills, Brum and Anderson Public Relations, Cy DeCosse Creative, Inc., Recipes Unlimited, Edina Magazine, The Orion Group, Job Boss, Inc., Tony Sandler of Sandler & Young, The Pillsbury Company, CompCare Publications, Corporate Report, Minnesota Association of Commerce & Industry, Metropolitan Woman, Chicago Cutlery, J. Olson, Machine Company, Inc., Com-Tel, Byerly's, Military Lifestyle Magazine, GEICO Insurance, Deluxe Check, National Car, Webb Co., Paul Brink & Assoc., Woman's Club of Minneapolis, Doubleday, Strategic Marketing Resources, Inc., Concordia College Language Villages, University of Minnesota, Children's Medical Foundation, Southside Family Nurturing Center, French Meadow Bakery, Job Box Software, Strategic Team Makes, Frozen Images, Edina Country Club, and International School of Minnesota.

L

PATRICIA C. LEAF   651-437-1198
11138 East 230th Street   Hastings 55033
CONTACT: Patricia Leaf
E-MAIL: leafpat@aol.com

586 / Writers - Editorial

SERVICES: Full-service writing, editing and marketing on an as-needed basis. Types of Writing: Corporate publications, news releases, news and feature stories, profiles, editorial research, promotional pieces, collateral material and newsletters.
SPECIALTIES: Interior Design, Personality Profiles, Engineering and Architecture. Special Event Planning, Media Relations.
PRESIDENT/CEO/OWNER: Patricia Leaf

M

BETH MATTSON-TEIG 612-972-3436
2920 Nelson Road Delano 55328
FAX: 612-972-3917
CONTACT: Beth Mattson-Teig
E-MAIL: bcmattson@aol.com
TYPES OF WRITING: Magazine and newspaper feature writing, business-to-business, and other promotional and business communications.
WRITTEN FOR: CityBusiness, Corporate Report Minnesota, National Real Estate Investor, Shopping Center World, Midwest Real Estate News, Banker's Review, Cherbo Publishing Group.
SPECIALTIES: Business writing, particularly commercial real estate, finance and banking.

P

MARGERY PETERSON, FREELANCE WRITER 651-731-0591
625 Hillwood Court St. Paul 55119
CONTACT: Margery Peterson
E-MAIL: interplay@uswest.net
SERVICES: Types of Writing: Brochures, newsletters, press releases, holiday cards, web pages and other marketing and promotional materials. Journalism, articles.
SPECIALTIES: Creative concepts using humor and unique angles.
CURRENT/RECENT CLIENTS/PROJECTS: Written For: Architecture and construction, health, fitness and medical, consumer products, education, the arts, environment, government, and service industries.

PROFESSIONAL EDITORS NETWORK OF MN 651-690-0881
(PEN)
PO Box 19265 Minneapolis 55419
CONTACT: Molly McBeath - 651-690-0881 or Barbara Schue - 651-690-5577
CAPABILITIES: Organization of staff and freelance editors, writers and allied professionals who meet to share professional knowledge and experience; group also serves as a clearing house for information about job and educational opportunities, and publishes a directory of freelance editors, writers, and proofreaders.
SPECIALTIES: Membership requirements: Annual fee covers expenses and meetings. Meetings: Informally organized: monthly (except July and August) on the second Tuesday of the month. 100 members, approximately.

S

SANDRO R. SABO　　　　　　　　　　　　　　　651-681-9262
2230 Bent Tree Lane　　　　　　　　　　　　Mendota Heights 55120
FAX: 651-681-1591
CONTACT: Sandra R. Sabo
E-MAIL: srsabo@aol.com
TYPES OF WRITING: Marketing and educational materials, brochures, and magazine articles.
SPECIALTIES: Corporate communications and non-profit materials.
CURRENT/RECENT CLIENTS/PROJECTS: Medtronic, American Society of Association Executives, Dayton Hudson Corporation, Means! Magazine, Lamaze Family Magazine, Field Force Automation Magazine.

PAT SAMPLES　　　　　　　　　　　　　　　763-560-5199
7152 Unity Avenue North　　　　　　　　　Brooklyn Center 55429
FAX: 763-560-5298
CONTACT: Pat Samples
E-MAIL: psamples@pioneerplanet.infi.net
SERVICES: Writer and editor for marketing, internal communication, book-length projects, and program materials, primarily for educational, health care, social service, and other non-profit and governmental organizations. Curriculum design and writing. Script writer and producer for educational videos.
CAPABILITIES: 23 years of experience. Excellence in managing large projects, helping clients with conceptual development and refinement, and working efficiently and collaboratively to meet deadlines and produce quality work.
CURRENT/RECENT CLIENTS/PROJECTS: Hazelden; Search Institute; Lutheran Brotherhood; Family Service America.
PRESIDENT/CEO/OWNER: Pat Samples

T

DORRINE TURECAMO　　　　　　　　　　　　952-929-4402
3111 Heritage Drive #12　　　　　　　　　　　　Edina 55435
CONTACT: Dorrine Turecamo
E-MAIL: idpoat@aol.com
SERVICES: Editing, writing, ghostwriting books, articles.
CAPABILITIES: Author, ghost writer, leading national magazine articles writer, book and magazines editor, business management columnist, business management consultant. University faculty instructor in "writing for publication" and "creative writing".

588 / Writers - Editorial

V

SUSAN VANCLEAF   763-475-2145
18525 22nd Avenue North   Plymouth 55447
FAX: 763-478-8740
CONTACT: Susan VanCleaf
E-MAIL: svancleaf@aol.com
SERVICES: Writing and photography for internal and external audiences, public information, public relations and educational uses. Print, video and websites.
CAPABILITIES: Twenty years experience. Has written for and/or shot still photos for newspapers, education, health-related organizations, city government, businesses. Video producer, writer, videographer for municipal and educational access TV. Special interests in environment and health. Knows basic HTML.
CURRENT/RECENT CLIENTS/PROJECTS: City of Plymouth; Minneapolis Public Schools; Valley Casting; Advance Machine Co.; Mayo Foundation for Education and Research.
PRESIDENT/CEO/OWNER: Susan VanCleaf

W

NEAL WALLACE, WRITING, CONSULTING, RESEARCH   612-884-1632
8901 Lyndale Avenue South #202   Minneapolis 55420
FAX: 612-884-7726
CONTACT: Neal Wallace
E-MAIL: nealx007@tc.umn.edu
TYPES OF WRITING: Marketing communications and planning consulting, specializing in commercial construction field, architects, engineers, contractors, attorneys, and building materials producers.
CAPABILITIES: Photography, research including construction technology, project case histories, guide specifications, technical brochures, news release.
WRITTEN FOR: Inspect, Inc., Dalco Roofing & Sheetmetal, Inc., West Materials, Breck School; Owens Corning Fiberglas Corp.; Styrotech, Inc.; Specialty Systems; Kavaney & Associates, Ltd.; Attorneys at Law; Construction Arbitration and Mediation Services Inc.; Construction Industry Cooperative Committees of Minnesota; local and national construction industry publications.

WORDS & DEEDS, INC.   952-835-4731
5511 Southwood Drive   Bloomington 55437
FAX: 952-897-1721
CONTACT: Connie L. Anderson
E-MAIL: wordsdeeds@aol.com
SERVICES: Professional profiles, brochures, newsletters, interviewing, write business articles, sales letters, edit and write.
CAPABILITIES: Write for banks, clinics, real estate, mortgage, community groups, design, college, political candidates, professional speakers, business coaches and businesses of all kinds.
CURRENT/RECENT CLIENTS/PROJECTS: Contributing writer to several business publications.
PRESIDENT/CEO/OWNER: Connie L. Anderson

THE WRITE APPROACH 651-698-1634
1019 Fairview Avenue South St. Paul 55116
FAX: 651-690-3253
CONTACT: Arlene Appelbaum
SERVICES: Book writing, book editing, manuscript editing, editorial research, idea development, consulting, feature writing for newspapers and magazines, publications, newsletters, brochures, news releases.
CAPABILITIES: In business since 1980 providing creative writing and editing services for a variety of companies and non-profit organizations.
SPECIALTIES: Biography and ghosted autobiography books; how-to books; business books; feature writing; human interest feature articles; general reporting articles with feature aspects; people profiles; nature, cultural and artistic writing; publication writing; civic organization and social service agency writing.
CURRENT/RECENT CLIENTS/PROJECTS: Visions Communications; Devine Multi-Media Publishing, Inc.; Voyageur Magazine; MacFarlanes; St. Paul Pioneer Press; Highland Villager; National Athletic Director; Minnesota Business Journal; American Jewish Would; Corporate Report; Minnesota Jewish Life; JCC Circle; Minnesota Language Review; St. Paul Winter Carnival Associates; St. Paul Convention Bureau; The Lexington Restaurant; Jewish Community Center of St. Paul; Temple of Aaron; United Jewish Fund and Council; Willwerscheid and Peters Mortuary; St. Paul Civic Center, and a variety of other individuals and companies.
PRESIDENT/CEO/OWNER: Arlene Appelbaum

Paul Schersten – Writer

"Wit as needed. Substance and style guaranteed."

➔ Emmy-nominated writer for *Mystery Science Theater 3000* with an M.A. in Public Affairs

➔ Magazine journalism – books – television and screenplays

➔ Experienced advertising and corporate writer – print and broadcast

From frozen food to politics...
"I can write that."

Ph. 612-925-3205   pscherst@ix.netcom.com

Writers - Technical

A

NANCY S. ALCOMBRIGHT   651-452-2394
2236 Bent Tree Lane   Mendota Heights 55120
CONTACT: Nancy S. Alcombright
TYPES OF WRITING: Project proposals, communication plans, technical marketing materials, training materials, technical reports, articles; writing projects that require definition and organization development.
CAPABILITIES: Health care and pharmaceutical; physician, dentist and patient education; owner is a chemical engineer with health care product development and marketing experience.
CURRENT/RECENT CLIENTS/PROJECTS: Technical and non-technical audiences; pharmaceutical, biopharmaceutical, consumer packaged goods, information technology, and chemical companies.

B

BENDER ASSOCIATES, INC.   952-226-1200
5651 180th Street East   Prior Lake 55372
FAX: 952-226-1201
CONTACT: Shereida Bender
E-MAIL: sbender@benderassocinc.com
SERVICES: Custom design, development and production/delivery of training and technical documentation; web site design; business communications consulting. We can design complete training curricula, documentation and communications plans, or can work on one element of a larger project. We also provide project management and coaching services for documentation and training projects.
CAPABILITIES: Experienced in working with insurance/financial industry, manufacturing, telecommunications, retail, governmental, law enforcement, and agriculture clients. Primary focus is business computing/communications; specifically custom software applications and the documentation, training and communications associated with their development and implementation. Expertise in a wide variety of media -- print, computer-based, web-based, video, audio, etc.
CURRENT/RECENT CLIENTS/PROJECTS: Current/recent projects include: managing/producing documentation associated with Y2k certification for industrial and environmental clients, managing/coaching the documentation team associated with a major insurance client's system re-engineering efforts; coordinating communications and documentation for a major governmental system integration design effort; producing product documentation for a laser sensor manufacturer.
PRESIDENT/CEO/OWNER: Shereida Bender

BUSINESS AND SCIENCE WRITERS, INC.   651-642-9999
2311 Ione Street   St. Paul 55113
FAX: 651-645-2372
CONTACT: David Gardner, full-time professional communications consultant.

TYPES OF WRITING: Technical, scientific, and business communications for high-technology corporations, government agencies, universities, and businesses large and small. Corporate communications-including mission statements, annual reports, newsletters for employees and potential clients, press releases, policy manuals, and market research reports. Corporate marketing-including sales brochures, product literature, collateral materials, advertisements, business proposals, and feature articles for local, national, and trade publications. Technical manuals-including installation, training, operation, maintenance, service, and parts manuals. Software manuals-including thoughtfully designed interactive help systems, on-line documentation, and paper-based manuals. Web text of all kinds.
SPECIALTIES: Designing user-friendly interactive help systems for large and medium sized corporations in the information technology, computer and telecommunications industries. Writing that precisely meets your particular needs.
CURRENT/RECENT CLIENTS/PROJECTS: Large range of clients from Fortune 100 companies to small businesses.

F

STEVEN V. FITCH & ASSOCIATES   651-483-0961
4103 Brigadoon Drive   Shoreview 55126
CONTACT: Steven V. Fitch
E-MAIL: fitch006@tc.umn.edu
SERVICES: Types of Writings: Business to business technical marketing communications and training materials include brochures, datasheets, newsletters, direct mail, trade journal advertising and trade magazine features. QuarkXPress, and FrameMaker, desktop publishing on PC. Technical writing include on-line help screens, software user guides, operating manuals and maintenance manuals. Written for: Healthcare, education, mental health, refrigeration, financial and computer hardware and software.

H

HIGH POINT CREATIVE, LLC   651-426-4012
4583 Shady Lane   St. Paul 55110
FAX: 651-426-6699
CONTACT: Kate Huebsch
E-MAIL: kate@highpointcreative.com
WWW: highpointcreative.com
SERVICES: Copywriting and full project management for business-to-business and consumer brochures, catalogs, direct mail, websites, newsletters, speeches and presentations, PowerPoint shows, special events, marketing and internal communication pieces. A special interest in "translating" high-tech products and services into compelling and effective copy for non-technical readers.
CAPABILITIES: Marketing communications with an emphasis on strategic development and effective writing.
CURRENT/RECENT CLIENTS/PROJECTS: 12 years in business serving financial services companies, industrial manufacturers, health care organizations and community not-for-profit organizations.
PRESIDENT/CEO/OWNER: Kate Huebsch, President/Owner; Maiya Willits, Creative Director

592 / Writers - Technical

I

INNOVATIVE PROGRAMMING SYSTEMS, INC.   952-835-1290
9001 Poplar Bridge Road   Bloomington 55437
CONTACT: Karen M. Hess, Ph.D.
TYPES OF WRITING: Technical, proposals, textbooks, workbooks, documentation, policy and procedures manuals, annual reports, corporate histories, journal articles, etc.
WRITTEN FOR: EMA, Inc.; Braun Intertec; Northern States Power; West Publishing Company; John Wiley and Sons, Inc.; C.C. Thomas and Company; Custom Publishing; Pennwell Books; Van Nostrand Publishing.
SPECIALTIES: Textbooks.

INTERIM TECHNOLOGY CONSULTING   612-543-3300
1550 Utica Avenue South #945   Minneapolis 55416
FAX: 612-542-1419
CONTACT: Tom Shaughnessy
E-MAIL: tomshaughnessy@interim.com
WWW: interim.com/technology
SERVICES: Information design, instructional design. User interface design, usability engineering and web design.
CAPABILITIES: Web design, web-based training, web-based health systems, knowledge management system design, customized training solutions, user documentation and technical writing.
CURRENT/RECENT CLIENTS/PROJECTS: Jostens, Best Buy, US Bank, United Health Care, Medtronic, Northern States Power, Computer Network Technology, Deluxe Corporation, NCS, State of Minnesota.
PRESIDENT/CEO/OWNER: Stuart Emanuel, President

J

JF THIBODEAU, INC.   651-488-0610
490 West Street   Taylor Falls 55084
P.O. Box 425
CONTACT: Joe Thibodeau
SERVICES: We offer: Design and development of technical documents; design and development of online Help systems; project management relating to technical information projects.
CAPABILITIES: Extensive technical and business writing experience including user manuals, system architecture and design documents, business plans, sales proposals, and technical training materials. Experience creating online Help systems that coordinate with other software product technical documentation. Advanced project management expertise and credentials.

CURRENT/RECENT CLIENTS/PROJECTS: Over 20 years experience in technical communications. Primary markets include software development, Internet-based systems, telecommunications, and computer hardware engineering. Our typical client is a computer software/hardware engineering company doing system development either for direct sale or on contract to an end customer. Recent projects include: design and creation of Technical System Overview documents for a large e-commerce infrastructure provider; data model documentation for a major Internet-based sales configuration tool; user manual and online Help system for a distributed Internet security administration system; research project documentation for development of Internet tools.
PRESIDENT/CEO/OWNER: Joseph F. Thibodeau

K

DAVE KOCH
2256 Overlook Drive
FAX: 952-884-1560
CONTACT: Dave Koch
PAGER: 612-306-5009
WWW: dave.koch@worldnet.att.net

952-884-1560
Bloomington 55431

CAPABILITIES: 15 years of Technical Writing experience, and worked in the following industries: computer software and hardware, accounting, banking, point-of-sale, Smart Cards, telecommunications, and web sites.
SPECIALTIES: MS-Windows 9x/NT; MS-Word 6/95/97/2000, RoboHelp/RoboHTML 2000, WebHelp 3, Flash 4, FrontPage 2000, Acrobat 4, PhotoShop 5.5, Firewords2, CorelDraw 9, FrameMaker 5.5.6, and Visio 5.

M

MAHER FINANCIAL MEDIA
P.O. Box 205
FAX: 651-433-3543
CONTACT: Jim Maher
E-MAIL: mahermedia@aol.com

651-433-4647
Marine on St. Croix 55047

SERVICES: Editorial development and research for companies in the financial services industry. Provide content for brochures, newsletters, broker/representation communications, websites, training materials.
CAPABILITIES: Special knowledge on financial topics, including investments, insurance, financial planning, estate planning, retirement plans.
CURRENT/RECENT CLIENTS/PROJECTS: Zurich Kemper Life Insurance, American Express Financial Advisors, Met Life, Reliastar Financial, Fortis Financial, Allianz Life Insurance Company, First American Funds.

MEDIACRAFT, INC.
2315 Benjamin Street NE
FAX: 612-781-6898
CONTACT: Kerry Cork
E-MAIL: kscork@aol.ocm

612-789-9478
Minneapolis 55418

594 / Writers - Technical

SERVICES: Types of Writing: Design, develop, and produce multi-media training programs and promotional materials for business and industry, training manuals, workshop and seminar materials, audio and AV scripts, computer- assisted instruction, product information, company newsletters and promotional brochures.
SPECIALTIES: Creative sales training, technical and financial training, employee and management training programs. 22 years of experience.
CURRENT/RECENT CLIENTS/PROJECTS: Carlson Companies; 3M; G & K Services; First Bank; Encyclopedia Britannica; Frank B. Hall; Southern Bell; Longman Financial Services; Control Data Corporation; Fingerhut Companies, Inc.; Lutheran Brotherhood; Life USA; KTCA's Newton's Apple.

R

R.D.O.   612-755-3896
12832 Polk Street NE   Blaine 55434
FAX: 612-623-6580
E-MAIL: robert_d_ogden@graco.com
SERVICES: Technical manuals, training guides, promotional materials, and presentations.
CAPABILITIES: IBM and Mac format. Word, Word Perfect, Ventura Publishing. Interleaf and FrameMaker capabilities. Visio and PowerPoint presentations.
CURRENT/RECENT CLIENTS/PROJECTS: Anoka-Hennepin School District 11 - Technology Plan, Air Quality Plan.
PRESIDENT/CEO/OWNER: Robert D. Ogden

T

2KOOL STUDIOS   651-773-8717
PO Box 28094   Oakdale 55128
CONTACT: Bruce Bethke
CAPABILITIES: Contract technical writing service: we do it all, from brochures and user manuals to training videos & multimedia presentations. We're exceptionally good at delivering high-quality creative work on short to insane schedules.
SPECIALTIES: Specializing in windows and web help systems, online tutorials, Macromedia Flash, Graphics and Web application user-interface design and prototyping.
CURRENT/RECENT CLIENTS/PROJECTS: Portfolio and client list available by request.

TC2 COMPANY   612-922-8864
5324 Irving South   Minneapolis 55419
CONTACT: Les Barry
E-MAIL: les.barry@tc2.org
SERVICES: Information research & analysis, writing, editing, layout, illustrations and photography. Start-to-finish development including interfacing with prepress, printers, web developers/hosts, etc.

Writers – Technical / 595

CAPABILITIES: Communicating technical information about engineered products, processes, services, and businesses. New business/venture research, analysis and planning; product/project and marketing management. Three decades of experience providing services to technology-oriented companies. Professionals who know their way around, who get up-to-speed quickly, who work hard, who work smart, who don't make a lot of mistakes (fewer false starts & less rework), and who do good work with minimal supervision. Team players who work well with all levels of personnel, customers and suppliers; while maintaining complete confidentiality.

CURRENT/RECENT CLIENTS/PROJECTS: Recent projects included training materials, manuals, instructions, specifications, reports, competitive comparisons, scripts, articles, questionnaires, charts, diagrams, business plans, e-commerce needs assessments, and implementation plans.

PRESIDENT/CEO/OWNER: Les Barry

TWIN CITIES TECHNICAL COMMUNICATIONS COMPANY   612-922-8864
5324 Irving Avenue South   Minneapolis 55419
CONTACT: Les Barry
E-MAIL: info@tc2company.com

TYPES OF WRITING: Technical materials including manuals, training aids, sales aids, competitive comparisons, letters, reports, booklets, scripts, articles, newsletters, price lists, speeches, overhead transparencies and related items, other materials including business plans, new product development and commercialization plans, and marketing plans.

WRITTEN FOR: Organizations that have engineered products, services, and processes and need to communicate to customers, users, operators, employees, management, sales marketing, service, support, distributors, dealers, and investors.

SPECIALTIES: Specializing in content -- clear, concise, understandable, simplified content. Other services include product and project management, marketing management, and general management.

W

CLEMMER G. WAIT, TECHNICAL WRITER   651-698-9451
PO Box 4162   St. Paul 55104
CONTACT: Clemmer G. Wait
E-MAIL: c.wait@worldnet.att.net

SERVICES: Technical and advertising writer, medical writing and transcription, illustrative photography, continuation using DOS-based word processor

CAPABILITIES: Descriptions of mechanical and industrial processes, descriptions of construction and materials, aviation, medial and procedure writing, advertising copy writing, critical editing.

CURRENT/RECENT CLIENTS/PROJECTS: Control Data; Beryl D'Shannon; Weiser & Scott; Cray Research; Lab-Volt-Bolt; Univeristy of Minnesota

WHITE PLUME COMMUNICATIONS
1267 Van Buren Avenue #101

651-646-7359
St. Paul 55104

CONTACT: Judy Nollet
E-MAIL: janollet@minn.net
SERVICES: Clear, concise writing matched to the medium: Web, CD-ROM and other interactive computer-based platforms, as well as video and print. All types of business communications for training and marketing.
CAPABILITIES: Because I understand all aspects of multimedia production, I know how to provide programmable-ready scripts that work for the client as well as the development team. I've completed advanced graduate work in interactive media and have more than 20 years of experience writing and producing audiovisual and multimedia scripts, as well as ancillary print materials.
PRESIDENT/CEO/OWNER: Judy Nollet

ON THE WEB AT

gosilverbook.com

INDEX

A

A & N CRIST COMPANY, INC	147
A B DILLON	11
A LA CARTE MARKETING COMMUNICATIONS	571
A LIGHT COMMUNICATIONS	11
A-1 PRINTERS, INC	440
AARON & MCCANN ADVERTISING PHOTOGRAPHY	394
AARON-STOKES MUSIC, LTD	369
ABF DISPLAY COMPANY	151
MELISSA A. ABRAMS, INC	461, 583
ABSOLUTE MUSIC	369
ABSOLUTE PHOTOGRAPHY	426
ACADEMY FOR FILM AND TELEVISION AT CARYN INTERNATIONAL STUDIOS	286
ACCENT PRODUCTIONS	191
ACCI	111
ACCI AMERICAN CUSTOM COMPUTER	174
ACTION MAILING SERVICES, INC	136
ACTORS PLUS/VOICE PLUS	83, 361, 554, 560
ADAMS' PRODUCE	11
ADTECH COMMUNICATIONS GROUP	58, 111, 218
ADTRACK, INC.	379
ADVANCED AUDIO VISUAL	83
ADVENTURE GRAPHIC DESIGN	251
ADVERTISING FEDERATION OF MINNESOTA	286
ADVON INCORPORATED	431
AFTERWORDS WITH MIKE KAPEL	571
AFTRA/SAG TWIN CITIES LOCAL	286
AIRGRAPHICS 1	251
AKERLIND & ASSOCIATES CASTING	218, 361
NANCY S. ALCOMBRIGHT	591
ALDATA	136
BRUCE S. ALLEN, INC.	151, 219, 454
ALLIANCE FRANCAISE OF THE TWIN CITIES	287, 554
ALLOUT MARKETING, INC.	11, 301, 331
ALPHA VIDEO	83, 219
ALT BUSINESS SERVICES	130
ALTERNATIVE VIDEO SOLUTIONS	84
AMBASSADOR PRESS	440
AMERICAN BUSINESS FORMS AND PROMOTIONS	431
AMERICAN HOW-TO	476
AMERICAN JEWISH WORLD	476
AMERICAN MARKETING ASSOCIATION	287
AMERICAN SNOWMOBILER	476
AMERICAN SOCIETY FOR TRAINING AND DEVELOPMENT	167
AMERICAN SPIRIT GRAPHICS CORPORATION	440
AMOS/SMITH PHOTOGRAPHY	394
AMT COMMUNICATIONS/ANN M. THOMPSON	191, 563
AMUNDSON COMMUNICATIONS	571
AMUNDSON MARKETING	136, 301, 530
GREG R. ANDERSON COMMERCIAL PHOTOGRAPHY	394
ANDERSON MARKETING RESEARCH	344
TERRY ANDERSON PHOTOGRAPHY	394
GREG. R ANDERSON	420
ANDERSON, NIEBUHR & ASSOCIATES, INC.	344
ANDERSON-MADISION ADVERTISING, INC.	12
THE ANIMAL CONNECTION	361
ANIMAL TALENT POOL	362
ANIMUSE.COM	12, 58, 70
ANTARCTIC RESOURCES	292
JAN APPLE AGENCY RELATIONS CONSULTANT	331
NEIL APPLEQUIST	70, 130
AQUENT PARTNERS	280
ARCHITECTURAL ART BY KOHLRUSCH	70
ARIA PRODUCTIONS	191, 219
FRANK ARISS DESIGN	251
ARMOUR PHOTOGRAPHY	12
ARMSTRONG PHOTOGRAPHY	395
JIM ARNDT PHOTOGRAPHY, INC.	395
THE ARNOLD GROUP	13
THE ART FARM ADVERTISING, INC.	13, 428
ART OF COPY	573
ART REP SERVICES	66
ART WRITE COMMUNICAITONS	572
ARTESIAN CREATIVE COMPUTER SERVICES	130
ART-TECH PRODUCTIONS, INC.	151, 428, 454
AS SOON AS POSSIBLE, INC.	112 130, 174, 179, 558
ASI IMAGE STUDIOS	70
ASI SIGN SYSTEMS	379
ASIAN PAGES	476
ATLANTIC PRESS	558
AUDIO/VIDEO PRODUCTIONS	191
AURORA PHOTOGRAPHY, LTD.	395
AURORA PICTURES	191
AVA GROUP INC.	13, 313
AVA GROUP, INC.	313
AVALLO MULTIMEDIA & CREATIVE SERVICES	130

B

B & B PROMOTIONAL ADV. INC.	530
B J LARSON	71
B R PRODUCTIONS, INC.	514
BABS CASTING	220
BABY TIMES	477
NANCY BACHER, ARTIST REPRESENTATIVE	66
BACK MCKAY	563
BADIYAN INC.	167
BALLOON ASCENSIONS UNLIMITED	379
BANBURY STUDIOS	424
BARD ADVERTISING, INC.	13
BARSUHN DESIGN INCORPORATED	275
BARTLETT STUDIO, INC.	251
BASSETT CREEK STUDIO	220
BAU, INC.	71, 112, 252, 527
BBDO MINNEAPOLIS	13
BEARD COMMUNICATIONS, INC.	503
BEASLEY PHOTOGRAPHY	395
THE BEAUDRY GROUP	71, 220, 455
BEAVERS POND PRESS, INC.	496
PETER BECK PHOTOGRAPHY	395
DOUG BEKKE	71
MICHAEL FRANCIS BEMIS, FREELANCE WRITER	563
RAOUL BENAVIDES	396
BENCH & BAR OF MINNESOTA	477
BENDER ASSOCIATES, INC.	590
BENSON COMMUNICATIONS, INC.	56, 501
THE BENYAS AD GROUP, INC.	14, 302, 314, 332
THE BENYAS DESIGN GROUP	252,384
THE BENYAS GROUP	63, 72, 131, 558
RUTH A. BERGENE, WRITER	564
RAYMOND BERG'S MUSIC WORKS	369
BERKLEY PHOTOGRAPHY	396
BETHANY HOUSE PUBLISHERS	496
BEYLERIAN DESIGN	113
BEYOND MARKETING THOUGHT	332
WALTER BIEGER ASSOCIATES	284
PATRICIA BILCIK	389
BILITZ DESIGN, INC.	284
BIRD DOG & RETRIEVER NEWS	477
BLACK & WHITE PHOTOLAB, INC.	248
BLACK CAR MARKETING	302
BLACK DIAMOND MARKETING	302
BLAZE MARKETING GROUP, INC.	14
ROGER BLOOM PHOTOGRAPHY	392
BLUE EARTH PICTURES, INC.	192
BLUE MOON PRODUCTIONS, INC.	220, 424, 514
THE BOB PETERSON GROUP	14, 303
JAN WILLIAM BOER	72
BOERNER, INC.	303
BOHEN COMMUNICATIONS	564
BOLIN MARKETING AND ADVERTISING	333

Index / 599

THE BOOK	477
BOOKER COMMUNICATIONS	192
BOWEN CREATIVE COMPANY	63, 174
BOZELL KAMSTRA	15, 461
BRADLEY JOSEPH	370
MARK BRADLEY	160, 583
BRAEMAR PRINTING, INC.	441
BRAINCO: THE MINNEAPOLIS SCHOOL OF ADVERTISING	535
DARRELL BRAND/MOVING IMAGES, INC.	193
PER BREIEHAGEN PHOTOGRAPHY	396
GERALD BRIMACOMBE	424
P. H. BRINK INTERNATIONAL	84, 555, 559
NANCY S. BROWN	345
ROB BROWN COMMUNICATIONS	461
BROWNE & BROWNE MARKETING, INC.	15
BRUCATO & HALLIDAY, LTD.	462
BRUCE WILLITS DESIGN	275
BRW, INC.	252
BRYTE SPOT STUDIO	514
ROBERT BUCKNER DESIGNS & SUCH	72
BUDGET PR	462
MIKE BURIAN PHOTOGRAPHY	396
BUSCH & PARTNERS, INC.	478
BUSINESS & TECHNOLOGY GRAPHICS	152
BUSINESS AND INDUSTRIAL MARKET RESEARCH CORPORATION	105
BUSINESS AND SCIENCE WRITERS, INC.	590
THE BUSINESS EDGE	303
BUSINESS EXPRESSIONS, INC.	131
BUSINESS INFORMATION TECHNOLOGIES, INC.	109
BUTTONS ON BRISTOL/ADAMS PROMOTIONAL GROUP	431

C

C J OLSON MARKET RESEARCH, INC.	333, 345
CABLE IZ	56
CABLE PHOTO SYSTEMS	392
CABLE12/NORTHWEST COMMUNITY TELEVISION	101
MAGGIE BELLE CALIN	537
CALLAHAN & COMPANY PHOTO, INC.	397
LEAH CAMPBELL PHOTOGRAPHY	397
CAMPBELL MITHUN	16
CANDYLAND PONY SERVICE	221
CANNON CREATIVE RETOUCHING	527
CANTON COMMUNICATIONS, INC.	17
CANTWELL COMMUNICATIONS	193
CAPTIONMAX, INC.	193
CARL FRANZEN IS A WRITER	564
CARLISANO COMMUNICATIONS	462
CARLSON - VOHS COMMUNICATIONS	572
CATHERINE CARLSON ARTIST	527
CARLSON CUNICO, INC.	17
DAWN CARLSON	160
THE CARLSON PRINT GROUP	442
CARMICHAEL LYNCH, INC.	17
PAT CARNEY STUDIO, INC.	253
CAROLRHODA BOOKS, INC.	496
CARR CREATIVES	314
JEANETTE CARRELL ART DIRECTOR	63
BRENT CASEY, INC. PHOTO/FILM STYLING	221, 389, 537
CASWELL PHOTOGRAPHY	113, 397, 528
LAUREL CAZIN PHOTOGRAPHY	397
CBIG (CHILDRENS BOOK ILLUSTRATORS GUILD)	73
CELSKI COMMUNICATIONS	314
CENTRAL CONTAINER CORP.	152, 283, 380, 384, 429
CENTRAL PRINTING COMPANY	432
CG BOOK PRINTERS	93
CHANCE/NELSON & ASSOCIATES, INC.	18
CHARLIE WALBERG CREATIVE SERVICES	63, 253
CHARS WORDSHOPPE	160

CHARTHOUSE INTERNATIONAL LEARNING CORPORATION	194
JOANN CHERRY	398
CHERYL WALSH BELLVILLE PHOTOGRAPHY	398
CHURCHWARD BENSON DESIGN, INC.	253
JEAN CHURILLA, ADVERTISING ARTIST	63
CINE SERVICE	221
CINE SOUND 2	222, 515
CITY PAGES, INC.	478
CITY VISIONS	398
CITYBUSINESS, THE BUSINESS JOURNAL BOOK OF LISTS	478
CITYBUSINESS: THE BUSINESS JOURNAL	479
CITYLITES USA, INC.	380
CITY'S BEST MARKETING, INC.	18, 303, 315
CLARITY COVERDALE FURY, INC.	18
CLASSIC IMPRESSIONS	183
CAROL CLAY	573
CLEAN LINE GRAPHICS, LLC	131
CLEARVISION PRODUCTIONS	194
CLICK COMMUNICATIONS CORP.	315, 333
CML MARKETING SERVICES, INC.	346
CMS, INC.	134
THE COAST	370
COCHRAN COMMUNICATIONS NETWORK	315
COGSWELL DESIGN COMPANY	253
BOB COLE PHOTOGRAPHER	398
THE COLLATORS, INC.	93
COLLECTOR CAR PROPS	455
COLLEEN SZOT WONDERFUL WRITER, INC.	137, 222, 565
RAPP COLLINS WORLDWIDE	137, 304, 316
COLOR ARTS	536
COLOR PRINTING	442
COLORHOUSE	113, 131, 175, 179, 528
COMMERS PRINTING, INC.	442
COMMON LAW PUBLISHING, INC.	479, 496, 503
COMMUNICATIONS UNLIMITED VIDEO PRODUCTIONS	194
COMO CONSORTIUM, LTD.	19
COMPASS INTERNATIONAL RESEARCH & INFORMATION SERVICE	346
COMPLIMENTS, INC.	389
COMPUTER USER	479
CONCEPT GROUP INC.	19, 138, 316
THE CONCISE WORD	160
CONFERENCE COORDINATORS INTERNATIONAL	184
JUDITH CONNER DESIGN	73
TOM CONNORS PHOTOGRAPHY	398
CONSUMER MARKETING & PROMOTIONS, INC.	432
CONSUMER RESEARCH CORPORATION	346
CONTACT INK CORPORATION	147
CONUS PRODUCTIONS & SATELLITE SERVICES	85, 125, 195, 223, 292
COOK RESEARCH & CONSULTING, INC.	347
COOKHOUSE RECORDING STUDIOS, INC.	515
COOKING PLEASURES	479
GLORIA COOPER CALLIGRAPHY & DESIGN	73
CORPORATE INCENTIVES OF AMERCIA	432
CORPORATE MEDIA SERVICES	195
CORPORATE MEETINGS CONSULTING	184
CORPORATE REPORT FACT BOOK	497
CORPORATE REPORT MAGAZINE	503
COSTUMES & CREATURES	455
COTTAGE COMMUNICATIONS, INC.	317
CRAIG PERMAN PICTURES	399
CRASH & SUES	59, 114, 223, 515
CRC, INC.	20, 317, 384, 530
CREATIVE BUSINESS INK	565
CREATIVE CADRE, INC.	280
CREATIVE COMMUNICATIONS CONSULTANTS, INC.	20
CREATIVE CONSULTANTS	573
THE CREATIVE EDGE FILM & VIDEO PRODUCTIONS, INC.	195
CREATIVE PUBLISHING INTERNATIONAL	501
CREATIVE RESOURCE CENTER/CRC, INC.	20, 317, 384, 530

600 / Index

CREATIVE VENTURES, INC.	317
CREO INTERNATIONAL - INTERNATIONAL AND CROSS CULTURAL COMMUNICATIONS	555
THE CULLINAN GROUP	21, 304, 531
CUSTOM BUSINESS VIDEO, INC.	196
CUSTOM CASSETTE, INC.	516
CUSTOM RECORDING STUDIOS	516
CYD WICKER STUDIO	74

D

D.S. ADV. ETC.	21
D.W. ET AL.	21, 94, 305, 333
STEVEN DAHLMAN PHOTOGRAPHY	420
JACKIE DALTON	223
MELISSA DALTON	224
DANGER STUDIOS	196
TODD DANIELS MARKETING & ADVERTISING	22, 184, 305
DANNER PRESS CORPORATION	443
JEFFREY DARREL ADVERTISING	22
DAVIES DESIGN	64
SHARON DAVIS MAKE UP ARTIST	224
DAYTOURS & CREATIVE EVENTS	184
DEBNER PUBLICATIONS	161
DECKER PUBLICATIONS	503
DEEG PRODUCTIONS	318
DELITE OUTDOOR ADVERTISING, INC.	380
DEMOTT ADVERTISING	22
DESIGN COMMUNICATIONS	254
THE DESIGN COMPANY	254
DESIGN WRITE COMMUNICATIONS	463
DESIGNABILIA	254
DESIGNSTEIN	22
TOM DEVENY & ASSOCIATES	56
DICK BOBNICK ILLUSTRATION, INC.	74
DIGIGRAPHICS, INC.	114, 153
DIGITAL EXCELLENCE, INC.	516
DIGITAL MANN	528
DIGITAL PEOPLE	254, 280, 551
DIGITAL PICTURES, INC.	224
DIGITAL REFLEXIONS	114
DIMENSION CREATIVE	66
DIS MEET PEOPLE	55
DK&Y	23
DOCUMENT RESOURCES	443
DORN PRODUCTION MANAGEMENT SERVICE, INC.	443
DOWN ON THE FARM	183
DOWNING COMMUNICATIONS	132
STEVE DOYLE PRODUCTIONS	196
DOZZI PHOTOGRAPHY, INC.	399
DR. OF PROPTOLOGY	456
DRAGON DOOR PUBLICATIONS	480
DRAWING CARD	283
DREAMSTITCHER CUSTOM COSTUME	456
JEANNE DREW SURVEYS	347
CHERYL DRIVDAHL	161
DROEGE PHOTOGRPAHY	420
JOHN DU CANE	573
ANDREA J. DUCANE	224
DUERR & TIERNEY, LTD, ART OF THE WEST	480, 497, 504
JANE DUGAN EDITORIAL SERVICES	161
DUPLICATION FACTORY, INC.	225
DYNOPRESS, INC.	443

E

E J SIGNS	381
E. K. QUEHL COMPANY	23
E. LIVINGSTON & ASSOCIATES	23, 334
EAGLE DIRECT/EAGLE GRAPHICS, INC.	138
EATON & ASSOCIATES DESIGN COMPANY	255
ECHO BOYS, INC.	370
ECLECTIC MUSIC/MARKETING & PUBLISHING	94
EDW DESIGN	255

EFFECTING CREATIVE CHANGE IN ORGANIZATIONS (ECCO)	168
EIII PRODUCTIONS, INC.	196, 371
ELECTRONIC INTERIORS, INC.	225
ELLER MEDIA COMPANY	357
ELLIOTT HOUSE ADVERTISING GROUP	24
DAVID ELLIS PHOTOGRAPHY, INC.	399
ELLIS PHOTOGRAPHY INC.	399
FAYE ELLISON	389
EMERALD GRAPHICS	179
EMERGE MARKETING	334
JAMES ERICKSON PHOTOGRAPHY/DIGITAL IMAGING	400
SUSAN ERICKSON	281
ERNSTER PUBLIC RELATIONS	463
ESCHER ILLUSTRATIONS	74
ESK MARKETING RESEARCH	347
EURUS INC.	556
TONY EVANS, PHOTOGRAPHER	400
EVOLUTIONARY ILLUSTRATION & DESIGN STUDIOS	74
EXCEL DEVELOPMENT GROUP, INC.	250
EXECUTIVE TYPING SERVICES	107
EXHIBITS PLUS	153

F

4FRONT PRODUCTIONS	256
45 DEGREES/MINNEAPOLIS	256
FABER SHERVEY ADVERTISING	24
AARON FAHRMANN	392
FALLEK AND ASSOCIATES	24
THE FALLS AGENCY	24
FAME - A RETAIL IMAGE MANAGEMENT FIRM	256
FAMILY TIMES, INC.	480, 504
FARINACCI & ASSOCIATES, INC.	197
FARROW MEDIA SERVICES	197
FAST FOOTAGE	292
STEVE FASTNER	75
BILL FELKER	22
FFI MAGAZINE	481
FIELD DRESSING	39
FILM FOOD	22
FINNEY COMPANY	49
FINS PUBLICATIONS	49
STEVEN V. FITCH & ASSOCIATES	574, 59
MOE FLAHERTY	22
FLEMING DESIGN	25
FLOATING HEAD	371, 56
FLYING COLORS INCORPORATED	85, 22
TOM FOLEY PHOTOGRAPHY	40
FORM & CONTENT	5
FORMAT MAGAZINE	4
FOUR STAR PARTNERS	3
LIZA FOURRE PHOTOGRAHICS	4
FOX COMMUNICATIONS, INC.	
FOX STUDIO LTD	
FRANCISCO PHOTOGRAPHY	3
FRANEYDESIGN	2
FRANKE + FIORELLA	94, 318, 3
KIMBERLY FRANSON MODEL/ACTOR AGENCY	226, 3
FREELANCE CONSORTIUM	
FREELANCE CREATIVE SERVICES	281,
FREESTYLE PRODUCTIONS, INC.	85, 125, 185, 197,
JANA FREIBAND PHOTOGRAPHY	
FRETHEIM & FRIENDS	75,
STEVE FRIEDERICHSEN, INC.	
FROGTOWN TIMES	
LINDA FROILAND	
JENNIFER CLARK FROST - PHOTOGRAPHERS REPRESENTATIVE	
FTL PUBLICATIONS	
BETH FULLER DESIGN	
PAT FUNK COPYWRITER	
FUTUREPAGES, INC.	

G

G & J PATCH AND PIN	433
GABRIEL DIERICKS RAZIDLO	26
GEOFFREY CARLSON GAGE, LLC	26, 95
GAGE MARKETING GROUP	306
GALLAGHER MEDIA, INC.	27, 357
KENNETH GAMMELL	227
GARDENING HOW-TO	481
JON GARON CREATIVE, INC.	371, 574
GEHLHAR PHOTOGRAPHY	401
GENERAL LITHO SERVICES, INC.	139, 444
GERMAN LANGUAGE SERVICE	556
GILLIES CREATIVE	575
GILLIES GROUP, INC.	334
SUSAN GILMORE PHOTOGRAPHER	420
THE GISLASON AGENCY	299
BARBARA J. GISLASON & ASSOCIATES	290
GOFF & HOWARD	463
THE GOLD BOOK	482
THE GOLD BOOK/ARIZONA	482
GOLD FISH COMMUNICATIONS	318, 575
STAN M. GOLDSTEIN	567
GOOD AGE	482
GOOSE GRAPHICS	64
GOPHER SIGN COMPANY	381
GOPHER STATE LITHO CORPORATION	445
GOVERNMENT TELEVISION NETWORK	550
GRAF ADVERTISING	27
GRAHAM BROWN PHOTOGRAPHY	401
CHRIS GRAJCZYK PHOTOGRAPHY	401
GRANDPARENT TIMES	483
GRAPHIC EXHIBITS, INC.	153
GRAPHIC IMPRINTS, INC.	433
GRAPHIC RELIEF	28, 64, 139, 282
GRAPHXPOINT	319
HEIDI GRAYDEN	390
GREAT GARMENTS	433
GREATAPES CORPORATION	86, 227, 228, 517
GREEN LIGHT CONSULTING, INC.	584
GREEN MAN PYROTECHNICS	228
THE GREENE SHEET	86, 228
GREENHOUSE GROUP	162
LAURIE GROSS	64, 258
JEFFREY GROSSCUP, PHOTOGRAPHER	293
GROSSMAN DESIGN ASSOCIATES	275
GROUP DESIGN, INC.	258
GROUP ONE RESPONSE MARKETING	335
GRUGGEN BUCKLEY	28, 428, 525
GULENCHYN, INC.	228
GUTHRIE THEATER COSTUME RENTALS	229, 456
GV GRAPHICS, INC.	180, 445, 453

H

HAAG DESIGN, INC.	258
HABERLE COMMUNICATIONS	464
MIKE HABERMANN PHOTOGRAPHY, INC.	402
TODD HAFERMANN PHOTOGRAPHY	402
HAKALA COMMUNICATIONS INC	584
HALL KELLEY, INC.	259
HALSEY CREATIVE SERVICES, INC.	402
DAVID HALSEY	576
LARS HANSEN PHOTOGRAPHY	402
HARMONY BOX	229, 517, 541
GRETCHEN HARRIS & ASSOCIATES	403
HARRIS WAREHOUSE & CANVAS SALES	154, 457
SUE HARTLEY PHOTO	403
HARTWIG MUSIC AND SOUND	371
PATRICIA C HASWELL	162
HATLING & THOMAS	28
HAUCK MARKETING	335
HDMG DESIGN, POST & EFFECTS	59, 115, 229
HEALTH CARE COMMUNICATIONS, INC.	29

Index / 601

HEDSTROM/BLESSING, INC.	29, 96, 259, 319, 386, 532
HEINRICH ENVELOPE CORPORATION	140
HELLMAN ASSOCIATES	260
HENDLER - JOHNSTON, LLC	29, 260
RALPH W. HENN, PUBLIC RELATIONS,	162
RALPH HEPOLA	372
HIEBEL & ASSOCIATES	320
HIGH POINT CREATIVE, LLC	140, 320, 438, 576, 591
HOBAR PUBLICATIONS	498
HOFFMAN COMMUNICATIONS INC	320
MICHAEL A HOHMANN AND COMPANY	335
HOLDEN GRAPHIC SERVICES	140, 445
JOHN HOLDEN	576
THE HOLLYWOOD-MADISON GROUP	110, 362
BRIAN SCOTT HOLMAN	403
THE HOLTON GROUP	168, 577, 584
HOPF & HOPF PRINTING, INC.	446
SANDEE HORK PHOTOGRAPHY	426
KATHY HORWATH, MARKETING SERVICES	336
HOUSE OF CINEMAGRAPHICS	230
DAVID HOUSEWRIGHT	578
HSC SCENIC SERVICES, LTD	75, 154
MARK HUFFINGTON PRODUCTIONS	198
LINDA HUHN & RICHARD JOHNSON PHOTOGRAPHY	403
HUMMEL PHOTOGRAPHY	404
HUNT ADKINS, INC.	30
HUSOM & ROSE PHOTOGRAPHICS	293
MELINDA HUTCHINSON	230

I

IDEAL PRINTERS, INC.	446
ILLUSION GRAPHICS & COMMUNICATIONS	115, 175
IMAGE GROUP	404
IMAGE ONE STUDIOS	404
IMAGETECH SOLUTIONS, INC.	116, 248
ImageTrend	260
IMAGINALITY, INC.	275
IMPACT MAILING	150
IMPRESSIONS	198
IMPRESSIONS INCORPORATED	446
IN THE GROOVE MUSIC	372
INDEPENDENT DELIVERY SERVICE	141
INDEPENDENT FEATURE PROJECT/NORTH	230
INDEX GROUP	336
INDIGO INK COMMUNICATIONS	567
INDUSTRIAL EQUIPMENT NEWS	504
INFINITY DIRECT, INC.	30, 141, 176, 261, 446
INFOJO	116
INFORM RESEARCH SERVICES	105, 294
INFORMATION AGE COMMUNICATIONS	578
INFORMATION SPECIALISTS GROUP, INC.	348
INHOUSE MEDIA	87, 125
INITIO, INC.	30
INNOVATIVE PROGRAMMING SYSTEMS, INC.	592
INTERACTIVE GAMES	546
INTERACTIVE PERSONALITIES, INC.	60
INTERFACE GRAPHICS	116
INTERIM TECHNOLOGY CONSULTING	592
INTERNATIONAL & ETHNIC COMMUNICATIONS, INC.	31, 557, 560, 567
INTERNATIONAL ASSOCIATION OF BUSINESS COMMUNICATORS	287
INTERNATIONAL EDUCATION SYSTEMS	543
INTERNATIONAL RESEARCH & EVALUATION (IRE)	105
INTERNATIONAL TELEVISION ASSOC. (ITVA)	287
INTERSECT, INC.	31
INTUITIVE	517
IPARES, LTD.	87, 116, 134, 169, 261, 321
IRISH GAZETTE	483
IRRESISTIBLE INK, INC.	142
ISA PROMOTIONS, INC.	123, 434, 532

602 / Index

J

J MILLER ASSOCIATES	543
J R CASTING	199
JACKIE URBANOVIC, ILLUSTRATION	76
SCOTT JACOBSON STUDIO, INC.	404
JAGGED EDGE	231
DAN JAGUNICH	231
JALIVAY & ASSOCIATES	185, 336
JAM ADVERTISING, INC.	32
JAMCO MARKETING GROUP	306
JAPS OLSON COMPANY	447
JEDD, MARCIA/MJ & ASSOCIATES	348, 584
JEDLICKA DESIGN	386
JF THIBODEAU, INC.	592
JG STUDIOS	405
JGI COMMUNICATIONS	32
JIM STOKES COMMUNICATIONS	568
JKL STUDIOS	117, 180, 528
JODEE KULP DIGITAL DESIGN	261
JOHANNES GASTON DESIGN, INC.	284
JOHMAR FARMS	231, 363, 457
JOHNNYS ILLUSTRATIVE DESIGN	76
JOHNSON ADVERTISING, INC.	32
CLIFF JOHNSON MARKETING	337
CURTIS JOHNSON & ASSOCIATES	405
JOHNSON GROSSFIELD, INC./PROMOTIONAL MARKETING	532
JEFF JOHNSON PHOTOGRAPHY	405
JOHNSON PRINTING & PACKAGING	447
JOHNSTON DESIGN OFFICE	276
JOLA PUBLICATIONS	483
SUSAN JORGENSEN	300, 390
BEVERLY JOVANOVICH FREELANCE WRITER	585
JUNTUNEN MEDIA GROUP	117, 126, 169, 199, 231, 294
JUNTUNEN MOBILE TELEVISION	232

K

K L PUBLICATIONS, INC.	483
K· M· T COMMUNICATIONS	321
K2 ASSETS	360
KABLOOE DESIGN, INC.	285
STEVE KAHN CREATIVE	578
KARWOSKI & COURAGE - PUBLIC RELATIONS	464
KASM AM/FM	509
KAT WOMAN PRODUCTIONS	199
KATE AM/KCPO FM	509
JOE KATZ MODELS	363
KAUS AM/FM	509
KBEW AM/FM	509
KBMW	509
KBPR FM	509
KBSB FM	509
KBUN	509
KCRB FM	510
KDG INTERACTIVE	170, 276, 322
KEELER PHOTOGRAPHY	405
THE KEEP, INC.	232
TIMOTHY D. KEHR ADVERTISING	295
FRED KELLER COMMUNICATIONS	185, 464
KENDALL PHOTOGRAPHS	406
KENNEDY & COMPANY	32, 358
KERKER MARKETING COMMUNICATIONS	33, 465
KETCHUM METZ, INC.	465
KGWB	510
KIKV FM	510
KILROY'S	457
KIM HORECKA, MAKE-UP ARTIST	390
KIMM PUBLISHING	498
HEATHER RANDALL KING	585
KING PRODUCTIONS	232
KINGSBURY STUDIOS	406
KITA ASSOCIATES, INC.	504
KITCHENER PRODUCTIONS	200
KJLY FM	510
KKBJ AM/FM	510
KKIN/KEZZ	510
DAVID KLAUSSEN	200
KLBB/KLBP AM	101
KLIZ AM/FM	510
KLKS FM	510
KLLZ FM	511
KLP, INC.	67
BRUCE KLUCKHOHN	406
KMSK FM	511
KNFX AM	511
KNITTIG DESIGN, INC.	76, 262
IRV KNOWLEN DESIGN/ILLUSTRATION	77
MARY ANN KNOX	447
KNUTSON PHOTOGRAPHY, INC.	406
DAVE KOCH	593
DAVID W. KOEHSER	290
KOHNSTAMM COMMUNICATIONS	465
ROD KOMIS PHOTOGRAPHY	406
KOSKINEN VIDEO INC.	200
KQPR FM	511
KRIVIT PHOTOGRAPHY	407
KRJB FM	511
BILL KROLL	77
KRS DESIGN	262, 538
KRUEGERWRIGHT	262
KRWC AM	511
KSCR AM/FM	511
KSTQ FM	511
KUEHN CREATIVE	578
TIMOTHY KUHLMANN	578
KENNETH L KUNKLE, ATTORNEY AT LAW	290
CYNTHIA KURKOWSKI	458
KV GRAPHICS	277
KVBR AM/FM	512
KXDL FM	512
KXRA AM/FM	512
THE KYDD GROUP (TKG)	322
KYRS FM	512

L

L A STUDIOS, INC.	407
L A, INC.	323
LA TERESA IMAGE CONSULTING & MODELING SCHOOL/AGENCY	363
LA VOZ	484
LABEL PRODUCTS, INC.	447
LABELLE & ASSOCIATES	33
JAMES M. LAING & ASSOCIATES	142
DEBORAH LAKE/WITTA MAKE-UP ARTIST	233
LAKESHORE WEEKLY NEWS	484
LAMAR ADVERTISING COMPANY	381
LANCE LEWEY ADVERTISING AND PHOTOGRAPHY	34
LANGUAGEPOWER PUBLICATIONS	484
LAPINSKI PRODUCTIONS, LTD.	201, 233
LARKIN INDUSTRIES	448
LARKSPUR STRINGS	183
LARSEN DESIGN + INTERACTIVE	263
LARSON & ASSOCIATES	34
ART LARSON PHOTOGRAPHY	407
JIM LARSON	579
LASER GRAPHICS, INC.	382, 434
LAVENDER MAGAZINE	485
LAWRENCE FRIED	233
LBF, INC.	407
PATRICIA C. LEAF	585
LEAPFROG ASSOCIATES	96
LECY DESIGN, INC.	263

Index / 603

LEE PICTURES, INC.	201
LEHMANN PRODUCTION SERVICES	201
LERNER PUBLICATIONS	485
LETS PLAY, INC.	485
LET'S PLAY, INC.	486, 505
LIFETOUCH VIDEO CREATIONS	88, 201
LIGHTHOUSE CREATIVE	568
LIGHTHOUSE, INC.	234
LIGHTING IN A JAR STUDIOS	234
LIGHTNING IN A JAR STUDIOS	407
LIGHTS ON MINNEAPOLIS	234
PAT LINDQUIST & ASSOCIATES, LTD.	466
THE LINK	466
JOHN LINN PHOTOGRAPHY	408
LINN UNLIMITED, A PRODUCTION COMPANY	202
LIONOWL FILMS	202
LIPSERVICE, INC.	364
LLEWELLYN PUBLICATIONS	486
LOCATION AND BACK, LTD.	234
TOM LOCHRAY INC.	77
LONG RUN PRODUCTIONS, LTD.	88
STUART LORENZ PHOTOGRAPHIC DESIGN STUDIO	408
LOUD NEIGHBORS	372, 518
LOW AND INSIDE	486, 545
LUDLOW ADVERTISING	34, 55
PAUL LUNDQUIST PHOTOGRAPHY	408
WADE C. LUNEBURG	186, 300
LYNCH JARVIS JONES, INC.	34, 337, 348
LYNN TEMPORARY	552

M

MACCABEE GROUP, INC.	466
MACHALEK COMMUNICATIONS, INC.	487
MACHINE DREAMS INCORPORATED	126
MACLEAN & TUMINELLY	264
DAVID MADERICH	235
MAGNETIC PICTURES	235
MAGNETO COMMUNICATIONS	35, 97
MAGOFFIN ASSOCIATES	424
MAHER FINANCIAL MEDIA	593
MAHONEY MEDIA GROUP, INC.	202
MAINSTREAM COMMUNICATIONS, INC.	88, 127, 186, 235
MAINSTREET GROUP, INC.	35, 142, 149
MAJERES GRAPHIC DESIGN	264
MAJOR GROOVE MUSIC COMPANY	373, 518
MAMMOTH MARKETING COMMUNICATIONS	35
MANUAL-MATIC, INC.	176
MANUSCRIPTS DIVISION	295
MARACOM CORPORATION	448
PETER MARCUS PHOTOGRAPHY	420
MARK*NET	142
MARKERT PHOTOGRAPHY	408
MARKET RESOURCE ASSOCIATES, INC.	352
MARKET VISION	352
MARKETING MIDWEST, INC.	358
MARKETING SOURCE USA	307
MARKETING WORKS	337
MARKETRAIN	36, 307
MARKGRAF & WELLS ADVERTISING & MARKETING	338
JOHN MARKOVICH PHOTOGRAPHY	409
MARLOR PRESS, INC.	487
CHRISTINE MARTIN CONSULTANTS	391
MARTIN ROSS DESIGN	264
MARTIN/BASTIAN PRODUCTIONS	127, 203, 543
MARTIN/WILLIAM - I GROUP	143, 264
MARTIN/WILLIAMS ADVERTISING	36
MARVY!	409
CHAR MASON & ASSOCIATES	186
MASON ILLUSTRATION	67
MASTER COMMUNICATIONS GROUP, INC.	171, 203, 323
ALAN MATHIOWETZ PHOTOGRAPHY	409
MATNEY & ASSOCIATES, INC.	236
MATRIX VIDEO, INC.	203
MATRIXVIDEO, INC.	236
MATT BLAIR'S CELEBRITY PROMOTIONS, INC.	187
BETH MATTSON-TEIG	586
MAX STUDIO	323
SANDY MAY PHOTOGRAPHY	409
MCARTLAND	118
MCCARTHY-KERN PUBLIC RELATIONS	467
JOY MCCOMB	163
MCCOY & ASSOCIATES, INC.	204
MCGRAW-HILL HEALTHCARE INFORMATION GROUP	506
MCMAHON STUDIO PHOTOGRAPHY	409
G & W MCNAMARA PUBLISHING, INC.	487, 505
MCNAUGHTON INCORPORATED	307
MCSMITH PACKAGE & DISPLAY, INC.	387
MEDIA LOFT, INC.	89, 187, 236
MEDIA MAXX COMMUNICATIONS	89
MEDIA NETWORKS, INC.	57
MEDIA PRODUCTIONS, INC.	187, 204, 324
MEDIACRAFT, INC.	593
MEDIAONE	236, 549
MEDIATECH	36, 358
MEDVEC-EPPERS ADVERTISING, LTD.	37, 324
MIKE MEEHAN COMPANY	429, 525
MEETING PROFESSIONALS INTERNATIONAL	188
J. T. MEGA, INC.	38
MEIROVITZ & COMPANY	38
LOIS MEISCHPHOTO/FILM STYLIST	391
MENTEN MUSIC, INC.	204
MENTZER MAKE-UP & HAIR DESIGN	237
MERCHANT & GOULD	291
MEREDITH MODEL & TALENT AGENCY	364
MERIT PRINTING	448
MERRIAM PARK POST	487, 505
MESH CORPORATION	307, 324, 338
MESSAGE IN MOTION	205, 568
METRO PROMOTIONS	434
METROPOLITAN HODDER GROUP	205
MEUSEY COMMUNICATIONS	506
MEYER MARKETING, LTD.	38
MGRAPHICS	163, 569
MIDWEST BADGE & NOVELTY COMPANY, INC.	435
MIDWEST INDEPENDENT PUBLISHERS ASSN.	288, 487, 498
MIDWEST MEDIA ARTISTS ACCESS CENTER	237
MIDWEST STAFFING GROUP, INC.	552
MIKE JONES FILM CORP.	205
MIKE REED ILLUSTRATION	77
CYNTHIA MILLER CREATIVE CONCEPTS & COPY	579
PAT MILLER PHOTOGRAPHY	421
MINNEAPOLIS PUBLIC LIBRARY	295
THE MINNEAPOLIS TELECOMMUNICATIONS NETWORK	101
MINNESOTA BRIDE MAGAZINE	487
MINNESOTA CLIPPING SERVICE	123, 467
MINNESOTA FILM BOARD	205
MINNESOTA GUIDEBOOK TO STATE AGENCY SERVICES	488
MINNESOTA HISTORICAL SOCIETY RESEARCH CENTER	296
MINNESOTA LAW & POLITICS	488
MINNESOTA LINK	467
MINNESOTA MEDICINE	488
MINNESOTA MEETINGS & EVENTS	506
MINNESOTA NEWSPAPER ASSOCIATION	57, 468
MINNESOTA PARENT	506
MINNESOTA SCHOOL OF COMPUTER IMAGING	171, 288
MINNESOTA STATE BAR ASSOCIATION	506
MINNESOTA WOMENS PRESS	488
MINNESOTA'S BOOKSTORE	489
MIRAGE ADVERTISING (FORMERLY RUDISILL ADVERTISING, INC.)	39
THE MISSISSIPPI RAG, INC.	507
MITCHELL PHOTOGRAPHY	424
THE MNN RADIO NETWORKS INC.	102
MODERN MUSIC	519

604 / Index

MODERN PRESS	448
MODERNISTIC, INC.	154, 429, 449, 536
MOLGREN RESEARCH ASSOCIATES, INC.	352
MOMENTUM DESIGN, INC.	265
MONJA MARKETING	308
MONTAGE	149, 547
MOORE CREATIVE TALENT, INC.	365
MOTION PICTURE PROJECTIONISTS AND VIDEO TECHNICIANS	89
MOTION PICTURES, INC.	206
MRA GROUP	352
MRC PUBLIC RELATIONS, INC.	468
MTM ADVERTISING	39
MULTI-AD SERVICES, INC.	176
MULTIMEDIA	128, 172, 206, 265, 325
MUSIC AUDIO SOUND SERVICES	237
MUSICAL MARKETING	373
MWA DIRECT, INC.	308

N

NAMETAG INTERNATIONAL, INC.	353, 378
THE NANCEKIVELL GROUP	265
LISA NANKIVIL	78
NATIONAL ASSOCIATION OF GOVERNMENT COMMUNICATORS - VOYAGEUR CHAPTER	288
NATURAL SOUND RECORDING STUDIO	373, 519
NED KANTAR PRODUCTIONS, INC.	183, 365
MARGARET NELSON & ASSOCIATES	580
PAUL NELSON PHOTOGRAPHY	410
NEMER, FIEGER & ASSOCIATES, INC.	39, 468
PETER NEUBECK VIDEO	206
NEVILLE & ASSOCIATES	172
JOHN NEVILLE	580
NEW RESIDENTS GUIDE	489
NEW SCHOOL, INC./E-STRATEGY	469
RAYMOND NIEMI PRODUCTION SERVICES	238
NITEWRITER ADVERTISING	40
C A NOBENS ILLUSTRATION & DESIGN, INC.	78
NOCTAGRAPHICS: COMPUTER ILLUSTRATION AND DESIGN STUDIO	266
JOHN NOLTNER PHOTOGRAPHY	410
NORTH AMERICAN FISHERMAN	489
NORTH AMERICAN HUNTER	490
NORTH WOODS ADVERTISING	40, 308
NORTHCOTT BANNER CORPORATION	155
NORTHWEST COMPUTER SERVICES	155, 181
NORTHWOODS COLOR	181
NUTS, ltd	365
THE NYCOR GROUP	190, 553
NYGARD & ASSOCIATES	40, 97, 266, 309, 325
NYGARD SET DESIGN	156, 430, 538
PAUL NYLIS PHOTOGRAPHY	410
NYSTROM PUBLISHING COMPANY, INC.	490

O

OAKWOOD PRODUCTIONS	89
OASIS ART STUDIO	78
O'CONNOR & WALTER	326
OEU'VRE CREATIVE SERVICES	188
ROBIN OGDEN REPRESENTS	68
OLAUSEN PHOTOGRAPHY	410
OLD ARIZONA	238
DENNIS P O'LEARY, INC.	41
OLSON AND COMPANY	41
KRUSKOPF OLSON	42
SUSAN OLSON FOOD STYLIST	238
OMNI ADVERTISING, INC.	42, 132
ONLINE PRODUCTIONS, INC.	239
ORANGESEED DESIGN	42, 267
ORCHESTRATED CREATIVE SERVICES	267
ORFIELD LABS, INC.	519
ORMAN GUIDANCE RESEARCH®, INC.	353

OTTO'S ART STUDIOS AND GALLERY	78
OUTSMART MARKETING	353

P

PADILLA SPEER BEARDSLEY	469
TYLER PAGE	79
PAPAS ART STUDIO	79
PAR CONSULTING, INC.	449, 533
PARACHUTE DESIGN	43, 268
PARKER PHOTOGRAPHIC	411, 421
PASSION FRUIT COMPANY	239
PATHWAY BOOKS	498
PATRICIA GARDNER DESIGN, INC. (PLEASE SEE SPOT DESIGN)	268
REBECCA PAVLENKO PHOTOGRAPHY	411
PENSCRIPTIONS	79
PERIMETER PRODUCTIONS, LTD.	207
MARY PERKINS	79
GEORGE PETERS DESIGN & ILLUSTRATION	268
GLENN PETERSON, INC.	411
J M PETERSON & ASSOCIATES	339
JAN PETERSON	239
MARGERY PETERSON, FREELANCE WRITER	326, 586
PETERSON MILLA HOOKS	43
PETTERS LEWMAN STUDIO	411
PGA TOUR PARTNERS	490
PHOTOGRAPHIC SPECIALTIES	113, 156, 177, 248, 430
PHOTOLAB IMAGING CORPORATION	118, 157, 177
PICAS AND POINTS, INC.	268
PINNACLE VIDEO PRODUCTIONS, INC.	207
PINS DIRECT	435
PIXEL FARM, INC.	60, 119, 240
THE PLACE IN THE WOODS	499
POGO PRESS, INC.	499
POINT CLOUD, INC.	119
POINT2POINT COMMUNICATION SOLUTIONS, INC.	128, 207
THE POLL GROUP	310, 470
POPULAR FRONT STUDIO, INC.	119, 412
POSL PHOTOGRAPHY, INC.	412
ANN POTTER & ASSOCIATES	106
POTTER PRODUCTION SERVICES	107
PR NEWSWIRE	470
PRECISION GRAPHICS, INC.	449
PRECISION POWERHOUSE	60, 90, 120, 240, 326, 438, 521, 541
PREMIERE SCHOOL OF SELF-IMPROVEMENT AND PROFESSIONAL MODELING, INC.	366
PRENTICE CREATIVE, INC.	269
BARB PRYBYL COMMUNICATIONS	327
PRINTER PROS	450
PRINTS CHARMING (DBA BUTTONS ON BRISTOL)	536
PRISM STUDIOS, INC.	157
PRO/PHASE MARKETING, INC.	135, 143
PROFESSIONAL COLOR SERVICE, INC.	120, 157, 249, 450, 529, 540
PROFESSIONAL EDITORS NETWORK OF MN (PEN)	163, 586
PROFESSIONAL SERVICES MARKETING	339
PROMEDIA PRODUCTIONS, INC.	208
PROMOTIONAL SYSTEMS GROUP, INC.	144, 435, 533
PROMOTIVISION, INC.	208
PROP RENTAL SERVICE	458
PROPAGANDA	240, 458
THE PROSPER GROUP, INC.	107
PROSPERA DESIGN	123, 277
PUBLIC ISSUE MANAGEMENT, LLP	470
PUBLIC RELATIONS SOCIETY OF AMERICA, MINNESOTA CHAPTER	471
KENDALL PURDY GROUP	98
PUSH MEDIA GROUP	120, 208, 240

Q

Q SOUND PRODUCTIONS, INC.	374
QUIRK PUBLISHING	502
QUIRK'S MARKETING RESEARCH REVIEW	507

Index / 605

R

R RANDOLPH STUDIO	366
R.D.O.	594
R.E.M. VIDEO & EVENT COMPANY	90, 209, 439, 520
RADARMS	458
RADIO K/KUOM-AM	512
RAINBOW MARKETING, INC.	44
RAINY LAKES PUZZLES	250
RAJTAR PRODUCTIONS	391
KRISTI K. RAZINK	44, 359
RDO MARKETING	340
REACTION STUDIOS	412
READEX	354
REAL PRODUCTIONS	241
REALGOOD CREATIVE	241
RECREATIONAL PUBLICATIONS INC	507
BARBARA REDMOND DESIGN, INC.	65, 269, 278
PATRICK REDMOND DESIGN	278
SUSAN REED DESIGN	269
REELWORKS ANIMATION STUDIO	61
RELAY HOUSE, INC.	102
REPRO PRINTING, INC.	450
RESOURCES AND COUNSELING FOR THE ARTS	499
DAVE RESTUCCIA PRODUCTIONS	209
THE RESUME SPECIALIST	569
REZERVOIR	270, 278
PENNY RICH GALINSON	241
RICH IMAGE VIDEO, INC.	209
THE RICHARD DIERCKS COMPANY, INC.	61, 210
RICHTER CASTING	366
ROBERT J. RIESBERG ANTIQUES	241
RILEY HAYES	44
RISDALL LINNIHAN ADVERTISING	44, 310, 340, 471
RMS PUBLIC RELATIONS	472
ROBBINS ISLAND MUSIC	210
DIANE ROBINSON	210
GORDON ROBINSON & ASSOC., INC.	45
KELLY E. ROGERS PHOTOGRAPHY	425
ROSSOW COMMUNICAITONS	327
STEVE ROUCH PHOTO	421
ROUTE 3	374
RUDISILL ADVERTISING, INC. (NOW MIRAGE ADVERTISING)	45
RUMJUNGLE MEDIA, INC.	102, 129, 211, 242
RURIK	80
RUSSELL & HERDER	46
RUSTEN MARKETING GROUP, INC.	341
RUTABAGA RAGS	436
R-W & ASSOCIATES - MANAGEMENT CONSULTANTS	341
GREG RYAN/SALLY BEYER	296
RICH RYAN PHOTOGRAPHY	412
RYBAK & ASSOCIATES	569

S

SA ADVERTISING	436
SAARI & FORRAI PHOTOGRAPHY	422
SANDRO R. SABO	587
SANDRA R. SABO	164
SAGA ADVERTISING & MARKETING	46
THE SAGE GROUP, INC.	328, 472
SALES BY PHONE, INC.	147
SALES EFFECTIVENESS TRAINING	172
PAT SAMPLES	587
SAN FRANCISCO BRIDE	490
THE SANDCASTLE GROUP	46
SARA JORDE PHOTOGRAPHY	392
SATIN STITCHES, LTD.	242
SATISFACTION MANAGEMENT SYSTEMS	342, 354
SCC ON LOCATION	242
SCENIC PHOTO!	296
SCHALL PRODUCTIONS	211
RON SCHARA	211
SCHMIDT COMMUNICATIONS	500
PETER SCHMIDT PHOTOGRAPHY	413
STEVE SCHNEIDER/PHOTOGRAPHY	413
JOEL SCHNELL PHOTOGRAPHER	413
SCHUBERT & HOEY OUTDOOR ADVERTISING	382
SCHULTZ-WARD PRENTICE	46
VICKI L SCHUMAN	328
SCIDMORE, HERSOM & OTHERS	47, 270
SCROUNGERS, INC.	459
BETHANNE M. SCULLY	570
SEATTLE BRIDE	491
SEATTLE MAGAZINE	491
GRETA SEBALD CREATIVE, INC.	270
SECRET AGENT MAN	68
SENIOR TIMES	491
SENNSATION TELEPROMPTER LLC	243
SENSE OF DESIGN	47
7· 30 CREATIVE	47
MICHAEL R. SEVERSON	243
SF PRODUCTIONS	243
SHAFER & FELD, INC.	451
SHA-KAR 9 ANIMATION	61
PAUL SHAMBROOM, PHOTOGRAPHER	413
SHAMROCK PICTURES, INC.	212
SHANDWICH INTERNATIONAL	342, 472
SHANNON DESIGNS	65
JOEL SHEAGREN PHOTOGRAPHY	414
KELLY SHIELDS PHOTOGRAPHY	414
TIMOTHY SHOLINE HEDGES	328
SHORE TO SHORE COMMUNICATIONS	473
FREDERICK SHORT	80
SHOULTZ & ASSOCIATES ADVERTISING, INC.	48
SIDE BY SIDE MARKETING	48
R. MYLES SIEGEL PHOTOGRAPHY	393
SIGHTLINES	243
SIGNS & GRAPHICS	382
SIGNTIFIC	158
RICH SILHA	249
RICH SILHA PHOTOGRAPHER	422
THE SILVER BOOK	491
DIANE SIMS PAGE	354
SINKLER PHOTOGRAPHY	414
SIR SPEEDY PRINTING & COPYING	451
SAL SKOG PHOTOGRAPHY	414
SKYLINE DISPLAYS INC	124
SKYWAY NEWS	492
SKYWAY PUBLICATIONS, INC.	507
SLIPSTREAM MUSIC	375, 521
SMITH COMMUNICATIONS	328
SMITH HOUSE PRESS	500
RICHARD HAMILTON SMITH PHOTOGRAPHY	415
SMYTH COMPANIES	48
DEBORAH SNYDER, CREATIVE REPRESENTATIVE	68
SOLDIER BRANE	244
SONS OF NORWAY	492
SOUND80	521
SOUNDBITES/MICHAEL R. SEVERSON	244
SOUTHWEST JOURNAL	492
SPANGLER DESIGN TEAM	279, 387
SPECTRUM STUDIO, INC.	80
MYLES SPICER & ASSOCIATES	342
SPORT EVENTS, LTD.	188
SPOT DESIGN	271
SPOTNIK	164
ST. JOHNS PUBLISHING, INC.	500
STAFFORD PHOTOGRAPHY	415
STAGES THEATRE COMPANY, INC.	459, 493
STANISLAW PHOTOGRAPHY	415
STANLEY WAI - GRAPHIC DESIGN OFFICE	271
STATE REGISTER	493
ALEX STEINBERG PHOTOGRAPHY	422

606 / Index

STEVEN LINDER PHOTO	80, 415
STEVEN WEWERKA PHOTOGRAPHY	393
KATHY A. STEWART	81
GREG STIEVER	212, 244
STOCKHAUSEN INK	544
LEE STOKES ADVERTISING ARTIST, INC.	529
STONE CIRCLE PRODUCTIONS	212, 244
LINDSAY STRAND ASSOCIATES, INC.	473
THOMAS STRAND STUDIO	415
STRANDESIGN STUDIO	271
STRINZ CREATIVE, INC.	581
STROTHER COMMUNICATIONS GROUP	474
MAKI STRUNC PHOTOGRAPHY, INC.	416
STUDE-BECKER ADVERTISING & COMMUNICATIONS	49, 271
STUDIO	416
THE STUDIO CENTRAL, INC.	416
STUDIO ONE, INC.	81, 272
STUDIO STOCK	297
STUDIO X	416
STUDIO Z IMAGERY	61
STUDIOCRAFTS, INC.	158, 245, 538
SUN NEWSPAPERS	493
SUNSHINE PHOTO, INC.	249
B SUTER GRAPHICS AND DESIGN, INC.	272
JERRY SWANSON PHOTOGRAPHY	422

T

2KOOL STUDIOS	594
TAD WARE & COMPANY, INC.	49
TADPOLE PARADE	189
TAG TEAM FILM & VIDEO, INC.	91, 212, 245
TAJ STUDIOS	177
TAKE 1 PRODUCTIONS	91, 213, 245
THE TALENT CENTER	561
TALENT POOLE TALENT AGENCY	367
TALENT TEMPS, INC.	553
TANAKA ADVERTISING	49
TANDEM COMMUNICATIONS	272
TANGLETOWN RECORDING STUDIOS	375, 520
TARTAN MARKETING	50, 99, 145, 311
TASTY LIGHTING SUPPLY	246
TC2 COMPANY	593
THE TCI GROUP	355
TDI	382
TEAM CREATIVE	273
TECHNICAL REPRODUCTIONS	182, 427
TECHNICAL WRITING AND EDITING	164
TECMARK, INC.	343
TEENER'S THEATRICAL DEPARTMENT STORE	459
TELEDIRECT	547
TELEPHONE SALES ASSOCIATES	546
TELE-PRODUCERS, INC.	213
GLENN TERRY, FINE ARTIST	81
THAMAN & ASSOCIATES, INC.	50
CRAIG THIESEN	81, 121
THE THIRD EYE	359
THIS BOYS FREE	375
THOELE PRINTING COMPANY	451
THOEN & ASSOCIATES ADVERTISING PHOTOGRAPHY, INC.	417
W J THOM COMPANY	436, 533
THOMAS DESIGN GROUP	273
SUSAN THOMPSON, PR	474
THOUGHTS UNSEEN	376
3SCORE MUSIC/ETC.	376
CHRISTINE TIERNEY	82
TILKA DESIGN	273
TIMELINE COMMUNICATIONS, INC.	213
SYLVIA TIMIAN	164
TOBYS TUNES, INC.	522, 297

SCOTT TONEY/CREATIVE ALLIANCE	65
TOP FLIGHT MARKETING	121
BETH TORGERSON COPYWRITING AND PROJECT MANAGEMENT	581
TOTAL MARKET COVERAGE, INC.	359
TPT MAGAZINE	494
ANDREE TRACEY	82
TRACK RECORD STUDIOS	522
TRACK SEVENTEEN PRODUCTIONS, INC.	522
TRADITIONS CLASSIC HOME FURNISHINGS	460
TRAIL MIX INC.	246
TRAINING DYNAMICS	173
TRANSTOP MINNESOTA, INC.	383
TRAVEL GRAPHICS INTERNATIONAL	533
TRELEVEN PHOTOGRAPHY, INC.	393
TRIANGLE PRINTING COMPANY	451
TRILOGY MARKETING GROUP	92, 436, 534, 561
TRIPP ADVERTISING	51
TROUPE AMERICA, INC.	189
TUNDRA FILMS	214
TUNHEIM GROUP	214
DORRINE TURECAMO	587
JENNIFER TURNER-BRAND	246
TWIN CITIES EMPLOYMENT WEEKLY	494
TWIN CITIES LUTHERAN NEWSPAPER, INC.	508
TWIN CITIES PARENT	494
TWIN CITIES TECHNICAL COMMUNICATIONS COMPANY	595
2 HEADS COMMUNICATION	582

U

U. S. LICENSING GROUP	298
ULTRA CREATIVE, INC.	51, 273, 387, 534
UNCLE PETE'S COLORING BOOK	82
UNDERTONE MUSIC, INC.	376
UNFORGETTABLE MODEL	367
UNIVERSITY MEDIA RESOURCES	214
UNIVERSITY OF MINNESOTA COLLEGE OF CONTINUING EDUCATION	173
UNO HISPANIC ADVERTISING DESIGN	52
UPFRONT PRODUCTIONS	122, 124, 158, 178, 182, 274, 329, 343, 452, 494, 525
ALVIS UPITIS PHOTOGRAPHY	417
US BANCORP PIPER JAFFRAY	124

V

VAL-PAK OF MINNESOTA	145
RON VAN ZEE PHOTOGRAPHY	417
VANBAR PRODUCTIONS	215
SUSAN VANCLEAF	588
VAVRICKA JUNTTI & COMPANY	329
VEE CORPORATION	159, 246, 460, 527, 540
VENTURES MAGAZINE	508
VENUS DIRECTIONS	215, 548
VIDEO ASSIST SUPPORT SERVICES	246
VIDEO HOME SERVICES	215
VIDEOMED, INC.	216
VISIONQUEST PHOTOGRAPHIC ARTS CENTER	417
VISUAL MUSIC & SOUND, LTD.	522
VOICE MATTERS(*!)	562
VOICE PLUS/ACTORS PLUS	367, 562
VOLKART MAY & ASSOCIATES	148
VOLTAGGIO JOHNSON	388
VOYAGEUR PRESS	500

W

CLEMMER G. WAIT, TECHNICAL WRITER	595
NEAL WALLACE, WRITING, CONSULTING, RESEARCH	588
TAD WARE PHOTOGRAPHY	418
WATERS MOLITOR	99, 312
DIANA WATTERS PHOTOGRAPHY	426
WBCS, INC.	133

WBJI FM	511	WINNERS MARKETING COMMUNICATIONS	330
WCCO-TV	103	WISE BUY MEDIA	53
WDGY RADIO	513	WJJY FM	513
WEBER PHOTOGRAPHY	418	WMNN NEWSRADIO 1330	103
WEHMANN MODELS/TALENT, INC.	368	STEVE WOIT PHOTOGRAPHY	418
WEICHERT FINANCIAL RELATIONS, INC.	475	WOLD PHOTOGRAPHY	418
WELLAND LAIKE COMMUNICATION	52, 475	WOLF MARINE, INC.	247
WENTINK PHOTOGRAPHY	418	WOODLAND PRODUCTIONS	247
HEATHER WEST PUBLIC RELATIONS	475	WORD TECH SECRETARIAL SERVICE	108
WFTC-TV	103	WORDS & DEEDS, INC.	588
WG COMMUNICATIONS	216	WORDS AT WORK	312
WHITE PLUME COMMUNICATIONS	596	WORDSCAPE COMMUNICATION	165
WHITEWOLF ENTERTAINMENT, INC.	103	WORKING WORDS	165, 582
WHITNEY MORSE	53	WOW AND FLUTTER MUSIC AND SOUND	523
WHITNEY WORLDWIDE, INC.	146, 355, 437	THE WRITE APPROACH	589
GARY WICKS	216	WRITING ON POINT, INC.	582
WIESE PHOTOGRAPHY AND DESIGN	423	WWWI AM	513
WILD SOUND	523		
WILHIDE & COMPANY	53	**Y**	
JAN WILLEM BOER	69		
WILLETTE MPLS PHOTOGRAPHY	418	MARGARET LABASH YOUNG	165
MORGAN WILLIAMS & ASSOCIATES, INC.	274, 274		
WILSON GRIAK	216	**Z**	
WILSON PRODUCTIONS	217	ZEBRA PHOTOGRAPHY	419
WINDFLOWER PRODUCTIONS	247	PEGGY ZETAH, LTD.	274
WINDOW FASHIONS MAGAZINE	495	THE ZIMMERMAN GROUP	54
		SALLY E. ZORICH & ASSOCIATES	355
		BILL ZUEHLKE PHOTOGRAPHY	419

Phone Numbers

Phone Numbers

Phone Numbers

Phone Numbers

Phone Numbers

Phone Numbers

Phone Numbers

Phone Numbers

Phone Numbers

Phone Numbers

Phone Numbers

Phone Numbers

Phone Numbers

Phone Numbers

Phone Numbers

Phone Numbers